HARDPRESS.NET
HOME OF HARD-TO-FIND BOOKS

The Phrenological Journal and Science of Health
by Unknown

Address:
HardPress
8345 NW 66TH ST #2561
MIAMI FL 33166-2626
USA
Email: info@hardpress.net

F. Jos. Gall.

Drawn for Vol. 2 N° 1 of the Am. Phren. Journ.

Lith. of Tho. Sinclair, N° 79 S. Third St. Phila

THE

AMERICAN

PHRENOLOGICAL JOURNAL

AND

MISCELLANY.

" Res non verba quæso."—COMBE.

"One fact is to me more positive and decisive than a thousand metaphysical opinions."—SPURZHEIM.

" This is truth, though at enmity with the philosophy of ages."—GALL.

VOL. II.

PHILADELPHIA:

PUBLISHED BY THE PROPRIETORS.

AND FOR SALE BY

HASWELL, BARRINGTON & CO. PHILADELPHIA; L. N. FOWLER, NEW YORK; J. J. HASWELL & CO. NEW ORLEANS; WEEKS. JORDAN, & CO. BOSTON; AND WILEY & PUTNAM, LONDON.

1840.

CONTENTS. *

' A critical index of Volumes I. II. and III. of this Journal will be pre-
ed, and appended to the close of our next volume.

THE

AMERICAN PHRENOLOGICAL JOURNAL

AND

MISCELLANY.

| Vol. II. | Philadelphia, October 1, 1839. | No. 1. |

amp

ARTICLE I.

BIOGRAPHY OF DR. GALL.

THE discovery and early history of all principles in science are identified, to some extent, with individual life and character. And a full and minute account of the former cannot be given, without involving, more or less, the merits of the latter. For as there necessarily exists a relationship between the agent and the subject, in bringing each into public notice, so in recording a history of its results, this connection should be duly acknowledged and fairly stated. We propose, therefore, to present in this article, a brief history of the life of Dr. Gall, with a critical analysis of his character, and some few remarks upon his merits, in connection with the nature and importance of his discoveries. The facts stated in this biographical notice are derived from the most authentic sources.

François Joseph Gall was born in the village of Tiefenbrunn, within the district of the Grand Duchy of Baden, on the ninth of March, 1758. His father was a merchant by profession, and a man of considerable distinction and character for his circumstances. Scarcely any information whatever can be gleaned from the writings of Gall, or from any other source, respecting the character of his mother, or the history of his brothers and sisters. It appears that his parents were professors of the Roman Catholic religion, and, for some reasons, had intended him for the service of that church. His education was therefore early attended to, and his studies directed in accordance with his future pursuits.

In the ninth year of his age, Gall was placed by his parents under the care and tuition of an uncle, who was a clergyman, residing at a place not far distant, called the Black Forest. Here he remained for some years, a diligent and successful scholar. Afterwards, he prosecuted his studies for some time at Baden, then at Brucksal, and

VOL. II.—1

also at Strasburgh.   As a student, Gall was distinguished more for
originality and solidity of talent, than for display and brilliancy.   As
a scholar, he was respectable, but excelled most in branches involving
principles of science and philosophy.   He was passionately fond of
the studies of nature, and frequently resorted into the country and the
forests to make observations on butterflies, insects, birds, and other
tribes of the animal kingdom.   This spirit of enquiry and observation
was undoubtedly the key which opened to him the way to his future
discoveries.   Having arrived at the age of manhood, it was necessary
for him to make preparations more directly appertaining to his profession.   Though his parents had intended him for the church, yet his
natural dispositions were averse to such a course ; and having become
already interested in studies connected with medical science, he was
led to turn his attention to the healing art.

Vienna, at this time, contained the most distinguished medical
school which could be found in the interior part of Europe.   Hither
Gall repaired, while in the twenty-third year of his age.   Here he
enjoyed very superior advantages for obtaining a thorough knowledge
of his profession ; and his future career evidently shows that they
were neither neglected nor unimproved.   After completing his studies
at the University, Gall entered upon the practice of medicine in Vienna.
In the year 1796, he commenced giving public lectures on his new
discoveries respecting the functions of the brain.   We will here present a brief account of the manner in which he was led into this
course of discovery and investigation.

" From my earliest youth," says Dr. Gall, " I lived in the bosom
of my family, composed of several brothers and sisters, and in the
midst of a great number of companions and schoolmates.   Each of
these individuals had some peculiarity, talent, propensity, or faculty,
which distinguished him from the others.   This diversity determined
our indifference, or our mutual affection and aversion, as well as our
contempt, our emulation, and our connections.   In childhood, we are
rarely liable to be led astray by prejudice ; we take things as they are.
Among our number, we soon formed a judgment who was virtuous or
inclined to vice, modest or arrogant, frank or deceitful, a truth-teller
or a liar, peaceable or quarrelsome, benevolent, good or bad, &c.
Some were distinguished for the beauty of their penmanship ; some
by their facility in calculation ; others by their aptitude to acquire
history, philosophy, or languages.   One shone in composition by the
elegance of his periods ; another had always a dry, harsh style ;
another reasoned closely, and expressed himself with force.   A large
number manifested a talent or a taste for subjects not within our
assigned course.   Some carved, and drew well ; some devoted their

leisure to painting, or to the cultivation of a small garden, while their comrades were engaged in noisy sports ; others enjoyed roaming the woods, hunting, seeking birds' nests, collecting flowers, insects, or shells. Thus each one distinguished himself by his proper characteristic ; and I never knew an instance, when one who had been a cheating and faithless companion one year, became a true and faithful friend the next."*

Gall had observed that those scholars with whom he found the greatest difficulty in competing in *verbal* memory, were distinguished for large prominent eyes. He made very extensive observations on this point, and was finally led to suspect that there must be some necessary connection between memory for words and the size and projection of the eye. "In following out, by observations, the principle which accident had thus suggested, he for some time encountered difficulties of the greatest magnitude. Hitherto, he had been altogether ignorant of the opinions of physiologists, touching the brain, and of the metaphysicians, respecting the mental faculties, and had simply observed nature. When, however, he began to enlarge his knowledge of books, he found the most extraordinary conflict of opinions prevailing ; and this, for the moment, made him hesitate about the correctness of his own observations. He found that the moral sentiments had, by an almost general consent, been consigned to the thoracic and abdominal viscera ; and that, while Pythagoras, Plato, Galen, Haller, and some other physiologists, placed the sentient soul, or intellectual faculties, in the brain, Aristotle placed it in the heart, Van Helmont in the stomach, Des Cartes and his followers in the pineal gland, and Drelincourt and others in the cerebellum.

"He observed, also, that a great number of philosophers and physiologists asserted, that all men are born with equal mental faculties ; and that the differences observable among them are owing either to education, or to accidental circumstances in which they are placed. But being convinced, by facts, that there is a natural and constitutional diversity of talents and dispositions, he encountered, in books, a still greater obstacle to his success in determining the external signs of the mental powers. He found that, instead of faculties for languages, drawing, distinguishing places, music, and mechanical arts, corresponding to the different talents which he had observed in his schoolfellows, the metaphysicians spoke only of general powers, such as perception, conception, memory, imagination, and judgment ; and when he endeavoured to discover external signs in the head, corresponding to these general faculties, or to determine the correctness of

* Introduction to the " Anatomie &c. du Cerveau."

the physiological doctrines regarding the seat of the mind, as taught by the authors already mentioned, he found perplexities without end, and difficulties insurmountable.

"Dr. Gall, therefore, abandoning every theory and preconceived opinion, gave himself up entirely to the observation of nature. Being physician to a lunatic asylum at Vienna, he had opportunities, of which he availed himself, of making observations on the insane. He visited prisons, and resorted to schools; he was introduced to the courts of princes, to colleges, and the seats of justice; and whenever he heard of an individual distinguished in any particular way, either by remarkable endowment or deficiency, he observed and studied the development of his head. In this manner, by an almost imperceptible induction, he conceived himself warranted in believing that particular mental powers are indicated by particular configurations of the head.

"The successive steps by which Dr. Gall proceeded in his discoveries, are particularly deserving attention. He did not, as many have imagined, first dissect the brain, and pretend by that means to have discovered the seats of the mental powers; neither did he, as others have conceived, first map out the skull into various compartments, and assign a faculty to each, according as his imagination led him to conceive the place appropriate to the power. On the contrary, he first observed a concomitance between particular talents and dispositions, and particular forms of the head; he next ascertained, by removal of the skull, that the figure and size of the brain are indicated by these external forms; and it was only after these facts were determined, that the brain was minutely dissected, and light thrown on its structure."*

It was thus not until after more than twenty years of observations, and with the best facilities for making researches, that Gall first ventured to present his peculiar views to the public. He had, during most of this time, extensive practice as a physician at Vienna—ranked high as a man of science—associated with the first men of the place and the nation, and was connected with several public institutions. His lectures were continued from 1796 to 1802, and were attended by audiences the most intelligent and respectable. Many distinguished strangers, as well as some of the foreign ambassadors at the court of Vienna, encouraged him in his labours privately, and honoured him with their attendance publicly. Prince Metternich was a pupil of Dr. Gall, and afterwards renewed his acquaintanceship with him in Paris, during his residence there as ambassador to Napoleon. Con-

* From the Biography of Gall, by the editor of his works on the Functions of the Brain.

siderable interest was now created on the subject. Several scientific gentlemen, who had heard his lectures, published reports of them in different periodicals and works. Some, through ignorance and preju-dice, opposed his discoveries. It was represented to the emperor, that Gall's views were injurious to good morals and dangerous to religion. This opposition arose from two sources. First, from the influence of Dr. Stifft, then physician to the emperor, and president of the medical faculty. It is stated on good authority, that Dr. S. was a man of no talent as a physician, but a great politician and intriguer. The second source of opposition arose from the over-whelming influence of an ignorant, bigoted, and corrupted clergy.

Accordingly, an edict was issued, on the ninth of January, 1802, by the Austrian government, prohibiting all private lectures, unless a special permission was obtained from the public authorities. Dr. Gall presented to the officers of government a very able remonstrance in defence of his views, and in favour of public lectures on the same; but it was all in vain, and the efforts of his friends in his behalf were equally unavailing. Gall, finding that all prospect of communicating and defending publicly his new discoveries, in Austria, was cut off, determined to seek a country whose government was more liberal and tolerant. He had now passed the meridian of life—(being in the forty-fifth year of his age)—had spent the best of his days at Vienna, and there hoped in peace to live, labour, and die; but TRUTH was dearer to him than ease, pleasure, wealth, or honour. Few can con-ceive the immense sacrifice which he must have made in giving up an extensive professional business and public confidence, in breaking away from the society of all his acquaintances and relatives, and leaving what had then become more valuable, in his estimation, than all the rest, the greater portion of his craniological specimens, which he had been more than thirty years in collecting.

On the 6th of March, 1805, Dr. Gall left Vienna, accompanied by Dr. Spurzheim, who had now been with him nearly five years. They first visited Berlin, and afterwards continued their tour—repeat-ing their lectures and anatomical demonstrations in more than thirty towns of Germany, Prussia, Holland, and Switzerland—until they arrived at Paris, in the month of November, 1808. In these travels, says Gall, "I experienced every where the most flattering reception. Sovereigns, ministers, philosophers, legislators, artists, seconded my design on all occasions, augmenting my collection, and furnishing me every where with new observations. The circumstances were too favourable to permit me to resist the invitations which came to me from most of the universities. This journey afforded me the oppor-tunity of studying the organisation of a great number of men of

:minent talents, and of others extremely limited, and I had the advantage of observing the difference between them. I gathered innu nerable facts in the schools and in the great establishments of educaion, in the asylums for orphans and foundlings, in the insane hospitals, n the houses of correction, in prisons, in judicial courts, and even in laces of execution; the multiplied researches on suicides, idiots, and nadmen, have contributed greatly to correct and confirm my opinions."

It was during this tour, that Gall made his celebrated visit to the rison of Berlin, and to the fortress of Spandeau. Here the practical application of the new doctrine was put to a searching test. The nterest excited by the novelty of the scene, was not greater than the astonishment produced by the results of the process. On the 17th of April, 1805, Gall visited the prison of Berlin, in company with the directing commissaries, the superior officers of the establishment, the nquisitors of the criminal deputation, the counsellors, assessors, medical inspectors, &c. &c. In their presence, he examined over wo hundred prisoners, picked out and arranged into separate classes, hose convicted of murder, robbery, theft, &c.; and stated many hings remarkably correct concerning their previous history and character, as well as respecting the particular kind and degree of crime for which they then were imprisoned. His visit at the fortress of Spandeau was no less interesting. Here he examined over four hundred convicts, and was equally successful in detecting their crimes, and delineating their characters. Reports of these visits were published at the time in several periodicals, and created no little sensation in various parts of Europe.

Frem November, 1807, Gall made Paris his permanent residence. In the months of November and December, Gall, assisted by Spurzheim, delivered his first course of lectures in that city. "His assertions," says Chevenix, in the Foreign Quarterly Review, "were supported by a numerous collection of skulls, casts, heads, &c.; and by a multiplicity of anatomical and physiological facts. Great, indeed, was the ardour excited among the Parisians, by the presence of the men who, as they supposed, could tell their fortunes by their heads. Every one wanted to get a peep at them; every one was anxious to give them a dinner or a supper; and the writer of this article actually saw a list on which an eager candidate was delighted to inscribe himself for a breakfast, distant only three months and a half; at which breakfast he sat a wondering guest."

In 1808, Gall and Spurzheim presented a joint memoir on the anatomy of the brain to the French Institute. A committee was appointed to report on the same, with Cuvier at its head. The French nation, at this time, was sore on the subject of quackery, and were suspicious of foreign innovations. The influence of the first consul, Napoleon, was now almost omnipotent over the Parisians, and he had signified his decided disapprobation of the new views of the German doctors. The report of Cuvier before the institute was unfavourable to the discoveries of Gall and Spurzheim, though it is stated that he was fully convinced of the truth of their discoveries, and acknowledged it in private. But such was the influence of Napoleon's opposition, and other leading men, as well as the unsettled state of the French government, and its relations to other nations, that phrenology made very slow progress in Paris.

In 1809, Gall and Spurzheim commenced publishing their magnificent work, entitled " *The Anatomy and Physiology of the Nervous System in general, and of the Brain in particular; with Observations upon the possibility of ascertaining several Intellectual and Moral Dispositions of Man and Animals, by the Configuration of their Heads.*" Four volumes, folio, with an Atlas of 100 plates. Price 1000 francs.

This great work was continued, by their joint exertions, to the completion of two and a half volumes, and was ultimately finished by Gall in 1819. In the mean time, he delivered several courses of lectures, which were attended by respectable audiences, composed mostly of medical students, and literary and scientific men. Spurzheim left Paris, 1813, for Great Britain; and ever after that period, they prosecuted their researches separately.

The two following accounts, describing the person, circumstances, habits, &c., of Dr. Gall, will be read with interest by all, but more especially by those already interested in phrenological science. In the year 1826, there appeared in the Birmingham Journal the following communication, from a correspondent who was then on a visit in France.

" I found Dr. Gall to be a man of middle stature, of an outline well-proportioned; he was thin and rather pallid, and possessed a capacious head and chest. The peculiar brilliancy of his penetrating eye left an indelible impression. His countenance was remarkable—his features strongly marked, and rather large, yet devoid of coarseness. The general impression that a first glance was calculated to convey, would be, that he was a man of originality and depth of mind, possessing much urbanity, with some Self-esteem and inflexibility of design.

" After presenting my letters of introduction to him, at seven o'clock in the morning, he showed me into a room, the walls of which were covered with bird-cages, and the floor with dogs, cats, &c. Observing that I was surprised at the number of his companions, he remarked, 'All you Englishmen take me for a bird-catcher; I am sure you feel surprised that I am not somewhat differently made to any of you, and that I should employ my time in talking to birds. Birds, sir, differ in their dispositions like men; and, if they were but of more consequence, the peculiarity of their characters would have been as well delineated. Do you think,' says he, turning his eyes to two beautiful dogs at his feet, which were endeavouring to gain his attention—' do you think that these little pets possess pride and vanity like man?' 'Yes,' I said; 'I have observed their vanity frequently.' 'We will call both feelings into action,' said he; he then caressed the whelp, and took it into his arms; 'mark his mother's offended pride,' said he, as she was walking quietly across the chamber to her mat; 'do you think she will come, if I call her?' 'Oh yes,' I answered. 'No, not at all.' He made the attempt, but she heeded not the hand she had so earnestly endeavoured to lick the moment before. 'She will not speak to me to-day,' said the doctor.

" He then described to me the peculiarity of many of his birds, and I was astonished to find that he seemed familiar also with their dispositions (if I may be allowed the word). 'Do you think a man's time would be wasted thus in England? You are a wealthy and a powerful nation, and as long as the equilibrium exists between the two, so shall you remain; but this never has, nor cannot, exist beyond a certain period. Such is your industry, stimulated by the love of gain, that your whole life is spun out before you are aware the wheel is turning; and so highly do you value commerce, that it stands in place of self-knowledge, and an acquaintance with nature and her immense laboratory.'

" I was delighted with this conversation; he seemed to me to take a wider view in the contemplation of man than any other person with whom I had ever conversed. During breakfast, he frequently fed the little suitors, who approached as near as their iron bars would admit. You see they all know me.' said he, 'and will feed from my hand, except this blackbird, which must gain his morsel by stealth before he eats it; we will retire a moment, and in our absence he will take the bread." On our return, we found he had secreted it in a corner of his cage. I mention these, otherwise uninteresting, anecdotes, to show how much Dr. Gall had studied the peculiarity of the smaller animals.

" After breakfast, he showed me his extensive collection; and thus ended my first visit to the greatest moral philosopher that Europe has produced; to a man, than whom few were ever more ridiculed, and few ever pursued their bent more determinately, despite its effects; to a man, who alone effected more change in mental philosophy than perhaps any predecessor; to a man, who suffered more persecution, and yet possessed more philanthropy, than most philosophers."

The other communication is from the pen of Dr. Elliotson, formerly professor in the University of London. Says Dr. E.——" I have seen Dr. Gall—seen much of him, and had repeated conversations with him on phrenological points, and on the history of his discoveries. He lectures in Paris, to a class above one hundred, at the Athenée Royale. His course consists of sixty or seventy lectures, and he spends several days in dissecting. When at the end of the hour, he asks whether he shall proceed? the audience applaud violently, and he often continues two, and upwards of three hours. Dr. Gall ranks high in Paris; he is physician to ten ambassadors—has great practice —is considered a *savant*—and bears himself, and lives handsomely, like a gentleman.

" Gall's head is magnificent; and his countenance, dress, and manners, with the depth, continuousness, liberality, and simplicity of his remarks, show you that you are in company with a profound philosopher—a perfect gentleman—and a most kind-hearted friend. He is perfectly free from affectation or quackery; *pursues truth only, regardless of all consequences; and has sought it at an immense expense, and free from all interested motives. He knows the importance and reality of his discoveries; and though perfectly modest and simple, forms the just estimate of himself that posterity will form, and feels secure of immortality.* I advised him to write some popular work, but he objected; said he had written for the studious only—for those who desired to understand the subject thoroughly; that he had composed a work for posterity, and must leave to others the occupation of writing for loungers. It was delightful to see the good old man every day sitting on his sofa, or sitting up in bed (for he was ill at the time), surrounded by his friends, all listening to him, while he spoke knowledge in the most amiable manner, attending to every question, and allowing some more voluble, though not less admiring than the rest, to interrupt him, patiently resuming his arguments when they had finished. He is incessantly meditating and observing; telling them that much remains yet to be done, and mentions points upon which he wishes them to make observations, for the purpose of solving various difficulties."

The person of Dr. Gall was well-proportioned; in stature, he was five feet two inches, with a large chest and strong muscles; his step was firm, and his look vivid and penetrating. His features, though not handsome, possessed a mild and pleasing expression. He acquired no mean reputation as a physician, as well as a writer and philosopher; and, independent of the respect shown him by all parties, he realised from his profession a handsome fortune. His skill as a physician may be inferred from the following fact. " In he year 1820, a gold medal was presented to him, executed by M. Barre, an eminent artist in Paris, by order of Count Potosky, a ·ich Polish nobleman, who took this method of expressing his deep gratitude to Dr. Gall, who had cured him of an old and dangerous malady, for which he had in vain consulted the best medical men in Paris. On one side of the medal is the head of Dr. Gall, an admirable ikeness; and on the other is Esculapius, standing at the bed-side of .he patient, chasing away with one hand the birds of darkness, and crushing a frog, the symbol of ignorance, under his right foot. Behind Esculapius is an altar, with a skull placed upon it, to denote the particular kind of study to which Dr. Gall was devoted."

In March, 1828, at the close of one of his lectures, Dr. Gall was seized with a paralytic attack, from which he never perfectly reco-vered, and which ultimately carried him off, the 22d of August, 1828, in the seventy-second year of his age. His remains were followed to the grave by an immense concourse of friends and admirers, five of whom pronounced discourses over his grave, as is the custom in France on such occasions. A gentleman in Paris, who was not a phrenologist, writing about this time on various topics to Dr. A. Combe, of Edinburgh, expresses himself as follows:—"You will, I am sure, be more affected by the death of Dr. Gall, than by any political event. In truth, it is an immense loss to science. What-ever opinion we may form of the system of that illustrious man, it must be acknowledged that he has made an immense stride in the sciences of medicine and of man. You must have been satisfied with the homage paid to his memory by the side of his grave, by whatever distinguished men Paris possesses." Dr. Fossati, in his funeral dis-course, has the following touching paragraph:—"What an irreparable blank do I perceive in the scientific world by the death of one man!— a blank which will long be felt by all the friends of science and of sound philosophy. But what a man have we lost! what a genius was his! what a happy organisation nature had given him! Yes! Dr. Gall was one of those privileged individuals whom the Creator sends upon the earth at the interval of ages, to teach us how far human intelligence can reach!"

It remains now for us to enter into a more critical analysis of the mental powers of Dr. Gall; in doing which, we propose to apply phrenological principles. And there is reason to believe that the results of such an application will not be less interesting to the reader, than honourable to the genius of the distinguished discoverer of the true science of mind.

The head of Dr. Gall was large, measuring, above the eyebrows and at the top of the ears, twenty-two inches and two lines in circum ference ; and fourteen inches and nine lines from the root of the nose to the occiput. The several regions of his brain were generally well-developed, though some organs were considerable larger and more active than others. The organs of Amativeness, Philoprogenitiveness, Adhesiveness, Combativeness, and Destructiveness, were all well developed. He always showed great fondness for children and pets, as well as sympathy for helpless and dependent objects generally. And while he was never distinguished for ardour of attachment, and enthusiasm of feeling, yet the friendships of few were stronger, more sincere and constant. He was possessed of no ordinary share of energy and force of character, which strikingly marked his whole career of discovery, in overcoming the greatest obstacles, and encountering the most bitter opposition. Still, notwithstanding the consciousness of his mental superiority, and the certain conviction of the truth of his doctrines, he was rarely, if ever, known to exhibit an improper or wrong manifestation of the faculties of Combativeness and Destructiveness to his opponents, or to any others with whom he had intercourse, amid the various scenes and changes through which he was called to pass. It is believed that very few can be found in the annals of history who have displayed, under like circumstances, greater liberality of feeling and magnanimity of mind.

The organs of Secretiveness and Cautiousness were rather large. His whole life was characterised by great prudence, caution, and forethought. He evidently saw, in the early part of his career, the true nature and vast importance of his discoveries, and therefore proceeded, step by step, with the greatest care and deliberation. In several attempts to deceive him by false reports, and impose upon him by improper subjects for examination, he showed no ordinary degree of shrewdness and sagacity. But while he was acute and penetrating, he was frank and honest ; and was too conscious of his intellectual strength, and the justness of his cause, ever to resort to cunning or fraud for obtaining his ends.

The organs of Self-esteem and Firmness were very large, and formed conspicuous traits in his character. Few persons ever possessed more real self-respect, and a greater love of independence, than Gall. We will here quote a striking passage from his remarks on the former faculty, in which he has given a remarkably correct delineation of himself. "There are certain men," says he, "with minds sufficiently strong, who are so deeply impressed with a sense of their own value, and so independent withal, that they know how to repel every external influence which tends to subject them. As far as practicable, they choose the freest countries to live in, and devote themselves to an employment that renders them independent, and exempts them from the caprices and favour of the great. That domination over their inferiors, which becomes slavery under an absolute master, would be insupportable to them. The honours and distinctions that are withheld from merit, while they are lavished on insignificant men, are but humiliations in their eyes. If they prosper, it is only by their own exertions; like the oak, they are sustained by their own efforts; and it is to their own resources that they would be indebted for all they possess." But notwithstanding Gall's large organ of Self-esteem, he had too much good sense, and too well-balanced a mind, to render him insolent and overbearing. It was undoubtedly, in part, the influence of this faculty in creating a due sense of respect and estimation for himself, according to real merit, that supported him in the prosecution of his arduous and discouraging labours. But perhaps he was equally, if not more, indebted to Firmness for the success of his researches. For without that constancy, or rather obstinacy, with which he pursued the same ideas, the same observations, and the same investigations, it would have been impossible for him to have carried his new science to the point where he left it.

The faculty of Approbativeness was extremely weak, and had comparatively little or no influence on his character. He was as indifferent to the praise and approbation of men, as he was to their blame and censure. He laboured, disinterestedly, for the good of science—for the love of truth, and under the full conviction that his views would triumph in the end, over all error, prejudice, and opposition. "We could recall," say some of his associates, "a thousand anecdotes to prove that his vanity was not very susceptible. How many times have we seen him laugh at the squibs of the little journals, and unaffectedly despise the gross abuse which they heaped upon him. Let us cite one fact, which will answer for many others. When Gall was at Berlin, the celebrated poet Kotzebue profited by the occasion, in learning of him the technical terms of his science, and such ideas and principles as he could best turn into ridicule. He composed a very ludicrous play, called *Craniomania*, which was immediately performed at the theatre; Gall attended the representation, and laughed as heartily as any of them."

The organs of the perceptive faculties, as a class, were only fairly or ordinarily developed. Individuality was probably the strongest of these, though this was far from constituting a marked trait in his character. He was led to make observations, and study nature, rather from a desire to understand *principles*, than to know *facts*. The faculty of Locality was decidedly weak. It was with the greatest difficulty that he could recognise or remember localities.

While a boy, he frequently got lost, and was never fond of the study of geography; as a physician, he often forgot the residences of his patients, and never took pleasure in traveling, for the sake of merely seeing places. The faculty of Language was fair. Gall understood several different languages, and could converse in them with ease and fluency, yet was not verbose, and always had great antipathy to all questions about mere words, grammatical discussions, compilations, &c. His memory of words, names, persons, and *things*, generally was poor; but for principles, relations, and analogies, it was good. His love of Order was very weak. It is said that his house and office presented, generally, a complete scene of disorder and confusion. His perception of Colour was also extremely weak. He was frequently deceived upon this point, and had to rely principally on the judgment of others. He had scarce any taste for music, or the fine arts; was very deficient in the science of numbers, and was comparatively destitute of taste or talent for mathematics, geometry, architecture, mechanics, &c. &c.

The organ of Wit was well developed. Few could more clearly discern and better appreciate the witty and ludicrous than Gall. And though he never resorted to the weapons of wit, ridicule, and sarcasm, in answering the cavils and objections of his opponents, yet his reviews and controversial writings display a keenness of satire, and a shrewdness of remark, that can rarely be found. The weapons which he used were not pointed with the shafts of prejudice, envy, and malignity. They emanated rather from the honesty, the nobleness, and the magnanimity of a mind which relies in self-defence solely on the inherent power of truth, and the intrinsic goodness of its cause.

The organs of Imitation and Ideality were rather moderate. It is related that he was somewhat fond of representations, exhibitions, &c., and had considerable ability himself to copy, to imitate, and to act out; but this was by no means a leading trait in his character. And as for poetry, or the productions of Ideality, he had but little taste or genius. His manner of living was far removed from outward display and show; his habits were simple and plain; and the style of his writings, though not flowery or highly polished, yet indicate good taste and judgment.

But the superiority of Gall over most men, arose from the great size and activity of reflective intellect. His portrait evidently shows that this region of the head was very prominent. He manifested these faculties in early youth, by a spirit of eager and constant enquiry to understand *principles*—to know the *why*, the *wherefore*, and the *reason* of things, &c. It was a strong desire of this kind which so forcibly excited and urged on his perceptive powers to make observations, and to collect facts. And had not his mind been early, thoroughly, and correctly disciplined in the processes of observation, analysis, and induction, it might have been as purely abstract and speculative in its productions as that of Kant, or any other metaphysician. We may here notice the powerful influence which early mental habits may have in the direction and formation of character.

The organs of Comparison and Causality were both very large; though his writings, perhaps, indicate a larger development of the former than of the latter. There is probably no study that requires the more constant exercise of the faculty of Comparison, than that of phrenology. The student can scarcely proceed a step in observing and studying its facts or principles without employing it. He must first discover the relations of agreement and disagreement between the objects of his examination, and then search for affinities, comparisons, and similes, between the relations of other objects or principles. The discovery and early advancement of the science were necessarily almost one continued process of comparison of organisation with faculties; and of the faculties of man with those of other animals. And no one could have been better adapted to such labours than Gall; and it is needless to say, that no one since has ever made even an approximation to the extent and amount of his researches.

The portrait of Gall indicates a fair development of the coronal region, though not so great a predominance of the organs of this region, as those of some other portions of the head. The sentiment of Benevolence was probably the strongest. Dr. Fossati, in his discourse over the grave of Gall, was led to make the following remarks: "I have not yet alluded to the qualities of his heart—to the deep sentiment of justice, and the warmth and constancy of benevolence, by which he was distinguished. Time does not permit me to dwell on these qualities; but artists, young physicians, and many unfortunate persons of every condition, now testify by their tears the loss of a benefactor; and they do not expect soon to meet with another man who will lavish kindness with less ostentation, and greater readiness, good nature, and simplicity. These cannot sufficiently deplore his death; but they will make way for a moment to those rich patients, to princes, to the representatives of kings, whom his art restored to health, and allow them to bear witness before posterity how often Dr. Gall came to implore their aid in solacing and assisting unfortunate but deserving men of talent, whom his own means were inadequate to relieve. Let these personages tell us, too, whether Gall ever solicited their protection for himself, or if he did not always beg it for others! And you, also, relatives and friends, who have lived with him in the intimacy of domestic life, add your voice to mine, and say if he ever refused his help to a suffering being?" The latter part of the paragraph refers to a charge brought against Gall by his enemies for being selfish in pecuniary matters. But there is reason to believe that there was more of falsehood than truth in the accusation.

The views of Gall respecting God and religion, were no less philosophical than original. " Every where," says he, " and in all times, man, pressed by the feeling of dependence by which he is completely surrounded, is forced to recognise at every instant the limits of his power, and to avow to himself that his fate is in the hands of a Superior Power. Hence the unanimous consent of all people to adore a Supreme Being; hence the ever-felt necessity of recurring to Him, of honouring Him, and rendering homage to His superiority." Thus Gall recognised God like a philosopher. He was indignant only against the abuses that men practised upon the credulity of the people ; against those who make of religion a refinement of power, of ignorance, of slavery, and corruption. He was indignant against the persecutions which sectarians of different faith carry on against their fellow-men, in the name of God and religion. He was indignant against all these abuses, because he loved the human race, and desired its happiness.

We shall now close this article by presenting some statements respecting the merits of Gall as a discoverer and a philosopher. It has been our object thus far, in giving the history of his life and the analysis of his character, to state *only matters of fact*. While, on the one hand, self-respect and regard to duty, growing out of the relations which man sustains to his fellow-men and to his Creator, forbid that we should, either through ignorance or prejudice, mete out praise to any one beyond the measure of true merit and desert ; on the other hand, truth and justice imperiously demand that the claims of real merit and worth should be duly acknowledged and correctly stated. Though there is good reason to believe, that in no sphere whatever are the principles of justice oftener and more flagrantly violated than in this.

The influence of ignorance and prejudice, of envy and pride, of bigotry and dogmatism, are almost omnipotent; and have been repeatedly arrayed in all their magnitude against some of the most splendid discoveries ever made, as well as against the greatest benefactors of the world. The principal agents concerned in these discoveries have suffered all manner of obloquy and reproach—have been branded, while living, with epithets the most abusive and opprobrious —and have gone to their graves comparatively unknown and unrewarded, leaving it for posterity to vindicate their claims, and do justice to their names.   The treatment to Dr. Gall, and the reception of his doctrines, have not differed materially, in spirit and character from the history of the discoveries of Gallileo and Jenner, of Harvey and Newton.   We might enter into a particular statement of facts, in confirmation of this remark, but our present design and limits will not permit such a digression.

The following testimonials will show what have been the opinions of some, *at least*, respecting the character and merits of Gall, who personally knew him ; and of others who are thoroughly acquainted with the nature, and can appreciate the importance, of his discoveries. The first is from M. Hufeland, one of the most scientific men that Germany has produced for the last century.   His opinion of Gall and his discoveries is as follows :—" It is with great pleasure, and much interest, that I have heard this estimable man himself expound his new doctrine.   I am fully convinced that he ought to be regarded as one of the most remarkable phenomena of the eighteenth century, and that his doctrine should be considered as forming one of the boldest and most important steps in the study of the kingdom of nature.

" One must see and hear him, to learn to appreciate a man completely exempt from prejudices, from charlatanism, from deception and from metaphysical reveries.   Gifted with a rare spirit of observation, with great penetration, and a sound judgment—identified, as it were, with nature—become her confidant from a constant intercourse with her—he has collected, in the kingdom of organised beings, a multitude of signs of phenomena, which nobody had remarked till now, or which had been only superficially observed.   He has combined them in an ingenious manner—has discovered the relations which establish analogy between them—has learned their signification—has drawn consequences and established truths, which are so much the more valuable, that, being based on experience, they emanate from nature herself.   He ascribes his discoveries solely to the circumstance of his having given himself up ingeniously and without reserve to the study of nature—following her in all her gradations, from the simplest results of her productive power to the most perfect. It is an error, therefore, to give this doctrine the name of a system, and to judge of it as such.   True naturalists are not men to form systems.   Their observations would not be sufficiently accurate, if they were prompted by a systematic theory, and realities would not square with the various limits of their notions.   Hence the doctrine of Gall is not, and cannot be, any thing except a combination of instructive natural phenomena, of which a part consists at present only of fragments, and of which he makes known the immediate consequences."

Dr. Roget, in the "Encyclopædia Britannica," speaking of the discovery of Harvey on the circulation of the blood, has the following remarks :—" On its being made known to the world, it met with the most violent opposition ; and so inveterate were the prejudices of the public, that the practice of Harvey was considerably diminished in consequence of his discovery. It was remarked, that no physician who had passed the age of forty would admit the truth of a doctrine so much at variance with all the systems in which he had been educated. Envious of his growing reputation, many of his cotemporaries had recourse to all kinds of sophistry, with the view of detracting from his merit. They at first vehemently contested the truth of the doctrine ; but afterwards, when forced to admit it by the decisive evidence adduced in its support, they changed their ground of attack, and alleged that the merit of the discovery did not belong to Harvey, the circulation having been known even to the ancients. But vain were all the efforts of envy and detraction to lessen that fame which will command the admiration of all future ages." Nearly all these facts (though penned by an *anti-phrenologist*) are equally true in relation to Gall. Some ingenious writers, after opposing Gall's doctrines with the greatest hostility, and with all the sophistry and arguments which they could command, have attempted to arrest from him the claims of discovery ; and maintain that they belong to other philosophers. It has been asserted in the Edinburgh Review, as well as elsewhere, that Gall borrowed much of his knowledge from Reil and Loder, two celebrated German anatomists. But it so happened, that the authors of these statements were not aware of the opinions which these very anatomists had previously expressed on this subject. In the sixth volume of Dr. Gall's large work on the "Functions of the Brain," &c., at page 303, the following extracts are given from a publication by Professor Bischoff, who was well acquainted with Reil and Loder. "The worthy Reil," says Professor Bischoff, "who, as a profound anatomist and a judicious physiologist, stands in no need of my commendation, has declared, in rising above all the littleness of egotism, ' that he had found more in the dissections of the brain performed by Dr. Gall, than he had conceived it possible for a man to discover in his whole lifetime !'"

"Loder," continues Professor Bischoff, "who certainly does not yield the palm to any living anatomist, has expressed the following opinion of the discoveries of Gall, in a letter to my excellent friend, Professor Hufeland. ' Now that Gall has been at Halle, and that I have had an opportunity not only of being present at his lectures, but of dissecting along with him, sometimes alone, and sometimes in the presence of Reil, and several other of my acquaintances, nine human brains, and fourteen brains of animals, I consider myself to be qualified, and to have a right, to give an opinion regarding his doctrine.   The discoveries of Gall in the anatomy of the brain are of the highest importance; and many of them possess such a degree of evidence, that I cannot conceive how any one with good eyes can mistake them.'   After enumerating several discoveries respecting the interior structure of this organ, Loder continues—'These alone would be sufficient to render the name of Gall immortal; they are the most important which have been made in anatomy, since the discovery of the system of the absorbent vessels.   The unfolding of the brain is an excellent thing.   What have we not to expect from it, as well as to the ulterior discoveries to which it opens the way?   I am ashamed and angry with myself for having, like the rest, during thirty years, sliced down hundreds of brains, as we cut a cheese, and *for having missed seeing the forest on account of the great number of trees which it contained.*   But it serves no purpose to distress one's self, and to be ashamed.   The better way is to lend an ear to truth, and to learn what we do not know.   I acknowledge with Reil, that I have found in Dr. Gall more than I believed it possible for a man to discover in his lifetime.' "

The two following testimonials are from individuals who commenced their investigations on phrenology with the strongest prejudices, but probably now understand the science, in all its bearings, better than any other two men living.   They are therefore competent judges of the merits of Gall.

Dr. Vimont, a distinguished French anatomist, commenced his labours with the express purpose of refuting the doctrines of Gall and Spurzheim.   After immense exertions, he was obliged to declare himself a phrenologist, by means of the very facts which he had collected to subvert the science.   It is stated that he had two thousand facts, more than twelve hundred skulls, sawn open, wax casts of fifty brains, and three hundred designs, drawn out with the greatest accuracy.   He worked indefatigably during six years, and expended upwards of twelve thousand francs in procuring his specimens.   Dr. Vimont, in his large work on Comparative Phrenology, after speaking of the works of Gall, expresses his opinion of him thus:—"I saw that I had made acquaintance with a man removed above his fellowmen; one of those whom envy is always eager to thrust aside from the position to which they are called by their genius, and against whom she employs the weapons of cowardice and hypocrisy.   The great qualities which seemed to me to render Gall conspicuous, were extensive cerebral capacity, great penetration good sense, and varied acquirements.   The indifference which I at first had entertained for his writings, was soon converted into a feeling of profound veneration."

Mr. George Combe, in his "System of Phrenology," page 625, pays the following just tribute of respect to the memory of Dr. Gall. "The discoveries of the revolution of the globe, and the circulation of the blood, were splendid displays of genius, interesting and beneficial to mankind; but their results, compared with the consequences which must inevitably follow Dr. Gall's discovery of the functions of the brain, (embracing, as it does, the true theory of the animal, moral, and intellectual constitution of man,) sink into relative insignificance. Looking forward to the time when the real and ultimate effects of Dr. Gall's discovery shall be fully recognised, I cannot entertain a doubt that posterity will manifest as eager a desire to render honour to his memory, as his cotemporaries have shown to treat him with indignity and contempt. Like many other benefactors of mankind, he has died without his merits being acknowledged, or his discoveries rewarded by the 'great in literature and science' of his own age; but he possessed the consciousness of having presented to the world one of the most valuable discoveries that ever graced the annals of philosophy, and enjoyed the delight of having opened up to mankind a career of improvement, physical, moral, and intellectual, to which the boldest imagination can at present prescribe no limits. This appears to be the reward which Providence assigns to men eminently gifted with intellectual superiority; and we may presume that it is wisely suited to their nature. A great duty remains for posterity to perform to the memory of Dr. Gall."

ARTICLE II.

PHRENOLOGY AND DIVINE TRUTH.

BY H. T. JUDSON, M. D., NEW YORK.

THE relation which exists between phrenology and revelation is a very interesting one, and one which has not yet received all that attentive consideration which its importance demands. It is desirable, we think, that each should hold its proper relative place in our regard, and that we should not expect the one to disclose such truths as properly belong to the other. Phrenology is not the Gospel, nor does it pretend to be. All that is incumbent on its defenders is, to show that it does not contradict the Scriptures, and is not in opposition with the best interests of mankind. It does not reveal the nature of mind itself, nor pretend to decide upon its existence separate from matter. We know that the brain and the mind are connected during this life, and phrenology no more leads to materialism than any other system of philosophy which admits this connection.

Phrenology wisely leaves our enquiries respecting immortality, and our future destiny, to be answered by a knowledge of a different kind, derived altogether from higher sources, even from the writings of holy men of old, inspired by the spirit of truth. Thus the Gospel comes in and dispels every doubt; for by it life and immortality are brought to light. A person may believe in phrenology, and disbelieve in revelation, just as one may receive any other system of mental philosophy and still be a skeptic; or, on the contrary, he may be persuaded of the truth of phrenology, and at the same time, cordially, the doctrine of Scripture. All we wish to contend for on this point, is that there is no logical discrepancy between believing in the Bible and believing in phrenology. The present writer fully and firmly believes in both and during study and observation, for nearly twenty years, has seen nothing to alter or lessen his faith in either.

Admit, in the first place, that phrenology unfolds the true constitution of the human mind, and then, in addition, receive all that the Scriptures teach respecting sin, redemption, forgiveness, regeneration influence of the Holy Spirit, eternal life, and evangelical obedience and you will have the highest and noblest exhibition of the wisdom and goodness of the Creator in the formation of man, and in providing for all his wants as an animal, moral, and intellectual being. Now no mere system of philosophy will reveal all this, and phrenology comes short in common with the rest. Hence the need of Divine Revelation; and blessed is he who is not offended in it. Phrenology is, in our opinion, matter of human research, resulting in science; the Gospel is a revelation from God of the most momentous and interesting truth, worthy of all acceptation.

Some philosophers have said that "man is a spirit." We think this is going too far; and that of the Almighty alone—that great and all-pervading spirit—can this be truly predicated. "God is a spirit," is the sublime announcement of his being and character, made by Him who came into the world to make known the nature and perfections of the Eternal. But we are ready and willing to allow that there "is a spirit in man," which, by the will of its Author, is incorruptible and immortal. Phrenology by no means asserts that mind is composed of matter, or that it cannot exist and act independent of matter, but merely that in this present life it is manifested only through the organs of the faculties in the brain. It does not compel us to deny its existence as a separate entity, or to question the immortality brought to light in the Gospel. Phrenologists of sound reasoning powers are as sincere believers in the truth of Christianity as any other class of philosophers. Phrenology, therefore, does not lead to materialism, nor will it conduct its votaries to any thing but truth.

We believe that the brain is a congeries of organs, each of which organs is subservient to a particular function of the mind, and we regard this discovery as one of great value, and destined eventually to have great influence on education, legal study, medicine, and the general welfare of the human race; we at the same time are free to acknowledge that our understanding of the mind is imperfect, and in all probability it will always remain so, more or less, but we claim that phrenology has shed not a little light over the mental and moral constitution of man, and unfolded to him the true principles of his being. And this is high praise, and sufficient to immortalise the names of its discoverers—GALL and SPURZHEIM. When we reflect upon the capacity of the mind—when we remember its wide range of noble thoughts and pure feelings—when we anticipate its future destiny in the realisation of its aspiring hopes, we cannot but value highly the inestimable benefits which these gifted individuals have bestowed on their species, in revealing the mental constitution. Here is the region of truth, but all around us is a wide and stormy ocean; the region of false and deceptive appearances, where floating clouds indicate apparently the position of new countries, but while they delude the mariner with the hope of discoveries, they involve him in endless adventures from which it is difficult for him to escape, and which never lead him to the possession of truth and certainty.

Having showed that phrenology does not stand opposed to the Scripture doctrine of immortality, we shall offer a few remarks upon the objection of fatalism, which is sometimes brought against our science. Here we might content ourselves with saying, that neither phrenology, nor any other system of philosophy, throws any very clear light over the disputed question of the freedom of the will. All we know, is that every effect is determined by some cause, and the cause of volition is motive acting on the will. The will follows the strongest motive, and thus presents us with an opportunity to urge the most powerful arguments upon the intellect, when we would modify or change the feelings or conduct. Is this fatalism? For example, if a person injures another, Combativeness and Destructiveness would prompt to revenge; but by reminding the sufferer of the excellence of Benevolence and the dictates of conscience, we might persuade him to forgive, and in this manner the superior sentiments would have the supremacy. So far phrenology could go; but the Gospel, by referring

the injured person to the precepts and example of the Saviour, woul
present still higher and more powerful motives, and therefore mor
effectual ; yet it is evident that the will is, in either method, move
and directed by motives of some kind presented to the understandin;
This is the sum of all we know on this subject, and the warm dispi
tations of philosophers and theologians cannot advance our knowledg
to any practical advantage.

Men have been influenced on this point by their feelings, rathe
than by their reason ; and it is not wonderful that contention respec
ing free-will, grace, predestination, and kindred topics, should hav
been more ardent than their real importance warrants. We aim
keeping this article free from any taint of sectarianism, and therefor
shall enter no further into the controversy ; but be content wil
observing that, although we may believe, as phrenologists, in th
freedom of the mind in moral subjects, yet there may be a questic
whether this freedom extends to spiritual and holy things. This di
tinction, perhaps, has not been sufficiently attended to by those wl
have contended either for or against free agency. Practically, phren
logy teaches us to give our moral power the ascendency, and
subdue and regulate our lower propensities. It is useless to deny th
we possess inclinations which sometimes entice us to evil, as all exp
rience proves their existence. Phrenology professes to be establishe
on facts, and boldly asks her opponents to refute her positions t
showing that what she thus claims as facts are not facts, or to nullit
her arguments by proving that she draws illogical inferences fro:
those facts. This is surely not an unreasonable demand.

Are we to be told, at this period in the history of physiology, th
there is no dependence of mind on matter ? A single example w:
suffice to illustrate a principle, and we select one from M. Richeran
who, by-the-by, is not favourable to our science. "A woman, abo
fifty years of age, had an extensive carious affection of the skull ; th
left parietal bone was destroyed, in the greatest part of its extent, ar
left uncovered a pretty considerable portion of the *dura-mater*, |
membrane covering the brain. Nothing was easier than to ascerta
the existence of a complete correspondence between the motions (
the brain and the beats of the pulse. I wiped off the sanious matt
which covered the *dura-mater*, and I at the same time questioned tl
patient on her situation ; as she felt no pain from the compression (
the cerebral mass, I pressed down lightly the pledget of lint, and c
a sudden the patient, who was answering my questions rationall;
stopped in the midst of a sentence ; but she went on breathing, ar
her pulse continued to beat. I withdrew the pledget, she sa
nothing ; I asked her if she remembered my question ? she said no

Seeing the experiment was without pain or danger, I repeated it three times, and thrice I suspended all feeling and all intellect.'' So much for Richerand. The brain presides over the animal motions so far as those motions depend on volition, and is also essential in its integrity to the regular activity of the intellectual and moral faculties, while the mind and body form one person. We see no danger in this admission to the interests of morality or religion, but think that phrenology harmonises in many respects with the precepts of Christianity, in inculcating forbearance, justice, kindness, charity, and other virtues. Let us endeavour to discover and to cultivate truth of every kind, and we need not fear that there will result any conflict between natural knowledge and Divine Revelation.

In order to show that our views are not singular, and unsupported by the authority of other phrenologists, as well as for the justice and truth of the observations, we extract a few paragraphs from the "*Constitution of Man.*'' "The relation between Scripture and phrenology,'' says Mr. Combe, "appears to me to be the following:

"The communications of the Bible may be divided into two great classes—the one relating to matter which the human intellect could never by its own powers have discovered, and the other consisting of descriptions of beings existing in this world, and of rules of duty to be observed by those beings, which appear to me to be subjected to the examination of every ordinary understanding. To the former class belong the character and offices of Jesus Christ; while in the latter are comprehended human nature itself, such as it now exists, and all moral and religious duties which bear relation to human happiness in this world.''

"The Calvinist, Arminian, and Unitarian, entertain views widely different regarding the character and offices of Jesus Christ. The doctrine of the natural law and phrenology can throw no light whatever on the subject, and therefore it would be a mere waste of words to mix up a discussion of the one with a treatise of the other; and this observation is equally applicable to every announcement in the Bible regarding matters which are not permanent portions of ordinary nature.''

"The Bible, however, contains numerous descriptions of human character, and numerous rules for the guidance of human conduct; all of which may be compared with the constitution of the mind as it is revealed to us by observation, and with the inference which may be drawn from that constitution concerning its most becoming and most advantageous mode of action. The result of this comparison appears to me to establish the harmony between phrenology and Scripture.'

ARTICLE III.

PHRENOLOGY SUPPORTED BY SCIENTIFIC MEN.

It is very evident, from many notices of phrenology in books an periodicals, as well as from frequent observations made both publicl and privately, that there are large numbers in the community who al entirely unacquainted with the present state of the science, and th character of its advocates. And this remark includes not only th ignorant and unlettered, but applies with equal force to many who al deservedly distinguished for their talents and attainments in the high walks of life. In most cases, there may be some reasonable apolog for want of knowledge on this subject, but there can be no vali reason for exposing this ignorance in a manner which neither re: self-respect or regard to truth can approve, nor true wisdom an philosophy sanction. We hope the time is nearly past in our country when this science is to be condemned, without the least show of argu ment or knowledge on the subject; or when its advocates are to t branded as quacks and unscientific men. Such unqualified assertion: and groundless charges, reflect no credit on the integrity or intell gence of their authors.

That our readers may know something about the standing an character of the advocates of phrenology in Great Britain, we al induced to present the following facts. At the meeting of the Britis Association, last year, for the advancement of science, large numbel of phrenologists were present, as members of that body. This asse ciation meets annually, and comprises the most scientific men i England, Scotland, and Ireland. It is divided into several sections, i each of which committees are appointed to make reports on the stal and prospects of the various departments of science. During th sitting of this society at Newcastle, 1838, a public meeting was calle by the phrenologists present, and arrangements were made for forn ing a phrenological association, which should meet at the same tim and place with the British Association. These explanations al deemed necessary, in order that the reader may understand som statements and allusions made in the following extract from the 58t number of the British Phrenological Journal.

The claims of phrenology to be ranked amongst the sciences wei discussed in a notice of Mr. Noble's work, in the last volume of th journal, and were shown to be valid. The proposal to form an asse ciation exclusively for the advancement of this science, has induce us now to give a finishing blow to an old objection, still frequentl brought against phrenology, but which it would be well for the opponents of the system to cease adducing in the present day; because, being no longer true, it must often recoil upon him who urges it against the phrenologists. This is the false assertion, that few or no persons of ability, or of any scientific reputation, lend countenance to the phrenological doctrines. There was a time when the assertion might have been made with truth in this country. Twenty years ago, scarcely a dozen names of passable repute could have been drawn from the list of British phrenologists. Perhaps Leach and Parry were amongst those best known at that time; but even then several other persons had commenced their phrenological studies, who have since risen to eminence. The objection has now quite ceased to be true, and never was a valid reason for rejection. But ideas will still linger among the less informed, (both the novices and those whose increasing age causes them to drop into arrear in their knowledge,) long after they have been given up by more intelligent persons; and accordingly, scores, perhaps hundreds, still successfully reiterate this assertion as the readiest means of getting the subject dismissed in contempt from the minds of others, whose want of correct information upon it thus renders them the blind dupes of confident defamers.

Phrenologists may now boldly meet the objection by a counter statement; and if the contempt of phrenology, formerly shown by scientific men, deterred other persons from attending to the subject, the respect evinced by several of them at the present day should have the effect of recommending it to attention. In a recent number of this journal, we quoted the Monthly Magazine, which roundly asserted, that "not a single man of sterling genius, not a single literary or scientific person of real eminence, has deigned to become a promoter of phrenology; nay, amongst the *thousands of so-called phrenologists*, scarcely a dozen of them could cut a respectable figure in any assembly of *third-rate talent*." In the present number we have quoted the admission of an opponent (Dr. Roget), probably more competent to speak on this matter than is an anonymous tale-writer in a magazine, to the effect that "*many* men of eminent talents and extensive knowledge" have avowed their belief in phrenology. These must have place amongst the "so-called phrenologists;" and to admit or to deny the fact of men of talent being found amongst phrenologists, would thus seem to depend pretty much upon the information and veracity of the writer. But what is to be the test of "real eminence" in science or literature? Or of respectability of figure, sufficient for an "assembly of third-rate talent?" Before proceeding to suggest some tests applicable to Englishmen, amongst whom we do not altogether relish the invidious duty of choosing a jury of *respectables*, we shall copy a dozen names from the list of members of the Phrenological Society of Paris, as published on its institution, in the year 1831 :—

ANDRAL, Professor in the Faculty of Medicine of Paris.
BLONDEAU, Dean of the Faculty of Law of Paris.
BROUSSAIS, Professor in the Faculty of Medicine, and First Physician of the *Val-de-Grace.*
CLOQUET, Professor in the Faculty of Medicine of Paris, Surgeon to the Hospital of Saint Louis.
COMTE, Professor of Philosophy in the Athenæum.
DAVID, Sculptor, Member of the Institute.
JULLIEN, Editor of the *Revue Encyclopédique.*
LACOSTE, King's Counsel.
LENOBLE, Head of the department of Public Instruction.
PONCELET, Professor in the Faculty of Law of Paris.
ROYER, First Secretary at the *Jardin des Plantes.*
SANSON, Surgeon to the *Hôtel Dieu.*

Here, in one phrenological society, during its first year, were the full dozen of persons surely respectable enough for " an assembly of third-rate talent;" and we have some notion that amongst these twelve there are included more than " a single literary or scientific person of real eminence." If not, we must enquire what test our magazine-writer would apply by way of discovering the presence of "real eminence" or " third-rate talent?" And now for the tests at home. Are the professorships in British Universities to be esteemed as any evidence of ability or knowledge, in the persons filling them? The following names may be adduced as examples made apparent by this test :—

DR. ELLIOTSON, Professor of Medicine, London.
DR. GREGORY, Professor of Chemistry, Glasgow.
DR. HUNTER, Professor of Anatomy, Glasgow.
DR. NICHOL, Professor of. Astronomy, Glasgow.
REV. DAVID WELSH, Professor of Divinity, Edinburgh.
MR. WHEATSTONE, Professor of Natural Philosophy, London.

Is the holding of similar appointments in Ireland to be taken as a test? The following names may then be added :—

DR. EVANSON, Professor of Medicine, R. College of Surgeons.
DR. JACOB, Professor of Anatomy, R. College of Surgeons.
MR. LLOYD, Professor of Natural Philosophy, Dublin.
MR. LONGFIELD, Professor of Political Economy, Dublin.
DR. MAUNSELL, Professor of Midwifery, R. College of Surgeons.
DR. MONTGOMERY, Professor of Midwifery, College of Physicians.

Are we to seek amongst the Fellows of the Royal Societies of London or Edinburgh, for persons supposed to be competent to pass muster with other scientific men? We again name half a dozen in example of this test :—

Mr. Bindon Blood, F. R. S. E.	Dr. Patrick Neill, F. R. S. E.
Dr. W. T. Edwards, F. R. S. L.	Dr. D. B. Reid, F. R. S. E.
Sir G. S. Mackenzie, F. R. S. L. & E.	Mr. H. T. M. Witham, F. R. S. I

Are we to seek amongst the fellows of other chartered and scientif societies in England, for men likely to " cut a respectable figure i any assembly of third-rate talent?" If so, add the following name to those given above :—

Mr. John Buddle, F. G. S.	Capt. Maconochie, F. G. S.
Dr. T. J. M. Forster, F. L. S.	Mr. W. C. Trevelyan, F. G. S.
Mr. William Hutton, F. G. S.	Mr. H. C. Watson, F. L. S.

Are members of the Royal Irish Academy held of any weight i the question? Then add the following :—

Dr. James Armstrong.	Mr. Richard Carmichael.
Mr. W. W. Campbell.	Professor Harrison.
Mr. Andrew Carmichael.	Dr. Henry Marsh.

Is the authorship of approved works, more particularly those cor nected with the medical or political philosophy of mind, any test o ability and fitness to judge the merits of a science of mind, founde on organisation? The following half dozen writers may be named :—

Dr. E. Barlow, author of Essays in the Cyclopædia of Practical Medicine
Mr. W. A. F. Browne, author of Lectures on Insanity.
Mr. R. Cobden, author of the Treatises by a "Manchester Manufacturer.
Sir W. C. Ellis, author of the Treatise on Insanity.
Mr. C. Maclaren, editor of the Scotsman.
Dr. W. Weir, lately co-editor of the Glasgow Medical Journal.

If we may also refer to the editors of esteemed medical periodicals or other able journals, *countenancing* phrenology, then we cite th editors of the following :—

The Analyst.	The Lancet.
The Brit. and For. Med. Review.	The Medico-Chirurgical Review
Chambers's Edinburgh Journal.	The Naturalist.

And whilst alluding to editorial personages, we shall give the name of the six gentlemen who, at different times, conducted the forme series of the Phrenological Journal, before it came into the hands o its present proprietor. For ability and general information, they wi not sink in a comparison with any other of our half dozens :—

Dr. Andrew Combe.	Dr. Richard Poole.
Mr. George Combe.	Mr. William Scott.
Mr. Robert Cox.	Mr. James Simpson.

Our ambition rises as we write, and though the first intention wa that of giving only a dozen names, the enumeration beyond ha already quadrupled the first dozen, and, could space be convenientl allowed, we should be tempted to quadruple these forty-eight. If w

have omitted the names of many able phrenologists in Britain ar
elsewhere (indeed, as phrenologists, more able than some of thos
who are included), or of men eminent in other departments of knov
ledge who countenance phrenology, it has been occasioned by th
impossibility of naming all, and by the limitation into groups of half
dozen each, according to the several tests proposed.

Whilst we are thus excluding several very able phrenologists, v
have still no hesitation in saying, that the preceding forty-eight nam
belong to persons, who, taken together, are as respectable for inte
lectual ability and general information, as would be any forty-eig
selected chemists, geologists, botanists, zoologists, or cultivators
other sciences respectively. Try the phrenologists on other subjec
than mere phrenology ; and also try the chemists, the geologists, tl
botanists, the zoologists, on other subjects than mere chemistr
geology, botany, or zoology (as the case may be), and we are wide
mistaken if the phrenologists would not be found at least the compee
of the latter. It may be said that these are not all of them perso
particularly devoted to the study of phrenology. This would
true ; but let one dozen devoted phrenologists be selected from tl
forty-eight, and subjected to the same ordeal with one dozen of tl
chemists, &c., and the result would be still more in favour of tl
phrenologists. But, notwithstanding this willingness to submit t
supporters of phrenology to any equal test in comparison with othel
we must still maintain that the proper estimate for scientific men,
the ability and success with which they pursue their own espec
studies. It would be as ridiculous—nay, it would truly be *mo*
ridiculous—to measure the abilities of a phrenologist by his kno
ledge of chemistry, as to estimate the talents of a chemist by l
phrenological information.

Before concluding these remarks, we shall yet resort to one oth
test, afforded by the last meeting of the British Association, as givi
very conclusive proof that *other* scientific men do look on the phren
logists as proper associates for themselves in their scientific investig
tions. That the proposed phrenological association, mentioned
the preceding article, should have been commenced exclusively l
members of the British Association *for the advancement of scien*
is in itself something very like evidence that phrenology is zealous
supported by persons evincing a considerable interest in other scie
tific studies ; because the British Association has hitherto shunn
the subject of phrenology, and has thus repelled rather than attract
phrenologists, who must have joined the association from otl
motives than the love of this department of science. But me
membership of that association is so much a matter of course to tho

desiring it, that it cannot be looked upon as any indication of the
individual members being received as fit associates of their co-members
Yet, when we find the phrenological members sitting on the com
mittees, or filling higher offices in the management of the sections
(which is the *scientific*) business of the association, it must be regarded
as indisputable evidence that they have claims to respect on othe
grounds than those of their phrenological acquirements ; that they are
not phrenologists alone (which, in our eyes, is their highest qualifica
tion), but are also the fellows of other scientific men in their own
several departments.   In looking over the list of office-bearers in the
Sections, published in the Athenæum, we recognised the names of
several persons publicly known as phrenologists, and also those of
some others who express favourable opinions of the science in private
society.   The latter we shall not enumerate, lest it should be unplea
sant to the parties ; but the names of the sixteen following gentlemen
have been before the public on other occasions than the present, as
those of persons favourable to phrenology ; and some of whom are
well known to be particularly devoted to the study of that science.

> Mr. J. Buddle, Vice-President of Section C.
> Mr. W. Cargill, Secretary of Section F.
> Mr. B. Donkin, Vice-President of Section G.
> Mr. J. Fife, Vice-President of Section E.
> Mr. T. M. Greenhow, Secretary of Section E.
> Professor Gregory, Committee of Section B.
> Mr. J. I. Hawkins, Committee of Section G.
> Mr. W. Hutton, Committee of Section C.
> Mr. W. Morrison, Committee of Section E.
> Dr. P. Neill, Committee of Section D.
> Professor Nichol, Committee of Section A.
> Dr. D. B. Reid, Committee of Section B.
> Mr. W. C. Trevelyan, Secretary of Section C.
> Mr. H. C. Watson, Committee of Section D.
> Professor Wheatstone, Committee of Section A.
> Mr. H. T. M. Witham, Committee of Section C.

As there are seven sections, the average of publicly avowed phreno
logists exceeds two on each committee.   Were we to add others
whom we know to be favourable to the doctrines, but whose names
we have not seen publicly connected with them, the average would
exceed three on each.   It is to be borne in mind, however, that such
a test is highly disadvantageous to phrenologists, because, while
there is no *section for phrenological science*, its cultivators can be
received only on the score of their other attainments ; and this, as
before remarked, is a very trying test for scientific men who usually
achieve eminence by devoting their attention to some single depart
ment almost exclusively.   Accordingly, none of the sixteen persons
named in this list are at the summit in the respective departments in

which they are placed, because they are not so exclusive in their studies.   Were we to single out the acknowledged head of any other science, in general attainments and philosophical character of mind he would not excel our indisputably first phrenologist—MR. GEORGE COMBE.

Let it be remembered, that we are very far from upholding the ability and respectability of all phrenologists "so-called."   Phrenology having become popular, and being (in the eyes of the ignorant) a sort of mysterious fortune-telling, lots of disreputable charlatans make use of it for their own purposes of gulling others; and probably three-fourths of the public (but self-elected) teachers of phrenology are persons who would be shunned, not by men of science only, but by every man of respectability and gentlemanly feeling.   The cause of this lies with the public, who encourage them by offering a premium to empiricism and knavery.   It is the same in politics, in medicine, and in religion; only that the recognised bodies of statesmen, of physicians, and of clergy or ministers of sects, throw the quacks more into the background.

ARTICLE IV.

CASE OF MENTAL DERANGEMENT.

To the Editor of the American Phrenological Journal.

Sir,—

I have been informed by Dr. Estes, of this place, that he has, in his correspondence with you, mentioned a case of mental derangement, the history of which fell under my observation in conducting the defence of a suit at law, and that you think it is of sufficient importance to merit a place in your Journal.   In accordance with the doctor's request, I will give you a brief history of the case.   The persons from whose testimony the facts were gathered, are resident citizens of the county of Noxubie, Miss.   The attending physician, Dr. Caleb Greenwood, is a gentleman of intelligence, and experience in his profession.   It is much to be regretted, however, that his enquiries in the case in question were made with an eye single to his own profession, and that his acquaintance with phrenology was not sufficient to induce him to invoke its aid in ascertaining the nature and tracing the progress of the disease; nor to watch over the manifestations of the disease with a view of throwing light upon the science.   Aided by an acquaintance with phrenology, with his intelligence and nicely discriminating powers of mind, the doctor could hav given to the world one of the most beautiful illustrations of the truth of the science which has ever been published. The other witnesses examined were plain people, of high moral excellence.

The person diseased was a negro boy, about nineteen years of age. He had from birth been the property of the family of Calloways, in Noxubie county. Upon the death of the father of the family, it became necessary for his adminstrator to sell the boy. Francis Calloway, son and administrator of the deceased, accordingly sold him at public auction, on the 6th of January, 1837, and, to enhance his price, warranted him to be sound in mind and body. Abner Calloway, also a son of the deceased, became the purchaser. The suit spoken of was instituted by the administrator to recover the purchase money. The sole defence set up, was that at the time of the sale the boy was not sound in mind.

Mrs. Harber, (formerly Miss Calloway,) a daughter of the deceased, testified that she had known the boy from his birth, he had grown up to manhood in her father's family; from a child he had manifested an excellent disposition—had always been humble, obedient, submissive —had never been known to be impudent or insolent to any of the family—and had been uniformly kind and benevolent to his fellow-servants; that for the first time which had come to her knowledge, he broke through his good conduct about ten days before the day of sale. At that time he became quarrelsome and turbulent among the negroes on the farm, whipped the women and boys, and was disposed to fight on every occasion. Mrs. Harber found it necessary to interfere; she told the boy that if he did not desist, she would have him punished as soon as Mr. Harber returned home. Upon this, he used insolent and threatening language towards her. The witness stated that she was astonished at his conduct; that she attributed it, however, at the time to the influence of sudden passion, but after his subsequent disease and death, she had no doubt that the fatal malady had then made its first aggression. Several other witnesses were then examined, whose names I do not recollect. They concurred with Mrs. Harber in the character which she gave the boy. They knew nothing more than what took place on the day of sale. The boy on that day seemed to be sound in every respect; but after he was bid off, he sprang from the block on which he had been placed, exclaiming that he was as big as Jesus Christ, and behaved otherwise in an unusual manner. The witnesses were surprised that the boy should so far depart from his accustomed humility and decorum; none of them, however, thought at the time of attributing it to a diseased affection of the mind; but after the boy was taken with his subsequent derangement, they believed that he must on that day have been under the influence of disease.   The remaining part of the boy's history was given by Dr. Greenwood, Mrs. Harber, and two other witnesses, whose names I do not recollect.   Ten or twelve days after the sale, the boy left his work, came home with his hands clasped behind his head and neck, and complained of pain in the back part of his head. He was sent to Dr. Greenwood, who then happened to be in the neighbourhood.   Bleeding gave the boy relief, and the doctor sent him home without examining into the nature of his disease.   About two weeks after this, the doctor, who lived at a distance of ten miles, was called on to attend him.   Upon examination, he found that the boy was labouring under sub-acute inflammation of the posterior portion of the brain, attended with constant priapism.   Some days after this, the boy was seized with a similar passion for fighting to that spoken of by Mrs. Harber.   It differed from it, however, in violence and duration.   He became excessively rude and troublesome among the other negroes, fighting every one who gave him the slightest provocation ; whipped the women, and beat the young negroes cruelly. His owner, incensed at his conduct, punished him severely.   His passion for fighting instead of being subdued by punishment, dethroned reason, took under its control the reins of the propensities, and drove furiously onward, until all were lost in an ungovernable desire to kill every person who came into his presence—without regard to age, colour, or sex.   A desire to kill continued to be his ruling passion up to the hour of his death, which happened about ten weeks from the time first spoken of by Mrs. Harber.   Dr. Greenwood informed me that at every visit which he made to the boy after he first discovered his disease to be inflammation of the brain, the boy was labouring under priapism.   In a post-mortem examination, Dr. Greenwood found a quantity of water infused upon the brain, and a portion of the brain highly inflamed.   The doctor used a drawing of Spurzheim's head, mapped off into phrenological divisions for the purpose of pointing out to me the parts affected.   He pointed to Amativeness as being the most highly inflamed, next to Combativeness, and lastly to Destructiveness.   Amativeness was the seat of the disease, as was evinced by the presence of the pain in that region of the brain, and by constant priapism.   His passion for fighting appeared when Combativeness was invaded, and his desire to kill indicated that Destructiveness was also inflamed.

This case at the same time furnishes undoubted evidence of the truth of phrenology, and sets forth the science as furnishing the best means of tracing the progress of mental disease.

Respectfully, &c.,

RICHARD EVANS

Columbus, Miss., Sept. 1839.

ARTICLE V.

MEDICAL JURISPRUDENCE OF INSANITY.

BY A. DEAN, ESQ., ALBANY, N. Y.

The value of science, to the great mass of mankind, is derived fro the practical applications of which its truths are susceptible. Th learner may acquire it for its own sake, and receive the rewards o his toil in the pleasures that await the action and the acquisitions o his intellect. But God has not rested the progress of the race upo the simple desire of the mind for knowledge. He has also bestowe strong incentives, the effect of which is to render truths, apparentl the most abstruse, available for the most common purposes. He ha not left the astronomer satisfied with comprehending the movement of the universe, and the machinery of the heavens, until he coul bring that knowledge to earth, and give to human history an unfailin chronology, and open to industry and enterprise a path-way over th depths of the ocean. He has not left the investigator of that subtle but powerful agent of nature, electricity, to repose in quiet upon mere knowledge of its properties, until he could turn that knowledg to useful purposes, and protect, by a simple rod, from its destructiv action, all the delights that centre in his home.

The time has arrived when mind, equally with matter, presents it claims for consideration, not alone with the view of being studied i itself, but also in reference to its practical bearings. Among the mos prominent of these is insanity, or mental alienation; including as wel idiocy and imbecility, as the more active forms of mania. This sub ject is acquiring additional importance in proportion to the advanc of civilisation. The disease is, with very few exceptions, wholl confined to civilised nations. The causes that possess the mos efficiency in its production, are found the most active where man ha made great advancement. Its prevalence, as well as that of all ner vous diseases, in this country, is alarming. The proportion of insan in the United States has been set down as one in eight hundred. I some of the New England states, as one to two hundred and fifty The entire number of the insane in the United States has been com puted at fifty thousand.

There are many causes of a moral nature that are peculiarly opera tive in the production of this disease in this country. The grea freedom of thought and action allowed by law; the spirit of emulatio and rivalry, so rife among our citizens; the ever acting and changin scene of our politics; and, perhaps, more than all other causes com bined, that spirit of speculation that despises the ordinary means o accumulating property—that contemns the regular salutary laws impressed by God upon the condition of things—that seeks to crowd the events of years into the brief space of moments, and perils often the slow accumulations of a life upon the hurried transactions of an hour, are some, among the moral causes, that here push the different faculties into an unnaturally excessive action—that destroy their harmony of movement, and leave, bereft of its own guidance, the mind of the hapless sufferer. These are causes that exist, and must continue to, in the very nature of our institutions. They are interwoven in the frame-work of all our leading and original plans of policy, and are as utterly inseparable from our habits of thought, of feeling, and of action, as is the dead stillness of intellectual and moral death from the iron grasp of unqualified despotism.

The constant operation of these causes, followed by effects correspondingly extensive, loudly requires an examination into the nature and forms of mental alienation, with the view of applying to them sound and correct legal principles.

It is a melancholy truth that, until recently, the subject of insanity, neither in its causes, nor its curatives, nor the variety of its forms, nor the legal principles applicable to them, does not seem to have been properly understood. It has been regarded more especially as a judgment of God; as beyond the reach of remedies; as an infliction that should rightfully exclude its subject from all the privileges of social intercourse, and all sympathy with human feelings. In courts of justice, the plea of insanity has met with a cold reception. It has been there regarded rather as an attempt to escape the merited results of crime, than as furnishing a true reason why its consequences should not be visited upon its perpetrator. Many, it is to be feared, have been the miserable victims who have been doomed to expiate on the scaffold the acts, not crimes, which the derangement of their faculties has occasioned.

A brighter era for the insane, however, is fast opening. The last fifty years have probably done more for them than all the previous experience of the world put together. A new and more rational philosophy of mind has inspired more correct views in reference to its complex phenomena. It has been made a thing of observation as well as a creature of consciousness; and our knowledge of its different powers and capacities has been derived both from our feeling them in ourselves, and our perceiving their action in others. The fundamental error upon which all the old metaphysicians proceeded, of considering mind as a single general power, equally capable of efficient action in any direction, has been productive of innumerable mischiefs in metaphysics, in morals, in criminal legislation, in medical jurisprudence. Men rarely act right who reason wrong; and th erroneous judgments formed of mind and of men; the action of legis lative bodies, in the protection of rights by the punishment of wrongs the strong effort to embody the common sense of mankind in th correct application of sound legal principles to aberration of mind have all been so tinctured with that radical error, as to give rise t injurious consequences in the action and progress of society an civilisation.

Fortunately we have at last succeeded in discovering in the scienc of mind the elements of a system, definite in its proportions, under standable in its nature, harmonious in its results. The consequence attendant upon this discovery, render it of the first importance. No the least amongst these are the new views men have been led t entertain in regard to insanity. Its varied forms of exhibition wer anomalies for which the old metaphysical systems could neve account. They were totally inadequate to explain the operations ol mind in health, much more in disease. Whether the man though and felt, or the idiot simply vegetated, or the maniac raved, were alik inexplicable upon those numerous metaphysical systems that substitutec hypothesis for truth, consciousness for observation, and fancy for fact

No one can reasonably expect to comprehend derangement of minc without first understanding its healthy, normal action. At the founda tion of every thing mental, whether healthy or diseased, we recognis this great truth—that the mind is *not* a single general power, possess ing, originally, capacities every way equal; but is made up of a grea number of independent powers and faculties, each being a power, o: an instrument of thought or of feeling, possessing its own constitution its own specific function, and being independent of every other, excep as to its modes of operation, and certain mutual and reciprocal rela tions established between all. This truth is of vital importance ii reference to mental aberration, and to the legal consequences attachec to it.

It follows, as a resulting consequence, that each faculty does no necessarily manifest itself simultaneously with the others; that each may rest or act singly, and, what is of vast importance to medica jurisprudence, that each may singly preserve its own proper state ol health or derangement.

With the view of understanding aright the divisions introduced inte the forms of insanity, it is proper to remark that the entire mind, con sisting of intellectual, sentimental, and impulsive powers, is primarily divided into two great departments, intellectual and affective or moral the first including all the faculties that form ideas, and the second all those that feel emotions and furnish impulses.

The intellectual department is divided into two; the first including those faculties that perceive, that furnish facts and premises; the second, into those that reflect and reason, that make inferences and arrive at conclusions.

The affective or moral department has a similar division; the first including those faculties that impel, called the propensities; the second, those that experience emotions called the sentiments. Those included under the division of propensities are, 1, Alimentiveness, which gives the instinct of hunger and thirst; 2, Amativeness, producing physical love; 3, Combativeness, inspiring the desire to combat; 4, Destructiveness, impelling to destroy; 5, Secretiveness, giving birth to cunning and secrecy of movement; 6, Acquisitiveness, or the propensity to acquire; 7, Constructiveness, giving the desire to construct; 8, Imitation, producing the propensity to imitate.

The principal of the sentiments are, Self-esteem, giving the sentiment of self; Attachment, or Adhesiveness, inspiring social friendly feelings; Approbativeness, which experiences pleasure on receiving the approval of others; Cautiousness, inspiring fear; Conscientiousness, or the sentiment of right and wrong; Benevolence, giving birth to the feeling of general philanthrophy; Veneration, producing the sentiment of reverence; Hope, which lights up the future with buoyant expectation; Wonder, which delights in the marvellous; Wit, originating the mirthful; and Ideality, producing the sentiment of the sublime and the beautiful.

The intellectual faculties are as numerous as are the ultimate results, or simple definite elements afforded by external things on a careful and searching analysis, each faculty taking cognisance of each result. The faculty of Individuality, for example, takes cognisance of individual existences; that of Eventuality, of events; that of Causality, of the relation of cause and effect.

There are certain modes of activity in which some or all the faculties have a common action. The intellectual faculties—

1. *Perceive.*
2. *Remember* what they have *perceived.*
3. *Conceive* or *imagine* what they have *remembered.*
4. *Associate* what they have *perceived* and *remembered.*

The reflective powers possess judgment; and all the faculties in common possess *Consciousness*, which reveals to themselves their own operations.

Mind, in its healthy state, may well claim for itself much attentive consideration. A human being is a spectacle sublime in contemplation. Tenanting a globe every way adapted to his wants; linked by his physical constitution to the animal tribes, whom he subjects to his dominion, and compels to administer to his necessities; bound to his home and his species by those domestic and social ties that grow with his growth, and strengthen with his strength; and connected with high orders of intelligence, by those moral and religious bonds in which the moral elements of the world are bound together, he stands forth, in the perfection of his primitive powers, a glory, a wonder, and a marvel. His enquiring spirit has recognised no limits to investigation. He has questioned nature in her private work-shop, and attempted to wrench from her the secrets of existence under its ten thousand modified forms. In the volume of nature and life, he has deeply studied the hidden things of death and destiny.

In its state of aberration, mind presents an object of equally intense interest. Whether demented in idiocy, or frensied in madness, it claims investigation and legal protection.

The immediate seat of the disease is in the mind's organs—the brain. We infer this—

1. Because it is most reasonable in itself. As far as our experience extends through living nature, whatever is subject to disease is also subject to death. Indeed, death is the natural termination of disease. And even if it were not, there is nothing in the death of the body in itself calculated to cure a diseased mind; and hence no reason why it should not remain equally deranged after, as before, death.

2. Because it is then in harmony with all other diseased affections.

3. Because many of the causes producing it act directly on, or through the medium of the brain. Idiocy is often congenital, and results from defective development of the brain, or it may arise from structural derangement. Blows or injuries on the head may be productive of insanity.

4. Because of many of the physical phenomena attending insanity. The increased pulse, the furred tongue, the peculiar cast of countenance, and the preternatural heat, either of the whole brain or the particular organ affected, all indicate physical disease.

5. Because of the morbid phenomena often discoverable in the brains of those who have been afflicted with insanity. Necroscopical investigations have often resulted in the discovery of structural changes in the brains of the insane. This is more particularly the case when the derangement has been the cause of death.

While the primary seat of the disease is to be found in the material organ, yet the symptoms that indicate its existence are chiefly mental; and in their exhibitions partake of the nature of the faculty whose function is disordered. They consist in the aberration, exaltation, suppression, derangement, or perverted action of the primitive powers: and are, therefore, as numerous as are the faculties, and as various and diversified as they admit of morbid modes of action in their functions.

In judging of the existence of insanity in any given instance, we are to compare the mind alleged to be insane, not with other minds, but with itself in its sane state. Where the cautious become daring; the timid, bold; the humane, cruel; the peaceful, combative; or wherever any marked change becomes obvious, in any of the exhibitions of mind, a strong inference is furnished of disease in some one or more of the organs, and perversion of the corresponding faculties. Although this change is a strong proof of aberration, yet it is not equally certain that such aberration is always characterised by change. That will depend much upon its cause. Where external agents produce the disease, such as heat, blows, &c., we shall be likely to find derangement accompanied by change. But a faculty may become insane from the intensity of its own action. It may be exercised so violently through the medium of a large organ, as finally to push itself beyond a healthy state, and thus effect a pathological change in the organ. In this case there may be no very obvious change of character, except that the faculty or faculties affected, will throw off all control, and, becoming irresistible in their action, exhaust in their own morbid displays all the phrenic or mental energies.

Wherever insanity has been defined, it has usually been in reference to its mental characteristics. Such definitions fail to throw light upon the real nature of the disease. In a medico-legal point of view, however, it is important to become acquainted with it as a mental disease, with the view of being enabled to judge of its disabling effect on the mind, and how far it should be allowed to exempt its subjects from the performance of their duties. It seems difficult to find a definition that will cover all its phenomena. It has been defined, in a very general manner, to be an aberration of the manifestations of the mind from their state of health; but this is too general to convey any definite idea. Dr. Spurzheim defines insanity to be an aberration of any sensation or intellectual power from the healthy state, without being able to distinguish the diseased state; and the aberration of any feeling from the state of health, without being able to distinguish it, or without the influence of the will on the actions of the feeling. In other words, the incapacity of distinguishing the diseased functions of the mind, and the irresistibility of our actions, constitute insanity. This may be true, universally, so far as relates to irresistibility of our actions; but there are undoubted instances where the insane impulse to do evil co-existed with the consciousness of the impulse, and of its evil tendency. Neither will it cover those forms of mental alienation in which there is deficiency, not derangement, in the action of the faculties.

Insanity, as related to medical jurisprudence, is a disqualifying disease. When once clearly established, it incapacitates from the enforcing of rights, disables from the performance of duties, and releases from the fulfilment of obligations. Its divisions and forms should be considered in reference to its legal bearings.

Its primary divisions are two. In the one, the powers and faculties are so defective from weakness, or incoherence, as to incapacitate. In the other, the exalted or perverted action of one or more of them, constitutes the derangement, and renders the individual irresponsible for his actions. In the first division are included idiocy, imbecility, and dementia. In the other, the active forms of mania, both intellectual and moral, general and partial.

Idiocy is that condition of mind in which the reflective, and all, or a part, of the affective faculties, are either entirely wanting, or possess a very slight power of manifestation. It is in most cases congenital, and therefore incurable. So uniformly is this the fact, that the common law makes a distinction between idiots and lunatics, considering the first as incurable, and the last as likely again to attain the possession of reason.

One uniform characteristic of idiotism is a faulty conformation of brain, the organs of mind being either preternaturally small or enormously large. The convolutions are observed to be less thick, less deep, and less numerous, particularly in the anterior lobes. The brain is often found of about the same dimensions with that of a new born infant; that is, about one fourth, fifth, or sixth, of the cerebral mass of the adult in the full enjoyment of his faculties. The forms of idiotic brains are observed to possess about as much variety as those of adults. Indications of idiocy are also derivable from the features, from the unsteady, glaring, objectless eye, thick lips, open mouth, and limbs often crooked, or otherwise defectively formed. There is considerable variety exhibited in the power of manifesting mind possessed by idiots. They have generally more or less of the propensities, particularly the lower ones, such as Amativeness, Secretiveness, Combativeness, and Destructiveness; sometimes some of the sentiments, such as Self-esteem and Approbativeness; and occasionally is to be found, the power of exercising some of the intellectual faculties, particularly those taking cognisance of names, numbers, and historical facts. Almost all the varieties of idiocy are to be found among the Cretins of Switzerland. While some are to be found among them whose life is simply automatic, there are others who manifest particular faculties, and exhibit a taste for music, drawing, &c. Some attempt poetry, succeeding, however, in nothing but the rhyme; others may be learnt to read and write, but without any adequate conception of their purposes.

Imbecility is a state or condition of mind above idiocy, but inferior to the amount of power ordinarily possessed. It consists in a preter natural deficiency, either in the intellectual faculties or in the senti ments, or in both, coupled frequently with the strong action of one or more of the propensities. Imbeciles have some use, although a limited one, of speech; display some indications of intellect, feelings and affections; the senses appear dull and feeble in receiving impres sions. The power of thought and attention is diminished. They exhibit great varieties of character and inclination. Some are change able, others fixed. They seem to lack depth both of feeling and reasoning. They have no apprehension of the remoter relations and higher purposes of things. They have no settled plan or purpose and no final aim or subject.

Imbeciles, in regard to their intellectual operations, may very pro perly be divided into two classes. The first will include those who are the most defective in bringing their minds to act upon the materials furnished; the second, those who experience the most difficulty in acquiring the materials on which judgments are based. The firs arises from a want of *reflective* power; or, according to Hoffbaner from a lack of *intensity* in mental action; the last, from a simila want of *perceptive* power, or from lacking the *intensity* of Hoffbaner The result in both cases is unsoundness of conclusion: in the first because all that should go to form it has not been duly weighed and adequately considered; in the last, because all has not been properly perceived or apprehended.

There are various degrees of imbecility. The first degree is characterised by an inability to form a judgment respecting any new object, even when the necessary data are furnished, and the question is not one possessed of intrinsic difficulty. The same difficulty is no experienced in reference to objects long known.

In the second degree, objects that had been familiar, create more or less confusion in the mind. There seems to be a want of power pro perly to discriminate times, places, and accidental circumstances.

In the third degree, the imbecile is unfitted for all matters tha require any thing more than the mechanical action of the faculties He possesses generally an irritable and suspicious temper, and a strong disposition to talk to himself.

The fourth degree is characterised by a clouded state of the intellect and great irritability of temper.

The fifth degree borders directly on idiocy. There is a nullity of intelligence, indifference to objects, and inability even to be affected by passion. Imbeciles, whatever be the class to which they properly belong, are incompetent to judge and decide correctly when it becomes necessary to weigh opposing motives. They cannot carry the action of their minds beyond the circle of objects with which they are habitually surrounded. Some are incapable of embracing more than a single idea at a time, which they must dismiss before they can pass to the consideration of another. Many can never arrive to the comprehension of complex ideas. They have very improper motives of property, of laws, society, government, and justice. The lower propensities, having little to restrain them, often possess relatively greater activity than other mental faculties. Hence many are inclined to incendiarism, to destroying life, to stealing, and to indulging in loose and vicious conduct. Many more of these than we are aware of, fall into the hands of justice, and are punished they know not why.

One rather remarkable feature in imbecility should be particularly taken notice of, and that is, the fact that its manifestation is more in the *conduct* than the *conversation*. The latter, if confined, as conversation generally is, to familiar every-day topics, may give rise to no suspicion of imbecility, because the common perceptive faculties, if very moderate in strength, will be enabled, with even a small language, to embody and present conceptions of common objects in a correct and unexceptionable manner. But when an *act* is required to be done, which does, or should, represent the joint action of all the faculties, if a deficiency exist, it cannot well avoid being made apparent.

The exhibition of imbecility is, in many respects, very similar to that of childhood. There is in both the same frivolity of pursuit; the same fondness for, and stress upon, trifles; the same general inertness of mind, paucity of ideas, shyness, timidity, submission to control, and acquiescence under influence.

The conflicting testimony of witnesses, in regard to the existence or degree of imbecility possessed in any given case, arises, in most instances, from the varying opportunities of observation, coupled with the erroneous assumption that the mind is a single general power, possessing originally equal capacities. One has been favoured with the exhibition of faculties comparatively sound, and hence infers the sanity of the individual. Another has been only in a situation to witness the display of faculties that are weak or perverted, and hence judges the same person to be an imbecile. In this manner, the most opposite and conflicting statements are often obtained from different, honest and intelligent witnesses.

ARTICLE VI.

CAN THE FUNCTIONS OF ORGANIC MATTER BE ASCERTAINED FROM ITS STRUCTURE ?

To the Editor of the American Phrenological Journal.

Sir,—

Though, since Jeffrey surrendered up his pen, and retired from the field, under the mortification and despair of a vanquished chieftain, but little of talent, argument, or any other form of intellectual resource, has been brought by anti-phrenologists against our science, there has been manifested by them no lack of cunning, stratagem, and delusive expedient. And to operate on the " million" toward whom their efforts are directed, the latter instruments are far the most powerful, efficient, and dangerous. The reason is plain. By the discerning and intellectual, trickery can be detected, exposed, and rendered harmless ; but it seduces the uninformed into all kinds of delusion.

One of the most common, plausible, and disgraceful expedients to deceive, as respects phrenology, is made up of anatomical and physiological pretension. Plausible, however, as it is, and often effectual in its action on the minds of the multitude, in the view of those who are competently informed, it is a fallacy as shallow, and as easily unmasked and overthrown, as any that can be imagined. It is the pretence avowed by many anti-phrenologists of being able to disclose physiology by anatomy—of being able, I mean, to detect the function of a portion of organised matter, by its anatomical structure. The following extract from Dr. Sewall's " Lectures," will exemplify my meaning :—

" In pursuing the investigation," says he, " I shall enquire,

" 1, How far phrenology is sustained by the *structure and organisation of the brain*."

In this sentence, the purport of the writer evidently is, to palm on those who know no better, the belief that he can detect and communicate to others the functions or modes of action of the living brain, by an examination of its organic "structure" when dead. And Professor M'Dowell, of Cincinnati, makes the same pretension in his *verbal* attacks on phrenology. He has not yet ventured to commit his discourses on the subject to the press, though publicly challenged to do so. Other anti-phrenological combatants have attempted to sustain themselves by the same stratagem.

Is this pretension of Dr. Sewall, Dr. M'Dowell, and others, true ? Can either, or all of them—can the united intellect and exertion of all the anatomists and physiologists now living, or that have ever lived, discover and announce the function of the brain, by any examination of its organic structure they can possibly make? No, they cannot—*they know* that they cannot; else is their ignorance of anatomy and physiology consummate, as far as the point in question is concerned—or they are enthralled by a delusion that might well be called madness.

Though this topic has already, on sundry occasions, been noticed in a manner sufficiently satisfactory to qualified judges, it has not yet, as far as I am informed, been fully discussed as an isolated question. It has been considered only in the light of an appendage to some other more prominent subject. The consequence is, that it has not been brought out in full relief, and has therefore failed to make on the public mind the impression it might have made, if treated by itself. Instead of thorough conviction, it has probably produced nothing beyond supposition. It is under such view of the matter that I purpose making it the subject of a few remarks in this communication.

The function of the brain, like the function of every other form of living organised matter, can be ascertained only in one of two ways; by observation, or by learning from its structure its *modus agendi*. For the attainment of such knowledge, no third channel is open to us. Nor does any difficulty exist in determining which of these two modes is preferable—I should rather say, *alone practicable.*

All enlightened and substantial physiologists (and they constitute the only competent judges) prefer the former mode, convinced of the utter impracticability of the latter, which they therefore leave to the adoption of the uninformed, the misinformed, and the visionary—to such anti-phrenologists as Dr. Sewall and Dr. M'Dowell—perfectly satisfied that by men of that caste alone will it ever be adopted. And by those gentlemen it *is* adopted, and constitutes one of their main *arguments* (I beg pardon of all enlightened physiologists for applying so solid and respectable a term to so flimsy an expedient)—it constitutes, I say, one of those gentlemen's main arguments against phrenology. They assert that they can disclose the function of the brain (in other words, its modus agendi) from its "structure and organisation." I, on the contrary, in concurrence with all anatomists and physiologists of any distinction, assert that they cannot. And thus the question between us is at issue. Nor does the matter end here.

I further pronounce Drs. Sewall and M'Dowell so ignorant of the works of nature, that they cannot tell, from its structure and organisation, the function or modus agendi of the simplest form of living matter. Let them try their skill on a seed or a nut, to which they are strangers—respecting which they have previously learned nothing from observation, reading, or report. Will they be able to tell, from an examination of its organic structure, how it will grow, and what sort of vegetable it will produce? Boundless as is their confidence in their penetration and sagacity, they will not so far expose their conceit and folly, as to hazard to this question an affirmative answer. Or, from an anatomical or physiological examination of a strange plant, can they predict what kind of blossom and, fruit it will bear? No, they cannot; nor will they pretend to such foresight. To make a trial of their skill on the animal kingdom:

Can they tell us, from its structure and organisation, why a polypus feeds and acts in all respects like a polypus, a star-fish like a star-fish, a crab like a crab, a booby like a booby, or even a *goose like a goose*? They will not pretend to such profundity of insight. To come up to the system of man, with which they ought to be better acquainted:

Can they predict, from its organic structure, why one human nerve subserves sensation, and another, motion? or why one sensitive nerve is tributary alone to vision, another to hearing, a third to taste, a fourth to smell, and a fifth to touch? To no knowledge of the kind will they pretend. Can they tell, from their organic structure, why a muscle only contracts and relaxes, a gland secretes, or the lungs arterialise and vitalise the blood? why, from the same kind of blood, one gland secretes saliva, another, urine, a third, pancreatic juice? why the liver alone secretes bile from venous blood? and why the stomach alone can convert food into chyme? Nothing of all this can they do; nor do they pretend to it. Yet do they affect to discover, from its "structure and organisation," whether the brain, the most delicate and complicated portion of the system, can subserve the purposes of phrenology. Whether one compartment of it be the seat of animality, a second, of the moral and religious sentiments, and a third, of the operation and display of the intellect. After a grave and affectedly wise examination of its structure, they proclaim one portion of brain unfit to be the organ of Benevolence, another, of Veneration, a third, of Conscientiousness, a fourth, of Firmness, a fifth, of Hope, a sixth and a seventh, of Wonder and Ideality; and in the same spirit do they deny the functions of all the other organs, merely because their structure does not please them. Thus do they presumptuously attempt to decide on that which is known to the Deity alone. For as he alone is the Creator of living organised matter, to him alone are the forms of action, from an acquaintance with their structure, of the different kinds of organisation known.

Drs. Sewall and M'Dowell are understood to admit the brain, as an integral mass, to be the organ of the mind—the whole brain of the whole mind—but deny its *different portions* to be the *special organs* of the *different faculties* of the mind.

For this admission, as intelligent men, they must have a reason—certainly they ought to have one. What is that reason, and whence is it derived? Have they discovered the entire brain to be the organ of the entire mind, from an examination of its structure? or are they indebted for the discovery to observation alone? To the *latter* source unquestionably do they owe their information. In truth, to the *former* they have never applied, nor even dreamt of seriously applying for the discovery alluded to. Stronger still. They are utterly unprepared for an investigation so delicate and intrinsic, and involving such a thorough knowledge of anatomy and physiology. Of such want of preparedness, moreover, they are themselves conscious. They know, and if interrogated by an individual sufficiently enlightened in medical science, will not deny, that they are destitute of every element of fitness for an enquiry demanding such an amount of science—an amount to which neither Bichat, Cuvier, nor any other human being, ever made pretence—*conceited and boastful anti-phrenologists excepted.* And to whom do they make their boast? To the high-gifted and enlightened of the land, who are competently informed in anatomy and physiology? Far from it. With that class of individuals they have neither intercourse nor companionship. Their boast is intended only for those individuals who have no knowledge of the subject boasted of, and whose ignorance of it they are anxious to perpetuate. For their object is, not to spread abroad the light, and freedom, and vigour of knowledge, but the darkness, debility, and thraldom of the uncultivated and deluded mind—uncultivated, I mean, as relates to the true principles of mental philosophy. Into their reasons for the pursuit of a course so exceptionable, I shall not enquire. For that they must account before a higher and more unerring tribunal than any to which I can to summon them.

In conclusion: for Drs. Sewall and M'Dowell, or any other vain and boastful anti-phrenologist, to assert that they can tell, by an examination of the structure of the brain, whether it is fitted for the purposes of phrenology, is an arrogant and presumptuous assumption of knowledge, which, in the present state of science, no mortal is privileged to claim. It is a daring invasion of the province of the MOST HIGH, who alone, as already stated, is the author of living organised matter, and who alone knows, from its structure, the peculiar suitability of given forms of it for the performance of given kinds of action. Unite the entire wisdom and sagacity of all the anti-phrenologists on earth, and they will not, in the lump, be able to decide, *on the ground of mere organic structure,* whether muscle, gland, membrane, or brain, is best fitted to serve as the organ of the mind—or whether either of them is suited to so important a purpose.

The design and modes of action of all living organised matter, we learn, I repeat, from observation alone. Through that channel only we learn that the eye and its appendages are intended and organised for the purpose of vision, the ear for hearing, the tongue and nostrils for tasting and smelling, the stomach for digesting food, the lungs for arterialising the blood, and the heart and blood-vessels for the circulation of that fluid throughout the body. To such an extent is this true that, without observation, the vital economy of our own systems would be as utterly unknown to us, as is that of the beings who inhabit the sun, or any other orb within the scope of the universe.

If the sentiments contained in this article are true—and the entire clan of anti-phrenologists is challenged to refute or even to question them—how indignant and blighting is the sentiment of reprobation that should be directed against those writers and declaimers, who falsely profess to disclose the functions of the brain, by an examination and analysis of its organic structure! Amidst all the charlatanica pretensions and quackery of the age, no form of imposture is more flagrant than this, or should more certainly cover its professors wi irretrievable disgrace!

Respectfully yours,
CHARLES CALDWELL.

Louisville, Ky., August 10th, 1839.

MISCELLANY.

Mr. Webster in London.—Extract from a letter to the editor of the New York Mirror, from a London correspondent.—"Were you to ask me who was the greatest lion now in London, I should say, unhesitatingly, Daniel Webster. He is fêted and dined without intermission Artists are besetting him to sit for his picture, and *phrenologists are crowding to get a sight of his wonderful cerebral developments. Webster is one of those men who carry the stamp of greatness unequivocally upon their brows. No one can see him and doubt his intellectual preeminence.*"

Letter to Dr. Sewall on the Merits of Phrenology.—The following amusing and singular letter, which purports to come from the Emperor of China, appeared in the New York Evening Post, September 6th. It requires no comments on our part to explain its design and application. Those of our readers who have seen the second edition of Dr. Sewall's Lectures, and the commendatory letters attached to it, or have read the review of the same in the preceding number of the Phrenological Journal, cannot misunderstand the meaning of this letter. We copy it entire, with a few prefatory remarks, which accompanied it in the Post.

"Since the second edition of Dr. Sewall's work, 'Errors of Phrenology Exposed,' was published, the following letter has been received. It came too late to be printed along with the letters of Mr. John Quincy Adams,

Dr. Ruel Keith, and other distinguished men, prefixed to the volume itself. The Evening Post is, therefore, requested to give it a place in its columns. It is proper to observe that, in the Chinese language, the word 'Barbarian,' which occurs frequently in the letter, has a signification very much resembling the word 'foreigner' in English. All who are not subjects of the Celestial Empire are 'Barbarians,' in the court language of China; and the term is not intended to be offensively applied.

"We, Whang-Ho-Ching, Brother to the Sun and Moon, Cousin of the Stars, Grandfather to the Comets and Meteors, Supreme Ruler of the Celestial Empire, and only Fountain of Universal Truth, to the learned Barbarian Thomas Sewall, M. D., Professor of Anatomy and Physiology in the city of Washington, District of Columbia, in the United States of America, greeting:

"Thou hast done well, oh learned Barbarian, to lay at our feet thy production entitled 'An Examination of Phrenology, in two Lectures;' for we are the fountain of all science. Thou askest our judgment on thy grand proposition, 'the brain is a unit.' We condescend to inform thee that we have never enquired into the dark mysteries of the human skull, but in virtue of our high relationship to the Sun and Moon, it belongs to us to know all things without study; and also, in matters recondite and strange, to judge infallible judgment even without knowledge. Learn, then, that in the Celestial Empire, men distinguished for their stupendous wisdom have no brains at all. It is only in the desolate outskirts of the universe, in regions far removed from the dazzling glories of the Celestial Kingdom, that brains are known to exist; and there they darken the sublime and immaterial spirit. We, and our treasurers and sub-treasurers; our postmasters and collectors; our mandarins and judges, district and supreme, men of surpassing wisdom; our wives and concubines, and the ten thousand millions of subjects who live on the breath of our Celestial nostrils, are all brainless. Hence the greatness and glory of the Celestial Empire. Know, then, that the great son of science, Confucius, before whom all barbarian sages are ignorant as unborn babes, hath written 'a hen's head to a wise man, a big head to a fool; small heads shall be exalted, because they are light; large heads shall be abased, because they are heavy and full of brains.' In the Empire which encircles the Universe, and is endless as time, we cut off all heads that are large, because they are troublesome. Hence our everlasting peace.

"But oh, most learned Barbarian, we chide the presumption of thy friends. Know that it belongs to us alone, in virtue of our high prerogative, to judge infallible judgment without knowledge. To Barbarians this is not vouchsafed, yet a certain Barbarian, who, in thy pages, indicates his existence by the hieroglyphic marks, 'J. Q. Adams,' speaketh as one possessing wisdom, concerning the uses of the brain; nevertheless this barbarian saith, 'I have never been able to prevail on myself to think of it, as a serious speculation.' We, the great Wang-Ho-Ching, rebuke the barbarian Adams. It belongs to us ALONE to judge infallible judgment without knowledge.

"We rebuke, also, the Barbarian whose marks are 'John M'Lean,' who useth these words: 'I am, in a great measure, unacquainted with the anatomy of the parts involved in the question; but I have always supposed that there was a tenancy in common in the brain.' Make known to this Barbarian that he insults our Celestial Majesty by his presumption, and surely in his brain wisdom has no tenancy. It belongeth to the brother of the sun and moon alone, to judge righteous judgment without knowledge. Thou stylest this Barbarian, 'Judge of the Supreme Court of the United States.' Truly hath the heaven-eyed

Confucius written, 'Darkness envelopeth the Barbarian.' How otherwise could a Barbarian Judge pretend to judge without knowledge.

"We rebuke, also, those who are known among Barbarians by the hieroglyphic marks, 'John Sargeant,' 'H. L. Pinckney,' 'S. Chapin,' 'Justin Edwards,' 'Moses Stewart,' and 'Ruel Keith.' Touching the brain, they have all usurped the Celestial prerogative, which belongs to us alone—they have pretended to judge infallible judgment without knowledge. Verily, Barbarian brains obscure wisdom and engender presumption.

"We commend the Barbarian whose marks are 'Daniel Webster.' He judgeth *cautious* judgment, as behoveth all Barbarians. He saith, 'Of the value of the physical and anatomical facts which you state, I am no competent judge; but *if* your premises be well founded, the argument is conclusive.' Our great interpreter of the Barbarian tongues, Hungi-Fuski-Chang, read to us lately, forth of a Barbarian book, these words—'A *second Daniel* come to judgment.' We condescend to greet this 'second Daniel.' His wisdom is worthy of a mandarin of the Celestial Empire. 'If the brain be good for nothing, then good for nothing is the brain!!' Has not this Barbarian read the pages of the sublime Confucius? Only from the deep fountains of his inspired volumes could such discreet wisdom penetrate the mind of a Barbarian, obscured by a brain.

"We instruct our interpreter, Hungi-Fuski-Chang, to render this our epistle into thy Barbarian speech, lest our Celestial wisdom, radiating with too intense a brightness, should extinguish thy feeble and Barbarian mind, clouded by that 'unit' styled by thee a brain.

"Given at our Palace of the Moon, in the year of the Celestial Empire, the seven hundred and fifty-fourth thousand; and of our reign, the 399th year.

"(Signed,)   WHANG-HO-CHING.

Seal of the

FIGURE.

{ A large man, with a small head, sitting on a white cloud, the sun beneath his right arm, the moon beneath his left, a tiara of comets around his head, and a firmament of stars beneath his feet. His countenance is radiant with self-complacency, good-nature, and foolishness. }   (Signed)   FUM, Chancellor.

Celestial Empire.

"A correct translation.   (Signed)
                              "HUNGI-FUSKI-CHANG,
                          "Interpreter of the Barbarian tongues."

Mr. George Combe, we learn, was to commence a course of lectures on phrenology in Hartford, Ct., September 27th.

We understand that Rev. J. A. Warne is to commence an extended course of lectures on phrenology in this city, October 4th.

Mr. S. Colman, of New York, is about issuing from the press, Mr. Combe's lectures, as reported by Mr. A. Boardman.

Our next number will contain articles from Professor Caldwell, A. Dean, Esq., President Shannon, and others. Several miscellaneous notices are necessarily deferred.

THE

AMERICAN PHRENOLOGICAL JOURNAL

AND

MISCELLANY

| Vol. II. | Philadelphia, November 1, 1839. | No. 2. |

ARTICLE I.

PHRENOLOGY VINDICATED AGAINST THE CHARGES OF MATERIALISM AND FATALISM.

BY CHARLES CALDWELL, M. D.

PART I.

THE charges of materialism and fatalism, though, when strictly scrutinised and fully understood, among the most groundless and frivolous in their nature that have been preferred against phrenology, are, notwithstanding, the most pernicious in their effects, and have constituted the most stubborn and obstructive barriers to the dissemination of its truths. The reason is plain. They are addressed to the feelings which are blind and credulous, instead of the intellect which, being the mental eye, can see and examine, doubt and determine. Hence they have excited the fears, and awakened and alarmed the prejudices of the community, and called into the conflict an honest conscience (the conscience of the public), without the lights by which it should be guided.

Nor, to the minds of a vast majority of those whose ears they reach, are the charges referred to destitute of plausibility. Far from it. To detect their fallacy, and trace through its ramifications their mischievous tendency, without aid, requires much more of attention and accuracy of research, than the great body of the people will bestow on them ; and also, perhaps, more of sagacity and knowledge than they actually possess.

On the community at large, this rooted and pervading dread of the evils of phrenology operates injuriously in a two-fold way. By their groundless fears of its demoralising tendency, thousands and tens of thousands are induced to keep aloof from the science themselves, and to use their influence to make others do the same. It need hardly be observed, that persons of this description, being altogether ignorant of it, cannot rationally entertain in relation to it either opinion or belief. Those states of mind, to be worthy of the names bestowed on them, must be the product of evidence. And, from the individuals alluded to, evidence is excluded by the ignorance which their fears and prejudices throw around them. Notwithstanding this ignorance, however, its concomitant want of evidence, and all other disqualifications which follow in its train, those individuals do entertain and exercise what is to them tantamount to confirmed opinion and belief; because it effectually prevents them from enquiring, and thus shuts and bars against them the door of knowledge. Hence their ignorance of phrenology, reducing their minds, as respects that science, into a state of inaction, perpetuates itself. Artful anti-phrenologists, moreover, constantly resort to it, in their declamations and intrigues, with a view to cover the science with odium.

On another portion of the community, the fears and shadowy suspicions which they harbour (in open defiance of the lights which should dissipate them) in relation to the pernicious tendency of the science, produce an effect still more to be lamented. They seduce them to surrender up their judgment and positive conviction, to be made the sport of their vague apprehension of evil.

The persons here referred to, acquire an acquaintance with phrenology sufficient to give them a knowledge of its leading facts and principles, to none of which can they offer an objection. Nor do they even pretend to object. They are really, and in spite of themselves, convinced of the truth of the science; but they shrink, notwithstanding, from what they still regard as its demoralising consequences. They do not, therefore, adopt it as a creed, avail themselves of its benefits, or recommend it to others. On the contrary, their measures are the reverse, signally unreasonable, and culpably inconsistent with moral courage. They allow themselves, by the phantoms of their timidity, to be so far warped and perverted in sentiment, and so deluded in judgment, as to believe that *truth*, the favourite creation and highest attribute of the God of truth, can be productive of evil! Though I shall not pronounce this irreverent view of things altogether blasphemous, that it is deeply blameworthy will hardly be denied. Those who harbour it through the blindness of fear, seem ignorant of the fact, that *all truth is essentially useful*, if correctly understood, and skilfully applied. They forget, moreover, that doubt on this subject is *virtual infidelity*. Yet if reason and common sense do not unite in pronouncing it so, I am mistaken in their decision. In what respect, I ask, is it more erroneous and culpable, to doubt the usefulness or dread the mischief of truth, when revealed in the Word of the Creator, than when revealed with equal clearness in his Works? Let others answer the question. My skill in casuistry is unequal to the task. That in either case the act is fraught with irreverence toward the Deity, from involving a doubt of his wisdom or goodness, or both, and is therefore wanting in religion, cannot be questioned. Yet, by many anti-phrenologists, who are sufficiently ostentatious in their profession of religion, it is hourly perpetrated.

Of these cases, neither is more strongly portrayed than truth and the interest of science and morals abundantly warrant. In form and colouring, they are depicted as I have witnessed them. Perhaps nine tenths, or more, of all the anti-phrenologists I have conversed with on the subject, have belonged to one or the other of these two classes. They either had not ventured to approach the science as enquirers, and were therefore utterly ignorant of it, or, having acquired some knowledge of it, and been convinced of its truth, they still rejected it in fact, on account of what they dreaded as its hostility to the interests of morality and religion. In illustration of this, and in confirmation of the principle on which it rests, no single incident, perhaps, can be more pointed and powerful than the following one, in which I had myself an immediate concern.

A gentleman of great distinction and worth, and one of the most amiable men I have ever known, after having held much conversation, and attended a brief course of lectures on phrenology, became a proselyte to its truth. At the time of this event, he was distant from home, and had nothing to consult but his own splendid and masterly intellect. Not so, however, on his return to his family. To his wife, a woman of earnest piety, and great accomplishments of mind and person, he was peculiarly attached. To her he communicated his views of phrenology, and attempted to convince her of its truth and usefulness. But the effort was worse than fruitless. It alarmed her fears. She fancied that she detected in the science the fatal elements of impiety and irreligion. The fears of the wife were reflected back on the husband. So deep and tender was his affection, and so manly his magnanimity, that he could not bear to be a source of pain to a being so dear to him. The consequence was, that phrenology lost, through this groundless apprehension, a powerful advocate. From that period, the gentleman could never be induced again even to converse on the science. Yet his regard for truth withheld him from ever assailing its evidences.

Another less numerous, but more passionate and intolerant body of unbelievers, have not confined their assaults to the supposed injurious effects of phrenology. Their warfare has been materially different, in both its form and its object, more vindictive in its spirit and bearing, and pushed to a much more exceptionable extent. It has been rude, personal, and repulsively malignant.   Not content with a crusade against doctrines, this band of belligerents have fiercely attacked, also, reputation and standing, with a view to compass their object, by covering with odium the advocates of the doctrines which they deem objectionable.   Hence, while emptying against them their deeply drugged vials of condemnation, invective, and abuse, they have denounced phrenologists as materialists and fatalists, heretics and demoralisers, and therefore enemies of the human race.   Of this class of vilifiers, I regret to say, that no inconsiderable proportion has consisted of members of some religious denomination—clergymen or laymen, or both united, characterised by much more of zeal than judgment, and much better versed in militant creeds and sectarian wrangles, than in either the history or the science of nature.   Cased in prejudice, warped in feeling, and restricted in intellect, by their tortuous artifices, and narrowing and perverting courses of enquiry and thought, such litigants are peculiarly disqualified to sit in judgment on physical questions.   Their long-settled and engrossing dogmas, moreover, entangled with rigid professional habits, and a caste of belief exclusive and limited, too often unfits them for liberal research of any description.   Such men, I say, have figured as the most rancorous foes, and the most vehement anathematisers of phrenology and its advocates.   True, a few of them, less ferocious, or more artful than the rest, while fulminating in wrath against the science, have assumed at times a milder, and, as they no doubt would have it thought, a more merciful and charitable tone toward what they miscalled its *deluded* votaries.   They have admitted that phrenologists *may* be honest in their intentions—perhaps are so; but that, in *their* opinions, they *must be* and *are* deplorably mistaken.   In a special manner, that, from some cause, they are so blinded as to cause and effect, or perverted in their mental vision, as to be disqualified to judge of the nature and tendency of the doctrines they advocate. That though phrenology, in its consequences, tends palpably and directly to mischief, its cultivators, who have bestowed years on the study of it, are too dim-sighted to be sensible of that mischief.   In a word, that however commendable phrenologists may be in their purposes, their pursuits are condemnable, and they themselves intellectually dull and imperceptive, and therefore unfit to be the authors and guides of their own course of action, and the arbiters of their own destiny.   I shall only add that, apart from all other considerations, charges such as these are in no small degree injurious, from their unfortunate effect on the human temper, and on social intercourse. They estrange men from each other, and chill their mutual affections and charities, if they do not produce between them actual hostility.

To impute to a body of men, whether truly or falsely, dishonesty or folly, never fails to offend them, if it does not excite in them open enmity toward their indiscreet and indelicate accusers. But that charges to this effect have been, for the last forty years, broadly and uninterruptedly preferred, by fanatics and their adherents, against the votaries of phrenology, has been already intimated, and cannot be denied. And the grossness and repulsive nature of the practice, not to say its malignity and viciousness, are among the evils and disgraces of the day. Hence the unkindness of feeling, not to call it resentment, that has prevailed between phrenologists and their opponents; and the spirit of harshness and rancour, with which their controversy has been conducted. Their conflict has been that of incensed gladiators, mutually bent on overthrow or destruction, rather than of calm and deliberate enquirers, conscientiously labouring for the establishment of truth.

Such are some of the products of the belief, that phrenology favours materialism and fatalism; and the evil and discredit of them are sufficiently striking. That their extinguishment would be eminently beneficial to the cause, and subservient to the usefulness of the science, cannot be doubted. It would render the study of it much more general and effective, and the results of that study in an equal degree more abundant and available for the welfare of the community. For these reasons, and with such resources as I can bring to the task, it is my intention, in this essay, to contribute my part toward the vindication of the science from the specified evils which have been laid to its charge. And first from that of

MATERIALISM.

This, as heretofore stated, when subjected to analysis and strictly examined, is one of the most frivolous and indefinite, mystified and unintelligible charges, that can well be imagined. Hence it is one of the most difficult to be practically treated, and satisfactorily settled. Its levity, and near approach to nothingness, render it all but untangible. An attempt to grapple with it bears too close a resemblance to grasping at air, or striking at a shadow. The enquirer wastes his strength in a fruitless struggle to find in his subject something on which to fasten his mind, and bring his exertions to bear on a reality. All before him is a flitting phantasmagoria, which appears but to vanish, and give place to another as shadowy as itself. Nor is the most intractable difficulty yet specified. Far from it.

While the enquirer is threading his way through the entanglements of materialism, he is instinctively led, by a law of his mind, to seek knowledge through contrast, and thus makes an attempt on the subject of immaterialism. And, as far as human powers are concerned, that is literally an attempt on *nothingness.* No more are our faculties calculated, or intended by HIM who bestowed them on us, to investigate that subject (if subject it may be called) than is our eye to see the inhabitants of Saturn, or our voice to converse with them. Consummately mad as was the mad Knight's assault on the windmill, it was sober sense, compared to the formal attempt of a philosopher to run a tilt with immaterialism. When will man, in his transcendental visions, and fanatical reveries, escape from insanity! Immaterialism a theme to be discussed and illustrated by such faculties as we possess, or to serve in any way as a source of knowledge to us! It is as utterly untangible to us, as the wildest chimera of a crazed imagination. To our efforts to sound or fathom it, it is an ocean not merely without shore or bottom, but without substance or its shadow—a thing of inconceivable emptiness—the very void of a void! As soon shall we measure immensity itself, and make in person the circuit of creation, as form respecting *immaterial things* a single idea.

In truth, it is discreditable to the science of an advanced period in the nineteenth century, which is boastfully pronounced the age of reason, common sense, and practical knowledge, and when theory is professed to be discarded for fact—it is discreditable that at such a time, and under such circumstances, the subjects of materialism and immaterialism should be brought into question, and spoken of as themes of interest and importance—worse still, as matters essential to morality and religion, on which the good order and prosperity of temporal affairs, and an eternity of wo or felicity depend! That such abstractions (I was near saying *nihilities*) as *substance, essence,* and *entity,* were dreamed of and dozed on in the cloisters of the fifteenth and sixteenth centuries, when nearly all of mental exercise was *abstraction* and hypothesis, is not surprising. But that such philosophical foolery should be practised now, is matter of amazement, and shows that we have but partially escaped from the superstitions and phantasies of the "dark ages." But unmeaning as the enquiry is, and unsatisfactory as the issue must necessarily prove, the effort to say something on the subject must be made, because it is expected and promised, and shall be therefore commenced, without further delay. And in the course of it, the matter, frivolous as it is, shall be treated as if it were worthy in itself of serious consideration.

Were I to introduce the discussion by asking the question, What is the precise meaning of materialism, as a charge against phrenology? I doubt exceedingly, whether one in every thousand of those who are in the habit of preferring it could answer the question in a way to be understood—or whether half a dozen in a thousand would answer it alike. No doubt those who first imputed materialism to phrenology had, or believed they had, some meaning in their words. Not so however, with a vast majority of their disciples and followers. They have learned the imputation, as a battle-cry, from their leaders; and they now exclaim, "materialism, materialism!" as literally by rote and with as little meaning, as would the parrot or the magpie. True they imagine the term to be of terrible import. But what that impor is, very few of them with whom I have conversed have any but the most crude and indefinite notions.

Of materialism there are several forms, which, on various occasions, and for different purposes, writers and speakers have referred to and considered. Of these, that which denies to man the possession of an immaterial, immortal, and accountable mind, appears to be the form which is charged against phrenology as one of its evils. But the charge, as will be made to appear, is as "baseless" as any other "fabric of a vision," which words can express or fancy conceive.

Phrenologists neither deny the immortality and accountability of the human mind, nor are in any way opposed to them. On the contrary, they accede to both, and that in perfect accordance with the principles and doctrines of the science they profess. But as respects the substance of the mind—the thing, I mean, of which it is formed—they say nothing; because they know nothing. Yet have they just as much, and as accurate knowledge on the subject, as the most sagacious and the wisest of their opponents. But they have less of pretension and self-conceit, and being much less captious and difficult to be pleased, they are not so prone to murmurs and fault-findings. They are less inclined, I mean, to except to any of the works of creation, or to usurp a share in the superintendence or direction of them. Under a full conviction that their minds are made out of the substance best suited to the purposes for which they were created, be its *essence* what it may, they are content with them as they have received them from their unerring Creator. And had He chosen, in his wisdom, to form them out of a different substance, their content would have been the same. Their confidence in the Deity, his designs and operations, is boundless.

Of enlightened and reflecting anti-phrenologists (if they can be induced to reflect with seriousness on the subject), I ask the cause of their deep hostility to materialism in the abstract? Is there in the doctrine, when fairly interpreted and fully understood, any thing incompatible with the immortality or accountability of the human soul? or in the slightest degree unfriendly to them? I reply that there is not, and defy refutation. The supposed incompatibility and unfriendliness are but notions—groundless notions, arising from a misconception equally valid, he can, if he please, hold matter accountable also. Indeed, if I mistake not, we are taught to believe that he does so. The bodies of the wicked are doomed, after the resurrection, to suffer in common with their spirits, in consideration of their having co-operated with them in the commission of sin. And, on contrary grounds, the bodies of the righteous are also to participate in the enjoyment of bliss.

That the Creator can, then, if he please, attach to the human mind, as a material substance, accountability as well as immortality, will not be denied. Nor does any one know that he has not done so. He has no where told us that he has not; nor has he furnished us with powers to make the discovery ourselves, by curiously prying into his works. To take a less abstracted and more practical view of this subject:

Is any conceited spiritualist so presumptuous as to assert positively that the Creator *has not* formed the human mind out of matter? By such assertion, he fairly implies that he possesses so intimate and thorough an acquaintance with the mind, as to know certainly of what substance the Creator *has* formed it. But a pretension of the kind would be in an equal degree audacious and groundless. In plainer and stronger terms, it would be impious and false.

Does any one contend that the Deity *could* not make the mind of man out of matter, and still attach to it immortality and accountability? That would be a notion no less groundless and culpable; being, it would be a denial of the Deity's omnipotence. And no one will be guilty of impiety so flagrant.

Who will venture to assert that the Creator *ought not* to make the mind of man out of matter? No one, surely. Or if so, his presumption is still more consummate and impious; because he dares to interfere with the designs and counsels of the Creator. He rebelliously aspires to

> ———"Usurp the balance and the rod;
> Rejudge his justice; be the God of God!"

Thus, fair and harmless, then, in the eye of reason and philosophy; and, stronger still, thus, fair and harmless, in the eye of common sense, stands the misunderstood and much abused doctrine of materialism. Against its truth, no rational and solid objection can be raised. Nor against its moral principles and tendency can any accusation be justly preferred. That, if it be not misapplied, or in some way abused, it is unproductive of mischief, is perfectly certain. And every form of misapplication and abuse, whatever be the nature and value of the thing thus dealt with, is sure to be in some shape productive of evil.

If, then, reason and philosophy, common sense and morality, find nothing erroneous or blameworthy in materialism, how stands the matter in the view of the Christian religion? In precisely the same attitude. Materialism is no anti-christian doctrine. Nor is immaterialism adopted, or in any way countenanced, by unsophisticated Christianity. When correctly construed, the New Testament does not hint at either the one or the other—much less does it pronounce either to be an element of orthodox belief. In the substance or essence of the human soul, that production takes no concern. Its immortality and accountability, with its purity or corruptness, are all it affirms, and all to which it attaches the slightest importance. And, as already intimated, these attributes are as compatible with a material essence, as with an immaterial one.

True, the New Testament speaks of the *soul* and the *body*, the *flesh* and the *spirit* of man. But what of that? When these terms are traced to their origin, and have their actual meaning developed, they seem to be employed to discriminate between one form of matter and another—between that which is gross and impure, and that which is subtle and refined—much rather than between something material and something immaterial. By no Greek and Latin scholar will this be denied. The same terms (*pneuma* and *psuche*) which, in Greek, signify soul or spirit, signify also *air* or *wind*. Of the Latin tongue, the same is true. *Spiritus* denotes at once the air we breathe, the wind that fans us, and the spirit which presides over our movements and thoughts. Wherefore is this? The answer is easy. Because spirit and wind are attenuated and subtle; not because one of them is material and the other immaterial. In truth, there is not in the writings of the evangelists or apostles a single clause or word that hints at immaterialism; much less that enjoins it as an article of belief. If there be, it has escaped my notice; and I therefore respectfully ask for the chapter and verse of either of those productions in which it may be found. I shall only add, that were a belief in the immateriality of the human spirit as essential to sound Christianity, as most religionists now pronounce it, some intimation to that effect would have doubtless been given by the Messiah himself, or by some of his apostles. But they are silent on the subject. Wherefore, then, are those who profess to be their followers so boisterous and intolerant? Nor is this all.

The primitive fathers of the Christian church (those, I mean, of the first and second centuries), some of whom were contemporaries of the longest lived of the apostles, and no doubt saw and conversed with them—those venerable and holy patriarchal Christians were probably as orthodox in their creeds, and as spotless in their lives, as the most zealous and sanctimonious sectarians of the nineteenth century. Yet they knew nothing of the doctrine of *immaterialism*. At least they have left behind them nothing to testify to that effect. They were neither speculative metaphysicians nor visionary transcendentalists. They were Christians—firm, thorough-going, fearless Christians, clinging to their faith and worship, in the midst of danger, persecution, and death. Their endeavours were, not to detect the essence of their souls, but to regulate their tempers, and improve their piety. Theirs was *peaceful* and *practical*, not theoretic and militant Christianity. It was Christianity of the sentiments and affections, not of cold dogmatism, cavil, and opinion. Its fruits were humility and charity, beneficence of conduct and uprightness of life; not denunciation or persecution, malediction or abuse. Nor was it, I think, until the third or fourth century, that immaterialism was broached as a Christian doctrine. And then it was derived from the writings of Pythagoras and Plato, especially from the seductive creations of the latter. And those by whom it was first adopted and transplanted, were no doubt the metaphysical Christians of the day, who had more in their constitution of Causality and Wonder, than of Veneration and Conscientiousness.

Immaterialism, then, I repeat, is not a doctrine of Christian origin. It is a pagan dogma, engrafted on Christianity by metaphysical refinement and logical subtlety. Whether it be true or false, is a problem which involves the consideration of substance and essence, and cannot be solved. Nature has bestowed on us no faculties for such disquisitions. Nor, as already stated, do the Scriptures contain any revelation to enlighten us on the subject. But had a belief in immaterialism, I repeat, been essential to Christianity, and to our eternal welfare, as immortal beings, such revelation would certainly have been made to us. To say nothing of the tender and indulgent attribute of *mercy*, the *justice* of heaven would not have doomed us to perish through ignorance.

Wherefore was the scheme of redemption revealed to us? The reply is easy; because the reason is plain. Our mental exertions could not reach it. Without the aid of revelation, therefore, it must have lain endlessly concealed from us. Yet could our faculties have detected that as readily as immaterialism.

From the foregoing considerations, I feel justified in the inference, that the doctrine of materialism cannot be shown to be either groundless, irreligious, or immoral; and that, therefore, a belief in it can lead to no form of mischief, either now or hereafter. Error in some shape can alone prove mischievous. Materialism is but a bug-bear to frighten the timid and unthinking; or a dream of the fancy, to feed prejudice and repress enquiry. And for these purposes it has been used with a degree of success eminently injurious to the cause of truth, the promotion of science, the liberalisation of the human mind, and the welfare of man.

But grant the truth of the worst that anti-phrenologists and fanatics can say of materialism, and phrenology does not suffer by the admission. The reason is plain. Between that science and the doctrine I have been discussing there is no necessary connection. Phrenology, I mean, is not more directly and essentially chargeable with materialism, than any other scheme of mental philosophy. For every such scheme partakes of the doctrine; and phrenology does no more.

Notwithstanding all I have said on the subject, most phrenologists concur with their opponents in relation to the nature of the human mind. They believe it to be immaterial. And on this point I am no dissenter. Though I profess to know nothing certain respecting the substance of mind, whether it be material or immaterial, I am persuaded that it is something exceedingly different from the gross material which composes the body. I believe, moreover, that it is not, like the body, liable to change, decay, and dissolution; but that its condition is permament, and that it is an heir of immortality.

Phrenologists, however, farther believe, that the mind, though the superior portion of man, does not *alone* perform any of the phenomena denominated mental. In every action, whether it be one of voluntary motion, sensation, or thought, it calls into requisition, and employs, as its instruments and ministers, the corporeal organs. In some actions more organs; in others, fewer are necessarily engaged.

By a fair analysis and exposition of the subject, it can be made clearly to appear, that mataphysicians and anti-phrenologists themselves are compelled to explain a large majority of mental phenomena, if they attempt to explain them at all, on the same principles with the advocates of phrenology. To illustrate and confirm this position by a reference to facts:

The external senses of seeing, hearing, tasting, smelling, and feeling, together with the faculty of speech, are as literally mental operations, as perception or reasoning. So are the affections and sentiments, and every form of voluntary motion. In the correctness of this statement, all men who have spoken or written on mental philosophy concur in opinion. It is therefore universally regarded as true.

But metaphysicians and anti-phrenologists agree with the rest of the world, that the mind, as an immaterial organless substance, and in its exclusive and solitary capacity, can perform none of these functions. It must employ as its instruments the necessary forms of organised matter. It cannot see without an eye, hear without an ear, taste and smell without a tongue and nostrils, feel without sensitive nerves, speak without organs of speech, nor perform voluntary motion without suitable muscles. And these instruments, I say, are all made of matter.

By metaphysicians and anti-phrenologists, the affections and sentiments are also referred to material organs. But by them this reference is made to the heart, stomach, and bowels, in which they contend that the affections are seated; while by phrenologists it is made to certain portions of the brain. But as respects the external senses, speech, and muscular motion, the parties concur in belief. To the performance of the whole of them, the same material organs are acknowledged to be indispensable.

Thus far, then, as respects materialism, phrenologists, anti-phrenologists, and metaphysicians, go hand in hand. And, except as regards the sentiments and affections, their harmony is complete. Here, however, they separate, for reasons which shall be rendered: and their separation is wide. Nor do the spirit and principles productive of it admit of compromise. There is no middle ground on which the parties can meet. One or the other must ultimately abandon its position; and no gift of prophecy is requisite to foretell by which party the surrender will be made.

Metaphysicians and anti-phrenologists contend that man possesses certain purely spiritual faculties, which have no shade of dependence on matter. Pre-eminent among these are reason, conscience, and veneration, or a sentiment of piety and homage.

On the ground of this immaterial or " purely spiritual" hypothesis, phrenologists and their antagonists are openly at issue. To the exercise of the faculties just cited, phrenologists maintain that matter is as necessary, as it is to voluntary locomotion, speech, or the external senses. They assert that reason cannot exist without the organs of Comparison and Causality, veneration or piety without the organ of Reverence, nor conscience, or a sense of right or justice, without the organ of Conscientiousness. Nor do they rest their doctrine on mere assertion. They illustrate and prove it from four distinct sources:

1. Inferior animals entirely destitute of the organs in question, are equally destitute of the corresponding faculties. 2. Idiots who, by a defective organisation of the brain, are denied the organs of Comparison, Causality, Veneration, and Conscientiousness, are incapable of reasoning, and possess neither a sentiment of reverence nor of justice. They certainly make no manifestation of such attributes. 3. An injury done to the brain by accident or disease, deranges or destroys the reputed "spiritual" faculties just enumerated, as certainly and completely, as it does those of seeing, hearing, feeling, or moving.

Indeed, it sometimes extinguishes the higher and so-called "spiritual" faculties, while the senses remain uninjured.

Let the accident be a severe blow on the head, and the disease be apoplexy. In either case the individual falls, and every mental faculty vanishes. He retains no more of reason, reverence, or conscience, than he does of sense, speech, or the power to walk; and usually no more of the three latter than a marble statue. Why? Because they are all alike the product of mind through the instrumentality of the brain as its organ of action; and that organ is now unfit for action. Nor, without the aid of the brain, can the mind any more manifest those faculties, than the brain can without the aid of the mind. 4. Other things being equal, the degree of strength with which men reason, and the intensity with which they feel, and exercise veneration and a sentiment of justice, are proportionate to the size of the corresponding organs. In proof of this latter position, the noted Rammohun Roy was a remarkable instance. Though most of his cerebral organs were large, and his mind powerful, he was exceedingly deficient in the organ of Veneration; and the corresponding sentiment was equally wanting in him.

Where, then, is the "pure spirituality" of faculties, which, the mind itself being untouched, are thus extinguished by an affection of matter? Let anti-phrenologists answer. The hypothesis is theirs; and they are bound to defend it, and prove it to be sound, or to abandon it as untenable. And the former measure being impracticable, the latter is the only alternative left them, as men of reason, ingenuousness, and conscience. As well may they assert the "pure spirituality" of hunger and thirst, as of reason, reverence, and conscience. The one set of mental conditions is as palpably dependent on material and appropriate organs as the other. And an injury done to those organs, deranges or extinguishes both sets alike. In a word, composed as human nature is, of body and spirit, in every act that man performs, whether of sensation, intellection, or voluntary motion, his mind and his matter are indispensable to each other. They are indispensable, also, to his *natural* existence, as an acknowledged member of God's creation. Separate them, so as to withdraw one of them but for a moment from him in any of his operations, and during that moment he is man no longer, but a new monster, which creation disowns—as literally denaturalised as were the Houyhnnms or Yahoos of the Dean of St. Patrick! And with such monsters have metaphysicians and anti-phrenologists peopled and deformed a creation of their own, from the days of Aristotle to those of Gordon, Jeffrey, and their satellites. Fortunately, however, such a spurious creation has nothing in harmony with that which the Deity pronounced 'very good."

If the foregoing facts and statements be true, (and opposition to their truth is set at defiance,) there is no scheme of mental philosophy, worthy of the title, which does not essentially partake of materialism. And phrenology does nothing more. It is not pure materialism, any more than the mental philosophy of Locke or Beattie, Reid, Stewart, or Brown. It is what it ought to be, semi-material, and nothing more. It " renders unto Cæsar the things that are Cæsar's"—concedes to mind, as well as to matter, what justly belongs to it. But to neither does it give, in intellectual operations, a monopoly of influence. For, as already stated, a large majority of phrenologists subscribe to the doctrine of the immateriality of the mind; though they pretend to no definite knowledge on the subject. Nor should any body else ; for, as heretofore alleged, no such knowledge is attainable by man. From a consciousness of this, many enlightened and pious Christians, even Christian ministers, have frankly acknowledged that materialism may be true ; and that they do not hold a belief in it inconsistent with orthodox Christianity. To this acknowledgment, I have been myself a witness.

Having, as I trust, in the preceding pages, sufficiently vindicated phrenology from the charge of such materialism as is either repulsive or dangerous, I shall now endeavour to show that still greater injustice has been done to the science, by the weightier and more calumnious accusation of FATALISM.

(To be continued.)

ARTICLE II.

CASE OF FRACTURE OF THE SKULL, AND THE SUBSEQUENT PHENOMENA.

The following pathological fact occurred, a few years since, in the city of New York. The fact possesses peculiar interest, as connected with phrenology, in throwing additional light upon the functions of the brain, and its relations to the cranium. As, we believe, it has never been recorded in any medical work or scientific journal, we are induced to present our readers with the particulars of the case, as they were published at the time in the daily newspapers. The statement was drawn up by a committee, appointed by the New York Phrenological Society, and is as follows:—We have kindly been permitted to copy the following extract from a report, recently made to the New York Phrenological Society by its secretary, as one of a committee appointed to investigate the phenomena connected with the fracture of a skull, and the subsequent manifestations. The subject of this committee's examination was a small child of Mr. James Mapes, which, at the time of the accident alluded to, was two years of age.

About two years since, this child, whilst leaning out of the dormant window of the three story brick house, No. 42 Green street, unwittingly lost its balance, and was precipitated headlong to the pavement below. Before reaching the sidewalk, she struck against the iron railing of the steps, by which her skull was most horridly fractured. On removing her to the house, she was supposed by her parents, and the distinguished medical gentleman, Dr. Mott, who had been called, to be irrecoverably injured. Another physician, who had been called, felt desirous to perform an operation, deeming it possible to procrastinate the dissolution; and, by removing the pressure of the skull upon the brain, to effect a temporary restoration of the child's faculties. This would, it was thought, afford a transient satisfaction to the parents at least.

The operation was accordingly undertaken, first by trepanning and afterwards by sawing transversely across the skull, and then laterally, so as to remove a portion of the skull three and a half by four inches square. It was found that the membrane had not been ruptured, and, consequently, that the cerebral organs were uninjured, except from the concussion. The scalp having been carefully laid back and secured, the child soon recovered, and indicated even more than its wonted manifestations of mind.

The most remarkable fact in this case was, that the child previous

VOL. II.—5

to the accident—evidently from some mal-conformation—had not manifested the intellectual powers common to children of that age, whereas, on its recovery from the physical disability, it exhibited extraordinary acuteness of perception and strength of the reflective faculties. The sentiments were also remarkably active and susceptible. The committee, on placing the hand upon the integuments immediately covering the brain, and requiring the child's mind to be exercised by a process calling into activity compound emotions, at once perceived the agitation into which the brain had been thrown by the mental effort. The perturbations were rapid and oftentimes violent. Different faculties were called into activity by varying the kind of subjects presented to the mind of the child, and variations in the agitation of the brain followed the change of subject. The motions of the brain were sometimes like the vibrations of a string when violently struck, and at other times like the more equal undulations of a wave.

It is quite apparent in this case, that the faculties, whose cerebral organs were situated directly beneath the cranial fracture, were mostly affected by the accident, and also, that the cause of mental imbecility, previous to that circumstance, is attributable to the pressure of the skull on the brain. This is found to be no very uncommon circumstance. Numerous cases are recorded in the medical books of a similar nature. The agitation of the brain on the excitement of the mind, corresponded exactly with a case of Sir Astley Cooper's, in which the brain being exposed, and the patient made to exercise his mind powerfully, the brain was protruded, by the mental effort, some lines above the skull, but which receded on the relaxation of thought. A case of a similar kind also occurred in this city some time since. A lady having been confined for insanity in the Lunatic Asylum, was visited one day by her husband. Whilst he was in the room, conversing with the keeper, his wife, watching the opportunity, escaped from the door, and springing into her husband's wagon, drove off with so much rapidity, as to render her being overtaken quite impossible. Dashing down the streets, she came to her former residence ; when rapidly turning her vehicle into the yard, it was upset, and she thrown head first against the wall of the house, by which her skull was fractured. No other material effect, however, was produced, *save the complete restoration of her mind to sanity, and healthful action;* and, of course, to the enjoyment of her family and friends. This is but one of many cases, proving insanity to be oftentimes the result of pressure upon the brain, and that always, as a consequence, insanity is caused by the disease or derangement of that organ.

ARTICLE III.

BY A. DEAN, ESQ., ALBANY, N. Y.

Another form of mental deficiency occurs in *dementia*. This is characterised in all its stages by a general enfeeblement of all the faculties. This is not, like idiocy, congenital, but occurs as the sequel of many diseases, and often at or near the close of life. It is distinguishable from that general decay of mental power that often accompanies extreme old age, by the *incoherence* with which it is accompanied. Persons, places, times, and circumstances, occur disjointedly, apparently without any order of sequence, or bond of association. Objects are mistaken, times confounded, and circumstances strangely confused. There is a want of fixed data from which to reason. The organs of thought lack the vigour necessary to the integrity of their functions.

There are reckoned four degrees of dementia. The first is characterised by a loss of memory. Events that are recent make little or no impression. They are much less vivid than the ideas of early impressions.

The second is accompanied by a loss or diminished action of the reasoning power. Either the reflective faculties that direct reason become impaired, or the perceptive, that furnishes the material, and the affective, that afford the stimulus, act with diminished energy.

The third is attended by an inability to comprehend the meaning of any principle or proposition, however simple, accompanied usually by a physical activity.

The fourth consists in a loss of instinctive action, the mode of existence becoming merely organic.

The incoherence characterising dementia, is widely different from that which usually accompanies mania. The first consists in the *diminution*, the last in the *exaltation*, in the action of the same faculties. The failure of memory in the one, is owing to the obliteration of past impressions, as soon as they are made from a lack of power to retain them. In the other, to the crowding into the mind new ideas, and mingling and confounding them with those of the past.

INTELLECTUAL MANIA is characterised by delusion or hallucination, which may be either, 1. Where there is a belief in facts that never existed ; or, 2. When facts that do exist are carried to enormous and unfounded lengths.

GENERAL INTELLECTUAL MANIA is accompanied with the utmost

confusion and disorder in the action of the intellectual faculties. The greatest possible excesses occur in rapid and disordered succession.

The insane very frequently entertain a full and unshaken conviction of their perfect sanity.

In this form of insanity the ordinary laws of association appear to be suspended. There seems to be a destruction or perversion of that influence which, in a healthy state, is mutually exercised by the faculties over, or in relation to, each other. The mind appears to have lost its control over itself.

One great difference observable between intellectual and moral mania is, that the first is the most manifested in the exaltation or perversion of ideas, the last in singularity and eccentricity of conduct. It is apparent that conduct is mostly influenced by the affective faculties, while ideas are derived solely from the intellectual. Intellectual mania is often complicated with moral mania.

PARTIAL INTELLECTUAL MANIA consists in the perverted or deranged action of some one, or a limited number, of the intellectual faculties. The derangement of those faculties that discern the relations of things, is the easiest perceived, and the most certainly constitutes insanity. Many of the perceptive faculties may be greatly impaired, and yet the soundness of the others may preserve the integrity and sanity of the mind.

The subject of partial intellectual mania is himself generally conscious of his derangement, and often succeeds for a long time in concealing it. The first appearance is usually in the entertainment of some strange and fantastic notion, against which the verdict of common sense would be unqualifiedly rendered. This is often connected with some error of sensation, and more frequently still with the prior habits of the individual. It is sometimes confined to a single topic; and at others, takes a wider range, and embraces within the circle of its action many ideas and relations.

In the present state of our knowledge, it is impossible to mark out, with any degree of precision, the boundaries that limit the insane delusion. So that the enquiry, how far insanity on any one topic ought to disqualify the whole mind, cannot be satisfied in general, and only as the application is made to particular cases. The reasoning powers of the monomaniac, or subject of this partial mania, on subjects not connected with his delusion, do not appear to be impaired.

MORAL MANIA occurs when the organs of the affective faculties become diseased, and their functions perverted or deranged. This also has a twofold division.

GENERAL MORAL MANIA consists in a general perversion, exaltation, or derangement of function of the affective powers. While the reasoning faculties remain unimpaired, the moral maniac is apt to take violent antipathies, to harbour unjust suspicions, indulge strong propensities, and affect singularity in dress, gait, and phraseology.

No delusion or hallucination accompanies this form of mania. It seems as if the passions had thrown off the dominion of reason.

No distinctive character can be affixed to this form of derangement. It may, successively or together, exhibit every possible display of propensity and passion. It frequently involves a perversion of intellect, and is then complicated with delusion.

This form is often accompanied by an entire perversion of character. The pious become impious; the prudent, imprudent; the liberal, penurious; and the virtuous conduct of a long life may be succeeded by acts possessing all the deformity of the most atrocious vice.

PARTIAL MORAL MANIA consists in the perverted, exalted, or insane action of one or more of the affective faculties. The propensities and lower sentiments are most frequently the subjects of this derangement.

The propensity of Amativeness is often deranged in its action; and it then gives rise to impetuosity of desire, gross obscenity, contempt of decency, and a headlong rush into the indulgence of morbid and unnatural appetites.

The other propensities the most frequently deranged, are Acquisitiveness, Combativeness, and Destructiveness. The last is the most frequent in its occurrence, and the most fearful in its displays. It appears under two forms: the one leading to incendiarism; the other, to the destruction of life.

The homicidal monomaniac sometimes appears influenced in his destructive acts by motives avowed, but inadequate, and often irrational. Others destroy without any acknowledged or discernible motive, the individual seeming impelled to the commission of destructive acts by a blind irresistible impulse. The destruction is either indiscriminate, or lights upon those who stand in the nearest and tenderest relations to the monomaniac. This form of mania is often complicated with physical disease; and, in females, is often connected with those changes in the system produced by parturition, menstruation, and lactation.

The sentiments the most generally deranged, are those whose functions give rise to Self-esteem, Love of Approbation, and Cautiousness. The last, in particular, is a fruitful source of partial moral mania. It produces settled gloom, startling apprehensions, terrific fears, and all that host of terrible phenomena embodied in the term despair.

There are other forms of mental aberration. Such as that leading to the commission of suicide, that involved in febrile delirium, and

hat to which drunkenness gives rise, which require not here to be
particularly considered.

A knowledge of the different forms of insanity is of no other use to
he medical jurist, than to enable him to apply properly the legal rules
ntended to cover their various and complicated phenomena.   For
hat purpose, however, such a knowledge is essential, as without it a
proper application could not well be made.

Legal rules can be only binding upon beings possessing sufficient
apacity to undersand them, and sufficient free moral agency to give
r withhold their obedience.   It is, therefore, perfectly obvious that
either the idiot nor the insane can ever be subjected to the obligations
hey create, or the duties they impose.   The one lacks the power of
omprehending; the other, freedom of acting.   The one is exempt
rom an intellectual defect; the other, from a moral difficulty.   The
ne is to be sought in the understanding; the other, in volition.

Although this position will be readily conceived, yet the great diffi-
ulty lies in applying the doctrine.   It is not so well settled what
onstitutes idiotism and insanity in a sufficient degree to exempt from
ie action of legal rules.   It is apparent, that the degrees are about as
arious as the different cases that arise; and hence the utmost skill
nd discrimination are requisite to judge of the propriety of their
xemption.

In the infancy of jurisprudence, no other distinctions in mental
berration seem to have been organised, than those possessing the
10st obvious characters.   The great, and, indeed, only distinction
1at seems to have been first regarded, was that of mental deficiency;
r idiotism on the one hand, and that of furious mania on the other.
he Roman law protected those only whose understandings were
eak or null, and those who were restless and furious.   The early
rench law was nearly to the same effect.

The English common law originally recognised two forms of
ental alienation, and termed the one idiocy, and the other lunacy.
oth were included under the general term, *non compotes mentis.*

In endeavouring to give these terms a meaning, by designating the
ass of persons to whom they should apply, Lord Coke, the early
gan of the common law, says there are four kinds of men who may
said to be non compotes mentis.

1. An idiot, who is such from his infancy.

2. One that becometh such by sickness, grief, or other accident.

3. A lunatic that hath sometimes his understanding, and sometimes
)t.

4. He that by his own act depriveth himself of memory and under-
anding, as he that is drunken.

No attempt is here made at the description of mind to which the terms idiot and lunatic should apply. It still remained to be determined what degree of mental destitution should constitute the idiot, and what perversion of understanding or moral power was necessary to divest lunacy of responsibility. The early definition of an idiot, is of a person "who cannot count or number twenty pence, or tell who was his father or mother, or how old he is, so as it may appear that he hath no understanding of reason what shall be for his profit or what shall be for his loss." Thus the protection of idiocy could only embrace the most extreme cases, and those only of intellectual deficiency, without any reference to that extensive class of powers included in the affective department. The least observation should have furnished the conviction, that most of those included within the class of idiots are possessed of a limited portion of intellectual power, varying in degree from the most marked cases of congenital deficiency, up to that limited possession of intellect, designated by the term imbecility.

The legal mode of determining the fact, whether idiocy or lunacy in any given case existed, has been by the issuing, execution, and return of a commission of lunacy. The finding of idiocy or lunacy was early attended with very different consequences. Idiocy was, in presumption of law, a perpetual infirmity; and therefore the return of that for ever thereafter divested the person of his civil rights. Lunacy was considered a curable disease; and the return of that, therefore, only incapacitated during its continuance.

It was at length discovered that all cases of mental alienations could not be embraced within the terms, idiots and lunatics. This led to a change in the form of the writ, and the terms, "non compos mentis," "insanæ mentis," "unsound mind," have been employed as terms more general, and capable of including a greater number of phenomena.

The commission issues to commissioners named in it, and directs them, through the aid of a jury, to ascertain and return the fact stated in the commission. The return, or finding, must be strictly confined to the facts or things enquired of, and can include no others.

Formerly, no person could himself allege his unsoundness of mind, as a defence from the consequences of his own acts, "because," in the language of the ancient law, "no man is allowed to disable himself, for the insecurity that may arise in contracts from counterfeit madness and folly; besides, if the excuse were real, it would be repugnant that the party should know or remember what he did." But although the individual himself could not plead his disability, in avoidance of his acts, yet his heirs and personal representatives might.

That doctrine, however, has ceased to be law; and under a more enlightened system of public policy, it is now rendered unnecessary to delay until the death of the individual, before his acts done under the influence of unsound mind can be avoided.

Mere mental weakness alone, without aberration, furnishes at law no sufficient reason in avoidance of an act. It is considered, however, as laying a very proper foundation from which fraud and imposition may be the more easily inferred. The proof of aberration lies always with the party who alleges it. Once established, its continuance is presumed; and an entire restoration, or a lucid interval is necessary to be proved, before any acts done can be valid.

Much has been said and written in regard to what constitutes a lucid interval. The proof of it is now required to be direct and clear. It must be shown to be something more than a mere cessation or suspension of the symptoms of disease. It must be a partial restoration; an interval in which the mind, having thrown off the disease, has recovered its general habit. Not merely one, but a succession of rational acts are required to be shown. The evidence in support of a lucid interval, should be as strong and demonstrative of that fact, as where the object of the proof is to establish the aberration. It should be constantly borne in mind, that the cerebral organs, through the medium of which the mental faculties are exercised, may retain an irritable habit for some time after the removal of the primary cause of the disease; and this should present a strong claim for consideration, whenever extraordinary acts or crimes have been preceded by a diseased state of any of the organs.

One singular feature in the law, relative to the insane, cannot fail of exciting the surprise of reflecting men, and that is the difference made in its application to criminal and civil responsibility. The same degree of mental aberration will not excuse criminal, which is allowed to civil acts. Why, if any difference was to be made, property should come to be regarded more favourably than life, and more worthy of protection, is hardly conceivable.

Another anomaly in jurisprudence, is the different kinds or degrees of force that are attached to the same kind of evidence in civil and criminal cases, viz. the evidence derivable from the act itself. In civil cases, a "rational act rationally done," is regarded as evidencing the rationality of its source. An act, on the contrary, which the common sense of mankind condemns as irrational, is allowed to furnish a presumption of mental aberration. Judicious or unnatural dispositions, in a last will and testament, go far to establish or invalidate it. In criminal cases, the enormity and unnatural character of the act, as that of a parent's killing his child, is often insisted on as affording evidence of the greatest possible degree of guilt, instead of being regarded as the offspring of insane impulse.

Some leading cases have occurred in the progress of jurisprudence, which furnished the occasions for laying down principles relative to the insane. In the case of Arnold, which occurred as early as 1723, Judge Tracy affirmed the law to be that a madman, in order to be exempt from punishment, must be totally deprived of his understanding and memory; so as not to know what he is doing any more than an infant, a brute, or a wild beast. According to this case, the lowest degree of idiocy alone would exempt from punishment.

A more rational doctrine came to be entertained in the year 1800, as exemplified in the celebrated trial of Hadfield, for shooting at the king of England. The speech of Lord Erskine, on that occasion, furnishes a fine specimen of judicial eloquence, and is eminently successful in establishing some great and important truths in relation to the insane. The following are among the most essential of the positions established :—

1. That it is the reason of man that renders him accountable for his actions, and that the deprivation of it acquits him of crime.

2. That the law will not measure the sizes of men's capacities, so as they be compos mentis.

3. That a person is accountable for his criminal acts in cases in which he is not for his civil. This doctrine, a more enlightened period cannot fail of essentially modifying.

4. That a total deprivation of memory and understanding is not required to constitute insanity.

5. The important principle then, for the first time, brought distinctly into view; viz. that there is irresponsibility where there exists hallucination, and that punishment should not be administered where the act is derived from, or is based upon, an unfounded delusion—the baseless assumption as true of what really does not exist. And,

6. That the act complained of, should be the immediate unqualified offspring of the disease.

The great merit of this case consists in extending the protection of law, as well to embrace the delusions of the insane, as the intellectual destitution of the idiotic.

From the earliest periods in the history of jurisprudence down to the most recent, the great desideratum has been the establishment of certain tests, by means of which the fact of insanity could be certainly ascertained, if it existed. The test, which seems to have been among the first adopted, and which has certainly been the most undeviatingly adhered to, is that which consists in the capacity of distinguishing right from wrong. The great importance of this capacity, considered relatively to the elements that go to constitute crime, renders it but little surprising that it should have been so early adopted, and so pertinaciously adhered to. To those, however, who reflect, it must be obvious, that as this is entirely dependent upon a primitive faculty of the human mind, which, like every other, possesses independence in the exercise of its function, it cannot really be considered as evidence in proof of any thing beyond its own healthy or deranged action.

A knowledge of right or wrong implies two things :—

1. A perception or recognition by the mind, of those actions or things, in regard to which right or wrong may be predicated.

2. The feeling of what is right or wrong in reference to such actions or things.

The first is the work of the intellectual, particularly of the perceptive, faculties ; the second is the special function of the faculty of Conscientiousness.

The conclusions, upon which I think we may safely rely, in reference to this test, are the following :—

1. That it is to be regarded as one, but not the only, test.

2. That its absence, either from an original lack, or from an idiocy in that particular, renders the individual so imperfect, as to divest him of the elements of accountability.

3. The perversion of that special faculty by disease, or. derangement, produces the same result, by acting in the same general manner.

4. An original want, or material lack, of the perceptive faculties, by rendering it impossible that the facts, actions, or, in more general terms, the material, should be furnished upon which man's moral nature was framed to act, renders the mental constitution so defective, as to take away all accountability. And,

5. The perception of the perceptive or reflective faculties, or of both, by derangement, in consequence of which mental delusions exist, possessed of such strength that the moral faculty is utterly powerless when applied to them, also absolves from all responsibility for crimes.

Another test, upon which much reliance has been placed, is the *design* and *contrivance* sometimes displayed in the commission of a criminal act. The peculiar trait of character denominated *cunning* has often been noticed prevailing, to a great extent, among the insane. The degree of confidence, we may safely attach to this test, will not appear very considerable, when we remark,

1. That designs and contrivances, so far as relates to the adoption of means calculated to accomplish an end, is the work of the intellectual faculties, and is, therefore, perfectly consistent with the existence of moral mania. And,

2. So far as cunning, secrecy, adroitness of manœuvre are con cerned, they are referable to the special faculty of Secretiveness which, like all the other special faculties, possesses its own separate states of health and disease.

Another test, which has been assumed as infallible in determining the existence of insanity, is the presence of *delusion or hallucination* by which is meant the assumption by the mind of things as *realities* which in fact have no existence as such. To estimate properly the value of this criterion, we must consider its source. It is referable solely to the intellectual faculties, because they only form ideas. Its presence, therefore, indicates intellectual mania, either partial or general.

The affective faculties, however, never form ideas, and hence are subject to no delusions. Their action, therefore, may be perverted and insane, and yet there would be no delusion. The just inference from all this is, that its presence furnishes proof of the existence of some form of intellectual mania, while its absence affords no evidence to negative the existence of moral mania.

From all this, we are enabled to conclude that there is no certain infallible test, by which the presence or absence of insanity can be determined. It is a disease of the material organs of mind, and the aberration of mind is symptomatic of that disease. It is to be judged of, therefore, from a careful consideration of all the symptoms, and an attentive examination of the phenomena of mind, both in its states of healthy and deranged action.

ARTICLE IV.

THE NECESSITY OF REVEALED RELIGION, PHRENOLOGICALLY ILLUS- TRATED.

In an address by James Shannon, President of the College of Louisiana, delivered before the Philomathic Society of that Institution, on the 5th of February, 1839, Jackson, La.

FELLOW-MEMBERS OF THE PHILOMATHIC SOCIETY,—

Called by your politeness to the honour of appearing, on this occa- sion, before the public as your orator, I surely need not apologise for selecting a subject of a *grave* and *instructive* character. To those who are engaged, as we all are, in the development and training of the human mind, whatever is calculated to throw light on its funda- mental faculties cannot be uninteresting.

The pre-eminent value of self-knowledge, in its various departments and practical bearings, has long been admitted. All our enjoyments originate in harmony with the laws of our organisation; and the infraction of those laws is the fruitful source of human suffering. Hence, whoever would advance the perfection and happiness of the human race, *must do it in accordance with unchanging laws*, to which all nature, rational as well as irrational, has been subjected by the Creator of the universe. Every pang that is alleviated, every tear that is wiped from the eye of misery, indicates, on the part of the intelligent agent, a knowledge, to a certain extent, of the curious mechanism with which, and upon which, he operates for the accomplishment of his benevolent purpose. How important, then, is the study of man to all, who either seek happiness themselves, or nobly aspire to the *god-like* honour of promoting to the utmost the happiness of their fellow-men.

These principles are equally applicable to man, whether we consider him as a physical, organic, intellectual, or moral being. All, however, will admit, that some of man's faculties rank higher than others in the scale of relative importance. To the perfection of man, as man, all his faculties are alike essential. But it will hardly be contended by any reflecting mind, that those powers, which we possess in common with superior natures, are not relatively more important, than those which we possess in common with the brutes. None, perhaps, will question the propriety of classing some sentiments as *superior*, and others as *inferior*. Nor will any deny, that intellect and the moral feelings are superior to the animal propensities; and, consequently, that the former should regulate and control the latter.

The paramount importance of a correct knowledge of the human organisation is beautifully exemplified, and impressively admitted, in the great attention which, in all civilised nations, *is now*, and for many centuries *has been*, most justly paid to the various branches of the healing art. What benevolent mind could contemplate, without pangs of unutterable distress, the total extinction of all those lights which, even within the last century, have been thrown on man's physical organisation by the votaries of medical science, in order to alleviate animal suffering, and to promote animal enjoyment. Dark, unutterably dark and gloomy, would be the night of hopeless misery by which such an event must inevitably be succeeded.

If, then, a correct knowledge of our organisation, so far as the mere animal nature is concerned, be of unquestionable importance, how vastly more important is the knowledge and cultivation of our highest faculties! Strange! passing strange! that, in all ages, so much care should have been expended on man's *animal*, and so little on his *moral* and *intellectual* nature.   Let us hope that the *age of reason*—an age in which things will be esteemed and cultivated in proportion to their real value—has begun to dawn on our hitherto deluded world.

Phrenology teaches, (need I say, *demonstrates?*) that man possesses by nature *intellectual* and *affective* faculties ; the former of which *know*, the latter *feel*.   It teaches that the affective faculties include various subdivisions, occupying different points of elevation in the scale of relative importance—the propensities, or appetites, at the bottom, and the moral and religious sentiments at the top of the scale.

Thus, by patient and laborious induction, it proves that man is, *by the necessity of his nature*, a religious being ; that his religious faculties are the highest and most authoritative with which he is endowed ; and, consequently, that those infidel philosophers are egregiously in error, who maintain that religion is the unsightly work of priestcraft, rather than a noble structure, the foundations of which have been laid deep, broad, and *ineradicable*, in the organisation of man by the hand of the great Architect.

Now, to the reflecting mind it must be obvious, that if the Deity created man with religious faculties, he must have designed that those faculties should be cultivated.   Deny this, and you slander Jehovah with having formed this part, at least, of man's organisation in vain.

Again : As all man's faculties are designed, by their proper action, to contribute, each in its own sphere, to the perfection and happiness of his being, and as the religious faculties are the highest and most authoritative, it follows, by necessary inference, that supreme dignity and enjoyment can be obtained in no other way than by the cultivation and supremacy of our religious nature.

Once more: As the abuse of any organ degrades man, and involves him in the loss of happiness, to a greater or less extent, in proportion to the relative importance of the given organ, it is evident that *the deepest degradation and misery*, in which man can possibly be involved, result from the abuse of his religious organisation.

Were not this inference intuitively plain, we might refer, in proof of its correctness, to the universal wretchedness and debasement of the blinded devotees of idolatry and superstition.

From the foregoing reflections it must be obvious, that no questions are so completely identified with man's highest dignity and most exquisite enjoyment, as those which regard the proper cultivation of his moral and religious faculties.   Supreme dignity and happiness, as I have already said, cannot be obtained except in the supremacy of the religious and moral feelings ; but that supremacy will not of itself secure the desired object.   *Veneration* is probably as active in the worshipper of Juggernaut, as it is in the most devout Christian.

The religious feelings of Saul had as much control over him when he was engaged in persecuting the disciples, as subsequently, when with heroic fortitude he braved every danger, nobly defied even death itself, and, in the depth and holy ardour of his devotion, exclaimed— "God forbid that I should glory, save in the cross of our Lord and Saviour Jesus Christ, by whom the world is crucified unto me, and I unto the world."

If, then, the religious feelings, even while their supremacy is maintained, may nevertheless be misdirected, and in this state involve men in the deepest degradation, wretchedness, and crime, it follows that the question, *which, in point of intense interest, should absorb all others*, is simply this :—

In what way shall the religious organisation be cultivated, so as to harmonise with the designs of Infinite Benevolence to elevate and dignify our nature, to exalt us to the highest attainable happiness, and to the utmost limit of GOD-LIKE ELEVATION ?

Let us occupy a few moments in the investigation of this subject.

None of man's faculties can, with any propriety, be called abstractly either good or bad. They all contribute, as has always been said, to his perfection and happiness, when properly directed, and to his degradation and unhappiness, when misapplied.

The feelings, or affective faculties, are *all blind*, act solely with reference to their own present gratification, and cannot, of themselves, discriminate what mode of activity will avoid evil, and secure the greatest amount of good. This is as true of the religious sentiments, as of the animal propensities.

Take an example. The action of Veneration is a blind impulse to worship, it knows not what, but something at the time regarded as great or good. Hence, some have blindly venerated *loathsome reptiles*, and even *leeks* and *onions*. Others, to the present day, devoutly worship the impostor Mahomet. And others, still, as a religious act, immolate their children ; or, in deep adoration, prostrate themselves beneath the ponderous wheels of the Juggernaut, and are crushed to death.

Hence, we see very clearly that the highest activity of the religious faculties, unless it is directed by intellect properly enlightened, may be productive of the deepest misery and degradation.

But intellect alone will not suffice for the accomplishment of the desired object. To the truth of this proposition, history bears ample testimony. She most unhesitatingly affirms, that, throughout all ages, she has never known a single instance of a people left without revelation, that was not wholly given to the most debasing idolatry. Frequently, too, the most enlightened nations—as Egypt, Greece, and

Rome—were engulfed the most deeply in all sorts of licentiousness and idol-worship.

As a general rule, wheresoever men have been left without the light of revelation, " they have become vain in their imaginations, and their foolish heart has been darkened." In the strong language of Paul—" Professing themselves to be *wise*, they became *fools;* and changed the glory of the incorruptible God into an image made like to corruptible man, and to birds, and four-footed beasts, and creeping things."

With these undeniable facts staring us in the face, who can say that *revelation is not necessary* to elevate man's whole nature to the perfection and felicity of which he is capable; and for which his organisation proves that he was benevolently designed? Inasmuch as happiness is supremely desired by all, whoever denies the necessity of revelation, must maintain that man is able, by the unaided light of nature, to determine, with unerring certainty, what course of conduct will infallibly conduct him to the greatest amount of happiness of which he is capable. If this cannot reasonably be affirmed, then none can reasonably say that revelation is unnecessary.

But some may be disposed to ask, Is it possible that a revelation would be given? We think it is; and for the following reason. Is it not more manifest, that the eye was designed for vision, or that the ear was intended for hearing, than it is evident to the unbiased mind, that all man's faculties were designed for the production of happiness, and of nothing else.

Now, if a revelation be necessary for the accomplishment of that object, which God evidently had in view when he organised man as he has done, it is not merely probable that such a revelation would be given; but it is even in *the last degree improbable that it should be withheld.* This is no more than to say, that it is in the last degree improbable that the Deity would neglect to take such measures as are in the nature of things indispensable for the accomplishment of his benevolent designs.

So palpably deficient is the light furnished by natural religion, and so obviously necessary, under all the circumstances of the case, is revelation to guide man to perfection and felicity, that even pious and reflecting heathens have been led to expect that the Deity would, some day or other, bestow on the human race such a guide, to conduct man to the consummation of his being.

This revelation, in itself so necessary for the accomplishment of the Creator's benevolent designs, and, therefore, in the nature of things so probable, is given in the *inspired volume.* The Christian Scriptures contain a perfect system of religious doctrine and duty; a system, in its hopes, fears, and prescriptions, so completely adapted to man's whole nature, so evidently calculated to conduct him to the consummation of his being, as to demonstrate most undeniably its divine origin. When science shall have clearly disclosed man's whole organisation, and when Christianity, *freed from the rubbish of the dark ages*, shall have been correctly understood, I apprehend that its divine origin will be as little questioned by the *philosophic*, as it is now by the *Christian* world.

The correctness of the foregoing principles being admitted, it follows that, in order to produce the highest style of man, the animal propensities must be kept in subjection to the moral and religious faculties; and these, again, must be habitually cultivated under the guidance of intellect properly enlightened by the Christian Scriptures. Let this course be generally pursued, and such a flood of glory will at once be poured upon our sin-worn earth, that the morning stars will again sing together, and all the sons of God shout aloud for joy.

Here, however, it must be admitted, that we are presented, at the outset, with a difficulty of no inconsiderable magnitude. Dogmas the most contradictory, and, not unfrequently, the most absurd, have been deduced from the Christian Scriptures. Practices, too, that were not merely unjustifiable, but even malignant and diabolical in their nature, have been justified under the pretext of Christian duty and religious zeal. So undeniable are these truths, that the "odium theologicum," or *sectarian hate*, has become as truly (I might say, *lamentably*) proverbial in modern times, as was "Punica fides," or *Carthaginian faith*, in days of yore. Hence, it may be inferred by some, that, after all, this boasted revelation can be a guide only in name; whereas, practically, it is of little or no value.

I apprehend that this difficulty, though at first view by no means inconsiderable, will, on closer inspection, prove to be much less than many may imagine, and certainly not at all insurmountable. Let us enquire very briefly whether the difficulty in question can possibly be obviated; and if so, then in what way.

In this stage of my remarks, it is taken as granted that the Christian Scriptures are what they profess to be, a revelation from heaven, given to man for the purpose already specified, viz. to conduct him to the highest attainable happiness; and the question at present before us may be stated in the following way :—

Are the Christian Scriptures such a system as is capable of being certainly applied for the accomplishment of that purpose for which they were given?

Or it may be stated more fully thus: Is the Christian revelation capable of being *certainly understood* by those to whom it is addressed? And, when so understood, does it admit of a practical application?

That it is capable of being *certainly understood*, is necessarily implied in the very idea of its being a revelation. A revelation incapable of being understood by those to whom it is addressed, is as direct a contradiction in terms, as a *revelation* UNREVEALED. To affirm, therefore, that it is *unintelligible*, is to affirm that it is *no revelation*.

Again, in the very nature of things, it must be such as to admit of a practical application. In all our conceptions of revelation, this much at least is undeniably implied, viz. that it is a system of *instruction* and *motive*, rendered necessary by man's ignorance and tendency to err, and that it is designed to conduct him in the path of duty, dignity, and enjoyment.

Now, to suppose revelation incapable of being applied *successfully* to the accomplishment of the very end *for which it was given*, must appear, to the enlightened and pious mind, a very singular charge against its Author of either *incompetence* or FOLLY.

From the foregoing considerations it must be obvious, that the Christian Scriptures *are capable* of being *certainly understood* by those to whom they are addressed, and of being *successfully applied* for the accomplishment of that end for which they were given. It follows, too, that being so applied, they "are ABLE to make men *wise unto salvation*"—to conduct them to the perfection of their being—to the highest attainable dignity and happiness in this world, and to *glory inconceivable* in the world to come.

It must not be forgotten, however, that when these high and holy capabilities are predicated of the Christian Scriptures, they are predicated of *them alone*, in *their true import*, and not of *any thing*, or *every thing*, into which *men may be pleased to convert them by their vain imaginations*. This truth is self-evident; and, therefore, it would be, indeed, passing strange, if it should appear to any rational being to require proof.

Hence it is manifest, that the *diligent* and *honest-hearted study* of the Christian Scriptures is of paramount importance to all who would attain to the highest possible dignity, perfection, and happiness—who would nobly aspire to be not merely *angelic*, but even *god-like*.

Christianity never was intended to operate as a talisman, or an incantation. It can only operate in so far as it is understood, and reduced to practice. Its effects are truly sublime—a bright reflection of the glory of its Author. It can raise a world lying in wickedness, from the deepest abyss of misery and degradation, and restore it to holiness, to happiness, to God. But that any individual may be thus restored to a blissful connection with the throne of the Eternal, he must be not merely a hearer, but also a DOER of the word.

Hence the vast importance of the most perfect liberty of conscience. Unless in a very restricted sense, God never gave the conscience of any human being in keeping to any other. Every human being is for himself individually responsible to the common Judge of all. And, *that he may be so, his conscience must be free.* Hence the man that would interfere, in the slightest degree, with the most perfect liberty of conscience, constitutes himself by that very interference a *traitor against God*, and against the highest interests of him whose liberty is thus restricted.

On the necessity of following at all times the dictates of an unrestricted conscience, and of having that conscience properly enlightened, the opinion of Burlamaqui is so correct, and, withal, so appropriate, that I cannot forbear to quote it.

" But what must we do," says he, " in case of an erroneous conscience ?

" I answer, that we ought always to follow the dictates of conscience, even when it is erroneous, and whether the error be vincible or invincible.

" But it does not thence follow, that we are always excusable in being guided by the dictates of an erroneous conscience. This is true only when the error happens to be invincible. If, on the contrary, it is *surmountable*, and we mistake with respect to what is commanded, or forbidden, we sin either way, whether we act *according* to, or *against*, the decisions of conscience. This shows (to mention it once more) what an important concern it is to enlighten our conscience ; because, in the case just now mentioned, the person with an erroneous conscience is actually under a melancholy necessity of doing ill, whichever side he takes."

A truer sentiment than the foregoing, Burlamaqui never uttered. I fear, however, that on this subject, so far at least as the practical part is involved, there still remains much to be learned, even in enlightened and republican America.

Thus we see that it is absolutely impossible for any person to be permanently benefited by the Christian Scriptures, except in so far as he studies them honestly for himself, and for himself diligently reduces them to practice. The paramount importance of such study and such practice, is still farther illustrated by existing facts.

We find the so-called Christian world divided into a vast number of rival and conflicting sects. advocating an equal number of jarring and irreconcileable dogmas. Now, it is self-evident, that out of every hundred who differ on any point, at least ninety-nine must be wrong.

Therefore, without once enquiring who is right, or who is wrong, the divided state of Christendom makes it *intuitively plain*, that no human being can safely follow the opinions of another in religious matters; and that *he who does not, regardless of the opinions and wishes of others, investigate and act for himself on this all important subject, in this very neglect, sins against the plainest dictates of wisdom, duty, and self-interest.*

Neither will it do to say, that these differences have existed mainly among the unlearned, but that the learned have been in general more nearly agreed. The very reverse of this would be much nearer to the truth. Whoever will give himself the trouble to examine, may find that divisions have originated mainly, if not solely, with the learned Rabbis; and that among the *unlearned* there has been comparatively *little diversity of sentiment*, except so far as has been occasioned by a blind adherence to the dogmas of their leaders. This goes to show, that an honest heart, and a teachable child-like disposition, are much more certain to find the path of truth and duty, than great talents and learning, connected with *inordinate self-esteem*, or *love of approbation.* Hence the correctness of the Redeemer's sentiment, when he spake of some things that were "hid from the *wise* and *prudent*, and revealed unto *babes.*"

In short, you may select almost any truth or duty, taught in the Scriptures, in language so plain and unequivocal, that "he who runs may read, and the wayfaring man, *though a fool*, need not err therein," and you will propably find, that, in relation to *that truth*, or *that duty*, there *is*, or *has been*, as much *controversy among the* LEARNED, as about any other point.

Hence the danger, as well as the folly and criminality, of allowing others, learned or unlearned, friends or foes, to judge for us, or dictate to us, on religious subjects. And hence, too, the wisdom and importance of treating this matter in accordance with its real merits, as the chief business of our lives, our highest interest, our paramount concern.

From the foregoing reflections it is manifest, that the man who neglects to cultivate his religious faculties, acts even more unwisely than he who, possessing both eyes and ears, obstinately refuses to *behold the loveliness of nature*, or to be *charmed* with her *ceaseless* and *exquisite music.*

This, however, is not the worst view of the picture. All our faculties *will*, and *must* act. If their activity, therefore, is not directed into a proper channel, it will of necessity take an improper course. Hence, ALL MEN HAVE SOME RELIGION. And let the vaunting nfidel say what he please to the contrary, HE, too, HAS HIS RELIGION, and his God; and that God he worships with *a heart as sincere*, and with *a devotion as deep*, as that with which the Christian worships the God of revelation.

It will readily be granted, that the God, or CHIEF GOOD, supremely venerated, differs widely with different characters. The idol of some is a golden calf. Others worship the bubble *reputation*. Of others, still, "their god is their *belly*"—(perhaps the *intoxicating cup*)— " whose glory is in their shame, who mind earthly things."

The results, too, upon the character and prospects of the worshipper, are as diversified as the objects of worship. In all ages, the character of men has been mainly conformable to the character of their gods. If mammon be the god, or *chief good*, supremely venerated, the character will be progressively *covetous*. If LUST be the object of adoration, the worshipper becomes supremely *lustful*. If RUM and ROWDYISM be selected as the idol, who can fail to recognise the disgusting likeness in the *fetid breath*, the *bloated face*, the *nose* of almost *crimson hue*, the *besotted intellect*, and the *swinish conduct* of the *imbruted worshipper?*

This influence of a man's religion upon his character, is by no means accidental. It is the natural and necessary consequence of principles, well established in the philosophy of mind, but on which it would now be unseasonable to expatiate. It is sufficient for our present purpose to know, that the character of every individual will of necessity harmonise with the character of his god, or CHIEF GOOD. If that be noble, his character will be noble likewise. And if that be *earthly, sensual*, or *devilish*, such will his own character inevitably be.

This singular view of the subject demonstrates the pre-eminent value of the Christian religion, and its immense superiority over all other religious systems. Besides addressing the most powerful motives that can be conceived of, to *hope, fear, gratitude*, and to all the strongest and highest principles of our nature, Christianity presents for our ADMIRATION, IMITATION, and WORSHIP, a BEING of spotless purity and unbounded excellence. No marvel, then, that he who *is baptized into Christ* is a NEW CREATURE. If he were not, it would be as strange as if *fire* should *cease to burn*, and *water to drown*.

This tendency of Christianity, and its adaptation to the fundamental principles of our nature, I consider Paul as recognising in the following passage—" But we all, with open face beholding, as in a glass, the glory of the Lord, are changed in the same image from glory to glory, even as by the Spirit of the Lord."

How sublime the prospect, how glorious the destiny, by which we

are thus allured to the consummation of our being! In compariso
with this, *how poor, how contemptible,* the highest object of earthl
ambition!

Young gentlemen, from the foregoing reflections, it is apparent tha
man is, by the *necessity of his organisation,* a RELIGIOUS BEING; tha
his religious faculties are the highest and most authoritative wit
which he is endowed; that these faculties will act either to his per
fection and felicity, if properly directed, or to his degradation an
misery, if misapplied; and that, in order to raise him to the highes
possible elevation of dignity and enjoyment, their activity must b
guided by intellect, enlightened by the Christian Scriptures.

Your choice, then, is not, cannot be, between *religion* and N
RELIGION. If your religious faculties are not employed in rendering
supreme homage to the living God, they are supremely devoted t
some other object, selected as your idol; regarded and worshipped a
your CHIEF GOOD.

The only alternative, therefore, that is left you is, whether you
will have a *true* or a *false* religion—one that will accomplish the sub
lime purposes of the Divine Architect, in elevating and beautifying
our whole nature; or one that will defeat those purposes, sensualise
and brutify your highest aspirations, and involve you in the deepes
degradation and wretchedness, both at present, and throughout the
whole duration of your future existence.

In such circumstances, can any thing short of *idiocy* or *madnes*
hesitate what choice to make? On one hand, the path of duty, dig
nity, and enjoyment, endlessly progressive, opens wide before you
inviting you to enter, and be *for ever* and *inconceivably happy.* Or
the other, folly's gates expanded wide invite you to *wallow* in the
mire of sensuality, be transformed *into brutes,* and sink deep, and stil
deeper, in brutality and wretchedness for ever.

Make, then, your election; and be it such as you shall neve
regret; such as will send a thrill of joy through all the myriads o
holy beings that adore and worship around the throne of God.

ARTICLE V.

ON MENTAL EXERCISE AS A MEANS OF HEALTH.

That there is an intimate connection between the mind and the
body, and that each exerts a powerful influence over the state of the
other, all readily admit. The experience and observation of every

one, will afford abundant evidence of this fact, as well as ample testimony of the importance of being acquainted, as far as possible, with a subject which so vitally affects human happiness. Many facts have been observed on this point for centuries, but, till lately, very little definite or tangible knowledge has been possessed which could be rendered available to any practical purposes. The researches of modern science, particularly the discoveries of phrenology, have thrown a vast amount of light on the mutual relations which exist between the mind and the body. And though we may not be able to comprehend the precise nature of this relationship, yet we can understand, to a considerable extent, the conditions or laws by means of which each, reciprocally, affects the other. If we would, therefore, secure the great object of our existence, as well as promote the happiness of our species, the dictates of duty, no less than of wisdom, should incite us to study those laws, and to avail ourselves of all the helps which either science or experience can throw in our way.

A distinguished physician of Edinburgh communicated, some years since, to the " Phrenological Journal," several interesting articles " *On Mental Exercise as a means of Health.*" We propose to present our readers with the substance of these articles, either in a condensed form or by means of extracts. With this acknowledgment, we proceed to the subject, without making any farther reference or giving quotation marks.

No principle in physiology is better established than that the proper exercise of every organ promotes, not only the vigour and health of that organ, but also of the entire system. And according to the importance of its functions, as well as the nature of its relations to other organs, will be the effects of its proper, excessive or deficient exercise on the whole body. This remark applies with peculiar force to the brain, as the organ of the mind.

In the first place, we shall find that a disuse of its functions, or, in other words, *inactivity of intellect and feeling, impairs its structure, and weakens the mental powers which it serves to manifest.*

It is by the deliberate employment of this principle that the law, without knowing it, subdues even the most violent and obdurate criminals. Placing a man in solitary confinement, without books, without occupation, and without light enough to see distinctly around him, is neither more nor less than withdrawing all means of activity from his cerebral organs. Its influence in diminishing their activity and power is so speedy and so terrible, that few natures, however rough, fearless, or brutal, are able to withstand it for many days, and few criminals who have undergone it once, will ever rashly expose themselves to it a second time. So much does this discipline weaken the mind, that the most unruly and ferocious ruffians, upon whom severity and blows had been expended without effect, have come forth subdued and tractable. The inference obviously follows, that to strengthen the brain and nervous system, we must exercise them regularly and judiciously, just as we would do the muscular system, to give it tone and vigour. If we neglect to do so, we may use any other means we like, but our efforts will be fruitless, and debility of body and weakness of mind will continue to increase, and to aggravate each other.

If we look abroad upon society, we shall see innumerable proofs of what is here advanced. When a person is confined to an unvarying round of employment, which affords neither scope nor stimulus to one half of his faculties, his mental powers, for want of exercise to keep up due vitality in their cerebral organs, become blunted, his intellect becomes slow and dull, and he feels any unusual subjects of thought as disagreeable and painful intrusions. But let the situation of such a person be changed; bring him, for instance, from the solitude of the country to the bustle of the town, give him a variety of imperative employments, and place him in society so as to supply to his cerebral organs that extent of exercise which gives them health and vivacity of action, and in a few months the change produced will be surprising. Animation and acuteness will take the place of former insipidity and dulness. We ought not to suppose that it is the mind itself which becomes heavy and feeble, and again revives into energy by these changes in external circumstances; the effects arise from changes in the state of the brain. Regular exercise conduces to its greater health and activity, and the mental manifestations are influenced by its condition. The following examples place the effects of exercise in a striking point of view:—A young military officer, who lately commanded a small detachment. spent three years in Canada in a remote station, where he was completely detached from all society of his own rank. During all that period, he was obliged to pass his time in listless sauntering, shooting, or fishing, without the excitement to his various faculties which is afforded by the society of equals. The consequence of this compulsory mental apathy, and the corresponding inactivity of brain, was, that, on being relieved at the end of that time, his nervous system had become so weak and irritable, that he feared to meet even with the members of his own family, and for months would never venture to walk out to take necessary exercise, except in the dark. And it was only at the end of several months that the renewed stimulus of society and employment restored the tone of his nervous system so far as to allow him to regain his natural character of mind, and to return to his usual habits of life. A gentleman, with whom I have the pleasure of being personally acquainted, was stationed for some years up the country in India, completely secluded from the society of ladies. The party being pretty numerous, the officers contrived to pass their time agreeably enough; but this gentleman said, that on his return to Calcutta he felt so great an aversion to female society, that he would rather have faced a tiger than gone into a drawing-room resplendent with youth and beauty. After becoming familiar, however, with this situation, his faculties recovered their tone, and the fair sex exhibited to his mind all their wonted graces and attractions.

Another very appropriate example may be found in the case of a nervous young lady, whose education has communicated nothing but accomplishments—who has no materials of thought, and no regular and imperative occupations to interest her and *demand* attention—who takes no active part in promoting the welfare or comfort of those about her—who looks to others for support and sustenance—and whose brain, in short, is half asleep. Such a person has literally nothing on which to expend half the nervous energy which nature has bestowed on her for better purposes. She has nothing to excite and exercise the brain, nothing to elicit activity; her own feelings and personal relations necessarily constitute the grand objects of her contemplations; these are brooded over till the mental energies become impaired, false ideas of existence and of Providence spring up in the mind, the fancy is haunted by strange impressions, and every trifle which relates to self is exaggerated into an object of immense importance. The brain, having literally nothing on which to exercise itself, becomes weak, and the mental manifestations are enfeebled in proportion, so that a person of good endowments thus treated will often exhibit something of the imbecility of a fool. But suddenly change the circumstances in which such a person is placed. Suppose, for example, that her parents lose their health or fortune, and that she is called upon to exert her utmost energies in their and in her own behalf—that, in short, her mental faculties and brain, her intellect and her moral and social feelings, are blessed with a stimulus to act; the weakness, the tremors, and the apprehensions, which formerly seemed an inborn part of herself, disappear as if by enchantment, and strength, vigour, and happiness, take their place, solely because now God's law is fulfilled, and the brain with which he has connected the mind, is supplied with that healthful stimulus and exercise which he ordained to be indispensable to our comfort and welfare.

An additional illustration will be found in the case of a man of mature age and of active habits, who has devoted his life to the toils of business, and whose hours of enjoyment have been but few and short.   Suppose such a person to retire to the country in search of repose, and to have no deep moral, religious, or philosophical pursuits to occupy his attention and keep up the active exercise of his brain—the latter will lose its health, and the invariable result will be ennui, weariness of life, despondency, and nervous diseases in their most distressing forms.   This arises solely from the brain being left unexercised and unexcited, till, like the eye without light, its powers of action become so far enfeebled, that derangement even of the general health ensues from the deficient and vitiated supply of nervous influence which is then sent to the rest of the body.

The wonderful effects of a change from inactivity to bustle and employment is well known in common life, and is explicable only on the principle of strengthening the brain and mind by a due exercise. In nine cases out of ten, a visit to a watering-place, or a journey through an interesting country, restores health more by giving healthy excitement to the mind and brain, than by the water swallowed or the locomotion endured.   And it is proverbial of weak and delicate persons, that under strong excitement they will exert not only double muscular force, but even prove superior to the effects of miasma and contagion, to which, when excited, they would have been the first victims.   In the army it is proverbial also, that the time of fatigue and danger is not the time of disease.   It is in the inactive and listless month of a campaign that crowds of patients pass to the hospitals. In both these cases it is active exercise giving strength to the brain, and through it healthy vigour to the body, which produces the effect.

This law of our constitution seems to me one of the most beautiful of the many admirable arrangements of a wise and beneficent Providence.   We are gifted with many high and noble powers of thinking and of sentiment, which are, in this world, in close dependence on our bodily frame.   If we exercise them duly, we promote directly the growth, nutrition, and health of the corporeal organ, and indirectly the health of the whole system, and at the same time experience the highest mental gratification of which a human being is susceptible, viz. that of having fulfilled the end and object of our being, in the active discharge of our duties to God, to our fellow-men, and to ourselves.   If we neglect them, or deprive them of their objects, we weaken the organisation, give rise to distressing diseases, and at the same time experience the bitterest feelings that can afflict humanity—ennui and melancholy.   The harmony thus shown to exist between the moral and physical world, is but another proof of the numerous inducements to that right conduct and activity, in pursuing which, the Creator had evidently destined us to find terrestrial happiness and comfort.

Seeing, then, that the brain and nervous system cannot, any more than the muscles, be strengthened without well-regulated exercise, we come next to enquire what are the functions which their different parts perform, as it is well known that each can be kept in activity only by employing it on its own objects. Phrenology enables us to answer this question with sufficient accuracy for our present purpose. It reveals to us the various faculties of intellect, sentiment, and propensity, which are primitive powers of the mind; it points to the different nerves of sensation and of motion, going to the various organs by which life is sustained, and to the numerous muscles, bones, ligaments, and instruments of sense and of locomotion, which put us in relation with the external world and with our fellow-men, and it shows us that, to produce a full effect, all of these must be duly and regularly exercised; but as to notice all of them would embrace much too wide a field, I shall at present confine myself to the functions performed by the brain, as the material instrument or organ of mind.

It is an axiom in physiology, that every part must be exercised upon its own objects. if we wish to develope or strengthen its powers. A man may read and understand rules of arithmetic and all the definitions of Euclid, but if he do not practise them, he will never become an expert arithmetician or mathematician. A man may read and understand directions for drawing, or chiselling, but unless he put his own hand to the work, and accustom his mind to guide it to his pnrpose, he will never attain excellence as a painter or sculptor, or even ordinary command over its movements. Now, the purely mental faculties, being connected during life with material organs, are subjected exactly to the same law; and, therefore, unless the intellectual faculties and moral feelings be duly exercised directly, and for their own sakes, neither they nor their organs will ever acquire promptitude, strength, or healthy development. Education rests on this fact; and the intellectual acuteness and facility which we acquire, by a judicious exercise of the mental powers, the soundness of judgment, promptitude of action, and command over our feelings, which we obtain by being thrown upon our own resources among our fellow-men, and obliged to act according to our own perceptions of what is right, are unequivocal proofs of the advantages of attending to this law of our nature. The moral feelings do not differ in this respect from the intellectual faculties; they require direct education and regular activity to bring them to maturity, quite as much as the intellect does; and it has only been from blindness to this fact, that their proper culture and direction have hitherto been so little attended to. We shall see presently how very imperfect existing systems of education are, in regard not only to the moral sentiments, but even to intellect itself, which has been the chief object of attention with teachers and directors of education.

If phrenology be true, (and here I must take its truth for granted,) the great mass of the brain is connected with the operation and manifestation of the various propensities and moral sentiments which furnish us with impulses to action and with restraints on conduct, and a comparatively small portion is dedicated to the intellectual powers. Let us see, then, how much of the brain is exercised in the acquisition of those branches of education which occupy almost exclusively the whole time of young ladies. At school, French, Italian, geography, arithmetic, music, dancing, and drawing, are the grand employments, whatever may be the capacity of the individual for any or all of them; and at home, novels, poetry, and the lighter sorts of reading, fill up the vacant hours. Analysed phrenologically, all these very pleasing accomplishments have reference to the faculties of Language, Locality, Number, Tune, Time, Form, Size, Eventuality, and Comparison, but to some of these only indirectly; so that, when we compare the aggregate mass of the organs corresponding as to these faculties, which modern education seems to consider embracing the whole mind, in its real relation to the whole mass of the brain, we find that it will amount to certainly not more than *one tenth part*, thus leaving *nine parts* to shoot forth just as chance and circumstances may direct, or to lie inactive altogether. And thus, be it observed, we deliberately deprive the body of that healthful and stimulating nervous energy which an active and efficient brain can alone bestow; and while we rear a mind that remains a stranger to the highest interests which ought to occupy its powers, we rear a body which remains also enfeebled and suffering in consequence of their neglect. The ordinary occupations, habits, and mode of life of our young ladies, therefore, obviously do not afford sufficient employment and healthy stimulus to a large portion of the brain, and more important faculties of the mind; and consequently few of those who are delicately formed ever become so robust physically, so happy mentally, or so useful in society, as their nature and constitution are really capable of attaining. The intellectual faculties of a rational being require something higher and more useful in practical life than mere accomplishments; and unless they are presented with objects worthy of their notice, something that at the same time rouses, exercises, and braces their higher feelings, they become dull and languid. The mental alacrity, happiness, and bodily vigour, which are constantly observed to follow full and *imperative* occupation of mind, and actively-employed affections, even in persons feeble by nature, are palpable illustrations of the benefits and necessity of exercise to strengthen the mind, and of the close dependence of it on the state of the organisation—a point which, I am afraid, is not sufficiently kept in view.   If the intellect is not provided with interests external to itself, it must either be inactive and become weak, or work upon the feelings and become diseased.   In the former case, the mind becomes apathetic, and presents no ground of sympathy or fellowship with its fellow-creatures; in the latter, it becomes unduly sensitive, and shrinks within itself and its own limited circle, as its only protection against every trifling occurrence or mode of action which has not relation to itself.   A desire to continue an unvaried round of life takes strong possession of the mind, because to come forth into society requires an exertion of faculties which have been long dormant, which cannot awaken without pain, and which are felt to be feeble when called into action.   In such a state, home and its immediate interests become not only the centre, which they ought to be, but also the boundary of life; and the mind being originally constituted to embrace a much wider sphere, is thus shorn of its powers, deprived of numerous pleasures attending their exercise; the whole tone of mental and bodily health is lowered, and a total inaptitude for the business of life and the ordinary intercourse of society comes on, and often increases till it becomes a positive malady.

If the parents or guardians of young persons so situated be themselves possessed of talent, but want either the knowledge of human nature, or the tact requisite for drawing out the faculties of those under their charge, the evil is aggravated rather than diminished, because the natural veneration which the young feel for talent in their seniors, keeps them too far from that equality which is essential to friendly confidence and encouragement.   Girls of a sensitive mind thus situated, will often suppress their own thoughts, and do injustice to their own powers, when with more confidence they would have displayed much energy, and engaged in many active pursuits.   From timidity, and the want of independence which it engenders, such persons rarely act up to the limits of their faculties, and yet are habitually judged of as if they did.   In accordance with this observation, it is no rarity to see them, on the occurrence of circumstances which call forth their faculties, evince a degree of activity and vigour of judgment which previously no one suspected them to possess.

That exercise of the various feelings and intellectual powers is one of the most efficient tonics to the nervous system, is proved by another striking fact.   Every person who has either attended invalids, or been an invalid himself, must often have remarked, that the visit of a kind and intelligent friend is highly useful in dispelling uneasy sensations, and in promoting recovery by increased cheerfulness and hope.   The true reason of this is simply, that such intercourse interests the feelings, and affords an agreeable stimulus to several of the largest organs of the brain, and thereby conduces to the diffusion of a healthier and more abundant nervous energy over the whole system. This, in fact, is an important medical principle, according to which medical men endeavour to act systematically, when they often seem to be merely passing the time ; and it is this which makes it so desirable, even for his own power of relieving disease, that the medical man should be always the friend as well as the professional adviser of his patient.   The extent of good which a man of kindly feeling and a ready command of his ideas and language can do, is much beyond what is generally believed ; and if this holds in debility arising from general causes, in which the nervous system is affected not exclusively, but only as a part of the body, it must hold infinitely more in nervous debility and in nervous disease ; for then, indeed, the moral management is truly the medical remedy, and differs from the latter only, that its administration depends on the physician, and not on the apothecary—on the friend, and not on the indifferent attendant.

What, therefore, seems most wanted, in addition to judicious exercise, regimen, and other points on which I cannot touch here, to strengthen the nervous system and general health of delicate and nervous young ladies, is a mode of life and of occupation that shall give full scope to the intellectual powers, and healthy excitement and activity, and a right direction to the affective faculties or feelings ; and in forming any arrangements for this purpose, we must take for our guide the grand rule of *exercising the faculties we wish to employ upon their own immediate objects*, as no other stimulus is half so efficacious or grateful as this.   It would be as absurd to think of cultivating our powers of vision by listening attentively to sounds instead of looking upon the face of nature, and examining the colours, forms, and qualities there presented to the eye, as it would be to think of cultivating Causality by reading poetry, or Benevolence, Justice, and Veneration, by studying logic.   The intellectual powers, therefore, must be applied each to their own objects ; and the moral sentiments and propensities must be kept in activity by contact and communion with the sentiments and propensities of our fellow-men, and not left to the listless dulness to which either seclusion or fashionable society would condemn them.

MISCELLANY.

Outlines of Physiology, with an Appendix on Phrenology, by P. M. Roget, M. D.—This is the title of an octavo volume of 516 pages, recently issued from the press in this city. It is composed of two articles, originally prepared by Dr. Roget for the "Encyclopædia Britannica." Their present republication is introduced to the public with a brief preface and numerous notes, by an "*American editor.*" The article on phrenology, including nearly fifty pages, appears in the form of an appendix. Dr. R. has been an unbeliever in phrenology ever since its first introduction into Great Britain; and it would be very strange, if a man of his age, circumstances, and relations to the public, when once having committed himself decidedly and unequivocally against it, should take any other ground but that of an open opposer to the science.

In his treatise on physiology, page 449, Dr. Roget states the fact, that no physician over forty years of age would admit the truth of Harvey's celebrated discovery of the circulation of the blood ; so in relation to the truth of Dr. Gall's discovery of the functions of the brain, though there may be many honourable exceptions to the above historical fact, yet we presume *Dr. Roget will never be enrolled among that number.*

Notwithstanding Dr. R.'s objections to phrenology have been repeatedly answered in Great Britain, yet they are republished in this country with the evident design of prejudicing the public against the science—a thing which they are peculiarly calculated to effect, both from the well-known reputation of their author, as well as from his misrepresentations and plausible mode of reasoning. Since this is the fact, we shall present a thorough and extended review of the work in a future number of the Journal. We are gratified to find that it has already met with some strictures in the September number of the Eclectic Journal of Medicine.

——

The Literary Examiner and Western Monthly Review, published at Pittsburg, Pa.—The August number of this periodical contains a critical and able review of Dr. Sewall's lectures against phrenology, as well as an extended notice of the famous letter of J. Q. Adams. The writer displays a thorough knowledge of anatomy, physiology, and phrenology ; and completely exposes the sophistry and misrepresentations of these two anti-phrenologists. We should be pleased to notice this review at length, did our limits permit, and had not the same subjects already been discussed in this Journal; and, as it is, we cannot refrain from copying the following excellent paragraph in commendation of Phrenology :—

"This science studies man only as a living agent, confining its enquiries to his organisation and its resulting phenomena. Strictly Baconian in all its parts and processes, it pushes its investigations no farther than the safe ground of observation and experience, and pretends only to examine the proper subjects of rational enquiry. Of all the systems of mental philosophy that recognise the truth of the Christian Scriptures, it alone deserves the high praise of rejecting all ontological hypotheses, and reverently leaving to revelation its proper province of unfolding the condition of the soul in a future state. It is the only science of mind which consists exclusively of facts and phenomena, and their classified arrangement, dealing only with the certainties which sense and reflection are competent to attain, and walking cautiously by the sound rule, that first causes and the intimate nature of things is the wisdom of God—observation and legitimate deduction, the proper knowledge of man."

Southern Literary Messenger.—This monthly periodical, which is deservedly popular, and has an extensive circulation in the southern states, is furnishing its readers with the full reports of Mr. Geo. Combe's lectures on phrenology, as they first appeared in the New Yorker. Each number contains a report of one lecture. We doubt whether the editor of the Messenger could select matter more interesting and instructive to the great mass of its readers; and in confirmation of this remark, we observe that several papers, in their recent notices of the work, have spoke of its value in high terms, with special reference to the full reports of these lectures.

W. Lawrence, F. R. S., Professor of Anatomy and Surgery, London, makes the following statement in his lectures on physiology:—"I consider the difference between man and animals, in propensities, feelings, and intellectual faculties, to be the result of the same cause as that which we assign for the variations in other functions, viz. difference in organisation; and that the superiority of man in rational endowments, is not greater than the more exquisite, complicated, and perfectly developed structure of his brain, and particularly of his ample cerebral hemispheres, to which the rest of the animal kingdom offers no parallel, nor even any near approximation."

Usefulness of Phrenology to the Treatment of Insanity.—Very great improvements have been made within twenty years in the treatment of the insane, and in the management of lunatic asylums. It is now generally admitted, that mental derangement of every kind and degree is the result of a diseased state of the brain; and it has been found, by actual experiment, that this disease, like others, is curable to a very great extent by the application of proper remedies. Nearly all cases of mental alienation, if taken in season and properly treated, are now found to result in the restoration of health to the body, as well as of sanity to the mind of the patient. Once the insane were regarded universally as incurable, and comparatively no exertions were made to promote their happiness or prolong their lives. The important changes which have been brought about in this respect, are attributable in no small degree to the lights which phrenology has shed upon medical science. But this unfortunate class of our fellow-beings, as a body, have scarcely yet begun to enjoy its healing and beneficial influences. The next fifty years will witness far greater changes and improvements in the treatment of the insane, than have occurred during the last half century.

For some time past, several lunatic asylums in Great Britain have been under the superintendence of medical gentlemen who have availed themselves of the helps of phrenology. And it has been found, we believe, in every instance, that the number of cures has been greater, and the general management better, in these institutions, than in those superintended by persons entirely ignorant of the science. There is evidence to believe, both from experience as well as philosophy, that, ultimately, all hospitals and asylums for the insane will be managed by superintendents who understand the principles and application of phrenology. Dr. James Scott, of the Royal Hospital at Haslar, England, recently gave, in a public document, the following testimony of the utility of the science:—"I unhesitatingly give it as my deliberate conviction," says he, "that *no* man, whatever may be his qualifications in other respects, will be very successful in the treatment of insanity in its various forms, if he be not well acquainted with practical phrenology; and I will add, that whatever success may have attended my own practice in the Lunatic Asylum of this great national establishment, over which I have presided as chief medical officer for many years, I owe it, almost exclusively, to my knowledge of phrenology."

Phrenology in Louisiana.—It appears that there is a strong and increasing interest on the subject of phrenology in various parts of this state. At Jackson, where is located the college of Louisiana, a large and flourishing Phrenological Society has for some time existed, which embraces the president and professors of the college, as well as many of the students. In No. 10, Vol. 1, of the Journal, we presented our readers with an excellent address, delivered before this society by President Shannon; and we have the pleasure of presenting them with another address from the same source in the present number of the Journal.

We learn, also, that Professor H. H. Gird delivered, last year, an address before the Phrenological Society of the same institution, which is spoken of in high terms. Will some friend of the science send us copies of the Feliciana Republican for February, 2, 9, and 15, containing this address? Meanwhile we copy for our readers its concluding paragraph from an exchange periodical:—

"For this trait, for its tendency to diffuse the noblest kind of knowledge, I am a *warm* friend to phrenology. It shuts not itself in the scholar's cell, its sphere is not the narrow bounds of the professor's lecture-room; it goes forth strong in the consciousness of its truth and simplicity, and addresses itself to all who are willing to hear. It calls men together, it teaches them to study themselves and their fellow-men, and to apply their knowledge to useful and benevolent purposes under the guidance of the Holy Spirit of Christianity. It is not extravagant, then, to apply to its authors and propagators the eulogium bestowed on Socrates. Like him, they have brought philosophy down from heaven, and caused her to dwell once more in the abodes of men."

The celebrated Dr. Physick, who for many years stood at the head of the medical profession in this country, was, in the year 1821, *President* of the Philadelphia *Phrenological* Society.

A very scientific gentleman recently stated, in a public lecture, that, from a critical examination of paintings, statues, busts, &c., he was fully convinced of the truth of this fact: viz. that *all the signers of the Declaration of American Independence were men possessing large heads.* Can any one furnish us with definite information, respecting the general size or particular development of the above class of individuals, or of any of the great leaders in the American Revolution?

Several interesting articles on phrenology have appeared in the recent numbers of the "Boston Medical and Surgical Journal," which we shall notice more particularly hereafter.

THE

a

AMERICAN PHRENOLOGICAL JOURNAL

AND

MISCELLANY.

| Vol. II. | Philadelphia, December 1, 1839. | No. 3. |

ARTICLE I.

PHRENOLOGY VINDICATED AGAINST THE CHARGES OF FATALISM.

BY CHARLES CALDWELL, M. D.

PART II.

In the consideration of this intricate and much vexed question, it is not my purpose to endeavour to prove that the will of man is *free*, in the loose and unlimited interpretation which the term may receive. Such freedom, transcending the bounds of rational liberty, would be wild licentiousness. It would be incompatible with subjection or definite responsibility to any form of law. But this is not true of the human will. In the performance of his voluntary actions, man is as strictly under the control of the laws of his moral and intellectual nature, as the streams are under the influence of gravitation in their descent to the ocean, or the planets in the performance of their journeys around the sun. Nor are the laws which govern the movements of mind less definite, positive, and unchangeable, than those which govern the movements of matter. Were the case otherwise, to reason as to the grounds and motives of human conduct would be impossible; and all efforts to that effect would be futile. Let the actions of man be free from the guidance of affective causes and controlling influences, and by no extent of experience or depth of wisdom could they be foreseen, or reasonably calculated on from one moment to another. A moral and intellectual chaos, with the confusion accompanying it, would every where prevail. When I say that I will or will not perform a certain deed, my meaning is, that I purpose to obey a motive which now influences me. And some motive must always influence us, else are we aliens and outlaws from the system of nature, violators of its harmony, and totally dissimilar to every thing else within the compass of creation.

In the sphere, however, for which he is intended, and within whose imits alone he can act, man is sufficiently free for all the purposes of noral agency and personal accountability.   In his selection and pur-ruit of a line of conduct, as well as in the performance of individual ictions, he feels himself free from any hampering control ; though he ilso feels that, in whatever he does, he is influenced by some cause. And between that cause and the action he performs, there is as natural ind positive a bond of law, as there is between a falling body and the 2arth which attracts it.   Were the case otherwise, man, I repeat, would be an anomaly in creation, all things else being governed by aw, and he being lawless.   To this, even the actions of the Deity form no exception.   They are circumscribed and determined by the law (if it may be so called) of his own nature and perfections.   He cannot swerve from truth, justice, or goodness, because they are elements of his moral essence, and form a kind of fate, which bind him to maintain them pure and inviolate.   Much less can man so far control his nature, as to become independent of the motives and influences which are ordained and fitted by his Creator to govern his actions.

My object, then, I say, in the present disquisition, is not to prove the abstract and positive freedom of the human will ; but to show that there is nothing in phrenology more inconsistent with it, than is found in other doctrines of moral action.   On the contrary, I hope to make it appear that, on the principles of that science, a more satisfactory exposition of Free Will can be given, than on those of any other scheme of mental philosophy. . Without farther preface, therefore, I shall engage in the enterprise.   In this attempt, the truth of the science will be regarded, not as a postulate *to be* demonstrated, but as a theorem demonstrated already.

Phrenology shows that the human brain is composed of thirty-six or thirty-seven distinct and specific organs, each being the seat or instrument of a mental faculty, also distinct and specific.   These organs and faculties, however, are not independent, but exercise over each other a modifying and, to a certain extent, a controlling influence. They are not only, moreover, essentially different in their nature and tendency ; some of them have bearings so directly opposite, as to be checks on one another, should any of them threaten to run to excess in their action.   All these faculties are useful, and therefore valuable in themselves, equally consistent, under proper regulation, with morality and virtue, and necessary to the completion of the human mind—necessary, I mean, to fit man for the world he lives in, and to qualify him for the duties of the station he occupies.   Vice and crime, therefore, are not the necessary product of the human faculties.

They are but the incidental fruit of only a few of them, when abused or misapplied. And the mind is so constituted, as to be able to prevent such abuse or misappliance, provided it be suitably educated and disciplined. For it must be borne in remembrance, that the mental faculties are susceptible of great alteration by training. They can be strengthened or weakened, according as the condition of the mind requires for its amendment the one or the other.

Another truth essentially connected with this subject, and which the enquirer therefore should never forget, is, that some persons receive from nature a much stronger propensity to vice than others. This is verified by all observation, and cannot therefore be disputed, much less denied. The propensity is in many cases a strongly-marked constitutional quality. Even in members of the same family, educated alike by precept and example, this difference of propensity is in numerous instances exceedingly striking. From their early infancy, some of the children are marked by ill-temper, and, as soon as they are capable of action, are addicted to mischief, cruelty, and vice. They delight in teazing or in some way annoying, perhaps tormenting, their brothers and sisters—in puncturing servants with pins, needles, or penknives—in inflicting pain and mutilation on domestic or other animals—and even in the tearing or burning of wearing apparel, the breaking of glass windows, and the destruction of household furniture.

In their dispositions and characters, the other children of the family are not only different, but directly the reverse. They are mild in their tempers, affectionate and kind to every thing around them, and pained at the very thought of giving pain or offence, or of injuring property.

In another instance, some children of a family are irritable and passionate, resolute and fearless, perhaps enamoured of danger, and, under resentment, prone to combat. Of these heroes in miniature, the brothers and sisters are slow in resenting injuries, peaceful and timid, and inclined to shrink from danger, rather than to seek it.

In a third family, some children are covetous from their cradles. They greedily, and by instinct, grasp at every thing within their reach, always illiberally, and at times unjustly; and, having gained possession of the object desired, they selfishly apply it to their own gratification, regardless of the wishes or wants of their associates. Others, again, of the same family, reared under the same roof, and the same external influences, manifest a spirit of unmixed kindness, generosity, and disinterestedness. Regardless, apparently, of their own gratification, their chief object seems to be the gratification of others. I should speak more philosophically, were I to say, that their gratification consists in gratifying their companions. For the attainment of this, they cheerfully and even joyously distribute among their playfellows whatever they possess, that they may minister to their enjoyment. Some children, again, are prone to secrecy and concealment, equivocation, deception, and open falsehood; while others of the same household are frank, confidential, and communicative, and prefer punishment to a departure from truth. In a special manner they never permit their innocent comrades to sustain blame, or incur a penalty for faults which they have themselves committed.

By no one of observation and experience in life will this statement be denied. On the contrary, its correctness is fully established, by facts and scenes of hourly occurrence. My reference for illustration and proof has been to children, because their native dispositions have not been yet materially changed by the influence of education. And the inference to be drawn from the contrast presented is, that, though all men may be, by nature, more or less prone to vicious indulgences, the propensity is far stronger in some than it is in others. And this is in accordance with the lessons of Scripture on the same subject.

For these different degrees of propensity to vice, phrenologists assign an intelligible, and, as they believe, a veritable cause. Each propensity is the product of a specific organ of the brain; and, other things being equal, its strength is proportionate to the size of that organ. A large organ, a strong propensity, and the reverse. It is, moreover, to be borne in mind, that, in common with muscles and other parts of the body, the size and strength of cerebral organs can be greatly changed by education and training. And while suitable excitement and exercise invigorate them, inaction and want of excitement debilitate them. At pleasure, therefore, cerebral organs, when too strong, may be enfeebled, and strengthened when too weak. Thus may the balance between the organs be maintained. Though it is not contended that this balance can be in all cases rendered sufficiently complete for the security of morals, and the promotion of virtue, it can be made highly available in the amendment of the disposition, and the prevention of crime.

In the view of anti-phrenologists, this doctrine is eminently objectionable; because, as they assert, its issue is inevitable and unqualified fatalism. If, say they, man has a material organ of crime, that crime he must commit, as certainly as he must see with his eye, hear with his ear, or breathe with his lungs.

This objection being utterly wanting in strength, or candour, or both united, is no better than a cavil. The answer to it is correspondingly plain and easy. Man has no organ of crime; nor does such a doctrine make any part of phrenology. He has several organs which may lead to crime, unless they are prevented from acting to excess, or if they be abused or misapplied. And what is there that may not, by misuse, be productive of evil? But, as already mentioned, all excessive action, and all abuse and misapplication of the organs, which alone produce crime, may be in most instances easily prevented. The natural action of every organ, when under due regulation, is useful and necessary. The inference, therefore, which anti-phrenologists draw by analogy, from our eyes, ears, and lungs, is groundless and futile. We do not see, hear, and breathe, with those organs only *when* or *because* their functions are inordinate and excessive. On the contrary, it is the *natural* state of the organs alone that it is salutary to us. Their excessive or preternatural state is injurious, precisely as is that of our cerebral organs. Our physical, moral, and intellectual soundness and comfort, consist in the correct regulation and condition of them all. It is a departure from such condition of them that does mischief. But this subject may be presented in another point of view, no less fatal to the doctrine I am opposing.

That man brings into the world with him a propensity to vice, has been already represented, is a tenet of Christianity, and will not be denied. In his mind or his matter, therefore, that propensity must be rooted. There is no third place of deposit for it. Anti-phrenologists plant it in the mind; phrenologists in the brain. Are the former sure that their location of it furnishes the best guaranty against fatalism? Let a fair analysis of the matter be made, and the question will be answered.

There are but two modes in which full security against the evils of a vicious propensity can be attained. The propensity must be eradicated by a change in the substance in which it is located, or it must be counterpoised and neutralised by a virtuous propensity. Is the substance, in which the propensity to vice is located, mind or spirit? Then must the mind or spirit be changed and improved either wholly or in part, else will the evil propensity be permanent. Is the seat of location matter? Of it the same *is true*. It must be altered and amended in its condition, otherwise the vicious propensity which it harbours and cherishes will flourish.

But the mind or spirit of man is believed to possess neither separate portions nor distinct localities. It is held to be perfectly simple and indivisible. It cannot, therefore, in the way of improvement, be changed *only in part*. It must be changed *in toto*, or not changed at all. But, as respects a substance simple and *partless*, change and annihilation *are the same*. Such a substance cannot be in the slightest degree altered, without an absolute extinguishment of its identity. In

e nature of things the case cannot be otherwise.   A moment's reflec-
on on it will render the truth of the position self-evident.   Hence it
 already so clear and palpable, that an attempt to illustrate it farther
 ust fail.   Let a single effort, however, to that effect be received for
 hat it be thought worth.

A particle of light, or of caloric, is regarded as a simple body.
 hange either, and it is necessarily converted into something else.
: is a particle of light, or of caloric, no longer.   Change even a blue
 ty of light, consisting of a line of simple particles, into a red or an
range ray, and its identity is destroyed.   It is a blue ray no longer;
or does it manifest any characteristic properties as such.   Of any
 ther simple and indivisible substance the same is true.   The slightest
 lteration in it is unconditional annihilation.   To extinguish in an
 ndividual, therefore, a propensity to vice, change his mind or spirit,
 n the slightest degree, and, as far as that substance is concerned, you
 tterly destroy his personal identity.   You effect in him a complete
 netempsychosis.   Not more radically would you extinguish his
 dentity, by metamorphosing his body into that of a stork or an ibis.

But suppose the case were otherwise   Admit that the spirit may
 e somewhat changed and reformed, and still remain the same spirit,
 what do anti-phrenologists gain by the concession?   Do they, in fact,
 ain any thing by it?   Let them answer these questions for them-
 elves.   And to try their ingenuity farther in the solution of problems,
 shall propound to them a question or two more.   Are they sure that
: is easier to change and improve the condition of a depraved simple
 pirit, than of an organ of compound matter?   Do they really know
 hat such condition of spirit can be changed and improved at all?
 No, they do not; because they have never witnessed the pheno-
 nenon; nor can they form the slightest conception of it.   Having no
 hadow of acquaintance with the nature, or any of the attributes of
 pirit, they know nothing respecting its susceptibility of change, the
 neans of operating on it for the purpose of changing it, or the mode
 n which those means should be employed.   To say every thing at
 nce, they are utterly ignorant of the whole concern; because it is
 eyond the comprehension of the human faculties.

Will anti-phrenologists deny or even controvert any one of these
 llegations?   Will they assert that they can, by education and train-
 ng, so far improve the human spirit, as to convert it from a feeble to
 strong, or from an immoral to a moral one?   Will they even hazard
 neir reputation, by declaring their positive knowledge that education
 perates on the spirit at all?   If so, they hold their reputation by so
 ail a tenure, that they will certainly lose it.   They do not know,
 or does any body else, that he experiences in his spirit the slightest

change by any form of education he can receive. On the contrary, here is strong reason to believe that he does not. That his organised matter is changed by education, cannot be doubted; because the fact is susceptible of proof. But that the human spirit is precisely the same after education that it was before, is a position which, though not perhaps demonstrable, there is much more reason to believe than to doubt. As already stated, if it be in any way altered, no matter whether for better or worse, its identity is destroyed.

Such are some of the defects of the hypothesis maintained by anti-phrenologists and metaphysicians, respecting the moral improvement of man by education and example. They implant vicious propensities in the spirit, from which they are utterly unable to remove them. They know not that the spirit can be changed; they are ignorant of any means by which a change in it can be effected; nor were such means in their possession, would they know how to use them. As respects any form of mental improvement, therefore, education, conducted on their notions, would be wholly unavailing. They radicate in the spirit the scions of vice, which nothing but the Creator of the spirit can pluck out. No human means can reach them.

On the principles of this hypothesis, (if, indeed, principle can be predicated of a thing so incongruous, vague, and unintelligible,) fatalism is complete. Unless supernatural agency come to his aid, each individual must be in the constant commission of his besetting sin. For the extinguishment of the propensity giving a proneness to it, his spirit cannot be changed except *miraculously;* nor has it any separate portion, in which a virtuous and countervailing sentiment can reside. But to allege that a vicious and a virtuous disposition can inhabit the same point of either spirit or matter, is rank absurdity. In truth, to represent the human spirit as an indivisible substance, possessing at once, within its own compass, a heterogeneous mass of vices and virtues (for human virtues have an existence as well as human vices)—a representation of this sort is not only unintelligible and contradictory, it is unqualified nonsense. So replete is it with folly, and so repulsive to common sense, that, when thus analysed, stript of its garb of superstition and prejudice, which has so long concealed and protected it from derision, and exhibited in its naked form and fallacy—when thus dealt with, no one will have the weakness to adopt and defend it. Yet has it been the doctrine of metaphysicians since the days of Aristotle, and is the doctrine of anti-phrenologists at the present day. And I repeat, that, as far as it deserves any name, it is unsophisticated fatalism. And the reason of this assertion has been already rendered. The doctrine, if it can be so called, infixes in the spirit of man an active principle of vice, from whose destructive influence no earthly means can rescue it. All hope of amendment, therefore, from human efforts being thus extinguished, our race has no alternative, under this scheme of philosophy, but to sin on, in utter despair of sublunary aid, and looking for the means and the process of reform *exclusively from above*. But on the fallacy, unchristian character, and ruinous tendency of this hypothesis, it were a waste of time in me to dwell any longer. I shall therefore decline all farther consideration of it, with the single remark, that if, by a thorough examination of the subject, metaphysicians and anti-phrenologists can convict me of a single error in preferring against their scheme of philosophy the charge of fatalism, it shall be instantly renounced. Meantime, as relates to such charge, let the doctrines of that philosophy, as just represented, be fairly contrasted with those of phrenology, and the issue be marked.

Here, in their characters and bearings, all things present themselves under not only a different, but an opposite aspect. Phrenology offers no such disrespect and injustice to the Deity, through an accusation of his works, as to admit of the existence of a human propensity, one of the constitutional elements of man, *vicious in its nature*. Such an admission would virtually pronounce the Creator to be the author of unqualified evil. Our science only admits that certain propensities belonging to man may become sources of vice, through the fault of their possessor, who negligently allows them to run to excess in their action, pampers and urges them to such excess by improper practices, or in some other manner misapplies or abuses them. And all these things he does voluntarily and of choice, having it amply in his power to prevent or avoid them. In this case, I say, no shade of imputation is thrown on the Deity, as if he were actually the author of sin; whereas it is impossible, as might be easily made to appear, to defend from that irreverent and impious charge the doctrines of anti-phrenology. But, without farther remark on the errors and mischiefs of that fast-fading scheme of mental philosophy, I shall again turn to its opposite, and, as respects the charge of fatalism preferred against it, bring its doctrines more strictly to the test of observation and experience, reason and common sense.

According to the doctrines maintained in phrenology, none of the mental faculties of man, in their natural and well-regulated condition, as already mentioned, are tributary to vice; and but a few of them can become so, even in cases of excess, misapplication, and abuse. These are Amativeness, Destructiveness, Combativeness, Acquisitiveness, and Secretiveness; and they have their seats, not in simple spirit, but in compound material organs, whose vigour of action, if likely to become excessive in degree, and vicious in its issue, can be restrained and overruled in a manner to be presently described.

From this enumeration it will be perceived, that all the faculties which, by their excess or abuse, may minister to vice, belong to the animal compartment of the brain. In opposition to these, or at least as a balance to bridle their impetuosity, and prevent their propensities from running into vice, may be arrayed the reflective faculties, all the strictly moral faculties, and the most powerful of those that may be called semi-moral. By this antagonism of mental powers, the mind can be held in a state of equilibrium, as relates to vice and virtue; or rather, as will presently appear, a preponderance toward the latter may be easily imparted to it.

The restrictive faculties, more especially referred to as being best qualified to withhold the mind from vice, and incline it to virtue, are Causality and Comparison, Benevolence, Veneration, Conscientiousness, Self-esteem, Cautiousness, Love of Approbation, and Firmness. And these are also seated in cerebral organs, most of them comparatively large and powerful; and they may all be materially augmented in size and strength, by suitable training. It might be correctly added, that, in many cases, Hope, Wonder, and Ideality, unite their influence to that of the more strictly moral and the reflective organs, in the prevention of vice, and the promotion of virtue.

Such, in its relation to morality and immorality, vice and virtue, is the constitution of the human mind. It possesses *five* faculties which *may*, by excess, neglect, and abuse, lead to vice, and *eight*, at least, of about equal strength, whose *only* tendency is toward virtue; and another which, in co-operation with the latter, gives them steadfastness and perseverance. In addition to these, three more, as just mentioned, co-operate occasionally in the same good cause. And it is repeated, that the organs of the faculties which *may* minister to vice can be enfeebled not a little, and those of the faculties which, from their nature, *must* subserve the cause of virtue and sound morals, in an equal degree invigorated, by a judicious and well-concerted scheme of education and training. Thus may the balance in favour of virtue be made greatly to preponderate.

If a mind thus constituted and disciplined can have any liability or propension to fatalism, it must be to a fatalism of virtue, rather than of vice. Its leaning must be toward moral rather than immoral actions. Any one of the strong moral faculties will be as likely as any one of the animal to become the ruling passion of the individual, and sway his conduct. And when the reflective and all the moral faculties unite and co-operate, they must necessarily predominate in influence and action over any one or two, or even all of the animal

aculties, and not only restrain their propensity to crime, but prove,
n their own joint power, a certain and abiding fountain of virtue.
'or the more complete illustration and establishment of this point, a
rief analysis of it will be sufficient.

Suppose an individual with Destructiveness so largely developed
s to give him a propensity to the shedding of blood. His con-
ederacy of antagonising organs, if duly cultivated and strengthened,
rill be more than sufficient to restrain him from crime. They are as
ollows :—

Benevolence, in the emphatic language and subduing tones of
lemency, kindness, and mercy, implores him to do no injury to the
bject of his malice, and to inflict no pain on his connections and
riends. Veneration solemnly warns him, in the name of all that is
acred and holy—especially as he regards the precepts, example, and
njunctions of the wise, the good, and the revered of all ages, climes,
nd countries, and the commands of his God, with the penalty
nnexed in case of violation—to withhold his hand from the medi-
ated deed. Conscientiousness, in a manner no less stern and man-
latory, admonishes him to abstain from an act which is not only
njust, and flagrantly wrong in its own nature, but which can hardly
ail to visit him in future, whether sleeping or waking, with the con-
lemnation of repentance, and the agonies of remorse. Self-esteem
ssures him that he will forfeit, and irrecoverably lose, whatever sen-
iment of self-respect and personal dignity he may have hitherto
ossessed, and will pass the remainder of his life under a deep and
vithering sense of self-degradation. Approbativeness will remon-
trate with him on the loss he must sustain in the regard of his
ellow-men. Cautiousness, invoking him to beware, will alarm him
or his personal safety and welfare. The reflecting faculties will
lace before him, in colours of blood, the fearful and ruinous conse-
uences of the deed of guilt. And Firmness, uniting with these
irtuous associates, will give stability to their resolution, and perseve-
ance to their efforts. And I repeat, that Hope, Wonder, and
deality, being much more akin to good than evil, and much more
ratified with beauty than deformity, will not fail to unite in the
raiseworthy association.

Such is the confederacy of moral and reflecting organs and faculties
hat may be arrayed against a single animal organ, each of them indi-
idually being nearly, and some of them entirely, equal to itself, in
ize and strength, to withhold it from crime. And they can effect
heir purpose as certainly and easily, as seven or eight men, each
qual in strength to the intended offender, can, when resolutely deter-
nined on it, prevent a single man within their reach from perpetrating

murder. And the same confederacy may be brought to act again any other animal organ, and stay its movement, when about to plun; into some immoral and forbidden deed.

Is Acquisitiveness about to lead to theft, swindling, or any oth form of felony or fraud ? These acts are odious to the same orgai with murder, and will, on the same principles, and with the san salutary result, be opposed by them. Is Combativeness on the e' of a lawless quarrel, or a mischievous riot? Does Secretivene meditate deceit or duplicity, treachery or open falsehood? Or do Amativeness urge to an act of profligacy and dishonour? In eith case, the combination of the higher organs to preserve peace ar morality, and to prevent crime, is the same. And, provided tho organs are trained and invigorated, as they are and ought to be, the success is certain. It is as certain, I repeat, as is that of eight stror and resolute men over a single man, not superior in strength to eith of them, in the following case :—

The party is assembled in the same room. A stranger enters, whom one of them is hostile, and whom he is determined assassinate, the others being privy to his felonious design. That it perfectly in their power to prevent the deed, provided they act oppo tunely and in concert, will not be denied. With equal ease, mor over, could they restrain the individual from the commission of an other crime or misdemeanour, were his purpose known to then And the propensity of an organ to vicious indulgence is never co cealed from him who possesses it. If he falls into his besetting si therefore, he cannot excuse himself on the plea of ignorance. H cannot, I mean, plead that his superior organs were not apprised (the lawless propensity of the inferior one. His consciousness suf ciently advises him of the fact.

Thus simple and efficient (I might say *perfect*) is the system (moral checks and balances which phrenology recognises and present and the mode of establishing it which it so plainly teaches. Is enquired of me what that mode is? I reply, that it consists in givii to the moral and reflecting organs and their faculties an ascendency power and influence over the animal ones, by cultivating and strengt ening the former by exercise, and restraining and moderating tl action of the latter, in case they be inordinately and dangerous vigorous.

Am I asked again, in what way the animal organs of the brain m be reduced in power, when they threaten to become a source (annoyance and crime? I reply, in the same way in which any oth organ of the body may be reduced in tone, and weakened in actio Protect those organs from every form of unnecessary exercise ar excitement, and thus keep them tranquil, which may be effected without difficulty, and the work is done. Their power is diminished, and their excess prevented. Not more certainly are the muscles strengthened by exercise, and enfeebled by inaction, than the organs of the brain. By judicious exercise is every portion of the body invigorated, and by withholding exercise debilitated. This is a maxim as incontestably true, as that things equal to one and the same thing are equal to one another.

In phrenology, then, I repeat, there is no fatalism. Or if there be, its cast is *moral*. For, under such a scheme of education and training, as may be easily accomplished, the confederacy of faculties leaning toward virtue is much more powerful than any single faculty, whose excess of action may lead to vice. And the animal faculties, especially when their propensities are inordinately strong, do not act confederately, but seek each one its own individual gratification.

As far as concerns the vindication of phrenology from the charges of materialism and fatalism, I might here close my paper. But I have promised a few remarks of a more direct and pointed character on the subject of Free Will; and to the fulfilment of that promise I shall now proceed, with the settled design that my remarks shall be brief. And first, of the meaning that should be attached to the term Will.

Metaphysicians and anti-phrenologists consider the will as a distinct faculty of the mind, possessing a control over certain other faculties. Phrenologists, on the contrary, regard it as only a function or mode of action of the intellectual faculties; for to that class of faculties alone does it belong. It is nothing, therefore, but a power of applying those faculties at pleasure to certain selected purposes and pursuits.

As respects itself, however, the will is not so free as to be arbitrary. It is controlled, as already mentioned, by causes under the denomination of motives. And those motives govern it in its actions, as certainly and uniformly, as gravitation governs the movements of the running stream, and the falling body.

Am I asked what these will-controlling motives are? and whence they are derived? I answer, they are propensities or appetites, in the form of desires; and are furnished by the affective *faculties* of the mind—I mean, by the animal propensities and the moral sentiments. It is in some shape for the gratification of these, that the intellectual faculties will to act, or *not* to act. Provided, therefore, the affective faculties be suitably educated, and correctly inclined, the intellectual faculties, in providing means to gratify them, by meeting their desires, will necessarily minister to the establishment of sound morals and the promotion of virtue—and the reverse. Are the affective faculties so uneducated, or so badly educated, that those belonging to the animal compartment of the brain are loose and unbridled in their propensities, and preponderate over those of the moral and reflecting compartments? In such a case, the intellectual faculties become the panders to evil and licentious passions, and minister to vice. In each instance, the affective faculties, though they have no will of their own, furnish the motives which govern the will, and, through the instrumentality of it, throw the intellectual faculties into action. To exemplify this proposition:

An individual, in whom Conscientiousness and Benevolence are predominant faculties, is introduced to a family that has suffered wrong and oppression, and been reduced by them to poverty and bitter distress. A strong desire is awakened in him to redress their wrong, by having justice done to them, and to relieve their sufferings, by offices of kindness and acts of beneficence. And to this desire his will conforms. Hence to furnish means for the accomplishment of his intention, his intellectual faculties are immediately at work. Are the sufferers still agonised by the actual contact of the rod of injustice? That rod he indignantly snatches from the hand of the oppressor, and thus disarms cruelty of its power to injure. Are they broken-heartedly and hopelessly languishing in a dungeon? He throws open their prison door, and restores them to light, and liberty, and joy. Are they in want of food, and clothing, and a place of shelter and residence? He provides them with all, and does not leave them until their comforts are complete. While thus engaged, though his will is under the control of his moral faculties, he feels that it is free. And, under that impression, he would severely condemn himself, did he refuse to obey the virtuous impulse. In this way do the affective overrule to their purposes the intellectual faculties.

In another person, who is defective in Conscientiousness and Veneration, the predominant faculties are Acquisitiveness and Combativeness. He is in need of money, but being too idle and unprincipled to resort to the resources of honest industry, his boldness determines him to gratify by robbery his lawless cupidity. Here, again, the will conforms to the overruling propensity. Accordingly, the intellectual faculties being put into requisition, suggest the time and place most suitable for the ambush, and provide the weapons to be employed on the occasion. Nor is the will under the slightest degree of constraint, though actually controlled by the master propensities. In proof that it is not constrained, if, instead of one traveller *unarmed*, four or five *well-armed*, and carrying with them immense wealth, approach the place of the robber's concealment, though his Acquisitiveness burns with ardour for the booty, he notwithstanding shrinks from an attack. Why? Because his Cautiousness, taking the alarm, warns of the danger of an encounter with so formidable a party, and assumes, for the time, the control of the will.

In a third case, an individual being unprincipled from a lack of the moral organs and faculties, is strongly marked with Acquisitiveness and Cautiousness, and is defective in Combativeness. Such a man possesses the elements of a thief, and will basely purloin what he has not the courage to procure by the pistol. Here, again, the will is influenced by the dominant propensities, unbridled Acquisitiveness pointing to the property to be gained, and Cautiousness to the mode of gaining it.

In every other voluntary transaction, whether virtuous or vicious, the mental machinery concerned is the same. The affective faculties furnish the motives to action, and lead the intellectual faculties through the medium of the will to prepare the means.

In conclusion, though I do not pretend to have completely solved, in the foregoing pages, the problem of Free Will, because I deem such solution impracticable, I trust I have shown it to be fully as compatible with phrenology, as with any other scheme of mental philosophy. And that, perhaps, should be the summit of my aim. But in alleging that it is much more compatible, I might safely defy metaphysicians and anti-phrenologists to put me in the wrong.

Phrenology unquestionably furnishes, through the affective faculties, the motives between which the will may choose, in a much more simple and intelligible manner, than any other scheme of mental philosophy with which I am acquainted. In truth, I know of no other scheme in which the existence and operation of such motives is intelligible at all. The hypothesis, that the motives, and the will, and the memory, and the judgment, and the imagination, are all seated in the mind, which is even less than a partless indivisible point—such an hypothesis amounts to a mental labyrinth, which I have neither the sagacity to thread, nor the courage to attempt it.

ARTICLE II.

MEDICAL JURISPRUDENCE OF INSANITY.—NO. 3.

BY A. DEAN, ESQ., ALBANY, N. Y.

Each form of mental alienation has its own legal consequences, rather presents its own peculiarities, to which legal rules are applie The legal consequences of that form which consists in deficiency mind, may be summed up in an avoidance of the act, when tl deficiency is sufficient in reason to justify it.

There is a difficulty occurs in applying the law to this extensi class of cases. This arises from the fact, that all such cases must l judged of by persons in the possession of the ordinary comme faculties; and who, therefore, can derive from their own consciou ness no aid to assist them in forming their conclusions. Such mu obviously be incapable of arriving at a correct judgment of a conditic of mind of which they can form no adequate conception from the lig of their own experience. Hence there is, in all these cases, gre danger of committing injustice from the assumption of an erroneo standard of judgment.

So far as regards responsibility for crimes, one material and a pervading principle never must be lost sight of; and that is, that tl law always primarily regards the *intent to injure*, and that in refe ence to the kind of injury legitimately deducible from the act.

When we examine the elements of *injurious intent*, with a vie to a rigorous analysis, we find them embracing the following coi siderations, viz.—

1. A perception by the intellect, and an appreciation by the mor forces, of the relations in which rational beings stand towards eac other.

2. A sufficient strength and activity of the propensities to enab them to furnish their impulses to circumvent, combat, destroy, commit some other mischief upon another human being.

3. Sufficient of intellectual power to perceive the relevancy means to ends, and the mischievous or ruinous results to which tho impulses, if followed, would naturally lead.

4. A sufficient strength of moral power, or of the faculty of coi sciousness, to feel the deviation from right, and to know that the contemplated is a *wrong*, and not simply an *injury*.

A fatal defect in either one, or all these elements, would render tl individual irresponsible for his actions. The questions, therefore, be settled, in all cases of alleged incapacity from mental deficiency, are—

1. Are the relations of human beings perceived?

2. Are the impulses sufficiently strong that lead to the act?

3. Are the nature of the means employed, and the end to be accomplished, understood?

4. Are the moral results *felt* to be *wrong?*

One of the principal difficulties in the way of arriving at correct conclusions, in all these cases of mental deficiency, has been the groundless assumption that the imbecility, or defect from deficiency, must be confined to the intellectual department, without any reference to the moral or affective. Nothing can be more erroneous than such an assumption. There is nothing in the nature of the affective or moral powers to exempt them from the action of the same laws and influences as the intellectual. Dr. Woodward, the intelligent principal of the insane asylum at Worcester, Mass., has remarked in one of his annual reports, that in some cases there seems to be something like *moral idiocy*, or such an imbecile state of the moral faculties, from birth, as to render the individual irresponsible for his moral conduct.

The ascertainment of the degree of imbecility is necessary for the purpose of a correct application of the law. As the first degree consists principally in inattention, or absence of mind, in regard to objects generally known, its existence can furnish no legal excuse for any act done under its influence.

In the second degree there is less responsibility than in the first. Not only is the general capacity diminished, but there is also a greater proneness to sudden emotions and fits of passion. The general power of exercising control over the manifestations of sentiment, propensity, and passion, is diminished or impaired.

In the third degree of imbecility, the individual cannot safely be entrusted with the management of his own property, and should, therefore, be subjected to guardianship, or to the appointment of a committee.

Jurisdiction over idiots and lunatics has been exercised by courts of equity. That jurisdiction was long confined to those two classes of alienation. It came at length to be extended, and to embrace all those cases of imbecility where the individual was confessedly incompetent to manage his own affairs. Cases in which the exercise of this power is often required, occur towards the latter periods of life, when the organs of mind have become enfeebled, and the faculties act less efficiently in consequence of defects in their material instruments.

The execution of conveyances of real estate, and of last wills and testaments, has furnished the most frequent occasions for the examination and decision of questions of imbecility. The last, as they are generally among the latest acts of life, have been by far the most productive of these occasions. In all cases of contested capacity to dispose by will, the enquiry becomes material, what was the nature and seat of the disease, if any, which prevailed at the time of executing the instrument.

All those diseases that primarily affect the organs of mind, are the most likely to incapacitate, and hence their existence should in all cases create a doubt as to the capacity. All lethargic and comatose affections and apoplexy, expending, as they do, their primary energies upon the brain, very frequently deprive the unfortunate subject of the capacity to make a valid will. Those diseases, on the contrary, which primarily affect organs other than the brain—such, for instance, as the pulmonary consumption—generally leave unimpaired to the latest period the action of the mental faculties.

. The execution of a valid will requires the testator to be of sound disposing mind and memory, so as to be capable of making a testamentary disposition of his property with sense and judgment, both in reference to the situation and amount of such property, and to the relative claims of the different persons who are, or might be, the objects of his bounty. In determining the validity of a will, it is proper to consider—

1. Its provisions. If they are judicious and discreet, a presumption is raised in its favour.

2. The circumstances attending its execution. The situation of the testator, his associates, the influences to which he is, and has been, subject.

3. Whether the instructions and directions have come from the testator himself, voluntarily, or have been derived through some other medium.

4. Each faculty should be enquired of by itself, and its own particular strength or weakness determined.

General intellectual mania, involving, as it does, the perverted or insane action of the entire intellect, is attended with those hallucinations, or unfounded delusions, that, to a greater or less extent, destroys the ability to act upon the commonly received principles of human action. The law, therefore, wisely takes the maniac from his own guidance, and while it divests him of his rights, releases him also from his duties. It allows him the use, but not the abuse of his property, and holds him irresponsible for any aggression he may make upon liberty or life, because he lacks the elements of accountability, which are essential to constitute crime.

A different rule, however, seems to prevail in reference to the civil elations of the maniac. He is held legally responsible to make good, luring his lucid interval, whatever injury he has caused to the property of another, while acting under the influence of any insane delusion. This is upon the principle, that as some one is to suffer the loss, it should be he, though innocent, who causes the injury, rather than he other, who has no agency whatever in its production.

Cases involving the greatest difficulty in their decision, are those of partial intellectual mania, in which there is insanity of one or more faculties, or a mental alienation on one or more topics, while, in every other respect, the mind appears to be sane. This is generally termed monomania. Whether intellectual mania of this limited and partial character, does or does not invalidate an act, depends on the intimacy of the connection that subsists between the act and the peculiar derangement. Where the act obviously proceeds from, or is intimately connected with, the insane delusion, the actor is clearly irresponsible, because in respect to such an act he has ceased being a free agent.

A mental disorder, operating upon some particular subjects, so far as those subjects are concerned, is attended with the same effects as a total deprivation of reason. But partial derangement should not be extended beyond its own morbid phenomena; and in all doubtful cases, the enquiry should be reduced to the single point, whether the act complained of in fact proceeded from a mind fully capable, in respect of that act, of exercising a free, sound, and discriminate judgment.

There is often much difficulty in determining what is really embraced within the morbid circle of action; besides, the delusion itself is very subject to change. In estimating the character of an act, we must admit for that purpose the truth of the insane delusion under which it is performed, and then its relation to its cause will generally be apparent. This arises from that law of causation, so universally operative in all the movements of mind, which connects, with bonds so indissoluble, the act with the ideas and motives instrumental in its production.

The sound rule, in regard to this form of insanity, is to establish,

1. The delusion, which must be something entertained as true, which is really false in fact.

2. The act sought to be invalidated must be directly traceable to the delusion, and either actually produced by it, or so intimately connected with it, as to lead to the presumption that it never would have occurred had not the delusion existed.

The same degree and extent of partial insanity, that absolves from contracts, ought also to relieve from the consequences of criminal acts.

The irresponsibility of mind for acts committed under the influence of moral mania, proceeds upon a principle entirely different from that which prevails in cases of intellectual mania. In moral mania there is no delusion; the intellectual faculties may remain as perfect as they ever were, and yet the derangement, or perverted action of the affective or moral powers, embracing the propensities and sentiments, may destroy the control of the individual over himself and his actions.

To estimate actions properly, we must understand them. They are volitions of mind carried to their ultimate limit. In the normal healthy state, an action is evidence of two things.

1. Of the existence of a perfect volition in the mind.

2. Of the ability to manifest itself externally, through the medium of the material organisation.

Volitions are formed under the influencing power of motives, which are presented to, and appreciated by, the affective or moral powers of man. The impulses furnished by the propensities, aided and directed by the emotions and dictates proceeding from the sentiments, are the primary springs of all volitions and actions. The intellect neither impels, guides, or directs; it simply furnishes the material, and enlightens. A volition, and the act by which it is evidenced, is the joint result of the action of the affective faculties, in reference to the materials furnished by the intellectual.

We certainly ought not to hold a being responsible for an action, unless all its essential elements are complete. This cannot be the case, if all or any one of the affective faculties are fatally defective, or deranged in their functional action. Without moral liberty, there can be no responsibility for crime. The true test to determine, in any given case, the existence of moral liberty, is to ascertain whether the volition and the action are or are not *irresistible*. If they are so, all punishment would be not only useless to the offender, but two of its principal purposes could not be answered. It would neither tend to amend the person punished, nor be productive of a salutary effect upon others, by way of example.

To determine the *irresistibility* of an act, reference must be had directly to the act itself. Its attendant circumstances must be examined, as also the things and events that preceded and succeeded it. The presumed influences that were brought to bear upon the actor must be scrutinised, and the agreement or contrast of the act itself with his previous character examined. A presumption of insanity arises, if there is observed to be a want of ordinary care and caution—as if an act of a flagitious character be committed in a public place, in open day, and in sight of witnesses.

The records of criminal jurisprudence have furnished many cases n which much doubt existed as to criminal liability. When, however, death has been caused through the resistless promptings of insane impulse, there are usually many circumstances indicating its true origin or cause. In the first place, the destructive act is motiveless. The unfortunate subject is generally a wife, a child, a parent, or the first living being who presents himself. The accomplishment of death is the immediate object. Nothing beyond it is at all regarded. All within reach are often sacrificed. None of the conveniences of time, place, and circumstance are consulted. The homocidal monomaniac performs his deeds of death as if controlled by some severe and unaccountable destiny.

In all these respects the criminal pursues a different course. He has in view some definite object—some ulterior aim. Death is with him a means, not an end. He is a creature of motive. He sheds no more blood than is necessary for the accomplishment of his object. Time, place, and weapons, are suited to his purpose. His movements are all consistent, and indicate a plan, regularly commenced, and successfully carried out. Thus a correct knowledge of mental operations, and their development in character, cannot easily fail of leading to tolerably correct conclusions as to whether the act proceeded from a sane or an insane mind. If the act is utterly inconsistent with all the previous developments of the character, it affords strong evidence of insanity, unless the destructive propensity have become morbid and deranged in consequence of its own excessive action.

On a careful review of the whole matter, it is humiliating to witness how trifling has been the real attainment made in the jurisprudence of mental alienation. There is a want of definiteness, a lack of precision, in all the knowledge we now have on that subject. Until recently, sufficient attention has never been paid to facts; nor are facts now observed with sufficient accuracy in this country. In Europe, particularly in France, in the large and well-regulated institutions of the insane, which attest the enterprise and humanity of that lively people, much attention is paid to the different forms of mental alienation. Pinel, Esquirol, and Georget, have successively rendered to humanity a service which future times can only repay by holding them in grateful recollection. Observed facts, to possess value, must be connected with general reasonings. The insane manifestations of the faculties can never be thoroughly understood, until their respective functions in health are well ascertained and definitely settled. The more accurately the true philosophy of mind comes to be understood, the more perfect may we expect our codes of morals, and the more settled, certain and satisfactory, our maxims of jurisprudence.

ARTICLE III.

ON THE PRESENT MODES OF MEASURING THE HEAD, AND THE ADVAN
TAGES OF A NEW INSTRUMENT.

For the American Phrenological Journal.

As the human head—exclusive of the face—differs in most indi
viduals—and especially in children—but little in magnitude, and stil
less in form, from the encephalon, it is a problem of some interest u
determine the exact size and shape of the former. The instrument
already in use, and even the eye of the practised observer, will giv
an approximation sufficiently near to establish the main doctrines of
phrenology. But the problem is not solved as rigidly as it must be
if phrenology is to take a place among the more exact sciences
Who can state, numerically, the *position* of a single organ? I an
acquainted with no instrument hitherto used, with which this is pro
fessed to be determined. How, in geodæsical operations, do we
determine the figure and magnitude of the earth? The mere measure
ment of linear distances on its surface affords no sufficient data. I
is necessary to combine this measurement with that of the *angula:*
position of different stations. The callipers for measuring the head
are like a chain, without a theodolite or transit instrument, fo
measuring the earth. It does not even approximately determine the
length of any cerebral fibres, except those which have a low and
lateral direction, and terminate near the ears. The craniometer which
has been used, supplies this deficiency, but is equally destitute of any
provision for determining the *position* of parts.* The positions of
organs are often defined by their contiguity to others; and a descrip
tion of the head too much resembles that of land in some deeds of ou
American ancestors—every man's farm bounded by those of his
neighbours.

If the mental powers are modified by the depth of the convolutions
or the thickness of cineritious substance, or the texture of the brain
these modifications would equally affect the conclusions to be draw
from any mode of measurement. So far are they from rendering a
exact and proper mode objectionable, that it is by this alone that the
existence and total amount of such modifications—separately indeter
minable as they are during life—can ever be arrived at.

* A plate of this instrument may be seen in Combe's smaller work on phreno
logy.

'The upper extremity of the medullar oblongata being the radiant point of the encephalic fibres, if—as is generally maintained by Combe and others—the powers of the different pyramidal bundles, or organs, have a relation to the lengths of the axes and the areas of the bases of these spheroidal pyramids, these are the data important to be determined by measurement. The ordinary craniometer—an instrument too much neglected—determines the length of the axis at any point of the surface assumed to be the centre of the base of an organ. But suppose phrenologists to differ, and the views of all to change in regard to the number and location of organs—and this has taken place to a certain extent—then the recorded numerical results of previous measurements are not available for comparison with subsequent ones, nor those of one phrenologist for comparison with those of others.

But if, in addition to the indications furnished by cerebral prominences, and the somewhat vague and empirical reference to certain great landmarks on and near the skull, we determine and record the angular distance of each station of measurement from two determinate co-ordinate planes at right angles to each other, we then have three times as many data as are furnished by the ordinary craniometer, and are able to deduce from them the three grand numerical results required by phrenology as an exact science; to wit: 1st, the lengths of the axes of the pyramids; 2d, their positions; 3d, the distances between the middle points of their bases, and, consequently, the extent of the bases. The ordinary craniometer gives but one single result; viz. the length.' The callipers give but one; viz. the base.

An instrument which I have constructed, and exhibited to the New York Phrenological Society, determines the position on the same principle as the astronomer determines that of a star, by its altitude and azimuth, its right ascension and declination, or its latitude and longitude.

Without a precise reference to co-ordinate plans, uranography could not have become an exact science, but must have remained with few other guides than the more empirical ones of the early astrologers, the uncouth figures of men, animals, and monsters, still seen—to use Mr. Herschell's expression—"scribbled over" artificial globes. I will not compare these to phrenological maps and busts, as it regards their utility or the artificial character of the divisions, but I must in regard to their availableness for the purposes of numerical comparison.

My instrument consists essentially of two graduated semicircles in planes at right angles to each other. The one answering to the ungraduated semicircle of the ordinary craniometer. The other is

attached to the axis of the former; and the centre of this additiona
semicircle, or circle, (for this may be a complete circle,) correspond:
to a point in the axis of revolution of that which sweeps over the
head, and by the graduations of which the angular distances from it:
extremities are indicated. The graduations on the smaller semicircle
indicate the angular positions of the plane of the larger semicircle
from a determinate plane of reference. The larger semicircle is made
sufficiently large to sweep over the head, when the direction of it:
axis of rotation passes through the point of divergence of the encephalic fibres. This position of the axis may be given by two rods.
sliding at the extremities of the semicircle, and pressing respectively
at the root of the nose and at a point near the occipital protuberance.
The contrivance necessary for fixing them in this position need not
be detailed. Instead of this, the rods may be introduced into the ears;
but the anterior posterior position of the axis appears more eligible
than the transverse one through the meatus auditorius, for two
reasons; viz. the axis may be made to pass more nearly through the
point of divergence of the cerebral fibres, and the application of the
instrument is not disagreeable. For similar reasons, the mastoid processes are eligible points of application. This instrument may also
be employed as callipers. In using it as a craniometer, its radius
must be known; and then the length of the fibres at any part—plus
the thickness of the skull and the integuments—is ascertained, simply
by reading off, on a graduated sliding rod, the complement of the distances between the head and the circumference of the large semicircle.
The position of the plane of the latter is read off on the smaller
graduated semicircle, a dot place on the forehead or temple being
used as a fixed index.

With this instrument, the true lengths of the fibres or organs are
given in inches and parts of an inch, and their positions in degrees;
and a comparison of these two classes of results will give the breadth
of the base of an organ, or at least the half sum of two contiguous
bases, also the direction and distance of the centre of the base of any
organ from that of any other organ, or from any point so considered
in the present state of phrenology. A great variety of interesting
conclusions may be expected to result from such comparisons.

In the phrenological reports, as usually given, one of two methods
is adopted, and both have some disadvantages. One is to express the
size of the organs by such vague terms as "full, large, rather full,
full +," &c. The other is to give the linear distance between
different points on the surface of the head. The statements of the
former have no reference to an invariable standard, and are essentially

vague. The measurements of the latter are liable to several objections. The distances are by some measured in a straight line; by others, along the convex surface of the head. By some they are measured from one point, by others from another; so that scarcely any two are comparable. The ear is not unfrequently selected, and is one of the most advantageous points on the surface; but this does not give the measure of the organs. One of the most usual methods is to give the distance between the corresponding points of opposite sides, as from Cautiousness to Cautiousness, Ideality to Ideality, &c., and no doubt many readers are led into the belief that these are the measures of those organs, for I see no care used to guard against such a conclusion. Whereas, in fact, this only gives double the base of a right-angled triangle, of which the hypothenuse is the length of the organ, and the other side unknown. The problem of course not only remains unsolved, but indeterminate for want of data which such measurements can never furnish.

In deducing inferences from measurements of the same head in different directions, allowance is of course to be made for the normal and average difference between the lengths of the different fibres. For example, those of the cerebellum are much shorter in almost every individual than those of the anterior lobes of the cerebrum. The standard human head is not a sphere; and allowance for its deviation from this form, is always required in estimating the relative power of different cerebral organs in the same individual, and equally required whether we have aimed at arriving at the lengths by a perfect or imperfect instrument, or by no artificial instrument at all. Such an instrument as I propose, appears to be necessary for determining, by numerous observations, the very data which phrenology requires in making these allowances, and which—if phrenology were out of the question—would form an interesting addition to our knowledge of the anatomy of the head. I allude, of course, to the mean proportions of the lengths of the different fibres. A comparison in this respect might be made between races, sexes, and ages, as well as individuals. The use of such an instrument as the above, in connection with observed mental manifestations, would contribute to the solution of several other interesting problems. One is the effect on the powers of any organ, produced by the relative deficiency of circumjacent organs, and the consequent narrow prominence or bump. which forms an essential element in the vulgar conception of phrenology, and the precise influence of which, as compared with that of absolute length of fibre, even scientific phrenologists have never, so far as I know, attempted to determine. In the present state of phrenology, this instrument, considered with reference to the application of the science instead of its advancement, will be at first chiefly useful in measuring the corresponding parts of the brain, or organs of the same name in different hands.

B. F. J.

ARTICLE IV.

REVIEW OF DR. VIMONT'S WORK ON COMPARATIVE PHRENOLOGY.*

A Treatise on Human and Comparative Phrenology, accompanied by a Grand Atlas in folio, containing 120 *Plates, executed in the best style.* By J. VIMONT, Doctor of Medicine of the Faculty of Paris, Honorary Member of the Phrenological Societies of Paris and of London. (With an Epigraph.) Second edition. Brussels, 1830, pp. 558, royal octavo.

L'orgueil, la superstition, la crainte, ont embarrassée la connoissance de l'homme de mille préjugés que l'observation doit détruire. La religion est chargée de nous conduire dans la route du bonheur qu'elle nous prepare au-delà du temps. La philosophie doit étudier les motifs des actions de l'homme pour trouver de le rendre meilleur et plus heureux dans cette vie passagère (G. Leroy, *Lettre Philos. sur l'homme et les animaux*). Second edition. Bruxelles, 1836.

As we are not aware that either a full review, or an analysis even, of Dr. Vimont's great work on Human and Comparative Phrenology, has yet been given by any journalist on this side of the water, we shall endeavour on the present occasion to supply this omission, making, the while, such incidental remarks as may seem to grow out of the subject before us. If, in the performance of this latter part of our task, we should press a little hard upon certain doctors of law and divinity, judges and politicians, including an ex-president, we hope to be excused on the plea of self-defence against those who, for the nonce, have taken into their heads to masquerade, in the garb of philosophy, and under their assumed characters, to elbow somewhat rudely those who differ from them in opinion.

Dr. Vimont, a physician of Caen, in Normandy, and the author of the work before us, gives, in an introduction, the causes of his beginning the course of study and the series of observations which ended in his adoption of the doctrines of phrenology. These we shall present to our readers as briefly as possible.

* From the Eclectic Journal of Medicine for August, 1839, edited by Dr. John Bell.

In 1818, the French Institute having offered a prize for the best memoir on the anatomy of the brain in the four classes of vertebral animals, Dr. Vimont resolved to apply himself to this subject of enquiry, and to submit the result of his investigations to that learned body.   In 1820, he was already master of a considerable collection of anatomical facts, the more valuable, in his opinion, because they had been made with great care and fidelity.   Hitherto, his observations had been restricted to the anatomy of the nervous system; and although he was desirous of ascertaining at the same time the functions of this system, and felt that he had a richer collection of facts than Haller and Vicq d'Azir, he found it at the time impossible to detect the relations between the encephalic mass and its functions. "I was struck, nevertheless," continues Dr. Vimont, "with the kind of conformation of brain exhibited by certain birds and quadrupeds. I may cite, for instance, the migratory birds, sixty of the brains of which were in my possession, and those of carnivorous quadrupeds, which I had studied with still more care, and which I preserved in spirits of wine.   It was impossible for me to believe that with such numerous varieties of organisation there should not be connected special faculties; but how to ascertain these faculties, unless, before all, I were to make a long study of the manners and habits of animals. I began, accordingly, to read with ardour the most celebrated works on the subject, and in order to judge of the accuracy of the authors, I determined to raise a great number of animals, and to study their manners, to note their most remarkable ways, and to compare my own observations with those made by these illustrious men."   Pliny and Buffon were read; the first with a feeling of admiration at the prodigious extent of mind displayed in his Natural History, enriched as it was by the accumulation of facts by a still greater genius— Aristotle.   Buffon disappointed Dr. Vimont, who saw in him great beauty of style, but who felt that he was reading the production of a poet rather than that of a naturalist.   This is, we believe, the verdict of impartial judges generally on the merits of Buffon.   Linnæus gave more satisfaction to our author, by the greater exactness of his anatomical descriptions, whereby he marked out the course, following which the cultivators of the natural sciences have been most successful. Reference is next made, in terms of approbation, to two authors who are not sufficiently known, viz. George Leroy and Dupont de Nemours.

Dr. Vimont had not at this time any knowledge of the works of Dr. Gall; and he little believed, then, that they would furnish him with the dominant idea for the direction of his numerous researches. All that he had heard and read, was calculated to exhibit Gall in the light of a charlatan, and to deter him from paying any attention to the labours of this celebrated man. *Still, however, he was not willing to condemn him without hearing him.* This commendable resolution, and yet one of common sense and common justice, might be imitated advantageously by many of our pseudo-critics, D. D.s and LL. D.s, and even sundry M. D.s, teachers, and lecturers, and authors of lectures we wot of. But what was the result of Dr. Vimont's impartial enquiry? "No sooner had I read his (Gall's) works," says Dr. V., "than I saw at once that I had made acquaintance with a man removed above his fellow-men; one of those whom envy is always eager to thrust aside from the position to which they are called by their genius, and against whom she employs the weapons of cowardice and hypocrisy. The qualities which seemed to me to render Gall conspicuous, were extensive cerebral capacity, great penetration, good sense, and varied acquirements. The indifference which I at first had entertained for his writings, was soon converted into a feeling of profound veneration." But this conversion did not make Dr. Vimont a blind follower. Continuing a course of independent observations and experiments, he discovered that although Gall had opened the true road, and had made great advances in it, yet that he had not marked it out with all the requisite distinctness for future travellers. It is in the department of comparative anatomy that Gall is most open to criticism.

Dr. Vimont, then, in place of contenting himself with retaining his original prejudices against Gall and phrenology at one period, or of eulogising the science and its founder without stint and limitation at another, set about supplying the deficiencies which he believed to exist in both; whilst he took no pains to conceal the fact, that through them he had been placed in the true path both of cerebral physiology and of mental philosophy. He was not satisfied with giving merely a plausible statement of phrenology, and then introducing exceptions and special pleadings in the form of an alleged refutation of the science— a refutation, the fallacy and absurdity of which had been already fully exposed by Gall himself. With the delicate tact of his nation for perceiving the ridiculous, he could not think of displaying such ill-timed pleasantry as to elicit from the dignitaries of the church, doctors of the school of law, popular members of the Chamber of Deputies, and some flash *litterateurs*, testimonials in favour of certain anatomical and physiological exceptions. Even if he had been so inconsiderate as to seduce these persons to give publicity to their own ignorance, the Parisian press would soon have shown the absurdity of a set of men exerting themselves as either judges or umpires on a scientific question, the very elements of which they never learned.

It was reserved for an anti-phrenologist in our own country to be instrumental in inducing such a display of absurdity. The exhibition is certainly a novel one, in this nineteenth century, and in the United States of America—that of a scientific question being determined by votes, without any reference to the qualifications of the voters.* But of this more anon. We continue for the present our account of the steps pursued by the French author, in order to arrive at a knowledge of the truth.

In 1827, nine years from the time when he began his studies and observations on the brain and nervous system generally of animals, and on their habits and manners, Dr. Vimont sent to the institute a memoir for the prize of physiology, in which he introduced a portion of his numerous anatomical and physiological investigations. This memoir, of which honourable mention was made, was accompanied by twenty-five hundred heads belonging to animals of different classes, orders, genera, and species; fifteen hundred of which were those of animals whose habits were perfectly known to him. In addition, he sent also, moulded after the originals, four hundred copies of brains in wax, and an atlas of more than three hundred specimens of the cerebral system, and of its bony case, represented with the greatest fidelity.

In the prosecution of his experimental enquiries, Dr. Vimont, as already stated, brought up a large number of animals, whose dominant faculties he noted daily. The tribes of dogs and cats furnished him with a great many observations. He availed himself, at the same time, of those which were contributed by reflecting and truth-loving men; and conversed much and often with hunters and others, who, by their situation, were enabled to note the most remarkable traits of animals. By arranging and comparing these observations, Dr. Vimont was put in the route of what he justly believes to be true experimental physiology. We have not here the narrow limits marked out by the scalpel; but the wider and more philosophical domain of the mental acts of the cerebral system of animals—acts determined and appreciated in a truly physiological condition of the organs—very different from that painful and convulsive state during vivisection, in which they are not cognisable.

All this must seem to be a very needless trouble, if not a very absurd course of proceeding, to the metaphysician, who, sitting in his closet, writes from his imagination of the differences between man and animals, and talks of the reason which is characteristic of the

* See the commendatory notices appended to the second edition of Dr. Sewall's two Lectures on Phrenology. Boston, 1839.

former, and instinct of the latter. If, on the other hand, the course of experimental enquiry pursued by Dr. Vimont, and advocated and began by Gall, is admitted to be the true one, that alone by which we can attain a knowledge of the various instinctive feelings and limited intellectual combinations of animals, it must be speedily evident that a similar process of observation is the right one to guide us in our study of man's mixed nature. It was not until 1825 that Dr. Vimont began the study of the psychological manifestations of man, and applied himself assiduously to test the value of the numerous facts collected in the works of Gall. In 1827, our author for the first time heard Gall lecture at the Athæneum, in Paris. In 1829, Gall being then dead, Dr. Vimont gave a course of lectures on human and comparative phrenology, which was well received, and elicited expressions of pleasure from men of intelligence, who were his auditors. He subsequently went to London, with the view of acquiring a knowledge of the language, the better to enable him to ascertain the state of the physiology of the brain in Great Britain. When there, he read carefully all the numbers then published of the Phrenological Journal, and also the volume of the Phrenological Transactions.

Having placed before our readers the grounds on which they may justifiably give their attention to Dr. Vimont, we proceed, next, to indicate the nature of his testimony, which they will find is not given at random, nor from tradition or hearsay, but is the result of his own carefully and long-conducted observations. He was conversant with physiology, as it is usually taught in the schools, and was master of the common literature of his profession, when he began to devote himself more especially to the study of the anatomy and physiology of the brain. In this latter he spent no less than nine years of his life, noting anatomical facts, observing and comparing mental phenomena, and the relation between the latter and the former—and with what results? A full confirmation of the doctrines of phrenology, and the distinction of being called charlatan and ignoramus by men in other professions, who never gave as many hours to the subject on which they complacently dogmatise as he did years; by men, in fine, who scarcely know the difference between cranium and cerebrum, or between the latter and its meninges, and who probably never carried the study of mental philosophy beyond the reading of a few chapters of Locke and Stewart, and the committing to memory a few definitions of terms, which, after all, are not the representatives or exponents of either man's intellectual or moral faculties or nature.

Dr. Vimont devotes the first chapter of his work to some general considerations on the study of the functions, in which, after deducing some of the various speculations on the part of the brain which was supposed to be the common centre of mental action, he shows that Bonnet had, sixty years before Gall, distinctly stated the plurality of cerebral organs, and that they are destined for the manifestations of feeling and intellect.

The second chapter is on the processes employed by physicians and naturalists to appreciate the extent of the intellectual faculties of man and animals. Those of Camper, Daubenton, Cuvier, and Soemmering, are noticed by Dr. Vimont, who gives a decided preference over all of them to the method adopted by Gall. This last, as the reader knows, consists in a careful examination of the entire form of the head, and of each of its several parts. *" By this means we are able,"* says Dr. Vimont, *" with some exceptions to be afterwards made known, to appreciate the development, and consequently the action of the organs of the intellectual and affective faculties of both man and animals."* This is the part of phrenology to which the term craniology or cranioscopy has been applied, and which certain young misses, collegiate smatterers, and even grave pundits, have chosen to regard as phrenology itself, and as the beginning and end of a study of the several faculties of the mind, as well as of their determinate range and combined or balanced action. As his work is intended both for the general and professional reader, Dr. Vimont enters into very full preliminary details respecting the membranous and bony envelopes of the brain of man, and of the vertebral animals in general. He passes in review the hairy scalp and the cranium ; and he describes minutely the several bones of which this latter consists. Of the scalp he says, that in man it is so accurately fitted to the cranium, and of such a thickness, as to present no obstacle to our ascertaining the form of the head from which the hair has been removed. In some cases, however, as in idiots and in athletic subjects, it is so thick as to prevent our determining the volume of the cranium by simple inspection of the skin. Pressure by the fingers on the head will apprise us of the modification from this cause. Sometimes there is a fulness and laxity of the cellular tissue between the skin and skull, particularly near the orbits, which might impose upon the eye were we to trust to it alone. Here, as in the former case, a firm touch and some traction of the skin will enable us to detect the fallacy.

On the subject of the cranium, Dr. Vimont remarks, that man, of all vertebral animals, exhibits the greatest development of its anterior region. He investigates the crania of man, of quadrupeds, and of birds, and illustrates and explains his text by a great number of engravings, for the accuracy of which he vouches. The edition now before us is a Brussels one ; pirated, and therefore not to be so fully relied on, in regard to the engravings, as that published in Paris, under the immediate supervision of the author himself.   Even with this drawback, the plates of the former are calculated to command attention, and to give us a high opinion of the untiring industry of the author.   Dr. Vimont examines the skull under several points of view. First, the upper part or arch, or vault; secondly, the lower part or base; and, thirdly, of sections made vertically.   When speaking of the two tables of the skull, he mentions their separation, at times, at the anterior region of the vault constituting the frontal sinus; and he points out the obstacle which this presents, when it is of any extent, to our ascertaining with precision the development of the cerebral organs situated in this region, from the appearance of the external surface of the cranium.   No such difficulty exists respecting other parts of this bony case; " so that, with the exception of some morbid states to be noticed hereafter, we can have an accurate idea of the volume of the region of the brain which it covers by a simple inspection of its external table, the internal table being perfectly parallel, and the degree of elevation of the one corresponding strictly with that of the other."   It is not meant by this assertion, that the minuter divisions made by the convolutions of the brain are indicated by the external configuration of the cranium.   This is prevented by the thickness and firmness of the dura mater in the human subject, and by the thickness of the diploe between the two plates of the skull. " But it is not the less true," continues Dr. Vimont, " that when a portion of the cranium is developed, the portion of brain corresponding with it is also developed; and this is what the phrenologists understand by the relation between the development of the external table and that of the brain."

The base of the cranium in the human subject offers, according to our author, three distinct regions; viz. the anterior, middle, and posterior.   But it is by a vertical section of the skull of both man and animals that we are able to see at once, 1st, the extent and figure of the cranial cavity; 2d, the various degrees of thickness of the sides of the skull, from the root of the nose to the termination of the occipital bone, and consequently the greater or less separation of the frontal laminæ constituting the sinus at this region; 3d, the depth of the cavity which indicates a proportionate development of the cerebral parts lodged in its sides.

The vertical section of the cranium of the human subject is of an ovoid figure, having more extension behind than it has before.   The two laminæ which form it are, inclusive of their intermediate spongy tissue, about two lines, or the sixth of an inch in thickness.   The portion of these plates which corresponds to the inferior region of the frontal bone, and that in which the occipital crest is met with, are the thickest.   That answering to the cerebellum is the thinnest, not being more than half a line through.

Here we have the expression of a fact of general occurrence, just as we would state any other anatomical fact, without supposing that the accuracy of the proposition could be impeached by pointing out a morbid state of the part, and that the occurrence of the latter was proof conclusive against the former.   As well might the increased thickness of the skin in elephantiasis be adduced in opposition to the fact of its general and average state, as the instance of thick skulls brought by Dr. Sewall, to show that there is no average standard of thickness of the human cranium.   The copies which he gives in his lectures, were the skulls procured, with one exception, from the museum of a friend, (Dr. Smith, of Baltimore,) who had these precisely because they were exceptions to the common standard; they were pathological, not simply anatomical specimens; and Dr. Sewall traveled from the record, in introducing them to confirm his negative position.   Whether it be an evidence of that remote sympathy which one sees every now and then without being able to account for it, we cannot pretend to say; but it would seem that the learned gentlemen who certify to Dr. S.'s triumphant philosophy, have an evident leaning to the anatomy illustrated by these thick skulls, in preference to that which is taught, in all the works on the subject, by the current and general examples from the healthy and thinner skulls.   It would hardly be a greater deviation from the anatomical standard, and the rules of logic, if Dr. Sewall were to procure some fractured skulls, and exhibit them as proof that the common division of the bones of the cranium by sutures was inaccurate, and its retention empirical.   We give him this hint very cheerfully, which he may turn to account for the third edition of his lectures.   The certifiers in his favour will doubtless be as eager in the advocacy, then, of cracked skulls, as they now are of that of thick ones, in order to put down the heresy and absurdities of phrenology.   The argument would be just as fair and valid in the former as it is in the latter case.

Dr. Vimont enters into a description, also, of the vault, base, and vertical section of the skulls of the vertebral animals in general.   In the following chapter, we have a comparative account of the bones which enter into the construction of the cranium in man and other animals, and a designation in that of the former, of the prominences and processes of the bones which are liable to deceive the student in his craniological enquiries.   The details on this subject are ample, and possess, in an anatomico-physiological point of view, great interest, which is increased by the varied pictorial illustrations of the atlas. They will be found to have a far higher value, scientifically, than the superficial and inaccurate summary given in Dr. Sewall's two lectures; and if read and studied by his *learned* certifiers, these gentlemen would then see that they had passed the *pons asini* of phrenology, and would feel some compunction at the self-complacency with which they had been induced to certify to erroneous concluding postulata, before they had acquired a knowledge of even the elements of the science.

Among some of the anatomical axioms with which Dr. Vimont concludes the sixth chapter of his work, are the following :—

The form of the cranium of the vertebral animals varies wonderfully in volume, according to the classes, orders, genera, and species. Each species has a type peculiar to itself, and which prevents our confounding it with any other. We find, however, great individual differences in volume; differences which explain those of the extent of action of the nervous system in the members of the species.

The form of the cranium being given, it is easy to ascertain, by its exterior, that of the encephalon, with the exception of some diseased states, and the presence of the frontal sinus in the adult man and in some species of animals.

Man has, of all the vertebral animals, the anterior portion of the cranium the most fully developed. After him, come the elephant, the ourang-outang, the dog, hare, and monkey. Parroquets, the species of the genus *corvus*, and geese, have this region tolerably developed. The turkey, the barn-yard fowl, and several species of water-fowls, are among those birds which exhibit it in the least degree of development.

The complete development of the cranium only takes place at an epoch remote from birth; its growth is generally more rapid in animals than in man, in whom it is not completed until his twenty-fifth and even sometimes thirtieth year.

The internal surface of the cranium presents, in a great number of classes, orders, and genera, depressions corresponding with the reliefs or convolutions of the brain.

Birds, of all the vertebral animals, are those the external surface of the crania of which most closely corresponds with their cerebral structure; this is owing to the thinness of the plates of the cranium, and to their perfect parallelism. After birds, came the *rodentia*, then the small *carnivora*.

Birds present also the greatest symmetry in the form of their cranium. The higher we rise in the scale, the less this symmetry is met with; and in man it is least evident of all.

Age brings about notable changes by diminishing the size of the cranium, and in its thickness and density.

In chapter eight, Dr. Vimont describes the brain of the human subject, and of quadrupeds and birds, in the most important anatomical points of view. Without pretending to repeat, or even to give a summary of his description, it will be sufficient to indicate an important inference, deduced from the vast collection of facts which he had observed, and which, by the way, is in harmony with those laid down by many distinguished physiologists, in addition to Gall and Spurzheim. It is, says Dr. Vimont, a general law of nature, that the more extended and complex the functional acts, the more complicated are the parts designated for their performance. The brain is an example of the truth of this proposition. Man, of all animals, has a brain of the most complicated structure; then, in the order enumerated, are quadrupeds, birds, reptiles, fishes, and insects.

(To be continued.)

ARTICLE V.

REFLECTIONS ON THE DEATH AND CHARACTER OF DR. SPURZHEIM.*

> Far may we search before we find
> Such kindly heart, such noble mind."—SCOTT.

The disappointment of human hopes is a trite theme, and the obituary record of an oft-told tale. But there is something startling, almost appalling, in the death of Dr. Spurzheim—something to make the most unreflecting pause, and think, and feel! Just as he had entered on his labours in our country, a new field, where he was ardent in his expectations of doing great things for the cause of truth and human improvement, he has been called upon to give up his trust, to resign the spirit which seemed as if it had not felt one breath of decay steal over its clay tenement. And who can calculate the loss to society when such a mighty mind, devoted to doing good, is removed from our earth?

It is only when feeling a perfect trust and confidence in the ways of our heavenly Father, that we can be reconciled to his providence when removing those who are labouring to make the world better and

* This article is copied from No. 12, Vol. V, of the "Ladies' Magazine and Literary Gazette," published at Boston, December, 1832. It is, perhaps, sufficient praise to state that these reflections, so just and appropriate, emanated from the pen of *Mrs. Sarah J. Hale*.

happier. But all who had the high privilege of hearing Dr. Spurz
heim lecture, will recollect how often and how fervently he urged th
duty of entire submission to the Divine laws. It seemed his constar
aim to impress on his audience the necessity and the happiness o
cultivating this humble spirit—of saying, in reference to all even
and circumstances, "*Father, thy will be done.*"

His own death is an event which most deeply tries the faith of hi
friends. Why he should have been taken away, when so able and s
ardent to perform his part, and when with such long observation an
severe study he had matured a system which promises so much fc
science and education, and which he only, of all living men, seeme
capable of explaining and enforcing, is to our short-sighted ke
incomprehensible. The mind almost refuses to believe that one s
perfect in life's best energies should be dead.

"Dead, dead! when there is on our earth
  Such waste of worthless breath!
There should have gone ten thousand lives
  To ransom him from death!—
Ay, twice ten thousand might have gone,
  Nor caused the blank that's left by *one.*"

Short biographical sketches of Dr. Spurzheim, and notices of hi
sickness, death, and the funeral honours paid him by our lamentin
citizens, have appeared in many of our papers.

We have seen no description, however, which has done justice t
the character of Dr. Spurzheim. Great men are too often rated onl
by the standard of mind. The brilliancy of genius, without referenc
to the manner in which it is displayed, is worshipped. Dr. Spurz
heim was great in goodness as well as talent. It was this combinatio
of philanthropy and philosophy, rendered active by the enthusiasti
temperament of genius, and effective and useful by a judgment s
quick and discriminating that it seemed almost like the spirit of prc
phecy, which gave him his immeasurable superiority. There need
no surer proof of this superiority, than the influence he had obtaine
during the little time he resided among us. He had been in Bosto
but about ten weeks, and in that short space he had literally " gaine
the hearts of the people." Those who saw and heard him, and i
that number is comprised our best and most eminent people, gav
him not merely their admiration, but their esteem, reverence, an
love. They felt he was a friend of the human race, and that i
honouring him, they honoured the noblest of human virtues—benevo
lence.

Dr. Spurzheim was a phrenologist; that is, he devoted himself t
the study of the human mind as it is manifested in the affective an

ntellectual faculties of man.   In the pursuit and establishment of his
heory, he was actuated by the noblest and purest motives.   He
sought to improve our systems of education, as the sure and only
means of perfecting the character of the human race.   The principles
or which he contended seemed to him all-important.   They involved
he knowledge of human nature, and the art of education ; and he
aboured, and as we may say, died, in the cause of phrenology ; for all
agree that it was his over-exertion and zealous desire to benefit others
which caused him to neglect himself, and thus gave to his disease the
fatal ascendency over his constitution which terminated his life.   The
best and most heartfelt tribute, then, which we can render to his
memory, will be to examine carefully and cordially the principles he
held thus dear and sacred.   This can be done, for he has left works
which embody his peculiar sentiments, and which will soon be pub-
ished in this city.

There are reasons which should make my own sex revere his
character and be zealous in studying his doctrines.   He was the friend
of woman.   He entertained exalted views of the great benefits which
would result to society and the world, from the influence of female
ntellect, judiciously cultivated and rightly directed.   And it was to
be an intellectual and moral help meet for man that he would have
her trained.

In a conversation with the editor of this magazine, respecting
emale education and the best mode of introducing improvement into
our systems, he remarked :—

" Excepting Christianity, phrenology will do more to elevate
woman than any other system has ever done.   It gives her a participation in the labours of mind.   She must understand its principles,
and practise them in the nursery.   And her influence it is which
must mould the minds of her children, and thus improve the world."
' If," continued he, " I possess any excellence of character, I owe it
all to my early training.   In the first place, my mother gave me a
good physical education—then she cultivated my moral feelings, and
he taught me to *think*.   I owe every thing to my mother !"

Those only who have seen his face when suddenly kindling with
he enthusiasm of intellect and benevolence, and the smile that broke
over his features, which seemed the gush of heart, soul, and mind,
n the cause he was advocating, can understand the expression of
ountenance that accompanied these words—" I owe every thing to
my mother."   The effect on my own feelings will never be forgotten.
Here was this great and good man, before whom our best and wisest
men were proud to come for instruction, laying all his honours on the
altar of filial piety, and ascribing all his excellences to the influence

of his mother. What a triumph for woman, and what a responsibility such influence should impose on our sex!

In thus highly appreciating the character of woman, Dr. Spurzheim is entitled to her confidence, so far as the examination of his principles of education, and the particular manner he has suggested for the improvement of society, is concerned. He wished no one to adopt these principles without scrutiny. He asked to be trusted for his own purity of purpose and honesty of assertion; the belief in phrenology, he always insisted, could only be justified by personal observation and study.

To his writings, therefore, and the exertions of our citizens who are earnest to promote the cause of human improvement, we must now be indebted for instruction in this new science. We shall hear his voice no more. The charm of ease, simplicity, and attractiveness, his manner could impart to subjects the most abstruse, difficult, and dry, is dispelled; but truth, he always insisted, would prevail; and if the principles he inculcated were true, what a great responsibility rests on the people of Boston and Cambridge! They only, of all our waiting nation, have been privileged to hear the teachings of Dr. Spurzheim. They know his generous purposes, his exalted views; and it is for them to build his monument—not with perishing marble merely, but by disseminating the truths of his philosophy, and encouraging the practice of that universal benevolence which made such a prominent feature in his system. In this work ladies can surely do something.

ARTICLE VI.

CASE OF SUICIDE.

To the Editor of the American Phrenological Journal.

London, October 18th, 1839.

Dear Sir,—

Allow me to call the attention of your readers to a singular phrenological coincidence, presented in relation to the extraordinary suicide which has recently taken place in this city.

I allude to the case of Margaret Moyes, the young woman who threw herself from the monument in September last, the particulars of which have doubtless appeared in the American newspapers. I am not aware that any examination of her head took place after the event, and, indeed, I presume that, from the injury which the back part of the skull sustained, an examination would have been almost impracticable; but it is quite evident, from the testimony of the witnesses interrogated before the coroner, that the organ of Self-esteem was in a state of the greatest excitement, and that a morbid action of this sentiment was the proximate cause of the act of self-destruction. This will be sufficiently shown by the selection of a few scattered sentences from the evidence of the witness who was best acquainted with the deceased and her family.

"Mr. Moyes has a large family of daughters growing up, and lately the necessity has been seen of some of them going from home to get their living."

"The determination of some of the daughters, and among others the deceased, being sent out to situations, was come to a month or six weeks ago."

"Margaret was the first for whom a situation was to be found."

"It is difficult to say whether the dejected state of her mind proceeded from the illness of her parent, or from the prospect of going out to earn a livelihood."

"It was intended to give her a situation in a confectioner's shop."

"On the subject of going out to a situation being mentioned to her, I heard her say—'*I take it to heart; I cannot get over the feeling*—and yet *I'm aware it is the right course.*' "

And the following is from her sister's evidence:—

"The *idea* of going out into the world to get her living *preyed upon her mind.*"[*]

It was also shown by the evidence, that she was not impelled to the peculiar mode of her death by the circumstance of casually passing the monument at the time when the thought of suicide had occurred to her mind, but that she deliberately left her home and walked to that structure, which was at a distance of several miles from her father's house. The mode of her death, therefore, was evidently a matter of choice and consideration—the result of some prevailing impulse of her mind which could not be overruled, and which urged her to ascend to, and plunge from, some tremendous height. Bearing these facts in mind, the following remarks on the functions of the organ of Self-esteem, extracted from Mr. Combe's System of Phrenology, are worthy of the most attentive consideration.

* The Spectator newspaper, one of the most philosophical productions of the London press, under date 13th October, publishes an article which has been suggested by the prevalence of suicide in this country with a view of tracing its causes, and quotes the above evidence as illustrative of the effect of a morbid self-esteem.

"Having studied the sentiment of pride as a primitive ment
quality, and its organ, in the human race, Dr. Gall wished to asce
tain whether his observations would be confirmed by the low
animals. He therefore examined the heads of such of them as w
are accustomed to call proud—the race-horse, the cock, and peacoc
He did not find in any of these a remarkable development of th
cerebral parts corresponding to the organ of Self-esteem in man; b
he found a considerable development of these parts in animals i
which he would never have thought of looking for it—that is to sa
in those which voluntarily remain in the higher regions of the ai
living on mountains, and other elevated situations; for example, i
the roebuck, the chamois, the wild goat, and certain species of eagl
and falcons; and what struck him most was, that the parts in questio
were the more developed in proportion to the greater height of th
dwelling places of the animals. Dr. Gall himself was astonished i
this observation. That a *predilection for physical heights* should, i
animals, depend on the same organ as that to which the sentiment c
self-esteem is referrible in man, appeared to him at first altogeth
improbable and inadmissible; 'yet,' says he, 'I have laid down th
rule to communicate the progress of my observations, as well as th
manner in which they have given rise to my opinions.' He accor
ingly enters into some interesting observations on the various dwellin
places of animals, and states, that in the heads of all of them whic
have their abodes in high places, there is an eminence which entirel
resembles the organ of Self-esteem in man."

In confirmation of the above, it may be remarked, that a case is o
record of a Monsieur B., in whom the organ was naturally very larg
and who was accidentally wounded by a nail in this part of the brai
" While labouring under the influence of the wound, he felt himsel
as it were, *elevated above the clouds*, and *carried through the ai
retaining at the same time, and also manifesting during his conv
lescence, the same proud and haughty manners which had disti
guished him in health."

I am, dear sir,

Very faithfully yours,

M. B. SAMPSON.

ARTICLE VII.

PHRENOLOGICAL DEVELOPMENTS OF JOSEPH CINQUEZ, ALIAS GINQUA.

Mr. Editor,—

Inasmuch as the Africans, recently cast upon our shore, hav created considerable excitement in various parts of the country, have thought it might be interesting to present the public, throug your Journal, with a brief sketch of the phrenological development and character of their leader, viz. Joseph Cinquez or Ginqua. O the 5th of September, I visited New Haven, where the Africans wer then confined, and made a critical examination of Cinquez's head. also took in plaster of Paris an exact likeness of his head, which i now deposited in my cabinet, and may be examined by any perso: who will call at No. 135 Nassau street, New York. The followin cut, taken from this cast, will perhaps convey to your readers correct view of the outlines of Cinquez's head.

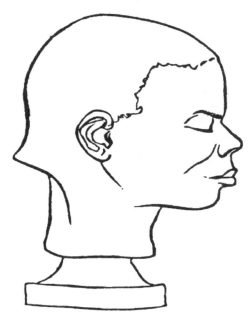

His head is peculiar in shape, being long and high, but narrow The base of his brain is inferior in size; consequently the lowe animal propensities do not constitute the leading elements of hi character. His temperament is very favourable to mental and phy sical exercise, being nervous bilious, with a fair portion of the san guine.   He is rather tall and spare, but well-formed, and adapted for great physical and mental exertions.   His appearance indicates a strong constitution, and great powers of endurance.   He has very fine pliable hair, thin and soft skin, with strongly-marked nervous and locomotive powers.   His head measures most in the region of those faculties giving a love of liberty, independence, determination, ambition, regard for his country, and for what he thinks is sacred and right ; also, good practical talents and powers of observation, shrewdness, tact, and management, joined with an uncommon degree of moral courage and pride of character.

Amativeness, Adhesiveness, Combativeness, Destructiveness, Alimentiveness, and Acquisitiveness, are only fairly developed, and would have but a common or ordinary influence in the formation of his character.   The organs of Self-esteem and Firmness are very large, and would form leading traits in his character.   I should not infer that he was *naturally* cruel, malicious, or even selfish, except in relation to his liberty and his rights.   But while he is not revengeful or ill-natured, he has too much pride and love of self to become subject to the will of others.   He could not be trifled with, with impunity ; his indignation is extreme, and he would not easily give up the object of his pursuit.   His thoughts and feelings are protracted and connected, owing to his large Concentrativeness and Firmness. Inhabitiveness is large, and would render him much attached to home and country ; his domestic organs being only fairly developed, he would not be particularly warm-hearted, social, and fond of friends or company—had much rather have influence and power than friends, and, at times, might be tyrannical and dictatorial, yet withal, has much humanity, kindness, and sympathy, for the happiness of others.

His intellect is generally well-balanced, and better developed than most persons' belonging to his race.   Still he is quite deficient in those faculties giving natural refinement, delicacy of feeling, imagination, powers of adaptation, and construction.   His general memory and practical talents, I should think, might be good.   He has the requisite faculties for rendering him a close observer of men and things, and a good judge of human nature.   Though Causality is not very strong, yet, having rather large Secretiveness and Cautiousness, he would be shrewd, artful, and a very good manager.   He would have great self-possession in times of danger, and might easily conceal, by the expressions of his countenance, all appearance of his real feelings or designs, so that it would be difficult to find him out, or detect his plans.   His faculties admirably adapt him to take the lead, secure power, and command the respect of others, as well as render him capable of exerting a controlling influence over the minds of those like the native Africans.   His cerebral organisation, as a whole, I should think, was also superior to the majority of negroes' in our own country.

Yours, &c.
L. N. FOWLER.

New York, November, 8th, 1839.

MISCELLANY.

Phrenology in Hartford, Ct.—Mr. Combe delivered a course of lectures on phrenology in this city during the month of October.   We copy from the "Hartford Times," of November 2d, the following interesting statement, giving an account of the reception of these lectures, together with the views which some of the most intelligent, scientific, and moral citizens of Hartford entertain respecting the science.

"At a meeting of Mr. Combe's class, held at Gilman's Hall, on Friday evening, October 25th, immediately after the delivery of the last lecture of his phrenological course, the class was organised by calling the Rev. Dr. Totten to the chair, and appointing Wm. Jas. Hamersley secretary.

"On motion, a committee was appointed to draft resolutions for the consideration of the class.

"The committee consisted of the Rev. T. H. Gallaudet, Erastus Smith, Esq., and Dr. A. Brigham.

"The committee having reported, the following resolutions were discussed, and unanimously adopted:—

"*Resolved*, That we have derived great pleasure and instruction from the interesting lectures of Mr. Combe.

"*Resolved*, That, from his able exposition of phrenology, we have learned numerous facts in relation to intellectual, moral, and physical education.

"*Resolved*, That we consider his exposition of the subject of importance in teaching us the functions of the brain, and believe that beneficial results will be witnessed from the application of its principles to the education of youth, to legislation, jurisprudence, and the treatment of the insane.

"*Resolved*, That a committee of five be appointed to convey to Mr. Combe these resolutions of his class, and also an expression of thanks for the gratification his lectures have afforded them.

"The committee appointed in accordance with the last resolution, consisted of the Rev. T. H. Gallaudet, Erastus Smith, Esq., Dr. A. Brigham, the Rev. S. Hovey, and Professor Stewart.

"On motion, adjourned.

"SILAS TOTTEN, Chairman.

"WM. JAS. HAMERSLEY, Secretary."

Application of Phrenology to Education.—We find, in the July number of the British Phrenological Journal, a report of an interesting discussion before the Aberdeen Phrenological Society, on the application of the science to education.   Mr. Connon, who had applied its principles with great success for several years, is represented to have made the following statement :—

"He entered into a very interesting detail of the principles by which he was guided in conducting the school under his charge. Phrenology, he said, had been useful to him in two respects. First, by affording indications of the natural talents and disposition of each individual scholar, it had facilitated his labours in a very high degree. But it is, he said, in the clear insight which phrenology gives into *what ought to be the object of education*, and *the proper method of conducting it*, that he had found its chief value to consist. It enabled teachers to carry out the fundamental principles of education with a precision which he believed could not be attained by any who are ignorant of its truths. He then alluded to the principle of *sympathy*, as one of supreme importance in the art of teaching—the principle, that whatever feeling, desire, propensity, &c. &c. the teacher manifests, the same will be generated in corresponding strength among his pupils. If the teacher uniformly maintains the supremacy of his own moral sentiments and intellect above his lower animal feelings, his pupils will manifest the same faculties, if, on the contrary, he indulges his animal propensities—say Combativeness and Destructiveness—his pupils cannot help manifesting the same passions."

We copy only a part of Mr. C.'s remarks. The great advantages of a thorough knowledge of mental science to an instructer, must be obvious to every reflecting mind. But until the functions of the brain are correctly understood by teachers, and the true laws, which regulate the exercise and development of the cerebral organs, are recognised and obeyed, any and every system of education must necessarily be *imperfect* and *empirical.*

———

Dr. Buchanan in Florida.—In our first volume, we presented several notices of the operations of this gentleman, in behalf of phrenology. Some time since, we received a letter from Dr. B., dated Pensacola, Fa., June 20th, 1839, containing the results of some observations, which must be interesting to the advocates of the science generally. Our limits prevent us from copying the entire letter, but we will give the more important extracts, and the substance of the remainder in our own remarks. Dr. Buchanan suggests the propriety and desirableness, that phrenologists, in various parts of the country, should communicate, from time to time, to this Journal, the results of their observations, and give an account of the progress and state of the science in the vicinity of their residence and operations. By this means, there would be more personal interest and unity of action among phrenologists themselves; the public would become better acquainted with the principles and progress of the science, as well as the number and character of its advocates, and, what is not unimportant, a correct and minute history of phrenology in this country would thus be transmitted to posterity. We would, therefore, solicit communications of the above character, and promise to make such a disposal of them, as, in our judgment, will best subserve the interests of the science. The letter of Dr. B. continues as follows:—

"Having just returned from a pleasant excursion in Florida, I will venture to give you some desultory reminiscences of the last few months. I have found in the public mind some lingering remains of the prejudice against our science, which was once universal; but this prejudice, when it is accompanied by curiosity and mental activity, is rather beneficial than otherwise, for it increases the amount of collision, argument, and excitement; and intellectual excitement must result in the discovery of additional truth.   Phrenology is so demonstrable a science, that all who sincerely wish to discover truth—all who have sufficient strength of mind to lay aside prejudice and adopt a newly demonstrated truth—are apt to become its zealous votaries whenever it is fairly brought before them.   I am often asked the question among strangers, 'Do you make many converts to phrenology ?' My usual reply is, that I hope not, for I should regret to think that there were *many* in such a condition of mind as to require conversion.   Surely there would be no occasion for *converting*, if every man took care to investigate subjects thoroughly before forming an opinion.   Still, I have sometimes to witness the conversion of those who have set themselves against the truth, because they know not what it is.   As far as the sphere of my operations extended, I found few indeed who did not ultimately regard phrenology as an admirable and important science.   As far as I came into contact with the community, public opinion seemed decidedly favourable, and instead of finding my profession a mere subject of jest, I was frequently received with the attention and honour which are usually bestowed on politicians alone."

Dr. B. here gives some description of the Indian hostilities, and the war carried on at the present time in Florida by the Seminoles.   He also gives an account of several ancient mounds, and makes the following interesting remarks respecting some skulls which he obtained from them :—

"The heads which I obtained from these localities are mostly below the white average in point of size, and rather irregular as to the character of the developments.   A few are quite good, and others extremely bad. Conscientiousness is, indeed, more frequently defective than you will ever find it among the whites.   Conscientiousness and Benevolence are the organs that most frequently fail in Indian crania, while Reverence has usually a fine development.   I do not recollect ever seeing an Indian head defective in Reverence.   The strictness with which their traditionary laws are enforced, their reverence for the aged, and their habitual gravity and dignity of deportment, are ample illustrations of this faculty; while their treachery and broken treaties, their system of warfare and horrid massacres, illustrate well the deficiency of Benevolence and Conscientiousness.   Nor can we suppose that these deficiencies are solely acquired by their mode of life.   Even if they originated in that way, we know that they would be transmitted to their progeny, and thus become congenital.   I observed, in the heads of children and infants, forms quite as unfavourable as in the adults.

"The heads of the chiefs appear quite superior.   Coa-harjo, the chief of a band of Creeks who joined the Seminoles, came in a little more than a year ago, and was preparing to emigrate.   While his band was at Walker's town, on the Apalachicola, with the United States agent, Coa-harjo was treacherously murdered by Lewis, one of the Indians of the village, and his men were soon alarmed by one of the whites, who enjoyed a salary as an interpreter, and was therefore interested in the prolongation of the war.   Fearing treachery in the whites, they fled and joined the hostiles.   Having obtained the skull of Coa-harjo, who was regarded as a trusty and honourable man by the whites, I found it to present a noble, and, indeed, beautiful form.   The frontal and coronal regions have a predominance, and the organs of Inhabitiveness and Adhesiveness are moderate.   It would be an interesting investigation to discover whether these are large in the body of Seminoles, who have so long maintained possession of Florida against our government.   Had

Coa-harjo lived, his band would have gone with him to the west. The Indian Lewis, by whom he was stabbed, lingered about home, expecting him to recover. Upon his death, Lewis was immediately, according to the Indian custom, dragged from his cabin and shot by a party who came to execute justice. The skull of Coa-harjo makes a fine contrast with that of Lewis.

"Vacca Pechassee, the old chief at Walker's town, has been dead five or six years. His skull presents large developments, and much more of Comparison, Causality, and Philoprogenitiveness, than is usual. He lived in plenty, and, I believe, took his name of Vacca Pechassee, or Master of Cows, from the number of his herds. Practical phrenologists are familiar with the influence of Philoprogenitiveness in giving us a fondness for animals. Perhaps the poor development in this organ in many Indian heads, may be one great cause of hindering their advance to civilisation. The pastoral mode of life to which Philoprogenitiveness would tend, being a common, if not necessary, intermediate step between the hunting and the agricultural stages. The skulls of Vacca Pechassee and Coa-harjo, placed among a group of ordinary Indians, would naturally suggest the idea that they were 'born to command,' by their general superiority."

"It is now more than three years since I suggested to Mr. Fowler that there must be some unknown organs between the intellectual and the moral. Since that time, I have seen nothing to change the opinion, but have met with as many striking illustrations of their functions as of any other faculties. My views do not very materially differ from those which he has published. The organ above Comparison I have found to give the sense of emotion, and that above Causality, the sense of design. Both combined, give a knowledge of character, and an insight into the workings of other men's minds. Whatever theoretical objections may be found to this view, it will be found *practically* true. But as I have given my views upon this matter elsewhere, I shall not here repeat them. One of the greatest intriguers and shrewdest politicians in this territory, I found to have these organs large, especially that of design. Another, who stands above reproach, is an intellectual and observant man, but I told him (on account of this deficiency alone) that although well calculated for business, he would suffer and probably be cheated, from his incapacity to understand and manage men. This was considered remarkably true, and well evinced in his life. Besides their utility in the study of character, these organs are necessary in giving expression, and therefore important to the actor, orator, painter, caricaturist, &c.

"In conclusion, let me call the attention of phrenologists to a mode of investigating character which has not received sufficient attention. That it should not have been urged upon us by those close observers of nature, Gall and Spurzheim, is indeed surprising. I do not at this moment recollect any passage in their writings, recommending the method to which I allude. The growth or change of the encephalic mass is always well accommodated by the osseous structure of the head. Whenever an organ declines, the deposite of bone which ensues obliterates its digital impression in the skull, and continues to follow it on inward. When an organ increases, the skull yields by absorption at the spot against which it lies, and then, by a general growth over it, accommodates the development and displays it externally. This process is continually going on as our faculties are increasing or declining. Our character is seldom left by circumstances precisely at the spot at which it was placed by nature. It is seldom that all our organs receive a sufficient and uniform degree of cultivation; hence almost every skull will display some evidence of growth or decline. The deep digital impressions and cranial thinness over active organs, or the smooth internal surface and great thickness at the spot of inaction, will show very plainly the changes or cultivation which the character has undergone. If the skull is not opened, we can ascertain very easily, by inserting a taper* at the *foramen magnum*, the comparative activity of the organs. When a skull is presented me for examination in public, I do not venture to pronounce upon its character until I have tried it in this manner.

"The regions of the greatest activity will be plainly indicated by the translucency of the skull, and the total opacity of other spots will mark the extent of cerebral inactivity or atrophy. For instance, the skull of a negro woman (in my possession) who murdered her own child, and cut it open with an axe, exhibits an entire atrophy of the brain, except at the spots of Firmness, Acquisitiveness, and Destructiveness. These three sites exhibit a translucency; but at the site of the other organs, the atrophy is such as to make the skull not only thick and opaque, but the heaviest that I have ever seen. The character and the skull are equally monstrous.

"In the skull of Coa-harjo, the organ of Conscientiousness does not show any remarkable external development, but illustrates his character by the internal proofs of its activity.

"In the head of Jesse Goodman, a degraded creature, who murdered his wife, there is an entire opacity of the superior portion of the frontal bone, showing a decline of Benevolence, Ideality, and the reflective organs.

"In the skull of a Mexican soldier, from San Jacinto battle-field, Hope and Combativeness appear very active, and the moral organs feeble. In the head of a negro, who killed his overseer, and died without any repentance, the organs of Benevolence and Reverence appear the most inactive. In the head of another, who bore the character of a faithful and humble servant, there are plain digital impressions, and a distinct translucency at the organ of Reverence. In the head of a murderer, executed in Louisiana, there is a most unusual thickening over the moral organs, which is particularly striking at Benevolence; while in another, whom I know to have been a kind, benevolent man, there is a distinct translucency at the site of Benevolence, as well as a good development externally. The same individual was remarkable for his love of animals and pets. I do not find quite so large a development of Philoprogenitiveness as I expected; but at the situation of Philoprogenitiveness, or the occipital bone, usually the thickest part of the skull, there are two remarkable translucent spaces, showing the vigour of the organ. In the head of a French nobleman, who died in the commission of a felony, there is a poor development and general opacity of the coronal region. But it is needless to detail my illustrations. 'Ex uno,' &c.

"This mode of investigation is very striking to those who are unaccustomed to it, and gives to the lecturer important additional means of illustrating the science, and investing it with interest to his auditors. It is still more striking in its results. In the study of living character, the indications of the developments are assisted by pathognomony and the conduct of the individual. But in the skull we have almost as great an assistance in the indications which it gives of the activity or inactivity

* As this may smoke and burn the skull too much, it is best to insert a large glass tube with the superior extremity closed, so as to resemble a long slender cupping glass. By thrusting the taper up this, the skull will be preserved from injury.

of the faculties.   We are often enabled to know precisely what were th
governing powers of the individual in the latter periods of his life, an
even to take a retrospective glance at his history.   The external table o
the skull presents us his congenital or natural character, and the interna
his ultimate or acquired one.   The interval between the two, the spac
of transition, is the history of his life."

Phrenology in the Western States.—Our science has been makir
very commendable progress for many years in the western states.   W
have numerous facts in confirmation of this statement, and shall prese
them, when convenient, in the Journal.   Within a few months, a ve
interesting series of articles on the subject have appeared in the "Bann
and Pioneer," a religious paper, devoted to the Baptist denominatio
published at Louisville, Ky., and having an extensive circulation in th
west.   The articles were prepared by one of its editors, J. M. Peck, A. M
of Rock Spring, Ill., who is the author, we believe, of several public
tions.

In one of those papers, after some remarks on the brain, as the orga
of the mind, being a fundamental principle in phrenology, he makes th
following very appropriate and important observations :—

"If this theory be adopted by the teacher of youth, the divine, th
jurist, and the physician, a field of interesting practical application
open.   The various metaphysical theories heretofore adopted must b
overhauled, examined, and made to conform to this doctrine.   Preache
of the gospel will have less room to build their theological speculatior
on abstract mind and metaphysical theories.   When they think, rea
converse, and preach about the soul, they will have due regard to i
connection and bearing upon man's animal nature.   They will ende:
vour to learn something about the structure and functions of the brai
and the nervous system, and the different effects that different states c
the brain and nerves have upon the mind.   They will regard and addres
man, not as mere soul, or mere body, but as a complex being, possessin
a bodily and mental nature, both of which are affected by religious im
pressions, and concerned in all moral and religious actions, yet both cor
stituting one and the same being, called MAN.   Physicians will find a
interesting field of exploration, especially in reference to that class c
diseases that affect *mind*, and they will aim to remove the unhealth
action by operating directly upon the animal economy, and restoring i
functions to a healthy state.

"The jurist will find this subject has very important relations to h
department, that due and proper allowance should be made in all tho:
criminal cases where obliquity of mind and conduct evidently resu
from a diseased brain.

"But instructers of youth, more than all other persons, have occasic
to make themselves acquainted with the relations that exist betwee
man's material, moral, and intellectual nature, and that the whole bein;
in a proportionate degree, demands his attention; and that great care
necessary to preserve healthy action in the brain and nervous systen
while he is aiming

"'To rear the tender thought,
And teach the young idea how to shoot.'"

Crania Americana.—This great work, (by S. G. Morton, M. D., o
Philadelphia,) which has been many years in the way of preparation,
now published and ready for delivery.   In Vol. I., page 385, of the Journa

we gave a particular description of the leading characteristics of the work, to which we would refer the reader. Since that notice, we have had the pleasure of receiving several names as subscribers for the work, and should be happy to receive more, as we understand the number of copies are not quite all engaged. It should be remembered, that the work is published for *subscribers only*, and that it will never be deposited in bookstores for sale. If any persons, therefore, wish to procure a copy, they should forward their names and address immediately to the publisher, J. Dobson, No. 108 Chestnut street, Philadelphia.

As a part of this work is strictly phrenological, and is very important in its bearings on the science, it is our intention to draw somewhat largely from its pages for the Journal. But for the present we can refer only to one topic. We observe in the Preface, that in consequence of the author's receiving some valuable specimens of crania too late for the work, as well as from a desire to institute a more extended comparison between the five different races of men, it is his design to issue a *supplementary volume*. In this volume, the capacity of the anterior and posterior chambers of the skull will be given, and also numerous anatomical and phrenological measurements. To make a fair comparison, a very extended series of crania will be necessary, "and the author respectfully solicits the further aid of gentlemen interested in the cause of science, in procuring the *skulls of all nations*, and forwarding them to his address in this city." We hope this request will be faithfully responded to. The results of an investigation here proposed, will be of the highest importance. To illustrate this remark, we will present our readers with some striking facts on the subject, contained in the Crania Americana, page 260. The author obtained from correct measurements of skulls, without selection, the following results:—The mean internal capacity of

52 skulls	of the	Caucasian race	was found to be	87	cubic inches,
10	" "	Mongolian	" "	83	" "
147	" "	American	" "	82	" "
18	" "	Malay	" "	81	" "
29	" "	Ethiopian	" "	78	" "

It will be observed, that here the comparison is made between the *whole* internal capacity of the skulls; but when we have the capacities of the anterior and posterior chambers given, the results will be far more striking and important. But even in the present case, with the above comparison, we find that the Caucasian race, which is the most civilised, and is, in every respect, superior to the others, possess, on an average, heads *four cubic inches* larger in capacity than either of the other races, harmonising most strikingly with the fundamental principle in phrenology, that size, other things being equal, is a measure of power.

—

Lectures of Rev. J. A. Warne, A. M.—The lectures of this gentleman on phrenology, in this city, consisting of twenty in number, and commenced early in October, are now in a state of progress. The general objects of these lectures are to give the history of the science, and discuss, at length, its principles in their application to morals, education, insanity, jurisprudence, &c.; entering, at the same time, into a full and minute analysis of each faculty, in its uses and abuses. We shall revert again to Mr. W.'s lectures when they have closed.

THE

AMERICAN PHRENOLOGICAL JOURNAL

AND

MISCELLANY.

| Vol. II. | Philadelphia, January 1, 1840. | No. 4. |

ARTICLE I.

Outlines of Physiology: with an Appendix on Phrenology. By
P. M. ROGET, M. D., Secretary to the Royal Society, Professor
of Physiology in the Royal Institution of Great Britain, &c. &c.
First American edition, revised, with numerous notes. Philadelphia: Lea and Blanchard, (successors to Carey and Co.,) 1839.
8vo. pp. 516.

To notice the whole of this volume is not our intention. Our concern is with the Appendix only; and chiefly with but a part of that;
the other part having been already sufficiently examined, and satisfactorily replied to, in the Edinburgh Phrenological Journal, and elsewhere.

The portion of the Appendix thus already analysed, appears to have
been written and published by Dr. Roget in 1818 or '19. The portion which we purpose to analyse is of a much later date, having probably been composed by him in 1837 or '38. Be its date, however,
what it may, the preparation of its author for writing it does not seem
to have been either ample or mature. Our reason for saying so,
being as follows, is to ourselves satisfactory. Our readers will
receive it for what they may think it worth.

In April, 1838, Dr. Roget wrote to a friend of ours, then in Great
Britain, but now in the United States, assuring him that "between
1819 and that month (April, 1838) he (Dr. Roget) had never read one
word on the subject (phrenology), and never made one observation
on it." And yet, in the course of that same year (1838), that same
writer published against the science another tirade, as bitter and condemnatory as hostile feelings and disrespectful language could render
it. And that article constitutes the subject immediately before us.

But before commencing our analysis of the article, let us briefly
but candidly enquire, what, at the date of that publication, must have

been *the amount of our author's knowledge* (or rather, what was *necessarily the depth of his ignorance*) of the then existing condition of phrenology? By this enquiry, we shall attain no inconsiderable acquaintance with his unfitness for writing on it.

From 1819 until 1838 is a period of *nineteen years*, during which, at least tenfold as much had been written, said, and effected by observation, experiment, and general research, to throw light on phrenology, as had been previously done, from the commencement of the science. And of that entire mass of instructive materials, Dr. Roget, by his own acknowledgment, is *utterly ignorant.* Assuredly he *was* so in April, 1838; and his preface, announcing the publication of the article we are considering, is dated " October 20th, 1838," *only six months afterwards!* Let it, moreover, be farther observed and borne in mind, that in that preface he represents his occupation and disposition to be such as to allow him, in his own words, "neither the *leisure* nor the *inclination* to engage in controversies" on the subject of phrenology. In plain terms, he neither employed the means, nor possessed even a willingness, to inform himself in the science.

From his own confession, then, literally interpreted, Dr. Roget was *necessarily* and *intentionally* ignorant of the state of phrenology at the time of his second attempt to refute it. So obvious is this, and so futile, not to say contemptible, does such proceeding, under such circumstances, render his sophistry and cavils on the subject, that were it not for the name he has attained in other branches of knowledge, we should entertain toward him, as an anti-phrenologist, no other sentiment than indignation and scorn for his deceptiveness and audacity, and pity for his weakness. And this would induce us to be silent and regardless of all he could say. Perhaps even now it would better become us to pass him unnoticed, under a conviction that, in the full meaning of the expression, he " knows not what he does," and that *his* anti-phrenological *power* is but *impotence.*

For nineteen of the busied and most prosperous years of the friends and fast-multiplying advocates of phrenology, in Europe and America, he sealed up in relation to it every inlet to knowledge, and thus, as respected all its concerns, continued in a state of lethean apathy, or virtual hybernation. And at the end of that period, awaking, like Rip Van Winkle, from his slumber of a lifetime, and dazzled into blindness by the effulgence around him, plunges again into his anti-phrenological perversities. From the absolute puerility, moreover, of his efforts to suppress it, he seems to consider phrenology as still in the same state of comparative infancy in 1838, in which he had left it in 1819; and therefore resorts again to the same worn-out and oft-repelled contradictions of it. He is wholly imperceptive of the growth

healthy condition in the meridian of life—no more than the decaye
and palsied limb of an octogenarian does of the same limb, when pei
fectly healthful, at the age of thirty-five! And we need scarcely add
that it is the healthy adult brain to which phrenology especiall;
alludes, when it asserts that there is a correspondence in it betwee
magnitude and power. Though the science derives evidence an
strength from that viscus, at every age, and in every condition
whether morbid or sound, it is more substantially sustained, we say
by its phenomena in health.

In a heedless and unhappy moment, Dr. Roget has made a studie
effort to mislead his readers, by palming on them the notion tha
comparatively few physicians are believers in phrenology. Than thi
a more groundless and futile allegation can hardly be inculcated, o
even imagined. *"But few physicians are believers in phrenology!"*
Why there can scarcely be found, in Christendom, a thoroughl;
educated and enlightened physician, under the age of forty-five, wh‹
is not more or less of a phrenologist. Indeed, "thoroughly educated"
without it he cannot be; for phrenology is but another name for th‹
anatomy and *physiology* of the brain. And without an acquaintanc‹
with these, no man deserves the title of physician. Why? Becaus‹
the brain is the leading viscus of the system, of whose anatomy an‹
physiology next to nothing was known, until light was thrown o‹
them by the labours and disclosures of the founders of phrenology.

True, every cultivated and extensively informed physician may no
be versed in the *details* and *uses* of the science, especially in it
application to the detection of character. But he understands it
fundamental principles, and believes in their truth. As respects th‹
mere *trading* portion of the profession—those, we mean, who deal i‹
medicine, as they would in button-making—to gain by their dail;
labour their daily bread, regardless alike of science and letters—as t‹
this class of "medicine-men," no matter what they do or do no
know, or what they believe or disbelieve. Philosophy disclaim
them; and the world is neither benefited nor to any extent influence‹
by their thoughts or their actions. This corps of "mediciners,'
therefore, with all their appurtenances, we freely consign to the keep
ing and training of Dr. Roget, his friend, Dr. Prichard, and hi
American editor, and such other anti-phrenological chieftains as ar
ambitious of enlisting such soldiery, and enrolling them in their ranks
We are willing to dispense with their service. Nor do we expect o
covet the aid or companionship of the elder members of the professio‹
of medicine, whose notions are antiquated, and whose minds hav‹
taken rust, and become, by inaction, too rigid, decrepit, or both, t‹
keep pace with the progress of knowledge. These knights of th‹

blunted lance, also, whom modern science has disbanded as unfit for service, but who still case themselves in a panoply of prejudice, and trumpet their own doings in by-gone days, we cheerfully quit claim to, and cordially commend them to the invalid and motley bands of Drs. Roget, Prichard, Sewall, and their comrades in the crusade against phrenology. With us, " SIMILIA SIMILIBUS—*Birds of a feather*, &c."—is a favourite motto. And it will becomingly grace the banner of Dr. Roget, his subordinates, and retainers.

But the vast and rapidly multiplying hosts of soundly educated and enlightened physicians, from the age of forty-five and downward, who, both in mind and body, are in the summer-vigour, or the spring-time of life—these untold legions, ·who, as soldiers of truth, contend for principle and the advancement of science, have arrayed themselves under the flag of phrenology, and are determined and invincible.

We could refer to sundry other topics, on which our author has equally violated truth and justice. But we shall no farther pursue so repulsive a task.

It was our intention to offer a few remarks on Dr. Prichard's " Researches into the Physical History of Mankind," a work from which Dr. Roget has liberally extracted. But circumstances permit us not to execute our purpose. We take the liberty, however, of observing, that those two members of the holy alliance are, in some respects, very strikingly alike. *" Par nobile fratrum"* would be a suitable motto on their flag of conspiracy against the doctrines of phrenology. In the arts of mystifying and prevaricating, ill-intentional but impotent satire and caricature, and insidious deception in its Proteus-like modifications, they rank with the most vindictive spirits of the day. We speak of them as anti-phrenologists. In no other respect have we any concern with them. In proof of the accusation here preferred against them, we ask the reader's deliberate attention to the two following extracts from their anti-phrenological philippics.

"It is not enough," says Dr. Roget, "as Dr. Prichard very justly observes, to have a few chosen coincidences brought forward by zealous partisans, who go about in search of facts to support their doctrine, and pass by, or really cannot perceive, the evidence that ought to be placed in the opposite scale. The principles of the system ought to be applicable in every instance. The phrenologists, however, aware of numerous and striking exceptions, elude their evidence by asserting, that when a certain portion of the cranium and of the brain is greatly developed, while the faculty there lodged has never been remarkably distinguished, it nevertheless existed naturally, though the innate talent, for want of proper cultivation, has never been displayed; the predominant organic power was never discovered by the owner, though according to the principles of the doctrine, with this organic power a proportional impulse to exertion, or an instinctive energy is combined, which communicates of itself a strong and irresistible tendency to particular pursuits.　When, again, a strongly marked propensity, or a decided talent, has been manifested without any corresponding amplitude of structure, it is in like manner pleaded, that by sedulous exercise and culture, a natural deficiency has been overcome.　Thus the phrenologist avails himself of a double method of elusion; his position, like the cave of Philoctetes, affords him an escape on either side; and in one direction or another he contrives to baffle all the address of his opponents."

This malicious tirade deserves no other comment, than the unceremonious declaration that it is *untrue*.　Nor, of this, do we deem it possible, that either its author or extracter can be ignorant or even doubtful.

The following extract from the essay of Dr. Roget, manifests a like spirit of caricature and falsification, and is as barren of every thing either solid or useful, and as imbecile and pitiful, as phrenologists can wish it.

· "Let it be borne in mind, then, by the practical enquirer into the truth of phrenology, that he will not be esteemed qualified to verify its doctrines, unless he be previously deeply versed in the new system of psychology, can assign to each of the thirty-five special and primary faculties of the soul its sphere of operation, and has acquired a readiness in unraveling their multifarious combinations, so as to analyse, by this subtile metaphysical chemistry, all human qualities into their proximate and ultimate elements, refer all actions to their proper innate impulses, and assign the proportions of the various ingredients which are mixed up in the formation of the character of each individual.　No one is competent to excel in this new branch of philosophy who doubts the possibility of appreciating the intensities of moral or intellectual qualities by geometrical measurements, on scales divided into tenths and hundredths of inches.　The young and ardent phrenologist, who after having applied his callipers to the skull subjected to his examination, and taken a note of the dimensions of each of the thirty-five organs, proceeds to verify his observations by comparing them with the character of the possessor of those organs, will never fail to meet with *wonderful coincidences*, sufficient to give him the greatest satisfaction, and confirm him in the persuasion that he possesses the real key to the secrets of nature in the hitherto recondite science of mental philosophy.　A moderate share of dexterity in reconciling apparent discrepancies will suffice to ensure a preponderance of favourable evidence; since, fortunately, there have been provided in the brain different organs, sometimes of similar and sometimes of opposite properties, capable, by a little adjustment of *plus* or *minus* on either side of the equation, of furnishing the requisite degrees of the mental quality sought for, and of thus solving every psychological problem.　We shall suppose, for instance, that he is inspecting the head of a person known to have given credit to the prophecies of a weather almanac; he finds, on reference to the 'System of Phrenology,' that a belief in astrology is the offspring of No. 16, that is, *Ideality;* so that if this organ happen to be sufficiently large, the phenomenon is at once accounted for.　But if it be not, our phrenologist will have another chance; for he will probably discover it to arise from the dimensions of No. 15, which inspires *Hope*, the source of the *propensity to credulity*. Habitual *irresolution* may result either from the magnitude of No. 12, or the diminutiveness of 18; thus affording very great convenience for making our observations of the character square with those of the dimensions of the organs, and *vice versa*. If, again, the magnitude of the organ of *Combativeness* accord with the manifestations of pugnacity given by the individual, it is well, and we need enquire no farther, but set it down at once as an irrefragable proof of the accuracy of phrenological determinations. Should the correspondence, however, not prove satisfactory, the organ being large, for instance, and the manifestation small, we have then further to examine the dimensions of the organ of *caution*, the influence of which is to moderate and check the operation of the former; and we shall perhaps find this organ sufficiently large to account for the phenomenon. Both these organs may be large, or both small, or the first may be small and the second large, or the converse; and other modifications of action may result if either one or both be only of moderate size, allowing great latitude of choice in the assignment of motives. Should we be so unfortunate as to exhaust all the combinations without meeting with the success we desire, there is still an abundance of auxiliary faculties of which we may avail ourselves with advantage. If we were to explain the fact of the individual in question having accepted a challenge, he might have been inspired by *Combativeness*, whose voice was 'still for war,' or goaded on by *Destructiveness*, to fight that he might destroy; *Firmness* may have urged him to persevere by the consideration that he had previously resolved it, and *Concentrativeness*, by riveting his attention to the subject, may have screwed his courage to the sticking place; or he may have been prompted by *Imitation* to follow the example, or by *Approbation* to gain the applause of his friends. We have also to take into the account the countervailing influence of faculties which are pulling in the opposite direction, and qualifying the combined powers of the former incentives. And should *Cautiousness* not be in sufficient force, we are to consider the power of *Conscientiousness*, which preaches forbearance, meekness, and forgiveness; of *Veneration*, which appeals to the high authority of religion and of law; of *Benevolence*, restraining the hand from inflicting pain and death; of *Approbation*, who qualifies her sanction by raising other voices condemnatory of the deed; and last, though not least, the *Love of Life*, which recoils with instinctive dread from the possible catastrophe. Drawing, then, a diagram of all these component moral forces, in their proper directions, and suitable proportions, it will not be very difficult to obtain by this artificial dynamico-phrenological process, the exact resultant which corresponds with the actual fact to be explained."

This contemptible ebullition of trash and temper, is itself the best and most condemnatory comment *on* itself. We decline, therefore, offering any other. "Ephraim is joined to his idols—let him alone!"

If, then, Dr. Roget's assault on phrenology is thus utterly false and deceptive in spirit, and thus stale, common-place, and oft-refuted in matter, wherefore has it been reprinted in the United States? To this question we call on the editor of the reprint for such a reply as truth will sanction and candour approve. But lest he be slow in accepting our invitation, or decline it altogether, we shall, as best we may, respond to it ourselves.

walking, from partial genius, the development and decay of the
different faculties of the mind at different periods of life, the differ-
an,

ole,
web
ction.

cing
y.

he ..
inferre
vented
them
as respec
science thi.
and gloriou.
that man can

walking, from partial genius, the development and decay of th
different faculties of the mind at different periods of life, the differ
ences between the mental characters of man and woman, and espe
cially from monomania—these facts, with many others that might b
referred to, and which defy refutation, are not derived from analogy
These come from a much less questionable source. Nor have anti
phrenologists, either single-handed or embodied, ever dared to mee
them, and manfully grapple with them. They have distantly assailed
and miserably caviled at them—and nothing more. Nor will the;
ever attempt more. The reason is plain. The foe is too formidable
and would instantly vanquish them. In such a conflict, their cobwe:
armour of prejudice and sophistry would afford them no protection
Nor is this all.

We caution Dr. Roget to beware of disparaging and denouncin;
analogy, and endeavouring to divorce it from its union with philosophy
We venture to admonish him to this effect, on a two-fold ground. Ii
the first place, reason, experience, and common-sense, will put ii
their joint plea, and bar the success of his effort against analogy; an(
in the next, were success to be achieved by him, it would b(
disastrous, if not fatal, to the entire Newtonian system of astronomy
For on analogy alone is that system founded.

An apple fell on the astronomer's head. That accident led him t(
reflect on the cause of the movement of ponderous bodies, in thei
descent toward the earth from elevated positions. To that cause h(
gave the name of gravity, or the principle of attraction. Nor did h(
stop here. That would have been unworthy of his great intellect
which possessed and practised reason in its widest range, and utmos
depth, and confided in its decisions. Hence he inferred, *by analogy*
(for he had no other data,) that the same power which drew an appl(
toward the earth, drew the earth toward the sun. And not the eartl
only, but all the other planets belonging to the solar system; an(
their satellites toward themselves. And in proof of this inference n(
experiment was or could be made. Nor was this the only inference
on which the astronomer was compelled to rely. Holding a globula
body by a string, and applying force to it, in the requisite direction
he found that it moved in a circle around his hand. Hence he agaii
inferred, by analogy, the existence of a *projectile power*, which pre
vented the primary planets from falling into the sun, and propelle(
them around their orbits; and did the same to the secondary planets
as respects their primary. And yet would our author exile fron
science this principle of analogy, on which is erected the most sublim(
and glorious system of philosophy that the world has witnessed, o
that man can conceive.

True, in the details and final adjustment of his system, Newton brought in aid of analogy all the enginery of his mighty calculations. But analogy furnished not only the fulcrum, on which alone that enginery could work; it furnished also the source from which it was drawn. Without analogy, therefore, existence would have been denied to the whole concern.

Of phrenological analogies the same may be affirmed. They do not constitute the only props and muniments of the science. Far from it. They are aided and fortified, as already stated, by masses of facts, as unequivocal and solid as any that observation has ever collected, or experiment disclosed. Some of these are the facts already referred to, as being deducible from dreams, monomania, partial genius, and other phenomena that were then enumerated. Those phenomena, which, on all other grounds, are wholly inexplicable, can be easily and satisfactorily explained on the theory of the multiplex character of the brain. Yet that theory, or rather the facts which maintain it, our author virtually opposes, by asserting that phrenology is supported by analogy alone.

But we cannot thus proceed any farther in holding a grave and analytical examination of the general mass of Dr. Roget's essay. It is not worthy of such respect and labour. It is a production as obsolete, inane, and unsatisfactory, as we have ever perused. Sewall's lectures are not more so. It contains nothing to interest us, in the abstract, either in its favour or disfavour—imparts not to us an idea, nor awakens in us a thought, that we would wish to remember. Dealing almost exclusively in general imputations and assumptions, and containing neither points, facts, nor principles, it sets analysis at defiance. It is a thing of mere temper, words, and pretences—asserts or denies doggedly, and sometimes vehemently, and condemns by the lump. But it never argues nor attempts to prove, except by the arbitrary dictum of the writer—never selects from phrenology a proposition or a principle, contests it fairly, and endeavours to subvert it by an onset of reason, or an adduction of evidence. It strives to bring the whole science into disrepute, not by showing it to be either false in principle, or mischievous in effect, but by sneering allusions, insidious allegations, and groundless charges, with a view to render it a mark for the ridicule, prejudice, and odium of the bigoted and the uninformed. To attempt to close, in the form of grave and vigorous discussion, with a thing so vaporous and meager in the product of intellect, and so abundant in the offspring of hollow pretension and conceit, is like grasping at a shadow, or buffeting the air. Notwithstanding, however, this general vacuum as to fact and thought, there

are in our author's paper one or two topics more, on which we shal
offer a few remarks.

With a view to make it appear that great mental powers have no
necessary connection with a large brain, he asserts that the brain of
Sir Walter Scott was "small," and in proof of this, refers to a state
ment to that effect in the writings of Mr. Lockhart, his biographer
This assertion is worthy, perhaps, of more attention than all the
others which the "secretary, &c." has hazarded. Let it be freed
therefore, from what is unsound or suspicious in it, placed in the
balance, and accurately weighed.

However high and imposing the authority of Mr. Lockhart may be
deemed on many subjects, it is not possible for *us*, *in the present
case*, to receive it as authentic. We should regard such reception as
thoughtless in the extreme. And for this incredulity the following
are our reasons, which the reader will accept for what he may deem
them worth.

Being the son-in-law of the deceased, and entertaining for him the
warmest attachment, and the most exalted veneration, it is by no
means probable (we *might* say it is hardly *possible*) that Mr. Lockhart saw and examined his brain. Such a step would bespeak in
him much less of delicacy and sensitiveness than we think he
possesses. He could have been seduced into it by nothing short of a
spirit of curiosity, both useless and unbecoming. Nor is this all.

Admitting, for the sake of the argument, that Mr. Lockhart insensi-
tively acted thus, he did so to no efficient purpose. Not being versed
in the inspection of dead bodies, he was not, in such a case, a competent judge of comparative size. The brain, moreover, when diseased and softened, (and Sir Walter's brain *was* diseased,) collapses
when removed from the skull, and, *in appearance*, loses its size.
On some ground, therefore, the biographer was deceived. Nor will
it surprise us to find that that ground consisted in the examination
being held, and the report made out and delivered to Mr. Lockhart
by an *artful anti-phrenologist*, who, to give a momentary support to
a fast-sinking cause, did not scruple to misrepresent, and practise
deception. Such a stratagem would be in perfect keeping with *anti-
phrenological morality;* which may be pronounced identical with the
Punica fides of the Romans. Should this charge offend any self-
conceited or high-blooded anti-phrenologist, he may find, notwithstanding, ample justification of it in the worse than Grecian deceptiveness of his tribe.

Nor do we think it probable that Mr. Lockhart himself would
scrutinise very rigidly the character of the report respecting the size
of the brain of his kinsman. He is understood to be an anti-

phrenologist. Provided, therefore, the report was so shaped as to favour the views of himself and party, he would be likely to receive it without scrutiny, and publish it without scruple.

Be this, however, as it may, we deem it next to impossible that Sir Walter's brain was actually "small." The *brain* of that wonder and ornament of his race, we have never seen. But we *have* seen his head; and that was large—in our view, *very large*—though not equally so in each of its regions. It had not the dimensions of the head of Lord Bacon, nor those of the heads of Sir James Mackintosh, Mr. Hume, Mr. Webster, or Lord Brougham. It was not the head of a philosopher; nor *was* Sir Walter a philosopher, his reflecting organs being inferior in cast to his moral and perceptive ones. It was a head of vivid, strong, and acute perceptiveness, wide and fruitful observation, brilliant and towering fancy, and spotless integrity. And in its owner these attributes were happily blended. It was the head of a man of genius; and such pre-eminently was the great novelist.

We saw Sir Walter in the prime of his life. And not the united asseveration of all the anti-phrenologists on earth could induce us to believe that his brain was then small. Such a belief would have been in contradiction of the express representation of nature on the subject. It would have been to convert in fancy one of the most plainly and strongly characterised of men into a perfect anomaly—a positive outcast from the principles and rules that control the dimensions and proportions of the human system, and from the settled conformity known to exist between the size of the head and the size of the brain, as well as between the exterior and interior of other parts of the body, when all are healthy and natural. To the naked assertion, therefore, that the brain of the "great unknown" was "small," no credit can be safely given; nor can any inference be fairly drawn from it prejudicial to phrenology.

That, in the decline of his life, the size of Sir Walter's brain might have lessened, is not perhaps improbable. Such changes in that viscus have certainly occurred; especially in cases where it was the seat of some chronic disease. Under that form of suffering, the brain, in common with other organs, is diminished at times by the process of absorption. And such was unfortunately the condition of the Scotish minstrel. In his latter years his brain was seriously disordered, and not a little debilitated, as appeared from the fallen character of his writings at that period. If at the time of his death, therefore, the organ was "small," it had been rendered so by the diseased affection which had been preying on it for years. Hence it afforded, *then*, no just criterion of the size it had possessed, in a and strength it had acquired in the long space of nineteen years. In this hallucination, he resembles not a little that celebrated personage, Dominie Samson, who, because he had known Harry Bertram when a child of three or four years old, continued to call him "little Harry," when six feet in height, and at the age of twenty-three! And so does our time-defying and improvement-contemning author consider and treat our science as "little phrenology" in 1838, because he deemed it infantile in 1819, the last time he had thought of it.

On contemplating this long-practised supineness and neglect of Dr. Roget, we read with astonishment and condemnation the following clause in the preface of his American editor.

"It will be seen that *farther examination* (of phrenology) *in the interval of many years*, which has elapsed since the publication of the sixth edition of the Encyclopædia, has not induced him (Dr. Roget) to modify his sentiments on this head."

What shall we say of this broad and bare contradiction between our author and his editor? and how reconcile so fatal a collision? The former confesses that he has altogether *neglected* phrenology for nineteen years; while the latter avers that he has employed that "interval" in "farther examination" of it! In which of the two, the *master* or the *man*, shall enquirers confide? or will they allow themselves to be duped by a confidence in either? To such a question, an enlightened public will be at no loss for a suitable answer. From that source, therefore, let the answer come. Nor can it fail, we think, to come with the blight of a sirocco on the work we are examining. And that it will also impair the credibility of the editor, can hardly be doubted. But to consider our subject in another point of view :

From the entire cast and tenor of his conduct toward phrenology, it is abundantly evident that Dr. Roget's object, in the essay before us, is not faithfully and conscientiously to *try* the science, but tyrannically to *condemn* and *execute* it unheard, regardless alike of its innocence or guilt, merit or demerit, and of the positive mandate of justice on the subject. Is it demanded of us why we thus accuse our author? Our reply is ready. Because he refuses, with the coldness of the icy north, and the insensitiveness of its granite, to listen to either evidence or advocacy in behalf of phrenology ; and persists in his refusal for nineteen years, (though its cause, during that period, is exciting deep interest and earnest sympathy in most parts of Christendom,) and then pronounces against it his sentence of condemnation ! If any star-chamber proceeding ever surpassed this in premeditated disregard of right and mockery of justice, we know not where the record of it may be found !

Will this imputation be accounted by the friends of our author, and the foes of phrenology, unceremonious and harsh? Be it so. Our object is neither affected mildness, undeserved courtesy, nor counterfeit compliment. It is *truth*, in plainness, without reserve, and regardless of consequences. And we contend that the imputation preferred by us is indisputably correct. In proof of it, we fearlessly appeal to the facts of the case. Those who are solicitous to receive courtesy and observance, ought themselves to practise them.

Nor, in this view of the matter, has our author any shadow of cause to complain of us, in the capacity of phrenologists, since he, as an anti-phrenologist, affects to treat the science with a sneer bordering on rudeness, from the beginning to the end of his sophistical essay. In no single instance does he discuss the subject of his paper with the ingenuousness of a fair and liberal mind, or the dignity of a philosopher. Availing himself of his elevated standing and connections in science, his disposition and effort seem to be, to hector presumptuously over those who dissent from *his* dicta, (as Bridgewater writer, " Secretary to the Royal Society, Professor of Physiology in the Royal Institution of Great Britain, &c. &c.,") and from the time-worn dogmas of other gowned and titled authorities. But had the professor ten royalties for each one that now bedecks him, and on which he founds his spurious right to dictate and condemn, it would not, in this common-sense, matter-of-fact period of the world, in the slightest degree avail him—except, indeed, with those who value the shadow more highly than the substance. Science recognises no titles, save those which she herself bestows on such of her votaries as have advanced truth, extended the limits of her own empire, and benefited man by their talents and labours. Least of all, does she recognise a "royal road" to her temple, or sanction a royal claim (*because* it is royal) to minister at her altar. Nor will any of her true disciples suffer themselves to be superciliously driven by frowns or jeers, or lured by false logic, either *out of her* service, or *into* the service of those who derive their titles from sources merely artificial, and therefore illegitimate. Their delight and practice are, to appeal to reason, and acquiesce in the issue of observation and experience, neither distorted by prejudice nor perverted by design. Never, however, will they do else than regard with indifference, or repel with disdain, every effort of their opponents to assail them with ridicule, annoy them through ignorance, or injure their cause, by studied misrepresentation. Whether or not our author has been concerned in any or all of these practices, it is our purpose to enable our readers to judge. And we shall, without farther preface, engage in the task.

To show that the object of Dr. Roget is not to do justice to phreno-

logy, by fair discussion, giving an impartial statement of evidence fot
it and against it, but, as far as possible, to discredit and degrade it, by
sneering and sarcasm, we shall submit to the reader a single extrac
from the essay we are examining.

Toward the close of the last century, or the beginning of the pre
sent, (we have forgotten the precise year,) Dr. Gall opened in Vienn;
a course of lectures on the science. No sooner did the doctrine(
which he taught in his lectures become a subject of discussion in the
society of the place, than the priesthood made war on them, and pro
cured a suppression of them, by an interdict of the government. A
respectable body of strangers, however, sojourning in Vienna at the
time, petitioned the court in behalf of the doctor, and were successfu
in having the interdict so far modified, that permission was grantec
him to lecture to *them.* Of this occurrence, Dr. Roget gives the
following contemptuous narrative :—

"They (the strangers) formed a strong party in his (Dr. Gall's)
favour, and made such interest at court, principally through the
medium of the foreign ambassadors, that the doctor was again per
mitted to resume his prelections, on condition that he delivered them
to foreigners only; as it was *wisely* considered that *their* being
exposed to the *dangers of knowledge* would not be of any material
consequence to the state, as long as care was taken that the infection
did not spread farther; *the emperor kindly preserving the bliss of
ignorance to the exclusive enjoyment of his Austrian subjects.*"

This might, perhaps, be alleged to be a double-pointed jeer, directed
alike at his majesty of Austria, and the discoverer of phrenology.
Subsequent passages of the essay, however, make it clearly appear,
that the aim was more especially at the latter individual.

In proof of Dr. Roget's entire ignorance of the history and presen'
condition of phrenology, he has not adduced a single objection to it
which had not been previously urged, perhaps, a score of times, anc
as often refuted by the advocates of the science. Of this descriptior
is the following trite and unfounded assertion; which, made by hin
first in 1819, is still pertinaciously and doggedly defended by him.

"The truth is, that there is not a *single part* of the encephalor
which has not, in one case or other, been *impaired, destroyed, o1
found defective, without any apparent change in the sensitive, intel
lectual, or moral faculties.*"

This assertion is in several respects very strikingly at fault. Ir
the first place, it is *untrue.* In the estimation of all men, anti-
phrenologists excepted, this would be fatal to it. To many, if no1
most of *them,* however, it would seem recommendatory, rather than
otherwise; for they deal in little else than untruth. In the second

ace, it has been repeated and reiterated by all ranks and descrip-
ons of anti-phrenologists, from the *savans* of the beer-house, to those
" the " Royal Society" and the " Royal Institution," until, by such
'omiscuous hackneying and prostitution, it has grown insufferably
usty and offensive.   And thirdly, it is so puny and untenable, that
child may refute it.

 In the range of pathology there is not a single fact more conclu-
vely established, than that an injury done to the cerebellum affects
:ry obviously, and, at times, most distressingly, the sexual pro-
ensity.   Is the cerebellum severely concussed and paralysed?   That
·opensity is enfeebled, suspended, or destroyed,   Is inflammation
:cited in the cerebellum ?   The propensity is always invigorated,
id sometimes fired to the rage of satyriasis.   This truth has been
itnessed by hundreds of physicians, and is familiar to every tyro in
irenology.

 That an injury done to the brain, a little above the eyes, impairs
e memory for nouns substantive, especially for proper names, is as
ell known, as that an injury to the eye-ball impairs the vision.   By
ι event of this kind, we have known an unbeliever in phrenology
·nverted into an advocate of it.   From the infliction of a severe con-
ission of this sort, a lady, well known to us, lost for a time her
emory for the name of every article of food, and every cooking
ensil, in her kitchen; while her other faculties remained unimpaired.

 Again: an entire want, or a great deficiency, of that portion of
·ain which lies under the superior region of the frontal bone, is well
iown to withhold the reflective faculties, and to entail idiocy.   This
uth, sustained, as it is, by facts unquestioned and innumerable, Dr.
oget will not himself have the contumacy to contradict.

 The perception and remembrance of *place*, moreover, have been
ipaired or destroyed, by injuries inflicted on that portion of the
ain, which, on phrenological principles, constitutes its organ.
milar facts in relation to other organs could be easily adduced.
ut such things, amounting to nothing but truisms in phrenology,
ust be dwelt on no longer.   Yet do they prove conclusively the
norance or obstinacy, or both, of our author, as an anti-phrenologist.
or are all his defects and obliquities in this respect yet summed up.

 He very strenuously objects to phrenology, because, as he alleges,
is supported by nothing more substantial than *analogy.*   This is a
istake.   Analogy is not its only basis, although some of the argu-
ents in favour of it are analogical.   Nor, to whatever extent he may
·uggle to discredit those arguments, is it in his power to refute them.
it the facts confirmatory of the doctrines of phrenology, (and they
e numerous,) derived from the phenomena of dreaming and sleep-

Dr. Roget's book, as its title indicates, consists of two parts: one on physiology; the other against phrenology. Of these, the latter has been republished by the editor, because he is hostile to the science, and wishes to discredit it. Destitute, however, of the courage to attack it with his own weapons, and under his own name, he draws the materials and means of assault from the armory of Dr. Roget. Thus does he show himself to be, like another Englishman we could name,

"*Willing to wound, but yet afraid to strike;*"

or like the *English* knight of *swaggering* renown, who, thinking " discretion the better part of valour," sent his soldiers to be " peppered," where he did not dare to go himself; or like the no less prudent and sagacious knight Sir Hudibras, who hath thus bequeathed to us his wisdom on the subject—

"He that from battle" (*stays*) "away,
May live to fight another day."

Thoroughly schooled in these maxims, our author's editor shrinks himself from the danger to which he exposes his friends. As far as he is concerned in giving character to the times, well may it be proclaimed, that " the age of chivalry is gone."

That the physiological portion of the work has *some* merit, we are not inclined to deny. That that merit, however, is alone sufficient to justify a reprint of it, may well be doubted. It is so very a skeleton, as to be nothing else, we suspect, than the text-book, or syllabus of the lectures of its author. But, by the reprint, the editor has created an opportunity, no doubt very gratifying to him, to make very numerous references to *Dunglison's Physiology;* a work which we have reason to believe had not been previously much referred to as authority.* Were any of our readers so curious of further information on this subject, as to ask us what interest the editor has in so often quoting, as authority or for additional explanation, Professor Dunglison's Physiology? we would hazard, perhaps, but little in alleging, in our reply, that he participates in the profits of the sale of that work. To refer to it, therefore, is to make it known, give it currency, and multiply its purchasers. Should this be denied, we

* In proof of the exalted estimation in which the editor holds Dunglison's Physiology, as a work of authority, he has referred to it, in his foot notes, near *thirty times! !* We counted the references until the number amounted to *twenty-four or five*, and then broke off our count, to attend to something of more consequence; intending, however, to renew the process on some future holiday, when we shall be without a more agreeable and useful employment.

hall probably feel constrained to speak in relation to it more in
letail, and state our reasons for the conjecture we have offered. In
till plainer terms, we know who the editor is, and could openly
ame him, were the act allowable; and his views in the reprint are
oo plain to be mistaken. To convince him of this, we are confident
hat the following remarks, in another publication, which he also
dits, are from his pen.

  " The truth or falsehood of phrenology is not to be established by
ngry declamation, but by calm and unprejudiced observation. Facts
m both sides numerically arranged—over and over again observed
ind recorded by unbiased observers——can alone settle this disputed
)oint of physiology, for such it is. No study—using the term in the
ense of thinking or of musing—can lead to a decision; nor can it be
acilitated by personal invective, or undue ascription of improper
notives to either party."

  " Calm, temperate, and courteous discussion on a subject of science
nay tend to the developement of truth."

  These sentiments, we say, come from the pen of Dr. Roget's
ditor; and in most of them we fully and heartily concur, and should
)e sincerely rejoiced to see such of them as are correct and practical
arried into effect. They invite from us, however, a few further
emarks.

  Who, we respectfully ask of the worthy editor, first began with
' angry declamation?" the phrenologists or the anti-phrenologists?
ind we reply, the *latter*. Nor will the editor contradict us. When
Dr. Gall was mildly and courteously communicating to his classes, in
Vienna, the facts he had collected by " calm and unprejudiced obser-
ration, ' he was assailed by the priesthood, not merely with " decla-
nation and invective," but by *fierce denunciation*, until, at length, at
he instigation of that fraternity, he was compelled by the Austrian
;overnment to close his lecture-rooms, and suspend his instructions.

  Who, after this act of *anti-phrenological tyranny*, spent several
rears in the further collection of facts, by " calm and unprejudiced
)bservation," practised in most of the large cities of continental
Europe, under toils and perseverance that have never been surpassed?
t was Drs. Gall and Spurzheim, the founders of phrenology,   Who
vas it that afterwards, in Great Britain, with the temper of fanatics,
ind in language but little more refined than that of Wapping or
3illingsgate, abused and denounced these same two illustrious philo-
ophers, as " German doctors"—" fools"—" ignoramuses"—" char-
atans"—" mountebanks"—and " impostors?"   It was the intolerant
ind persecuting *anti-phrenologists* of the kingdom—and we might
ay, of the *whole* kingdom—for there was scarcely a pulpit, press, or

rostrum for debate, in any portion of Great Britain, that did not, at one period, unite in the infuriated clamour. Nor was there, at this stage of the contest, a single angry or retaliating word returned by the two great phrenologists, or their friends and followers.   And as to the "undue ascription of improper motives," that uncharitableness is practised in hundreds of instances by anti-phrenological writers needs no proof.   Even the two extracts we have taken from Dr. Roget's essay, abound in such "ascriptions."

As respects the learned editor's admonition, to collect " facts on *both sides*" of the question, that appears to us to be a blunder— something strongly resembling a bull.   It would come from an Irishman, therefore, with a better grace than from an *Englishman.* True and pertinent "facts on both sides" of a controverted point in science cannot exist.   The notion is ludicrous, implies a contradiction, and brings nature into discrepance and conflict with herself. One fact in philosophy can never oppose another.   Fictions and groundless assertions may clash with each other, and also with facts. But nature is never at variance with herself.   In the controversy between the friends and foes of phrenology, as far as our acquaintance with it extends, the latter have arrayed against the facts of the former, nothing more philosophical than assertion and fiction, invective and abuse.   If the editor knows of any case in which means of controversy other than these have been employed by his party, we shall be gratified at being informed by him, at what time it occurred, and where the record of it may be found.

" Calm, temperate, and courteous discussion on a subject of science may tend," says the editor, " to the developement of truth." This is true, and is much more valuable than all the other sentiments our extract from him contains.   Let it, then, be reduced to practice, and the issue be recorded.

We have already asserted, and now repeat, that neither Dr. Roget, his editor, nor Dr. Prichard, has heretofore selected a single principle, doctrine, or fundamental proposition in phrenology, and, in a fair argumentative contest, attempted its refutation.   They have caviled, skirmished, manœuvred, and availed themselves of stratagem, and nothing more.   We shall now afford them an opportunity to aim at something higher, and thus achieve for themselves, if they can, as anti-phrenologists, a more honourable reputation, by a manly effort to overthrow the science which so much annoys them.   The following are some of the main pillars of that science, which being broken or beaten down, the superstructure must fall.   We respectfully invite them, therefore, singly and collectively, as the Samsons of their party, to attempt the overthrow of this superstructure in science.

1. In the present condition of man, the brain is the organ of the mind, in all its operations. Without the aid of that organ, the mind can no more perform a single action, than the organ can, without the co-operation and aid of the mind.

2. The brain is not a single organ, but an aggregate of many organs, each being the seat or instrument of a special faculty. And these organs, though intimately connected, and influencing each other, as parts of the same whole, perform each its own function, without mutual interference, hindrance, or control.

3. As are the size and configuration of the brain, so are the size and configuration of the skull. By a skilful examination of the head, therefore, the form and dimensions of the brain may be ascertained.

4. Other things being alike, the size of a single cerebral organ is the correct measure of its strength; and the size of the whole brain is a measure equally correct of the strength of the brain as an aggregate—and consequently of the scope and power of the mind, which it subserves.

5. The positions of the several cerebral organs, and the mental faculties connected with them as instruments, are known.

6. The brain consists of two hemispheres, each containing the same number of separate organs, and each organ resembling its corresponding one, in faculty and function. In case, therefore, an organ in one hemisphere be injured or destroyed, the function may still be performed, by its correlative organ in the other hemisphere; in like manner, as when one eye is injured or destroyed, we see with the other; while the same is true of the nostrils and ears.

Such, we say, are some of the propositions on which phrenology essentially rests; and should all or either of them be overthrown and demolished, the science must be surrendered. We again, therefore, invite Dr. Roget, Dr. Prichard, or Dr. D——, the editor, or all of them united, to select at option one or more of these propositions as points of attack. Let the assault by those chieftains be fair and philosophical; free alike from outbreaks of temper, exceptionable language, groundless and unworthy insinuations, efforts to deceive and mislead by misrepresentations and stratagems, and all other forms of discourtesy, sinister dealing, and disrespect; let this invitation be accepted by our opponents, (with the privilege, if they please, to enlist, as auxiliaries, Dr. Sewall and his retainers, the Hon. John Q. Adams, the Hon. Judge M'Lean, and company,) and

they will not fail to be met by an antagonist, prepared to maintai
the truth of phrenology in a spirit and manner alike unexception
able.   And let an enlightened and impartial public be judge of th
issue—the refusal of either party to engage in the tourney, to b
regarded as a defeat.

ARTICLE II.

ORGAN OF MUSCULAR MOTION.

For the American Phrenological Journal.

The experiments which have been made by Flourens, Bouillaud
Magendie, and others, have induced many persons to suspect tha
muscular motion might have some direct connection with the cere
bellum ; and upon this point, Mr. Combe has arrived at conclusion
which I can now demonstrate to be true.   He says—

" The great size of the cerebellum, the circumstance of its latera
portions not bearing the same relation to the middle part in al
animals, and also the results of some late experiments, have sug
gested the notion that it may not be a single organ, but that
although Amativeness is unquestionably connected with the larges
portion of it, other functions may be connected with the other part
This seems not improbable ; but as we have no direct evidence in
proof of the fact, or in illustration of the nature of these suppose
functions, it is unnecessary to do more than announce the proposi
tion as one worthy of investigation. · If I might hazard a conjecture
founded on such facts as are known, I would presume the middle
portion to be the organ of Amativeness, and the two lateral portion
to be those of motion.   The middle portion springs from the same
roots as the organs of the other propensities, while the latter por
tion, by means of the *pons varolii*, are placed in connection with
the *corpora pyramidalia*, from which originate the organs of the
intellect that preside over motion."

It has been so generally believed that a large cerebellum, indi
cated by great breadth between the mastoid processes and a large
neck, gave evidence of a large organ of Amativeness, that I wa
greatly surprised, four years since, to find the space between said
processes and the neck to be quite small, (the former measuring
only 3½ inches,) in a boy, fifteen years of age, who died, in the
charity hospital of New Orleans, of the consequences of onanism

The middle portions of the cerebellum were greatly developed downwards, measuring 1¼ inches below the inferior margin of the crucial ridge. A similar developemont of the cerebellum obtains in he skull of a Mr. Kennedy, who was executed for the perpetration of a rape. As the facts in this case are interesting, and as my examination of the skull may have a happy influence on some, I have extracted both from the Southern Democrat, as reported by Dr. Johnson, of Claiborne, Ala.

" In May, 1837, the well-known phrenologist, Dr. W. Byrd Powell, came to Claiborne, and having heard much of phrenology, and the astonishing precision with which Dr. P. is said to delineate character from an examination of the skull, and being prevented by professional duties from having examined the claims of the science upon our belief, I determined to test the skill of the doctor, by submitting to his inspection the skull of a man whose character was well known to me. After attentively regarding the skull for a few minutes, he proceeded to describe the temperament and complexion of the man, and then entered upon the leading traits of his character.

" His Amativeness, said he, is enormously developed, and although he was cautious and timid, he thought his moral powers were too small to enable him to restrain its improper manifestation. This he regarded as the leading trait of his character. He considered him to be base and cowardly in his disposition, and greatly deficient in every species of moral refinement. Intellectually, he regarded him as strongly marked with mathematical and mechanical powers, and qualified for their practical manifestation.

" The subject of the above remarks was named George Kennedy, born in Annapolis, Md. He was a good practical surveyor, and a carpenter by trade—an ingenious mechanic. In illustration of his Amativeness, which the doctor regarded as his ruling passion, we have the following facts. At the age of fourteen years, he was known to attempt the violation of a girl seven years of age. At the age of eighteen, he attempted the same offence upon a girl nine years of age. At the age of twenty-two, he married an amiable and respectable girl, with whom he lived four years. Shortly after his marriage, his wife detected him in making a similar attempt upon a servant girl in his chamber. At the age of twenty-five, he violated a girl ten years of age, in the state of Virginia, for which he was hanged. A few minutes before his death, he confessed that his greatest desire through life was such an intercourse with female children. He was such a coward, that the boys bullied over him in the streets. As a phrenological illustration, I have presented the skull to Dr. Powell.

" The prompt and off-hand manner in which he gave the temperament, complexion, and character of Kennedy, by an examination of his skull, and the startling truths he disclosed, during a subsequent examination of my own head, removed all doubts from my mind, and left me impressed with the belief that phrenology will ultimately triumph over every obstacle, and maintain a high rank in the circle of science.

"R. JOHNSON, M. D."

The breadth between the mastoid processes of Kennedy is 3⅘ inches, and the depth of the central portions of the cerebellum is 1¾ inches. These two cases satisfied me that, although a broad cerebellum and a large neck might always be regarded as indicative of a large organ of Amativeness, still this organ may be large with a narrow cerebellum and small neck. They furthermore taught me to regard the central portions of the cerebellum as the amative organs, which, when well developed, cause the cunical muscles to have a backward developement.

Last summer, I obtained the skull of a Chickasaw Indian, who had, but a few weeks before he died, played ball successfully against three good players, upon a wager of $500. His cerebellum is narrow, measuring between the mastoid processes 3⅘ inches; but the lateral portions are greatly developed downwards and outwards, while the middle portions are as remarkably defective, presenting, with the preceding crania, a complete contrast.

Guided by these well-marked cases, I have made many observations, and now feel quite confirmed in the independent existence of an organ which produces a *desire* for muscular motion.

I have discovered that those persons who have a large endowment of this organ, are much adverse to confined or sedentary habits—they desire to be in constant motion. If Concentrativeness be well developed, they can fix their attention and confine themselves for a certain purpose, but this accomplished, they are again in action. This power exerts a powerful influence upon the entire character. I have seen persons with a large, well, and industriously formed head, and a good temperament, who were exceedingly lazy. I would have failed in giving the result of one man's organisation, but for this discovery. He was frequently known to sit all day on the bank of a river, with a fishing-line in his hand, without one small *nibble* to excite hope. He was a biped sloth—he walked as though he was a clumsy apparatus of human invention.

I am acquainted with a legal gentleman of very extensive acquirements and ambitious desires, who confesses that he has the greatest possible aversion to muscular exertion, but he brooks any amount of abour at his desk.	The organ under consideration is quite small with him.

I am satisfied, from observation, that an importunate condition of Amativeness, and a restless one of muscular motion, depend upon a lownward developement of these organs, which may obtain without much breadth of the cerebellum ; but more durable abilities depend ıpon a broad developement of these organs.	Both conditions are sometimes combined.

It is not my opinion that precision in the exercise of the muscles Jepends, in the least, upon the organ of muscular motion, but on the intellectual organs.	Nevertheless as persons, having that organ large, will exercise much, it may be safely presumed, other things being equal, that they will have the most thorough command of their muscles.

The phrenologist, in contemplating the function of this organ, must conclude that *ignorance* is the only apology that can be offered in justification of solitary and *sedentary* confinement for penal offences.

W. BYRD POWELL.

ARTICLE III.

PREDOMINANCE OF CERTAIN ORGANS IN THE BRITISH POETS.

For the American Phrenological Journal.

One of the most delightful, though not, perhaps, the most *useful*, of the thousand applications of which phrenology is susceptible, is the peculiar pleasure which may be derived from a perusal of the finer productions of literature.	" The thoughts that breathe, and words that burn," to the initiated, have an interest philosophical as well as poetical.	After exhausting the beauties of a poem, a new and strange interest springs up in the mind of the reader, and he is soon found deeply investigating the actual *causes* of the distinguishing features of the work ; he turns from the enjoyment of the well sustained image, to a fancy sketch of the *head* of its *author*, in whom he beholds a large developement, united with activity of the organ of Comparison ; and if the simile is also elevated and brilliant, he superadds that worshipper of pure beauty—Ideality.	The student of belles lettres will discover that when Comparison is equally large in two poets, but in one Ideality is very large, and the perceptive faculties small, and in the other the reverse is found, a striking difference exists in the *kind* of images employed. The poet possessing large perceptive faculties, generally likens one natural object to another, and seldom extends his flights beyond visible existences; while the other will be found diving deep into the regions of fancy, and seeking "The light that is not of the sea or earth, the consecration and the poet's dream." It is only in the airy analogies of imagination, he hopes to find the faithful representatives of his thoughts. When he seeks similitudes in natural objects, he rather appropriates the impressions they make upon the *fancy,* than their actual appearances. The possessor of large Wonder also affects the supernatural, but it is that which is *out of nature,* not necessarily *above* her. Scott is an excellent illustration of this, whose imaginative poetry is almost entirely the product of active Marvellousness. The poet of large perception and Comparison, and smaller Ideality, if he wish to describe the destruction of cherished prospects, he finds its likeness in flowers early nipped, blighted harvests, or in some obvious analogy furnished by perception. But if one of large Ideality be the writer, if he seek his images in nature at all, it will be as she exhibits herself in some *remote clime,* and in some *peculiar relation.* The following lines of Moore are in point:—

> "Oh for a tongue to curse the slave
>   Whose treason, like a deadly blight,
> Comes o'er the councils of the brave,
>   And blasts them in their hour of might!
> His country's curse, his children's shame,
> Outcast of honour, peace, and fame,
> May he at last, with lips of flame,
> On the parched desert, thirst and die!
> *While lakes, which shone in mockery nigh,*
> *Are fading off, untouched, untasted,*
> *Like the once glorious hopes he blasted!"*

The same writer, in his well known song of the "Araby's Daughter," has an image, the very child of large Comparison and Ideality!

> "Farewell! farewell to the Araby's daughter,
>   (Thus warbled a peri beneath the dark sea,)
> *No pearl ever lay 'neath Oman's green water,*
>   *More pure in its shell than thy spirit in thee."*

Indeed, the entire works of Moore are distinguished by great profusion of elevated comparisons; while the poetry of Byron is comparatively but little embellished by *direct* images. *All* his intellectual, and *semi*-intellectual organs, I think, must have been large, and hence the great depth and sublimity of his writing. Scott has

few similes remarkable for elegance, most of his figures being such
as had been used by all his predecessors, or were of easy occurrence,
such as—

> " No more on prancing palfrey borne,
> *He carolled light as lark at morn.*"

In Byron's higher flights, Comparison usually appears inwoven
with general reflection, as is strikingly illustrated in the following
soliloquy over a skull :—

> " Look on its broken arch, its ruined wall,
>   Its chambers desolate, and portals foul,
> Yet this was once ambition's airy hall,
>   The dome of thought, the palace of the soul!
> Behold through each lack-lustre, eyeless hole,
>   The gay recess of wisdom and of wit!
> And passion's host, that never brook'd control ;
>   Can all saint, sage, or sophist ever writ,
> People this lonely tower, this tenement refit ?"

Here we have a stately edifice, completely worked up in the description of a skull, while every line labours under its weight of thought.
This combination is exceedingly rare—the product of united Causality, Comparison, perception, sublimity, and Ideality !

There are readers of poetry who utterly confound the creations of
Marvellousness and Ideality ; and this error has been the cause of
much triumph to anti-phrenologists. A remarkable instance of the
kind occurred, it is said, with Spurzheim himself, who, in a large
private company, examined the head of the celebrated Coleridge.
He pronounced his Ideality relatively smaller than Causality or
Wonder ; as this organ was then thought to impart the power of
poetry, and as C. *had* unquestionably written *excellent* poetry, it
raised a considerable laugh at the expense of the philosopher, who
was thereupon introduced to the great living poet. The amiable
phrenologist joined in the merriment, and the opponents of his
science exulted in a victory. Like almost every *fact*, however,
which has been supposed to militate against phrenology, when
clearly investigated, it becomes confirmatory of its irresistible truth.
The poetry of Coleridge, (which, by the way, constitutes not one
third of his writings, published and unpublished,) is the legitimate
offspring of large reflective faculties and Wonder—the " Ancient
Mariner" draws its chief existence from the latter organ ; beside
which, the muses were only the play-fellows of Coleridge, while
metaphysics were his beloved study—his great hobby—and consequently his Ideality must have been much smaller than some of his
intellectual organs.

The poetry of *Crabbe*, remarkable as it is for vigorous description

and great condensation of thought, is equally so for its want of al
ideal beauty. His intellectual faculties were all favourably deve
loped, but his semi-intellectual, particularly sublimity and Ideality
must have been much smaller. These deductions, which I have
made from the perusal of his works, perfectly harmonise with a
portrait I have seen of him, in which the forehead is very full, bur
the region of the above named organs is comparatively contracted
All his readers know how anti-poetical are the mere subjects of his
poems; his muse wanders among the darkest and most hopeless
scenes of life, but it is not in the darkness of sublimity—she loved
to depict human suffering in frightful colours, and exhibit it unre
lieved by a single ray of light; neither was it in the trials of intel
lect, the fierce struggles of the *soul*, contending with the irreversible
decrees of destiny, whose lofty complainings furnish the rich mate
rials of the epic song, but she loved to dwell on *physical* pain, among
the groveling scenes of abject poverty, in the hovels of ignorance
and petty crime, or among the revelting spectacles of a village poor
house. None of the deep interest imparted by large Wonder, car
be found in any line he ever wrote—none of the fulgor of Ideality
—the grandeur of sublimity. It was the perceptive and reflective
faculties he chiefly exercised in writing, and the possessor of these
he always delights. Scott and Byron were both admirers of *Crabbe*
for they could both appreciate his masterly powers of description
His thoughts were among the last which wandered darkling across
the fast expiring intellect of the great unknown; and *George Fox*
it is said, derived consolation from the same source, when he lay
upon his dying bed. It was the *truth* of his poems which interested
these master minds; and yet his poetry is seldom seen in the
boudoir, or upon the centre table; and 1 have ever observed a dis
taste of his writings in all those whose Ideality predominated very
much above the intellectual organs. *Crabbe* could no more have
written "Lalla Rookh," than he could have leaped to the *moon*, and
Moore could as easily have accompanied him thither, as to have
written the Village Poor House. Many of your readers are doubt
less acquainted with the celebrated controversy as to whether Pope
was a poet? Could a good practical phrenologist, well acquainted
with the subject involved, have laid his hand upon the head of the
differen: parties engaged, I have no doubt he could have classified
the disputants with remarkable accuracy. From Bowles, who
originated the debate, through all the "lake school," as they were
called, Ideality or Marvellousness would have been found relatively
larger than in the heads of their opponents. Yet in every othe
respect their developements would have been widely dissimilar.

Wordsworth, who is ranked in this school, often seeks, like Crabbe, his subjects in the humble walks of life, but he frequently elevates them into the clouds; strips off the rags which disguise them, and presents them in all the *nakedness*, it is true, but still in the *beauty* and simplicity of *nature!*

W.

ARTICLE IV.

ON MENTAL EXERCISE AS A MEANS OF HEALTH.

(Continued from page 93 of this Journal.)

First, then, the intellectual faculties must be cultivated, and their cerebral organs strengthened and developed, by applying them directly to the study of nature, animated and inanimate, and to the study of the constitution of man himself, of the relation in which he stands to God, to his fellow-men, and to the various objects of the external world; and in all these studies, properly undertaken, many of his best sentiments will receive intense gratification, and many of his propensities find a legitimate, useful, and rational exercise. From experience as well as from observation I can say, that there is nothing so well calculated to give strength to the mind and expansion to the feelings, and healthy animation to the corporeal frame, as an acquaintance with the productions of nature, and with the general laws which regulate her operations, and the exposition of which constitutes the elements of the different branches of science. Nothing helps so much to give harmony and serenity of feeling as the contemplation of the omniscience, omnipotence, and beneficence of the Deity, as exhibited in the coincident and harmonious action of the great laws of nature. Nothing is so delightful as to trace them through the various departments of unorganised, organised, and living beings, in all of which their influence is conspicuous, and is yet strangely and wonderfully modified to their adaptation for a particular end. We then see them uniform and magnificent in their operation, and producing all the varied phenomena which lie open to our view, by a simple difference of the material to which they are applied, but acting in the production of the most trifling and unimportant change with as much regularity, harmony, and power, as in the most sublime and stupendous. Nothing conduces so much as this to take the mind out of itself, and to keep the feelings, as well as the intellect, in healthful play. Without some such knowledge, the mind never extends beyond the narrow circle of domestic events; all nature remains a barren wilderness, trivial occurrence assume an extravagant degree of importance, and from want of general principles are viewed, not according to their real merits, bu solely as they affect self—a standard which *must* vary as the differen perceptions and feelings happen to predominate at the moment hence a fruitful source of perplexity, uncertainty, and doubt, and the want of an abiding faith in the dispensations of a good and kind Providence.

In recommending a general acquaintance with science as a strengthener of the mind, I do not mean that young ladies should study chemistry, natural history, or natural philosophy, with the minuteness of a professional student, or that in society they should entertain their friends with discussions on the pressure of the atmo sphere, the composition of water, or the analysis of a mineral. This would be folly, not wisdom. But I mean, that a knowledge of the outlines of these sciences, such as an average capacity will deligh to acquire, will not only strengthen the intellect and its cerebra organs, and through these improve the health, but will be a source of pure and permanent gratification, even independent of its mos beneficial consequences on the general health. It withdraws the mind from self, it gives a pleasing confidence in the admirable arrangement of all nature's institutions, and, by the tendency which it imparts to connect ourselves and all our doings as links in the great chain of society, and not to regard ourselves as isolated and capricious agents, subject to chance alone, it gives a greater gene rosity and kindliness of feeling, and a more willing submission to any of the crosses or disappointments of life, from which we may never be able to escape; and it contributes to candour and openness in reasoning, and in argument where opinions differ. It is a matter of common remark, that where a man knows no science but his own profession, even allowing his general reading to be considerable there is almost always a limited *scope* of intellect, often clear enough and vigorous within its own immediate range, but timid, prejudiced, and inconsistent, in all beyond; but where, from a general know- ledge of two or three sciences, one perceives the same general laws ruling all things, the most admirable harmony and adaptation of all parts of the great universe to each other, not only does the intellect repose in implicit confidence, but at every step Veneration is carried back to the Creator, Conscientiousness is delighted with the dis- covery of every new truth, Benevolence is gratified by the increased power which it bestows of being instruments of good, and most of the other sentiments are also gratified.

Entertaining these views of the advantages of natural knowledge in strengthening the mind through the physical organisation, and in conducing to bodily health, I cannot omit to mention the science of mind itself as the most important and interesting; because, in fact, the basis of all others, and the true centre round which they all revolve, and on which all of them act. An accurate estimate of our own powers and capacities, and of those of others, not only contributes to peace of mind, but it gives strength to purpose, and confidence in addressing the good feelings of our associates. It enables us to appreciate qualities justly which we do not ourselves possess, and therefore are apt to underrate or make no allowance for; and it enables us to set a just value on the various motives by which conduct is influenced, and to cherish the highest. It unfolds the source of those unpleasant sensations and darker views which at times will come across the minds of the most placid. It deprives them of their sting, and leads us to anticipate and hasten their disappearance. It furnishes a scale by which to estimate pursuits and decide on conduct. It makes us know ourselves and our relations to others, and is the basis of practical philosophy, practical morality, and practical religion. So far as this acquaintance with the principles of mind is attainable, it is to be found only in phrenology; and, that I may not be misunderstood, you will allow me to say, that I have no wish to see young ladies going about examining heads, drawing characters, or making remarks on their neighbours' peculiarities, (although the worst of all this is too often done without phrenology,) or setting themselves forth in society as either disciples or champions, but I have a strong desire to see them taught as much of phrenology as should let them know what human beings are, what duties they have to perform, and how they will best secure their own happiness, and the improvement of the race. If, instead of definite and demonstrable knowledge, phrenology presented only the conflicting vagueness of metaphysical theories, I should never be found recommending its study to any one; but, having experienced and seen exemplified in others the benefits and peace arising from its practical uses, I cannot recommend it too strongly.

Your readers may perhaps think, that, in estimating thus highly the advantages arising from the study of natural knowledge, including therein the knowledge of mind, I am overlooking the importance of general reading and of general knowledge; but there is a reason for the plan I have followed, which is not without force. In chemistry, when two bodies are made to act on each other, and to produce a result different from both, we feel assured, that on all future occasions, by placing the same bodies in the same circumstances, we shall be able to procure the same results; but, before the chemist attempts any explanation of the compound action, he invariably sets about ascertaining the qualities which characterise each of the substances on which he is acting, and from his knowledge of these he deduces the chemical change resulting from their contact. Now this is exactly what we ought to do in treating the compound result —general knowledge—which is, in truth, a knowledge of events and occurrences in which *man has been the agent on the one hand, and other men, or the qualities of bodies, have been the powers operating on the other*, and which necessarily differ in their results, according to the different qualities of men, and of external bodies; and consequently, without previously analysing the human mind, and ascertaining its primitive properties, and without previously enquiring into the properties of external objects, we cannot by any effort arrive at a satisfactory explanation or understanding of the effects which each produces on the other, so as to be able with certainty to reproduce the result. The natural place, then, for the profitable study of general knowledge, seems to me to be after the mind has been already imbued with a knowledge of its own constitution, and with that of external nature; and I have therefore reserved the mention of it till now.

In regard to the second branch, or the exercise of the feelings and moral sentiments, and the improvement of the health resulting from the strengthening of their organs, and the consequent increase of nervous energy sent through the body, it is evident that, like the intellectual faculties, they must be exercised directly on their own objects. The feelings and moral sentiments are so many determinate impulses, given us by the Creator to act in a certain way towards those around us, and it is not necessary that some extraordinary situation should be waited for to give them full enjoyment. Benevolence, no doubt, is strongly excited by the aspect of misery and unhappiness, and impels strongly to the relief of the suffering object; but this is not its most common or its most useful field. In ordinary life it finds ample scope in charity to our neighbours, and in contributing to the happiness of our family-circle, and of our associates and dependants. Benevolence is much better occupied in adding a gleam of enjoyment, in removing little sources of irritation, in promoting concord among relatives, and in other kind offices of a similar nature, than in giving alms indiscriminately to all who demand them, or even in relieving occasional distress, where this is held to dispense, as it too often is, with all obligation to habitual forbearance and Christian good-will in the private relations. But how little is this most important faculty directly attended to or cul tivated in the way we see done with drawing or music, which, by incessant exercise, are brought into such a state of activity as ever after to enable their possessors to derive delight from their exercise, where the talents are possessed in a moderate degree! And what might we not expect from the systematic training of the higher sentiments on a similar plan in improving society, and exalting the happiness of the race! But it is evident, that the objects of Benevolence are our fellow-creatures, and consequently, if we restrict our intercourse and our sympathies to the limits of our own drawing-rooms, and take no interest in the progress of the race, or of the individuals composing it, we leave our best faculties in abeyance, and reap the reward of bodily debility and mental weakness and monotony.

Conscientiousness is another principle of the mind that requires direct cultivation, and that rarely receives it. It holds the balance between man and man, and is excited by the presentment of any difference of right between individuals, of any injustice, of any temptation offered by the other faculties, which may lead us to encroach on others. It gives a strong sense of duty, with which it is agreeable to act in conformity, but which it is painful and injurious to oppose. It gives weight and force to the impulses of the other sentiments, and, joined with Veneration, gives that faith in the beneficence and equity of the Deity, and in the immutability of all his laws, that forms the strongest encouragement to virtuous conduct and temporary self-denial. And here, again, living in society, engaging in the active duties of life, and acting justly amidst the conflicting interests of others, and not seclusion and privacy, are manifestly intended by the Creator as our proper sphere.

In like manner, Veneration, Hope, Adhesiveness, and all the other propensities and sentiments, suppose society, and active and daily participation in the business of life, to be the intention and will of the Creator. From this it is most evident, that the seclusion of the drawing-room, and the retirement of home, in which so many young ladies of a nervous and delicate frame pass their whole time, affords no sufficient scope for the due exercise of a great number of our most important and most grateful feelings; that the large mass of brain appropriated to these must thus languish in comparative inactivity and weakness; and that the general system, being thus deprived of its natural nervous stimulus from the brain, must share largely in the debility, and give rise to many complaints of an obstinate and intractable kind. How wretchedly, then, do those parents conceive of true happiness, of the true end of life, and of the true welfare of their children, who do not from their infancy direct their minds assiduously to the duties which they owe to others, and to the enjoyments to be derived from the performance of these duties, and inculcate as earnestly the theory of good conduct in promoting physical and mental comfort as they would do the advantages of eating when we are hungry, or of resting when we are weary! Wo expend time and money in attempting to cultivate the intellect; but we leave the moral feelings, the chief part of man, to the growth and direction of chance, as if they, blind as they are in their impulse, must necessarily go right of their own accord.

As to religion, I consider its consequences, in relation to futurity, of too momentous a character to be disposed of in the compass of an essay; but this much I must say, in a mere practical point of view, that the morality of Christianity is demonstrated by phrenology to be in perfect harmony with the nature of man, and to lead directly to happiness in this world. Phrenology points out faculties of Benevolence, giving a warm sympathy with, and desire for, the happiness of our fellows, which can reap full gratification only by being actively employed in promoting the welfare and alleviating the miseries of man. It points to a principle of Conscientiousness which has a direct reference to the active duties of life, and which can find no scope when secluded from society. It points to a principle in Veneration, which leads to the adoration of God, and to veneration for all his institutions, and a strong desire of yielding them obedience, and of rendering respect to every thing great and excellent. It points to Hope, to Firmness, to Cautiousness, and to many other faculties which are little called into exercise in the quiet retirement of entirely domestic life, but which, in the wider relations of society, find ample and pleasing scope.

On every principle, then, physiological, philosophical, moral, or religious, it becomes an imperative duty on those who are charged with the education of the young to do their utmost to draw out and invigorate the various mental and physical powers with which man is endowed, and not to leave any of them in passive weakness and languor where it can possibly be avoided.

Some object, that the study of any department of science, even of that of the human mind, is unfeminine and unbecoming; but who is the better judge here?—God, who gave the capacity that it might be used, or man, who tries to destroy it by its abuse and neglect? The same objectors hold it proper and feminine, that a lady who has no taste for music should waste five or six hours a day in its toilsome cultivation; but they think it wrong that she should take an hour of that time to acquire some useful and pleasing, but homely accomplishment. Your readers, however, are beyond the influence of such absurdities, and I shall not stop to notice any of the thousand and one equally frivolous objections made against female education.

The most rational objection which is likely to be started is, that the institutions of society do not yet afford the means of acting up to what reason points out as right. In this there is, unfortunately, too much truth, for education is only in its infancy; but still it is highly useful to draw public attention to the deficiencies of existing systems; and much may be done at home in the proper regulation of employments and of reading, and in fulfilling the ordinary duties of life towards all with whom we are connected above and below us. It thus becomes as imperative a duty to exercise and train the moral sentiments as to cultivate the intellect; to employ Benevolence in promoting happiness, in relieving suffering, in administering to the wants of others, and in seeking out deserving objects of compassion; to use Conscientiousness as the regulating principle between ourselves and others: to cultivate and direct Veneration to the worship of God and submission to his will, and to train every sentiment to healthy activity and vigour, by exercising it on its own objects. In those whose active sympathies never extend beyond their own families, the best feelings languish in painful inactivity, and both mind and body suffer; for it must never be forgotten, that in this world the state of the mind hinges of necessity upon that of the body, and is influenced by its every change. Improve the health and strengthen the tone of the one, and you will also improve and strengthen the other. The grand principle which lies at the foundation of education, moral and intellectual, is to exercise the respective faculties on their own objects, as it is only by exercise that the mental organs can be duly developed, nourished, and invigorated; and consequently, if, knowing this, we leave many of them unexcited and unemployed, and nervous debility remain, we ought to acknowledge that in so far we are falling short of our duty, and have no reason to be surprised at the nature of the result.

What, therefore, is wanted, is a system of education in harmony with the constitution of the human mind, and a mode of life and of occupation which shall give, not only full play to the intellectual powers, but also *healthy excitement and activity, and a direct direction to the moral, religious, and affective feelings.*

ARTICLE V.

CHARACTER OF EUSTACHE.

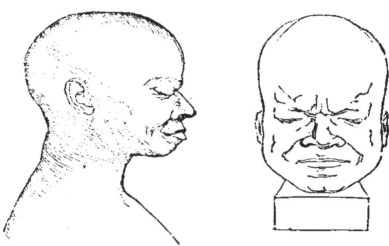

The above cuts are designed to present two different views of the head of a negro, by the name of Eustache, who was eminently distinguished for the qualities of virtue and benevolence. This individual died at Paris in the year 1835. Some years previously, the Paris Phrenological Society had obtained an accurate cast of his head, and forwarded specimens to the Edinburgh Phrenological Society, a copy of which was brought to this country by Mr. George Combe. Our object in introducing them in this article, is to show a remarkable developement of the coronal region of the head, and its corresponding manifestations in character. It is doubtful whether another such instance of pure virtue and disinterested benevolence can be found recorded in the annals of history. It is the more striking, inasmuch as the individual belonged to a race generally regarded as deficient in those qualities; and, besides, they were exhibited in the present case under circumstances of such ignorance and oppression, that we might naturally have expected traits of character directly the reverse. But we will let the facts speak for themselves.

The forty-second number of the Edinburgh Phrenological Journal gives the following account of Eustache, which is, in part, as indicated by quotation marks, copied from the Phrenological Journal of Paris :—

"On the 9th of August, 1832, this negro, when sixty years of age, obtained the *prize of virtue* from the Institute, on account of the devoted attachment he had displayed, in St. Domingo, towards his master, M. Belin. By his address, courage, and devotion, this gentleman, with upwards of four hundred other whites, were saved from the general massacre, and the fortune of M. Belin was several times preserved. 'The idea of murder,' says the reporter to the Institute, 'did not associate itself, in the mind of Eustache, with that of liberty. Placed among companions endeavouring to obtain, with the torch and the dagger, their bloody emancipation, and seeing his master in danger of being murdered amid the ruins of their burning dwellings, he hesitated not a moment. * * Incessantly occupied in warning the inhabitants of the conspiracies formed against them, (but without revealing the names of the conspirators,) and in devising a thousand stratagems to enable the proprietors to unite and strengthen their position, so as to make the insurgents abandon the idea of attacking them, he consorted with the negroes during the day, and in the evening went to give warning to the whites.' While Eustache resided at Paris, he was always busy in doing good. 'He never wishes,' says Dr. Broussais, 'to keep any thing. for himself; the profits of his industry, and the rewards which he has obtained, being on all occasions employed in relieving the miserable.' He has always preferred to remain in the condition of a servant, in order that he might turn to account his skill in cookery, and enable himself to do good to his fellow-creatures. The following characteristic trait is quoted from the report to the Institute before referred to. 'At Port-au-Prince, Eustache often heard his master, who was an old man, bewailing the gradual weakening of his sight. Now, had Eustache been able to read, he might have whiled away his master's long and sleepless hours, by reading the journals to him. It was therefore a matter of deep regret with him that he had never been taught to read; but this regret did not long continue. He secretly applied himself to study; took lessons at four o'clock in the morning, in order that the time necessary for the performance of his regular duties might not be encroached upon; speedily acquired the wished-for knowledge; and, approaching the old man with a book in his hand, proved to him, that if nothing seems easy to ignorance, nothing is impossible to devotion.'

"The bust of Eustache exhibits a prodigious developement of the organ of Benevolence; and we entirely concur in the statement of Dr. Broussais, that there is in the collection no specimen which can be in this respect compared with it. 'The organ,' says he, 'is so large that, though I were unacquainted with Eustache, I should, at the sight of such a head, exclaim—here is monomania of Benevolence. But I am better pleased to sum up, with M. Brifant, his life and his character in two words—*incorrigible generosity*.'

" We have measured the cast, and subjoin a note of its dimensions. It is proper to notice, that there was no hair on the head when the cast was taken.

Circumference, ...	22 inches.	
From Individuality to Occipital Spine, . . .	$14\frac{3}{4}$	"
" Ear to Ear, over top of head, . . .	14	"
" Individuality to Philoprogenitiveness, . .	$7\frac{3}{4}$	"
" Ear to Philoprogenitiveness, . . .	$4\frac{1}{2}$	"
" " Individuality, ...	$5\frac{1}{8}$	"
" " Comparison, ...	$5\frac{3}{4}$	"
" " Benevolence, ...	6	"
" " Firmness, ...	6	"
" Destructiveness to Destructiveness, . .	6	"
" Secretiveness to Secretiveness, . . .	6	"
" Cautiousness to Cautiousness, . . .	5	"

" It will be obvious to every phrenologist, from the foregoing table, that the head of Eustache was of very considerable size. In this respect, as well as in its form, it has quite the appearance of a European head. The organs of Veneration, Firmness, Philoprogenitiveness, Comparison, and Causality, are large, though not equal to Benevolence; Adhesiveness, Combativeness, Destructiveness, Secretiveness, Cautiousness, Conscientiousness, and Approbativeness, rather large, or large; Imitation and Wonder, where the head descends rapidly on both sides from Benevolence, moderate, or rather full. There seems to be a very fair developement of the organ of Language. And Benevolence, rising to a great height above Comparison, seems to tower above all the other organs."

The above account was published three years before the death of Eustache, when only a few facts were known concerning his life and character; and the regret was then expressed by the conductors of the Edinburgh Phrenological Journal, on finding so remarkable cerebral developements in the case of a negro, that a minute and extended history of Eustache had not been given. But since his death, this desideratum has been supplied, and, within the past year, the following history of Eustache has appeared in several papers in this country. We present it entire, as every phrenologist cannot fail, with the above data, to derive additional interest from the narrative.

"Eustache was born on the plantation of M. Belin de Villennue, situated in the northern part of St. Domingo, in the year 1773. In his youth, he was noted for avoiding light and vicious conversation, and for embracing every opportunity of listening to intelligent and respectable whites. Occupied in the labours of the sugar-house, in which he

became remarkably expert, he grew up respected by his master and
fellow-slaves. It was near the time of his attaining the age of manhood, that the revolution of St. Domingo broke out. He might have
been a chief among his comrades, but he preferred the saving to the
destruction of his fellow-men. In the first massacre of St. Domingo,
1791, his knowledge, intrepidity, and the confidence of his countrymen,
enabled him to save four hundred persons from death. Among these
was his master.

"Eustache had arranged for the embarkation of M. Belin, and
other fugitives, on board a vessel bound to Baltimore. In the midst of
terror and confusion, he bethought himself that his master would soon
be destitute of resources in the asylum to which he was about to be conveyed; and he prevailed upon upwards of a hundred of his comrades
to accompany them to the vessel, each bearing under his arms two large
loaves of sugar. These were stowed on board, and they set sail, but not
to reach the United States without a new misfortune. They were cap-
tured by a British cruiser, and a prize crew put on board. Eustache,
being a superior cook, soon rendered himself very useful and agreeable
to the officers of the prize in this capacity. Having gained their confidence, he was permitted to enjoy entire liberty on board, and he determined to use it for rescuing himself, his companions, and their property,
from their captors. Having acquainted the prisoners of his plan, and
found the means of releasing them at the moment of action, he proceeded, with his usual skill and assiduity, to prepare the repast of the
British officers; but soon after they were seated at the table, he rushed
into the cabin at the head of his men, with a rusty sword in his hand.
The officers were taken so completely by surprise, that they had no
weapons within reach, and no time to move from their places. Eustache
had got possession of the avenues and the arms, and he now told the
mess, whom he had lately served in so different a capacity, that if they
would surrender at once, no harm should be done to any of them. They
did surrender, and the vessel arrived safely with its prisoners and passengers at Baltimore.

"At that city, Eustache devoted the resources which his industry and
skill could command, to the relief of those whose lives he had saved.
At length it was announced that peace was restored to St. Domingo,
and thither Eustache returned with his master, who appears to have
been worthy of the tender and faithful attachment with which this
negro regarded him. But the peace of St. Domingo was only a prelude
to a more bloody tragedy than had been before enacted. M. Belin was
separated from his benefactor in the midst of a general massacre,
executed by the Haytian chief, Jean François, at the city of Fort
Dauphin. M. Belin effected his escape, while Eustache was employed collecting together his most valuable effects, and committing
them to the care of the wife of this avenging chief. She was sick in
his tent, and it was under her bed that the trunks of M. Belin were
deposited. Having made this provident arrangement, Eustache set off
to seek his master; first on the field of carnage, where he trembled as
he examined, one after another, the bodies of the dead. At length he
found the object of his search, alive and in a place of safety; and having
again embarked with him, and the treasure he had so adroitly preserved,
he reached St. Nicholas Mole. Here the fame of his humanity, his disinterestedness, and his extraordinary courage and address, preceded him,
and on disembarking, he was received with distinction by the population,
both white and coloured.

"On the return of peace and prosperity under the government of
Toussaint l'Ouverture, M. Belin established himself at Port-au-Prince,

where he was appointed president of the privy council. At this time, he had arrived at the decline of life, and had the misfortune to lose his eyesight. He now regretted that he had not taught Eustache to read. He expressed himself with much emotion on that subject, saying, 'how many heavy and sleepless hours of a blind old man might Eustache have beguiled, if he could read the newspapers to me.' Eustache mourned his father's bereavement, and his incapacity to console him. In secret he sought a master, and by rising at four o'clock, and studying hard, though not to the neglect of his other duties, he was able in three months to present himself to his master with a book in his hand, and by reading in it with perfect propriety, to give a new and surprising proof of the constancy and tenderness of his attachment. Upon this, followed his enfranchisement. But freedom did not change—it only elevated and hallowed his friendship for his late master; rather let us say, his venerable and beloved companion.

"Soon afterward, M. Belin died, leaving to Eustache a fortune which would have supported him in ease during the rest of his life. But the legacies of his friend came to the hands of Eustache only to be passed by them to the needy and unfortunate. At that time there was a vast deal of misery, and but *one* Eustache in the island of St. Domingo. If a soldier was without clothing and pay, a family without bread, a cultivator or mechanic without tools, the new riches of Eustache were dispensed for their supply. Of course these could not last long, and from that time until his death, in 1835, a period of near forty years, he maintained himself and provided for numerous charities by serving as a domestic. He lived and laboured only to make others happy. Sometimes he was found defraying the expenses of nursing orphan infants; sometimes administering to the necessities of aged relations of his late master; sometimes paying for instructing, and placing as apprentices, youths who were destitute and unprotected; and often giving to his employers considerable arrears of wages which they found it difficult, by a vicissitude of fortune, to pay. His remarkable skill as a cook enabled him to provide for all these expenditures, as it secured him constant employment in all the wealthiest families. His own wants were few and small.

" The virtues of this humble and noble-hearted negro could not long be hidden by the obscurity of his calling. In 1832, the National Institute of France sought him out, to announce to him that that illustrious body had paid to his worth the highest homage in its power, by awarding to him the first prize of virtue, being the sum of $1000. To this announcement, made by a member of the Institute, he replied with his habitual simplicity and piety, 'It is not, dear sir, for men that I have done this, but for my Master who is on high.' "

We have another circumstance to relate on this subject, which will afford not only new evidence, aside from the above facts, in proof of phrenology, but may serve to show the correctness with which its principles, in the hands of an experienced and skilful phrenologist, can be applied to the delineation of character About a year since, the bust of Eustache was presented to Mr. L. N. Fowler, 135 Nassau street, New York, and his opinion requested, when, without the slightest knowledge of the subject, and in the presence of T. D. Weld, S. Southard, and W. M. Chase, he gave the following opinion. It should be remembered, in reading this description, that phrenology professes to make known only the *natural* capabilities or the *strength* of the innate elements of mind, the manifestations of which must necessarily be more or less affected by external circumstances. Some allowance should therefore be made in the present case, as Mr. F.'s opinion was given on the supposition that the individual had enjoyed good advantages for intellectual and moral improvement. And there is abundant evidence to believe from the above narrative, that if Eustache had been educated, his *intellectual* character would have been as equally distinguished as his *moral*, and that the inferences of the phrenologist, even in this respect, were not incorrect. Besides, during the examination, and while the description was taken down, the bust was so covered that he supposed it, of course, belonged to a *white* person, and never knew, till afterwards, that he had been examining the bust of a *negro*. The stress laid upon the organ of Benevolence in this analysis, as forming the leading trait of character, is in striking accordance with the observations of the Edinburgh phrenologists, as well as with the facts in the case. The description given by Mr. F. is as follows:—

'The intellectual and moral organs are well combined, and would have the leading influence in his character. The leading feature in his moral character, is desire to do good; Benevolence being very large, distinguishing him for good nature and humanity. Religious from his youth, he was devotional, and had great respect for superiority, and things sacred and holy. He was very firm, but always willing to oblige. A man of principle, moral sense, and strong conscientious feelings. He was very domestic, affectionate and kind, strongly attached to children, and to home and place. He was both dignified and affable. A close reasoner; could connect his thoughts, and was not vascillating in his feelings. Was energetic and forcible when necessary; yet was more distinguished for good nature than temper. Very ambitious to be good and great, distinguished for benevolence, humanity, and virtue; fondness for improvement, and a love of the arts; for a philosophical mind, and a disposition to reason on moral subjects; for evenness of character, regularity, and circumspection, and a desire to fulfil all engagements and obligations. His talents were practical, and enabled him to carry into execution his plans. He was capable of being a good linguist, and of making great advances as a scholar; not marvellous or poetical; decidedly intellectual: had uncommon forethought and research of intellect; was a great reasoner—great planner; full of designs; not deficient in powers of intrigue; can plot and plan; uncommon share of ingenuity—never at a loss for means; systematic, disposed to encourage improvement in the arts; was original and somewhat eccentric.'

ARTICLE VI

*Lectures on Phrenology, by George Combe, Esq., including its appli-
cation to the Present and Prospective Condition of the United
States ; with notes, an introductory essay, and an historical sketch.
By* ANDREW BOARDMAN, *Recording Secretary of the Phrenolo-
gical Society of New York. Published by* S. Colman, No 8.
Astor House, New York.

The title of the above work will convey to the reader some idea
of its contents. Our principal object in noticing the work, is to commend it to the attention of all interested in phrenology. It is, in
some respects, decidedly the best elementary book now extant on
the science ; and we hope it will have an extensive circulation, as it
justly deserves. Mr. Boardman, the compiler, has performed valuable services for phrenology, and deserves the favourable regards of
its friends generally. In the first place, he communicated very full
reports of Mr. Combe's first course of lectures to the New York
Whig, and then, again, of the second course, to the New Yorker ;
from which papers, these reports have been copied, in part or entire,
into several other papers, so that by this means the claims of
phrenology have been presented to the consideration of many
thousands, which would not have otherwise been done. In the second
place, Mr. B. has reviewed and enlarged these reports, and, having
submitted them to the inspection of Mr. Combe, and received that
gentleman's sanction of "their essential correctness," has now presented them to the public in a handsome duodecimo volume of 389
pages. Besides, nearly one hundred pages of the work before us is
composed of original matter from his pen, and which we propose
briefly to notice.

The "Essay on the Phrenological Mode of Investigation" is an
able and philosophical article ; and constitutes a very appropriate
introduction to the work. Perhaps there is no feature of phrenology,
when contrasted with other systems of mental philosophy, more
peculiar in its nature, or more important in its results, than the fact
that it is an *inductive* science. It is well known that scarcely any
progress was made in the natural sciences till the seventeenth century, for the simple reason that the *true* mode of studying nature
was unknown. The general course which philosophers then pursued, was to start some *theory, speculation*, or *hypothesis* on subjects
of enquiry, and afterwards attempt to reconcile facts with their preconceived notions. Whereas, the only *true* mode of philosophising
is first to observe and collect facts on a subject, then establish the

correctness of these facts by their appropriate evidence, and classify
them according to their inherent properties or qualities, and afterwards deduce from them principles which must necessarily be true
in their nature, as well as susceptible of general application.   By
means of this process, and this *only*, can we arrive at truth in our
investigations.   We are induced to present a few extracts on this
subject, from Mr. Boardman's excellent essay.

"At the commencement of the seventeenth century appeared Lord
Bacon, one of the most remarkable men the world has produced.   With
'his supreme and searching glance, he ranged over the whole circle of
the sciences,' detected the absurdities of the schoolmen, and exposed
them with a vigorous and unsparing hand.   He dethroned the Aristotelian idol which had for ages received the blind fealty of a world, and,
fortunately for science and humanity, attempted not to substitute an idol
of his own, but pointed to nature as alone worthy of homage.   'Man,'
said he, in the opening sentence of his immortal work, 'the servant and
interpreter of nature, understands and reduces to practice just so much
of nature's laws as he has *actually experienced*, more he can neither
know nor achieve.'   Now this experience, Bacon maintained, must be
acquired by *observation*.   To observe facts, then, is the first great
business of the investigator."

"But we must bear in mind that isolated facts are of small value.
They must be brought together carefully and patiently ; must be rigidly
scrutinised and verified, compared and classified, for the purpose of
ascertaining some relation of sign and power, cause and effect, general
principle, quality, or mode of activity.   To achieve such results is,
indeed, the great object and triumph of the Baconian philosophy.   By
such observation, comparison, and classification, it has been discovered,
for example, that a certain state of the barometer indicates a certain
elevation above the level of the sea; that increase of heat causes bodies to
expand; that all the individual plants of the crow-foot tribe are more or
less acrid and poisonous; that the sun modifies the moon's influence on
the tides.   Or, to take another series of examples.   By this method it
has been ascertained that a large skull indicates a large brain, and that
a large brain causes a large skull ; that persons having a brain weighing
but one and a half pounds are invariably idiotic; that a predominant
coronal region gives a general tendency or disposition towards virtue ;
and that education has the power of modifying the constitutional tendencies of our nature.

"The fundamental error of ancient philosophy was the notion that a
general cause must be first *divined or conjectured*, and then applied to
the explanation of particular phenomena; they perceived not the plain
but momentous truth, that a general fact is nothing else than a fact
common to many individuals, and consequently, that the individual
facts must be known before the general fact can be stated.   Hence,
instead of first *ascertaining*, by direct observation, the relative velocity
of two descending bodies differing in weight, then of two others—persisting with new experiments until enough of instances had been
observed to justify an assumption of uniformity—Aristotle first *assumed*
a gross error as a general fact, and then *inferred* it of any two bodies
whatever.   His reasoning was correct, but his premiss was false.   He
attended to logics, but utterly neglected induction."

"By means of the inductive philosophy, man, in these latter days,
has been able to draw aside the veil of the inner temple, and become on

intimate terms with nature.' To it, chiefly, do we owe our superiority over the dark ages, for it cannot be supposed that all at once the human intellect gathered vigour, and emerged from childhood to manhood. No; it had lost its way, and become 'in wandering mazes lost,' and though vast powers were oftentimes displayed, yet as they were displayed in weaving webs of subtlety and conjecture, nothing was achieved. Like the arts of the posture master, the displays of intellectual power were wonderful, but of small profit, and, by enlightened reason, could be accounted only as 'fantastic tricks.' The inductive philosophy brought men back to the true path, and in that path advancement was not, as before, a departure from truth, but progress in it. No wonder, then, that we have surpassed our fathers, for, as Bacon well observes, 'a cripple in the right way may beat a racer in the wrong.'

"To this philosophy, then, do we owe the establishment of phrenology, a science pregnant with more important influences than the revelations of Galileo, of Harvey, or of Newton; making known, as it does, the material instruments of mentality, unfolding, as it does, the moral and intellectual constitution of man, and exposing, as it does, the secret springs of thought and impulses of action; furnishing man with a middle term, which will enable him, as it were, to throw his own and external nature into one mighty syllogism, and educe human duty and human destiny.

"The day is not far distant when it will be acknowledged by all, that no doctrines were ever established on a more extensive induction of rigidly scrutinised and verified facts, than were those of Gall. The length of time which he allowed to elapse between their dawn and promulgation; his entire devotion of life and property to their investigation; the bold but truth-loving spirit; the profound, comprehensive, discriminative, and practical understanding, every where manifested in his writings, place him at the antipodes of those speculative geniuses who spend their lives in weaving webs of sophistry for the entanglement of human reason. To make this evident, to show in a manner satisfactory to all candid minds, that phrenology is a discovery, and not an invention, that its doctrines are but the crowning stones to pyramids of facts, is the object of the present essay."

Our limits will not permit us to make farther extracts, or give even an analysis of the remaining part of this essay. The next article by Mr. Boardman, presents a brief "history of the rise, progress, and present condition of phrenology." Here, we have discussed the views which various writers and anatomists have entertained respecting the functions of the brain. The discovery, progress, and reception of the truths which phrenology discloses concerning the functions of this organ are clearly and correctly given. The merits of Dr. Gall, as a discoverer and philosopher, are ably and justly vindicated. We should be pleased to notice several points in this article, but cannot at the present time, though we may have occasion to refer to them hereafter.

The lectures of Mr. Combe, occupying the chief body of the work, are presented with great accuracy and minuteness. These reports certainly contain the substance of that gentleman's lectures; and, according to our best recollection, (and we had the pleasure of hear-ng these lectures delivered twice,) they are expressed in almost the precise words of the lecturer. The work contains valuable drawings, designed to show the location of the various organs and the physical signs of the temperaments, as well as numerous cuts, either to illustrate remarkable or deficient developements by way of contrast, or to represent particular personages, whose mental manifestations were in some way very striking and marked. As to the phrenological matter of these lectures, it needs no commendation from us. It emanates from the highest living authority on the science; and it is doubtful whether matter of equal value can any where else be found within so small a compass.

But in conclusion, we must dissent from the nature and tendency of some remarks in the Appendix by Mr. Boardman. If his premises and inferences are correct, the science can never be rendered available in its practical application to the extent for which its advocates have generally claimed for it. He has here made concessions which no other phrenologist, to our knowledge, has ever made, though many opponents of the science have repeatedly brought similar charges against it. We have neither the time nor the space, at present, necessary to examine this subject, and do it justice; yet on some future occasion we may attempt to prove, both by facts and arguments, that some statements in this Appendix are erroneous in their nature, and consequently injurious to the science.

MISCELLANY.

Laws of Hereditary Descent.—Probably there is no subject in the whole range of the sciences, more important in its bearings on the welfare of mankind, than that at the head of this paragraph. As we shall have occasion to discuss it, at some length, in the future pages of the Journal, it may be proper to offer first a few facts and general principles on the subject; and perhaps we cannot do this in better and more appropriate language, than by presenting a summary of Dr. Spurzheim's views, as they appeared, some time since, in the *Ladies' Magazine,* which are as follows:—

"Children participate in the bodily configuration and constitution of their parents, and also in their tendencies to particular manifestations of the mind, these being dependent on the individual parts of the brain.

"The qualities of the body are hereditary. There are family-faces, family likenesses, and also single parts, such as bones, muscles, hair, and skin, which are alike in parents and children. The disposition to various disorders, as to gout, scrofula, dropsy, hydrocephalus, consumption, deafness, epilepsy, apoplexy, idiotism, insanity, &c., is frequently in the inheritance of birth.

"Children born of healthy parents, and belonging to a strong stock always bring into the world a system formed by nature to resist th causes of disease; while children of delicate, sickly parents, are over powered by the least unfavourable circumstance.

"Longevity depends more on innate constitution, than on the skill c the physician. Is it not then astonishing that this knowledge, as a prac tical piece of information, is not taught and disseminated among youn; people? Indeed, it ought to be familiarly and generally known. Eve the unthinking must perceive that the enjoyments of life are rendere impossible, when diseases make their ravages in a family; and that lov for the most part ceases, when poverty takes up its abode in the house.

"There are many examples on record, of certain feelings or intel lectual faculties being inherent in whole families. Now if it be ascer tained that the hereditary condition of the brain is the cause, there is great additional motive to be careful in the choice of a partner in mai riage. No person of sense can be indifferent about having selfish c benevolent, stupid or intelligent, children.

"But it is said that men of great talents often have children of littl understanding, and that, in large families there are individuals of ver different capacities.

"As long as eminent men are married to partners of inferior capacities the qualities of the offspring must be uncertain. The condition of th mother is not valued as it ought to be, and yet it is a common observa tion that boys resemble their mother, and girls their father, and that mer of great talents almost always descend from intelligent mothers. Th physical education of both sexes deserves the greatest attention, and i is unpardonable to neglect that of girls.

"The degeneration of man is certain in families who intermarr among themselves. Uncles and wives, or first cousins, or cousins wh commit this error for several generations, have no children, or their pro geny is feeble in constitution of both mind and body.

"It is indeed a pity that the laws of hereditary descent are so muc neglected, whilst, by attending to them, not only the condition of singl families, but of whole nations, might be improved beyond imagination in figure, stature, complexion, health, talents, and moral feelings.

"'It is probable,' says Dr. Rush, 'that the qualities of body and min in parents, which produce genius in children, may be fixed and regulated and it is possible the time may come, when we shall be able to predic with certainty the intellectual character of children, by knowing th specific nature of the different intellectual faculties of their parents.'

"Three successive generations appear to be necessary to produce a effectual change, be it for health or disease. According to the laws c creation, therefore, it is said that 'the Lord visits those who hate hir (those who do not submit to his laws) to the third and fourth genera tion;' namely, by their hereditary dispositions.

"Such causes as produce what is called the old age of nations, deserv to be remarked. Luxury belongs to them, and its influence, if continue during several generations, weakens body and mind, not only of families but of whole nations.

"The Greeks, as appears from their customs, philosophy, and legisla tion, had particularly in view the beauty and vigour of the human con stitution. 'As we,' says Plutarch, 'are anxious to have dogs and horse from a good breed, why should we marry the daughters of bad parents? Plato speaks against marriages between relations. He, as well as Solo and Aristotle, considered also the age at which it was best to marry The ancient philosophers commonly fixed it between eighteen an twenty-four for a woman, and between thirty and thirty-six for a man. It is often the case that women who marry when very young, and bear a numerous family, become early victims to an exhausted constitution.

"It may be said that these considerations can never become practical rules of conduct for society at large. In the actual situation of things, perhaps this is true. But we must also admit that the laws of the Creator will not change to gratify our fancy. If we will not submit to his dictates, we have no right to complain of being punished by unavoidable, though disagreeable results.

"Christian principles are not sufficiently exercised in society; yet it is not, on this account, considered superfluous to teach them; and he who loves mankind, will wish for their promulgation. Now the laws of hereditary descent are in the same situation.

"The Supreme Being gave us understanding that we might perceive these laws; and having perceived them, it is our first duty to obey them as His dictates; and having done so, we may then, and not till then, expect His blessing to attend us. The special obedience to the natural laws of hereditary descent is an indispensable condition to the improvement of mankind; and nothing but ignorance, superstition, and prejudice, can oppose it."

We subjoin a few facts on this subject at the present time, and shall add others, as may be convenient. It happens, in the instances we now offer, that the inheritance of talent depended more on the maternal than the paternal side. It is a prevailing opinion, that this is generally the case, though it may be very questionable whether the laws of hereditary descent operate more effectively in the one case than in the other. Facts only can settle the question. The following cases present a variety, comprehending philosophers, poets, historians, and orators.

Lord Bacon: his mother was daughter to Sir Anthony Cooke; she was skilled in many languages, and translated and wrote several works, which displayed superior learning, acuteness, and taste.—Hume, the historian, mentions his mother, daughter of Sir D. Falconet, (President of the College of Justice,) as a woman of singular merit; and who, although in the prime of her life, devoted herself entirely to his education.—R. B. Sheridan: his mother was a woman of more than ordinary abilities. It was writing a pamphlet in his defence, which first introduced her to Mr. Sheridan, her husband. She also wrote a novel, highly praised by Johnson.—Schiller, the German poet: his mother was an amiable woman; had great relish for the beauties of nature, and was passionately fond of music and poetry. Schiller was her favourite child.—Goethe thus speaks of his parents: I inherited from my father a certain sort of eloquence, calculated to enforce my doctrines on my auditors; and from my mother, I derived the faculty of representing all that the imagination can conceive, with energy and vivacity.—Lord Erskine's mother was a woman of superior talent and discernment, and it was through her advice that he betook himself to the bar.—Thompson, the poet: his mother is represented as a woman of uncommon natural endowment, possessed of every social and domestic virtue, with a warmth and vivacity of imagination scarcely inferior to her son.—Boerhaave's mother acquired a knowledge of medicine, not often found in females.—The mother of Sir Walter Scott was a woman of great accomplishments and virtue; possessed refined taste, and wrote poetry at an early age.

Mr. Grimes in Albany, N. Y.—In the first volume of the Journal, we had occasion to present favourable notices of this gentleman's labours in behalf of phrenology, at Buffalo, N. Y., and Wheeling, Va. It appears that he has recently visited Albany, N. Y., and been quite successful in presenting the claims of the science to its citizens. We find in the Albany Argus of Dec. 4, the following statement in relation to the reception of Mr. G.'s lectures:—

"At the close of Mr. Grimes's lectures in the chapel of the Albany Female Academy, the class organised, by appointing Charles D. Townsend, M. D., chairman, and Thomas W. Olcott, Esq., secretary; whereupon Henry Green, M. D., introduced the following resolutions, which were unanimously adopted.

"*Resolved*, That we have listened with exciting interest to the lectures of Mr. Grimes, president of the Phrenological Society of Buffalo, on the science of phrenology.

"*Resolved*, That we believe Mr. Grimes has made new and important discoveries in phrenology; that his arrangement of the brain into three classes of organs, viz. the ipseal, social, and intellectual, together with their subdivision, into ranges and groups, is founded in nature, the anatomy of the brain, and the natural gradation of animals, as they rise in the scale of being.

"*Resolved*, That we are forced to believe that phrenology, as taught by Mr. Grimes, may be learned by persons of ordinary intelligence and observation, so as to be useful to them in their every day intercourse with society; that it is destined to improve our race, remodel the present mode of education, become useful in legislation, and in the government of children in families and schools.

"*Resolved*, That we not only esteem it a duty, but regard it a pleasure, to encourage talents, genius, and enterprise, wherever we discover them, and in whatever pursuit, if the object and effect is the improvement of mankind; that we regard Mr. Grimes as possessing the highest order of intellect—as original in his observations and deductions, and as destined to fill a distinguished place in the scientific world.

"*Resolved*, That we confidently recommend Mr. Grimes to the attention of our fellow-citizens in different sections of our extended country, believing they will find him an accomplished lecturer, a close, accurate, forcible reasoner, and inimitable in his illustrations of the science he so triumphantly advocates.

"*Resolved*, That Henry Green, M. D., and Professor M'Kee, of the Albany Female Academy, be a committee to present a copy of these resolutions to Mr. Grimes, and request their publication in the daily papers of the city.

"CHARLES D. TOWNSEND, M. D., Chairman.
"THOMAS W. OLCOTT, ESQ., Secretary."

——

The late Dr. Godman a Phrenologist.—Dr. Sewall, in his Eulogy on the Character of Dr. Godman, says of him, and deservedly, too, "it was his accurate knowledge of anatomy and physiology, and his uncommon power of teaching these branches of medicine, which gave him his strongest claims to our regard as a man of science." And again—"He always came to his subject as an investigator of facts; the zeal with which he sought information from this source (original observation) may be learned from a single incident, that in investigating the habits of the shrew-mole, he walked many hundred miles." Now this same Dr. Godman says, "As a general rule, it is safe to infer that the opponents of Gall and Spurzheim do not understand the exact nature of the case against which they dispute. At least no man, who ever set himself honestly to work to examine the subject fairly, has remained in opposition." And in another place he speaks of "the renowned, the indefatigable, the undefeated Gall." And again he says, "This is the foundation upon which the doctrines of Gall and Spurzheim rest—purely upon observation—and this is the reason why these doctrines have so triumphantly outlived all the misrepresentations and violence of opposition."

Pathological Fact.—The Public Ledger of this city contained, Nov. 27th, 1839, the following statement on phrenology. We have enquired into the particulars of the case, and would state, that our readers may rely upon the correctness of the facts as detailed below.—

"A few days since, Dr. Duffie, in presence of Dr. B. H. Coates, dissected the body of a female who, during her lifetime, had laboured under a peculiar monomania. When on her death bed, she was under the impression that every person who entered the room came with the intention of stealing. This conceit was carried to such an extent, that she even believed that a reverend gentleman, who paid her occasional visits during her illness, never entered the room but with an intention to purloin some of the small articles displayed and placed about the room. She also admitted to the doctor that, though placed far beyond the reach of want and penury, by her very respectable and comfortable sphere in life, yet her own desire to pilfer and purloin from others was so uncontrollable that she, notwithstanding her consciousness of doing wrong, actually could not resist this natural impulse of thieving from others whenever a favourable opportunity presented itself. On dissection of the head, the brain and its covering were ascertained to be greatly inflamed by the examining gentlemen; Dr. Duffie afterwards presented it to Mr. Fowler, the phrenologist, who, on Monday evening, embodied a full description of it into one of his lectures. Secretiveness, combined with Acquisitiveness, was said to be extraordinarily developed on her *cranium*, which organs, according to the phrenological system, denote a desire to steal. The organ of Benevolence was also largely developed, which is said to act in a kind of restraining manner on the organs already referred to. The brain was exhibited to the audience present at Mr. Fowler's lecture. At the time of her death, she had arrived at the age of thirty-seven years, and was the mother of eight children."

The above fact is only one out of a multitude in confirmation of the science. Mr. Fowler is well known as an excellent practical phrenologist. He has an extensive phrenological cabinet, which, in number, variety, and choiceness of specimens, exceeds, probably, any other in the country, unless it be that in the possession of the Boston Phrenological Society, which is made up chiefly of Dr. Spurzheim's collection. Mr. Fowler is delivering lectures every week through the winter at his rooms, which are well attended, and afford much practical information on the science.

Cerebral Organisation the cause of difference in Religious Views.—It is not our intention to discuss the subject heading this paragraph, though it is one exceedingly interesting in its nature, and vastly important in its application. Our object is merely to call the attention of the public to the fact, and leave it for others, to whom it more appropriately belongs, to investigate the subject. It is gratifying to know that the clergy are beginning to take more rational and correct views of mental science in its connection with theology. There are some excellent remarks on this subject in the October number of the "American Biblical Repository," from the pen of a distinguished professor in one of our theological seminaries. It will be perceived in the extract which we quote, that the writer lays too much stress on mere *temperament*, and that, with a knowledge of phrenology, he might have rendered the subject much clearer, as well as more forcible and striking. Religionists and divines have yet to learn, that difference in cerebral organisation is more frequently and generally the primitive cause of difference in religious views, than they now suspect; and that there even is a more intimate and striking harmony between the principles of phrenology and the essential truths of Christianity, than they or any others have ever yet conceived. Time will verify the truth of this remark, and show that it is not mere assertion.

In accounting for the cause of religious controversy and difference of opinion, this writer speaks as follows:—"It will soothe many agitated minds to reflect that religious disputes, instead of arising always from a want of conscientious regard to the welfare of the church, arise sometimes from so innocent a cause as the different temperaments of individuals. One divine has a phlegmatic temperament, and loves to insist on human passivity; another has a sanguine temperament, and loves to insist on human action and freedom; a third has a melancholic temperament, and is fascinated with the inexplicable mysteries of God's moral system; a fourth has a bilious temperament, and loves to combine the passive and the active, fore-knowledge and free-will. Now the phlegmatic theology, in its exclusive form, is erroneous; the sanguine theology is the same; and the melancholic, when uncombined with others, is unsound; but it is not philosophical to excommunicate men by the hundred and thousand, because they have a nervous temperament, or a bilious mode of reasoning. They may be all pious, equally so with their opposers, yet all imperfect, and their original prolific sin is, in this regard, a sin of the cerebral system, rather than of the voluntary emotions."

—

Rev. John Pierpont, of Boston.—The name of this clergyman is doubtless known to most of our readers. He is one of the most eloquent divines in New England, and, as a poet, has few equals in this country. When Dr. Spurzheim was in Boston, Mr. Pierpont attended his lectures, became deeply interested in phrenology, and has since not failed, in various ways, to manifest his interest in the science. During the past season, certain proprietors of his church, taking offence at his zeal and labours in behalf of the temperance cause, have (in order to effect his dismission) brought sundry charges against him, among which his advocacy of phrenology comes in for a share. His accusers, in the charge, allude to Dr. Spurzheim under the character of an "*imported mountebank,*" &c.; to which Mr. Pierpont eloquently and beautifully replies— "Shade of the lamented Spurzheim! forgive the man who thus dishonours thee. Dishonours *thee!* No; no man can dishonour any other than himself. Thou wast honoured in thy life as few in this land have been. Thou wast honoured in thy death and thy funeral obsequies as, in this generation, no other man has been. The munificent merchant of Boston, who gave thy bones a resting place in the sacred shades of Mount Auburn, and placed over them that beautiful copy of the tomb of Scipio, was content to cut thy name upon its front as thine only epitaph; feeling that wherever science was honoured, or philanthropy loved, no other could be needed." And again Mr. P. says,—"I was a hearer of Dr. Spurzheim, and have since been, and mean again to be, a hearer of the lectures of George Combe. To these two 'imported mountebanks,' feel myself more indebted for instruction in the philosophy of the mind, and upon the conditions of the healthy manifestations of the mental powers, than to all other men, living or dead."

Brain of the Elephant.—Some of the strongest evidences in proof of phrenology are derived from comparative anatomy. It was, undoubtedly, facts from this source, more than from any other, that produced conviction in the mind of the celebrated Dr. Godman. We find in an Address, by Dr. G., on Natural History, the following interesting remarks on the brain of the elephant. The scientific reader will perceive that they are in strict accordance with phrenological principles.

"The similarity in the proportion of the cavities for the anterior and middle lobes of the elephant's brain to those of the human skull, are strikingly obvious. The great magnitude of the anterior lobes, when compared with the posterior lobes and cerebellum, cannot fail to excite the attention of every competent observer, and would suffice, were the history of the animal unknown, to produce a conviction of the superiority of its intellectual character over that of the generality of quadrupeds. The remark has often been made, that the brain of the elephant is very small, compared with its huge bulk; this remark may have appeared to be of more consequence while the brain was regarded as the *source* of the nerves, than it can do, now it is well ascertained that the nerves *communicate* with, or *terminate* in, the brain, instead of being emanations therefrom. Perfection of intellect has nothing to do with size of brain, compared with corporeal bulk; but depends upon the *proportions* existing between different parts of the brain itself, and, as a general rule, upon the acuteness of the organs of sense. Where the proportions of the brain are comparatively excellent, as in the elephant, seal, &c., more of *mind* is displayed, although not more than one sense be remarkably good, than in animals having all the senses more acute, with a less perfect arrangement in the proportions of the anterior, middle, and posterior parts of the brain. It is remarked among men, that small, *well-proportioned* heads display, as a general rule, more of talent and energy, than the majority of large heads, having less perfect proportions between the conformation of the anterior and posterior parts. The difference between the mind manifested by large and small heads, equally well proportioned, may be stated to consist in difference of activity; the large head being slower in operation, but capable of greater continuance of effort, while the small one is quicker and more energetic, but sooner exhausted by mental exertion."

Lectures on Phrenology in Boston.—Mr. George Combe delivered in this city two courses of lectures on phrenology during the month of November—each course consisting of twelve lectures, and attended by audiences numbering somewhat more than three hundred. Mr. Combe delivered also at the Odeon, in Boston, about the first of December, three lectures on the application of the science to education. These lectures were attended by nearly six hundred persons, of which number there were more than one hundred and fifty teachers.

We also learn that he has been invited (and had made arrangements accordingly) to repeat the same course of lectures at Salem, Lowell, Worcester, and Springfield, Mass. It is well known that this state has always taken the lead in education, and that now its citizens are making special exertions to improve and elevate their common schools; and we are quite sure that they will be among the first to perceive and appreciate the important bearings which phrenology is destined to have on this subject.

THE

AMERICAN PHRENOLOGICAL JOURNAL

AND

MISCELLANY.

Vol. II.   Philadelphia, February 1, 1840.   No. 5.

ARTICLE I.

REVIEW OF DR. VIMONT'S WORK ON COMPARATIVE PHRENOLOGY.

(Continued from page 130 of this Journal.)

*A Treatise on Human and Comparative Phrenology, accompanied by
a Grand Atlas in folio, containing 120 Plates, executed in the best
style.* By J. VIMONT, Doctor of Medicine of the Faculty of Paris
Honorary Member of the Phrenological Societies of Paris and of
London. (With an Epigraph.) Second edition. Brussels, 1836
pp. 558, royal octavo.

*L'orgueil, la superstition, la crainte ont embarrassée la connoissance
de l'homme de mille préjugés que l'observation doit détruire. La
religion est chargée de nous conduire dans la route du bonheur
qu'elle nous prépare au-delà du temps. La philosophie doit étudier
les motifs des actions de l'homme pour trouver de le rendre meilleur
et plus heureux dans cette vie passagère* (G. Leroy, *Lettre Philos
sur l'homme et les animaux*). Second edition. Bruxelles, 1836.

The ninth chapter is a commentary on the anatomical propositions
of Gall and Spurzheim, and a critique on those of Serres.

In the following chapter, the author presents to our notice the
successive developement of the cerebro-spinal system of man and
vertebral animals, and the changes which are induced by age in this
system, and consequently in the functions dependent on it.

The rapid growth of the brain in the first few months after birth,
corresponds with that of the cranium in the same period. More
especially are these changes evident in the parts situated at the base
of the cranium: those, in fact, which are in direct anatomical connection with the senses, and some of the nutritive viscera and the
locomotive organs; and also those at the inferior and anterior part
of the frontal bone, which are the organs of those perceptive faculties
that are soon to be called into activity in the child. In the period
between the first dentition and the seventh year, the increase of fulness and consistence of the cerebro-spinal system of the young sub-

ject is most manifest.   It is at this time, also, that the intellectual and affective faculties exhibit more distinct features ; and a close observer may already distinguish those which will characterise the future man.

There is an obvious but less rapid augmentation in the size and consistence of the cerebro-spinal system of youth in the period between the seventh and fifteenth year from birth.   With a remarkable developement of the posterior region of the encephalon, and of the corresponding portion of cranium at the expiration of this period, which is the epoch of puberty, there is also a manifestation of new feelings ; notably of those which prompt to sexual intercourse, and at the same time a more decided expression of countenance and manner than before.   The intellectual faculties, though far from having acquired the power and latitude of range which they manifest at a later period, indicate with tolerable distinctness the extent of which they are susceptible in manhood.

It is only, continues Dr. Vimont, in the period between the eighteenth and fortieth year of his age that the cerebro-spinal system in man attains its entire developement ; it is also during this interval that the lineaments of the intellectual and moral being are distinctly defined, and that the affective faculties in particular have most power and duration.

After forty years of age, the system in question begins to lose its activity, as it does to be gradually diminished in volume, at the same time that it is increased in density.   There are of course great differences among individuals as to the readiness with which these changes take place, and the mental faculties manifest a decline.   On this text Dr. Vimont gives a short dissertation, which would go to show that progression in the sciences, and in human knowledge generally, has been sadly retarded by the undue ascendency which persons advanced in life have acquired by their being placed or retained at the head of literary and scientific institutions.   " Where is the man, of information and sincerity, who will not agree with us that the ideas and acquirements of those who have passed the sixtieth year of their age always turn in the same circle—that all their actions are purely mechanical and in routine."   In making the application of this fact to the state of mind of those who oppose phrenology, we do not mean to enquire into the age of the certifiers of Dr. Sewall's anatomy and philosophy ; but we may venture, without much risk of error, to say, that these gentlemen are too far advanced in life to begin a series of observations and enquiries in a new science, and to carry out the numerous and diversified induction from these, which are either in opposition to the creed of their earlier years, or are essentially foreign to their earlier studies and associations. Unacquainted with anatomy and physiology, how can they know whether Dr. Sewall's lectures are penned in ignorance, or with superficial knowledge, or intention to mislead? Ignorant, also, of the innate faculties of the mind, they never having studied man in reference to this important truth, nor noted the connection between organisation and function, between matter and mind, how can they be supposed, either to be able to appreciate the doctrines of phrenology, or to begin the study of them at this time? There was, indeed, a course which age in its wisdom is commonly supposed to be able to set to youth, and by which it rebukes youthful rashness and impetuosity; it is in a prudent forbearance to give an opinion until all the facts are present and studied, and compared during a suitable time and with becoming industry.

It is an interesting comparison, one full of instruction, that between the state of the brain of old persons, marked by its decay, its subjection to paralysis, congestion, and apoplexy; and of very young ones, marked by the increase of its growth, its vascularity, active circulation, and susceptibility; and then for us to note the diminution and feebleness of the faculties, the want of common sensibility, the difficulty of creating new impressions, or of stirring up the affections and exercising the intellect in the former, in contrast with the agitation, eagerness for novelty, ardour of feeling, and quickness of intellect in the latter. All this belongs to the physiology of observation—it is part of the study of the philosophy of mind, the truth of which cannot be either rejected or maintained by closet reveries and metaphysical jargon. What are we to think, then, of the piety of those persons, who can see naught in the study of the functions of the brain but "a subtle form of materialism and an auxiliary to infidelity?" for in these terms is phrenology spoken of by a president of a college, a D. D., whose name we forbear to repeat here, although he has gratuitously exposed his own ignorance and illiberality in the expression of his opinion of Dr. Sewall's lectures. It would comport admirably with this reverend doctor's metaphysical abstractions, and his idea of physiology, if a lecturer were to attempt to prove that the structure and organisation of the eye had nothing to do with optics and vision, and that the function of digestion could be very well understood without the least reference to the stomach. And yet neither of these propositions is a whit more absurd, and more adverse to inductive philosophy, than that which this reverend president of a college (save the mark!) would inculcate, viz. a study of the faculties of the mind without taking the brain into the account. If orthodoxy and piety are to be

measured in the inverse proportion of a knowledge of the circumstances under which our mental faculties originate, and are modified
and educated, either to good or to evil, then indeed should the
reverend doctor be sought after as the guardian of faith, and the
fount of morality. Dulness would then be the presiding deity, and
ought to be invoked in the words of the poet :

> " O ever gracious to perplex'd mankind !
>   Still spread a healing mist before the mind ;
>   And lest we err by wit's wild dancing light,
>   Secure us kindly in our native night."

Dr. Vimont has studied the progressive growth of the cerebro-
spinal system of animals from birth to maturity, as he had in the
case of this system in man.

The author devotes a chapter, 1st, to diseased crania; 2d, to alterations of the cerebro-spinal system and its membranes. He considers
the diseases of the cranium as of three kinds : 1st, Malformation, or
vice in the configuration ; 2d, An increase or diminution of the cal-
carious matter entering into the composition of the lines of the
cranium ; and 3d, An unusual number of the bones of which it is
formed.

Of the first, or vices of configuration, the two chief varieties are,
an atrophy or deficient growth of the cranium, coinciding with a
similar state of the cerebral hemispheres, and an opposite condition
of things in which there is excessive enlargement of the cranium,
following that of the contained brain.

The defective growth of the cranium may amount to an almost
entire absence of this part, as in acephalous foetuses, or to a deficient
developement, as in congenital idiots. In its morbid developement
in chronic hydrocephalus, by which the ventricles are gradually distended with fluid, and the convolutions effaced, so that the brain
assumes the appearance of a large membrane of a globular figure
filled with fluid, the cranium follows the developement of the brain
on which it seems to be moulded ; and in some cases the size of the
head is very great. Dr. Vimont mentions the case of a young man,
eighteen years of age, whom we have ourselves seen, at the Hospice
de Perfectionnement, whose head measured two feet nine inches in
circumference. Spurzheim describes one three feet in the same
direction.

These abnormal variations, in addition to the illustrations which
they furnish of the functions of the brain, show also how closely and
accurately the growth and configuration of the skull are dependent
on, and coincident with, these states of its contained organs.

Dr. Vimont, under the present head of abnormal configuration of the cranium, refers to the flat heads of the Caribs, tho round heads of the Turks, and to other national peculiarities in this respect, which we have not room to introduce here.

The bones of the cranium may exhibit different degrees of density or thickness without any change in the configuration externally. This state may be either natural, the effect of certain general affections which influence the nutrition of the whole osseous system, or the consequence of disorders of the brain, and particularly of those marked by derangement of the intellectual faculties, or insanity.

In some individuals of an athletic make, in whom the limbs, including the hands, are large, and the bones prominent, the cranium is also, Dr. Vimont thinks, notably developed, owing, in part, to its great thickness. This was the case with the skull of Dr. Gall himself. But, however the observer may be misled from such a cause, in the opinion which he might entertain of the size of the brain beneath, the configuration and general proportions of the former are still indicative of the proportional developements of the latter. A large frontal region, for example, will not cover a deficient intellectual organ; although it might indicate a larger endowment of these than is actually possessed. Age causes increase of thickness and of density of the skull, as do chronic diseases of the brain and of its membranes. Rickets, scurvy, and syphilis, also modify the state of this bony case. Dr. Vimont states that he has in his possession the skull of a young man, who died of pulmonary consumption of three years' duration, which towards the conclusion assumed a scorbutic character. The entire cranium does not weigh more than ten ounces; the external table is not more than a quarter of a line thick, and at some points had been completely absorbed. Syphilis, peculiarly destructive in its advanced stage to the osseous system, attacks, of course, at times, the cranium, producing great inequality of its surface, riddling its tables, as it were, and in parts increasing the hardness and thickness of its bones.

The accounts which some of the older anatomists have related of ossified brain are fabulous; and had their origin in confounding exostosis, or bony tumour projecting from the inner surface of the skull, with the brain itself.

Dr. Vimont thinks that alterations in the osseous structure of the cranium of animals are of rare occurrence, although their existence on occasions is not denied.

The second section of this chapter takes cognisance *of the alterations of the cerebro-spinal nervous system and of its membranes.*

Of these, we may notice the congenital deficiency of cerebral structure in idiots; the convolutions of whose brains are less distinct than in persons well organised, and to a certain extent are manifestly wanting.

The atrophy, or loss, by organic change, of a hemisphere, is recorded by more than one writer. The fact of the cerebral organs being double, as in the external senses, explains why, in the former as in the latter case, injury or destruction of the organ of one side is not incompatible with the display of the specific function by that on the other.

The only congenital deficiency of organisation seen in the cerebellum, is a diminution of the size and number of its lamellæ.

The accidental disorders of the cerebral system are very numerous. Room can only be found by Dr. Vimont for the specification of a few of them; for it is well known to the medical reader that volumes have been written on this subject, one of the most important and fruitful in pathological anatomy. In proof of the connection between the organisation of the brain and its functions, or the faculties of the mind, may be cited the effects of apoplexy. But it is also known, that consequent on an attack of this kind the intellect is sometimes only partially abolished, a result alone explicable on the admission of a plurality of organs of the brain, destined for a plurality of specific functions. If the brain were a unit, an injury of any one part of it would unfit it for the discharge of its functions, and of course for the manifestation of even a single intellectual faculty. But we find persons who have suffered from an apoplectic stroke, recover their intellect so as to appreciate justly the circumstances in which they are placed, and reason on them nearly as before, but who have lost, some the memory of proper names, and others of language in general. Mr. Hood gives the history of a patient sixty-two years of age, in whom there was gradually manifested an inability to make himself understood by those around him. He had lost the name of every object in nature; but he retained his knowledge of facts, was attentive to what transpired in his presence, recognised his friends and acquaintances as readily as ever; but their names, those of his wife and family, and even his own, were entirely forgotten. His judgment and reasoning powers generally appeared to be as good as before. Although he could not use words with any definite application, he was able to articulate distinctly, and to repeat names which he heard; but before he could repeat them a third time, they were lost as completely as if he had never pronounced them. He seized readily the meaning of a passage read to him, but he could not read it himself. His convalescence was marked by the acquisition of some general terms, to which he gave a very varied application. Time and space, for instance, he designated under the general term of time.   On being questioned one day about his age, he showed that he understood the question, but he was unable to give the answer.   When his wife said that he was sixty years of age, he assented, and asked what time it was?   Mr. Hood, not distinctly knowing what he meant, replied by telling the hour of the day; but the invalid made him understand that this was not the answer he wanted.   Mr. Hood then gave the day of the week; but still without satisfying him.   Having at last mentioned the day of the month, he intimated that this was the information he wanted, in order to enable him to reply precisely to the question asked by Mr. Hood respecting his age, which, he said, was sixty years and five days, or times, as he called it.

The patient, in whom this infirmity was first manifested on the 2d September, 1822, entirely recovered from it in the month of December of the same year.   But on the 10th of January following, he became suddenly paralytic on the left side; on the 17th, had an attack of apoplexy, and died on the 21st of the month.   An autopsic examination showed that there was an alteration of the cerebral substance of the left hemisphere, and that, at the part where it rests on the middle of the orbitar plate, there were two small cysts lodged in a depression, which seemed to extend from this point of the brain to the ventricle.   The right hemisphere did not exhibit any thing extraordinary.   (*Edin. Phren. Jour.*, Vol. III.)

The portion of brain lying over the orbitar plate, is that which was taught by Dr. Gall, on the strength of numerous observations made on healthy persons, to be the organ of Language.   Dr. Boillaud relates three cases of inability of speech suddenly coming on and continuing some time, but without the powers of perception and judgment being affected.   There are, Dr. B. thinks, evidences of palsy of the organ of speech, without any accompanying palsy of other parts of the brain.   This gentleman has collected the history of several other cases related by different physicians, the subjects of which had been seized with inability to speak, and in whom very perceptible structural changes were found at the lower lobule, near the anterior portion of the hemisphere.   There was no paralysis of the tongue, however, or inability to give it all the different and various movements required in vocal and articulate utterance.

Sanguineous effusions in the cerebellum have been accompanied, we will not say universally, but in a large number of cases, with erection and ejaculation of semen; and chronic irritation and change of the part noticed in persons who, during life, had manifested excessive, and even morbid, venereal propensity.   Similar coincidences have been noted in animals subjected to experiments by strangulation

The atrophy of certain parts of the brain has been followed by loss of function; and the suspension of function by destruction of the external organ of sense, has brought with it a decay of the cerebral parts corresponding. Loss of vision, for example, is the consequence, at times, of lesion and wasting of the anterior corpora quadrigemina; whilst, on the other hand, a wound of the eye, or inflammation by which its structure is altered, and the images of objects can no longer be impressed on the retina, will be followed after a time by an obvious diminution of the anterior corpora quadrigemina. A change of this nature has been effected in animals by putting out their eyes. The inferences from these facts are, first, the relation between certain parts (organs) of the brain and particular functions; and, secondly, the effect of exercise in preserving the former of their requisite fulness and density of structure.

Various morbid states of the brain are noticed by Dr. Vimont, but without any novelty or special application.

Mental disorders, to which the twelfth chapter is dedicated, is too extensive a theme for us to engage in at this time. Dr. Vimont points out the misleading influence of the systems of Locke and Condillac, to the standard and terminology of which medical writers attempted to adapt their descriptions of insanity; as when they would classify the varieties of this disease as so many disorders of judgment, or of imagination, memory, &c. Hence the strange contradictions into which some authors have been led by speaking, for example, of reasoning madness, which would be equivalent to saying that the patient is mad, and yet he is not mad. Well may we doubt that these persons were on the right path, when, in addition to such metaphysical mysticism, they attempted to find the causes of insanity in the colour of the hair, and of the eyes and skin, and in the temperament. Strange, indeed, than men, calling themselves observers, could not see that madness existed with every variety of the hair, eyes, and skin, and of temperament; and that it was to the brain, the material centre of all mental relations, to which they should look. Dr. Vimont may be thought to use language somewhat harsh, though it approaches unhappily too near the truth, when he says, "I am not afraid to assert publicly, after having read the treatises published up to this time on the disorders of the intellectual faculties, that they all seem to me to have been written by gossips, crones, and nurses; so much do they abound in contradictions, and in a jumble of popular notions and prejudices, characteristic of credulity and ignorance." From this general censure an exception ought to be made in favour of the work on Mental Derangement by

Dr. Andrew Combe, in which he has, to a certain extent, carried out the plan recommended by Dr. Vimont, viz. to observe the connection between the mental disorder and the lesions of the parts on which it depends; and to note all those disorders of the mind of a general nature, dependent upon a want of energy or of excessive excitement of the cerebral nervous system. In the first class we should find idiots, or persons of feeble intellect, who sometimes have a good conformation of head; and, in the second place, monomaniacs, whose cerebral organs, without being greatly developed, may be morbidly excited, and cause derangement of their corresponding faculties. The author (Dr. V.) carries out his inquiries on these points under the heads of *idiotism*, *monomania*, and *hypochondriasis*.

Here we pause, and suspend for a while any further analysis of Dr. Vimont's work on Human and Comparative Phrenology, although we have only gone through a part, and that not the larger of the two. It will have been seen by the reader, that although the author fully believes in the phrenological doctrines, viz. the plurality and distinct character of the affective and intellectual faculties, and the correspondence between these and cerebral organisation, and the manifestation of this latter by the configuration of the external surface of the cranium, yet he is not a servile follower of Gall and Spurzheim, or of Mr. Combe and others. Dr. V. acts the part of a true philosopher; he has assured himself that the system is a true one, and he does not feel inclined to reject or discredit it, because all the details recorded by his predecessors are not as accurate as could be desired, He affirms the truth and value of cranioscopy; even though there be frontal sinuses, sometimes thickened crania, and sometimes thick muscles covering a portion of the cranium. He affirms and demonstrates the harmony between the cranioscopical observations made on man and those on animals; not grounding his belief on the sizes and weights of the human brain relatively with those of the brain of animals, but upon the developement of the latter in particular regions. We may, hereafter, have an opportunity of showing, that although he differs from other phrenologists in respect to the functions of some of the cerebral organs, he is in accordance with them respecting the location of the classes and orders—those for the affective, and those for the intellectual faculties—and in believing that the only true basis of a system of mental philosophy which shall be applicable to education, jurisprudence, and the treatment of insanity is the physiology of the brain as indicated and taught by phrenology

All this may seem to be rank quackery to the worthy certifiers of the wisdom and power of the *ad captandum*, superficial, and unfair arguments and expositions contained in Dr. Sewall's two lectures

But if they should look a little into the subject, they would see that it partakes singularly of the aspect of a science, in its large array of facts, and the numerous and harmonious inference from these for the guidance of man in his individual capacity, and for the maintenance of his varied and important social relations. If the legal gentlemen who have committed themselves by a declaration of opinion, had paused a little, and not allowed their prejudices to bind them, like a retaining fee, to the advocacy of a singularly shallow plea, they would have found that the evidence is all on the other side— evidence of a distinct positive kind, in singular contrast with the gossiping, hearsay, and second-hand opinions of the metaphysical school. Teachers, heads of colleges, might, seeing how utterly barren has been their favourite philosophy through all time down to the present, look with a little more patience on a scheme of reform, which could hardly be carried into effect without some improvement resulting. Certain doctors of divinity and theologians might be counselled not to make their own ignorance the standard of science, nor their prejudices the test of other people's orthodoxy ; but rather to learn a little more of the wonderful mechanism and harmony of the works of the Creator, about whose wisdom, in the adaptation of means to ends, they sometimes discourse. More especially useful to them in their vocation, and as a check to hasty and intolerant judgment of the effect and tendency of what they do not at once understand, would be the study of physiology, and of natural science in general. With a knowledge of the commonest elements of anatomy and physiology, they would hardly commit themselves, as they every now and then do, by the utterance of such an absurdity as the accusation against phrenology of its fostering materialism. They are shocked, pious souls! at the idea of the brain being the material instrument of mind, and of its consisting of many organs on which depend the display of the mental faculties.

We would just remind such objectors, that their own creed of philosophy partakes fully as much of materialism as phrenology does. They may indeed discard the brain as useless ; but they will not venture to reject also the five senses. If they should ever descant on the knowledge of the colours, forms, distances of objects, on the beauties of the landscape, and the charms of art in statuary and painting, what are all these but phenomena resulting from the impression of matter on matter, of inanimate matter on animate matter. Is the mechanism of the eye spiritual or material? Could the mind perceive an external object, unless the image of the latter were impressed on the retina, which is the termination of the optic nerve—both of them portions of matter? But the process does not

end here; the material chain, of which one end is the eye, is con
nected at the other end with a certain portion of brain called th(
anterior *corpora quadrigemina*, the entireness of which is just a
necessary for vision as that of the optic nerve or of the globe of th(
eye. The man, therefore, who speaks of the eye seeing, or of th(
ear hearing, is just as much a materialist as he who speaks of th(
brain forming ideas of colours and forms, or of sound and harmony
Abrogate the five senses, and what would be the amount of ideas
the channels are all closed, and nothing can reach the mind, as th(
metaphysician would say, or the brain, as the phrenologist alleges
Each external sense has its own organic structure and mechanism
a mere modification in fact of matter: each sense depends for it
display of function on a particular portion of the brain; the optic
nerve with one, the auditory nerve with another, the olfactory with
a third portion, and so on of the rest. These nerves and the con
tiguous portions of brain have specific functions, each being acte(
on by its particular stimulus, and by it alone. Light will stimulat(
the retina and optic nerve, but has no effect on the auditory nerve
or the nerves of touch—as the retina in its turn is not susceptible o
the impressions which on the auditory give rise to the sensations o
sound. There is yet another series of nerves, connected also with
different parts of the brain, and distributed to various organs through
which these latter are moved. Without the aid of these, the ey(
would be fixed in its socket, its muscles would be powerless, and (
most limited range of vision would result. A knowlege of th(
functions of these several nerves—respectively of the senses, and fo
motion—was never acquired by an observation of their texture an(
structure, nor by any kind of observation, *à priori*. Nor, now tha
their functions are known, can we find any adequate explanation i(
differences of organisation. The thing is received as an ultimat(
fact, nor is any physiologist adventurous enough, in quixotic spirit
ualism, to deny that we see by means of the eye, and in virtue o
the connection of this organ with the brain; and that we hea
through the ear, and on account of its connection with the brain
merely because he cannot detect any notable differences betwee(
the optic nerve and the olfactory one, and between the two portion
of the brain with which they are severally united. Even Dr. Sewal
would not hesitate to teach this much physiology to the worthy pre
sidents of the college, and of the theological seminaries, who are s(
much alarmed at the materialism of phrenology. It is very true tha
the doctor would at the same time inculcate, and the worthy presi
dents would believe a materialism as positive and evident as that o
the phrenologists. The difference between the two schools consist

in this: Dr. Sewall and his friends would persuade us that a man can think, act, and have the affections of his nature, with the aid alone of that arrangement of matter which consists of the five senses, their nerves, and some of the minuter parts of the basis of the brain, connected with these nerves. The phrenologists, on the other hand, believe that the brain was not given by the Maker in vain, but that its hemispheres perform great and important functions, in completion of those of the inferior organic apparatus just mentioned. The organs of the brain are, they think, those of the internal senses; the eye, ear, &c., are the organs of the external senses.

We cannot say, then, of the two schools, that the one is, in its doctrine, spiritual, and the other material. Both admit the necessity of a material structure and organisation for the formation of ideas, and processes of thought: but the one denies in a great measure the necessity of a brain; the other admits it, and sees in it a complicated apparatus. Dr. Sewall and his friends, certain doctors of law and divinity, and distinguished politicians, &c., are advocates of what may, for distinction's sake, be called brainless materialism, and the philosophy of the external senses alone. For ourselves, and with all becoming respect for such authority, backed, as it is, by an ex-president and a judge of the Supreme Court, we still believe that the time has not yet come when a man can dispense with his brain, and walk, for occasional convenience, like St. Denis, with his head under his arm.

ARTICLE II.

ON THE PRIMARY FUNCTION OF THE ORGAN MARKED "?"

BY M. B. SAMPSON.

Phrenology being a system of philosophy of the human mind, and, as such, professing to throw light on all the primitive powers of human feeling, must, to a certain extent, remain in an imperfect and unsatisfactory state so long as any specific and inherent desire or affection can be shown to exist, as a uniform principle, in the mind of man, on the nature of which it can throw no light, or bring no collateral evidence or illustration.

The science has succeeded in winning the acceptance of some of the most comprehensive minds of the present day, by the clearness and simplicity of its rudimentary principles, among which there is none more in harmony with our perceptive and reasoning powers

than that which teaches us that man is provided with specia
faculties to adapt him to each physical and moral law of the worl
in which he is placed, and that it is upon the harmonious an
healthy action of such faculties that his happiness and safety ar
made entirely to depend. The phrenological system does no
embrace a single organ, the deprivation of which would not prove i
some way fatal to our physical or moral safety, or the functions o
which could be supplied by the action of any other faculty.

By the exposition of this view, much has been done to enlarg
our ideas of the plan of our existence, and of the ultimate destinie
of our race; but in estimating the effect of the various facultie
which have been hitherto ascertained, it remains to be seen if i
will give a full, harmonious and *complete* picture of the constitutio
of man, or if there still exist any emotions common to the huma
mind, and having reference to some moral or physical law of nature
for the manifestation of which phrenologists have failed to offer an
explanation, or to discover any organ in the brain.

There is a mental emotion peculiar to all men, and strongl
characteristic of many, which cannot be referred to the action o
any organ which has hitherto been located. An emotion whicl
takes root in the contemplation of that which we are accustomed t
consider as one of the most important laws of our moral destiny
and the absence of which would render us incapable of appreciating
even in the remotest degree, one of the most sublime attributes o
the Deity himself.

The sentiment to which I allude, is that which impels us to th
contemplation of ETERNITY.

That the perception of time is one of the peculiar conditions o
our relation to the external world, is not a more incontrovertibl
fact than that the tendency of our desires to an eternity of being i
a condition of our moral nature. If, therefore, among the percep
tive faculties we find an organ that adapts us to our destiny in time
we might well expect among the moral faculties to discover a
organ that should adapt us to our destiny in eternity.

Upon a full consideration of the primary functions of the variou
organs which up to the present time have been acknowledged, i
will be seen that there is not one to which this tendency of th
mind can be referred. It is impossible to attribute it to the actio
of " Hope," because the feeling is very frequently exhibited in it
greatest force by those in whom the sentiment of Hope is exceed
ingly deficient; and many individuals have been known, whos
thoughts of the future have been of a sad and desponding characte
yet to whom the idea of an *eternity* of pain seemed preferable t

that of utter extinction. Moreover, Hope does not point out the nature of the thing to be desired—it merely imparts the belief that the desires of the other faculties will be attained, and consequently, of itself, would never suggest a longing either for endless duration or ultimate extinction. If we turn to the organ of Marvellousness or Faith (?), we shall meet with the same result, for we have abundant testimony that this faculty is primarily intended to impart a belief in our spiritual existence, independent of our physical organisation, which renders us capable of a future state of being, but which (unless it can perform two functions) possesses no power of impressing upon us, as an irresistible sentiment, the idea that that state is to be eternal.

Moreover, many instances may be cited in which the abstract conception of eternity and boundless space seems to have been prominently manifested and dwelt upon with a delight that has been called forth by the simple and isolated idea. It seems to have been a marked characteristic of Byron's mind, as will be shown by the following passages, selected almost at random from his works. Cain thus apostrophises the wide expanse to which he is conveyed by his tempter :—

> "Oh, thou beautiful
> And unimaginable ether! and
> Ye multiplying masses of increased
> And still increasing lights! what are ye ?   What
> Is this blue wilderness of interminable
> Air?
> *   *   *   *   *
>   Do ye
> Sweep on, in your unbounded revelry,
> Through an aerial universe of endless
> Expansion, at which my soul aches to think,
> *Intoxicated with* ETERNITY ?"

And upon his return from his survey of those myriads of starry worlds,

> "Of which our own
> Is the dim and remote companion in
> Infinity of life,"

be thus replies to his brother's question, " What hast thou seen ?"

> "The dead,
> The immortal, the *unbounded*, the omnipotent,
> The overpowering mysteries of *space*—
> The innumerable worlds that were and are—
> A whirlwind of such overwhelming things,
> Suns, moons, and earths, upon their loud-voiced spheres
> Singing in thunder round me, as have made me
> Unfit for mortal converse."

Abel also addresses the Supreme Being thus—

> "Sole Lord of light,
> Of good, and glory, and ETERNITY!"

In Manfred, the same tendency is exhibited in almost every sentence.—His "joy is in the wilderness," and his spirit triumphs in all the sublimity of nature.

> "To roll along
> On the swift whirl of the new-breaking wave
> Of river, stream, or ocean, in their flow,
> In these my early strength exulted; or
> To follow through the night the moving moon,
> The stars and their developement; or catch
> The dazzling lightnings till my eyes grew dim,
> These were my pastimes   *   *   *
>   Then I passed
> The nights of years in sciences untaught,
> Save in the old time; and with time and toil,
> And terrible ordeal, and such penance
> As in itself hath power upon the air,
> And spirits that do compass air and earth,
> *Space*, and the *peopled infinite*, I made
> Mine eyes familiar with ETERNITY."

In the mind of Milton, this emotion must have held a very powerful sway. He found his happiness in " thoughts which wander through eternity," and he thus anticipated the day when " they that, by their labour, counsels, and prayers, have been earnest for the common good of religion and their country, shall receive above the inferior orders of the blessed, the regal addition of principalities, legions and thrones into their glorious titles, and in super-eminence of beatific vision, *progressing the dateless and irresoluble circle of eternity*, shall clasp inseparable hands with joy and bliss in over measure for ever."*

But perhaps its most perfect embodyment is to be found in the following anecdote of the celebrated R bert Hall, which I extract from a recent publication, entitled "The Life Book of a Labourer.'

" Upon the eternity of heaven he made, as I conceived, a memorable and striking remark. Would that I could record it with the fire, force, and freedom of the speaker! 'Sir, it is the perpetuity of heaven on which my soul reposes. If the Deity, sir, had assured me that I should be a dweller in the heavenly temple for any limited period, how long soever it might be, still, if it had an end, it would not be heaven! My thoughts, sir, would take wing beyond it. I should be continually harassing myself with the conjecture of what was to succeed beyond the end. This, sir, would mar to me all the

* A Treatise on Christian Doctrine, by John Milton.

melody of heaven. Its sweetness is its endlessness. Once in the heavenly temple, thence the saint goes out no more for ever.' "

All men delight more or less in whatever carries their existence forwards or backwards over the mere span of their actual and bodily life. Eternity having no end, can have had no beginning, and the faculty which would adapt us to a comprehension of its nature would therefore carry us to the *past* with the same force as it would exert towards the future. Accordingly, it will, I think, invariably be found that those who possess a tendency to let their thoughts dwell upon the one, will turn with equal ardour to the other. He who delights to trace his ancestry amidst the dust of ages, is most anxious to transmit his name to posterity; and the antiquary who ponders over the ruined tower, is most zealous to uphold and strengthen it, that it may stand as a monument through succeeding times. I am disposed to believe, that it is mainly to a faculty of this nature that the desire for posthumous fame may be attributed. To those who possess it, durability is always a paramount consideration; and in whatever they might undertake, either in literature or art, they would be buoyed up by the wish to produce something " that the world should not willingly let die."

Of course every idea connected with eternity partakes of the obscure; and the knowledge of the tendency which exists in the human mind to delight in this emotion, has often been turned to account by those who sought their own advancement, by appealing to the passions or prejudices of their fellow-men. In despotic governments, it is the practice to keep their chief as much as possible from the public eye; and the same policy has been pursued in many cases of religion. Almost all the heathen temples were obscure; and even in the barborous temples of the Indians at the present day, they keep their idol in a dark part of the hut, which is consecrated to his worship. In like manner, too, the Druids performed all their ceremonies in the bosom of the darkest woods, and in the shade of the oldest and most spreading oaks.

It may be said, that in these cases the object aimed at was to rouse a feeling of terror by the excitement of Cautiousness, but the object also was to gratify and chain the imagination. Now Cautiousness does not delight in the obscure, and although it may be excited thereby, it is excited only in a painful manner. Cautiousness is gratified only when we are in possession of a thorough knowledge of our situation, and of the certain means by which the continuance of our safety may be insured. If a shadowy and threatening figure were to approach, Cautiousness would endeavour to make it out, so that it might take the necessary measures of defence, while the mental feelings that is excited by the sublime would increase it mystery, and exaggerate its terrors.

It has been well remarked, that it is this power of carrying ou: thoughts to the indefinite and eternal, that aids in "exalting our idea of the Supreme Being, that removes it farther from humanity and c scattered polytheism, and makes it profound and intense as i becomes more universal." By its influence, we associate with ou: thoughts of God's power the idea that " if we fly into the uttermos parts of the earth, it is there also; if we turn to the east or the west we cannot escape from it ;" and while Veneration offers up the lan guage of adoration, it tells the worshipper that wherever it may be breathed, in the society of men, or on the solitary void of ocean, in the frozen stillness of an arctic night, or beneath the heat of the torrid zone, it will assuredly be heard by Him

> " Whose temple is all space.
> Whose altar, earth, sea, skies !"

If the foregoing remarks be correctly founded, the question tha may be addressed to phrenologists then arises, " In what part of the brain is the organ of this faculty located, or does your science with hold from it a local habitation ?" I believe that, in reply to this, i may be stated that the organ has been discovered—that almost al of its effects have been noted in an isolated manner by differen observers, each of whom has endeavoured to build up some partia theory out of the detached manifestations which had severally attracted attention, but who, failing to keep in mind that whateve: its primary function may be, it must be such as shall be in harmony with some great law of nature, have produced but partial anc unsatisfactory hypotheses.

In the phrenological bust, there is a space running laterally from the organ of Ideality, which is marked " ? " I propose to submit for the consideration of the reader, the various observations which have been made respecting its function.

Mr. Combe is disposed to consider it as imparting the sentimen of *Sublimity*. Speaking of Ideality, he says, " In some individuals the front part of this organ is most developed ; in others, the back part ; and from a few cases which I have observed, there is reasor to believe that the latter is a separate organ. The back part is lef without a number on the bust, and a mark of interrogation i: inscribed on it, to denote that the function is a subject of inquiry The back part touches Cautiousness ; and I suspect that excitemen of this organ in a moderate degree, is an ingredient in the emotior of the *sublime*. The roar of thunder or of a cataract, the beetling cliff suspended high in air, and threatening to cause ruin by its fall, impress the mind with feelings of terror; and it is only such objects that produce the sentiment of sublimity."

[I would here remind the reader, that the excitement of Cautiousness is evidently only an occasional effect, and not a cause of the emotion of sublimity. The most sublime object in nature, is the deep blue sky, gemmed with its innumerable and distant worlds, as seen when sailing at night upon a calm and unbounded sea; and although this awakens a deep sense of reverential awe, it has little of real terror in its nature.]

A writer in the London Phrenological Journal, Mr. Hytche, (No. 3, new series,) thinks that this organ imparts a love of *Antiquities.* He says, that upon examining with this view the heads of various persons, he "found almost invariably that a developement on the part of the head marked "?" was presented, which corresponded with the intensity or deficiency of the individual's love of the *past.*"

An earlier writer, under the signature J. K., (Vol. X, No. 53), had previously expressed a similar opinion—in confirmation of which, he quoted the following lines, as breathing the spirit of the sentiment to which he alluded:—

> " Eleven years we now may tell,
>   Since we have known each other well;
>   Since riding side by side, our hand
>   First drew the voluntary brand.
>   And though through many a changing scene
>   Unkindnsss never came between,
>   *Away those winged years have flown,*
>   *To join the mass of ages gone.*
>   Still days, and weeks, and months but seem,
>   The recollection of a dream—
>   So still we glide down to the sea
>   Of fathomless ETERNITY."—*Marmion.*

The words printed in italics will show how singularly applicable this quotation will be found to the more extended view which I have suggested. He goes on to say, "What seemed to strengthen my opinion that that part of the brain marked unascertained is the organ of a faculty which gives a tendency to the mind to look to the *past,* was the fact of its being immediately below another faculty which gives the mind a tendency to look to the *future.* At all events, my opinion respecting the functions of this organ is not inconsistent with its site."

[In reference to this, it is necessary to observe that the writer appears to labour under a misapprehension with regard to the function of the organ of Hope. I do not consider that Hope gives any specific *desire* with reference to the future. It gives a belief that all things will work together for good, and that, as I before observed the desires of all the other faculties will eventually be attained. I even a person desired that death should be to him nothing more than a dreamless sleep, then, however strongly some of the other facultie might resist the idea, I cannot help thinking that Hope, at least would whisper to his mind that his wish would be granted, and tha such a fate did in reality await him. If Hope is to be considered merely as an organ that "gives the mind a tendency to look to the future," it must very frequently find Cautiousness performing it part, and acting as a very sufficient substitute.]

In the last number of the London Journal, (October, 1839,) Dr Maxwell furnishes an interesting article on this organ, in which he states his belief that the primary function is to impart a *conservative* habit, and he proposes to give it the title of "Conservativeness." He has found it large in persons having a strong regard for *perma nence* and durability, and in those who have shown anxiety to retain and transmit their possessions unimpaired; and in connection with this subject, he alludes to the law of entail. It will readily be seen that this feeling, although it is only a subordinate one, is in perfec accordance with the view I have taken. Dr. Maxwell further says "This faculty appears to give the desire to retain, or rather a natural aptness to *preserve*, property, independent of the desire to acquire it;" and again, such is the desire and regard for durability, that it imparts that, with one in whom this organ is large, "a suit of clothes will last three times as long, as with it small." It evidently, according to Dr. Maxwell's view, gives an emotion of delight in the contemplation of that which is *lasting*. Eternity will last for ever!

The situation of the organ coincides most completely with the views which I have stated. It runs laterally from Ideality, which endues us with a sense of moral harmony (which can alone be truly permanent), and which, in its physical perceptions, delights in the compactness and smoothness of globular forms; while the only mate rial figure that has ever been found to aid the expression of our idea of eternity is derived from this, of the circle. On the other side the organ is bounded by Cautiousness, which checks the tendency that a large developement of it would give to penetrate into the dangers of the unknown dark, teaching us that although

"The wide, the unbounded prospect lies before us,"

yet

"Shadows, clouds, and darkness, rest upon it."

The following passage from Byron's Cain, will prove how com pletely the feeling of the sublime might be separated from that of

ution.   At the same time it shows how necessary the exercise of
ıe latter faculty becomes, when the former is actively excited.
ʼain, gazing on the distant worlds in space, exclaims,

> "Oh God—Oh Gods! or whatsoe'er ye are!
> How beautiful ye are! how beautiful
> Your works or accidents, or whatsoe'er
> They may be!   Let me die, as atoms die,
> (If that they die,) or know ye in your might
> And knowledge!   My thoughts are not in this hour
> Unworthy what I see, though my dust is:
> Spirit! *let me expire, or see them nearer.*"

I have made many observations on this organ, which have inva-
iably strengthened the idea which I now entertain respecting it.   I
ave found in all persons in whom it is largely developed, a never-
ıiling impression of the transitory nature of the present life—a dis-
osition, also, to revert to the past, coupled with strong considera-
ons for the future, and for the interest of those who may come
fter them—together with an enjoyment of all that is vast, un-
ounded, permanent, and grand.   I remember one instance of a
entleman who possessed a large developement of it, who told me
ıat although the thought of death was always present to his mind,
 was often welcomed, since he indulged a fancy that it might bring
im to a more exalted state of being, in which might be unveiled to
im the sublime knowledge of distant worlds, and the unbounded
ıysteries of space and eternity.

Perhaps I may be allowed to give an illustration of its effects,
om my own experience.

Last year, I visited the Falls of Niagara.   I approached them
om the Canada side, and on my first view of them was greatly dis-
ıpointed with respect to their sublimity, but agreeably surprised by
ıeir exquisite beauty.   After crossing the bridge over the rapids,
owever, I became fully impressed with their grandeur.   The
ıought of the countless ages through which they had rolled on,
ıen took possession of my mind; and now, whenever my recollec-
on turns to them, the same idea is always paramount, and I feel all
ıeir power when I contemplate that they are still rolling on, and
ill continue to roll on, with undiminished force, long after the pre-
ınt race, and many future dateless generations, shall have passed
lently away.

There is much to excite an emotion of this description in the
ıily operations of nature.   When we consider the permanence of
ıe laws by which the Creator upholds the universe, its endless
ıcay, and endless renovation—and when we call to mind, out of the
umerous illustrations that every where surround us, the simple fact,

that the rays of light which will this evening reach our sight from the nearest of the fixed stars, must, even at the velocity with which light travels, have left that star centuries ago, at the time when Alfred reigned in England, we may faintly approach to an estimate of the littleness of our present existence, and of the illimitable power of that great Being by whom the universe has been created and is upheld.

I conclude, therefore, that this organ is bestowed upon man to adapt him to the great *principle* of eternity. It is a noble requirement of his moral destiny!

London, November 1, 1839.

ARTICLE III.

REMARKS ON PHRENOLOGICAL SPECIMENS, CABINET, ETC.

The utility and value of specimens, to prove and illustrate the principles of any science, must be obvious to every one. In all the sciences which depend upon observation and experiment for proof and elucidation, we find those objects which appeal directly to the senses to be of the utmost importance. These objects may be either the products of nature or the creations of art. In many instances, we cannot multiply specimens of the former, nor even obtain them in that state or perfection which may be necessary for useful purposes, and therefore must resort to human agency and contrivance. Some of the sciences, such as geology, botany, zoology, &c., deriving their evidences from observation, must depend chiefly for support and illustration on the immediate productions of nature, either animate or inanimate; while other sciences, connected more directly with experiment, such as chemistry, natural philosophy, &c., are more dependent for proof and application on human agency. It becomes necessary, therefore, to have recourse to such means, both for studying and teaching those branches. And accordingly we find that the most zealous and efficient cultivators of science have always been deeply engaged in the collection of specimens appertaining to their several departments of study.

Phrenology, being also a demonstrative science, depends for proof and illustration upon objects which appeal equally direct to the senses. The evidences of its truth are of the most positive and irresistible character, and, when properly presented and canvassed, cannot fail to produce conviction in every unbiased mind. The materials for this purpose are, perhaps, as ample and diversified as those belonging to any other science. It summons in support of its truth, not only every individual of the human species, but even the greater part of the animal creation. Wherever there is *brain*, whether performing the functions of the feeblest instinct, or of the most exalted mental manifestations, we may find evidence of the truth of this science. The student who is somewhat familiar with its facts and principles, will find objects of interest and study on every side. But, as in other departments of knowledge, those who are inquirers or learners, must first become acquainted with the *elementary* principles of the science. For this purpose, not only books are wanted, but material objects which may be *seen* and *handled*. And in most cases these can be easily obtained. They may consist of skulls, busts, casts, drawings, paintings, wax prepara. tions, &c. They may be procured and possessed by individuals, societies, or public institutions.

The cultivators of phrenology have not been negligent in collect. ing specimens to prove and illustrate the principles of their science. Should a full and minute history of their labours in this respect be given, it would bear comparison with the results of the same number of cultivators of any other science, labouring under disad. vantages equally as great and discouraging. As phrenology has thus far been spurned from the notice of public institutions and associations, formed for cultivating science and encouraging its advocates, phrenologists have been compelled to labour in this field as *individuals*, in despite, too, of the most bitter opposition, and to make collections at the expense of the greatest personal sacrifices and exertions. We might allude to the labours of Gall, Spurzheim, Deville, and others, but it is unnecessary. It is true that, in some instances, collections have been made by associations, such as the Paris, London, and Edinburgh societies. But in order that such collections may be permanent, and become constantly increasing in extent and value, they should be connected with some public institu. tion, or national society, and enlist in their behalf as many indivi. duals as possible who are deeply interested in scientific researches.

We may revert to the discussion of this subject again, with par. ticular reference to the state and advancement of the science in this country ; but, for the present, must satisfy ourselves by introducing some excellent suggestions on the objects, materials, and arrange. ment of a phrenological cabinet, contained in a report drawn up by a committee of the New York Phrenological Society. This report we believe, has never been published, and it contains some observa tions which must interest phrenologists generally. The committee

was appointed by the president, Dr. J. W. Francis, and consisted c
Mr. A. Boardman, Dr. C. A. Lee, and Dr. B. Drake.   Their repor
was made to the society, February 28, 1839, and is as follows :—

*Report of the Committee appointed by the Phrenological Society o
New York to draw up a plan for a Phrenological Cabinet.*

The committee appointed to draft a plan for a phrenologica
cabinet, respectfully report :

That, in their opinion, the establishment of an extensive and well
arranged cabinet is an object worthy of the society's best efforts, fo
the following, among other, reasons—

1. By means of such a cabinet, the great phrenological principle
that " As is the brain, other things being equal, so is the menta
capacity of man," would be readily demonstrable.

2. Such a cabinet would enable the members to pursue phrenolo
gical investigations extensively at a small personal expense, thui
rendering membership extremely desirable.

3. Such a cabinet would form not only a centre of attraction, bu
a bond of union.   Nothing seems to unite men more closely or per
manently than common interest in property, the accumulation o
which is, indeed, the result of Acquisitiveness, but, in the case
before us, of Acquisitiveness acting under the control of intellect anc
the higher sentiments, for a purpose which affords them refinec
satisfaction.   In contemplating such a cabinet, Form, Size, anc
Individuality, would be gratified by the observation of the specimens
Order and Locality, by their arrangement ; Comparison would love
to dwell on the correspondence between cerebral developement anc
mental manifestation, and to note the dissimilarity of heads apper
taining to men distinguished by opposite mental characteristics
Causality would be agreeably exercised in recognising between the
developements of the brain and mental capacities the relation o
cause and effect ; while the higher sentiments would delight in these
studies, as a powerful means of human advancement.

In developing their plan of a cabinet, your committee will treat,

1. Of the *material* of which it should consist. ·
2. Of the *arrangement* of the material.
3. Of the *accommodations* for a cabinet.

Material.—The material of a phrenological cabinet should consist
principally of skulls, casts, plates, drawings, and preparations ; anc
here your committee would respectfully suggest the importance o:
discrimination in selecting specimens.   Every specimen should be
for the purpose of illustrating some fact or principle.   The value o
a cabinet cannot be inferred from its extent.

Your committee would suggest, too, that busts are unnecessarily large and unwieldy, inasmuch as the shoulders subserve no scientific purpose. The mere mask, too, is an unobjectionable form of specimen, inasmuch as the correlation of organs is so intimate, that to tell the influence of any organ whatever, the whole organisation should be known. Those forms of specimen which your committee think most appropriate, are the skull and entire head, the latter placed on a pedestal just large enough for its support.

Arrangement.—The great principle which has guided your committee in making the following suggestions, is, that the specimens should be so arranged as most readily to prove, and most clearly to illustrate, the principles and details of phrenology.

To prove that the brain is the organ of mind, and to illustrate, in a general way, the influence of form and size, your committee recommend that a series of casts and skulls be arrayed, commencing with those of idiots, progressing through intermediate grades, and terminating with those of the giant minds of the world.

To show the influence of the direction in which the brain lies, your committee would recommend that a series of contrasted specimens of known characters be arranged in groups, each specimen to resemble the others, of the same group, in general size, but to differ in the relative size of the three regions.

To show the difference of organisation on which the difference between the mental characteristics of the sexes depends, male and female skulls, human and comparative, might be arranged in contrasted pairs.

National skulls might be arranged, 1st, To furnish specimens of the crania of the various races, nations, and tribes of men; 2d, To illustrate in a more especial manner phrenological principles. For the first purpose, crania might be grouped in five classes; one for the skulls of European, a second for those of Asiatic, a third for those of African, a fourth for those of American nations, and a fifth for those of the natives of the islands of the Pacific Ocean. Each class having its appropriate subdivisions. For the second purpose, skulls belonging to nations widely differing in character should be placed side by side, that the correspondence of character and development might be manifest. Thus, the skull of the Englishman might be placed beside that of the Hindoo; and that of the timid Peruvian, whose opposition to the Spaniards was as the pecking of the dove against the kite, might be placed beside that of the Carib, whose indomitable courage and independence nothing but death could overcome.

Your committee would recommend that next in order should be

placed skulls of individuals differing in age, from infancy to senility; specimens of healthy skulls, and such as have suffered alteration from disease; of those that are of average and such as are of abnormal thickness, and specimens of frontal sinuses of average and of abnormal size.

Your committee recommend that in the next place the particular faculties should be illustrated. For this purpose, there might be formed as many groups as there are organs. And in each group, the organ to be illustrated might be shown in different stages of developement, from the highest predominance to the most striking deficiency.

Succeeding to these might be groups indicating the combination of faculties which give a tendency, fondness, and capacity for particular pursuits. The heads of poets, painters, musicians, mathematicians, warriors, and others, might be thus arranged.

Having finished the arrangement of whatever relates to human phrenology, the arrangement of specimens of comparative phrenology might succeed. These would be confined, of course, to vertebral animals, and might be arranged in four divisions.

1. Skulls of mammalia.
2. Skulls of birds.
3. Skulls of reptiles.
4. Skulls of fishes.

Each division being subdivided into its appropriate classes.

Besides this general arrangement, there might be special arrangements for the more striking illustration of phrenological doctrines; for example, arranged side by side might be the crania of such birds as sing, and such as do not; of such animals as build, and such as do not; and of the carnivora and herbivora. The skull of the woodlark or nightingale and of the woodpecker, that of the lion and of the beaver, and that of the cat and of the rabbit, might be thus contrasted.

The paintings, drawings, and engravings, might be, in part, suspended round the room, and in part arranged in portfolios. Your committee would particularly recommend the society to obtain a complete set of preparations and representations, illustrative of the nervous system. Especially a series of brains, human and comparative.

Such a cabinet would, your committee believe, be one of which not only the society, but the city, might be justly proud. To the phrenologist, it would form a tower of defence which the assaults of his enemies could neither overthrow nor injure; to the phrenological student it would afford the most powerful aid; and to all true

)vers of natural science, the most rational gratification and refined
elight.

The remarks in this report on the "accommodation" of a cabinet,
1anner of "collecting specimens," &c., being rather *local* in their
ature, and of less general importance, our limits compel us to omit.

ARTICLE IV.

ON THE HARMONY BETWEEN PHRENOLOGY AND REVELATION.

1r. Editor,—

The assertion has so often been made by the most competent
udges, that phrenology is not inconsistent with revelation, that it
eed not again be repeated.   Still it is worth while occasionally to
oint out the more striking instances in which the science, in its
elineations of human nature, is confirmed by those of Holy Writ.
'or though the enlightened and philosophical mind need no facts or
xamples to show that, as the God of *revelation* is also the God of
ature, the truths of the latter must necessarily be consistent with
hose of the former, yet the less instructed often find some indvidual
1cts, or single illustrations, the best means of stopping the mouths
f gainsayers, and of disproving the assertions of captious and short-
ighted objectors.

The Apostle Paul possessed a thorough education, and enjoyed
uperior advantages for observing and studying human nature.
Vith the greatest clearness, simplicity, and compactness of lan-
uage, he describes man and his characteristics just as he found
1em.   And they have always been the same.   Let us now com-
are one of his descriptions of man with those of phrenology ; and,
: I mistake not, we shall find, on an analysis of that full and
etailed enumeration of mental manifestations contained in the latter
art of the first chapter of his Epistle to the Romans, that what he
alls the man of "vile affections"—a "reprobate mind," &c.—
ossessed qualities precisely similar to those which phrenology
rould predicate, from the extreme abuses of certain very large or
eficient cerebral developements.   (See Rom. 1 chap. 26th verse to
1e end.)

That I may not occupy too much of your space, I will endeavour
) imitate the brevity of the apostle's description.   Instead of com-
ound manifestations, I place the principle word involved, directly

opposite to the faculty which aids chiefly to produce them—thus *envy* is the result of Self-esteem, Approbativeness, and Destructiveness, it is put under each ; much of the effects of combination is still left for the reader to supply, without its being pointed out.

Amativeness, very large, ungoverned—"Fornication," *v.* 29. "Sodomy," *v.* 26, 27.

Philoprogenitiveness, very small—"Without natural affection," *v.* 31.

Adhesiveness, deficient—Have pleasure in others of like character, *v.* 32

Combativeness, very large, ungoverned—"Debate, malignity," *v.* 29

Destructiveness, very large, ungoverned—"Envy, maliciousness, murder," *v.* 29. "Backbiting," *v.* 30.

Secretiveness, very large, ungoverned ⎱ "Deceit. blasphemy," *v.* 29
Cautiousness, " " " ⎰ "Backbiting," *v.* 30.
Self-esteem, " " " "Pride," *v.* 30. "Envy," *v.* 29
Approbativeness, very large, ungoverned—"Boasting," *v.* 30. "Envy," *v.* 29.

Conscientiousness, very deficient—"Covenant breaking," *v.* 31. "Full of all unrighteousness, wickedness, and maliciousness," *v.* 29.

Firmness, very large ⎱ "Implacable, unmerciful," *v.* 31.
Benevolence, deficient ⎰

Veneration, very small, &c.—"Disobedient to parents, haters of God,' *v.* 30.

Acquisitiveness, very large, unrestrained—"Covetousness," *v.* 29.

Constructiveness, ⎱ very large ⎱ moral sentiments ⎱ "Inventors of evil
Causality, ⎰ ⎰ deficient, ⎰ things," *v.* 30.

Intellectual Faculties, (as a whole,) deficient—"Without understanding," *v.* 31. Swept away by their propensities, They do what they know to be worthy of death, *v.* 32.

The reader will perceive that *every* idea, and almost every word, contained in those seven verses of Romans—and nothing else—are wrought into this most consistent and unmitigable bad character. The analysis might be carried still farther, and thus the harmony between the two descriptions rendered more perfect and striking but I must leave that process for the reader. The abuses of the propensities and sentiments are given by the apostle with the greatest minuteness and accuracy ; for it is *their* abuses chiefly that make character positively bad. The intellect is given in the whole group, for that was enough to show that, either from deficient strength or improper exercise, it could not easily restrain such propensities. Surely, every imagination of the feelings and thoughts of such must be evil, and that, too, continually.

E. C. B.

New York, December, 1839.

ARTICLE V.

ON THE USES OF PHRENOLOGY.*

In a former number, we pointed out the grand distinction between an instinctive and a rational being. An instinctive creature receives from the Creator, not only desires to pursue certain ends, but inspiration of the best manner of attaining them. In itself it is ignorant of the power and wisdom that direct its actions. A mother among the inferior animals is impelled, by pure instinct, to administer to her offspring that kind of protection, food, and training, which its nature and circumstances require; and so admirably does she fulfil this duty, even at the first call, that human sagacity could not improve, or rather not at all equal her treatment. The actions of these animals bear the strongest marks of wisdom, founded on perfect knowledge of their own nature and circumstances; but this knowledge does not reside in them, but is their Author. A rational being, also, is endowed with instinctive tendencies to act; but, instead of being directed by Divine wisdom towards the best manner of gratifying its desires, it has received intellectual faculties, by the employment of which, it may make this discovery for itself. Man is such a being: he is impelled by a variety of propensities and sentiments; but the privilege is conferred on him of discovering, by means of his intellectual powers, in what manner he should gratify these, so as best to promote his own happiness. The Creator, who constituted the desires and directed the actions of the inferior animals, knew the *nature* of the creatures, and of the external influence to which they would be exposed, and He adjusted the one to the other, so as to secure to them the highest enjoyment of which their natures are susceptible, in reference to the general constitution of the world. Man, to render himself happy as a rational being, must discover his own nature, and that of external objects, and form his institutions, and direct his actions, with the same wise reference to those which are displayed in the habits and actions of the inferior creatures, in relation to their nature and external circumstances.

A question of vast importance, in regard to man, presents itself at the very threshold of our inquiries. Of what elements is he composed, and with what powers is he endowed? If an agriculturist were desired to superintend the cultivation of an exotic plant of the highest value for human food, of the most exquisite beauty in form

---

* From the 26th number of the Edinburgh Phrenological Journal.

and colour, and suited, when brought to perfection, for the mos
admirable purposes of general utility, he would anxiously inquire
into the constitution of the plant, into its relation to particular soils
particular temperatures, particular degrees of humidity, and, in
short, into every property inherent in itself, and into every relation
which subsisted between it and external objects which might influence its condition; and he would treat it according to the dictates of
his soundest judgment, formed upon consideration of these particular
matters of fact. Man, as a being of creation, must be dealt with in
a similar way. It is quite certain, however, that down to the present day he has never been treated in this manner; and that, if
questions were put to a thousand individuals, selected indiscriminately
out of the most enlightened countries in the world, regarding the
general physical constitution of man, the elementary faculties of his
mind, including the objects of these faculties, the habits and occupations that are best calculated to favour the healthy developement of
his corporeal frame, and to invigorate and fill with enjoyment his
mental powers, and the great aim of his existence, the answers
would present that utter discordance and contradiction which betray
profound and general ignorance on every one of the topics here
mentioned.

This condition of ignorance is necessarily fatal to man's enjoyment as a rational being. In point of fact, human institutions of
every description have hitherto emanated from his instinctive feelings and desires, guided by mere glimmerings of intelligence; and
hence arise the general misery and feeling of disappointment which
so widely pervade society, the want of satisfaction in daily pursuits,
and the incessant demand for reform in church and state, which
every where is heard. Men, in whom the inferior propensities predominate, are discontented, because too many curbs exist on their
acquisitiveness, love of power, and general desire for animal indulgence. The institutions of society contain too much of morality and
religion to be in accordance with the nature of this class. Men,
again, in whom the higher sentiments and intellect predominate, are
unhappy because the pursuits which are forced on them by existing
manners, bear too closely a reference to mere animal gratification;
they desire society in which moral and intellectual pleasures shall
be the *aim*, and the pursuit of wealth only the *means*, of existence;
and they find around them only insatiable appetites for wealth and
ostentation, constituting the *objects* of life. This class finds among
mankind much desire for good, but preposterous notions of the
objects which constitute it, and of the manner of attaining it; it discovers, in the laws, much of justice and humanity, but still larger

nfusions of absurdity, injustice, and barbarism; in the political nstitutions of the country, much that is excellent, but still more that is defective, irrational, and calculated to foster the lower, and check the progress of the higher, principles of our nature. They are therefore discontented, and loudly demand reform and improvement.

This universal discordance proves that the nature of man is a mystery to man himself; to us it appears the natural result of his past and present ignorant condition; but we look to phrenology as the means by which a better order of things will, in due time, be introduced. It will require centuries to operate the change; but, in the history of the race, these are like days in the life of an individual. Some of our reasons for expecting this advantage from phrenology, are the following:—

To render man happy, his body must be maintained in a state of constant health. The nervous system, including the brain, is the fountain of all enjoyment in sensation and emotion, and it is most intimately connected with respiration and digestion. When all external stimulus is withdrawn, and the individual is thrown entirely back on his own sensations, he will experience a pleasing consciousness of existence when in perfect health; if he does not do so, if any sensation of weakness, listlessness, irritation, anxiety, or unhappiness, be experienced, the corporeal frame is not in its best condition; it is not in that state which the Creator, in endowing it with the susceptibility of happiness, intended it to be, and by bestowing reason on man, commanded it to be maintained. To secure health, the individual must exert his muscular frame for several hours every day in the open air, or at least exposed to a free circulation of air; he must observe the rules of cleanliness and temperance; he must exercise his moral and intellectual faculties several hours every day on pursuits congenial to their nature; and he must sleep in well-aired apartments, and neither for too long nor too short a time.

The institutions and manners of society at present render it absolutely impossible to fulfil these laws of our nature. Mechanics are compelled to labour with their muscles beyond what is serviceable to their moral and intellectual enjoyment; men in the middle ranks of life are confined within shops, counting-houses, or writing-chambers, so as to be denied muscular exertion adequate to maintain perfect health, and their pursuits have reference so exclusively to objects connected with the gratification of the inferior feelings, that no adequate stimulus or cultivation is afforded to their moral and intellectual powers; while ladies generally, and men in the higher ranks of society in particular, are rendered miserable through want of objects of interest calculated to excite them to that degree of bodily and mental exertion, without which the nervous system becomes a mass of disease, and the fountain of inexpressible suffering. The males of the higher classes, who seek to relieve themselves from this insanity and its consequent miseries, betake themselves to fox-hunting, horse-racing, prize-fighting, cigar-smoking, drinking, and seduction ; in short, through want of objects and pursuits calculated to gratify their rational nature, they abandon themselves to the indulgence of their animal propensities, and corporeal appetites— except a few, whose superior faculties carry them to literature, the improvement of their estates, the fine arts, or politics, as occupations.

Phrenology, if taught as an elementary branch of education, would undoubtedly remedy some of these evils. It would demonstrate to the senses and understanding of men,

1st, The intimate connection between sensation and bodily health ; and if this were rendered palpable to every capacity, men could not resist modifying their institutions and habits of life, so as to secure more of health and enjoyment from this source than at present. It would be felt as altogether inconsistent with the indubitable rights of human beings, to subject the lower classes to that degradation of their rational nature which is inseparable from excessive labour, and absence of moral and intellectual stimulus ; and it would no longer be reckoned a degradation on the part of the intelligent and refined, to submit regularly to that degree of muscular exertion which the Creator has rendered indispensable to health.

2dly, The fact that man is a rational and social being, would be practically acted upon. If this truth and its consequences were understood by the mass of society, it would be seen, that until social institutions, and the *leading* aim of *daily pursuits*, shall bear reference to the gratification of the *moral* and *intellectual powers*, happiness cannot be obtained ; and if this law of the human constitution were *generally* understood and recognised improvement would assuredly follow. In no country have human pursuits been regulated on this principle ; Britain is widely departing from it in her excessive exertions to acquire wealth. It ought never to be forgotten, that hitherto the most enlightened men have never known human nature as an object of science ; they have known it only through their individual feeling and experience, and been extremely ignorant of the influence of organisation on its exercise and enjoyments ; while the great mass of mankind, rich and poor, in every country, have never given it, and its wants and capabilities, one moment's consideration. The aim of life of most individuals has been determined exclusively by the pursuits and manners existing around them; they have viewed only that portion of the world and human nature, which lay nearest to themselves, and which was calculated to influence their private pursuits; and remained unconcerned about, and totally ignorant of, every institution and interest which existed beyond this limited sphere. Phrenology, when taught to youth, will instruct them concerning the nature of man, as it exists in the race, and as modified in individuals; it will prove to them the relative importance of the different faculties, enable them to form a just estimate of the relation of every pursuit and institution, first to these faculties, and secondly, to the general promotion of human enjoyment; it will demonstrate that the law of man's nature being that of a social being, individuals cannot be happy by confining their attention to their private interests, but must exert themselves to establish institutions and pursuits, formed with a due regard to the gratification of the highest elements of mind, otherwise that *all* will suffer.

3dly, Phrenology, by unfolding the functions and sphere of activity of the primitive faculties, will enable individuals to perceive that the Creator has really intended that man should enjoy existence as a rational being; and by the same means, it will afford them ultimate principles by which to judge of the truth of all doctrines, and the utility of all institutions, and to choose those which are best suited to the developement of their rational nature.

4thly, It will show that, to a vast extent, the mental qualities of individuals may be improved, by attending to the laws of physiology in the formation of marriages, and in the rearing of offspring; and,

5thly, That bodily disease, and consequent misery, may be greatly diminished by the same means. After an individual is instructed in the fundamental principles of physiology, and the most common laws of the transmission of bodily qualities, it is astonishing to what extent it becomes possible to trace the great calamities of life to ill-advised unions. Two individuals of consumptive families marry, and the children languish till the dawn of manhood, and die; two individuals belonging to families subject to fever and inflammation marry, and the children are carried off by acute diseases; two individuals of highly nervous temperaments marry, and the children die of convulsions, water in the head from over excitement of brain, or other diseases, clearly referable to the excessive exaltation of the nervous system; or one party possessing a favourably developed brain, marries one in whom the animal organs predominate, and some of the children inherit the inferior qualities, and bring sorrow and disgrace on their parents, and misery on themselves. Education is so defective, and human nature so little studied, that thousands of

individuals who are convinced of the truth of these remarks gene
rally, and who desire to act on them, find it impossible to obtain th
instruction necessary to enable them to do so. This state of educa
tion will appear intolerable when phrenology is more widely diffused

Persons who have never become acquainted with the springs c
human nature, and have no knowledge of their constitution and mod
of operation, conceive us writing mere fancies in delivering thes
opinions ; but wherever there is inherent penetration, mind is per
ceived to have fixed qualities, and powerful operating energies, a
well as matter, and confidence is felt that it may be improved an
directed. Let us not despair, therefore, of the fortunes of man.

The evils of the institutions and pursuits of society which we hav
pointed out, are not fanciful, nor are they inseparable from huma
nature. A few examples will show that they result from ignorance
We lately put the question to an excellent young man, about t
embark for India, what views he entertained of life, and the object
of his own existence ? The question was new to him. He had bee
well educated, in the common acceptation of the words, but he ha
never conceived that life had any higher aim than to acquire a for
tune, marry, rear a family, live in a fine house, drink expensiv
wines, die, and go to heaven. There was no provision in this lif
for enjoyment from the higher faculties of his nature. He was no
aware that these had any other functions to perform than to regulat
his conduct in the pursuit of the gratification of his inferior feeling:
This is the condition of mind in which almost all young men of th
upper and middle classes of society enter into active life, and nothin
can be well conceived more disadvantageous to their success an
happiness. Those who are religiously educated are not more fortu
nate ; because no sect in religion has yet addressed itself to the dut
of teaching, in a rational manner, the nature of man, the nature c
the different professions in life, and of the institutions of society, an
the relation of all these to the moral and religious faculties of th
mind ; without understanding which, no person entering upon activ
life can see his way clearly, or entertain consistent and elevate
views of duty, and the true sources of enjoyment.

This deficiency in knowledge is also remarkably exemplified i
young men born to large fortunes, who have succeeded in minorit
to their paternal estates, and on attaining twenty-one years of age
have been left to pursue their own happiness in their own way
Rational views of themselves and of human nature, and the institu
tions of society, would be invaluable to such individuals ; but the
have no adequate means of obtaining them. A story reached us, c
a young gentleman belonging to this class, not destitute of talent

and good feeling, who emerged out of the hands of his instructors in such a hopeful condition, that he devoted himself to horses and hounds, as usual; next, to coach-driving; he then married, and his post-connubial amusement was forming a float in the midst of a pond, placing cats upon it, and sending dogs to swim in and worry them.

In a speech which the young Duke of Buccleuch recently made at Dumfries, he stated that his guardians had taught him that the great duty imposed on him by his large fortune was to do *good.* This was an excellent lesson; but did they tell him *how* he could best accomplish good? If his grace were questioned on this point, we doubt much whether his intellectual perceptions of good, and the manner of pursuing it, would equal the fervency of his desires to attain it. We take the liberty to state, that, in our opinion, time dedicated to horses and hounds, beyond what is necessary for health, is not good, either to himself or his country; that the pursuit of political influence, with a view to support the existing imperfections in church and state, is not good; that idleness and frivolous occupations are not good; and that all external pomp, circumstance, and equipage, which is calculated to remove him from a knowledge of, and sympathy with, the general mass of cultivated society, are not good. On the other hand, it would be highly beneficial if he would set the example of pursuing knowledge, and applying it to useful purposes, so as to prove that he values the higher qualities of mind more than physical possessions; if he would patronise enlightened opinions; establish and support infant schools, all over his estates; promote the formation of a college in his native country, for educating the middle classes of society in general knowledge, applicable to practical purposes; endeavour to reform public institutions and the laws, so as to bring them as much as possible into harmony with the moral and intellectual faculties of man; in short, if he would view his wealth as a vast means for gratifying his Intellect, Benevolence, Veneration, Conscientiousness, and Ideality, and seek his supreme happiness in pursuits emanating from these faculties, he would do good effectually, and reap the highest reward, in the intense enjoyment of his rational nature. We cannot see a reason why, when a duke shall be born, in whom the moral and intellectual organs are large, and the temperament active, and whose education shall be conducted on the principles unfolded by phrenology, such a course of conduct should not be realised. It will then be acknowledged that the waste of life, fortune, and happiness, by the affluent, which characterises the present, as it has marked the past ages of the world, was owing in no small degree to ignorance of human nature, its wants and capacities.

In the higher ranks of life, family and ancestry are considered of great importance; nevertheless, daily instances occur of individuals sacrificing their prejudices on this head to wealth; and of aristocratical blood allying itself with mechanics or merchants, sprung from the lower walks of life, and ennobled only by wealth accumulated in these employments. The pride of ancestry arises from Self-esteem and Veneration, and has a legitimate as well as an illegitimate direction. In most of the countries of Europe, the founder of each great family was some feudal chieftain, of warlike and predatory habits, who, if he had done the same deeds in modern times, would have been designated as a robber and manslayer. On the principle that qualities of mind and body are transmitted by descent, it can be no honour to a mind which esteems its rational powers as the noblest, to derive its existence from such a source. The pride in such ancestry, which still exists, shows latent barbarism in the hearts of our nobility. Time and better education will render them ashamed of such progenitors. The real source of family pride ought to be that of a sound bodily constitution, and a moral and intellectual developement of brain, transmitted through many generations. It would be a real and positive advantage to obtain a husband or wife out of a family which had been distinguished for centuries for health and longevity, for handsome forms, agreeable features, kind, pious, and honourable dispositions, and great intellectual acumen. These qualities would render the domestic circle cheerful, animated, affectionate, and full of serene intelligence; they would command the world's respect and love, and insure success in every enterprise, so far as human virtue and sagacity could go. The admiration of ancestry, and the tendency to set a value on it, arise from instinctive feelings, and are given for the best of purposes; but the latter form of its gratification appears to us to be clearly that which alone satisfies man's rational faculties, and which, when enlightened, he will undoubtedly alone desire. The devices to found gratification of this feeling on entails and transmission of hereditary titles of nobility, without regard to the laws implanted in the human constitution, lead to lamentable failures and miserable results. No attention being given to transmit sound bodies and well constituted brains along with territory and titles, we see great landholders, whose acres have descended through centuries, wandering in beggary over Europe, while their rents are seized by creditors, who have supplied them with money squandered by them in sensual debauchery and in utter profligacy; earls and noble lords appear in a state of idiocy; and, in short, titles of nobility are found combined with incapacity and immorality of every form which the human imagination can conceive.   We repeat, that although individuals should fear and wish to avoid these calamities, instruction in human nature is so deficient, that it is almost impossible to be ce.tain of doing so ; and phrenology alone will supply this deficiency.

ARTICLE VI.

PHRENOLOGICAL CHARACTER OF WILLIAM LEGGETT, ESQ.*

BY L. N. FOWLER, NEW YORK.

Relative s ze of the organs on a scale from 1 to 7.

Amativeness, 6.	Concentrativeness, 5.
Philoprogenitiveness, 6.	Combativeness, 7.
Adhesiveness, 6.	Destructiveness, 6.
Inhabitiveness, 3.	Alimentiveness, 5.

* This analysis of character was prepared nearly two years before Mr. Leggett's death.   We have two objects in introducing it into the Journal: 1st. It affords learners of the science an opportunity to study the combination of the faculties, and see them applied in delineating the nicer, as well as the more prominent shades of character.   2d. This description is said, by those best acquainted with Mr. Leggett, to be wonderfully correct ; and, inasmuch as his character was strikingly marked, its analysis on phrenological principles is so much the more in'eresting.—ED.

Acquisitiveness, 2.
Secretiveness, 2.
Cautiousness, 6.
Approbativeness, 7.
Self-esteem, 6.
Firmness, 7.
Conscientiousness, 6.
Hope, 6.
Marvellousness, 2.
Veneration, 2.
Benevolence, 6.
Constructiveness, 6.
Ideality, 5.
Sublimity, 6.
Imitation, 5.

Mirthfulness, 6.
Individuality, 7
Form, 6.
Size, 6.
Weight, 5.
Colour, 3.
Order, 6.
Calculation, 6.
Locality, 6.
Eventuality, 6.
Time, 3.
Tune, 5.
Language, 5.
Comparison, 6.
Causality, 5.

Measurements of the Head.

	Inches.
From Individuality to Philoprogenitiveness, . . .	7.7
" Destructiveness to Destructiveness, . . .	6
" Meatus Auditorius to Firmness, . . .	6.2
" " " Individuality, . . .	5.2
" " " Philoprogenitiveness, . .	4.5

This measurement gives a predominance of brain in the region of perceptive intellect, and those faculties giving force of character, ambition, and powers of will and determination.

This individual has a full-sized head, and a very active, excitable mind. His physiological organisation is marked with a bilious, sanguine, nervous temperament. His head is very unevenly developed; he has an eccentric mind, having many strong and weak traits of character, the most striking of which are decision, energy, ambition, and critical observing power, with a want of prudence, reserve, respect, and credulity. His strong phrenological developements are Firmness, Combativeness, Approbativeness, and Individuality, all being very large, while Secretiveness, Acquisitiveness, Marvellousness, and Veneration, are small.

He lacks consistency of character and uniformity of feeling, because of the unequalised power and influence of the faculties; yet this inequality gives striking peculiarities which make the man, and are too plain to pass unnoticed by the phrenological observer. His very large Combativeness, Firmness, and Individuality, with large Destructiveness, Mirthfulness, and Comparison, in the absence of Secretiveness and Veneration, give him a power of expression which but few men possess. He can be sarcastic in the extreme; and having large Self-esteem, and small Secretiveness and Veneration, his remarks would be without qualification; and having large Conscientiousness, he would regard principles more than party or friends, and would speak his whole mind, let who would oppose him; and having made an assertion, he would withstand all opposition, and go all lengths to support it. It is not in his nature to yield in times of opposition, or manifest timidity or hesitancy in times of danger, for when excited he does not know what danger is.

He has both moral and physical courage, which in times of excitement may lead to recklessness, yet has but little faith or confidence in the marvellousness and spiritual, and is seldom troubled with feelings of devotion or respect. Ranks and titles of honour, as such, are of no account to him, and have no influence in biasing his remarks. In fact, he is a *real* democrat, phrenologically considered. He never stops at trifles, but makes thorough work wherever he begins, and friend or foe shares the same fate, when opposing what he thinks is true. His Firmness is too large, for when acting in connection with Combativeness and Destructiveness, it would have a controlling influence over his judgment, and gives too strong a bias to his feelings. Combativeness is too large, making him too radical, excitable, and forcible. He is too apt to think that others are opposing him; and while defending his opinions, his remarks are liable to be too strong and personal, if not abusive, to exert a healthy influence. Approbativeness has too much influence over the other faculties. He is too ambitious—is too anxious to out-say or out-do others, and will exert himself to the utmost to carry the day, and come off conqueror, and never leaves a stone unturned or a word left out, that would aid him in effecting his plans.

He is sincere and honest spoken—could not be a good hypocrite if he should try, for he has no desire to keep things in the dark, and would make but a poor attempt at concealing and representing things as they were not. He is not troubled with diffidence, and has a respect for that only which his judgment sanctions. He never takes *any* thing for granted, nor does he believe on the authority of others; for having small Marvellousness and Veneration, he cannot place sufficient confidence in others, but must have every thing proved as clear as that two and two make four, before he can believe, especially if the subject be in any way connected with religion. His strongest moral faculties are Benevolence and Conscientiousness. To do good and to do right, to love mercy and deal justly, is his religion.

He acts upon the principle that sufficient unto the day is the evil thereof; so that he never borrows trouble or magnifies his enjoyments, but takes things as they present themselves. He is no miser —he finds it difficult to keep property. His mind is not on money-making. He had rather not be bothered with the care of it, and is obliged to call to his aid other faculties besides his Acquisitiveness, in order to be prudent in the use of property. His Mirthfulness is *large*, giving a strong perception of the ludicrous, and disposing him to make many amusing and witty remarks. His jokes, however, are liable to be too practical, personal, and direct, to take well. He is a *very* great observer of men and things—but few things pass unnoticed—consequently he gets very distinct and definite ideas of what is passing around him. He is decidedly a *practical* man, and a *great utilitarian.*

His perceptive faculties being larger than his reflective, would make him a greater critic than reasoner, and enable him to criticise and demolish the principles of others, rather than create and sustain original ones. He has a good mechanical eye, and an excellent memory of countenances, of places, of facts, and things of a similar nature. The portion of brain between Ideality and Cautiousness, called Sublimity, is large, and its influence, joined with his temperament, should be marked, if there is any truth in the organ. His reasoning faculties are *very active* and strongly developed, and his perceptions should be clear, and his remarks *forcible*, and to the point. He has a fair command of language, yet he uses no more words than are necessary to convey his ideas; he should be more distinguished for condensing his ideas, saying much in a little, than for copiousness of expression. He is original in his manners, yet can act out, imitate, and represent, if he should make the attempt, and is very fond of tragedy—the deeper the better. His knowledge of colours, and of succession of time, is poor. He should be fond of the natural and exact sciences, as well as polite literature. His large Form, Size, Order, Individuality, and Comparison, would make him a critical scholar, and well qualified to read proof sheets. His social feelings are strong; he is quite fond of music, is much interested in friends, is warm hearted, polite, and gallant to the ladies, a devoted companion, an affectionate parent, and a strong partisan. All things considered, this is a very marked head, not because of its greatness, but on account of its many striking peculiarities.

ARTICLE VII.

In a late American edition of the works of Oliver Goldsmith, edited by Washington Irving, is a fair engraving of the author, by J. B. Longacre, from a painting by Sir Joshua Reynolds, whose accuracy in likenesses, added to his own intimacy with the poet, induces an entire reliance upon its faithfulness. In this engraving, the os frontis is finely developed. But the attention is chiefly arrested by the extraordinary protrusion of the organ of Locality, whose function, phrenology supposes, imparts the love and desire for travel. Now, if there be any one trait more strongly marked than another, in the author of the "Traveller"—if there be a fact of his personal history more strongly impressed upon the memory of his admirers than another—it is that well-authenticated one of his having actually accomplished the tour of Europe on foot!—of having, in spite of innumerable obstacles, of want of friends, influence, and money, and, as he himself terms it, "want of impudence," gratified the imperious demands of this organ by strolling from one end of Europe to the other, even when a smattering skill upon a flute constituted his principal means of support. That the inconveniences, the countless deprivations, and innumerable mortifications, attendant upon such a vagabond life, should have been incurred, and voluntarily incurred, by a man of education and refined taste, by one of his peculiar sensitiveness, is by no means a common occurrence, even among the eccentric class of men to which, as a poet and man of genius, he belongs. So unconquerable was this propensity for wandering, that even after he had attained an enviable rank among the greatest writers of his age, his restlessness, and great anxiety for further travel, formed a prominent feature in his character.—The well-known vanity of the poet may be ascribed to *morbid Approbativeness.* His selfish faculties, as a class, were rather small ; and his utter want of common prudence, is in harmony with the fact. But he also possessed, according to this engraving, strong social feelings; he had much of that organisation which phrenology says creates a *love of home, and its kindred* pleasures. How, then, it may be inquired, does this agree with the predominance of an opposing faculty ?   Let the poet himself reconcile the apparent contradiction in the following lines :—

"In all my wanderings round this world of care,
In all my griefs, and God has given my share,

> I still had hopes. my latest hours to crown,—
> Amid these humble bowers to lay me down;
> To husband out life's taper to its close,
> And keep the flame from wasting, by repose;
> I still had hopes, for pride attends us still,
> Among the swains to show my book-learn'd skill,—
> Around the fire, an evening group to draw,
> And tell of all I felt, and all I saw;
> And as a hare, whom horns and hounds pursue,
> Pants to the place from whence at first she flew,
> I still had hope, my long vexations past,
> Here to return, and *die at home at last*."

All the likenesses of the *poet Thompson* indicate, besides larg Ideality and perception, an unusual endowment of the organ c Language; and his great prodigality in the use of the latter faculty has been the chief target for the arrows of criticism. Dr. Johnso was accustomed, when any one was growing enthusiastic about th author of the "Seasons," to seize the poet's great work, read favourite passage, and after it had been warmly eulogised, infor the company that he had *omitted every other line*. Though thi smacks somewhat of the occasional injustice of the great lexicc grapher, it is not the less true that many passages may be found i the "Seasons" so exceedingly amplified, that entire lines can b expunged, with little injury to the sense or beauty of the paragraph

The following lines may be cited, rather, however, to show hov unjust Johnson's criticism might sometimes have been, though in th main correct. Upon the subject of disinterested goodness, the po sings—

> "But to the generous, still improving mind,
> [That gives the hopeless heart to sing for joy,]
> Diffusing kind beneficence around,
> [Boastless as now descends the silent dew,]
> To him, the long review of ordered life,
> Is inward rapture only to be felt."

The lines enclosed may be removed, certainly, without much affect ing the *mere sense* of the passage; but who, for the sake of conder sation, would wish away—

> "Boastless as now descends the silent dew,"

that truly poetical image of unostentatious benevolence. Man passages could be selected from the "Seasons," to which Johnson' criticism would much more justly apply, but the task is ungraciou and it is left for those who find equal pleasure in detecting faults a in discovering beauties—for those who will wander through who gardens, amid flowers of every hue and fragrance, to pluck an ugl weed, almost smothered in their sweets.

The head of the poet Gray, in an engraving now before me, was full in size, of delicate temperament, and well developed in the perceptive region; Ideality is not large.   The poetry of this author is essentially that of the man of talent, and refined taste, as contrasted with the man of genius; his imagery is generally referable to the cullings of the scholar who had wandered over every field of past literature, selecting with ingenuity, and afterwards combining with fancy and feeling.   He wrote but little poetry—his poetical writings scarcely filling a small volume; was all his life a student, constantly adding to his stores of knowledge, which were various and profound, but he *produced* little; and but for his correspondence, and the testimony of his friends, the world would have known comparatively nothing of his attainments.   When we would praise him, we resort to the "Elegy in a Country Church-Yard;" his "odes" are oftener praised than read.   His great acquirements are in striking harmony with his large perceptive faculties, which were manifested through his life, while his small volume of poetry indicates smaller Ideality.

W.

MISCELLANY.

Boston Phrenological Society.—This society held its anniversary meeting on Tuesday evening, December 31st, 1839, on which occasion George Combe, Esq., delivered an address.   The circumstances connected with the origin of this society—being formed immediately after the death of Dr. Spurzheim, as well as holding its anniversary partly to commemorate his birth, and having accidentally present the greatest living advocate of the science—were calculated to render the exercises peculiarly interesting.   As we are not yet informed whether this address is to be published, and finding a brief notice of it in the Boston Mercantile Journal, of January 2d, we are induced to copy it in part.

"In this address, Mr. Combe referred to the freedom which the citizens of this country enjoyed—thus presenting a favourable soil for the growth of philosophy—and contrasted the liberty enjoyed here, with the despotism of Europe, as exhibited in the conduct of the Emperor of Austria to Dr. Gall, the founder of phrenology, and the enmity of Napoleon to a system of mental philosophy which tended to show the true operations of the human mind.   He spoke of the inactivity of the Boston Phrenological Society at the present time, and ascribed it to the same cause which had produced a similar effect on like institutions in Europe, viz. a disposition to confine its operations exclusively to the practical and theoretical part of the science, and to neglect the application of its great principles to the more important purposes of life.

"He dwelt at some length on the importance of teaching children the principles of phrenology, and thought it might be taught with advantage in our public schools.   By giving them clear ideas of the connection between the mind and body—a knowledge of the local situation of the mental organs—the functions of those organs—their uses and abuses—children, even at an early age, could be made to co-operate with their parents and teachers in promoting their own education. In this way, good children would be rendered better, and bad children would become less bad. He well recollected how difficult he found it in childhood to determine what was right. His passions urged him on the one hand, and his moral sentiments on the other—and even if his better feelings prevailed, he seldom enjoyed the satisfaction of believing it to be a triumph of virtue. He described in just and forcible terms the great contrast which was found in the lessons of the Bible, and in the language and events of profane history ; and the importance of phrenology in learning a child to discriminate between the right and the wrong ; and to regard in their true character the actions of a hero and a conqueror. It would show him that, by the existence of the moral sentiments, it is plain that man is adapted to Christianity, and that by a close adherence to the laws of the Creator, he may realise virtue, intelligence, and enjoyment.

"He spoke of the effect of phrenology on religion—and exposed the fallacy of the idea which some persons entertained, that phrenology might tend to supersede religion. He believed that, like the discoveries of the compass and printing, the discovery of the true philosophy of the mind was destined to form a new era in Christianity. He explained the importance, among a people who were often called upon to act at a moment's warning in difficult and important cases, of having an instrument of moral analysis, prompt and correct, which would never fail them—and this he took phrenology to be. It would deprive the unjust man of his power, the unprincipled demagogue of his influence, and would prove a handmaid to religion.

"Mr. Combe alluded in a very feeling manner to Dr. Gall, the founder of phrenology, who, in his youth, disregarded the allurements of ambition and fortune, to devote himself to the science of mind. On the 9th of January, 1802, Dr. Gall addressed a petition to the emperor of Germany, explaining his doctrines, and requesting permission to teach them to his fellow-citizens. In this petition, he said that his doctrines would triumph—that no power on earth could prevent their success. He was forbidden to explain his doctrines, and went into voluntary banishment ; and now both of these individuals slept in death—but where was phrenology ? It prospered in France, and England, and in this country, and was conferring immense advantages on mankind. Francis of Germany, stripped of his crown, was but an ordinary individual ; but Dr. Gall would stand forth in history the equal, at least, of Galileo, Harvey, and Newton, and was destined to occupy a niche in the temple of fame, more illustrious than either of those eminent benefactors of mankind. Even Napoleon could not triumph over Gall. He was bitterly opposed to his doctrines during his life—but the cast of his head was one of the strongest proofs of the truth of Dr. Gall's opinions—and Napoleon dead, was constrained to pay homage to Dr. Gall.

"Mr. Combe paid a beautiful tribute to the memory of Spurzheim—'his teacher, his friend, and his benefactor.' He spoke of his monument at Mount Auburn—of the beauty of the design and execution, and the appropriateness of the inscription, viz. the single word 'SPURZHEIM'—and he said that posterity would connect with it the name of WILLIAM STURGIS, upon whom he had called that very day, to express to him the gratitude he felt, for his noble conduct in erecting this monument to the memory of that great philosopher."

A Test of Practical Phrenology.—In the fall of 1837, there occurred in the city of New York an interesting case where the truth and application of phrenology were tested by a practical examination. The results of the experiment were drawn up and published at the time, by a gentleman who is connected with the New York press, and is well known to the public. The account, as then published in one of the city papers, read as follows:—" A few days since, in company with a friend, we took Mr. O. S. Fowler, to examine the head of a person who was then in waiting close by. Mr. Fowler had no kind of knowledge of the person, either of his age, habits, or character; and he readily consented to make the examination blindfolded, while the individual was not to speak during the time. Indeed, the person to be examined and Mr. F. were entire strangers, and had no imaginable knowledge of each other; and the former, by the way, was a firm disbeliever in the science of phrenology. A gentleman present, who was also a disbeliever in the science, took down the examination of Mr. Fowler in his own words. It was as follows :—

" ' This gentleman has a most astonishing memory of almost every thing he has seen, read, or heard. He is by nature *a scholar of the highest order.* Has an unquenchable thirst for information—reads every thing he can lay his hands on, especially if it is in history or literature. Has a remarkable faculty for acquiring a vast amount of knowledge in a very short time. His faculty not only for collecting knowledge, but for concentrating it together, is astonishing. This is one of his intellectual forts—can learn to talk a language by hearing it, in a very short time. *I am certain that he is a natural linguist of the first class.*

" ' He is enterprising in a high degree—can be discouraged by no amount of obstacles. He is cheerful, and considered witty ; his remarks take admirably, and produce much laughter; his wit does not take as well when written as when he talks it, because he acts it out so, that he creates and keeps up a constant burst of laughter. His imitative power is great, makes himself all things to all men. He is pre-eminently social, and has an excessive fondness for the society of friends. He loves children and pets, and although exceedingly fond of travelling, loves home better. His mind dwells patiently upon every subject which engages it, till he has thoroughly finished the matter in hand. He has strong reverential feeling for the Deity, but is deficient in Conscientiousness, and would act from expediency, rather than from a sense of duty. Go where he will, he is very popular, and is regarded as one of the best hearted men any where to be found.'

"Thus far the description of Mr. Fowler. When it was concluded, the bandage was taken from his eyes, and he was introduced to the celebrated Professor Seixas, one of the most distinguished oriental scholars of the present age. Mr. Seixas, it is well known, though little over thirty years of age, has mastered, besides the ordinary classics, the Hebrew, Arabic, Chaldee. Persian, Syriac, and we know not how many other oriental, to say nothing of the German and other modern languages. And all these he has acquired without any instructions, not having attended any school since he was eleven years old. He is, also, the author of a Hebrew Grammar, a Chaldee Manual, and, we believe, has prepared for the press an Arabic and Syriac Manual; and, also, a Hebrew Concordance, which he informed us he had prepared, de novo, from his own knowledge of the Hebrew Bible. He committed the whole of the Hebrew Bible to memory when only eighteen years of age; and acquired a knowledge of the Latin language by first committing to

memory the whole of Buxtorf's Hebrew Grammar, a book of from fiv
to six hundred pages."

———

Phrenological Fact.—The following incident occurred a few month
since, between two strangers, while travelling in a stage-coach nea
Wheeling, Va. We have the names of both gentlemen, and will vouch
for the correctness of the statement. One is a clergyman; the other i
a merchant. The former describes the interview as follows:—"
remarked to a fellow-passenger, as one of our company withdrew, tha
I should like to have a phrenologist examine that individual's head
'Why so?' said my fellow-traveller. 'Because I think there is some
thing very peculiar connected with that man's character.' 'Why,
said my companion, 'do you believe there is any truth in phrenology?
I replied in the affirmative, and remarked that I professed to have some
knowledge of the science myself. 'Well,' said he, 'there is a very
great defect in me with reference to one thing, and if you can point ou
that deficiency, I must myself believe that there is some truth in the
science.' I looked at the intellectual region of his head, and, withou
applying my fingers, saw that his perceptive organs, as a class, were
well developed; I remarked to him that the organ of Order appeared to
be strongly developed, but that I should think he was quite deficient in
the faculty of Colour. 'That is the defect,' said he; 'it is impossible
for me to distinguish between colours. I have now been a merchant
about twenty years, and during all this time, I have never been able to
distinguish between colours. When a customer asks me to show him a
piece of black cloth. I frequently take down a red piece; and I cannot
possibly tell the difference between green, pink, white, blue, brown, or
black ribbon.'
"I then took a red handkerchief from my pocket, and held it up by the
side of my coat, and asked him if he could discern any difference; he
said he could see they were not both alike, but could not tell which was
black or which was blue, or red, &c.; and the only way he could infer
that my coat was black or blue, was from the fact that most men wore
coats of such a colour. 'I was wearing,' said he, 'some months since,
a black bombazet coat which needed repairing; I went into my store to
get something to match it, and I cut a piece off from a green roll of
cloth, and took the piece and the coat to my wife, to have her mend it.
'Why,' said she, 'do you wish a green patch to be put on a black coat?
When the stage company stopped to dine, I examined his head, and
found a distinct cavity where the organ of Colour is located; no kind of
developement could be discovered."

———

Beautiful Comparison.—The mammoth paper, called "Brother Jonathan," and published in New York, contained, December 21st, a very
sensible article on phrenology. After some appropriate remarks on the
dignity, nature, and importance of the science, accompanied with severe
censures on the course of those who prostitute it for the mere purposes
of *gain*, the editor closes the article with the following beautiful comparison:—

"Believers, then, as we are, in phrenology, we cannot say that we
believe in it as a *trade*. It is a science (so to speak) in *embryo*. It may
be likened to a noble edifice, the foundations of which are laid broad and
deep, upon the principles of unchangeable, eternal truth, and the superstructure of which, it must be the work of patient perseverance, deep
study, close observation, and rational philosophy to rear, range after

range, until it shall stand a firm and lasting monument, at once of the blessings arising from a careful cultivation of those powers of research, into the deep mysteries of our nature, wherewith God has endowed us, as well as of his benevolent providence, his fatherly kindness, and his consummate wisdom.   There will be quacks and sciolous pretenders around the edifice while it is rearing, with their handicraft tools, and dicacious mystifications ('blind leaders of the blind')—but as in the building of the great temple, the sound of the hammer and the axe must not be heard in preparing its massive ranges, as they rise, mind impelled, towards the sky, displaying to the world, at last, the true philosophy of that most wondrous work of the Creator—THE HUMAN MIND."

Lectures of Mr. Combe in Massachusetts.—It appears that the lectures of Mr. Combe have been quite favourably received in this state.   In the brief notice of his lectures in Boston, which we gave in our last number, a mistake occurred ; he delivered only *one* course in November, instead of *two*, as was then stated.   The public press of this city, we observe, have spoken in high terms of Mr. Combe's labours. Several papers take a decided stand in favour of the science.   We are induced to copy the remarks of one, which appear to be no less candid and appropriate, than they are just and merited.   The "Liberator," (a paper published weekly, and conducted with no ordinary ability,) contained, November 29, the following remarks :—

    " *Phrenology.*—We have been equally interested and edified in attending a course of lectures on this subject, by George Combe, of Edinburgh. This gentleman is widely known in this country, and in Europe, for his admirable work on the ' Constitution of Man,' and other publications. We have not yet had the pleasure of a personal introduction to him ; but, having listened to his exposition and vindication of the science of phrenology, we are quite certain that, as a philosopher, he deserves to take the first rank, and as a friend of humanity, he is entitled to universal commendation.   Before we listened to his teachings, we had no doubt as to the truth of phrenology ; but he has strengthened our convictions, and increased our interest in mental philosophy.   Simplicity is an essential element of true greatness of mind ; and it is a conspicuous trait in the character of Mr. Combe.   He is no orator, though a ready and accurate speaker.   The manner in which he handles his great subject is that of a master—clear, logical, felicitous, without art, and charmingly ingenuous. There seems to be no disposition, on his part, to *proselyte* those who attend his lectures ; but every thing is said and done with so much sincerity, every position is maintained with such consummate ability, every argument is so in accordance with good sense and right reason, and every objection is considered with so much candour, and removed with so much ease, that he must be a very inattentive or prejudiced hearer, who is not convinced that phrenology is destined to take the lead in the sciences, and is incontestibly true.
    " It is true this science has its unbelievers and its scoffers.   Were it not so, in its infancy, before it has vanquished all opposition, there would be just reason to regard it as either false or worthless.   But of what avail are scoffs and doubts arrayed against facts and arguments ? Blind men may not be able to discern any hues in the rainbow, any light in the sun ; and if they choose to question or deny the existence of these, their skepticism is pardonable, because they are sightless.   But what is visible, what is tangible, what is clear and palpable demonstration, may not be denied without folly, nor rejected without condemna-

tion. Phrenology is not supposition, guess-work, charlatanism, but self-evident, conspicuous, indestructible TRUTH. The heads of those who contemptuously repudiate it will often be found to furnish the strongest proofs of its authenticity. It is not an abstract theory, but practical reality. For a time, it may not excite general attention, or command universal assent; but it must ultimately be embraced by mankind—for it is indissolubly connected with the manners, the morals, and the physical and intellectual regeneration of the human race. Some, through ignorance or bigotry, have supposed it to conflict with Christianity; but it is far otherwise. It is the handmaid of religion, not its enemy. Whatever is true in nature, must be consistent with the moral government of the universe.

> 'What if the foot, ordain'd the dust to tread,
> Or hand to toil, aspir'd to be the head?
> What if the head, the eye, or ear repin'd
> To serve mere engines to the ruling mind?'

That these are 'mere engines,' or organs by which the mind acts, phrenology abundantly proves.

"But—*cui bono?* Of what utility is phrenology? Truly, if it be false, of no utility whatever, except to prove the credulity of mankind; but if it be true, how ridiculous is such a question! Is an accurate knowledge of mental philosophy, of the phenomena of mind, to be set down as useless? Of what utility is *truth?* '*The proper study of mankind is man.*' "

During the month of December, Mr. Combe delivered three lectures at Salem, Lowell, and Worcester, on the application of the science to education. These lectures, in each place, were attended by audiences numbering about three hundred. The "Massachusetts Spy," of Jan. 1, contained the following notice of Mr. Combe's lectures in Worcester:—

"The course of lectures on Mental Philosophy and Education, by George Combe, was delivered in this town last week. Although the weather was very unpropitious, the audience was large, and among them a considerable number from neighbouring towns, some of whom came from ten to fifteen miles, through bad travelling, to attend. On no former occasion, we venture to say, has the gratification of an audience, in this place, been of so high an order, and at the same time so complete. The principles of the philosophy which is taught, are stated and elucidated with a clearness which leaves on the mind of the hearer a strong conviction of their truth, while the importance of their practical application to the education of youth is so illustrated and enforced, as to invest the subject with a thrilling interest. We wish this course could be heard throughout the whole length and breadth of the land. A general knowledge of the principles inculcated, would shortly produce an almost entire revolution in our systems of education —a revolution to which the philanthropist must look forward with hope, as to the dawning of a better day, full of promise to our country and to the world."

—

Extract from the Letter of a Correspondent.—"All men are more or less under the government of phrenological laws—its opposers as well as advocates; none can escape from them. Or, in other words, all are influenced by the outward signs of inward power and action. Mental power has its material manifestation, as clearly evident, as bodily force. We become accustomed to associate the idea of mind, or the want of it, with outward appearances.   Is there a company of civilised men on earth, into which, if Channing or Webster should appear as strangers, they would not be received with respect?   Or into which, if an idiot, or a man much below the medium standard of intellect should come, his true rank of mind would not be almost instantly assigned him?   Certainly not.   But the mind itself is invisible—it is the outward signs only which are seen.   By having always these outward signs before us, we, without reflection, but by habit merely, learn unconsciously to associate the idea of mind, or its absence, with these signs; as uniformly as we do largeness of muscle with physical strength.

"It may be objected, that the respect spoken of above, would be caused by the expression of the face, and dignity of presence.   But it must be recollected, that this expression is nothing more than form and motion; or the face and features as acted upon or modified by the organs of the mind, and indicates the inward power and action, as certainly as the shadow does the substance, and can no more exist without it.   If it be said these appearances can be counterfeited, it only proves the reality and currency of the coin, whose stamp is thus imitated.   No one is ready to acknowledge that he ever mistakes the mock dignity of shallow self-conceit, for the calm expression of mental power.

"Children, and some of the lower animals, are much influenced by the outward signs, of the sentiments at least.   And the most perfect remains of ancient art which have come down to us, show their authors to have been keen observers of the connection between the outward size and form, and the power and attributes of the mind within.   The most perfect statues, and other representations of the imaginary beings of antiquity, conform, in the general developement of the organs of the mind, with the attributes assigned to those beings, or they are, in their leading outlines, phrenologically correct.   They never placed the head of Jupiter upon the shoulders of Adonis; or assigned to Venus that which belonged to the goddess of wisdom and valour.   E. B."

Health.—One of the New York papers recently contained this statement:—"Dr. Dewey remarked, in one of his lectures, that while other diseases had been constantly diminishing in this city for thirty years past, *those of the brain have increased twelvefold.*   This he attributed to the over action of the organ in their intense application to business, for which our citizen tradesmen are proverbial."   We here see the vast importance of correctly understanding the functions of this organ, in order to regulate its exercise so as to promote the general health of the body.   It will be found, too, on a candid and thorough investigation, that this viscus is composed of a *plurality* of organs, *each of which, in order to secure the greatest amount of health and happiness, must be harmoniously and properly exercised on its appropriate objects.*

Phrenology in the Family; or the Utility of Phrenology in Early Domestic Education.   By J. A. Warne.   This work has been republished in Great Britain, where we presume it will have an extensive circulation.

Mr. Combe is now lecturing at Albany, N. Y., and is engaged to deliver his next course of lectures at New Haven, Ct.

Mr. J. S. Grimes is lecturing on phrenology in New York city—the public press speak in high terms of his labours.

THE

AMERICAN PHRENOLOGICAL JOURNAL

AND

MISCELLANY.

| Vol. II. | Philadelphia, March 1, 1840. | No. 6. |

ARTICLE I.

REMARKS ON DR. ROGET'S OBJECTIONS TO PHRENOLOGY.*

Having recently met with a copy of *Roget's* "Outlines of Phy
siology, with an Appendix on Phrenology," I turned with consider
able interest to the *Appendix*, to see in what manner the science of
the brain had been treated, by so distinguished a personage as the
secretary to the Royal Society, professor of physiology in the Royal
Institution of Great Britain, author of a Bridgewater Treatise, &c.
The American editor of the work informs us, that the author is a
well-known unbeliever in phrenology, and that his published objec
tions to the doctrine have been regarded as too cogent to be per
mitted to pass unheeded:—wherefore it may fairly be presumed that
these objections are fraught with all the cogency of which the argu
ments on that side of the question are susceptible.

I have read them with some care and attention,—as a mere
amateur inquirer after truth and information, without any pretension
to an intimate acquaintance with the details of phrenological science
—and I must say, that I was forcibly impressed with what seemed
to me a disposition in the writer to evade the main points, or funda
mental principles of the doctrine, and to resort to doubts and cavil
lings, concerning the accuracy of subordinate facts and inferences

* The above communication was prepared for the Journal, before the write
knew that an article on the same subject was then in type. But as these remark
differ essentially, in many respects, from those in the article already presented, and
will afford our readers new evidence of the weakness, fallacy, and inconsistency of
Dr. Roget's objections to phrenology—who may fairly be considered the representa
tive of many others—we deem the communication well worthy of publication
The quotations from Dr. Roget's *own* work on physiology are quite appropriate
and savour somewhat of *phrenology.*—ED.

as taught, or suggested, by the advocates of phrenology.   The whole tenor of Dr. Roget's Appendix reminded me of those adroit efforts which we often witness among gentlemen of the bar, when they find the palpable evidence of a case against them, and are driven to the necessity of attacking and mystifying incidental matters, or of appealing to popular prejudices, in order to confuse the apprehensions of the jury, and divert their attention from the real merits of the question at issue.   The expedient is ingenious enough, but it is somewhat musty; and, at the present day, is rather obsolete, among reputable investigators of scientific truth.   If I understand any thing of the doctrines of phrenology, they are based on these positions: namely, that the *cerebral system* (*i. e.* the brain, with its elongations and ramifications) is the organ, or series of organs, on which all the intellectual phenomena are dependent, and by means of which all the operations of the mind are performed; that the native powers, capacity, and character of the intellect, depend upon the size, form, texture, and condition of the cerebral system; and hence, that the various developements of that system, as indicated to our senses, afford the means of ascertaining, to a certain extent, the intellectual character of the individual to whom it belongs.

The phrenologists aver, for instance, that the cerebral developements, in the man of intellect, and in the congenital idiot, are so palpably distinct and constant, that no man of observation can have failed to notice the fact, and no candid man can refuse to acknowledge it; and yet, it seems to me, if the opponents of the doctrine concede thus much, they virtually yield the whole ground—for the question then shrinks to a mere dispute about details.   The phrenologists also allege, that the various characters of individuals are indicated (with more or less certainty, according to circumstances) by the conformation of their respective heads; and that each particular conformation is owing to the size and active energy of corresponding portions of the *encephalon*—which portions are generally considered as so many distinct organs, or instruments, of the different intellectual faculties and sentiments.

These points are so many questions of *fact* and *inference*, to be determined by multiplied observation or legitimate deduction, and not by the preconceptions of Dr. *Gall*, nor the prejudices of Dr. *Roget*.   If the structure and condition of the cerebral system has any connection with, or influence over, the grade and character of the intellect, it seems to me to be neither irrational, nor illogical to suppose there may be *some* foundation for the doctrines of phrenology.   *How far* they are true, or to what extent they may yet be satisfactorily established, remains to be ascertained, by careful observation.   Dr. *Roget*, however, pronounces the whole affair, without any qualification, to be a " pretended science."

I propose to notice, in my desultory way, a few of his objections; and this I do, chiefly in the hope that it may induce some master-hand, among the contributors to the American Phrenological Journal, to take up the subject, and do it full and complete justice.

In the first place, then—as I have already intimated—Dr. Roget does not fully and explicitly meet the preliminary question, whether the brain be, or be not, the organ of the mind.   The *inference*, from the tenor of his objections, would seem to be that he holds the nega-tive.   If so, why does he blink the question?   Why not meet the phrenologists manfully, at the threshold of the inquiry, and deny them the basis of their system?   By courageously denying, wholly and at once, the functions usually ascribed to the brain, he would greatly abridge the discussion.   But he merely says, that " nothing like direct proof has been given that the presence of *any particular part* of the brain is essentially necessary to the carrying on of the operations of the mind.   The truth is," he continues, " that there is not a *single part of the encephalon* which has not, in one case or other, been impaired, destroyed, or found defective, without any apparent change in the sensitive, intellectual, or moral faculties."   He then refers to records of cases which are alleged to bear upon this point. We have not the means of testing the validity of these " cases ;" but if it be true, that "*any* particular part" of the brain can be dispensed with, it would be curious and satisfactory to know why *every* par-ticular part of such an anomalous organ might not be spared, with-out impairing the " operations of the mind."   At all events, why not give us an intimation *how many* of those " particular parts"—if any— are essentially necessary to the functions of intellect?   Time was, we are told, that when the brains were out, the man would die ; but it would seem, from Dr. *Roget's* researches, that the "operations of the mind" are not quite so dependent on the cerebral organs.

The doctor finds a " mass of facts" which, in his view, are abun-dantly sufficient to overturn the fundamental proposition of the phrenologists.   He treats with disdain the " feeble attempts of Dr. Spurzheim" to impeach the evidence afforded by those facts; but when phrenologists presume to talk about "facts," in support of *their* side of the question, he coolly observes, " we venture only to express doubts as to *the reality* of these facts !"   This is, indeed, a very con-clusive mode of conducting the argument—to say nothing of its courtesy and fairness!   No doubt, if the phrenologists admit all the doctor's facts, and surrender all their own, he will get on triumph-antly with his side of the controversy.   I incline to think, however, that questions of *fact*—either in real or "pretended science"—will scarcely be allowed to rest on the mere assertions or opinions of partisan disputants.   Men who seek for truth, will be apt to observe and verify facts for themselves; and even if the "operations of the mind" may be carried on without any particular portion of *brain*, it is altogether likely that some minds, in conducting their operations, will require a portion of *evidence* more satisfactory than mere cavillings, or prejudiced statements.   No honest man can desire to believe any thing but the truth.   Let the truth, then, be fairly and diligently sought for, by a careful observation and a candid scrutiny of all facts, or alleged facts, which bear upon the question at issue.

Dr. *Roget* scouts the allegation of *Spurzheim*, that "every one feels that he thinks by means of his brain;" and adds, "we doubt much if any one has naturally that feeling."   Whether we have this feeling "naturally," or whether it be acquired, it might be presumptuous, in the face of such a doubt, to undertake to decide; but it is an exceedingly prevalent opinion, on this side the Atlantic, that we *have* a consciousness, or "feeling," that our thinking transactions are performed in, or by means of, the brain.   Some of us find much thinking to be rather a fatiguing business; and after a laborious process of that kind, we are apt to be troubled with headach, and other evidences of a tired and over-exercised brain : in other words, we *have*, either "naturally" or artificially, a "feeling" that the cerebral system has been actively employed.   How they do their thinking in the royal institutions of Great Britain—whether by means of their brains, or by what other viscus—the doctor has not condescended to inform us.

But let us advert, briefly, to the evidences furnished by Dr. *Roget* himself, that the brain, or cerebral system, is entitled to be considered as our thinking apparatus.   When not engaged in controverting the doctrines of phrenology, he appears to be more ingenuous in his statements.   In his "Outlines of Physiology," he tells us that ' the functions of sensation, of voluntary motion, *and of thought*, are those which establish our mental connections with the external world; which enable us to acquire a knowledge of the existence and properties of the material objects that surround us; which awaken in us the operations of our own minds; which bring us in communication with other intellectual and sentient beings; and which enable us to react on matter, to exercise over it the dominion of the will, and to influence the condition of other beings which, like us, have received the gift of life, of sensation, and of intellect."   He further says, that "of the existence of our own sensations, ideas, thoughts, and volitions, we have the highest degree of evidence that human knowledge can admit—that of our own consciousness." He does not tell us whether we have this consciousness "naturally," or how; but he proceeds to inform us, that "the *nervous system*" (which is part and parcel of the cerebral system) "*is the name given to that assem blage of organs which perform the important functions of which we are now speaking.* The primary office of the fibres composing that system appears to be to transmit certain affections, which we may call *impressions*, from one part of that system to another; and more particularly to convey them both to and from *that particular part of the brain, the affections of which give rise to sensation, and accom pany our mental operations.*" This language seems to countenance the idea of the phrenologists, that the brain *has* something to do with the mental operations. But hear him again. "Such, then,' says he, " being the physiological connections which exist between the physical changes taking place in the brain, and the passive phenomena of the mind, *it is not an unreasonable supposition, that the voluminous mass of the cerebral substance which, in the human brain especially, has been superadded to the medulla oblongata, or to the immediate physical seat of sensation, is in some way subservien to that astonishing range of intellect, and combination of menta. faculties, which are found in man.* We may conjecture, also, *with much appearance of probability,*" he continues, "that in the lower animals, *the intellectual endowments, which mark several of the more intelligent races, are connected with similar, though inferior, expan sions of cerebral substance.*" If the doctor had not told us other wise, in his *Appendix*, I should have inferred from all this, that he held some, at least, of the doctrines of that "pretended science,' called *phrenology!* "All the mental phenomena," he further observes, " in which the mind is passive, have been referred by metaphysicians to the principle of association, and consequently may in as far as this principle is concerned, be connected with the physical changes above noticed. *Hence we find the memory, which is the direct result of that law, is more especially liable to be impaired by certain physical states of the brain, such as those induced by severe concussion, by fevers, and by the progress of age.*' Now, what is all this, I should like to know, but the language and doctrine of the phrenologists?

"That certain physical changes," says Dr. R., "take place in *some portion or other of the cerebral mass, in connection with various mental changes, we have the clearest evidence;* but of *the nature o* these physical changes we are wholly ignorant, nor does the presen state of our information afford a shadow of hope that we shall ever gain any more precise knowledge of them." So says the doctor and it may all be true; though it is by no means prudent or safe for any man, in view of the wonderful advances already made in science, to undertake to set "precise" limits to human attainments. Dr. *Lardner* committed a mistake of that sort, when he undertook to determine the *ne plus ultra* of steam navigation. But, admitting that we may not hope to gain a precise knowledge of "*the nature*" of those phenomena, does *that* go to demonstrate that the powers and capacity of the brain, to perform and promote intellectual operations, may not be ascertained, to some extent, by observing the connection of those powers with certain developements and conditions of that organ? If it does not, then is it premature—to say the least—to denounce phrenology as a "pretended science."

Dr. Roget, in another passage of his "Outlines," says expressly, that "*the brain has been very justly regarded as the organ of the mind; that is, the corporeal instrument invariably employed in the operations of the mind.*" Now, if the character of an operation may be in any mode, or degree, influenced by the condition of the organ, or instrument, which performs it—and if the condition or capacity of the organ can be ascertained, by observation of its size, form, or texture—then may phrenology be true, to a certain extent. If some itinerant pretenders—more familiar with human credulity than with the animal economy—undertake to teach more than is accurately known, *that is* the *misfortune* of the infant science, not its fault; and it is a misfortune, moreover, from which some of its elder sisters are not yet wholly exempt.

One more paragraph may be quoted, in this connection, from Roget's Physiology. "The affections of the mind," says he, "are very various and complicated; a great multitude of ideas and associations are treasured up in it, and constitute a variety of powers, of faculties, of propensities, of instincts, and of passions. *The conformation of the brain, which is the organ of the mind, is also very complex, and appears to consist of an assemblage of different parts, constructed evidently with extreme refinement, and arranged with great care, and with very elaborate design. The idea naturally suggests itself,*" he continues, "*that these different portions, recognised by the anatomist, may perhaps have some correspondence with the several faculties into which the phenomena of the mind have been analysed by the metaphysician.* This question has, indeed, been often started, and is quite distinct from that of the materiality or immateriality of the soul; *for it is perfectly conceivable that if the immaterial soul acts by means of material organs, and receiving impressions from these organs, its different operations may require different organs.*"

The statements in the foregoing paragraph seem to me to set forth plausible grounds for the doctrines of phrenology; and, at the same time, to vindicate the science from one of the most gratuitous and malevolent charges (viz. materialism) with which its prejudiced enemies have assailed it.

But, notwithstanding the admissions above cited, from his Outlines of Physiology, Dr. *Roget*, in his *Appendix*, still urges his objection against what he calls the ground-work of phrenological reasoning—namely, that the different faculties of the mind are exercised respectively by different portions of the brain—which, he says, is in no respect whatever established; and that the only arguments in its favour, which bear the least plausibility, are derived from analogy. I should rather consider *the ground work* of phrenology to be—as I have already stated—that the brain, being the organ of the mind may, by its size, form, and condition, indicate to the skilful observer, the powers and character of those intellectual operations of which it is the instrument.   Whether the cerebral system consist of a congeries of distinct organs, or whether its various developements be only parts of one organ, I hold to be a subordinate consideration, in reference to the fundamental principles of the doctrine.   If the intellectual powers depend upon certain cerebral developements, which are cognisable by our senses, *that* is a sufficient "ground-work" for phrenology.   If such be not the fact, then is it, in the language of Dr. Roget, a "pretended science."   But, if the main position be correct, it is sheer evasion and cavilling, to say that we do not know whether the alleged organs are *distinct*, or only *parts of one organ.   Either* may be true, without affecting the main question.   The doctrine of distinct organs is an *inference*, plausibly deduced from multiplied observations.   Who, I beg leave to ask, has refuted it?   It is well sustained by analogy, to which we may fairly resort for illustration, when arguing from the known to the unknown.   But Dr. R. contends that reasoning from analogy, in this case, is so loose and fallacious, that it may be applied to support either side of the question.   He has certainly demonstrated that there *may* be such loose reasonings, by citing the functions of the *stomach* to prove the unity of the cerebral organs.   He tells us, the stomach can digest different kinds of food; and yet, says he, we do not find *one portion* of that organ destined for the digestion of *meat*, and another for the digestion of *vegetables!*   And *this* he adduces as *analogical reasoning*, to disprove a plurality of organs in the cerebral system!   Could any one have anticipated such an argument from the author of a Bridgewater Treatise?   It seems to me to be about as apposite and conclusive, as if he had cited the functions of a *stove*, and edified us with the fact that the simple apparatus has the several faculties of consuming *oak* and *anthracite!* The doctor may well term analogy " loose" and " fallacious," if such be a specimen of the kind he deals in.

But let us see if the phrenologists have not some *analogies*, to sustain their views, of a more philosophical nature than that which Dr. R. finds in the digestive powers of the stomach. The cerebral system being " very complex"—(comprising the brain, with its convolutions and elongations, together with the organs of sense)—" the idea naturally suggests itself," that as the different nerves, or branches of the brain, have the faculty of originating distinct ideas, so may different portions of the great central mass, or sensorium, be appropriated to the performance of distinct functions ; or, according to the prenologists, these different portions may be considered as distinct intellectual organs. Dr. Roget himself tells us, that *" the nerve of each particular sense appears to have different specific endowments."* Is there, then, any thing so very " loose" or far-fetched, in extending the *analogy* to the cerebral mass, in which the nerves of each particular sense originate, and in supposing that the several portions of that mass have " different specific endowments ?" or that those " endowments" may vary in grade or energy, according as the several portions are respectively developed, and perfected in their organisation ?

But further : " From the experiments of the French physiologists, it would appear," says Dr. Roget, in his Outlines, "that in an animal *deprived of all the upper portions of the brain*, but in which the medulla oblongata is preserved, *all indications of the more complex operations of thought disappear*, but the animal still remains capable of executing such voluntary motions as are of an instinctive character ; as, for example, swallowing." If this be correct, it strikes me as somewhat more than " loose" analogy ; and as going directly to establish the doctrines of phrenologists.

Again : In speaking of the function of the nerves—in transmitting impressions from the organs of sense to the brain, which give rise to sensation—and in transmitting impressions of volition from the brain to the muscles of voluntary motion, which give rise to the contraction of those muscles, Dr. R. says the question has been often asked, whether *the same nervous filaments* which transmit the one class of impressions, are employed to transmit the other likewise; or whether *different portions of the nerve are appropriate to these different offices. The truth of the last of these propositions*, says the doctor, *may now be considered as being fairly established.*

If that be the case, I should like to know what there is so very

" loose" and unphilosophical in extending the *analogy* to the *brain itself,* and in supposing that different portions of that organ, also may be appropriate to different offices. After stating, that to Sir Charles Bell and Magendie belongs the merit of bringing forward decisive proofs of the reality of the distinction between nerves for sensation and nerves for motion, the doctor says, "it results from this discovery, that the transmission of impressions in opposite directions—that is, in one case from the extremities to the brain and in the other, from the brain to the muscles—is effected by different nerves, or at least by different sets of nervous filaments, and that no filament is capable of transmitting impressions both ways indiscriminately, but always in one particular direction. These two kinds of filaments are, it is true, conjoined together into one nerve but the object of this union is *not community of function,* but conve nience of distribution, the two kinds of filaments *still remaining dis tinct in their functions,* as they are likewise distinct in their origins.'

Again : Among some vertebrated animals—as the turtle, the ser pent, and the frog—" we find," says Dr. R., " that *isolated portions of the spinal cord perform functions analogous*" (that's the word *analogous!*) " *to those of the brain,*" &c. Is it " loose" and illogica to adduce evidence of this kind in support of the proposition, tha different portions of the *encephalon* may perform distinct functions Dr. R. mentions cases, in which he says we are " fairly entitled to extend analogy *to* other animals whose construction does not mate rially differ from that of man." Why not, then, " extend analogy' *from* other animals to explain the functions of kindred organs, in th human subject ?

But Dr. Roget contends that it is *equally conceivable,* that the phenomena of the cerebral system " should result from the imperfec or differently *modified actions of one organ,* as from the *separate activity of different parts* of that organ, whilst the other parts are inactive." Well, suppose it is; what then ? Does *that* disprove the fundamental principles of phrenology ? On the contrary, the sugges tion recognises their validity, and merely indicates a different mode of construing them. It is a sheer evasion of the main question. I the brain actually performs the functions ascribed to it by the phreno logists, and if its powers and capacities do really depend upon it size, form, and condition, what do the objectors to the doctrine gai by referring those functions to *modified actions* of an *unit ?* Does i explain any thing more logically or clearly, than is done by th theory of distinct organs? What do they mean by these *modifie actions ?* Can any one attach a definite intelligible idea to the term Can we conceive of any *modified action* of an olfactory nerve, fo instance, by means of which we may be enabled to perceive sounds or colours? Was it a *modified action* of the cerebral *unit* which gave to the blind man the idea that *scarlet* was something like *the sound of a trumpet?* If they understand the precise "nature" of these *modified actions* at the royal institutions of Great Britain, they have not been generous enough to show us how the functions of the brain may be more clearly explained by *such actions*, than they are by the doctrine of distinct cerebral organs. Neither have they been so obliging as to explain how, or why it is, that an injury done to *any portion* of a cerebral *unit*, does not destroy or impair *every faculty* in the same degree, or to the same extent. It would be satisfactory to hear those cavillers account for the phenomenon on more rational principles than those held by the phrenologists.

Every known fact, in anatomy and physiology, appears to sustain the leading or fundamental doctrines of phrenology. "The human brain is not only larger in its relative proportion to the body, than in any other of the mammalia, but its absolute size is greater, if we except only that of the elephant and of the whale. With these few exceptions, all the larger animals with which we are more commonly acquainted, have brains absolutely, and even considerably, smaller than that of man. Besides the prodigious expansion of the hemispheres, we may remark in the human brain a more elaborate structure, and a more complete developement of all its minuter parts. There is no part of the brain found in any animal, which does not exist also in man; whilst several of those which are found in man, are either extremely small, or altogether absent, in the brains of the lower animals."

These facts, and many others of a similar character, furnished by Dr. Roget himself, in his Outlines, all seem to afford good and sufficient grounds for the theory held by the phrenologists.

The doctor, nevertheless, objects to the proposition, that the *size* of an organ is, "in general, a criterion of the energy with which its function is performed;" and avers that it is "in itself extremely questionable." This is a fair subject for investigation; and the fact may, possibly, be one day ascertained to the satisfaction of candid observers—even if it should remain questionable to others. The superior "energy" of the cerebral functions, in man, is pretty generally admitted by philosophers; and the doctor has told us, in the passage just cited, that the human brain is not only *relatively larger* than that of other animals, but, with few exceptions, and those of the highest fabric, *absolutely larger* than in the lower animals. He notices, also, "*the prodigious expansion of the hemispheres*" as well as the more elaborate structure, of the human brain. Does not all this favour the idea of there being some correspondence or relation between the *size* and the *energy* of an organ? Do not the general sense and experience of mankind concur in the idea? What says the doctor himself, respecting the "energy" with which the function of the olfactory organs is performed? "*Every part* of the organ of smell," says he, "is *developed* in quadrupeds *in a degree corresponding to the greater extent and acuteness in which they enjoy this sense*, compared with man." Are we not, then, fairly entitled to extend the analogy to other organs, or portions of the cerebral system?

That the *form of the cranium* may be affected by the activity, and greater developement of different cerebral organs or portions of the *encephalon*, is by no means an improbable circumstance, especially in early life, while the ossification is yet incomplete. Numerous facts, both in human and comparative anatomy, demonstrate the moulding or modifying power, exerted by soft parts upon containing or contiguous bones, and testaceous coverings. Neither is it unwarrantable to suppose, that the habitual excitement of particular cerebral organs will enhance their energy, and promote their developement. Such excitement may be produced through the medium of the external senses, and may be sustained by reflection, or by presenting inducements and motives of various kinds, calculated to stimulate the intellectual organs. A similar power is also exerted by means of the sympathy, or reciprocal influences, existing between the brain and *other organs.* Every one is acquainted with the controlling influence which the state of the stomach, for example, has upon the passions, and even upon the moral faculties. Extreme hunger will not only produce mental irritation, but will render man selfish, unjust, and cruel. If long continued, it might perhaps effect a permanent change in the intellectual character. Certain it is, that the single circumstance of the presence or absence of some organs of the animal system, exerts a powerful and enduring influence, not only upon the character and disposition, but also upon the form and developement of the cerebral organs. This fact is strikingly illustrated by the results of early emasculation. The comparative developements of the bases of the cranium, and of the contiguous parts, in the steer and bull, for instance—as well as the difference in the characters and dispositions of the two animals— demonstrate the influences to which I have referred, in a way that can neither be doubted nor misunderstood. It is unnecessary to amplify on this point. The *facts* are palpable and notorious. Let the cavillers against phrenology furnish a better *theory* of them—if they can— than that afforded by the doctrines of GALL and SPURZHEIM.

W. D.

West Chester, Pa., November 16, 1839.

ARTICLE II.

PREDOMINANCE OF CERTAIN ORGANS IN THE BRITISH POETS.—NO. 3.

SHAKSPEARE.

To understand the author of Hamlet and Macbeth, is not easy; the poor and scanty materials of biography furnish few data; his own works show us all the world but himself—for Shakspeare was no *egotist*. Still it is only by a thorough acquaintance with the poet, that we can hope to be introduced to the man ; and if long and inti- mate communion with the works which form the brazen monument of his fame, may constitute one of the many requisites demanded for this analysis, the writer may at least escape the charge of arrogance in assuming the difficult task. Guided by some knowledge of the general operations of intellect, availing himself of the chart which the poet has himself furnished, with his way illuminated by science, he may sound, perhaps, some of the channels of this "oceanic mind." But, however the effort may fail, the poet cannot be involved in the blunder; the eagle's flight will not be less high, because he soars beyond our vision. Most of the efforts to analyse the intellect before us, have either turned too much upon his merely acquired information, or upon the mystic qualities of his genius, which, by some, have been represented as absolutely independent of all knowledge. Certain critics have enumerated the various kinds and degrees of his information, while others have dealt in the usual common-place matter about the indescribable operations of mind. He

is so accurate in the use of legal technicalities, says one, that he mu
have possessed the knowledge of the lawyer! He wrote so we
upon pathology, cries Æsculapius, that he was certainly intimate wit
the library of the physician! Such was his knowledge of the Bib
and polemics, says the divine, that he was even a good theologiar
The enthusiast of Shakspeare here steps in, seizes upon the
acknowledgments, and claims for his favourite the united wisdom
the divine, the lawyer, and the physician! But he has not yet create
a Shakspeare. All these qualities, in certain degrees, he indee
possessed. But he possessed something *more*. What was that
Now we approach the difficulty of our task. Glorious minds a
handed down to us in the annals of history; profound students
nature have been nurtured in our own lovely land. We can clai
the intellect that arrested the forked lightning in its course, an
directed it harmless from the habitations of man. But what sha
we say of Shakspeare? Shall we search the lexicon of eulogy, ar
conceal our ignorance under high sounding epithets? No: the
superlatives may commend, but they do not *describe*; they leave th
objects they praise as abstract and intangible as before—the questic
is not thus easily solved. Let us see how Coleridge, a man wh
blended the enthusiasm of the poet with the strength of the phil
sopher, answered the same question—" What shall we say of Shal
speare?" "Why even this: that Shakspeare, no *mere* child
nature—no automaton of genius—*possessed by* the spirit, not *posses
ing it*—first studied patiently, meditated deeply, understood minutel
till knowledge became habitual and *intuitive*, and at length brougl
forth that stupendous power which placed him without an equal
his own rank—which seated him on one of the two glory-smitte
summits of the poetic mountain, with Milton as his *compeer*, n
rival."

This is one of the very best pictures of the *progress* of a gre
mind; and beautiful and philosophical is the distinction betwee
possessing and being *possessed by* the spirit. There is here no ca
about knowledge that never was acquired—no claims of impossibili
—none of the mysticism so common in most attempts to describe th
divine attributes of genius. He traces the upward course of one
nature's most gifted sons; his mind he supposes intuitive, but
became so—wonderful as was its flight, he knows it was through th
regions of *real knowledge*. Still this is but a description of th
modes, the modifications of the great poet's mind; of the elemen
of that mind, there is nothing said. So far as mere *means* ma
modify and *improve* original forces of mind, these remarks of Col
ridge are highly discriminative; but before such means will ever t

employed, there must be certain impelling powers—certain imperious *wants*, naturally tending to such a course.   When we ascribe
the *results* of genius to wisely-chosen and well-adapted *means*, we
should not forget that we *assume* a capacity equal to great discrimination and enlarged comparison ; in short, to the power of reasoning.
"To study patiently," at least supposes a mind susceptible of improvement, and aware of its wants; " to meditate deeply," implies a high
order of the thinking principal ; " to understand minutely, and become
intuitive," absolutely demands an organisation *originally* active, of
extraordinary endowments, and *prone* to great exaltation and habitual
exercise.

Thus writes the ingenious author of the " Philosophy of the Human
Voice," while contesting the usual notions of the qualities of genius :
' Let those who are deluded by this mystic notion of genius, turn
from the impostors who cannot describe an attribute which they do
not *understand*.   Let them go to the great sachems of mankind, and
learn from the real possessors of it how much of its manner may be
described ; they will tell us that genius, in its high meaning, is
always enthusiastic—always characterised by its love of an object in
its means as well as its ends."   We have now before us one of the
greatest sachems of mankind, and purpose through him to learn the
nature of real genius—of genius in its high meaning.   It will be seen
that the phrenologist does not teach, as is so often laid to his charge,
that a mere conformation of brain is the only measure of knowledge
—for he, of all men, is most interested in the rational discipline of
mind ; and to this culture—pursued in harmony with a sound philosophy, as well as to original endowments—he looks for the most
enduring triumphs of mind.   " Genius, in its high meaning," says
the author above cited, " is always enthusiastic."   But this enthusiasm, is it not as various as the different attributes which constitute
it ?   Has any one an equal enthusiasm for all the arts and sciences ?
Could Bacon have written *Hamlet*, or Shakspeare the Novum Orga-
num ? or could either have composed the *Messiah* of Handel ?   The
philosopher of the human voice, could he have written with the same
power, the same profound analysis, upon *mechanics*, as he has done
in aid of a beautiful and useful art ?   But *enthusiasm is* an attribute
of genius, and " the love of an object, in its means as well as its end,"
it has ever cherished.   But is it necessarily *peculiar* to genius—does
t accurately define it ?   Who has more enthusiasm in his own pursuit than the intensely avaricious man, who has a greater love of his
object in its *means* as well as its end ?

Before entering upon the phrenology of Shakspeare, let us illus-
rate the description of Coleridge, and the nice distinction among

men of genius, by applying the principles of our science. An individual may have an unusual developement of certain organs which
constitute the genius for painting, poetry, or some particular art—
he is "*possessed by* the spirit." But in consequence of comparative
deficiency in reflective intellect—positive deficiency in firmness, and
some other qualities—in fine, for want of harmonious balance, he is
rather the "automaton of genius"—he does not *possess* the spirit,
gifted with the greatest powers he yet needs, the power of *will*,
that monarch of the mind that commands, moulds, and directs, all
these gifts to the attainment of certain ends. Such organisations
manifest great ability, but often leave the world without any adequate
memorial of their powers. Others, again, become the masters of
themselves, wield with effect the power they have, understand their
own strength, and attain an overruling consciousness. They "*possess*
the spirit," and seldom die before they are able to boast with
Horace, that "They have executed a monument more lasting than
brass." We will now briefly advert to those fundamental conditions
of phrenology which are found united in Shakspeare, intending to
give a more minute analysis in the course of this article. His head
was large, and strikingly developed in the intellectual region. His
temperament we may infer to have been mixed—a combination of
nervous, sanguine, and bilious; we refer to his works for the appropriate manifestations. His moral organs were unquestionably high
—referring again to his works—particularly Benevolence. Now let
the reader pause, and carefully examine the engraving which adorns
this article, considered the most accurate likeness extant. Mark
the unusual height, breadth, and *depth*, of the forehead; behold the
sweeping brow, indicating wonderful perceptive powers—the obvious
expansion of the reflective region—the language-lit eye—the surpassing benevolence—and on either side, above the temples, and partially
covered by hair, the dome where beauty sits weaving her glowing
thoughts—the graceful swell of *Ideality*—and, remembering that he
has before his eye one of the "foremost men of all the world"—the
poet who "exhausted worlds, and then imagined new"—ask himself,
whether this extraordinary correspondence of manifestation with
phrenological conditions be only a curious coincidence? But all
these conditions, implying, as they do, wonderful powers, and which,
in the very nature of organisation, could not be dormant, but would
delight by their manifestation, yet do not with the accuracy which
belongs to science, and is demanded by the subject, define the exaltation and fervid energy of this myriad-minded man, the grandeur, the
brilliancy, the ever-active wit, the profound discrimination, and the
harmony which reigned among all these, by means of which, they

to prove. We have heard of a volume compiled from his works by a physician, entirely relating to his own profession; and most writers on insanity illustrate their subject by large draughts from the same fountain. The poet seems to have known that the mysteries of the soul could be best studied and unravelled through the medium of its mortal instrument. Thus, at least, he did *study* it; and hence the accuracy, depth, and philosophic discernment, which characterise his writings, when man is the subject of reflection. We now approach, what we believe to be, the broadly-marked, the unmistakable distinction between the truly great poet and the elegant rhymer, who imagines the farther he departs from all that is *natural*, the higher he soars in sublimity; but nothing is more sublime than truth, and she is equally the object of the great poet and profound philosopher—in their mutual love of her, their characters gradually unite, and the line which distinguishes them, becomes less distinct. There is not, perhaps, a single instance of a really great poet, without the spirit of an elevated philosophy. "The poet's eye, in a fine frenzy rolling," often descries those great truths which the philosopher obtains only after forging long chains of deductions; but these truths become unto each other the materials for a world, which, so far as the mass of mankind is concerned, is equally *ideal* to *both*.

To talk of the ignorance of Shakspeare, as some do, in order to enhance his genius, is exceedingly unphilosophical; it is impossible a mind like his can be ignorant, even as relates to general information, or knowledge of books. The merely illustrative matter of the comprehensive thinker, must be drawn from an infinite variety of sources; and though the veriest groundwork of his mind, can only be amassed by one having an intuitive perception of the great truth, that all human knowledge is a circle, which, however marked and divided by technical and sophistical distinctions, has its centre in the contemplative man. The various methods of study are of little consequence, when we talk of master spirits, for the progress of all original genius is ever in accordance with its organisation. From Plato and Aristotle, down to the days of Bacon, omitting fortunate discoverers of half developed truths, whose intellectual stature has been much overrated—every consummate genius destined to leave its enduring impress and act upon the thinking world for ages, no matter what the medium through which he spoke—metaphysics, natural philosophy, or through a far-reaching and elevated poesy— has been scarcely more remarkable for the living truths he brought from darkness, than for the wide and various sources whence he deduced them. We have been too long content to measure knowledge by the standard of the schools, although the folly of doing so, has been repeatedly rebuked by the greatest of the race. Shakspeare belongs not to the class of partial geniuses. His was a mind, which, though possessed of the greatest facility in *acquisition*, was not content with the mere exercise of *memory*—using the word in its phrenologica lsense, as one of the lower modes of action of all the intellectual faculties—but assimilated, and was constantly tending to the higher state of thought—conception, the great creative power— the peculiar attribute of exalted genius. Man was to the bard of Avon, as a nucleus around which he gathered all that affiliated with the subject; and though in certain departments he was inferior to some of his contemporaries, it is probable that no intellect of his day experienced a higher and more sustained activity of all the intellectual faculties ascribed by phrenology to man. The proper aliment of each, having undergone the alchymic process of his ever-musing mind, might easily, without the trouble of careful selection, be arrayed before the readers of the Journal; but it would be something worse than supererogatory. We will, however, by short quotations, illustrate the philosopical manifestation of his very large Benevolence; for to the diffused and far-reaching spirit of this organ, united with others, we are indebted for his "language pictures" of the mental miseries of the great, as well as the physical sufferings of the lowest of his race. Thus does he penetrate into the anxious sleepless chamber of a king :—

> "Oh, sleep!
> Nature's soft nurse! how have I frighted thee,
> That thou no more wilt weigh my eyelids down,
> And steep my senses in forgetfulness?
> *   *   *   *   *
> Wilt thou, upon the high and giddy mast,
> Seal up the ship-boy's eyes, and rock his brain
> In cradle of the rude imperious surge;
> And in the visitations of the winds,
> That take the ruffian billows by their tops,
> Curling their monstrous heads, and hanging them
> With deaf'ning clamours in the slippery clouds,
> That with the noise even death awakes?
> Canst thou, oh partial sleep, give thy repose
> To the wet sea boy, in an hour so rude,
> And in the calmest and the stillest hour,
> With all appliances and means to boot,
> Deny it to a king?"

And thus he extends his sympathy to an humbler sphere. The lines are spoken by Lear, in the midst of a storm.

> "Poor naked wretches, wheresoe'er you are,
> That bide the pelting of this pitiless storm,
> How shall your houseless heads, and unfed sides,

Your loop'd and window'd raggedness, defend you
From seasons, such as these? O, I have ta'en
Too little care of this! Take physic, pomp;
Expose thyself to feel what wretches feel;
That thou may'st shake the superflux to them,
And show the heavens more just."

His works teem with similar examples; his benevolence embraced all human things—all suffering, whether it existed in the palace or the cottage—whether the heaving bosom was hid by the " robes and furr'd gowns," or exposed to the " peltings of the pitiless storm" by the " loop'd and window'd raggedness" of want.

If any student of phrenology wishes to observe and feel the manifestations of Ideality and Tune in their highest modes of activity, let him read certain portions of the " Tempest ;" and if he can arouse his own faculties to a perfect sympathy with the scenes, he will be transported to the " Enchanted Isle," the " delicate Ariel" will float in beauty before his eye, Prospero will wave his magic wand, and the air be filled with " all the linked sweetness of sound."

(To be continued.)

ARTICLE III.

PATHOLOGICAL FACT CONFIRMATORY OF PHRENOLOGY.

Mr. Editor,—

Sir,—As surgical and pathological illustrations of phrenology are not only of a more satisfactory character, but rarer than other classes of facts, I send you the following case, which I use in my lectures as a proof of the functions of Combativeness. The facts were communicated to me some years since by the attending physician. It occurred in South Carolina, but as to the exact date and locality, my memoranda are deficient.

A boy, nine or ten years of age, was riding a spirited horse. The horse started at full speed, and the boy was thrown off; as he fell, the back of his head struck against a stump, and also received a blow from the hoof of the horse, the effect of which double injury was what might be called an egg-shell fracture of the occiput. The occipital bone was crushed in, and the brain much injured. Dr Turner was called to attend the case; when he arrived, it presented a frightful appearance, the injury extending to the angles of the parietal bones on each side. The brain was exposed—a portion escaped from the wound, and a portion was removed in th treatment; in all, about a tea-cupful was lost. The case seeme indeed, a desperate one, but in a few weeks the lad recovered. D Turner, having remarked that the portion of brain which wi removed came chiefly from the organs of Combativeness on eac side, suggested that the lad would probably become a coward on h recovery.

During the first week or two, as he lay in a comatose or oppres condition, his dreams, or more properly delirious wanderings of th mind, presented images of terror, under the influence of which h frequently started from the bed, as if endeavouring to escape. Up his recovery, the usual debility of the convalescent probably pr vented any particular observations of its effects on his characte Two years afterwards, the doctor saw him. He was perfectl cured, and his mind, *intellectually*, was unimpaired; but his *ch racter* was changed. He was timid as the hare. He could not l induced to ride a horse; and even if he saw a horseman approachin in the road, he would run into the woods to escape. At an age i which boys are usually high-spirited and proud to show their ind pendence, he was destitute of the feeling, and seemed to lean up others. He would not even leave the house, and go a few hundre yards by himself, but was escorted about the farm by the negi women. He was quite intelligent, and able to converse over h own case in a full and satisfactory manner. He told a full story his dreams of terror during the first fortnight after the accident.

He was quite unsocial, and indisposed to mingle in the athlet sports of boys. His cerebellum was undeveloped, his manners wei timid and feminine, and his voice like that of the eunuch.

If this account should meet the eye of Dr. Turner, I wou request him to make out and publish a more complete account of th foregoing case, and his subsequent observations.

Permit me to suggest to practical phrenologists the importance another class of facts which may easily be collected, and which ai sometimes not less valuable than those furnished by pathology. refer to the materials to be collected from an accurate study of th various sensations in different regions of the head, connected wit cephalic action. The other day, a young man gave me a minu account of an apparition which he had pursued, until it made mysterious escape, and of others which followed him until became familiar with them. Seeing that he was sincere, I inquire into the condition of his perceptive organs, and found that he was certain periods liable to an affection in which there was pain alor the brows and just over the eyeballs. This generally terminate after a free bleeding at the nose.   Such affections of the perceptive organs may well be the foundation of popular superstitions, for it is difficult to resist the sincere and graphic accounts of those who are thus deceived, without being able to suspect the source of their delusion.

I have been fortunate in obtaining this class of facts; some of which, indeed, might not be credible to those who test every statement by its harmony with their preconceived opinions.   I feel confident, however, to assert that peculiar conditions, or excessive action of any organ, *will always be accompanied by a sensation of some kind at its site;* and that every true principle in the science of phrenology may thus be sustained *by the evidence of sensation.*

Yours respectfully,

Jos. R. BUCHANAN.

New Orleans, December 20, 1839.

ARTICLE IV.

ON HUMAN CAPABILITY OF IMPROVEMENT.[*]

Man, existing in a savage state, without arts and industry, can scarcely be recognised as a rational being; he manifests only instincts; and instead of subduing external nature to his will, he picks up from its surface, as the brutes do, whatever enjoyments it spontaneously yields, and submits in sullen patience to its adverse influences, till they pass away.   In civilised countries, on the other hand, he presents the most unequivocal evidence of the greatness of his rational faculties, by the sway which he exerts over physical nature; but even in these regions, when we examine closely into the condition of individuals, we discover that although the intellectual powers have achieved admirable conquests over matter, there is a deplorable deficiency of moral enjoyment; that although man has displayed the magnificence of his nature in triumphing over earth and sea, air and fire, and rendering them ministers to his will, he has not succeeded in infusing order and beauty into his moral condition; that his heart is often sick with anguish, while his eyes look on a lovely world as his own.   Some sects regard this as the necessary result of man's imperfect nature, and disbelieve in the possi-

[*] From the 39th number of the Edinburgh Phrenological Journal.

bility of his ever advancing by the use of reason so far as to do in the moral, what he has accomplished in the physical, world; call forth order, beauty, and enjoyment, where pain and sorrow at present reign. Other sects not only regard such an advance as attainable, but teach that the Creator has formed man as a progressive and improvable being, with the direct object of his arranging his institutions and conduct in conformity to the Divine law, and thereby attaining to real enjoyment. They maintain, that, without being animated by this conviction in our daily conduct, and without resorting to the study of human and external nature, under the reliance on the divine goodness which it produces, we cannot be said to live *with* God in the world.

Thus, two great parties may be said to divide the religious world. The one, with which we have a great sympathy, believes the physical, moral, and intellectual constitution of this world to be greatly disordered; many and bitter were the proofs of this truth afforded by the pains and sorrows attending our early life and education; and we are still far from imagining that this world is a perfect institution. The burning deserts of Africa, the frozen regions of the poles, the noxious swamps, and the stony wastes every where abounding, proclaim that physical nature is not perfect; while the mental blindness the heart's sickness, and the body's anguish, prove that human nature requires great amendment. The other party, however, contend, that the opinion generally entertained of the inherent defects and disorders of creation is exaggerated; and that there is a far greater provision made for human virtue and happiness in the functions and capabilities of nature, than is generally understood or believed; and that it is denying the Divine wisdom and goodness, to say that this world is essentially disordered in its constitution; that it is not arranged so as to favour virtue, but the reverse; that it is a world essentially wicked, against the seductions of which the pious require to maintain a constant struggle. They say, that, if we entertain these views as our theory of human nature, and act consistently, we shall be led to look with little interest on human science, and to listen with much incredulity to schemes for improving the dispositions, capabilities, and condition of the race, by teaching them the laws of the natural world, and inducing them to obey them. No system of political economy, of law, or of education, having for its object the promotion of human happiness and virtue, by a right ordering of the elements of nature, appears to be practical, according to the fundamental doctrine, that nature, physical, moral, and intellectual, is depraved and out of joint. Although *extra*-natural means of rectifying the disorder be admitted, these

means do not belong to the department of philosophy, and do not
fall within the sphere of reason; whereas every scheme having the
permanent improvement of man for its object, by increasing his
health, enlarging his knowledge, strengthening his moral affections,
amending his social institutions, and diminishing his passions, seems
to require that the elements of his nature should in themselves be
good; that they should be wisely adapted to each other and the
external world; and that happiness and virtue should be an attainable result of their due application and arrangement.

These unfavourable views of human nature are perhaps entertained
by some of our readers, while by many others they will be regarded
as altogether erroneous; and this difference of opinion is itself of
much importance.   A practical as well as a theoretical conflict is
permanently proceeding in society, founded on the two sets of
opinions now adverted to.   The belief in the right constitution of
the world is so far instinctive, that individuals of all ranks, when
they lay aside their sectarian peculiarities, combine cordially in promoting the study of science, the investigation of nature, the diffusion
of knowledge, and the amelioration of social institutions, on natural
principles; in full reliance that the great elements of the material
and moral world are really constituted with the design of favouring
happiness and virtue.   On the other hand, we are surrounded by
religious sects essentially founded on the opposite principle, of nature
being in disorder, and of the only means of rectification being such
as are afforded by an influence not belonging to this world's constitution, not cognisable by philosophy, and not falling within the sphere
of reason.   These sects, when they have acted in their proper character, have laboured for centuries to improve mankind by their own
peculiar means; we do not mean to say whether successfully or
unsuccessfully, but simply to call attention to the fact, that, in their
efforts, the exposition of the natural constitution of the human mind
of the external world, of their relations and capabilities, has formed
a very subordinate part. . They have greatly omitted to cultivate the
natural capabilities of the beings whom they have sought to improve
and nevertheless expected to accomplish this end without using the
means.   They have resembled the pious agriculturists of Scotland
of the olden time, who prayed for dry weather, when the natural
humidity of the atmosphere was damaging their crops with rain, but
omitted to drain their fields.   Their prayers were not successful
because they did not use the means which Providence had placed
within their own power for protecting their crops.   Their posterity
have applied their skill in draining, and have fitted their fields to a
greater extent to the climate, in consequence of which, fair crop

have been reaped in 1829 and 1830, after rains which would have spread absolute desolation over the fields of our ancestors. The enlightened tenantry of this age must enjoy a higher impression of the benevolence of the Creator, so far as it can be inferred from this single instance, than could be obtained by their predecessors.

If there has been an omission on the part of some of the religious instructors of mankind, in not making the most of the natural capabilities of man, as a preliminary condition to the efficacy of divine influence, we may expect to discover discrepancy between the magnitude of the exertions made by them for human improvement and the practical result. Accordingly, to a person of a plain understanding, nothing appears more extraordinary than the contrast afforded between the unwearied exertions of religious sects, and the fruit produced. Compare the sedulous teaching of religion to both sexes in youth, the powerful efforts constantly made to maintain its influence in adult age, with the wide dereliction of its principles in the practical affairs of life, and the deficiency is conspicuous. We do not find the principles of religion pervading all the employments of individuals, and the institutions of society. The daily occupations of the artisan, and of every other member of society, ought to be founded on, and regulated by, its principles. But let us look at the fact. Does the man, who commences at six o'clock in the morning to break stones on the highway, and who, exposed to heat, cold, or wet, as the heavens happen to send, labours at this occupation, with only two hours' intermission, till six o'clock at night, for six days in the week, from youth to old age, appear to be employed like a rational being, possessed of moral feelings and an immortal soul sent into this world to cultivate and improve these powers, in order to fit him for higher dignity and enjoyment hereafter? He appears more like a creature condemned to endure penance, but for what specific purpose, it is not very easy to discover. As the vivacity of his moral and intellectual powers depends on the condition of his brain, and as exposure to the rigour of a cold and variable climate in the open air, tends, by the laws of nature, to impede the action of this organ, the first fact that strikes us is the direct contradiction between the professed end of his existence, viz. his moral and intellectual improvement, and the arrangement of his physical condition. In the next place, as instruction and exercise of all the mental powers are required by nature as essential to moral and intellectual improvement, the second circumstance that attracts notice is the total absence or inadequate extent of such instruction and exercise. This forms a second contrast between his actual condition and the professed end of his existence on earth. Similar observations are applicable, under proper modifications, to the cases of the artisan, the operative manufacturer, the agricultural labourer, the merchant, the lawyer, the soldier, and statesman. If we look at the professional pursuits of one and all of these classes; at the principles on which they are conducted, at the faculties which they call into exercise, at the time which they engage, and at the *objects* which they present to the mind, and consider them in reference to the advancement of the individuals in moral and intellectual improvement, we cannot but be astonished at the imperfect adaptation of the external condition of many men to the professed object of their existence. We conceive that human nature admits of institutions and arrangements calculated to favour, in a far higher degree than those now existing, the developement of their moral and intellectual faculties.

It is justly assumed, that men are sent into this world to prepare, by the cultivation of their higher faculties, for a purer state of existence hereafter; yet, in many instances, their physical condition is opposed to it, and their occupations during nine-tenths of their waking dreams have scarcely any perceptible relation to their advancement in the knowledge of God and of his works, or in obedience to his laws. The professional pursuits of an operative tradesman, an extensive merchant or manufacturer, or a well employed lawyer, cannot be regarded as means for developing the rational powers of man, and fitting him for a higher sphere. So far as necessary to provide subsistence and comfort for his body, and to acquire leisure and means of cultivating his nobler faculties, they do conduce to this end; but viewed as the grand pursuits of life, they engross the mind, and become impediments to its moral progress. Besides, until these pursuits shall be founded on correct views of human nature, and be conducted on principles directly in accordance with the dictates of the moral and intellectual faculties, they must continue to obstruct, rather than advance, the improvement of man as a rational being. If nature does not admit of their being arranged, so as to favour this end, then human improvement is impossible: if it does admit of such an ordering of professional pursuits, then religious persons ought to view this as a preliminary condition, to be fulfilled before their other principles can become efficacious. In point of fact, artisans, merchants, and professional men in general, know as much, or often more, of moral, intellectual, and physical science, of religion and its practical power, and are purer in spirit, more Christian in temper and disposition, at eighteen than at sixty; though the very religion which they profess, teaches them that existence on earth is given to prepare them for religious, moral, and intellectual enjoyments in heaven.   In short, the double contradiction presses itself on our attention ; the life of busy men is at variance with the professed object of their existence on earth ; while, at the same time, the rectification of this system of society, and the better arrangement of the natural world, are objects very little attended to by those who profess these high views of human destiny and duty.

It appears to us extremely difficult to reconcile these contradictions, but we shall attempt to elucidate their origin.

The theologians who condemned the natural world, lived in an age when there was no sound philosophy, and almost no knowledge of physical science ; they were unavoidably ignorant of the elementary qualities of human nature, and of the influence of organisation on the mental powers—the great link which connects the moral and physical worlds.   They were unacquainted with the relations subsisting between the mind and external nature, and could not by possibility divine to what extent individuals and society were capable of being improved by natural means.   In the history of man, they had read chiefly of misery and crime, and had in their own age beheld much of both.   They were, therefore, naturally led to form a low estimate of human nature, and to expect little good from the cultivation of its inherent capabilities.   These opinions having been entwined with religious sentiments, descended from generation to generation ; and, in consequence, persons of sincere piety have, for several centuries, been induced to look down on this world as a wilderness abounding with briars, weeds, and noxious things, and to direct their chief attention, not to the study of its elements and their relations, in the hope of reducing them to order, but to enduring the disorder with patience and resignation, and to securing, by faith and penitence, salvation in a future life.   It has never been with them a practical principle, that human nature itself may be vastly improved in its moral and intellectual capabilities, by increasing the size of the anterior and superior regions of the brain, and diminishing the size of the lower and occipital portions ; which, nevertheless, the principles of physiology, and the facts ascertained by phrenology, warrant us in believing ; nor that human nature and the external world are adjusted on the principle of favouring the developement of the higher powers of our minds ; nor that the study of the constitution of nature is indispensable to human improvement ; nor that this world, and its professions and pursuits, might be rendered favourable to virtue, by searching out the natural qualities of its elements, their relationship, and the moral plan on which God has constituted and governs it.   Some philosophers and divines having ailed to discover a consistent order or plan in the moral world, have rashly concluded that none such exists, or that it is inscrutable. It appears never to have occurred to them that it is impossible to comprehend a whole system without becoming acquainted with its parts; these persons have been ignorant of the physiology of man, of the philosophy of man, of the philosophy of external nature and their relations, and nevertheless have not perceived that this extensive ignorance of the details rendered it impossible for them to comprehend the plan of the whole. Hence they have involved themselves in contradictions; for while it has been a practical principle with them, that enjoyment in a future state is to be the consequence of the believer attaining to a holy and pious frame of mind in this life; they have represented the constitution of the world to be so unfavourable to piety and virtue, that men in general, who continue attached to it, cannot attain to this right frame of spirit, or act habitually in consistency with it. They have not had philosophy sufficient to perceive that man must live in society to be either virtuous, useful, or happy; that the social atmosphere is to the mind what air is to the lungs; that while an individual cannot exist to virtuous ends out of society, he cannot exist in a right frame in it, if the moral atmosphere with which he is surrounded be deeply contaminated with vice and error. Individual merchants, for example, cannot act habitually on Christian principles, if the maxims of their trade be not Christain; and if the world be so unfavourably constituted that it does not admit of the rules of trade becoming Christian, then active life and practical religion are naturally opposed to each other. Divines have laboriously recommended spiritual exercises as means of improvement in this life, and of salvation in the next, but have rarely dealt with the philosophy of this world, or attempted its rectification, so as to render these exercises truly efficacious. Their minds have been infected with the first great error, that this world is irremediably defective in its constitution, and that human hope must be entirely concentrated on the next. This may be attributed to the premature formation of a system of theology in the dawn of civilisation before the qualities of the physical world, and the elements of the moral world and their relationship, were known; and to erroneous interpretations of Scripture in consequence, partly, of that ignorance.

Now, if phrenology is to operate at all in favour of human improvement, one of the most striking effects which it will produce, will be the lifting up of the veil which has so long concealed the natural world, its capabilities and importance, from the eyes of divines. To all practical ends connected with theology, the philo-

sophy of nature might as well not exist; the sermons preached a
century ago are equal, if not superior, in sense and suitableness to
human nature, to those delivered yesterday; and yet, in the interval,
the human mind has made vast advances in knowledge of the works
of creation. Divines have frequently applied philosophical discoveries in proving the existence and developing the character of the
Deity; but they have failed in applying either the discoveries themselves, or the knowledge of the divine character obtained by means
of them, to the practical purposes of virtue. This, however,
phrenology will enable them one day to do. In surveying the
world itself, the phrenologist perceives that the Creator has bestowed
elementary qualities on the human mind and on external objects,
and established certain relations between them; that these have been
incessantly operating according to their inherent tendencies, generally aiming at good, always desiring it, but often missing it through
pure ignorance and blindness, yet capable of attaining it when
enlightened and properly directed. The baneful effects of ignorance
are every where apparent. Three-fourths of the mental faculties
have direct reference to this world, and in their functions appear to
have no intelligible relation to any other—such are Amativeness,
Philoprogenitiveness, Combativeness, Destructiveness, Constructiveness, Acquisitiveness, Secretiveness, Self-esteem, and others; while
the remaining fourth have reference at once to this life, and to a
higher state of existence—such are Benevolence, Ideality, Wonder,
Veneration, Hope, Conscientiousness, and Intellect. To guide and
successfully apply the first class of faculties to the promotion of human
happiness, it appears indispensable that the faculties themselves, the
physical conditions on which their strength and weakness, inertness
and vivacity depend—the relations established between them and the
external world, which is the grand theatre of their action—and,
finally, the relation between them and the superior faculties, which
are destined to direct them, should be known; and yet, scarcely any
thing is known in a philosophical and practical sense by the people
at large, on these points. If we are correct in saying that these
faculties have, by their constitution, reference chiefly to this world,
then we maintain that useful knowledge for their guidance will be
afforded by the philosophy of this world; and that the wisdom which
is to reduce them to order, will receive important aid from studying
the constitution which it has pleased the Creator to bestow on them,
and the relations which he has seen proper to institute between them
and the other departments of his works. His wisdom and goodness
will be found to pervade them. He has bestowed on us intellect to
discover, and sentiment to obey, his will in whatever record its exist-

ence is inscribed, and yet little of this knowledge is taught by divines to the people.

Knowledge of the constitutions, relations, and capabilities of this world is indispensable also to the proper exercise and direction of the superior powers of our minds. In all ages, practical men have been engaged for three-fourths of their time in pursuits calculated to gratify the faculties which have reference to this world alone; but, unfortunately, the remaining fourth of their time has not been devoted to pursuits bearing reference to their higher faculties. Through want of intellectual education, they were incapable of deriving pleasure from observing nature and reasoning, and they were not furnished with ideas to enable them to think. Owing to the barbarism which pervaded society in general, there was no moral atmosphere in which their superior sentiments could play. Ambition, that powerful stimulant in social life, was not directed to moral objects, but generally the reverse. The hours, therefore, which ought to have been dedicated to the improvement of the higher portion of their faculties, were either devoted to the pursuit of gain, sensual pleasure or ambition, or spent in mere trifling amusements and relaxation. There was no practical onward purpose of moral and intellectual advancement abroad in the secular occupations of society; and the divines who formed public opinion, so far from discovering that this disorder was not inherent in the constitution of nature, and that Christianity, in teaching the doctrine of the supremacy of the moral faculties, necessarily implied the practicability of a state of society founded on that principle, fell into the opposite error, and represented the world as deranged in all its parts; as incapable, by the developement of its own elements, of rectification; and thereby added strength and permanence to the evils originating in ignorance and unguided passion.

We are far from casting blame on the exellent individuals who fell into these mistakes; they were inevitable at the time in which they lived, and with the lights which they possessed; but we point them out as errors which ought to be removed. We subjoin a few illustrations of the effects which a knowledge of human and external nature may be supposed to produce in improving the condition of man as an inhabitant of this world.

Divines most properly teach that it is sinful for the sexes to cohabit as husband and wife without having solemnly undertaken the obligations and duties imposed by the ceremony of marriage; that brothers and sisters, and uncles and aunts, cannot marry without sin; and that he that provideth not for his own, is worse than an infidel. In these particulars, the constitution of nature, and the precepts of divines, agree; but the following points, connected with the same order of duties, are generally omitted in the exhortations of the pulpit, and nevertheless, *it is impossible*, without attending to them, to avoid sowing the seeds of misery, producing physical and moral disorder, and directly counteracting the precepts themselves, which the divines deliver.

1. Very young persons ought not to marry; because, by the laws to which God has subjected our physical constitution, the offspring of very young parents are generally deficient in bodily and mental qualities, or both. The municipal law allows males to marry at fourteen, and females at twelve; and the divines take no cognisance of the sin of marrying at an unripe age; whereas nature, in this climate, is inimical to marriage before twenty or twenty-two in the female, and twenty-five or twenty-six in the male.

One consequence of marriages in extreme youth is, that the first born child or children are in general deficient in the organs of the moral and reflective faculties, and have an excess of the organs of the animal propensities. A single illustration of the consequences of such a union will suffice to show how deeply it may affect the order of the moral world. Suppose a British peer of forty, possessed of ordinary qualities, to marry an immature girl of seventeen, and that the first born child is a son. He would prove greatly deficient in moral and intellectual powers. The organs of the propensities would be large, and the anterior and superior portions of the brain, which manifest the higher faculties, would be relatively small. In consequence of this combination, his natural inclinations would lead him to prefer animal gratifications to study, and his innate consciousness of a low mind would render him sceptical of human virtue, and proud of his "order," as the only mark of superiority in his person over the base born vulgar. The law would give him the family estates and a seat in the upper house of parliament, and the customs of society invest him with a vast influence in his native country; but the low formation of his brain would render the high rank, the large property, the legislative voice, and the social influence, so many inlets of temptation to immoral conduct in himself, and so many instruments of perpetrating mischief to his fellow-men. The priest might give his benediction at his father's marriage, and his mother be unconscious of sin; but the Creator's laws being violated, His blessing would not fall on the first born. The children produced after the mother arrived at maturity, would manifest superior qualities. The result would be still more hurtful were old men to marry very young women; for bodily imperfection would then be added to mental imbecility. We state these cases hypothetically, to

oid the remotest chance of personal allusion; but we entreat any
ader who may be disposed to regard them as imaginary, to observe
ature, and he will acquit us of this charge.

Nature transmits the constitution of organs from parents to chil-
en, and health chiefly depends on the inheritance of them in a
und and vigorous condition. Small organs are, *cæteris paribus*,
ore feeble than large organs, and less capable of resisting the
ock of external influences of an unfavourable kind; or, in other
ords, they are more liable to disease from the ordinary atmospheric
anges, from moral depression, intellectual exhaustion, and other
uses. Nature, therefore, proclaims that two persons having both
eak lungs, weak stomachs, weak muscles, or weak brains, ought
ot to intermarry; the consequence will be, the production of an
feebled offspring, liable from birth to suffering and misery.

Now, our proposition is, that if it be the object of divines to
nder men happy on earth, to bring their whole being, animal,
oral, and intellectual, into the highest state of perfection of which
is susceptible, as a means of preparing them for heaven; and if
ese ends cannot, by the constitution of nature, be attained without
tention to the points alluded to, religious instructors, who confine
eir attention to performance of the ceremony of marriage, to
arding the forbidden degrees, and to the general precept of pro-
ding for offspring, omit nineteen-twentieths of the knowledge
hich is necessary to be taught, and to be practically acted on by
o sexes, before they can discharge their duties as rational, moral,
d religious beings, on the single point of marriage. Nay, farther:
e maintain that the points omitted, are fundamental and vital in
nportance; and that, while they are neglected, and beings are pro-
uced with enormous organs of the animal propensities, and small
gans of the moral and intellectual faculties, with feeble bodies and
herent bad health, practical Christianity, as a system not of words
d abstract contemplations, but of living action in the bosoms of
en, and in the transactions of society, cannot possibly be realised,
d moral order cannot be established in the world.

We repeat, that we do not blame the clergy for omitting this
struction; because they could not teach it till they possessed it
emselves, and saw its importance. We object, however, to their
tempting to excuse themselves after it is pointed out to them, by
leging that this is human science which it belongs to professors in
niversities, and not to Christian ministers, to teach. With the
tmost deference we would answer, that the clergy are the servants
f God, appointed to instruct the people in his laws and his will;
at while the book of Revelation is spread out in printed leaves, the

book of Nature is opened wide before them, also in the handwriting of the Deity; and that they are bound to read and to teach his law and his will, indicated in the one as well as in the other; and that it will only be when the truths of nature shall be communicated to the people as part of the Divine law and the Divine will, that they will take a living interest in them, and yield them a willing obedience. Nature has been neglected in clerical teaching only because it has been unknown. Within one generation, after a substantial education in natural knowledge shall have been communicated to the young, the prevailing style of preaching must be improved. Individuals, whose instruction is a little advanced, already perceive and lament its inefficiency, in consequence of not dealing in human nature in its living form.

2. Divines most properly teach us to contemn riches, and the vanities of life, to set our hearts on things above, and to be instant in prayer, serving the Lord—all which precepts are admirable in themselves, but utterly impracticable to the great mass of the people, while the present arrangements and habits of society prevail. To enable a man really to prefer the enjoyments afforded by active, moral, and intellectual faculties, to the animal gratifications which money may purchase, he must possess, *first*, vigorous, moral, and intellectual organs, and moderate animal organs; *2dly*, His higher powers must have been cultivated from youth, and stored with positive knowledge and pure moral perceptions, suited to their real nature; and, *3dly*, He must be surrounded by beings similarly constituted, similarly educated, and loving to act on similar principles. And we again most respectfully say to the clergy, that it is their duty to teach the people every branch of knowledge, and every practical observance, that may conduce to the realisation of these conditions, before they can expect their precepts to take effect. At present they issue the injunction to contemn riches, to men in whose brains the organs that desire the gratifications purchased by wealth greatly predominate; who live in society devoted systematically to the accumulation of riches; and who, without money, cannot effectually influence their fellow-men even in favour of religion and virtue; and still they complain that their precepts are ineffectual. As well might a husbandman who should sow seed in the desert, complain that he reaped no increase. Let the clergy insist on the absolute necessity of the *natural conditions* which the Creator has rendered indispensable to the practice of virtue being fulfilled, then sow holy precepts, and they shall not have cause to complain of the return.

These are mere illustrations of our position, that some sects have ome too hastily to the conclusion, that this world is wrongly constituted. Volumes would be requisite to develope the subject comletely, and to show fully its practical importance. In publishing hese remarks, we expose ourselves to the question, Who are we hat erect ourselves into authorities on the constitution of the world, nd become critics on the doctrine of venerable and illustrious ivines? We are in ourselves the least influential of men; but if he doctrine which we announce, be a correct interpretation of the onstitution of nature, a high authority supports the positions of vhich we are merely the humble expounders. If there be any truth n these positions, then, we humbly think that they warrant us in aying, that phrenology will one day produce a change in the sentinents and institutions of the world, beneficial to the Christian religion; nd that one of its first effects will be to lead the clergy to use means or producing the natural conditions, in individuals and society, which ire indispensable to practical Christianity, and then to hope for their loctrines being favoured with the divine blessing, and an abundant ncrease of fruit. The functions of the brain and the philosophy of nind have not been discovered to serve as mere laughing-stocks to vitless essayists. They are parts of creation of the very highest mportance, and we are warranted in saying, that the discovery of hem involves in its train consequences of the utmost interest to luman happiness.

Some pious persons may perhaps charge us with foolishness, if ιot atheism, because we advocate these views; but we retort on hem that, besides unintentionally, yet virtually, denying the Deity, ıs the governor of this world, they are practically strangers to the ıxtent of His power and goodness, displayed in sublunary creation. They see the beauties of the earth, and the magnificence of the ιeavens, as poets or painters behold them, but they do not per:eive or understand the constitution of human nature, and the relaions between it and external creation. They are strangers to the lesigns of the Creator manifested in these works in relation to man. Λ mystery hangs over them which they have not penetrated, and ιence, although they ardently desire to know God, they look for ıim almost exclusively in a spiritual world. We see and feel Him n us, and in every thing around us. Having obtained a knowledge ›f the faculties which He has bestowed, and discovered some of the :elations between them and creation, our eyes have been opened to a ›erception of a vast extent of design, wisdom, and goodness in the Creator, which was hidden from us until we obtained the light which :enders it discernible.

In conclusion, we observe, that while we do not contend for the absolute perfection of physical creation, or the perfectibility of man by natural means, we are humbly of opinion, that there are far more excellencies and capabilities in both than have hitherto been discovered; and that the study, evolution, and proper practical application of the natural elements of the physical and moral worlds are indispensable preliminaries, and most important auxiliaries to human improvement. It is one of the excellent characteristics of the Christian religion, that it is adapted to every state of society—to men scattered in wildernesses or thronged in crowded cities; and hence religion is shorn of her power and utility as a practical system of instruction, by whatever tends to widen her separation from science, philosophy, and the affairs of this world. The human faculties having proceeded from the Creator, are framed in harmony with the actual constitution of nature; and would kindle with zeal, and labour with delight in studying, unfolding, and applying it, if so directed; whereas they are restrained, cramped, paralysed, and enfeebled, by inculcating habitually maxims which cannot become practical, in consequence of the natural conditions on which they depend not being previously produced. This unfortunate habit of undervaluing the capabilities of the natural world, and neglecting the study of it, diverts the attention of the best minds among the people from the real road to improvement. In consequence of the constitution and moral relations of the natural world being too much neglected—while, at the same time, the Creator has rendered a knowledge of them indispensable to moral cultivation—preaching is inefficacious in improving the temporal condition of mankind, to an extent unprecedented in most human institutions. This conclusion is forced on us, when we compare the number, zeal, and talents of the teachers, the provisions made for their support, and the favourable dispositions of the people to profit by their instruction, with the actual benefits communicated by their preaching. When divines shall have become acquainted with the real constitution of the world, and the moral plan which pervades it, and shall have dedicated their talents to teaching these to the people, as preparatory for their other doctrines, they will find themselves and their instructions invested with a moral power and efficacy to which they have hitherto been strangers; and then, but not till then, will religion, science, philosophy, practical business, and recreation, appear resting on one basis animated by accordant spirits, coinciding in their objects, and contributing to one end—the improvement of man as a moral, intellectual, and religious being. These remarks apply exclusively to the temporal effects of religion. Its influence on the eternal interests of mankind is too sacred a subject for discussion in a journal devoted solely to philosophical inquiries.

ARTICLE V.

*rania Americana ; or a Comparative View of the Skulls of various
Aboriginal Nations of North and South America : to which is prefixed an Essay on the varieties of the Human Species ; illustrated
by seventy-eight plates and a coloured map.* By SAMUEL GEORGE
MORTON, M. D., Professor of Anatomy in the Medical Department of Pennsylvania College, at Philadelphia ; Member of the
Academy of Natural Sciences of Philadelphia, of the American
Philosophical Society, of the Historical Society of Pennsylvania,
of the Boston Society of Natural History, &c. &c.

The above title will convey to the reader some idea of the nature
nd character of this great work. It is not our present object to
resent a critical or extended review of its contents ; having given,
i Vol. I. page 385 of this Journal, a minute description of the
eneral plan and design of the work, and also another notice of it in
'ol. II. page 143, to each of which we would refer the reader.
'rom an inspection of the plates, and some portions of the work, we
id not then hesitate to speak of its value in the highest terms, and
thorough examination of its contents has now fully satisfied us of
ie correctness of our previous impressions.

The publication of the *Crania Americana* will constitute an inte-
esting and important era in the science of anthropology. It differs
ssentially, in many respects, from any other work ever presented to
ie public on natural history. Philosophers and historians have
itherto generally studied the nature of man, and described his cha-
acteristics, without sufficiently considering his physical organisation,
nd the intimate and necessary connection of this, with the manifes-
itions of mind. The consequence is, that most of the accounts
ecorded in history of the peculiar *distinctive* mental qualities of
idividuals, families, and nations, are, in their details, vague, indefi-
ite, and unsatisfactory. This remark is true, not only in reference
i the above class of writers, but applies with almost equal force to
iose who have devoted their attention more exclusively to studying
ian's physical structure and organisation. It is true, the labours of
ilumenbach, Buffon, Cuvier, and others, have greatly added to our
nowledge of the natural history of man, and of the varied exhi-
itions of his character in different ages and nations ; but how little
ght have all their observations and researches thrown upon his
iental qualities? While metaphysicians, guided by their own *indi-
idual* consciousness, have written volumes on the faculties or opera-
ons of mind, converting it into an abstract and speculative science,

naturalists have prosecuted their labours, comparatively ignorant, and certainly regardless, of the powerful influence of physical organisation over mind. Though, in many instances, they have been quite minute and precise in describing the complexion and general features of the face, yet they have almost invariably omitted any account of the relative size, or particular configuration of the cranium. And there is not a single instance in which they have ever given us the necessary data, from which correct inferences on this subject can be drawn. Blumenbach made some approximation to this, in his great work "DECADES COLLECTIONIS SUÆ CRANIORUM DIVERSARUM GENTIUM ILLUSTRATÆ." And perhaps it may not be out of place, here, to give some little account of this celebrated work, as it constitutes the only extensive collection of drawings of human crania which has ever been presented to the public, prior to Dr. Morton's.

The *decades* of Blumenbach came out in separate parts or fasciculi, which were in the course of publication during the space of forty years. The whole work contains about seventy plates, or drawings, of skulls; some few are drawn as large as life, but most of the drawings are evidently far below the natural size; and, at all events, there is such a want of accuracy and the requisite explanations, that no correct comparison can be instituted between these representations and the general size of the heads of nations or races to which they respectively belonged. Besides, we have no measurements whatever accompanying these plates; we know nothing concerning the internal capacity of the entire, or particular parts of the skulls here represented, nor of their diameters as taken in different directions. And though the author has recorded full and vivid descriptions of the general features and physical peculiarities of the different tribes or races represented in his work, yet he has not given us the least information concerning the relative size, or particular configuration of their crania. Not one word has he uttered illustrative of any coincidence or dissimilarity between the characters of individuals or races, and the size and shape of their crania, nor of the causes, uses, or consequences, of the physical differences in the skulls which are so well portrayed in his plates. The consequence is, these drawings of Blumenbach have never received much attention, and are almost valueless compared to what they might have been, had they been accompanied with proper measurements and descriptions. For it must be obvious to every reflecting mind, that illustrations of crania can rise in interest and value, only in proportion as the true physiology of the brain is understood and appreciated. It is not known how well Blumenbach was acquainted with the great truths unfolded by phrenology, concerning the functions of the brain, r in what light he viewed these discoveries, but this is certain, he once attended Dr. Gall's lectures in Germany, and could not possibly have been ignorant of his works on what was then called *cranioscopy*. But while Blumenbach has made no reference or allusion whatever to this subject, (and from what motives or reasons, we will not pretend to say,) he has not presented a single fact or statement in opposition to the discoveries of Gall. Whatever, therefore, may have been the *private* opinion of this distinguished physiologist, is a matter of no moment. Still, it is greatly to be regretted that he did not accompany his drawings of skulls with some data or measurements, from which others might deduce correct and important inferences, and thus turn this celebrated work to a far more valuable account than can possibly now be done.

But the author of the *Crania Americana* has pursued a very different course from Blumenbach. While it has not been his object to prove or advocate the principles of phrenology, he has not failed to give us descriptions of character and tables of measurements, which must render the volume invaluable to the student of mental science. The whole work may be considered in its design, nature, and character, as chiefly a contribution to the natural history of man, and to the science of anatomy in particular; but as it is strictly a treatise, professing to give accurate descriptions of the peculiar characters of certain portions of the human family, in connection with illustrations and measurements or their crania, it may be supposed to have important bearings on phrenology, to some of which we will now invite the reader's attention.

In the dedication of the *Crania Americana* (to John S. Phillips, Esq., who had rendered the author important services in preparing the measurements, &c.) we find this statement:—"It may, perhaps, be thought by some readers, that these details are unnecessarily minute, especially in the phrenological table; and again, others would have preferred a work conducted throughout on phrenological principles. In this study, I am yet a learner; and it appeared to me the wiser plan to present the facts unbiased by the theory, and let the reader draw his own conclusions. You and I have long admitted the fundamental principles of phrenology, viz. that the brain is the organ of the mind, and that its different parts perform different functions; but we have been slow to acknowledge the details of cranioscopy, as taught by Dr. Gall, and supported and extended by subsequent observers. We have not, however, neglected this branch of inquiry, but have endeavoured to examine it in connection with numerous facts, which can only be fully appreciated when they come to be compared with similar measurements derived from the other

races of men. Yet I am free to acknowledge, that there is a sin
gular harmony between the mental character of the Indian and hi
cranial developements, as explained by phrenology." Here we hav
the author's candid and explicit opinion on the science; it needs n
comment. The phrenological tables mentioned above, we shall refe
to after noticing other portions of the work.

The Crania Americana opens with an "Introductory Essay on the
varieties of the Human Species." This is decidedly the most critica
and philosophical production on the natural history of man, whicl
has ever appeared in this country. Our limits will not permit u
here to enter into a minute analysis or description of it; but, at th
same time, we cannot refrain from referring to two or three pecu
liarities which distinguish this essay from all other writings on th
subject, and which, in our opinion, greatly enhances its value. I
the first place, the descriptions of the different races and families o
men are drawn more in accordance with the true and distinctiv
elements of their nature—particularly with reference to mind—tha
what can be found in any other work on anthropology. In th
second place, there is such a description of the size and configuratio
of the skull, as to render the delineations of character far more inte
resting and valuable. And though the coincidences between the tw
may not be strictly phrenological in every particular, yet no on
acquainted with the general principles of the science can fail to per
ceive that a most striking harmony exists between the description
of the skull and the character given. As specimens on this point
we make the following quotations :—

In describing the five different races, the author uses this language
1. *The Caucasian, or European race.*—" The skull is large and oval
and its anterior portion full and elevated. * * * This race is distin
guished for the facility with which it attains the highest intellectua
endowments." 2. *The Mongolian race.*—" The skull is oblong-oval
somewhat flattened at the sides, with a low forehead. * * * In thei
intellectual character, the Mongolians are ingenious, imitative, an
highly susceptible of cultivation." 3. *The Malay race.*—" Th
skull is high and squared or rounded, and the forehead low an
broad. * * * This race is active and ingenious, and possesses all th
habits of a migratory, predaceous, and maritime people." 4. *Th
American race.*—" The skull is small, wide between the parieta
protuberances, prominent at the vertex, and flat on the occiput. *
In their mental character, the Americans (or Indians) are averse t
cultivation, slow in acquiring knowledge, restless, revengeful, an
fond of war, and wholly destitute of maritime adventure." 5. *Th
Ethiopian race.*—" The head is long and narrow, the forehead low

the cheek bones prominent, the jaws projecting, and the chin small.
* * * In disposition, the negro is joyous, flexible, and indolent ;
while the many nations which compose this race, present a singular
diversity of intellectual character, of which the far extreme is the
lowest grade of humanity." It should be remembered, that these
descriptions are general, and apply to the several races as a whole,
while there may be a great diversity in the character as well as in
the size and shape of the skull, among the different individuals and
nations composing each race.

As the Crania Americana will probably fall into the hands of few
of our readers, and it contains valuable facts on this subject, being
the fruits of great labour and research, we are induced to enrich our
pages with other extracts similar to the above. We cannot now
point out their connection with, or bearings on, phrenology, though
we may refer to them hereafter; in the mean time, some of our
readers may, perhaps, turn them to a valuable account. The quotations which we make, will refer particularly to the description of the
skull; our limits prevent us making copious extracts in relation to
character.

The author of this essay, following the classification of Blumenbach, considers each of the races under the head of distinct groups
or families, making in all twenty-two divisions. In the description of
the Germanic family, we find this account:—"The head is large and
spheroidal, the forehead broad and arched. * * * The moral character of the German is marked by decided personal courage, great
endurance of fatigue, firmness, and perseverance, and a strong
attachment to their families and their native land. Intellectually,
they are conspicuous for industry and success in the acquisition of
knowledge; with a singular blending of taciturnity and enthusiasm,
they rival all modern nations in music, poetry, and the drama ; nor
are they less conspicuous for their critical attainments in language
and the exact sciences." In describing the Celtic family, the author
says—"They have the head rather elongated, and the forehead
narrow and but slightly arched. * * * In disposition, they are
frank, generous, and grateful ; yet quick-tempered, pugnacious, and
brave to a proverb."

The Nilotic family include the modern and ancient Egyptians. A
writer, quoted by the author, says of the former—"Their heads are
a fine oval, the forehead of moderate size, not high, but generally
prominent." In alluding to the ancient Egyptians, the author makes
this statement—"Their heads were formed as in the Hindoo, thus
differing from the Caucasian only in being somewhat smaller in proportion to the body, and having a narrower and less elevated fore-

head. Mr. Madden, who speaks of having examined a great number of heads in the Theban catacombs, says 'that the old Egyptian skull is extremely narrow across the forehead, and of an oblong shape anteriorly. I never found one with a broad, expanded forehead.' There is a remarkable resemblance among the innumerable heads sculptured in the temples of the Nile; and one who is accustomed to examine them, becomes so familiar with the Egyptian physiognomy, that when other races are introduced, as the Jews and Negroes, the eye can mostly detect them. There is also a singular accordance in confirmation between the sculptured heads and the real ones taken from the Theban catacombs. Two prominent varieties are discernible in each; one of these has the rather low and narrow forehead above mentioned, while the other presents the full developement of the Caucasian head."

The Indostanic family is thus characterised :—" The head of the Hindoo is small in proportion to the body, elongated and narrow, especially across the forehead, which is only moderately developed. * * * The Hindoos appear by nature to be a mild, sober, and industrious race, warm in their attachments, and fond of their children. But their love of the marvellous, fostered as it is by a fantastic religion, is almost without a parallel among nations. They are of a timid disposition, and not inclined to cruelty, yet their avarice, which is extreme, leads them readily to commit murder for the most trifling acquisition. They practise deception with infinite art, to which falsehood and perjury form no obstacles." The character of the Hindoos is too well known to require farther extracts. We may here state, that some English phrenologists, who made a thorough examination in Calcutta, found a most striking harmony between the cranial developements of the Hindoos and their peculiar characteristics.

The skull of the Malay family is thus described :—" The forehead is low, moderately prominent and arched, the occiput is much compressed, and often projecting at its upper and lateral sides. * * * The Malays possess an active and enterprising spirit, but in their temper are ferocious and vindictive. Caprice and treachery are among their characteristic vices; and their habitual piracies on the vessels of all nations are often conducted under the mask of peace and friendship."

The following extract is copied from the description of the Chinese family :—

" The head is large, rounded, and somewhat conical, owing to a high retreating forehead. * * * The Chinese skull, so far as I can judge from the specimens that have come under my inspection, is oblong-oval in its general form; the os frontis is narrow in proportion to the width of the

face, the vertex prominent, and the occiput is moderately flattened. * *
The moral character of the Chinese is thus summed up by Dr. Morrison, whose opinion is derived from long and intimate acquaintance with these people:—'The good traits of the Chinese character, amongst themselves, are mildness and urbanity; a wish to show that their conduct is reasonable, and, generally, a willingness to yield to what appears to be so; docility, industry, subordination to juniors; respect for the aged and for parents; acknowledging the claims of poor kindred. These are virtues of public opinion, which, of course, are in particular cases often more show than reality; for, on the other hand, the Chinese are specious, but insincere; jealous, envious, and distrustful to a high degree. Conscience has few checks but the laws of the land; and a little frigid ratiocination on the fitness of things, which is not generally found effectual to restrain, when the vicious and selfish propensities of our nature may be indulged with present impunity. The Chinese are generally selfish, cold-blooded, and inhuman.' 'He might with great propriety have added,' says Mr. Ellis, 'that in the punishment of criminals, in the infliction of torture, they are barbarously cruel; that human suffering, or human life, are but rarely regarded by those in authority, when the infliction of the one, or the destruction of the other, can be made subservient to the acquisition of power or wealth.'

"The intellectual character of the Chinese is deserving of especial attention, although in letters, in science, and in art, they are the same now that they were many centuries ago. They have their national music and their national poetry; but of sculpture, painting, and architecture, they have no just conceptions, and their national pride prevents their adopting the arts of other countries. Their faculty of imitation is a proverb; and their mechanical ingenuity is universally known. 'That nation,' says Mr. Ellis, 'cannot be viewed with indifference, which possessed an organised government, an army, a written language, historians, and other literati, in a period so remote as to be coeval with the immediate successors of the inspired historian of the Creation, and the lawgiver of the ancient people of God.' They have a copious literature, both ancient and modern; they have possessed the art of printing for eight hundred years; and their written language, with the same characters that they use at the present day, is of extreme antiquity, not less, according to Remusat and others, than four thousand years.

"The civilisation of China is nearly as old as that of Egypt, and has probably remained stationary for thirty centuries; and, although it is based on a heartless religion, no doubt embraces as many both of the comforts and luxuries of life as the social institutions of Europe; at the same time that similar wants and indulgences, in these widely separated communities, are often gratified by very different, yet equally adequate, means. European civilisation has borrowed eagerly from China—the Chinese nothing from Europe. 'When the king of France introduced the luxury of silk stockings,' says Mr. Barrow, 'the peasantry of the middle provinces of China were clothed in silks from head to foot; and when the nobility of England were sleeping on straw, a peasant of China had his mat and his pillow, and the man in office enjoyed his silken mattresses. These were equally the luxuries of their ancestors, and they have not chosen to improve upon it. To prevent innovations, the laws prescribe for every thing, and a man must dress, and build, and regulate all his actions, according to a certain form. Hence it has been observed that unmovableness is the characteristic of the nation; every implement retains its original shape; every invention has stopped at the first step. The plough is still drawn by men; the written characters of their monosyllabic language stand for ideas, not for simple sounds; and the laborious task of merely learning to read, occupies the time tha might be employed in the acquisition of many branches of useful know ledge."

We have quoted the above facts respecting China, believing tha they involve important principles in the progress of civilisation, and wishing to suggest two or three thoughts which may, perhaps excite some inquiry and investigation on the subject. Man is according to the constitution of his nature, a *progressive* being. I was undoubtedly the design of the Deity in creating the laws whicl govern his physical and mental nature, and in establishing fixe: relations between these and the external world, that he shoul approximate to the perfection of his being in the same proportion a these conditions were understood and observed. A distinguishe philosopher has remarked, *that different degrees of civilisatio depend on the perfection of man's nervous system.* And this remark in our opinion, is based not only on the true principles of physiology but is confirmed by every fact which can be collected concerning th general state of society in different ages and nations. What is her meant by the perfection of the nervous system, evidently refers t the size and quality of the brain, as well as to all the condition which in any way affect the performance of its legitimate functions And this remark, too, must refer more especially to the *relative* siz of the anterior lobe, as compared with that of the middle and poste rior lobes of the brain. If we consider, now, the manner in whicl the nerves of motion and sensation are distributed to the differen portions of the brain, we shall find that they have a most importan bearing on this subject.

It has been proved by the discoveries of phrenology, that th nerves of motion, or *the voluntary nerves*, ramify the convolutions c the anterior lobe of the brain, whereas the nerves of sensation, o *the involuntary nerves*, ramify the convolutions of the middle an posterior lobes, which also receive a few nerves of motion, and only few, compared with the anterior lobe. According to these principle: what is called Will, as connected with free-agency, depends chiefl upon the anterior lobe; and, therefore, the propensities, feelings, an sentiments, manifested by the functions of the middle and posterio portions of the brain, must be governed principally by means of th intellectual faculties. There are, then, what may be considere *different degrees of free-agency;* or, rather, some individuals hav greater power than others, under the same external influences, t choose and pursue any given course of action. They have not onl a greater desire and capacity for knowledge, but more innate powe

to carry out that love of mental exercise, and independent thought
and action, which are absolutely necessary to enable an individual to
rise in the scale of being. Now, may not this principle be applied to
the state of a nation in its progress of civilisation? May not certain
cerebral developements favour an advance in the arts, sciences, literature, and every attainment which accompany civilisation? And is
it not a fact, that just in proportion as individuals or a nation have
risen in the scale of intelligence, they have possessed correspondingly
similar cerebral developements? But may there not be *such a proportion, as to size, existing between the anterior and the middle and
posterior lobes of the brain, and such invariable external influences
operating on the manifestation of the faculties connected with these,
as to keep a people or a nation in a stationary state of civilisation?
And may not such a state of cerebral organisation be transmitted for
centuries, by the laws of hereditary descent? And may not this have
been the case with China?*

We must defer farther remarks on the " Crania Americana" till a
future number.

ARTICLE VI.

Few persons are aware of the minuteness and accuracy with
which character may be delineated by a skilful and experienced
phrenologist. But, in order to do this, it should be remembered,
that the examiner himself must have *faculties adapted to such an
exercise*, as well as great experience in the application of the science,
and a thorough knowledge of all its principles. He should also be
made acquainted with the health, education, business, and, to some
extent, with the circumstances of the individual to be examined. A
knowledge of these conditions is necessary in order to judge of the
effect of external influences in developing character, as well as to
explain the *manner* in wh ch the faculties will be most likely to be
manifested. It requires, then, on the part of the examiner, such an
amount of care, experience, discrimination, and knowledge of the
science, as very few persons possess, or can easily obtain.

We have already presented several instances where the science
has been severely tested by practical examinations. Such tests
afford the most positive evidence of the truth of the science, as well

as of its utility.   The following case occurred about two years since in New York, an account of which was drawn up and published i the papers at the time, by a gentleman who is connected with th New York press, and is well known to the public.   The individu: examined, was a person who is extensively engaged in business, i quite active in promoting some of the benevolent operations of th day, and is *personally* known in many parts of the country.   We ar informed, that all who are, to any extent, acquainted with this ind: vidual, upon reading the description, have no difficulty in detectin at once the *original* of the portrait, though no name is given.   It i said, too, by his friends and acquaintances, that the correctness c nearly every trait of character as given in the description, might b as fully confirmed and illustrated, as in the few instances which ar presented in the form of notes.   Some allowance should be made fo the peculiar phraseology used in the description, it having bee given verbally, and without the least expectation of its being pub lished.   The account, as published at the time, was as follows:—

"In a social party, a few evenings since, in this city, the conversatio turned upon the subject of phrenology ; as usual, there was a differenc of opinion.   A regular set-to followed, and the question was eagerly dis cussed, till late in the evening.   One of the party was an elderly gentle man, a member of the society of Friends, whose well-known characte and history were marked and altogether *sui generis.*

"It was proposed to test phrenology by an experiment, and in com pliance with the importunity of both sides, this gentleman consented t undergo an examination the next day, in the presence of the contendin parties.   To make the test as perfect as possible, it was agreed that th examiner should be introduced into the room, and go through with th examination, blindfolded ; that the person examined should not spea during the process, as some inkling of the character might leak ou through the tone and volume of the voice, and the mode of utterance further, that no one in the room should make any remark or indicatio of any sort, during the examination, by which the operator could judg whether, in the opinion of those present, he had *hit* or *missed.*   Th well-known phrenologist, O. S. Fowler, was selected to conduct th examination.   At the time appointed, he was brought into the roon closely blindfolded, and his hands put upon the head of the subject.   / rapid writer, a stranger both to the operator and the subject, took dow the remarks of Mr. Fowler, as he made them, word for word.   We hav the original manuscript in our possession, and publish it because w believe it to be a perfectly fair and triumphant test of phrenology.

"It may be remarked, that Mr. Fowler, though blindfolded, and with out the least intimation from any quarter as to the traits of the indivi dual, drew his character and *peculiar* habits, not merely in generals, bu even in minute particulars, so true to the life, that the numerous acquaint ances of the gentleman examined, will be at no loss in at once recognisin; the individual from Mr. Fowler's description, which follows.   A multi tude of facts in the history of the individual might be stated, illustratin; the singular correctness of the description, but it would swell this notic beyond our limits—two or three will be thrown into notes at the bottom

as of its utility. The following case occurred about two years since, in New York, an account of which was drawn up and published in the papers at the time, by a gentleman who is connected with the New York press, and is well known to the public. The individual examined, was a person who is extensively engaged in business, is quite active in promoting some of the benevolent operations of the day, and is *personally* known in many parts of the country. We are informed, that all who are, to any extent, acquainted with this individual, upon reading the description, have no difficulty in detecting at once the *original* of the portrait, though no name is given. It is said, too, by his friends and acquaintances, that the correctness of nearly every trait of character as given in the description, might be as fully confirmed and illustrated, as in the few instances which are presented in the form of notes. Some allowance should be made for the peculiar phraseology used in the description, it having been given verbally, and without the least expectation of its being published. The account, as published at the time, was as follows:—

"In a social party, a few evenings since, in this city, the conversation turned upon the subject of phrenology; as usual, there was a difference of opinion. A regular set-to followed, and the question was eagerly discussed, till late in the evening. One of the party was an elderly gentleman, a member of the society of Friends, whose well-known character and history were marked and altogether *sui generis*.

"It was proposed to test phrenology by an experiment, and in compliance with the importunity of both sides, this gentleman consented to undergo an examination the next day, in the presence of the contending parties. To make the test as perfect as possible, it was agreed that the examiner should be introduced into the room, and go through with the examination, blindfolded; that the person examined should not speak during the process, as some inkling of the character might leak out through the tone and volume of the voice, and the mode of utterance; further, that no one in the room should make any remark or indication of any sort, during the examination, by which the operator could judge whether, in the opinion of those present, he had *hit* or *missed*. The well-known phrenologist, O. S. Fowler, was selected to conduct the examination. At the time appointed, he was brought into the room closely blindfolded, and his hands put upon the head of the subject. A rapid writer, a stranger both to the operator and the subject, took down the remarks of Mr. Fowler, as he made them, word for word. We have the original manuscript in our possession, and publish it because we believe it to be a perfectly fair and triumphant test of phrenology.

"It may be remarked, that Mr. Fowler, though blindfolded, and without the least intimation from any quarter as to the traits of the individual, drew his character and *peculiar* habits, not merely in generals, but even in minute particulars, so true to the life, that the numerous acquaintances of the gentleman examined, will be at no loss in at once recognising the individual from Mr. Fowler's description, which follows. A multitude of facts in the history of the individual might be stated, illustrating the singular correctness of the description, but it would swell this notice beyond our limits—two or three will be thrown into notes at the bottom.

It is due to Mr. Fowler to say, that he is no party to the publication of this statement. It has been prepared without his knowledge.

"*Mr. Fowler's Description.*—The *first* and *strongest* manifestation of this character is *efficiency*. The strong points are *very* strong, the weak points weak; so that he is an *eccentric* and *peculiar* character. The pole star of his character is moral courage. Pays no regard to forms or ceremonies, or established customs in church or state, and pays no homage to great names—such as D. D.'s, L. L. D.'s, Excellencies, &c. Has very little reverence, stands in no awe of the powers that be.* Emphatically *republican in feeling and character*—makes himself free and familiar with every one—will assert and maintain human rights and human liberty *at every hazard;* and in this cause will stake or suffer any thing. *This constitutes the leading feature of his character. Every other element of his character is blended into this.*

"I would consider him a very cautious man—*in fact* and in *appearance*, very imprudent, especially in his remarks on moral subjects. He is too apt to denounce those whom he considers in an error, and to apply opprobrious epithets, and censures them in the strongest terms and in the boldest manner. I have seldom, if ever, met with a larger organ of *Conscientiousness*. Has very little credulity. Does not treat his fellow-men with sufficient respect. He treats them with kindness and affection, but not with sufficient respect and courtesy. Nothing so much delights him as to advocate and propagate moral principles, no matter how unpopular the principles may be. He is capable of accomplishing more than one man in thousands. He is one of the closest observers of men and things any where to be found. Sees, as it were, by intuition, every thing that passes about him, and understands just when and where to take men

---

* "The following facts are a few of a multitude illustrating this trait. Some years since, this gentleman was in Dublin, and while passing a magnificent pile, was told that it was the palace of the Lord Lieutenant. At once, and in spite of the remonstrances of the friend who was with him, he strode in, unheeding the stares and scowls of pages and gentlemen ushers. Without a look to the right or left, he prosecuted his line of march till he came to the presence-room, where sat his lordship in state. 'I am an American,' said he, 'have heard much of the Lord Lieutenant, and thought I should like to see him, and take a look at his state residence.' His lordship, after an instant look of amazement, rallied and laughing, said to one of his gentlemen in waiting, 'Here, take this American and show him whatever he wants to look at.'

"At another time, he made his way into the English House of Lords, and with his broad Quaker hat on, ensconced himself in the midst of their pomp and circumstance. In an instant, rap, rap, went the rod of a special officer against his hat. 'Well, friend, what is thy business with me ?' 'Your hat, your hat,' roared the officer. 'My hat! what's the matter with my hat ?' 'Off, off with it immediately. Don't you know where you are ?' cried the man of the rod. 'Friend,' cried the imperturbable Quaker, 'I think thee must mean my *shoes*.' This was rather too much for their lordships, and the gravity of the surrounding benches relaxed into a burst of laughter at the expense of the dignitary of the rod, who slunk away into the crowd. So our friend, like William Penn before the king, wore his beaver without farther molestation.

"At another time he requested the mace-bearer to his majesty to unlock the door of the paling which surrounded the throne, that he might examine and sit down upon it. The mace-bearer indignantly refused, with an involuntary shudder at such a profanation. 'Well,' said our friend, 'thee may stand aside, then ;' and taking down the key, he unlocked the door, passed over the area in front of the throne, went up the steps, removed the costly covering, and sat down in sole possession of the chair of majesty while the stately official stood moveless as a statue, and gaping like a simpleton.'"

and things; just how and where to say things with effect. And in all he says, speaks directly to the point.

"He often says and does a great many severe and cutting things which, if any body else said, would get them at once into difficulty, and yet he says and does them in such a manner, that even his enemies, and those against whom his censures are aimed, cannot be offended with him.* He is always on the verge of difficulty, but never in difficulty and is hated mainly by those not personally acquainted with him. A personal interview, even with his greatest enemies, removes their enmity, because of the smoothness and easiness of his manners. Has at command a great amount of information on almost every subject well-digested, and makes an admirable use of this knowledge. Has a great many facts, and always brings them in their right place. His general memory of particulars, incidents, places, and words, is really wonderful. But he has a weak memory of names, dates, numbers, and colours; and never recognises persons by their dress, or the colour of any thing pertaining to them. He is a great story-teller. Tells a story admirably, and acts it out to the life. In telling anecdotes, is rather apt to magnify. Makes a great deal of fun, and keeps others in a roar of laughter while he is sober himself. Is indebted for his fun, as much to the manner as to the matter. He makes his jokes mainly by his happy comparisons, his striking illustrations, and the imitative power with which he expresses them.

"He possesses a great amount of native talent, but it is so admirably distributed, that he appears to have more than he actually possesses. He is considered enthusiastic; and by the world, generally, half crazy. His attachment to his friends is remarkably strong and ardent—yet he will associate with none but those whose moral character is unimpeachable. He makes himself free and easy with every one, and often lets himself down too much. This *constitutes a radical defect in his character*. He expects and anticipates a good deal—enters largely into things—is always overwhelmed with business—takes hold of every measure with spirit, and move where he will, cannot but be a distinguished man."

MISCELLANY.

Mr. Combe's Lectures in Albany, N. Y.—The Albany Argus, of February 10, contained the following account of Mr. Combe's recent course of lectures in that city :—

* "A few years since, a vessel, on board of which he was a passenger, was driven ashore and came near going to pieces. Most of the passengers were half frenzied with terror. One of them, a military officer of high standing, though evidently greatly alarmed, shocked the passengers with his boisterous and continued cursings and blasphemies. Our friend went up to him in presence of them all and laying his hand on his collar, and looking him full in the face, said, ' I have heard that thou art a very brave man, and from thy military exploits, suppose thou art brave in battle; but here thou art belching blasphemies to keep thy courage up while thy pale face and quivering lips show that thou art a coward. If thou has no regard for Deity thyself, don't shock, with thy impiety, those that *have*. Why general, thou behavest as though thou wast never in decent company, I am ashamed of thee.' These are believed to be the *very words used*. A clergyman on board afterwards said to him, if any other person on board had said those thing to him, he would have knocked him down. Instead, however, of personal violence the officer ceased his blasphemy, and afterwards treated his rebuker with marked respect."

"Chapel of the Albany Female Academy, February 7, 1840.

"At the close of Mr. Combe's course of lectures on phrenology, a meeting of the class was called, and on motion, Thomas W. Olcott, Esq. was appointed chairman, and the Rev. Dr. Bullions, secretary.

"Mr. Olcott stated the object of the meeting in a brief address, as follows:—

"'Ladies and Gentlemen: We have listened to the exposition of the principles of phrenology, by decidedly the most gifted and distinguished advocate and teacher of that science now living, and the object of the meeting now called, is to convey to Mr. Combe, on bidding him farewell, the assurance of the pleasure with which we have attended his class, and heard his lectures. The importance of phrenology, as a guide to health and physical education, most of competent judges will freely admit. The respected senior trustee of the institution in which we are now assembled, has long been an able and faithful champion of this branch of the subject; and Combe on Phrenology has been adopted as a text-book in this academy. If the science has not attained the accuracy of precision in details, yet its general principles are beginning to be acknowledged, and to occupy the attention of the most profound and cultivated minds. The proof of this fact, I have in the character of the audience before me. If the gentlemen have any remarks or resolutions to offer, they will now be entertained.'

"The following resolutions were offered by Rufus W. Peckham, Esq., and unanimously adopted:—

"'*Resolved*, That we have listened with deep and increasing interest to the lectures delivered by George Combe, Esq., of Edinburgh, on the subject of phrenology and its application.

"'*Resolved*, That we feel gratified, and in the highest degree instructed, by the clear and able manner in which the principles of that science have been explained, and that the facts and numerous illustrations with which Mr. Combe has fortified and enforced his principal positions, entitle them, in our view, to great weight and consideration.

"'*Resolved*, That the application made by Mr. Combe, of the science of phrenology to the explaining of life's complicated phenomena, and to the unfolding of the great principles upon which the physical education and the intellectual and moral culture of the young should be conducted, invest it with an interest, which, we believe, has not hitherto been properly appreciated; and we hope the day is not far distant, when every parent in this country shall be familiar with those principles.

"'*Resolved*, That, in our estimation, the American people are greatly indebted to Mr. Combe for his eminently successful efforts in promulgating doctrines so vitally essential to the proper developement of the physical and mental powers of man, and the increasing consequences of which can be realised in a manner adequate to their importance, only by coming generations.

"'On motion, *Resolved*, That Amos Dean, Esq., Dr. Hamilton, and Rufus W. Peckham, Esq., be a committee to wait on Mr. Combe, and present him with a copy of the above resolutions, and to request their publication in the daily papers of the city.

"'On motion of Amos Dean, Esq., *Resolved*, That a committee of three be appointed to draft and report a constitution of a Phrenological Society for the city of Albany.

"'Amos Dean, Esq., Dr. Hamilton, and Rufus W. Peckham, Esq., were appointed such committee.

"'THOS. W. OLCOTT, Chairman.

"'P. BULLIONS, Secretary.'"

THE

AMERICAN PHRENOLOGICAL JOURNAL

AND

MISCELLANY.

| Vol. II. | Philadelphia, April 1, 1840. | No. 7. |

ARTICLE I.

REMARKS ON PHYSICAL EDUCATION.*

BY J. L. PEIRCE, M. D., PHILADELPHIA.

The moral and intellectual education of children has, of late year claimed an unprecedented share of public attention. Schools an seminaries of learning, designed for both sexes and all ages, fro lisping infants, who can scarcely count two summers' suns, to tho of riper years and matured understandings, well versed in scienc and the richest attainments of classic lore, have increased with rapidity beyond all human conception. Instructors, calculated bestow honour on any country, and of whom Europe herself mig be proud, have come forward upon the stage of action, to rule th destinies of our nature by the influence they may now exert upc the minds of the rising generation. The opportunities for inte lectual and moral improvement, abstractedly considered, are withi the reach of all—and, under *this* view of the subject, the risin generation *should be* far better, wiser, and happier, than any whic has preceded it.

But, in the zeal manifested for intellectual improvement, is the no danger of our forgetting or overlooking the fundamental laws our own organisation? The manifestations of mind depend upc *organised matter*, and all matter is governed by certain inhere laws which cannot be violated with impunity; but whenever violate a punishment, proportioned to the nature and extent of the offenc

* These remarks constitute the substance of an address, delivered by Dr. Peirc three years since, before the Pennsylvania Lyceum. Believing that they invol important principles on the subject of education, especially when viewed in co nection with the *true philosophy of mind*, we have solicited their publication the Journal.—ED.

is, sooner or later, the inevitable consequence. But because the relation of cause and effect is sometimes of that character that they are separated from each other by a considerable interval of time, or their analogy and connection cannot be distinctly traced, their relationship is disputed, and the salutary influence of such institutions, on the part of our Creator, is rendered abortive. Interest and prejudice likewise have a most powerful influence over us, and blind our mental perceptions against the clearest truths of nature; and an unwillingness, and ofttimes a determination not to believe aught that conflicts with our preconceived opinions, closes the door to conviction. But notwithstanding this array against us, the principle remains incontrovertible, that every violation of a law of nature is followed by its appropriate and adequate punishment.

We have said that the manifestations of mind depend upon organised matter. This truth will not, I presume, in this enlightened era of the world, be doubted. If it should be, I would refer the sceptic to all approved medical and physiological works which treat of the nature and functions of the brain, in which he will find it amply confirmed. Neither shall we stop to inquire into the controvertible *nature or essence* of the mind itself. All that is sufficient for our present purpose, is the generally acknowledged fact, that it depends in this world upon organised matter for its manifestations. True, however, as this may be, it is equally evident that, in the systems of instruction usually adopted at the present day, this fact is entirely disregarded. The efforts of teachers are chiefly directed towards the improvement of the *mind*, the cultivation and expansion of the *intellect*, as if *it* were an *immaterial* principle whose developement, even at the earliest periods of existence, could be illimitably promoted without a violation of any law of nature. But this is far from being the case. In the cultivation and expansion of the faculties of the mind, we *act altogether upon organised matter ;* and this, too, of the most delicate kind—a kind which, while it serves as the mediator between body and spirit, partakes so largely of the nature, character, and essential attributes of the *former*, that, without its proper physical growth and developement, all the manifestations of the *latter* sink into comparative insignificance; so that, without a perfect organisation of the *brain*, the mental powers must be proportionally paralysed—without its maintaining a healthy condition, *they* must be rendered proportionally weak and inactive.

Now, inasmuch as man is a compound being, the healthy action of whose mental phenomena depends upon the sanity of his physical structure, a question naturally arises, whether, in the education of children, the cultivation of the mind should receive all our care, and

the body, upon which the mind is dependent, be left to chance f(
its preservation and improvement? Perhaps some may be ready t
ask, what care does the body require? If we provide it wit
suitable nourishment, and protect it from the inclemencies of th
weather, it progresses in its developement from infancy to manhoo(
without any especial attention being bestowed upon it. We answe:
first, that the greatest care which it requires is that of *preservatia
from injury*. Do nothing to it in opposition to the laws of i(
organisation. Expose not the delicate organ of vision to the brigl
glare of the meridian sun, else the stimulus, which nature has pr(
vided for its healthy action, will be too powerful for it, and blindne:
will be the consequence. Oppress not the stomach with foo
unsuited to its powers of digestion, else its function will be enfeeble
or destroyed, by what was designed for its nourishment and growtl
Excite not the circulatory system with artificial stimuli, else feve
and subsequent depression will be the certain result. And, abov
all, exact not too great an amount of duty from that most delicate (
all organs, which is the source of the nervous influence of the whol
body, as well as of the mental operations, else the health of the phy
sical structure, and the strength of the spiritual man, will have (
pay the forfeit of your indiscretion. These are severally the punisl
ments ordained by nature for the breach or non-observance of thos
laws which she has instituted for the preservation of our corpore:
frames. Secondly: Inasmuch as the vigour of the mind depends (
the health of the body in general, and particularly upon that portic
of it whence the nervous energy of the whole system is derived, it
in accordance with the dictates of reason and common sense tht
they should be sufficiently matured and strengthened in the
organisation, previous to their being called into active exercise, t
enable them to bear without injury the duties required of then
Hence we assume the position, that in infancy *physical* educatio
should supersede that of *intellect*, and afterwards that they shoul
proceed simultaneously together. The first years of life should t
appropriated to the developement of the body, without any particula
effort being made for the expansion of the mind—for it is by th
strengthening of the body that the mind becomes healthfully an
permanently invigorated. But if the mind is prematurely or to
strongly excited, you injure the organisation of the brain, an
thereby weaken its powers, both intellectually and physically. Th
is fully evinced by the circumstances, that we seldom, if ever, see
person of mature years, who has devoted his life, from an earl
period of his existence, to literary or scientific pursuits, who:
health has not, in a greater or less degree, been sacrificed to i(

ind also that we equally seldom see a child with a precocious intel-
ect live to adult age. But, on the contrary, where the physical
organisation has had time to become sufficiently matured before the
powers of the brain are called into undue exercise, by the active
stimulus of the mental operations, the health has continued unimpaired to the latest periods of existence. And these results are in
strict accordance with the laws of our organisation. The relationship of cause and effect can be distinctly traced in each of them,
and in the one where a law of our nature is violated, the punishment
follows as a necessary consequence, although years may elapse,
during which the individual may escape with apparent impunity.
And it is from this latter circumstance that arise the unwillingness,
the obstinacy, or the blindness, of many in tracing the connection
between them. Hence, also, the apparent correctness of the assertions of those who declare that the health of children is not injured
by the earliest and closest mental exertions, upon the most profound
subjects of investigation. But that they are mistaken, is, we trust,
fully apparent from the observations already made. As it is, however, a point of vital importance, we will devote a few minutes more
to its consideration.

Previous to the seventh year of age, children seem almost universally predisposed to diseases of the head. This is occasioned partly
by natural and partly by artificial causes. Among the former, may
be mentioned the extremely delicate structure of the brain, its rapid
developement, and its great vascularity, by which it receives a much
larger proportion of blood than any other organ of the body. These
conspire to keep it on the brink of disease, which is at times developed by the most trifling of artificial causes, among which may be
enumerated the gratification of a foolish pride, on the part of mothers
and nurses, in decorating the head of the infant, by which means it
is kept in a heated and ofttimes a feverish condition; and, also, the
liability of the head to injury by blows, falls, and other accidents. To
these may likewise be added the want of fresh air, and the greatest
indiscretions in diet, from which causes diseases are produced, which
become subsequently transferred to the head.

Now, whenever any portion of the human system becomes unduly
excited by an increase of that stimulus which is natural to it, the
blood rushes to that part, and produces a degree of irritation or
inflammation which, in a short time, deranges its functional or
organic action, thereby constituting disease. Thus, if the stomach
is oppressed with a mass of indigestible food, a derangement of its
powers very soon ensues, producing dyspepsia, colic, &c. If a
sudden or too strong degree of light is admitted to the delicate

organ of vision, how exceedingly painful is its first impression, anc
how terrible are its subsequent effects. What *food* is to the *stomach*
or *light* is to the *eye*, such also is *mental* exercise to that far more
delicate and important organ, the brain.   They are respectively the
proper and natural stimulus to each, and if the two former can be
injured by an error in kind or degree, far more liable is the latter
particularly in the early periods of his existence.   What judicious
mother would think of loading the stomach of the young and delicate
infant with that nourishment which is designed for the sturdy farmer
or the hardy daily labourer?   And do you think that that most deli
cate of all organs, the brain, can be loaded without injury with tha
food which is properly the portion of those of mature minds and cul
tivated intellects? Surely not! Now, inasmuch as nature provides
nourishment suitable for the digestive powers of the young, she also
provides, of her own abundant resourses, for their *intellectua*
nourishment, such food as will not unduly excite the delicate orgai
which she designs as its recipient.   There is no portion of the
human system that can bear undue exercise without injury, and
more particularly in younger life.   Let a young infant be accus
tomed to sustain its weight upon its lower limbs, before the bone
which connect them with the body shall have become sufficiently
consolidated, or shall have changed from their original cartilaginou
condition, and see how entirely destructive of their natural formatioi
will be the effect.   Notice the spinal column of the hod-carrier, who
may have commenced his business even long after the work of nature
shall have been completed in the formation and perfection of tha
bony fabric of the human frame, and see what changes of structure
will there be effected by such undue exercise.   Just so it is with the
brain.   By calling its powers too early into exercise, before its sub
stance shall have become sufficiently consolidated, an unnatura
excitement is produced, which causes a great flow of blood to the
organ.   This produces a degree of irritation, which, continuing for i
while, increases to inflammation—then a dropsy of the head ensues
which, sooner or later, terminates the career of the little sufferer
At other times, a tendency to convulsions, with all their baneful con
sequences, is the result.

But should the process be of a less summary nature, a greate.
activity or an enlargement of the brain ensues.   This gives the chili
an appearance of smartness and of precocity of intellect for a few
years, that excites the fondest hopes of the parent, and causes ai
increase of attachment which seems strengthened only to end in sad
and sometimes awful disappointment—for if life is continued, the
nervous energy of the brain becomes expended long before the child

arrives at years of maturity, and he then appears even duller than
his fellows who were formerly considered as his inferiors; or else,
the *nervous* system acquires a preponderancy at the expense of the
physical, and the child grows up with enfeebled health and debilitated body, with a temper irritable, peevish, and morose, hypochon-
driacal, subject to dyspepsia, affections of the heart, and scrofulous
diseases, and an innumerable host of ailments which result from such
infringement of the organic laws of nature; or else, that most dreadful of all earthly maladies ensues, a loss of those powers which give
to man the command over the rest of the animated creation—a loss
of his reasoning faculties.   What class of individuals is it, I would
ask, who are most subject to this terrible disease? Is it not the
philosopher, whose love of science carries him into the fascinating
regions of knowledge, until, deprived of sleep, deprived of food,
deprived of recreation, his brain becomes bewildered with the boundless expanse before him? As Dryden very beautifully observes—

> " Great wit to madness nearly is allied,
>   And thin partitions do these bounds divide."

Is it not the statesman, who, with an ambitious spirit seeking for
fame, and striving for the highest honours of his country, finds his
course marked with disappointment, and his fondest prospects blasted
for ever? Is it not the lover, who has indulged in dreams of halcyon
bliss whose realities he is never to enjoy? Is it not the religious
enthusiast, who can perceive nothing in the divine attributes but
eternal wrath and condemnation? These undoubtedly are the ones
whose minds are most apt to become affected. And why? Because
they suffer themselves to enter with so deep and intense interest into
the respective objects of their pursuits, that the excitement becomes
too great for the delicate organisation of that portion of their frame
through which every operation of the mind is manifested. If, then,
such an effect can be produced by an undue degree of excitement
upon the brain of those whose *organisation is perfected*, what must
be the effect of improper excitement upon the still more delicate
organisation of those brains in which the *nervous system naturally
predominates,* and which are readily affected by the slightest stimulus
that can be applied to them?

It should be remembered, that the brains of very young children
are not only of an extremely delicate nature, but quite imperfect in
developement and organisation.

Bichat, one of the greatest anatomists that ever lived, and to
whom the science is indebted for many of its most valuable discoveries, describes it as being at the seventh year " in a very soft con-

dition, and almost fluid under the finger." Meckel, another great anatomist, gives its weight at this period as "about ten ounces; " but," says he, " so abundant is its supply of blood in infancy, that its weight becomes doubled during the first six months. From the time it continues to increase more rapidly than any other organ of the body, although *it is not until the seventh year of age that all its parts are formed.*" At the period of adult life, the usual weight about three and a half pounds. Its consistency is, during this time also gradually increasing, and it thereby becomes more and more capable of performing, without injury, the all-important function which it is designed to fulfil in the great scale of creation, so that from the semi-fluid, or gelatinous condition in which it first appear it becomes gradually converted into a mass sufficiently solid to retain its form when deprived of the bony casement with which it is surrounded.

We do not mean to assert that a single instance of undue intellectual effort will occasion disease of the brain, any more than on instance of gluttony or dissipation will produce a permanent derange ment of the digestive organs. On the contrary, the recuperative powers of the system are constantly endeavouring to repair the injury, and, unless the laws of our organisation are repeatedly violated, the individual may escape with apparent, although no entire, impunity—for the punishment of the infringement of an organic law must and will ensue, although it may be mild in it operation, and of short continuance. But the constant or repeated violation of these laws must eventually be followed by consequence more or less serious and permanent, according to their nature and extent.

Now, in many instances children are sent to school at the age of four, three, and even of two years, when their *physical* power require all the *nervous energy* of the system in *their* developemen instead of having this nervous energy expended in producing a mor bid growth of the brain, and a precocious intellect which, sooner or later, must hasten the child's death—for it is seldom that we see child with a large head live to adult life. This is one great cause of the present generation being so much more weakly than were our ancestors. *Their* early years were spent in such a way that their physical powers could expand, and they became vigorous and healthy. But *we* task the minds of the young long before they are able to bear it, as if we thought they could gain no information except from books. *Nature, however, is the great and proper instructress of the young.* From her they can learn such things as are suited to their comprehension without tasking the mind, and thereby exciting the brain. In the construction of a dam along the course of the water stream, in the flying of a kite, in playing at marbles, yea, even in the falling of an apple, or the throwing of a stone, they can acquire as necessary and wholesome truths as any problem of Euclid or algebraical proposition can impart to them. But, when put to school at so early an age, they acquire a kind of parrot knowledge of many abstract propositions which they cannot understand, and relate many facts of history and of science for which their intellectual faculties are not at all adequate. This is fully evinced by the numerous publications of the present day, such as " Early Lessons in Geography," " Botany," " History," " Bible Lessons," &c., designed, as the authors express them, " particularly for children from two to six years of age ;" and such is the eager desire of the present generation for the accumulation of wealth, that, like the vender of ardent spirits, they care not how many bodies and minds are eternally ruined by the sale of such things, so that a small pittance is added to their filthy lucre. But let not parents be anxious for the early instruction of their children in such ways as will either task their memories, or produce a distaste or utter disgust for future literary acquirements. Let them not be uneasy lest they should be considered ignoramuses, in consequence of their unacquaintance with the alphabet during those years in which nature requires all the vital powers to perfect the organisation of that physical structure, so essential to their future health and intellectual vigour. Let them rejoice rather, if, as was said of the celebrated Adam Clark in his younger years, they are capable of rolling big stones, in preference to their manifesting a precocity of intellect and maturity of understanding which may, for a while, astonish the world, but which is a sure harbinger of mental disease, of bodily infirmities, or of premature death. And let me again state, that such early developement of the intellect very seldom continues to adult age ; for if the life of the child does not fall a sacrifice to this unnatural stimulus, his health becomes impaired, or else the nervous energy becomes expended by the time he arrives at the age of fifteen years, or thereabouts ; and afterwards he shows no signs of intellectual vigour beyond that manifested by the rest of his associates. But let me adduce the evidence of others in corroboration of the assertions I have made.

Tissot, a very able physician who lived in the time of Zimmerman, speaks thus:—" Long continued application in infancy destroys life. I have seen young children of great mental activity who manifested a passion for learning far above their age, and I foresaw with grief the fate that awaited them. They commenced their career as prodigies, and finished by becoming persons of very weak minds. The age of infancy is consecrated by nature to those exercises which fortify and strengthen the body, and not to study, which enfeebles and prevents its proper increase and developement." In another place he says, "Of ten infants destined for different avocatious, I should prefer that the one who is to study through life should be the least learned at the age of twelve."

The distinguished Hufeland, physician to the king of Prussia, in his valuable work on the Art of Prolonging Life, observes:—"Intellectual effort in the first years of life is very injurious. All labour of the mind which is required of children before their seventh year, is in opposition to the laws of nature, and will prove injurious to the organisation and prevent its proper developement."

Dr. Spurzheim, with whose researches into the moral and intellectual powers of man you are all more or less acquainted, says in his Essay upon the Elementary Principles of Education—"Many parents anxiously strive to cultivate the intellect of their children, and neglect to fortify their constitution. They believe that children cannot too soon learn to read and write. Their children, therefore, are obliged to remain many hours in school, breathing an impure air, while they ought to be developing the organs of the body by exercise. The more delicate the children are, and the more their affections and minds are precocious, the more important it is that the above error should be avoided; if it is not, premature death is often the consequence of this infraction of the laws of nature. *The mind ought never to be cultivated at the expense of the body, and physical education ought to precede that of intellect,* and then proceed simultaneously with it, without cultivating one faculty to the neglect of others—for health is the base, and instruction the ornament, of education."

Julien, a French writer, observes—"The course to be adopted with children for the first ten years of life, is neither to press nor torment them; but by plays, exercise of body, entire liberty, wisely regulated and good nourishment, to effect the salutary and progressive developement of the physical, moral, and intellectual faculties, and by continual amusement and freedom from chagrin, (which injures the tempers of children,) they will arrive at the tenth year without suspecting that they have been made to learn any thing; they will not have distinguished between study and recreation; all they know they will have learned freely, voluntarily, and always in play. The advantages obtained by this course are, good health, grace, agility, gaiety, and happiness; a character, frank and generous; a memory properly exercised; a sound judgment, and a cultivated mind."

I might add to these quotations similar testimonials from many of the most distinguished writers in Europe and America, but it is unnecessary. In proof, too, of the above positions, it might easily be proved, that not a few of the most illustrious names which adorn the pages of history, were of those who *first* cultivated their physical powers, and were by no means distinguished in early life for any manifestations of mind. Among this number, were Virgil, Demosthenes, Shakspeare, Gibbon, Scott, Byron, Davy, Newton, Franklin, and a host of others, whose names time will not permit me to mention. Parents should not, therefore, be discouraged if their children do not early afford any positive indications of genius or mental superiority.

(To be continued.)

ARTICLE II.

ON THE APPLICATION OF PHRENOLOGY IN THE FORMATION OF MARRIAGES.*

Being the substance of a Public Lecture, delivered by Mr. Alexander Smart, Secretary of the Dundee Mechanics' Phrenological Society.

In treating of the application of the principles of phrenology in the formation of marriages, it will be necessary to advert to the group of the social faculties, from which springs the impulse to the connubial union. The *first* of these is Amativeness. From this faculty the sexual feeling originates. The organ is generally larger in males than in females. Its size is known chiefly by the breadth of the neck from ear to ear; in new-born children it is the least developed of all the cerebral parts. It attains its full maturity between eighteen and twenty six years old, at which latter age it is equal to about one-seventh of the whole brain. When its developement is very large, it leads to libertinism and conjugal infidelity; but when under the guidance of the moral and reflecting faculties, it excites to mutual kindness, and the exercise of all the milder amenities between the sexes. The *second* is Philoprogenitiveness, or love of offspring. This faculty is in general much stronger in the

* From the 38th number of the Edinburgh Phrenological Journal.

female than in the male, and more so in some females than in others. In society, great differences are observable among individuals, in the manifestation of this feeling : some cannot endure the incessant and teazing prattle of children (as they choose to call it); while of others it is the highest delight to witness their innocent gambols, soothe them under their petty crosses, and caress them with the strongest demonstrations of affection. The feeling shows itself in the girl, in her early attachment to dolls; it continues to grow with her growth, and strengthen with her strength, long after she becomes

> " A happy mother, 'mid the smiles
>   Of ripened worth, and sunny beauty."

The last faculty of the social group is Adhesiveness, from which springs the instinctive tendency to attachment. Like Philoprogenitiveness, the organ is generally larger in the female than in the male ; and consequently, to use the words of a powerful phrenological writer, we find the feeling manifested " with a constancy and fervour in woman, which it would be in vain to expect from man. It has been truly said, that the most generous and friendly man is selfish in comparison with woman. There is no friend like a loving and affectionate wife. Man may love, but it is almost always with a view to his own gratification ; but when a woman bestows her love, she does it with her heart and soul."

These faculties minister highly to human happiness, when gratified in accordance with the dictates of the moral sentiments and intellect; but when not controlled by these higher powers, their gratification is pregnant with evil. If under the dictates of Amativeness and Adhesiveness, a partner be chosen of whom the other faculties do not approve, bitter days of repentance must arrive, as soon as the former feelings begin to languish, and the moral sentiments and intellect to receive offence from the qualities of the individual. On the other hand, if the domestic affections are guided by intellect to an object pleasing to itself and the moral faculties, these themselves will be gratified ; they will double the delights afforded by the domestic affections, and render the enjoyment lasting. Another principle is, that the manifestation of any faculty in others, stimulates to action the same faculty in us. Thus when any individual addresses us in the language of Self-esteem and Destructiveness, the same faculties are awakened in us, and we are impelled to return a correspondingly bitter answer; but let us be addressed under the influence of Adhesiveness and Benevolence, and our answer will partake of the warmth and affection arising from these feelings. Again, when any faculty becomes spontaneously active by being presented with its appropriate object, it calls other faculties of a like class into activity. It seems to be upon this principle that lovers are more amiable in each other's eyes than they appear to the rest of the world : for while in each other's society, the domestic faculties are called into a state of delightful activity ; these, again, rouse Ideality, Benevolence, Veneration, and Conscientiousness, which greatly heighten the delight experienced by them in their interviews with each other. I need not farther enlarge upon this part of my subject : each of you, probably, has either already experienced the delightful sensations hinted at, or will hereafter ; for the feeling is so universal, that we may triumphantly ask with the poet,

> " Where is the heart that has not bow'd,
> A slave, almighty love, to thee ?
> Look at the cold, the gay, the proud,
> And is there *one* among them free ?"

Some, possessing fine temperaments and a good endowment of the domestic and moral faculties, experience in these moments the most ecstatic joy. Moore has described it as a

> " Light, that ne'er will shine again
> On life's dull stream."

We may here remark, that these pleasurable feelings are denied to the sensualist. Milton has truly said, that " the embrace of harlots is tasteless, joyless, unendeared ;" and phrenology shows clearly how this arises—it is the momentary gratification of one or more of the inferior feelings, by which the moral faculties, with Self-esteem, and generally Love of Approbation, are wounded.

Having made these preliminary observations, I shall proceed to notice the principles upon which marriages are contracted in savage life and in the different orders of civilised society, and to point out how far these principles are in accordance with phrenology ; next, I shall attempt to lay down and elucidate some of these principles, give a summary of the whole, and conclude with an address to the youth of both sexes, upon the practical application of them as guides to conduct. I begin, then, with the native of New Holland. His mode of courtship is certainly unique—nor is there much danger of its being adopted in any other country. Goaded by the impulses of Amativeness, he provides himself with a club, endeavours to discover the retreat of another tribe—if a hostile one, so much the better—in the neighbourhood of which he lies in ambush until night overtake them ; and when, by the light of the fires, he discovers a female straying to any distance from the encampment, he rushes upon her from his hiding-place, levels her with his club, seizes her by the

feet, and runs with her to some secret spot, regardless of the injurie
which she may receive from her head striking against the roots c
trees or stones during the flight.   Every one must consider suc
conduct savage in the extreme, but it is in perfect accordance wit
the organisation.   All is animalised, and from a head and mind lik
his, much higher conduct cannot be expected.   Nor let us, on othe
grounds, too rashly condemn the untutored savage.   He, it is true
inflicts physical pain in the accomplishment of his purpose, but h
makes the amende honourable, by adhering to her as his wife, an
by using every endeavour to heal the wounds he has caused ; while
on the other hand, the European seducer, with all his intellectua
and moral superiority, in place of merely inflicting *physical* pair
abandons his victim to *mental* agony, and leaves her to the scorn c
an ungenerous and an unpitying world—a prey to " remorse, regre
and shame."   Happily, however, seduction is not a prevailing vic
among the humbler sons of toil ; it is a depravity which, it is to b
feared, the higher ranks of men will continue to practise until the
add to their wealth the nobility of virtue.   So much for love i
savage life.   Let us now turn to that of the nobility of our ow
country, of a sketch of which, as given in Mr. Fox's Repository,
gladly avail myself.   " When (the writer asks) the education c
their daughters is ended, what then remains for them ?   Are the
not led like lambs to the slaughter ?   Are they not put up for sal
at the fashionable shambles ?   where they are brought out to b
exposed to the highest bidder, with more real coarseness, thoug
disguised under the veil of hypocrisy, than it is the lot of femal
servants to undergo at a statue fair.   Are their feelings ever col
sulted—their likings or dislikings ?   Are they not bidden to sit, an
to walk, and to recline, in those modes which are most likely t
attract the eyes of the chapman ?   May they speak ere they ar
spoken to, and are they not required to overcome every feeling c
repugnance when a likely bidder appears, to make his offers ?   Ar
they not studiously instructed that marriage is not an affair of judg
ment, affection, or love, but merely a matter of bargain or sale; fc
the purpose of securing as much of wealth or station, or both, a
they can possibly achieve?   Are not the whole arrangements mac
with diplomatic caution, and is not a half concluded bargai
frequently broken off in consequence of a better offer ?   Disguis
this conduct as you will (adds the author), under the fine soundir
names of honourable alliance, excellent match, and other specion
terms, which have been invented to make interest look like affection
but such marriages, entered into by a female for wealth or statio
are at best but prostitution clothed in the robes of sanctity.   Ar

what is the result? The lordling is soon tired of his new toy, and
wanders in quest of fresh excitement, leaving his victim to her own
sad thoughts, and the consciousness that there exist desirable things
which neither wealth nor station can purchase." It is to be hoped
that this picture of our aristocracy is highly coloured, and not nearly
so universally true as the respected writer believes it to be. If it be
accurate, however, marriage amongst our nobility is nearly as much
an affair of the animal faculties as is the marriage of the New
Hollander. In the savage, the activity of Amativeness rouses
Acquisitiveness, Secretiveness, and Destructiveness; in the peer, it
excites Acquisitiveness, Self-esteem, and Love of Approbativeness;
while Benevolence, Veneration, and Conscientiousness, are kept in a
state of abeyance to these inferior faculties, and left ungratified.
And what is the result? Mutual loathing and disgust quickly ensue
—libertinism becomes the pastime of the peer; too often the
infidelity of his consort ensues; and the progeny of this unhappy
marriage inherit the powerful animal, and weak moral and reflecting, faculties of the parents. While such selfishness and ignorance
of the Creator's laws are to be found in what is called exclusive
society, we have little reason to wonder, if their inferiors in the
middle ranks partake in some degree of the same fashionable debasement; and accordingly we find, that the same pursuit after wealth in the
formation of the marriage compact characterises many of this class.
Hence the questions—"What money has she?—Is there any property?" are usually the first that are put by one who hears of the
marriage of a friend. Intellectual and moral considerations are
either given to the winds, or regarded as secondary to the acquisition of wealth. I do not mean that it is always so; but it will be
admitted that individuals of this class too generally consider a marriage wise or foolish, according as the dower is ample or deficient.
Nor can a favourable description of the conduct of the operative
classes be always given in this respect. It is a daily occurrence to
see a mere boy and girl, under the blind influence of the sexual feeling alone, *rush* into marriage, destitute alike of the means necessary
to enable them to sit down with comfort in their own house, and of
the judgment to retrieve a past error;—ignorant of each other's dispositions, unacquainted with the duties they have to fulfil, and destitute of the physical strength which might enable them to emerge
from poverty. Hence quarrels often ensue—home loses the attractions it ought to possess—want and all its attendant train of miseries
overtake them. Philoprogenitiveness is wounded by the death of the
children in infancy, from want of sufficient care and sustenance;—
Benevolence and Conscientiousness, also lacerated, give rise to feel-

ings of remorse, when reflection points to the absence of parental attention and moral training;—Self-esteem and Love of Approbation are rendered painfully active by the consciousness of inferiority;— life is embittered by domestic feud and the immorality of the off- spring, and shortened by excessive labour and irregular habits.   It is thus that marriages contracted for the direct gratification of the domestic faculties, without reference to the moral and intellectual powers, prove ultimately unsatisfactory, and pregnant with evil to both parties.   Happily, however, there are many exceptions to this picture in the humbler walks of life; because many estimable indi- viduals intermarry, as it were, by accident, without any previous knowledge of the principles which ought to regulate their choice. Some of these principles I shall now proceed to lay down and briefly illustrate.

Man, as an organised being, is subject to organic laws.   One of these laws is, that a healthy and vigorous constitution of body in the parents, is necessary to communicate existence in a perfect state to the offspring.   The progeny of too young or imperfectly deve- loped parents will be feeble, and probably short-lived.

Another organic law is, that mental talents and dispositions are transmitted by hereditary descent; or, more shortly, that "like begets like," subject to some important modifications; and that mental and moral endowments are determined by the form, size, and constitution of brain.   The temperaments indicate, to a certain extent, this constitution.   It seems a general rule, also, that the faculties which predominate in power and activity in the parents, when the organic existence of the child commences, determine its future mental dispositions.

The first of these laws will not be denied by any; yet, though of great practical importance, it is often, from ignorance, overlooked. An individual with weak lungs, indicated by a compressed chest, stooping shoulders, and other symptoms that may be known to him- self, should carefully avoid intermarrying with another so con- stituted; because the offspring will prove subject to pulmonary com- plaints that may carry them off in infancy; or if, by careful nursing, they should be enabled to survive that period, they will most probably fall victims to consumption before they attain maturity.   In like manner, with respect to any other constitutional malady to which we may be subject, we should avoid perpetuating it by an alliance with persons in a similar condition, because, in that case, it would descend in an aggravated state to the offspring.   These remarks are peculiarly applicable to that most deplorable of all maladies— insanity.   This, as is well known, descends, in many families, from generation to generation; and if individuals belonging to such families intermarry, it is more than probable that the offspring will be either weak in intellect or absolutely insane.

A knowledge of the temperaments is of great practical importance. Every one, therefore, should endeavour to ascertain his own; for, from the union in marriage of two individuals with very active temperaments, children will most probably be produced, having nervous systems still more predominant than those of the parents; and such children run a very great risk of dying in infancy from convulsions, or, if they survive, are peculiarly predisposed to high cerebral excitement, bordering upon insanity, in which there is great danger of its ultimately terminating. Again, the union in marriage of two persons of a lymphatic temperament, will give birth to offspring that will inherit the inertness of the parents, and will, consequently, be unfit to struggle successfully against the difficulties of life. Much more might be said on the importance of a knowledge of the temperaments, but I must refer to books on phrenology for farther information concerning them.

The organic law by which hereditary qualities descend to the offspring, is acted upon by every practical farmer with complete success in the rearing of his stock. Strange that it should never have occurred to such men, that they, as organised beings, are subject to the like laws, and that, if they desire to improve their own race, they have only to obey them. This law is also practically acted upon by the too-often immoral dog and cock fighters. More need not be said to establish its existence, because it is as universally admitted as it is disregarded in relation to man.

The next organic law is, that intellectual and moral endowment is determined by the size, form, and constitution of the brain—a fact of the utmost importance in leading to the choice of a suitable partner.

The phrenologist finds too many illustrations of domestic infelicity arising from ill-assorted unions. Thus, a young woman in whom the domestic and moral faculties were strong, and whose intellect was considerable, married a man about her own age, with great force of character, resulting from a large head, and with large animal and intellectual, but deficient moral, organs. During the first year or two of their married life they contrived to live peaceably; but, by degrees, the husband acquired dissipated habits, and neglected his domestic duties. His wife used every endeavour, by mildness and persuasion, to reclaim him, but, from his deficiency of the moral faculties, without effect. The two eldest children have taken up the mother's cerebral developement, and their lives have been exemplary and irreproachable; the young members of the family inherit the strong animal faculties, and deficient morality, of the father. The mother confesses she has had little moral enjoyment, and she feels that the remaining portion of her life is to be embittered by the profligacy of her children, and the unfeeling indifference of her husband.   Another instance may be given of a young man, whose father possessed great strength of character, by which he raised himself to the middle ranks of society.   The son, however, has a small head, with Acquisitiveness, Love of Approbation, and the reflective faculties, deficient.   Belonging by birth to the middle ranks, he married a very respectable young woman, entered into business, failed, subsequently contracted the lowest and most dissipated habits, and, after bringing his wife and family to destitution, contrives to secrete part of the charity she receives from her respectable connections, wherewith to regale himself and his low associates.   The parents have now three children, two of whom inherit very nearly the father's developement.   Had the mother been a phrenologist, it is not probable that she would have intermarried with him.

In another couple, where the husband has large organs of the moral faculties, with moderate intellect and large Combativeness and Self-esteem, while the other party has a small head, with excessive Self-esteem and Love of Approbation, there is a never ending contention about trifles.   They are total strangers to domestic tranquillity and fireside enjoyments ; nor, to all appearance, have they tasted domestic felicity for thirty hours together during the whole thirty years of their married life.   Happily for themselves, and perhaps for society, their children all died in infancy.   Too many instances might be given, demonstrative of the fatal effects of disregarding the operation of the organic laws in marriage ; but I shall conclude this part of the subject by referring, for several striking instances of it, to Mr. Combe's work on the Constitution of Man—a work that should be very generally perused.

I now proceed to give some facts strongly illustrative of the doctrine, that the faculties which predominate in power and activity in the parents, when the organic existence of the child commences, determine its future mental dispositions.   This is a doctrine to which, from its great practical importance, I would beg leave to call your serious attention.   It was remarked by the celebrated Esquirol, " that the children whose existence dated from the horrors of the first French Revolution, turned out to be weak, nervous, and irritable of mind, extremely susceptible of impressions, and liable to be thrown by the least extraordinary excitement into absolute insanity."   Sometimes, too, family calamities produce serious effects upon the offspring. A very intelligent and respectable mother, upon hearing this principle

expounded, remarked that there was a very wide difference in the
intellectual and moral developement between one of her children and
the others ; and accounted for this difference by the fact, that, during
pregnancy, she received intelligence that the crew of the ship, on
board of which was her son, had mutinied—that when the ship
arrived in the West Indies, some of the mutineers, and also her son,
had been put in irons—and that they were all to be sent home for
trial.   This intelligence acted so strongly upon her, that she suffered
a temporary alienation of judgment.   The report turned out to be
erroneous, but this did not avert the consequences of the agitated
state of the mother's feelings upon the daughter she afterwards gave
birth to.   That daughter is now a woman, but she is, and will continue to be, a being of impulses, incapable of reflection, and in other
respects greatly inferior to her sisters.

   The following is a melancholy instance of the operation of this
principle, which was communicated to me by a respectable medical
practitioner, and which I have since found, from inquiries in the
neighbourhood, and from seeing the subject of it, to be substantially
correct.   In the summer of 1827, the practitioner alluded to was
called upon to visit professionally a young woman in the immediate
neighbourhood, who was safely delivered of a male child.   As the
parties appeared to be respectable, he made some inquiries regarding
the absence of the child's father ; when the old woman told him that
her daughter was still unmarried, that the child's father belonged to a
regiment then in Ireland, that last autumn he had obtained leave of
absence to visit his relations in this part of the country, and that on
the eve of his departure to join his regiment, an entertainment was
given, at which her daughter attended ; during the whole evening, she
and the soldier danced and sang together ; when heated by the toddy
and the dance, they left the cottage, and after the lapse of an hour
were found together in a glen, in a state of utter insensibility, from
the effects of their former festivity ; and the consequence of this
interview was the birth of an idiot.   He is now nearly six years of
age, and his mother does not believe that he is able to recognise either
herself or any other individual.   He is quite incapable of making
signs, whereby his wants can be made known—with this exception,
that when hungry, he gives a wild shriek.   This is a case upon
which it would be painful to dwell ; and I shall only remark, that the
parents are both intelligent, and that the fatal result cannot be otherwise accounted for, than by the almost total prostration or eclipse of
the intellect of both parties from intoxication.   Numerous instances
might be adduced, wherein the temporary activity of certain faculties
not in general prominent in the parents, has caused strong endowments

in the offspring, and nothing but the fear of giving offence induces me to forbear citing many that have come under my own observation. It is well known, that the first born children of very young parents have usually a larger animal and less moral and intellectual developement than the younger branches of the family. Sometimes this is not the case, and the converse happens ; but this will be found to be the consequence of straitened circumstances, or other causes rousing the propensities of the parents into a state of unwonted activity, at the time of the production of the younger children. Marriage among near relations is also a breach of an organic law, and a fruitful source of evil ; but unions of this class are seldom contracted by individuals of *our* order. We find this law principally infringed by royal families, and others of the higher and middle classes, who, anxious to keep up their wealth and their caste, intermarry amongst each other, until mental imbecility results.

I now conclude with a few observations to the young of both sexes, founded on the foregoing views.

To my fair hearers, I would take leave to say :——Persevere in the acquisition of orderly, cleanly, and industrious habits ;——learn early to accommodate yourselves to the different dispositions of others with whom you may be associated ;——strive to acquire a knowledge of your own dispositions, and endeavour, as much as possible, to render your manner *habitually* agreeable and engaging ;——and when your estimable qualities, graces, accomplishments, attract the attention, or rivet the affections, of others, learn to be circumspect——act with great caution——be wary before you give encouragement. Consider that the happiness of yourselves, and the welfare of others, are dependent upon the choice you are about to make. Learn to know your own physical and mental constitution, and to judge of that of others aright. Remember that, if you contract an alliance with any one possessing an unhealthy constitution, that constitution will descend to your progeny, and, in all probability, consign them one by one to the grave, at the very time when they have become most endeared to you. Remember, also, that on the industry, honesty, sobriety, and affection, of him to whom you shall unite yourselves, depends your every temporal felicity. And remember that, unless your feelings, opinions, and sympathies, are in harmony with his, unhappiness will be your inevitable portion. "What," says Dr. Johnson, "can ·be expected but disappointment and repentance from a choice made in the immaturity of youth, in the ardour of desire, without judgment, without foresight, without inquiry after conformity of opinions, similarity of manners, rectitude of judgment, or purity of sentiment? Such is the common process of marriage. A youth and maiden meeting by chance, or brought together by artifice, exchange glances, reciprocate civilities, go home, and dream of one another. Having little to divert attention or diversify thought, they find themselves uneasy when they are apart, and therefore conclude that they shall be happy together. They marry, and discover what nothing but voluntary blindness before had concealed; they wear out life in altercations, and charge nature with cruelty." (*Rasselas*, chap. 29.) What, indeed, can be more productive of misery to a refined and educated woman, than the habitual society of a man addicted to grovelling pursuits, and who laughs at whatever she most highly esteems? Let not the countenance dressed up in smiles, nor the honeyed accents of a lover, enlist your affections in his favour before your judgment has been satisfied of his moral and intellectual worth. Regard not his behaviour towards yourself, but examine into his previous conduct as a son and a citizen. If you find that he has been regardless of the infirmities and wants of those to whom he owed his existence; that he could never brook parental restraint, or listen to the counsel dictated by affectionate regard; that he spends too much of his time in idleness, or that, though industrious, he spends too much of his money in the gin shop; that his associates are unintellectual, immoral, and dissipated;—shun him as you would a pestilence: but if you find that he has been dutiful to, and is esteemed by, his parents and the other members of the family; that he is industrious and sober; and that his associates are men of intelligence and moral worth, then will you have reason to believe that he may prove to you a faithful and affectionate husband, and fulfil all the duties of life with integrity and skill.

To the youthful aspirant towards manly usefulness and honour, I would now address myself. Acquire a knowledge of the physical and moral sciences, to fit you for the proper discharge of the duties of active life. Learn to know yourself, both as regards your physical frame and your intellectual and moral constitution. Physiology will unfold the former, and phrenology the latter. Study the laws which the Creator has established for the government of organised beings, and train your faculties to render them a willing obedience. Learn to look around you in the world, and note the consequences to others of their infringement of these laws, and the benefits that follow observance. Become acquainted with the institutions and laws of your country, and with the principles that regulate the population of a state. Cultivate a love of truth, and the moral courage necessary to follow it; for, be assured, that it can never lead to danger. Cherish a kindly feeling towards the whole human family. Let no distinction

of country or sect be made a pretext for indulging invidious feelings
but remember that it is not given us to be born where we please, and
that

> "True religion is a boon, which heaven
> To man, and not to any sect, has given."

Neither let inferiority of mental endowments in others prompt you to
despise them, nor be elated with the idea of your own capabilities and
acquirements; remember that the advantages you possess over others
in that respect, are purely a gift of the Creator, and that consequently
though you have been more fortunate, you are not the more meri
torious. Labour rather to improve those who are behind you, and do
not scorn to imbibe instructions from your superiors in moral and
mental attainments. Strive to acquire a knowledge of the duties you
may be called upon in after life to fulfil, either as citizens, husbands
or parents. Make phrenology in particular your study. Judge
not of the importance of the science from what my limited faculties
have been able to lay before you, but examine for yourselves the
writings of its intellectual and benevolent founders, and then look
abroad on society and draw your own conclusions. This you can
accomplish with a very trifling sacrifice of time and money, while the
benefit you will derive may be the means of insuring much of the
happiness of your future life, and will have the immediate effect of
exercising and rendering active your moral and intellectual powers
When you have acquired industrious and moral habits, and a know
ledge of those laws which the Creator has established for the moral
government of the world, endeavour to act in accordance therewith
Be especially on your guard that you do not infringe them in forming
the social compact; for the consequences will extend beyond your
self, and go far into futurity. And when a choice has been made in
accordance with the dictates of your superior faculties, let both partie
endeavour, by fulfilling every duty, to render yourselves mutually
agreeable; then will the joyful husband find by delightful experience

> "It is to lovely woman given
> To soothe our griefs, our woes allay,
> To heal the heart by misery riven,
> Change earth into an embryo heaven,
> And drive life's fiercest cares away."

ARTICLE III.

Lectures on Popular Education. By GEORGE COMBE. Second
American edition, corrected and enlarged. Published by Marsh,
Capen, Lyon & Co., Boston. 12mo. pp. 141.

It is now beginning to be generally admitted, that whatever other
merits phrenology may possess, it must have important bearings upon
he subject of education. It might be expected, *a priori*, that a science
which unfolds the primitive faculties of the animal, intellectual, and
moral nature of man, and their true relations to the 'external world,
would shed a vast amount of light on the education of these faculties,
both in relation to the *means* to be employed, as well as the *objects* to
e secured. The cause, which, of all others, has most retarded the
progress of education, defeated most frequently its designs, and produced the greatest diversity of opinions on the subject, has originated
from the fact, that the *true nature* of man has not been hitherto gene-
ally understood. This remark is more fully elucidated in the follow-
ng quotation from the above work :—

"Owing to the want of a philosophy of mind, education has hitherto
been conducted empirically ; and, instead of obtaining from it a correct
view of the nature of man, and of the objects and duties of life, each
ndividual has been left to form, upon these points, theories for himself,
derived from the impressions made upon his own mind by the particular
circumstances in which he has been placed. No reasonable person
assumes himself to know the philosophy of astronomy, or of chemistry,
or of physiology, without study, and without reaching clear, consistent,
and certain principles ; yet, in the philosophy of mind, the practice is
quite different. Every professor, schoolmaster, author, editor, and
pamphleteer—every member of parliament, counsellor, and judge—has
a set of notions of his own, which, in his mind, hold the place of a
system of the philosophy of man ; and although he may not have metho-
dised his ideas, or even acknowledged them, to himself, as a theory, yet
they constitute a standard, to him, by which he practically judges of all
questions in morals, politics, and religion. He advocates whatever
views coincide with them, and condemns all that differ from them, with
as little hesitation as a professed theorist himself, and without the least
thought of trying his own principles by any standard whatever. In
short, in the great mass, even of educated men, the mind, in judging of
questions relating to morals, politics, and social institutions, acts on its
merely instinctive impressions. and exhibits all the confliction and uncertainty of feeling, unguided either by principles of reason, or by facts
ascertained by experience. Hence, public measures in general, whether
relating to education, religion, trade, manufactures, provision for the
poor, criminal law, or to any other of the dearest interests of society,
nstead of being treated as branches of one general system of economy,
and adjusted on scientific principles, each in harmony with the others,
are too often supported or opposed on narrow and empirical grounds ;
and discussions regarding them, occasionally call forth displays of igno-

rance, prejudice, and intolerance, at once disgraceful to the age, and calculated greatly to obstruct the progress of substantial improvement. Indeed, unanimity on questions, of which the first principles must be found in the constitution of human nature, will be impossible, even among sensible and virtuous men, so long as no standard of mental philosophy is admitted to guide individual feelings and perceptions. Hence, when a young man educated as a merchant asks the use of any thing, the only answer which will thoroughly interest him, will be, one showing how much wealth may be acquired by it. The devoutly religious professor will acknowledge that alone to be useful, which tends directly to salvation; while the votary of fashion will admit the utility of such pursuits only as are recognised by the refined, but frivolous, and generally ill-informed circle, which, to him, constitutes the highest tribunal of wisdom. To expound, to such persons, principles affecting the general interests of society, and to talk to them of schemes for promoting the happiness of human beings, in their various conditions of husbands and wives, parents and children, masters and servants, teachers and pupils, governors and subjects, appears like indulging a warm imagination in fanciful harangued. They think that the experience of six thousand years is sufficient to show that a man is not destined, in this life, to be greatly different from what he has always been, and now is; and that any measures pretending greatly to improve his condition, however desirable, are not at all to be believed in by sensible and practical people. This state of things could not exist, if education were founded on a true system of human nature, and an exposition of its relations to the external world."

The truth and force of these remarks must be obvious to every one. It is quite evident that we have, as yet, but just begun to understand the *true nature* of education, and the great principles which must be applied in its successful attainment. It would seem to be no less the dictates of reason and common sense than of true philosophy, that the *being* to be educated must in the *first* place be correctly understood. But such a course is very far from being pursued at the present day. Parents, teachers, and guardians of youth, are, to a very great extent, profoundly ignorant of the laws which govern the physical and mental nature of man; and, until these laws are correctly understood and obeyed, any and every system of education must necessarily remain imperfect and empirical. But, in the mean time, these laws cannot be neglected or violated with impunity. Multitudes are still destined to disappointment, misery, and premature death, in consequence of the ignorance and prejudice existing in the community on this subject. It is true, some few are beginning to see a beauty and force, which they never before perceived, in the poet's saying, that

"The proper study of mankind is man;"

and they are compelled to acknowledge, too, that this study can be successfully pursued only by means of investigating the principles of physiology and phrenology. For on these two sciences only, can any rational system of education or philosophy of mind be based.

The work, whose title heads this article, contains a summary of views on this subject, which are of great importance, and should be thoroughly understood by all. We can notice only a few of the points discussed, and that, too, chiefly by quotations. Mr. Combe, after considering briefly man's position on the earth, and his relations to the external world, proceeds to show, as follows, that he is endowed by his Creator with faculties wisely adapted to his condition and circumstances in this world, and which, in order to secure his highest happiness, must be properly enlightened and exercised.

"Man, ignorant and uncivilised, is a ferocious, sensual, and super-stitious savage. The external world affords some enjoyments to his animal feelings, but it confounds his moral and intellectual faculties. Nature exhibits to his mind a mighty chaos of events, and a dread dis-play of power. The chain of causation appears too intricate to be unravelled, and the power too stupendous to be controlled. Order and beauty, indeed, occasionally gleam forth to his eye, from detached por-tions of creation, and seem to promise happiness and joy; but more fre-quently clouds and darkness brood over the scene, and disappoint his fondest expectations. Evil seems so mixed up with good, that he regards it either as its direct product, or its inseparable accompaniment. Nature is never contemplated with a clear perception of its adaptation to the purpose of promoting the true enjoyment of man, or with a well-founded confidence in the wisdom and benevolence of its Author. Man, when civilised and illuminated by knowledge, on the other hand, dis-covers in the objects and occurrences around him, a scheme beautifully arranged for the gratification of his whole powers, animal, moral, and intellectual; he recognises in himself the intelligent and accountable subject of an all-bountiful Creator, and in joy and gladness desires to study the Creator's works, to ascertain his laws, and to yield to them a steady and a willing obedience. Without undervaluing the pleasures of his animal nature, he tastes the higher, more refined, and more enduring delights, of his moral and intellectual capacities, and he then calls aloud for education, as indispensable to the full enjoyment of his rational powers.

"If this representation of the condition of the human being on earth be correct, we perceive, clearly, the unspeakable advantage of applying our minds to gain knowledge, and of regulating our conduct according to rules drawn from acquired information. Our constitution and our posi-tion equally imply, that the grand object of our existence is, not to remain contented with the pleasures of mere animal life, but to take the dignified, and far more delightful, station of moral, religious, and rational occupants of this lower world.

"Education, then. means the process of acquiring that knowledge of our Creator, of ourselves, and of external nature, and the formation of those habits of enterprise and activity which are indispensable to the evolution of our higher qualities, and to the performance of our parts, with intelligence and success, in such a scene as I have described.

"These views may appear to many persons to be so clearly founded in reason. as to require neither proof nor illustration; but there are others who are little familiar with such contemplations, and to whom a few elucidations may be useful. As the latter are precisely those whom I desire to benefit. I solicit the permission to enter into a few details, even at the risk of appearing tedious to the more enlightened among my hearers

"To understand correctly the constitution of the human mind, and its need of instruction, it is useful to compare it with that of the inferior animals.   The lower creatures are destined to act chiefly from instinct; and instinct is a tendency to act in a certain way, planted in the animal by the Creator, without its knowing the ultimate design, or the nature of the means by which its aim is to be accomplished.   A bee, for example, constructs its cell in conformity with the most rigid principles of mathematical science, according to which it is necessary that the fabric should possess a particular form, and be joined to other cells at a particular angle, in preference to all others, in order to give it the greatest capacity and strength, with the least possible expenditure of material. The creature has no knowledge of the principles of mathematics, such as man possesses; but it acts in accordance with them, by an impulse obviously planted in it by the Author of its being.   Man is not directed by unerring impulses like this.   Before he could construct a similar fabric, with success, it would be necessary for him, by means of experiment and observation, to become acquainted with the nature of the materials to be employed, and to form a clear conception of the whole design, previous to the commencement of his labour.   A mother, among the inferior animals, is impelled by pure instinct to administer to her offspring that kind of protection, food, and training, which its nature and circumstances require; and so admirably does she fulfil this duty, even at the first call, that human sagacity could not improve, or rather could not at all equal, her treatment.   Now these animals proceed without consciousness of the admirable wisdom displayed in their actions;— because they do not act from knowledge and design.   It is certain, that wherever design appears, there must be intelligence; yet the wisdom resides not in the animals, but in their Author.   The Creator, therefore, in constituting the bee, or the beaver, possessed perfect knowledge of the external circumstances in which He was about to place it, and of its relations, when so placed, to all other creatures and objects; and conferred on it powers or instincts of action, admirably adapted to secure its preservation and enjoyment.   Hence, when enlightened men contemplate the habits and powers of animals, and compare them with their condition, they perceive wisdom and benevolence conspicuously displayed by the Creator.

"Man, also, has received instincts which resemble those of the lower animals,—such as the love of sex, of offspring, of society, and of praise, the instinct of resentment, and many others; by the exercise of which, as I have said, he may maintain his purely animal existence, with very little aid from education.   But he is distinguished from the inferior creatures, 1st, By the possession of moral sentiments—such as the love of justice, of piety, of universal happiness; and, 2dly, By great superiority in the reflecting faculties, fitted to acquire knowledge of the modes of action of external objects, and of their effects."

"Many persons are not aware that human feelings are more blind than those of the lower animals, and that they lead to worse results when not directed by reason.   They imagine that if they possess a feeling strongly, such as the love of offspring, or the love of God, they cannot err in the mode of gratifying it; consequently, they act with all the energy of impulse, and all the blindness of infatuation.   A mighty change will be effected in human conduct, when the people at large become acquainted with the indispensable necessity of reason to the proper direction of their feelings, and with the fact that knowledge is the grand element, without which reason cannot be efficiently exerted.   Man, therefore, being an improvable being, has been furnished with reason, and been left to discover, by the exercise of it, his own nature, the nature of external objects and their effects, and to adapt the one to the other in his temporal sphere for his own advantage.   When he shall do so, and fulfil also his moral and religious duties, he will assume his proper station as a rational being. The only limit to this proposition is, that each of his faculties, bodily and mental, and every external object, have received a definite constitution, and are regulated by precise laws, so that limits have been set to human aberration, and also to human attainments; but, within these limits, vast materials for producing happiness, by harmonious and wise adaptations, or misery, by discordant and foolish combinations, exist; and these must be discovered and employed by man, before he can reach the full earthly enjoyment of which his nature is susceptible.

"I do not pretend to predicate *what* degree of perfection man is capable of attaining on earth by these means.   Looking at the condition of the inferior animals, I should not expect optimism; because disease, death, cold, heat, and famine, are incident to them all; but, on dispassionately comparing the enjoyments of the inferior creatures, in relation to their natures, with the past and present enjoyments of the human race, in relation to their superior capacities, I fear that man does not surpass them to the extent which he ought to do, if he made a proper use of the means fairly in his power of promoting his own happiness.   Comparing the civilised Christian inhabitants of modern Europe, with the ignorant, ferocious, filthy, and helpless savages of New South Wales, we perceive a vast advance; but I do not believe that the limits of attainable perfection have yet been reached even by the best of Europe's sons.*   All, therefore, that I venture to hope for is, that man, by the proper employment of the means presented to him, may arrive at last at a condition of enjoyment of his mortal existence, as great, in relation to his rational nature, as that of the lower animals is in relation to their natures.   This is no more than saying, that the Creator has made man as perfect as a reasonable being, as He has made the lower of animals perfect as instinctive creatures.

"I trust, then, that most of you will now concur with me in thinking, that if man, by his constitution, be an intelligent, moral, religious, and, therefore, an improvable being, he must be taught knowledge, and trained to apply it, as the first stage in his progress towards enjoyment.   In other words, he must be educated.

"Let us inquire, then, into the present condition of education, and afterwards consider how it may be improved."

Mr. Combe here proceeds to discuss at some length the merits of classical education, or the utility of devoting so much time, as is usually the case in most institutions, to the study of the languages. As this is a topic, connected with education, of great importance, we intend to present an article on the subject in some future number of the Journal.   Still, we cannot forbear quoting, at the present time, the following general remarks by Mr. Combe, on what should be the great objects of education.

"* A very instructive exposition of the evils arising from the improper physical education of the young, and of the means of substituting a better treatment, will be found in 'Health and Beauty, an Examination of the Laws of Growth and Exercise, by John Bell, M. D   Philadelphia, 1838.' "

"One great object of education, is the attainment of knowledge itself. If the season for obtaining real knowledge be dedicated to the study of languages, the individual will enter on active life in a state of qualification for practical business, similar to that of a lady for the practice of architecture, who has completed only her studies in drawing. He will be deficient in many acquirements that would be substantially useful for the preservation of his health, and the successful conducting of affairs. He will know nothing about the structure of his own body, and very little about the causes which support it in health or subject it to disease: he will be very imperfectly informed concerning the constitution of his own mind, and the relations established between himself and other beings: he will not be instructed in any science; know nothing of the principles of trade; be profoundly ignorant of the laws of his country, which he will be called on to obey, or even to administer; in short, he will be sent into society with little other preparation than a stock of prejudices gathered from the nursery, and of vague imaginations about the greatness of Greece and Rome, the beauties of classical literature, and the vast superiority of learned pedantry over practical sense.

"To discover the evils that arise from this misdirection of education, we have only to advert to the numerous cases of individuals who ruin their constitutions, and die in youth or middle age, not from the fury of ungovernable passions which knowledge could not subdue, but from sheer ignorance of the physical conditions necessary to health; or to the ruined fortunes and broken hearts clearly referable to the ignorance of individuals, of their own incapacity for the business in which they have embarked, of the characters of those with whom they have connected themselves, of the natural laws which govern production, or of the civil laws which regulate the transactions of men in particular states; and to ask, how many of these calamities might have been avoided, by instruction and by proper discipline of the mind in the fields of observation and reflection?"

Mr. Combe urges very earnestly and forcibly the study of the natural sciences, as being adapted to the nature of man's faculties, and to the relations which he sustains to the physical world, as well as to the duties which he owes to himself, to his fellow-men, and to his Creator. The study of anatomy and physiology is warmly commended. One of the benefits derived from a knowledge of these sciences, he alludes to as follows :—

"One great use of knowledge is the preservation of health. This, although greatly overlooked in established systems of education, is of paramount importance. Life depends on it, and also the power of exercising with effect all the mental functions. There are two modes of instructing an individual in the preservation of health: the one by informing him, as a matter of fact, concerning the conditions on which it depends, and admonishing him, by way of precept, to observe them; the other, by expounding to his intellect the constitution of his bodily frame, and teaching him the uses of its various parts, the abuses of them, the relations established between them and external objects, such as food, air, water, heat, and cold, and the consequences of observance or neglect of these relations. The former method, addresses the memory, chiefly; the latter, the judgment. The former comes home to the mind, enforced only by the authority of the teacher; the latter is felt to be an exposition of the system of nature, and deeply interests at once the intellect and affections. The former affords rules for particular cases; the latter, general principles, which the mind can apply in all emergencies."

The various uses of knowledge are then discussed at considerable length, under the following heads :—" Another use of knowledge is to enable us to exercise the mental faculties themselves, so as to render them vivacious and vigorous, and thereby to promote our usefulness and enjoyment." And again :—" A third use of knowledge is to qualify us to perform our duties, physical, moral, and religious in the best manner, and to reap the fullest enjoyment, here and hereafter, which Providence allots to those who best fulfil the objects of their existence, and yield the most perfect obedience to the Divine laws."

The third lecture is devoted entirely to female education, and contains many very excellent remarks. We regret that our limits preven us from making any quotations; but we would commend to the reader's attention, an article in Vol. I. page 316 of this Journal, titled " Woman in her Social and Domestic Character," which is from Mr Combe's pen, and constitutes, in part, the substance of this lecture That article is well worthy of a careful and attentive perusal, and a the time of its publication, was justly spoken of in high terms In concluding this notice, we earnestly recommend Mr. Combe's Lectures on Education to the attention of all our readers, and can assure them that they will never regret purchasing the work, and making a practical application of the principles which it inculcates.

ARTICLE IV.

PREDOMINANCE OF CERTAIN ORGANS IN THE BRITISH POETS.—NO. 3.

(Continued from page 260 of this Journal.)

The organ of Individuality in Shakspeare was largely developed its function is well known. It is the collector of isolated facts United with deficient reasoning powers, its action will be indiscrimi nate—it will still amass, but with no definite aim or object. In the head of our poet it became the accurate delineator of individual traits and gave life and body, and definite outline, to his inimitable concep tions. Exercised in harmony with Causality and Comparison, i formed the genius for observation, and aided the spirit of induction His knowledge of man was not confined to general attributes, all his descriptions being remarkable for the most delicate and characteristic distinctions and minute individuality; so much so, that the reader ever feels certain, that the portraits so faithful, so true to nature, mus surely have had a "local habitation and a name." A writer in the Edinburgh Phrenological Journal, in noticing this beauty, justly excepts to the criticism of Dr. Johnson, who says,—" The characters of other authors represent *individuals*, those of Shakspeare, *entire classes*." This supposed eulogium has been echoed and re-echoed, from the philologist's time to the present, by all who praise with more zeal than discrimination; but if it were *true*, it would reduce the corporeal presence of Falstaff, the actual tangibility of Hamlet, Lear, and Shylock, to the abstractions of the monomanias of Joanna Baillie. Shakspeare's characters smack, indeed, of the common stock, but they are ever so distinctly and beautifully individualised, that it is impossible to confound the revenge of Shylock with that of Iago, or Imogene's love with that of Juliet. In truth, Johnson knew very little about him; he has acknowledged that he never studied him, and that he never appreciated him, his commentations sufficiently prove. Profoundly versed in the scholastic poetry, a better or warmer critic of Dryden and Pope cannot be found, nor a more frigid, captious blunderer over the works of Shakspeare.

Language was wonderfully large and active, and was manifested not merely in acquiring foreign tongues, its usual direction when unaccompanied by higher powers, but in creating a just and glowing medium of his own, for all the infinite shades and delicate tracery of thought, and for all those combinations and varieties of human feeling and passion evoked by his other faculties. It is the *creative* power of this faculty we would especially dwell upon, which is shown, not in adapting new and peculiar words—for here the grammarian would equal or excel him—but in that nice and acute perception of the very spirit of his native idioms, and in the manner he has wrought them out into the perfect expression of all the passions which agitate, of all the sentiments which exalt, and of the richest dreams of grandeur, love, and beauty.

Who, acquainted with the real power of the poet in this respect, will not allow that he has affected infinitely more for the English language, than all the philologists who have grafted upon the hardy stock of Saxon growth, idioms, which as often weaken as they embellish its pristine strength and vigour? Our limits forbid examples, and we can only refer the reader to his works, where he will find the most powerful passages constructed almost entirely from words of Saxon origin, those expressive symbols which, artfully employed, impart so much force, point, and tripping vivacity to the thoughts.

Comparison, one of his largest intellectual organs, must have been exceedingly active, and, blended with his great perception, gave to his reasoning all the strength of the most accurate analogy, and to his descriptions, all the ornament which "the outward shows of sky and earth" presented to one whose eye was never closed to the beauties of nature.

Eventuality stored his mind with the incidents of all nations, ancient and modern, and supplied the rich resources of his historical plays.

Time does not seem to have been very energetic, and it may be noticed that *Action* was the only one of the sacred writers of the school he regarded; nor has his contempt of the Aristotelian dogma ever, we believe, been much regretted by those who prefer truth and nature to an adherence to artificial laws, which ought to have been abrogated when the emergency which created them had ceased to exist.

One of the most noticeable instances of the folly of this profound veneration of classic authority, may be found in Addison's Cato, when the "unity of place" is so rigidly observed as to convert it, though originally designed to add *probability* to the scene, into one of the most *improbable* fictions.

Veneration, so largely developed in our author, and acting in harmony with his lofty intellect and towering Benevolence, delights us by its beautiful and appropriate manifestation. Though writing under a monarchy, for such, in fact, was England in the age of Elizabeth, it is astonishing how seldom he perverted this noble endowment to servility and flattery. He venerates only what is venerable, and reserves his homage for the glories of nature, or the divine attributes of its author. In what page of theology shall we find a more exquisite picture of mercy than that put into the mouth of Portia?

> "The quality of mercy is not strain'd;
> It droppeth, as the gentle rain from heaven,
> Upon the place beneath: it is twice bless'd:
> It blesseth him that gives, and him that takes.
> 'Tis mightiest in the mightiest; it becomes
> The throned monarch better than his crown:
> His sceptre shows the force of temporal power,
> The attribute to awe and majesty,
> Wherein doth sit the dread and fear of kings;
> But mercy is above this sceptred sway,
> It is enthroned in the hearts of kings,
> It is an attribute to God himself;
> And earthly power doth then show likest God's
> When mercy seasons justice. Therefore, Jew,
> Though justice be thy plea, consider this,—
> That, in the course of justice, none of us

> Should see salvation: we do pray for mercy;
> And that same prayer doth teach us all to render
> The deeds of mercy. I have spoke thus much, ·
> To mitigate the justice of thy plea;
> Which if thou follow, this strict court of Venice
> Must needs give sentence 'gainst the merchant there."

In citing passages which may be rather familiar, the intelligen reader must remember our design, which is to illustrate, by well known examples, the phrenological developements of the bard. I would be easy to select others no less applicable, but which, from being less read, might not appear so well adapted to the subject Need we add a single word about his ever-active Mirthfulness? W fear even the slightest attempt to display the opulence of this faculty would be accepted somewhat as old Sheridan is said to have receive a present of the " Beauties of Shakspeare"—" Where," exclaime the veteran, " are all the other volumes?" We leave the reader therefore, to wander at his leisure with old Jack Falstaff, his com panions, Nym, Bardolph, and Pistol—to revel with Sir Andrew Ague-cheek, and listen to the amusing volubility of Touchstone, onl charging him not to leave the latter until the accomplished clown of courts and cities shall have consummated his nuptials with the rusti Audry. Thus far we have chiefly dwelt upon the intellectual an moral region, so strikingly large in the likeness. For the actual size of other portions of the brain, we must depend upon the relation which generally exists between one portion of the cranium an another, and the appropriate manifestations furnished by his writings. What, but large and active Adhesiveness, could have imparted life and reality to the Imogenes, Juliets, and Desdemonas? What, except Combativeness and Destructiveness, could have created hi spirit-stirring battle scenes? Or what, but the blighting force of the latter faculty, completely let loose for the purpose, could have inspired the fitting outburst of the misanthrope Timon, when, rushing from the city of Athens, he thus pours forth his withering curse and sweeping malediction?

> " Let me look back upon thee, O thou wall,
> That girdlest in these wolves!—dive in the earth,
> And fence not Athens! Matrons, turn incontinent.
> Obedience, fail in children! slaves, and fools,
> Pluck the grave wrinkled senate from the bench,
> And minister in their steads!
> *   *   *   *   Bankrupts, hold fast;
> Rather than render back, out with your knives,
> And cut your trusters' throats! bound servants, steal!
> Large-handed robbers your grave masters are,
> And pill by law!

> * * * * Son of sixteen,
> Pluck the lined crutch from the old limping sire,
> With it beat out his brains! piety, and fear,
> Religion to the gods, peace, justice, truth,
> Domestic awe, night-rest, and neighbourhood,
> Instruction, manners, mysteries, and trades,
> Degrees, observances, customs, and laws,
> Decline to your confounding contraries,
> And yet confusion live! Plagues, incident to men,
> Your potent and infectious fevers heap
> On Athens, ripe for stroke! thou cold sciatica,
> Cripple our senators, that their limbs may halt
> As lamely as their manners! lust and liberty
> Creep in the minds and marrow of our youth;
> That 'gainst the stream of virtue they may strive,
> And drown themselves in riot!"

We must not omit the poet's large Cautiousness and Wonder, which add so much thrilling interest to the dagger scene of Macbeth; nor the extraordinary *Imitation* which doubtless directed his energies to the drama; for various as are the objects to which this faculty may appropriately be directed, yet, to one in our author's circumstances, none could be more alluring than the theatre, where all the arts conspire

> " To raise the genius, and to mend the heart."

Thus we see *all* the organs which go to form a perfectly developed brain—*all* the propensities, sentiments, and intellectual faculties, were large, vigorous, and active; and supposing the possessor in the enjoyment of average health, any phrenologist would anticipate the magnificent results of such an organisation. For though there are many degrees between conception, however complete and perfect the embodiment, in passing through which, the poet, painter, and orator, find their greatest labour, anxiety, and despondence; though conception is the gift of nature, and embodiment oftener the reward of infinite toil, the ingenious employment of means, and an enthusiasm which no difficulties can abate, no dangers affright, no allurements betray, yet the phrenologist knows that the true heir of genius has entailed upon him with the gift, an eager restlessness which forbids all repose until the germ of beauty within him be cultured into bloom—until the materials of the grand and noble be brought into the stately and glorious edifice, which is to be at once the attestation of his obedience to the instinct of his nature, and the rich fruit of his industry.

ARTICLE V.

ELEMENTARY PHRENOLOGY.

BY O. S. FOWLER.

To present any science in a plain and simple manner, so that the amateur can readily and fully understand it, requires a better knowledge of its elementary principles than even to treat it learnedly and profoundly. Hence, scientific authors have generally been too philosophical and abstract, to be comprehended by the great *mass* of mankind, and writers on phrenology have too often fallen into the same error. Though they have *described* the different faculties, they have not *defined* them, whereas a clearer and better idea of their primary functions can be given in a very few brief definitions, than in pages of descriptions. Phrenologists have also *classified* the faculties, before the learner knew *what* was to be classified. These two defects the writer proposes to remedy, by substituting definitions for descriptions, as well as by showing what constitutional provision in man's nature, or in his relations to the external world, his mental faculties are adapted to, following, at the same time, what he has considered for many years an *improved* classification.

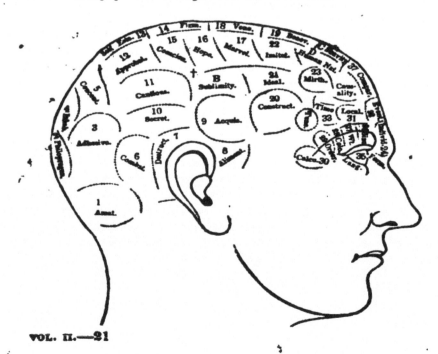

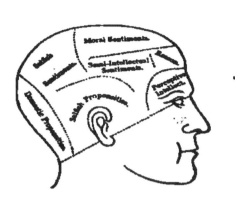
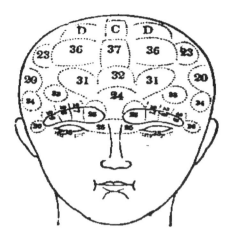

1. *Amativeness.*—Reciprocal attachment, and love of the sexes *as such;* with Adhesiveness, connubial love, and the matrimonial rela-tions. Adapted to man's condition as a reproductive being, and to the continuance of the species. *Abuses:* licentiousness, obscenity, &c.

2. *Philoprogenitiveness.*—Parental love; attachment to one's own offspring; love of children generally, pet animals, &c. Adapted to the dependent and helpless condition in which man enters the world, and to his need of *parental* care and protection. The organ is largest in the mother, on whom this duty chiefly depends. *Abuses:* spoiling children by excessive indulgence; idolising and pampering them, &c.

3. *Adhesiveness.*—Friendship; sociability; fondness for society; susceptibility of forming attachments; inclination to love, and desire to be loved; propensity to associate together in families and neigh-bourhoods. Adapted to man's capability of aiding and receiving assistance from his fellows, and to mutual happiness, by means of reciprocal affection. *Abuses:* too great fondness for company, indiscriminately; grieving excessively at the loss of friends, &c.

4. *Inhabitiveness.*—Love of home and country *as such;* attach-ment to the place where one has lived; unwillingness to change it; desire to locate, and remain permanently in one habitation; patriotism. Adapted to those advantages to be derived from having a permanent home, thereby preventing the evils of numerous and constant changes.

These faculties are called the *Domestic Propensities,* and constitute man a gregarious animal; render him a social and domestic being; create his family attachments and relations, terminating in the mar-riage state, and originating its duties and its pleasures. The proper, or improper, exercise of the domestic feelings have a most powerful influence on all the other faculties. When these organs are large, they cause an elongation and fulness in the middle and lower portion of the back part of the head; but when small, this part of the head presents a flattened and depressed appearance.

5. *Concentrativeness.*—Unity and continuity of thought and feeling power of connected and concentrated application to one, and but one thing at a time. Adapted to man's need of patient, prolonged, and thorough investigation of one thing, as well as of continued application to one subject, in order to complete any difficult or tedious undertaking or to arrive at correct results in complicated and abstruse matters *Abuses:* prolixity; tedious amplification of the feelings and menta operations, and inability to change one's occupation, or divert one's feelings. This faculty is referable to no particular class, but acts as a general regulator or modifier of all the other faculties.

6. *Combativeness.*—*Self*-protection; defence; resistance; defiance. resentment; spirit of opposition; determination; boldness; resolution; willingness to encounter; it originates the feeling implied in the phrase, "*let me and mine alone.*" Adapted to man's existence in a world. where difficulties are to be met and overcome, as well as where his person and his rights must be protected and defended. *Abuses:* pugnacity; a quick, fiery temper; a contrary, fault-finding, contentious disposition, &c.

7. *Destructiveness.*—Executiveness; indignation; sternness; harshness; a pain-causing, retaliating, exterminating disposition; hatred, and bitterness of feeling. Adapted to a state in which pain must be inflicted and endured, and many things must necessarily be destroyed. Man, in this world, is placed under the dominion of certain physical and moral laws. Without such laws, life would be valueless, and, without a penalty attached to their violation, that is, without the institution of pain, these laws would be null and void. Pain is, therefore, productive of good; and even necessary in man's present state of existence. *Abuses:* rage; revenge; malice premeditated; animosity; wars; cruelty; malignity; murder, &c.

8. *Alimentiveness.*—Appetite; hunger; desire for nutrition; gustatory enjoyment. Adaptation:—Man is an eating animal. By the laws of his nature, the exercise of both body and mind causes an expenditure of the vital energies. This expenditure presupposes a re-supply, or a speedy exhaustion would ensue, and this supply is received partly through the medium of the digestive apparatus, to which this faculty is adapted. *Abuses:* gluttony; gormandising; living merely to eat and drink; drunkenness—though this last vice depends much on the temperament, habits, &c. of the individual.

9. *Acquisitiveness.*—Love of possessing and acquiring property *as such;* the feeling of *mine* and *thine*—of claim and rightful possession;

an economical, saving, frugal disposition, which is pained by seeing
waste and extravagance.   Adaptation :—Man requires to lay by, in
store, at the proper season, the necessaries and comforts of life, such
as food, clothing, &c.   An exchange of property, also, between man
and man, is often beneficial to both, and even necessary.   Acquisitiveness has its counterpart in this demand for, and exchange of, property.
It tends to restrain that waste and prodigality, which the other faculties
would otherwise lead to ; promotes industry, as well as prevents idleness and vice.

10. *Secretiveness.*—Policy ; management ; evasion ; cunning ; acting under assumed aspects ; and disguising one's real sentiments and
purposes.   Adapted to man's need of this means of defence ; to the
necessity, sometimes, of his concealing his feelings, and of indirectly
effecting his purposes.   *Abuses :* hypocrisy ; deceit ; lying ; duplicity, &c.

These faculties are denominated the *Selfish Propensities.* They
stand intimately related to the body, being so located as to facilitate as
much as possible the intercommunication between them and the body.
Their primary adaptation is to man *as an animal*—to man in his
physical wants and conditions, giving rise to his merely *animal*
necessities, desires, and gratifications, thus begetting Selfishness, and
terminating solely on the interests and happiness of their possessor.
The organs of these faculties are located upon the sides of the head,
around the ears, and, when large, give it a thick and rounded appearance, and make the sides of the head *spherical ;* but when small, the
head is thinner, and more flattened in this region.   These faculties
receive their direction and modification chiefly from the relative influence of the sentiments and intellect.

11. *Cautiousness.*—Provision against want and danger ; solicitude
about consequences ; fear ; care ; anxiety ; taking precautionary measures ; fleeing from foreseen evils, &c.   Adapted to man's existence
in a world of danger, as well as to his need of care and foresight.
Abuses : procrastination ; irresolution ; timidity ; cowardice ; melancholy ; want of promptness and enterprise.

12. *Approbativeness.*—Regard for character and reputation ; desire
for a "good name," and to be esteemed ; love of praise, popularity,
fame, and notoriety ; pride of character ; feeling of shame ; ambition
to distinguish one's self.   Adapted to the praiseworthy and the disgraceful qualities of actions.   *Abuses :* vanity ; following the fashions
at all hazards ; extravagantly decorating the person ; making too great
display and show ; artificial manners ; formal politeness, &c.

13. *Self-esteem.*—Self-respect ; love of freedom, liberty, and independence ; self-confidence ; self-complacency and satisfaction ; high

sense of honour; love of power; nobleness; dignity; a high-toned manly feeling, which despises meanness and commands respect. Adaptation:—Man holds an elevated rank in the "great chain of being," especially in his mental and *moral* relations. This faculty gives him a consciousness that he is *what* he is, and disposes him to conduct in accordance with his high capacities and relations. *Abuses:* pride; egotism; swaggering pretensions; haughtiness; an aristocratical, domineering spirit, &c.

14. *Firmness.*—Decision of character; stability; fixedness of purpose, opinion, &c.; perseverance; an unwillingness to change. Adapted to man's necessity of meeting and overcoming difficulties, giving him fixedness, perseverance, &c. *Abuses:* obstinacy; wilfulness; a blind adherence to present opinions, and in opposition to reason.

This class of faculties, denominated *Selfish Sentiments*, like the selfish propensities, also terminate upon their possessor, and by disposing him to seek his own individual interest and happiness, make him selfish; yet their character and manifestations are far superior to those of the selfish propensities, especially when the religious and reasoning faculties are strong. They are located together in the superior posterior, or back part of the upper portion of the head. When these organs are large, this portion of the head is extended upwards and backwards; and when the moral sentiments are deficient, this region of the head is then conical.

15. *Conscientiousness.*—Moral principle; sense of justice; integrity; regard for duty; perception of right, and a feeling of wrong *as such*, and that right should be rewarded, and wrong punished; sense of moral accountability, of guilt and incumbency; love of truth; penitence for sin; disposition to reform; gratitude for favours; desire of moral purity and blamelessness of life. Adapted to the great principles of right and wrong, of duty and justice, established by the Creator in the very nature of things. *Abuses:* excessive scrupulousness; self-condemnation; making too little allowance for the faults and follies of mankind. This faculty enforces what the other faculties regard as right; does the fair thing between man and man, and makes one see and endeavour to correct his faults.

16. *Hope.*—Anticipation; expectation of future happiness and success; enterprise; cheerfulness; tendency of mind to magnify advantages, and to overlook or underrate difficulties. Adaptation:—Whilst the other faculties desire things, Hope assures us that they can easily be obtained; prompts the efforts required for obtaining the anticipated good, and prevents discouragement. *Abuses:* a visionary, chimerical, castle-building disposition, &c.

17. *Marvellousness.*—Faith; belief in special Divine Providence, and reliance upon it for direction; belief in spiritual existences and supernatural manifestations. Adapted to the supernatural portions of Divine revelation, and to the existence of spiritual beings. *Abuses:* belief in ghosts, witchcraft, &c.

18. *Veneration.*—Worship of a God; adoration of a Supreme Being; a disposition to observe religious rites and ceremonies; respect for religion and things sacred; regard for antiquity and deference to superiors. Adaptation:—Man is *naturally* a religious being, and has always had some object of worship. This faculty creates this sentiment of adoration, and adapts man to the worship of a Supreme Being. The existence of a Deity may be inferred, if not proved, from this source. *Abuses:* idolatry; superstition; respect for unworthy objects, &c.

19. *Benevolence.*—Kindness; sympathy for persons in distress; delight in seeing, and desire to make, sentient beings happy; willingness to make personal sacrifices to secure this end; generosity; benignity; humanity. Adapted to man's capability of relieving the miseries, and of promoting the enjoyment, of his fellow-beings. If man were incapable of experiencing pain, or of promoting human happiness, this faculty would have no counterpart. *Abuses:* giving alms to the vicious and undeserving; so great tenderness of feeling as to be overcome by the sight of suffering, &c.

These faculties, called the *Moral Sentiments*, create those religious and devotional feelings and emotions which enter so largely into the human character; humanise, adorn, elevate, and soften the nature of man; constitute man a moral and accountable being, and connect him with the moral government of God; create those moral duties and relations which exist between man and his Maker; and, also, between man and man. The organs of these faculties are located in the superior anterior, or the frontal portion of the upper part of the head, and, when large, throw a proportionally large amount of brain in this region, elevating and elongating this part of the head.

20. *Constructiveness.*—Mechanical skill; dexterity in using tools; ability to make, manufacture, build, contrive, and construct; skill in repairing articles; slight of hand in turning off all kinds of manual labour. Adaptation:—Man requires clothing and houses for the protection of his person; implements of husbandry; machines; tools of various kinds, and numerous articles, obtained either by means of the mechanical or fine arts. The conveniences and luxuries, to say nothing of the necessaries of life, flowing from these sources, are incalculable. Indeed, were it not for these, man would be compelled to live without garments and buildings, without carriages and internal

improvements, without household furniture, and, to a great extent destitute of books and the means of knowledge. Now there are certain laws to matter, by the knowledge and application of which various inventions and improvements may be made, that add greatly to man's happiness. But, unless man had some faculty by which h is enabled to perceive and apply these laws, they would be a dead letter to him, as they are now to the brute creation. Constructiveness is adapted to this necessity in man's condition for having things constructed, and to the existence of certain material laws, as well as to the practical application of principles in the sciences and the arts. *Abuses* wasting one's time and money in trying experiments, getting out useless patents, trying to invent perpetual motion, &c.

21. *Ideality*.—Good taste; refinement of feeling and manners delicacy; sense of propriety; fancy; love of polite literature, belles lettres, and a chaste and elegant style; that faculty which perceives and admires the beautiful, the rich, the exquisite, the sentimental, the perfect, and the fine arts generally; which gives impassioned ecstacy and rapture of feeling, elegance and beauty of style, and inspiration to poetry and oratory; softens down the rougher features of man's nature, and creates a desire for improvement and perfection. Adaptation :—Man is so constituted as to admire the beauties of nature and art, a handsome face and an elegant form, &c.; is delighted in contemplating the imaginative in poetry, fiction, romance, &c., and receives vast accessions to his happiness from the above sources. The faculty of Ideality also imposes great restraint upon the coarse, vulgar, and vicious manifestation of the passions, propensities, &c.; favouring the perfection of man's whole nature.* *Abuses :* ideal reveries; sickly sentimentalism; extravagant love of romance, poetry, the theatre, &c.; that sickly delicacy which is disgusted with the world as it is, and soars to dwell constantly in an ideal world.

22. *Imitation*.—Power of imitating and copying; of doing what one sees done; mimicry, &c. Adaptation :—Man is a *progressive* being. Individuals and generations copy from their predecessors (vices included), and then make changes and additions of their own, to be transmitted to those who succeed them. But were it not for this faculty, each individual, and every succeeding generation, would be compelled, to a very great extent, to begin *de novo*, originating every convenience and improvement. Moreover, man is obliged to communicate his ideas by means of certain *established* signs, which every one must copy. Children, too, learn a thousand fold more from *example* than from precept, doing what they *see* done. In this

* See page 275 and 279, Vol. I, of this Journal.

necessity for imitation in general, this faculty has its counterpart. The drama has its origin in this power. The faculty of Imitation also greatly aids in relating anecdotes, in powers of oratory, description, the arts, &c. &c. *Abuses:* mimicry; copying the faults of others; servile imitation, and following patterns to the exclusion of originality, and at the expense of independence, &c.

23. *Mirthfulness.*—Wit; perception of the absurd and ludicrous; disposition and ability to joke, make fun, ridicule; humour; pleasantry; facetiousness; intuitive perception of, and disposition to laugh at, that which is improper, ill-timed, out of place, unbecoming, &c. Adaptation:—To detect and expose to ridicule the preposterous, improper, absurd, &c.; thereby aiding the reasoning faculties in ascertaining truth by perceiving the absurdity of error, and correcting the exhibitions of all the other faculties by detecting, and holding up to ridicule, their improper or unnatural manifestations. *Abuses:* levity; making sport of serious things; ridiculing truth; laughing at the infirmities of the unfortunate, &c.

The faculties, called *Semi-Intellectual Sentiments,* are of a mixed nature, participating in the properties both of the sentiments and the intellectual faculties. They tend to the adornment and perfection of the human mind, by creating in it a taste and a talent for the fine arts and polite literature—for copying, constructing, manufacturing, and the like. Improvement seems to be the watchword of our race, and its spirit is manifested in those almost innumerable inventions and contrivances which so greatly augment our comforts, multiply our conveniences, and give new charms to our existence. These improvements result chiefly from this class of faculties. They are located partly between the forehead and the portion of the head covered by hair, and partly within the latter, giving, when large, a fulness and breadth to this portion of the head; but when small, the head, where the hair begins to appear, is narrower and flattened.

We come now to what are called the *Intellectual Faculties.* These have to do exclusively with objects and things, their physical properties and abstract relations. They create a thirst for information, and furnish the ability to acquire knowledge in general; take cognizance of facts and conditions, and remember them, and constitute what is commonly called the intellect, understanding, or judgment. The external senses, viz. sensation, sight, hearing, taste, and smell, are arranged by phrenologists under this class of faculties. Various and contradictory views have been entertained by different writers on the nature and operations of the external senses, and their relations to the mind. Phrenology has thrown a vast amount of light on this intricate subject, and it must be admitted, that the offices of the external senses can be fully and correctly understood, only by taking into consideration the true functions of the brain, as unfolded by the discoveries of this science. For a critical and extended analysis of these faculties, the reader is referred to Dr. Spurzheim's excellent remarks on this subject.

24. *Individuality.*—Observation of things as independent existences; curiosity to see and examine objects; disposition to regard physical things in their individual, isolated capacity. Adaptation:— Matter is divided into a great many distinct existences, called bodies, objects, things, &c., each of which has a personal identity of its own. On looking at any thing, say a book, the first impression that enters the mind, is its individuality or its *thingness*—that it is a certain something, which has an independent existence, called, generally, its *personality.* Now, this faculty constitutes the medium through which a knowledge of *things as such*, enters the mind, and is adapted to take cognisance of that great physical law, called the *divisibility* of matter.

25. *Form.*—Cognisance and recollection of the shape, superficies, configuration, and appearance of objects; observation and recollection of faces, of the expression of countenances, family resemblances, &c.; good eyesight. Adaptation:—Every physical substance, every particle of matter, has some *form* or shape. This is a *necessary* property of matter. By means of it, we are able to designate and recollect one object or one person from another. Infinite wisdom has wisely given *shape* or form to all bodies, and, at the same time, has given to man a faculty which enables him to perceive, and make a useful application of, this elementary property of matter.

26. *Size.*—Cognisance and recollection of magnitude, bulk, proportion, &c.; judgment of the weight of bodies, or their gravity, by observing their size. Adaptation:—Every physical thing that exists, occupies more or less *space*, and cannot exist without this condition. Magnitude or bulk is a *natural, necessary*, and *inherent* property of matter. The faculty of Size enables man to render this arrangement or elementary property of matter of incalculable service to himself. Without such a faculty, we could not perceive or know any difference in the relative size of different bodies.

27. *Weight.*—Intuitive perception and application of the principles of gravity; ability to balance one's self, to preserve the centre of gravity, and to judge of the weight of bodies by lifting them; ability to ride a fractious horse, to carry a steady hand, to throw a ball, stone, or arrow, straight, &c. Adaptation:—The laws of gravity pervade all physical nature, and, without some faculty to perceive and apply these laws, man would fall, and remain wherever these laws carry

him; would be unable even to stand, and much less to walk and labour. This faculty, then, adapts man to the great law of matter called inertia or gravitation.

28. *Colour.*—Perception of colours—of their various shades, hues, tints, &c.; delight and satisfaction in contemplating their diversified and harmonious applications. Adapted to that inherent property of matter called colour, by means of which man's happiness is greatly promoted in various ways, and he enabled to distinguish one thing from another.

29. *Order.*—System; physical arrangement; having a place for every thing, and every thing in its place. Adaptation:—" Order is heaven's first law." The whole universe is found to be a *perfect system* of things. Perfection of arrangement and perfect order characterise all the Creator's works. Man requires the application of this same principle in his business and various pursuits, in order to secure convenience, despatch, correctness, &c. Now, this faculty is adapted to the great law of order which pervades all the Creator's works, as well as to the necessity and utility of order on the part of man.

30. *Calculation.*—Intuitive perception of the relations of numbers or figures; ability to reckon figures and cast accounts *in the head;* numerical computation, having primary reference to the four fundamental rules of Arithmetic, as well as to what is called the Rule of Three. Adaptation:—We naturally *count* and *number* things; important advantages are derived from this capacity; no business transaction could be carried on without it, and nearly all exchanges connected with property or the value of things, depend very much upon it. This faculty adapts man to this necessity, which exists in the nature of things and in his relations to society.

31. *Locality.*—Cognisance and recollection of the relative positions of objects; fondness for geography; love of travelling; recollection of the looks of places, roads, natural scenery, &c. Adaptation:—Space exists and extends all around, both above and below us. Its boundaries man has never been able to fathom. Every material thing has of necessity a " local habitation," and occupies some particular place; and no two things can occupy the same space at the same time. Now, it is necessary that man should observe and recollect the *locality* of things, and it is this faculty which adapts man to his necessity.

These faculties, called the *Observing* or *Knowing Faculties*, store the mind with individual facts; furnish a general knowledge of things, their conditions, and qualities; collect statistical information; create a talent and a desire, proportionate to their size, for observing and knowing; and thus render very great assistance in doing every kind

of business. The organs of these faculties are located directly abov
the eyes—their principal medium of communication with the externa
world—and when large, cause the lower portions of the forehead
above the eyes, proportionally to protrude; but when these organs ar
small, this portion of the forehead is depressed.

We have now analysed all those faculties which have to do wit
the essential and *inherent* properties of matter, and, what is somewha
remarkable, we have found a phrenological faculty adapted to *ever*
inherent property of matter, and, vice versa, every inherent propert;
of matter adapted to some phrenological faculty. And we question
whether any naturalist or philosopher can point out a single elementary
property of matter which has not its counterpart in some menta
faculty, as proved and described by phrenology. Again: Natura
philosophy recognises the following inherent properties of matter
viz. "impenetrability," (Locality,) "extension," (Size,) "figure,'
(Form,) "divisibility," (Individuality,) "inertia," (Weight,) and
"attraction," which is only the principle of weight applied to the
integral particles of matter, and of which the faculty of Weight would
naturally take cognisance. In this catalogue, Colour, Order, and
Number, are omitted, and we would confidently appeal to every
philosopher, whether colour is not as much an inherent property of
matter as extension or figure—whether the numerical relations of one
two, three, and four, are not also inherent—and whether order is no
necessarily a *constituent* element of matter; or whether it is possible
in the very nature of things, for us to have clear and definite concep
tions of material bodies, without these three last conditions, viz. colour
order, and number, to each of which the faculties, Colour, Order, and
Calculation, are severally adapted. And *how*, we would ask, can
these facts be explained upon any other system of mental philosophy
but phrenology?

32. *Eventuality.*—Observation and recollection of action, pheno
mena, occurrences, what has taken place, and circumstantial and histo
rical facts; desire to witness and institute experiments; thirst for
information, and the news of the day; desire to hear and relate anec
dotes, and to find out *what is*, and know what *has been*, and see wha
will be. Adaptation:—Nature is one great theatre of action, motion
and change. These changes, called phenomena, are almost infinit
in number and variety. The whole vegetable and animal creation is
constantly passing through successive changes; and human life, from
the cradle to the grave, is made up of action and change. Innumer
able changes and events are constantly transpiring in the state of
society, as well as in the advancement of knowledge. Now, the

aculty of Eventuality adapts man to such a state of things, and greatly
favours his mental improvement.

33. *Time.*—Cognisance and recollection of the time *when*, of
duration, of the lapse of time, the succession of events; of dates;
keeping the beat in music and dancing, &c.   Adaptation:—Man,
instead of existing in a monotonous *now*, is the creature of succession.
One event happens *before* or *after* another, and Time is adapted to
his arrangement.

34. *Tune.*—Tone; disposition to sing; the musical faculty; sense
of melody and musical harmony; ability to learn tunes by note, and
to detect agreement or discord *by the ear*.   Adaptation:—There are
certain sounds, called *octaves*, which are musical in themselves, and
blend together harmoniously, producing melody, in a greater or less
degree, to the ears of all.   What is melody to the savage Indian, and
to the wild Hottentot, is also melody to the Swiss peasant and to the
musical Italian, as well as to the Anglo-Saxon.   Even the feathered
songsters employ the same octave that *man* employs, using notes that
are melodious to the human ear.   Now, these musical laws or sounds
exist, by means of which man's happiness is greatly promoted; and
we find the faculty of Tune adapted to this delightful arrangement in
nature.

35. *Language.*—Power of communicating one's ideas by means of
written and spoken language; memory of words; copia verborum;
volubility; versatility of expression; ability to learn spoken languages,
and to use such words as precisely express one's meaning.   Adapted
to the exchange or intercommunication of ideas between man and
man, thereby greatly promoting human happiness and improvement.

These faculties, called the *Semi-Perceptive*, perform a class of
functions intermediate between those exercised by the perceptive, and
those by the reasoning, faculties; and the location of their organs
corresponds with their character.   The perceptive faculties take cognisance of *material* objects, and their various *physical* properties,
such as their form, size, weight, colour, &c.; whereas, the semi-perceptive are of a more subtle nature, having to do with facts, and the
various phenomena produced by physical objects, and form, as it
were, a stepping-stone to the reasoning organs.   Eventuality, for
example, takes cognisance, not of physical objects, but their *actions*,
and the incidents and events thus produced; Time, of the particular
period in which these events occur; Language, of the vocal *sounds*
employed to name these objects; and *Tune*, of the *melody* of sounds
produced by them; and thus both the perceptive and semi-perceptive
faculties are employed as the subordinate agents of the reasoning

faculties, furnishing them with materials to scan, digest, and reflect and reason upon. Hence it would appear, that, in the mental economy, the functions of the semi-perceptive faculties are no less important than those of the perceptive, especially if we consider that they constitute as essential a part of the intellectual machinery, when viewed as a whole.

36. *Causality.*—Power of perceiving and applying the principles of causation; ability to plan, contrive, invent, adapt means to ends, take the advantage of circumstances, &c.; to create resources; to apply power most advantageously; to discover first principles, and trace out the connections and relations existing between causes and effects; to reason by drawing conclusions from given premises; to predict the result of given measures; disposition to investigate, and to seek the *why* and *wherefore* of subjects; a leading element of common sense; the *therefore* and *wherefore* faculty. Adaptation:—Every effect must have its cause, and every cause must have its effect. Like causes produce like effects. Without *some* power of perceiving and applying these laws of causation, man could not exist. Causality supplies this power, and is adapted to the arrangement of nature, called *causation.*

37. *Comparison.*—Power of induction and generalisation; of classifying phenomena, and perceiving and applying the principles of analogy; ability to discover the unknown from its resemblance to that which is known; and, also, error from its incongruity with truth, or from its opposition to facts; critical acumen; power of illustrating and explaining one's meaning; of referring to parallel cases, and of using comparisons, similes, figures of speech, &c. Adaptation:—In all the operations of nature, perfect uniformity exists. On account of the *resemblance* which one thing, or one set of things, bears to another, most of the phenomena of the natural world are capable of being grouped together into classes. That the principles of analogy really exist in nature, is demonstrated by every day's observation and experience. Hence we infer the necessity of a primary power of the mind, whose proper function it is to perceive and apply these principles.

Causality and Comparison are called the *Reflective* or *Reasoning Faculties.* They impart to the mind an intellectual power of a higher order than that given by the perceptive and semi-perceptive faculties, enabling man to invent, to think, and reason—to ascertain those abstract relations and bearings of things which neither observation nor any other mental power can reach. Most of the other intellectual faculties are possessed, in a greater or less degree, by some species of the lower order of animals, and some of them to a far greater extent than by man, yet none of these animals can *originate*

and *invent,* or to any considerable extent adapt means to ends. It is
Causality and Comparison which emphatically render man an *improvable* being—which give him the capacity and power of constantly *progressing* in knowledge and civilisation.*

MISCELLANY.

Pathological Facts.—The St. Joseph's Times, of Florida, contained
recently an account of the trial of a negro woman named Maria, charged
with the crime of killing her overseer. In the report of the trial, we find
this statement:—

"The death-bed declarations of the deceased, were also sought to be
used in evidence. He had received two severe blows with an axe on the
top of the head, cutting through the skull into the brain. The cuts into
the brain were each about four inches long, and so near together, that the
skull was broken between them. Deceased survived, notwithstanding,
about five weeks. During this period, he conversed intelligibly at times,
but though he could express his wants and recognise objects, he had lost
the power of calling names. He would say, 'I want to drink,' but he
could not say *water.* He was in the habit of drinking water, tea, coffee,
and milk, but never referred to either by name. The only individual he
attempted to name, was his wife, and he uniformly called her *Peter,*
though he had never done so before his misfortune. When asked who
it was that struck him, he replied, 'call over some names,' and when
Maria and her mother were named, said they did it. What organ of
the brain is essential to the recollection or calling of proper names? We
throw the question to the phrenologists."

This fact we would respectfully submit for solution, to those *antiphrenologists* who profess to believe that the brain, as a whole, is *the*
organ of the mind, or that the functions of the former have no connection
with the manifestations of the latter. Its solution, we think, will be
rather difficult on either hypothesis.

"There is residing in the city of Washington," says the Alexandria
Gazette, "a highly respectable and intelligent lady, rather advanced in
life, who, in 1837, experienced a slight shock of apoplexy. Up to that
time she possessed rather uncommon powers of conversation; was fluent,
and had a ready command of fine language. She had prominent eyes,
and her conversation indicated that the organ of Language, as the
phrenologists would say, was well developed. The attack of apoplexy

* In the first volume of the Journal, we presented two articles on the Elementary
Principles of Phrenology, intending ere this to have resumed the subject; and perhaps the series of articles then commenced may still be continued. We are well
aware that the numbers of the present volume have not been sufficiently *elementary*
and *practical,* and it is therefore with pleasure that we are now able, in part, to
supply this deficiency in the presentation of the above article. Mr. Fowler's
manner of treating the subject is very simple and lucid, and his views are the
result of extensive observations on the science.—ED.

destroyed all power of calling proper names, with a single exception, and which she has never recovered. She still converses fluently, so far as proper names are not concerned; but whenever a proper name occurs, she is arrested in her conversation, and cannot proceed until the name is suggested, when she instantly recognises the person or thing, and is enabled to go on. From this fact, would it not appear that man is endowed with two independent organs of Language, one for common words, and another for proper names?"

As phrenologists, we acknowledge our inability to give a satisfactory explanation to this fact. Some advocates of the science have considered the organ of Language as including in its functions names or nouns, which were both common and proper; others have thought that the use of *proper* names was connected with some other faculty. Farther observations, we doubt not, will throw additional light on this point, and reconcile any apparent discrepancies.

———

Antiquity of Phrenology.—The New Haven Record, Ct., of February 15, contained an article with this caption. It will be found, on a careful examination, that Dr. Gall was the *sole* discoverer of the true functions of the brain, and he alone should receive the merits. Still, many facts and opinions existed previous to his day, which harmonise most perfectly with his discoveries, such as the following, copied from the Record:—

"It is the common opinion that the science of phrenology is entirely of modern date; it is often claimed as a recent discovery which is to confer great benefit upon mankind. A classical friend at our elbow maintains that this is altogether a mistake—that the science is at least as old as the bard of Scio. Homer, he observes, distinctly tells us that Thersites had a conical head, and Jupiter had a wonderful forehead. Accordingly, the former was the most noisy, the most impudent, and the most self-conceited warrior, that ever went to Troy to fight for Helen: and the latter was the king of gods and men, and the highest counsellor. (See Ill. I. 528: II. 211—42, 478.)

"Aristotle, also, was undoubtedly very deeply versed in the science of skulls. In his treatise on physiognomy (Chap. VI.) he is of opinion that a conical head is a sign of impudence; and in this he perfectly agrees with his great predecessor Homer, and successor Gall.

"It would seem that Homer and Aristotle confined their observations to the anterior and upper portions of the human skull. But it was reserved for Apollonius of Rhodes to penetrate into the region of the passions. In his Argonautics, (Lib. III. 761—65,) he informs us that when Medea fell in love with Jason, the captain of the Argo, she felt a curious kind of uneasiness in the back part of the head, which, according to Apollonius, is considerably agitated when Cupid enters the heart, and which, according to Gall, is the seat of the tender affections."

———

Examination of a Skull.—The Worcester Banner, of March 3d, published at Snow Hill, Md., in giving an account of Mr. L. N. Fowler's phrenological examinations in that place, contained the following fact:—

"A human skull was handed him, and he was requested to state the character of its former owner, as developed by the various organs. The following we believe to be a correct report of his remarks.

"'*First*, This appears to be the head of a *male*.

"'*Second*, The organs of his intellectual faculties were small. The frontal lobe of the brain being narrow, and the fibres short.

"'*Third*, His moral faculties appear to have been weak; the coronal region being low, particularly Benevolence and Conscientiousness.

"'*Fourth*, The organs on the sides of the head were unusually developed. Destructiveness, Cautiousness, Secretiveness, Firmness, and Self-esteem, all appear to be large.

"'From these developements, I infer that he was a criminal—if so, probably a murderer. Phrenology, however, does not pretend to say what crimes a man has committed, but what he would be inclined to commit. He might have manifested some Veneration; if so, he was a superstitious man. He was a very selfish man, regarding his own wants and wishes more than those of others, and was self-willed. To sum up the rest in a few words, he was proud, stubborn, insubordinate, ambitious, avaricious, cunning, more desperate than courageous, depraved, and licentious. I regard it as decidedly a *bad head.*'

"We believe the above is an accurate summary of what was said upon the occasion. He also stated that if he were a murderer, he would be more likely to accomplish his purpose by stealth, having large Cautiousness and Secretiveness, than boldly and openly.

"Now for the facts of the case. The skull was that of a negro man who had murdered his master, or rather who was condemned and executed upon this charge. In connection with some other slaves of the same person, he had been punished very severely for theft. The master was waylaid, and killed at his own gate. The proud spirit of the negroes revolted at the punishment of their crime, and they sought revenge in the death of their master. Although the evidence against the negro executed for this crime, was sufficient, in law, to convict him, there remained, and still remains, on the minds of many, a persuasion of his innocence. To the last, he persisted in declaring his innocence of the crime for which he was condemned. At the same time he said he knew who did it, and was cognisant of the intention, and, in fact, was engaged in the plot—who committed the deed he would not tell. Such are the principal facts of the case, so far as we are acquainted with it. Upon comparing these facts with the character given by Mr. Fowler, from the developements of the skull, we think it must be acknowledged that phrenology fairly and triumphantly stood the ordeal to which it was subjected."

———

English Correspondence.—A gentleman connected with the Bank of England, in a letter, dated London, February 29, 1840, to the editor of this Journal, remarks as follows:—"Phrenology, I think, is making great strides in this country. Whenever I mention the subject, I find nine out of ten favourably disposed to it among young and intelligent people. You can scarcely pass by a chemist shop in London, without seeing a phrenological bust conspicuously displayed; and the sale of elementary works on the science is, I understand, enormously large. When, in conjunction with these facts, we take into consideration its more extensive popularity in France, and its very general practical application in the United States, we may believe that the position of those who now blindly oppose or obstinately refuse to listen to its principles, will not, in the course of five or ten years hence, be of the most enviable nature."

THE

AMERICAN PHRENOLOGICAL JOURNAL

AND

MISCELLANY.

| Vol. II. | Philadelphia, May 1, 1840. | No. 8. |

ARTICLE I.

DR. STOKES ON PHRENOLOGY.

Among the evidences indicating the advancement of phrenology we find that the science is beginning to be introduced and treated in a respectful manner, in some of the best medical works which now issue from the press. Many facts might be stated in confirmation of this remark; but it is our object to notice, at the present time, only one work on this subject, viz. "Lectures on the Theory and Practice of Medicine, by William Stokes, M. D." These lectures first appeared in the "London Medical and Surgical Journal," and have since been republished in this country among the standard volumes of the "American Medical Library." Dr. Stokes has sustained for many years a high rank in his profession in Great Britain, and is the author of several valuable works on medicine, as well as of numerous able articles in the English Quarterly Reviews and Journals. Dr. Dunglison, the American editor of these Lectures, informs us that the "author, from his situation, has every opportunity for confirming or disproving his theoretical considerations by the test of practice; he is well informed on every thing that has been done, and is doing, in various countries; and he possesses, withal, powers of discrimination and exposition with which few are favoured."

We have two objects in noticing the remarks of Dr. Stokes on phrenology: 1st, To call the attention of members of the medical profession to the importance of understanding the functions of the brain; 2d, To direct the attention of phrenologists to the intimate and necessary relations which pathological conditions of the brain sustain to phrenology.

It is a fact, no less lamentable than true, that the great majority of the medical profession have thus far been either entirely ignorant or regardless of the true physiology of the brain, in the treatment of disease. Their attention has not been directed to its nature and importance, while engaged in pursuing their professional studies, and, consequently, their future observations, and the practice of medicine, have availed them but little on this subject. While the functions of other organs of the body have been made the objects of special study, those of the brain have, in a great measure, been neglected. It might be inferred, *a priori*, from the position and anatomical relations of this organ, that it exerted a most powerful influence over the whole system, whether in a healthy or morbid condition. It is unnecessary to dwell here on the nature and number of diseases connected with the brain and nervous system, or to show, from their intimate relations to other organs, the powerful influence which they must necessarily exert over the whole body. No disease can be treated rationally and successfully without a knowledge of the functions of the organs involved, and just in proportion to the relative importance of such organs, will be the importance of correctly understanding their functions. And we need scarcely say that physicians, of all others, should understand the true physiology of the brain—the most important viscus in the human body.

No phrenologist can read the remarks of Dr. Stokes without being deeply interested. He will perceive that some of the strongest evidence, and most positive facts in favour of his science, are derived from pathology, and that arguments may be drawn from this source, which must silence for ever the cavils and objections of opposers. Dr. Stokes, in his lecture on "diseases of the nervous system," introduces the subject of phrenology as follows:—"The fact of delirium occurring so frequently in inflammation of the membranes of the brain, is of considerable importance, as showing, not that membranes of the brain have any thing to do with intelligence, but as supporting the opinion of those who believe the periphery of the brain to be the seat of the intellectual faculties; and here is a fact which, as far as it goes, is in favour of the doctrines of phrenology. If we compare those cases of cerebral disease in which there is delirium, with those in which it does not occur, we shall find that it is most common in cases where disease attacks the periphery of the brain—as in arachnitis. The cases in which we observe great lesions of the brain without delirium, are generally cases of deep-seated inflammation of a local nature, or inflammation of those portions of the brain which the phrenologists consider not to be subservient to the production of mental phenomena. This fact, also, would seem to confirm the truth of the opinion of the difference in function between the medullary and cortical parts of the brain. It is supposed that the cortical part of the brain is the organ of intelligence, while the medullary portion performs a different function. It is, however, a curious fact, that in delirium the inflammation is confined to the surface of the brain, and that, in cases of deep-seated inflammation, the most important symptoms are those which are derived from the sympathetic affections of the muscular system."

The above remarks not only confirm the doctrines of phrenology, but tend to throw light on many curious and hitherto inexplicable facts, concerning diseases or injuries of the brain, and their effects on the muscular system. This subject opens a most interesting and important field of investigation to the physician, and especially to the surgeon. Probably there is no department of pathology more inviting to inquiry, or which would prove more fruitful in its results. The remarks of Dr. Stokes on this subject are excellent, and we would earnestly commend them to the attention of all our medical readers.

In his lecture on "encephalitis," Dr. Stokes devotes several pages to the pathology of the brain, with particular reference to phrenology. As this, in our opinion, is the clearest and most condensed view of the principles involved on this subject, which can be found in any published work, we are induced to copy Dr. Stokes's remarks at some length. Besides, this Journal is read by, at least, between two and three hundred physicians, who should be thoroughly acquainted with the functions of the brain, as disclosed by recent discoveries; and, perhaps, no better authority could be cited on this subject than that of Dr. Stokes.

But, while we are highly pleased with the arguments adduced by him in support of phrenology, we must say that his censures on phrenologists for neglecting or undervaluing, in their researches, the pathology of the brain, are too severe, and, as far as our knowledge extends, they are *unjust*. It is true, there may have been some cases where phrenologists, not the best informed on anatomy and physiology, have discarded pathology, and attempted to defend the principles of their science independently of, and, possibly, in opposition to, facts deduced from morbid conditions of the brain. But this is by no means the case with the leading advocates of the science. Andral, whom Dr. Stokes himself often quotes as high authority in all departments of pathological anatomy, was for some time president of the Paris Phrenological Society, and perhaps it is not stating more than the truth to say, that there is not a more distinguished pathologist on the continent of Europe. We are not concerned, however, that the reproofs of Dr. Stokes, on this point, will do any injury.

After some general observations on diseases of the brain, and their effects, Dr. Stokes remarks as follows :—

To return again to the interesting consideration of great loss of cerebral substance with preservation of intellect, I have to remark, that this circumstance is one which some persons might quote against the opinion that the brain was the organ of intelligence ; and I believe this fact has been laid hold of by the opponents of phrenology, and put forward as a powerful argument against the truth of its doctrines. Thus, for instance, in the case of Mr. O'Halloran's patient, who lost a large portion of one hemisphere, and yet, with all this mischief, the powers of the intellect remained unimpaired ; it would not seem strange if a person should say, here is vast destruction of substance without any lesion of intelligence ; how then can the brain be considered as the organ of thought ? But let us look at this matter in its true point of view. In the first place, it is to be remembered that cases like this are rare—that they are to be considered as the exception, and not as the rule. I have already shown you, that it is a law of pathology that lesion of structure and lesion of function are not always commensurate. This law applies to the brain, as well as to all the other organs. To say that the brain was not the organ of intelligence, because in cases of extensive cerebral disease that intelligence was preserved, is false reasoning. A man will digest with a cancerous stomach ; is it to be argued from this, that the stomach is not the organ of digestion ? I have seen the liver completely burrowed by abscesses, yet the gall-bladder was full of healthy bile. I have seen one lung completely obliterated, and yet the respirations only sixteen in the minute, and the face without lividity. What do these facts prove ? Not that the health of organs is of no consequence, but that with great disease there may be little injury of function.

By reference to the original laws of organisation, we may (in some cases at least) arrive at an explanation of this fact. You know that organs are primitively double ; and we find, that though the fusion at the median line is produced by developement, yet that the symmetrical halves still, to a certain degree, preserve their individuality. Thus we see how the laws of organisation affect the phenomena of disease, and recognise a provision, acting from the first moment of existence, against the accidents of far distant disease.

Now, admitting that the brain is the organ of thought, we may suppose that, as in case of partial obstruction of the lung from inflammation, the remainder of the organ takes on an increased action, so as to supply the place of that which has been injured or destroyed. We know that if one lung be hepatised, the other takes on its functions, and carries on the process of respiration for a time. That this is the case, is shown, first, by life being continued, and, secondly, by the stethoscope, which informs us that the respiration of the lung, which has a double duty thrown upon it, is remarkably intense, proving the force of its action ; and it has been further established, that the lung which thus takes on a supplemental action may become enlarged and hypertrophied.   May not this also occur in the brain ?   There is no reason why such a pathological phenomenon, occurring in one viscus, may not also take place in another.   But the opponents of phrenology say, supposing the organ of causation to be destroyed, how can the person continue to reason ?   It strikes me that the only way in which we can account for this is, by supposing that other parts of the brain take on the functions of those which have been injured or destroyed. Nor is there any thing extraordinary or anomalous in such a supposition.   We see, almost every day, examples of this kind.   We see that in certain diseased states of the liver, accompanied by suppression of its secretion, its functions are assumed by other parts, and bile continues to be separated from the blood by the kidneys, salivary glands, and by the cutaneous exhalants.   Here is a remarkable case, in which the glands and other parts take on the performance of a function totally different from that in which they are ordinarily employed.   We find, also, that when the urinary organs are obstructed, urine, or its principles, are discovered in parts of the system where we should not at all expect them.   It is a well-established law, that when the functions of organs are suspended or destroyed, other parts will often take on the action of the injured viscus.   Now, supposing that a portion of the brain is to be looked upon as the organ of causation, and such portion is injured or destroyed, there is no reason why the remaining sound portion of brain should not take on, at least to a certain extent, in addition to its own, the functions of that part which has been injured.   If, independently of any phrenological views, we admit the brain to be the organ of thought, there is no reason why we should not admit that the loss of intellectual power, produced by lesion of one part, may not be supplied by an increase of activity in the remaining portions.   It is only by a supposition of this kind that we can account for the preservation of the integrity of mind in many cases of disease of the brain.   If we admit the phrenological doctrines, we can suppose that when one organ is injured, another may take on an additional function, and in this way preserve the integrity of the intellect ; so that, whether we reason from phrenology or not, the continuance of soundness of mind, in cases of injury of the brain, can be understood when you come to contrast it with other analogous pathological facts.   I again repeat, that it is not more extraordinary that, in case of local injury of the brain, the sound parts should take on a supplemental action, than that bile should be eliminated by the

livary glands, skin, and kidneys, or that the principles of urine
ould be discharged from almost every part of the system, or that a
:arious discharge from the roots of the hair should supply the place
the uterine secretion.

On this subject, one point should be always borne in mind, viz.
it we may be wrong in saying that a patient is *quite sane*, while he
still an invalid and in bed.   Unless we can show that, after his
:overy, and in his various intercourse with the world, he preserves
i original intelligence, it would be wrong to assert that there has
en absolutely no lesion of intellect consequent on the affection of
e brain.   While lying at ease in bed, and unaffected by any moral
muli, he may seem to possess a sound condition of mind ; he may
t out his tongue, or stretch forth his hand, when requested ; he may
ve an accurate account of his symptoms, and answer all the ordinary
edical interrogatories with precision.   But you are not, from this, to
nclude that he is perfectly sane.   Many persons, under these cir-
mstances, have died in bed, and appeared to preserve their intellect
the last ; but in such cases, the test of sanity, *intercourse with
e world*, could not be fairly applied, and hence I think that there are
t sufficient grounds to pronounce a decided opinion as to the real
ndition of the intellect in such cases.

Before I quit this part of the subject, I wish to make a few remarks
. the doctrines of phrenology.   There can be no doubt that the
inciples of phrenology are founded on truth, and, of course, highly
serving of your attention, as likely, at some future period, when
operly cultivated, to exercise a great influence over medical practice.
ie great error of the phrenologists of the present day, consists in
rowing overboard the results of pathological anatomy.   If a patho-
;ical fact is brought forward, as appearing to bear against the validity
their opinions, they immediately exclaim, "We dont recognise any
t or principle drawn from disease ; our science has to do with the
althy, and not the morbid, condition of the brain."   Now, this is
ogether absurd.   Phrenology, if true, is nothing but the physiology
the brain, and pathology is nothing but the physiology of disease.
irenology must be tested by disease as well as by health, and if it
es not stand the test of pathology, it is wrong.   If phrenology be a
ence founded on truth, if it is a true physiology of the brain, or of
it portion of it connected with mental phenomena, one of two results
ould obtain—either that it should be confirmed by pathology, or that
e difficulties, which pathology presents, should be explicable in a
inner consistent with the science.   The phrenologists, in my mind,
e doing a direct injury to the cause of their science, by their unne-
essary and ill-timed hostility to pathology.   It is idle to say, as they

do, that theirs is the science of health, and that it is unfair to apply to it the test of disease. From pathology is drawn a host of facts, from which the doctrines they profess derive their principal support. The mere phrenologist, who understands not, and despises, pathology, is nothing better than a charlatan, and professes a science which he does not comprehend. If he would recollect that the brain in a state of health is most, and in a state of disease least, adapted to the purposes of thought, he would see that this is one of the strongest arguments in favour of his doctrine, that the brain is the organ of mind. The more healthy it is, the fitter it is to discharge the functions of intellect, and vice versa; yet phrenologists are so absurd as to think that pathology has nothing to do with their science.

But besides confirming the doctrine that the brain is the organ of thought, there are innumerable facts drawn from pathology, which have a tendency to prove that particular parts of the brain are the organs of peculiar phenomena. We see an injury of one part of the brain, accompanied by a train of symptoms indicating some peculiar lesion of mind; we see an affection of another part, attended by a different class of phenomena. Here pathology, the science which phrenologists reject and despise, goes to establish the ground-work of their doctrines, that the brain consists of a congeries of parts, having each a separate and distinct function. We find, for instance, that disease of one portion of the brain affects the intellect; of another, the generative organs; of a third, the muscular system. What does this prove, but that the brain is not a simple organ, but composed of a congeries of parts, each of which governs a different part of the system, or ministers to a peculiar purpose? Now, what is this but what the phrenologists themselves wish to prove?

Further, the professors of phrenology have placed all their organs on the surface of the brain, and for this they have been loudly censured. Phrenology, it is urged, knows, or professes to know, nothing about the central parts of the brain, which must be equally important with the superficial, and have confined their investigations to the surface alone. Now it is a curious fact, that the pathology which they deny, in this instance, furnishes the best reply to this objection. I mentioned at my last lecture, that if we examine the symptom of delirium, we find that it characterises the inflammation of the periphery, and is commonly wanting in that of the deep-seated portions. In other words, mental alienation is the characteristic of the disease of that portion of the brain where the phrenologists have placed the intellectual organs. Here is a strong fact in favour of the doctrines of phrenology, derived from that science which the mere phrenologist throws overboard and despises. Again, according to the researches of some celebrated French pathologists, there are a number of facts to show that there is a remarkable difference between the symptoms of arachnitis of the convexity and of the base of the brain. This conclusion, which, after a most careful series of investigations, was adopted by them, is borne out by the results of my experience, and appears to me to be established on the basis of truth. They have discovered that arachnitis of the convexity of the brain is a disease characterised by prominent and violent symptoms, early and marked delirium, intense pain, watchfulness, and irritability. We have first delirium, pain, and sleeplessness, and then coma. But in arachnitis of the base of the brain, the symptoms are of a more latent and insidious character; there is some pain, and the coma is profound, but there is often no delirium. What an important fact for the supporters of phrenology is this, and how strikingly does it prove their absurdity in rejecting the lights derived from pathology! Here we find the remarkable fact, that inflammation of the arachnoid, investing the base of the brain to which the phrenologists attach, comparatively, no importance, is commonly unattended with any lesion of the intellectual powers, while the same inflammation on the convexity is almost constantly accompanied by symptoms of distinct mental alienation.

It is objected to the phrenologists that they know little or nothing of the central parts of the brain; that though these parts may be fairly considered to be of as much importance as any others, still they 'do not admit them to be organs of intellect. Now, what does pathology teach on this subject? It shows that we may have most extensive local disease of the central parts of the brain—that we may have inflammation, suppuration, abscess, and apoplexy, without the slightest trace of delirium. Indeed, there can be no doubt that the central portions of the brain have functions very different from those on the surface. They appear more connected with another function of animal life, muscular motion, and sensation. Then let us examine the phenomena of old age. Every one is familiar with the fact, that when a man arrives at an extreme age, he generally experiences a marked decay of intellectual power, and falls into a state of second childhood. Does pathology throw any light upon this circumstance? It does. From a series of ingenious and accurate investigations, conducted by two continental pathologists, Cauzevielh and Desmoulins, it has been found that a kind of atrophy of the brain takes place in very old persons. According to the researches of Desmoulins, it appears that, in persons who have passed the age of seventy, the specific gravity of the brain becomes from a twentieth to a fifteenth less than that of the adult. It has also been proved that this atrophy of the brain is connected with old age, and not, as it might be thought, with general emaciation of the body; for in cases of chronic emaciation from disease in adults, the brain is the last part which is found to atrophy; and it has been suggested that this may explain the continuance of mental powers, during the ravages of chronic disease; and also the nervous irritability of patients after acute disease, in which emaciation has taken place.

I might bring forward many other facts to show that phrenology is indebted to pathology for some of the strongest arguments in its favour; and I think that those phrenologists who neglect its study, or deny its applicability, are doing a serious injury to the doctrines they seek to establish. The misfortune is, that very few medical men have turned their attention to the subject; and that, with few exceptions, its supporters and teachers have been persons possessing scarcely any physiological, and no pathological, knowledge. Phrenology will never be established as a science until it gets into hands of scientific medical men, who, to a profound knowledge of physiology, have added all the light derived from pathological research. To give you an instance of the mode of reasoning of the non-medical phrenologists: In their drawing-room exhibitions, they appeal with triumph to the different forms of the skull in the carnivorous and graminivorous animals, with respect to the developement of Destructiveness; and all are horrified at the bump on the tiger's skull. But, as Sir H. Davy well observes, this very protuberance is a part of the general apparatus of the jaw, which requires a more powerful insertion for its muscles in all beasts of prey. Phrenology, as generally taught, may answer well for the class of dilettantis and blue-stockings, or for the purposes of humbug and flattery; but its parent was anatomy, its nurse physiology, and its perfection must be sought for in medicine. The mass of inconsequential reasoning, of special pleading, and of "*false facts*," with which its professors have encumbered it, must be swept away, and we shall then, I have no doubt, recognise it as the greatest discovery, in the science of the moral and physical nature of man, that has ever been made. I feel happy, however, in thinking that, of late, the science has been taken up on its true grounds, in Paris, London, and Dublin. Vimont's splendid work on Comparative Phrenology will form an era in the science. In London, Dr. Elliotson has directed the energies of his powerful mind to the subject; and in Dublin we have a Phrenological Society, of which Dr. Marsh is the president, and my colleague, Dr. Evanson, the secretary; and, under such auspices, much is to be expected.

ARTICLE II.

DISSECTION OF THE BRAIN.

An Examination of the Human Brain, by George Combe, Esq., in the Albany Medical College, on Saturday, 11 A. M., February 1st, 1840. Present, Drs. Hamilton, Boardman, Hoyt, Armsby, March, James M'Naughton, Professor Dean, Mr. Wm. Combe, Charles Olmstead, Esq., and David Cogswell, Esq. The two latter gentlemen, together with Dr. Hoyt, are residents of Syracuse.

Mr. Combe, while delivering a course of lectures on phrenology at Albany, N. Y., dissected a brain in accordance with the principles of the science, before the above named gentlemen. Several notices of this dissection have appeared in the Albany, Syracuse, and Utica papers, in some of which there were misstatements and remarks of a *personal* nature much to be regretted. We have collected the facts in the case, and present the following statement as a candid and correct account of the dissection.

The brain had been prepared by Dr. Hoyt, by having been kept in alcohol for some four or five months; and for the purpose of seeing for himself its true anatomical structure, as first shown by Drs. Gall and Spurzheim in their new mode of dissecting the brain, this gentleman had left home, and travelled one hundred and fifty miles to see Mr. Combe unfold the nervous tissues of the mental organs. Much praise is due to Dr. Hoyt for the pains he had taken in preparing a brain, and going the above distance to witness an examination of its structure, with particular reference to its functions. It should be remembered, that before the time of Drs. Gall and Spurzheim, the usual course of examining the brain was to cut it up into slices, like a ham or a cabbage-head, beginning the work of destruction upon the upper surface, and thus proceeding to the base; and this is the way pursued by the anti-phrenologists. To be consistent, they should dissect all parts of the body alike; that is to say, follow the tissues, and not cut them across, but unfold them as we would the parts of an orange—the same rule should be followed with the brain; and such was Drs. Gall and Spurzheim's method, and it is that of every phrenologist of the present day. We would here remark, that whenever a brain is placed in alcohol for dissection, it is highly important that the membranes be removed, in order that the spirit may have free access to all parts of the viscus, by means of which its fibrous structure will be rendered much more distinct in the dissection.

In the examination by Mr. Combe, the first thing exhibited was the decussating fibres at the roots of the pyramidal bodies, beautifully interlacing each other. He remarked, that with this knowledge of said fibres, we could now account for the effects of accidents upon the brain, occasioning paralysis of the opposite side of the body.

The next thing shown by Mr. Combe, was the fibres connecting the two lateral portions of the cerebellum, or little brain. These being removed, he then proceeded to demonstrate the fibres, proceeding forward to the anterior portions of the brain, and composing the intellectual organs. These fibres were shown passing through the *pons varolii* to the entire satisfaction of all present. Every medical man, either by word or nod of head, confessed that he saw with his own eyes these said fibres. They are highly important, inasmuch as they show the connection between the intellectual organs and the nerves of voluntary motion, and enable us to understand how, and in what manner, these instruments of motion are subservient to the will.

Mr. Combe showed Mr. Solly's commissure lying above the *corpus callosum*, connecting the posterior with the anterior portions of the brain. The justly distinguished Dr. M'Clellan, of Philadelphia, said, that before Mr. Combe's arrival in that city, "he used to deride phrenology, mentioning in particular to his class, that no communication was found to exist between the anterior and posterior portions of the brain. He found, however, that he had been laughing in ignorance of the existence of the superior longitudinal commissure." But he had the rare magnanimity to confess his ignorance to his class.

Mr. Combe then showed the *corpus dentatum*, and mentioned that the notable Dr. Gordon denied the existence of such a cerebral portion as that of the *corpus dentatum*.

Mr. Combe then proceeded to unfold the converging fibres. Here he said our opponents accuse us of making these fibres by scraping with the handle of the scalpel. He then scraped off a layer of these fibres from their bed, remarking at the time, that if these fibres be thus formed by mere scraping, it should be possible to produce the appearance of them in any direction; but he showed that when we try to do so, the result is quite different. He continued unfolding these fibres until he came even to the surface of the convolutions of the brain. Mr. Combe here explained how it happens, in cases of extreme distention of the brain from a collection of water within its folds, that a person will manifest no impairment of mental power. The water simply unfolds the convolutions. Most of the gentlemen present seemed very much delighted in having seen Gall and Spurzheim's method of dissecting the human brain. Some portions of it exhibited the fibrous structure more clearly than any plates or wax models could possibly do.

We present for serious consideration, the remarks of James Johnson, M. D., Physician Extraordinary to the late King of England, and editor of the Medico Chirurgical Review. "I have been long convinced," says he, "that the science of *mind* can only be understood and taught, properly, by those who have deeply studied the structure and functions of its material instrument, the brain. I am convinced, that in this world *mind* can be manifested *only* through the medium of *matter*, and that the metaphysician who studies mind independent of its corporeal organ, works in the dark, and with only half of his requisite tools."

ARTICLE III.

CASE OF MONOMANIA.

We copy from the London Medico-Chirurgical Review for April, 1831, the following fact:—"In a late clinical lecture at St. Thomas's Hospital, Dr. Elliotson alluded to a curious case of monomania, which we shall here notice. The patient was a female, thirty-one years of age, who had been admitted for a nervous affection, but who was soon found to be monomaniacal. The propensity was to injure some part or other of the body, by internal muscular efforts, and not by attempts at cutting or maiming. The part of the body that fell under the monomaniacal displeasure was never long the same, but varied from hour to hour—commencing in one part whenever it had ceased in another, so that she had no respite from this harassing propensity. Her judgment on all points was gone—she had no hallucination—and was conscious of the unnatural impulse which perpetually led to injure her own body. There was no reason to suspect a feigned disease. She had headach, drowsiness, sense of pressure on the head, as well as that of 'opening and shutting,' to use her own expression, behind the ears, and round the back part of the head. Dr. Elliotson considered this case as one illustrating the doctrines of phrenology—namely, that it was a case where the organ of Destructiveness was in an excited state, and consequently where the 'instinct carnassier,' as Gall would term it, was strongly called forth. Here, indeed, it was not a homicidal, but a suicidal, propensity that existed; yet the nature of both is the same. The peculiarity in the present case, which attracted attention, was the pain and throbbing just over each ear, and extending posteriorly round the head. Every gentleman who attended to the case, was witness of this phenomenon.

'This (says Dr. Elliotson) is a very striking phrenological fact,' and he goes on to state his belief in the general doctrines of phrenology. 'I have examined (says he) the subject of phrenology most carefully and unremittingly, and have seldom allowed a day to pass without making some observations upon it; and, after thus examining it for twelve years, I am more and more satisfied of the general truth of what Dr Gall has announced.' "

RTICLE IV.

REMARKS ON PHYSICAL EDUCATION.

BY J. L. PEIRCE, M. D., PHILADELPHIA.

(Continued from page 298 of this Journal.)

Perhaps I should not let pass unnoticed the reasons which are offered in vindication of early education.

Two excuses, very plausible in their character, and therefore the more to be guarded against, are generally rendered for infringements of the laws, which control our corporeal frames : the one is ignorance of those laws on the part of the guardians of youth ; and the second is the gratification experienced by teachers, in watching and promoting the developement of the intellectual faculties, and by parents in seeing their children manifest powers and acquirements superior to those belonging to their age. In reply to these excuses, we would remark, that under the civil government, ignorance of a law is never admitted as a palliation for an offence. If a man commits a wilful, deliberate murder, he suffers the punishment for his crime, notwithstanding his ignorance of the existence of a law upon the subject—and, in violating the organic laws in regard to the education of his children, the penalty is as sure to follow in the injury of their health as the ultimate sacrifice of their lives, by which means, however, THEY become the immediate sufferers instead of the parents, and the latter may not feel that moral guilt which is experienced by the criminal referred to.

Again : although the gratification may be great, on the part of parents and guardians, in witnessing the rapid advancement of their children in intellectual attainments, whereby some of them acquire a precocity of intellect, and become as prodigies in creation; yet, inasmuch as these acquirements are obtained at least at the risk, if not in every case the actual *loss* of the *health* of the children, it is unjustifiable, nay, it is actually criminal, on the part of parents and guardians of youth, to subject them to such a trying ordeal.

But, say teachers, we never witness the deleterious effects to which you allude. The children under our charge appear healthy and happy, and we endeavour to promote such a state by every means in our power. To such, we would repeat an observation we have already made, that in the laws which govern organic life, the *effect does not always immediately succeed the cause which produces it.* The progress of disease is slow in the outset, and the symptoms of cerebral irritation are at first scarcely discernable even to the most experienced eye ; it cannot, therefore, be expected that they will be noticed by one whose attention has never been particularly directed to the subject. Again, children, at the early period to which we allude, seldom remain for many years at the same school, and after they change, the former teacher loses sight of them, and is unacquainted with their future fate. But with parents the case is different. They can observe the progress of disease from the first evidences of cerebral irritation, through the subsequent stages of inflammation and dropsy, or other unhappy and, mostly, fatal termination ; but ignorance and prejudice prevent their tracing the effect to its proper cause.

That some great and powerful causes do prevail in destroying the health and lives of children, is fully apparent from our weekly bills of mortality, by which it appears that one half the deaths in our cities are of persons under seven years of age. How many of these are to be attributed to the causes to which we have referred, it is impossible for us to ascertain ; but that a large proportion of them owe the origin of their diseases to improper physical treatment, commencing with the earliest periods of existence, is so often illustrated by cases daily met with in our practice that we feel convinced of its truth. Another fact worthy of notice is, that in thickly populated districts the proportion of deaths among children is much greater than it is in the country. For this we shall indirectly account before we close our observations. With these startling facts before us, we may truly exclaim, that " none are so blind as those who will not see."

The object of education is to promote the happiness of the individual, and to render him a more useful member of society. But if our efforts are so misdirected that we either shorten his life, or ruin his health, so that he becomes a burden to himself and to society, we frustrate our own designs, as well as militate against the institutions of our Creator.

Perhaps some may now be ready to inquire, how the evils of which we have spoken are to be guarded against? We answer : Bear in mind that the physical powers require to be educated as well as the intellectual, and, as the vigour of the intellectual faculties depends upon the strength, and perfection and healthy condition of the body, and particularly of that part of it which is the seat of the nervou influence of the whole animal system, as well as the organ of all the mental operations, it follows, as a necessary consequence, that *physica* education ought to *precede* that of *intellect*, according to the position assumed at the commencement of our remarks. Man being a com pound being, we fulfil but half our duties, if we direct our attention to one portion of his nature, to the neglect of the other. Culpable indeed, should we consider that parent, who, surrounded by all the comforts of life, would suffer his children to grow up to years of maturity without bestowing one moment's attention upon the cultiva tion of their minds, let his care over their physical wants be ever so great—but familiarity has reconciled us to the equally culpable treat ment represented on the reverse of the picture.

Our remarks on this whole subject apply more especially to those residing in cities, villages, and thickly populated districts, than to people living in the country. The arguments urged in favour of sending children early to school do not, as a general rule, apply to the latter class of persons. *Their* pursuits are usually such as are conducted at their own homes. Their houses are located at a distance from each other, so that children can be kept separate from their neighbours, and free from the contaminating influence of their evil examples. Large yards are for the most part attached to the resi dences, where, with the additional advantage of fresh air, youthful sports can engage their attention, calculated to develope and strengthen the physical powers of the system, while they are in every respect free from the dangers incident to a city life. Habits of industry can, at the same time, be gradually instilled into their youthful minds, while their intellectual faculties will imperceptibly expand in propor tion to the physical growth and strength of that organ through which they are manifested. Hence we assert it as a general rule, that in the country it is unnecessary to use any measures calculated to excite the intellectual faculties of children, prior to their arriving at a period of life when the risk of injurious results will be avoided.

It may be said that we should thus permit children to grow up in ignorance, until they arrive at an age when their intellectual faculties become so blunted, as to render them afterwards incapable of being brought into active exercise. The *premises* we *deny*, and conse quently the *conclusion drawn from them* we consider to be *equally incorrect*. Ignorant of what? we would ask. Of a knowledge of *letters* and *words*, which, in nine cases out of ten, convey to their minds no definite ideas! They spend two, three, or four years to acquire by hard toil, and very frequently with a feeling of disgust, what in more advanced years may be acquired in six months, without

ie risk of that distaste for schools and science which effectually pre-
ents many of them for ever from making any considerable progress
i their studies.   We say that in nine cases out of ten this knowledge
onveys to their minds no definite ideas.   We make this assertion
om our personal knowledge of its truth.   Question them concerning
hat they have been reading, and you will most generally find that
ley know nothing about it—and where their intellectual faculties *are*
ufficiently matured to comprehend it, such children are the very
nes whose health will be injured by the course they are pursuing;
> that, in, the one case, you create an insufferable disgust for that
hich ought to afford them the greatest pleasure.   And, in the other,
ou destroy the health, happiness, and life of that charge, whose precious intellect should teach you a memorable lesson respecting the
ws of human organisation.

We have stated that the conclusion drawn from the premises we
onsidered to be equally incorrect.   We have shown that in propor-
on as the physical structure of the intellectual organ acquires perfec-
on and strength, in the same degree will be the vigour and efficiency
f those intellectual powers dependent upon it.   This we know is
enerally denied by those unacquainted with the physiological func-
ons of the human brain.   They argue that children who have
iceived the advantages of intellectual cultivation, manifest much
igher powers of mind than others whose education has been
eglected.   This we readily grant.   But let us take two children,
ie of whom has been to school from the earliest period of infancy,
id continued unintermittingly at his studies until he has arrived at
ie sixteenth year of his age—and the other, whose *physical* educa-
on constituted the chief concern of his parents until he arrived at his
iventh year, at which time his *intellectual* education commenced and
ogressed with the physical, under the direction of a competent and
idicious instructor, and when he shall have arrived at the age of the
rmer, his intellectual acquirements will be in every respect superior,
hile he will, at the same time, be in possession of a sound and
gorous constitution of which his companion may be justly jealous.
he nervous energy of the one will be exhausted, his strength
ipaired, and his enjoyment of life destroyed with the numerous
lments with which he will be afflicted, in consequence of his viola-
on of the organic laws of his nature; while the other will be in
ossession of every enjoyment derivable from a sound constitution
id well-cultivated intellect.   We make not these assertions igno-
ntly, but under a full knowledge and conviction of their truth.   We
ive witnessed them with our own eyes, we have experienced them
i our own person, and they have repeatedly been confirmed to us by

parents and teachers, who have likewise had experimental illustrations of their truth.

We have now come to a point which is undoubtedly the most diffi cult of any we have yet undertaken. We have shown some of the errors of the present existing modes of instruction, and have por trayed the evils arising from them; and as we must continue to dis approve of our schools, as at present organised, it is incumbent upor us to sketch some plan for an edifice to be reared upon the ruins of the superstructure which we have thus endeavoured to overthrow, and to give our views in regard to the mode in which the early periods of existence should be occupied. Were the whole community engaged in agricultural pursuits, situated as we have described in a former par of this address, we should refer to that for the requisite information, and consider our task completed. But as we are so frequently asked the question, how we would dispose of the children of that hard working industrious portion of the community, residing in our cities, who have to earn a subsistence for themselves and their families away from their own homes, where they can extend no care over their off spring from morning till night, and who would consequently be engaged in scenes of danger, vice, and crime, but for these institu tions—for the sake of such, we will extend our remarks farther. As regards the necessity of places of resort for such children, where they can be protected from the danger to which we have referred, there can be but one opinion. But the great object is, to have them so organised as to possess as few objections as possible. This is a task requiring deep reflection and experience; and as our views upon the subject have hitherto been confined to the evils of such institutions as now exist, and not to a substitute for them, it is scarcely to be expected that we should give more than the outlines of a superstruc ture upon which others may improve. But we trust that its founda tion may be laid upon a solid basis, against which the storms of adverse opinions and prejudices may produce no effect.

In the first place, suitable buildings should be provided in healthy, airy situations, similar to those recently erected by the controllers of our public schools, for the institutions under their care. Such of the rooms as may be appropriated for the purpose, should be provided with benches adapted to the various sizes of the children, with the seats of a height corresponding to their lower limbs, and with backs of an easy construction. By this means, many diseases of the limbs, chest, and spinal column, will be avoided, which owe their origin to the ill-constructed benches of our schools.

As we design the infant department more particularly as a place of safety, where the physical powers may be duly exercised and developed, rather than for the cultivation of the intellectual faculties, all exercises, designed to operate particularly upon the latter, should be made entirely subservient to the former. Such physical perform- ances, therefore, as are calculated to develope and strengthen the human frame, and suited to the age, strength, and agility of the chil- dren, should receive the first consideration. For this purpose, we would have one or more rooms furnished with such gymnastic apparatus as may be considered requisite, and, under the superintend- ence of suitable teachers or caretakers, these recreations · should frequently alternate with such others as may be directed. A portion of the apparatus should consist of mere instruments of play or amuse- ment, while others should be of a higher order, calculated to bring into active exercise the various muscles of the body. Other apart- ments should be furnished with every production of nature and art which would be at all suitable for the occasion. The various branches of trade, and the different kingdoms of the earth, should each be made to yield its quota, so that every school-house should be a museum of the most useful and interesting objects which could be collected together from the four quarters of the globe. These we would have constantly presented to the view of the children in the most familiar manner.

In the junior department, the children should be made acquainted with their names, and their most common qualities and uses—not by any particular intellectual effort, but by the exercise of their external senses upon them. The teacher selected for such a station, should have a mind well stored with interesting little anecdotes, connected with the names, the qualities, the properties, and the uses of the articles under consideration, and which should be narrated in the most familiar and interesting style, at all times avoiding terms or expressions unsuited to the capacities of children. As they advance in years and knowledge, they should also advance to the higher departments of the school, where they should be made acquainted with new properties of the same objects, and where new objects should also be presented to their consideration—not in the form of tasks or lessons, but altogether as amusements. From simple articles they should proceed to those more complex in their character, and adapted to their increasing power of perception and observation. They should then be made acquainted with their composition, not by committing names to memory and answering questions by rote, but by the exercise of their external senses. For instance, let them witness the operation of the manufacture of cotton fabrics from the change of the raw material, in its growing or pod state, through its various pro- cesses, until it is converted into the wearing apparel. And this should be exhibited to them, not in our large manufacturing establishments, where no distinct ideas could be obtained respecting it, but on a small scale in their own school-room. Neither would we have them witness the whole operation in one, two, or even three weeks; but let their minds become familiar with each successive stage, prior to their making a further advancement. So likewise in regard to the animal, vegetable, and mineral kingdoms. Make them acquainted, first, with the substance themselves, then with their different parts, and, ultimately, with their respective properties and uses, as far as they will admit of familiar illustration. Call their attention to the peculiarities of each, and to their general external characters. But, as regards the particular zone of the earth where they are produced, or the particular climate or country whence they are obtained, or the class, order, genera, &c., to which they belong, we must express our entire disapproval of any such unintelligible performances. That they are unproductive of the least shadow of good, is our most sincere belief; but, on the contrary, that they have an injurious tendency upon the physical and intellectual developement of those subjected to them, we have not the shadow of doubt. An exercise recently introduced into some of our schools under the name of "Calisthenics," we consider to be very beneficial in its character upon the physical structure of the human frame, and calls into action the various muscles more effectually than any other method with which we are acquainted. It serves as a pleasing recreation from other exercise, and, at the same time, gives grace, ease, and dignity, to the body, while it serves to impart the first principles of systematic instruction in the most pleasing manner in which it can be communicated.

We may here remark, that while the children are thus engaged in these innocent and useful amusements and recreations, ample opportunities will be afforded for instilling into their youthful minds practical lessons of morality, which will make a deeper impression, and be of far more utility to them, than the perusal of all the discourses which have been delivered upon the subject, from the creation of the world to the present time. No advice is so effectual as that which is delivered on a suitable occasion—on the impulse of the moment. Its force is then felt, and its truths duly acknowledged. And what season is so appropriate for inculcating the principles of love and affection, as when children are mingled together in the sportive recreations of youthful innocence? What opportunity so suitable for instilling into their minds the principles of justice, and virtue, and benevolence, as when their feelings of regard for each other, and each other's rights, are excited into active exercise? And what moment so

it for presenting to their view the baneful effects of improper conduct, whether it consist of unkindness to each other, or of deceit, or
of falsehood, or of theft, as when some one of their companions has
been guilty of one of these offences? Their feelings will become
tender on the occasion, and while they learn to detest the committal
of a wrong, they may be taught to pity the individual who thus suffers
on account of it.

As children advance in years and acquirements to that period when
their reasoning powers may safely be brought into active operation,
they may be led on to higher subjects, which may require a greater
exercise of their intellectual faculties. And when the period arrives
for them to turn their attention from substances to shadows, from
things to their signs, from real objects to the characters by which
they are represented, we should recommend a course very different
from that usually adopted in our schools. Instead of commencing
with the alphabet, which conveys no definite ideas to the mind of the
child, we would commence with words—words, with the signification
of which the child was already familiarly acquainted—and having the
representation of the thing signified attached to the word in the form
of a picture, he would soon acquire a knowledge of its other representation, viz. the word itself; and a few minutes' examination of the
individual characters of which it was composed, would so firmly
impress them upon his mind that they never would be forgotten. In
this way we would have him proceed, from simple words to those
more complex in their character, taking care to let the child possess a
thorough understanding of the meaning of each one that is presented
to his consideration. Let this be exemplified by his making repeated
applications of it in conversation. The first sentences that he attempts
to read, should be such as he can easily understand, and all his books
should be suited to his intellectual capacity, and calculated to interest
his feelings. We should then have no difficulty in teaching a child
to read understandingly, and he would feel the greatest delight and
pleasure in the pursuit.

But while he is thus advancing in intellectual acquirements, his
physical education should not be neglected. On the contrary, their
progress should be simultaneous, with a leaning of partiality towards
the developement of the corporeal frame.

We have thus given the imperfect outlines of a plan for the amusement and instruction of youth during the early periods of their existence. Of its superiority over those usually pursued in our schools,
we feel perfectly satisfied. By it, the great object aimed at in sending
children *early* to school is fully accomplished, without the evils
usually attendant upon it. Their physical powers, which we have

endeavoured to show should receive our first attention, are in this way duly exercised by every variety of innocent and appropriate performance which the ingenuity of their instructors can devise; and, consequently, their physical growth, and strength, and healthy action, are duly promoted, while their minds become disciplined and stored with a fund of the most useful kinds of *knowledge*, which they imperceptibly acquire in the form of amusement, without an undue exertion of their intellectual faculties—*knowledge*, of which most children, and too many adults, are entirely ignorant, but which, in every situation and condition of life in which they may be placed, will be of the utmost importance—*knowledge*, obtained as a substitute for an acquaintance with words and theories, which can be of no practical utility in the early periods of existence, but which are acquired at the risk of the health, the life, and the intellect of the children. We might have pursued the subject much farther, but we have already greatly exceeded the limits we designed occupying, when we commenced our remarks. If we have been successful in throwing out any suggestions that may be considered of use to the present or succeeding generations in lessening the amount of suffering, or saving a single individual from an early or an untimely grave, or if we have been successful in exposing the defects of existing institutions, or in hinting at any plan which may render knowledge more attractive, or its acquisition more easily attained, we have done all that we expect. It is to parents and instructors that we would particularly address our remarks. If their reason can be operated upon, and their feelings of affection for their young and tender charge, whose health and whose lives are undoubtedly dear to them, can be reached by these appeals to facts, and to the principles of their own organisation, we shall feel happy in the performance of our duty. If we have been unsuccessful in our endeavours, we shall have the satisfaction of knowing that our motives were pure, and that our best efforts were directed to the health, happiness, and welfare of our fellow-beings.

ARTICLE V.

History and Progress of Phrenology. By R. W. Haskins, A. M.

The above is the title of a small volume of 216 pages, recently published at Buffalo, in western New York. The object, as stated by the author, is "not to demonstrate what phrenology is, but rather to unfold, concisely, the history of its discovery and its progress."

This object appears to be very fully and faithfully carried out. The author seems no where to have forgotten, or overlooked, the broad distinction between the simple narration of historical facts connected with the origin and progress of a science, or great moral movement among men, and an exposition of the principles in which it essentially consists. He commences at a very early period in the history of mental philosophy, alluding to the idealism of Plato, the common-sense of Reid, the facial angle of Camper, the physiognomical deductions of Lavater, the phrenological discoveries of Gall, with the view of showing the gradual advance of mind in the attainment of a know-ledge of itself, and especially in the constantly improving means of that attainment, by gradually enlisting observation, as well as con-sciousness, in the discovery and elucidation of its powers and faculties.

He then proceeds to give rather a minute and detailed account of the means and method of discovery of the several organs and faculties enumerated by Dr. Gall, and of the additional discoveries and classifi-cation of Dr. Spurzheim. Of the incessant and invaluable labours of Dr. Spurzheim and Mr. George Combe, on both the eastern and western continents, and the numerous popular works they have pub-lished on the science, and its applications, we have here a brief but generally accurate account. Other phrenological writers, both Euro-pean and American, receive also their due share of attention. Among these, the long and efficient labours of Dr. Charles Caldwell, the first American phrenologist, justly claim and receive their proper share of attention. The proposed improvements of Mr. Grimes, in a work of his recently published, are briefly and succinctly stated. We are also treated with some highly entertaining and splendid specimens of the mode of warfare with which the science, at its earlier periods, was attempted to be demolished, and, in some instances, with the answers made to them. Mr. Haskins has certainly evinced a very extensive knowledge of the efforts made by phrenologists, and of the numerous publications, both elementary and periodical, relating to that science, that have at different times issued from the press, on this and the eastern continent. His style is extremely well fitted for historical communication, and conveys, with great clearness and perspicuity, a knowledge of the facts he designs to record. In some instances, he resorts to what might be deemed by many an unnecessary minuteness of detail, as in the case of introducing a paragraph from the "American Phrenological Journal and Miscellany," followed by remarks, some-what protracted, both of his own and Dr. Caldwell's. His quotations may also be thought by some both too long and of too frequent occur-rence, although, rightly considered, they form a part of his history. The reader of this little volume will, however, find himself possessed with very accurate ideas of the origin of the science; the obstacles it has had to contend with in its progress; the exertions of its advo- cates; the method and style of attacks that have been made upon it; the works that have been written in the unfolding of its principles; and the sources of information to which recourse may be had by those desirous of extending their knowledge of it.   As this is the first attempt we are aware of that has been made to present an entire his- tory of the science, we doubt not it will receive (as it really merits) a large share of attention from the American public.

ARTICLE VI.

PREDOMINANCE OF CERTAIN ORGANS IN THE BRITISH POETS.—NO. 4.

COLERIDGE.

Phrenology would say of Coleridge, in giving a condensed view of his character, that he was a man of extraordinary intellectual and moral powers, with not enough of the propensities to give him suffi- cient energy and vigour; that he possessed intense feelings, a tem- perament, which, though not the most active, was one of peculiar delicacy; that he was influenced by the purest motives in all his actions, and capable of labouring with much more of ardour and enthusiasm for the good of others, than for his own individual aggrandisement.   A reference to his actual life will confirm the truth of our science, and give him an elevated niche in that rare temple which history consecrates to the wise and good.

His Causality and Comparison were remarkably developed; to which may be attributed his exceeding fondness for metaphysics. He describes himself as delighting, even in boyhood, in the most abstruse speculations, seizing upon any one with whom he might

> ' Reason high
> Of Providence, fore-knowledge, will and fate;
> Fix'd fate, free-will, fore-knowledge absolute.''

Having convinced, or puzzled all about him, he would sally forth into the high road, and, by a species of metaphysical instinct, select from the wayfarers any one who wore a black coat, had dark brows, and a sallow face, and at once engage him in religious disputation; and woe to any travelling brother, whether Baptist, Methodist, or Presbyterian, who, when driven hard by the youthful champion, hoped to silence him by retailing the arguments of popular controversialists. The young polemic had read and sifted them all, and often overwhelmed his opponents with all kinds of ingenious queries, strange doubts, and startling deductions.

In his early manhood he visited Germany, and imbibed the philosophy of Kant; which, blended with other theories, and somewhat idealised, lost in him much of its severity, and became, when his hopes of the advancement of mankind were added to that mountain pile of withered prospects left by the disastrous events of the French Revolution, a solace and a charm. Nothing in his character is more beautiful than the philanthropy he still continued, even amid his own sad sufferings, to cherish to the last; and there can be little doubt, if phrenology had sooner displayed its beauties to the world, or he had not become entangled in the labyrinths of metaphysics, he would have discovered in its principles what he had sought so long in vain in every other system, and lent it the advocacy of his sincere and powerful mind. The moral and intellectual organs, as we have intimated, greatly predominated over other portions of his head, and with this fact before us, we shall have little difficulty in understanding why he was not a very popular author. Had he bowed to the prejudices of the day, or possessed the Combativeness and Destructiveness of Byron and Scott, his success might have been equal to theirs. More original in his conceptions than either, his mind was far more highly cultured and severely disciplined. Drinking from the wells of all knowledge, ancient and modern, and realising every dream of metaphysics, from Plato down to Kant, elegant learning, science, and art, conspired to polish, strengthen, and refine the genius which even they could not altogether eclipse. It is easy to suppose that a mind thus rich in wisdom, and endowed with moral perception no less acute and comprehensive than that of his intellect, would not readily assent to the conflicting theology of the schools, but would anxiously seek repose for his hopes in a religion pure and perfect, in its every principle, as the immortality to which it points.

He had won the right to think for himself upon all subjects, and exercised it without fear or favour. Thus he was as heterodox in religion as in politics and literature, and the very superiority and elevation of his mind, contracted, by the disparity it interposed between him and the bulk of mankind, its own legitimate influence. Neither church nor state, nor the public at large, would extend its patronage to one who could not, without some invidious reservation, subscribe to the entire creed, party, or prejudice of either; and the most gifted man of his day consumed his summer prime and vigour in the severest struggles of poverty, to lament at last in strains like the following:—

"Keen pangs of love, awak'ning like a babe,
Turbulent, with an outcry in the heart.
*　　*　　*　　*　　*　　*

Sense of past youth and manhood come in vain,
And genius given, and knowledge won in vain,
And all that I have culled in wood walks wild,
And all which patient thought hath reared, and all
' Commune with thee hath opened out but flowers,
Strewed on my corse, and borne upon my bier,
In the same coffin for the self same grave !"

We are aware of the indolence of which he is accused, but could never discover any thing else in the charge than the poor palliation of neglect. Its cold injustice is easily detected, when we remember that half his life was passed amid disease and hopeless struggles with his condition, and then recall his great acquisitions, his published writings, the many works projected with spirit and abandoned from the mere want of encouragement, the numerous fragments, and the brilliant thoughts scattered " like flower seeds by the far winds sown," which were found to be so full of truth and beauty, when reproduced to the public by the unconfessing plagiarism of some more favoured and popular author. Let us measure the powers of Coleridge by the standard of phrenology ; they will be high, indeed, and the result much nearer truth than that rendered by the uncertain test of modern criticism. When this science shall have been generally received and thoroughly understood, then will be found in its rich resources, abundant materials for furnishing literature with what it has never yet possessed—an unfailing standard, a true, unswerving test of merit. Especially, in its correct application, will it benefit that of our own country, hitherto so shamefully neglected. Guided by its light, future critics will discover, and present to public notice, many productions of sterling value, but which, from being offered to national sympathy without the charm of any foreign stamp, were suffered to sink into unmerited obscurity. Any one in the habit of reading works professedly critical, must often be amused, and sometimes pained, at their inconsistency and flat contradictions. So great, indeed, are these, and irreconcilable, as to show clearly they have in reality no settled standard of taste, but that each condemns or praises as his fancy, mood, prejudice, or more disreputable influences, dictate at the moment. Nor does the judgment thus rendered, accord with the most cultivated taste of the times in which it is given. The Edinburgh Review, indisputably the very first of the carping clan, has had most of its arrogant decisions, for many years past, reversed by the supreme court from which there is no appeal—the public. But, though unjust criticism cannot always utterly destroy, nor deprive the offerings of true genius of posthumous incense, yet it may withhold from living merit its just meed, by arresting the willing homage, without which its past labours appear vain and fruitless, and its future exertions altogether hopeless.   •

Should the Edinburgh Review happen to be fair and just in its comments, as the London Quarterly generally makes it a point to render a verdict directly opposite, where exists the criterion of final decision ?   A poem published some years ago, which excited considerable interest in all literary circles, was pronounced by one of these reviewers to be remarkable for the flow, fire, and facility of its versification, the happy management of its machinery, graphic vigour of its characters, and, in short, to be altogether a most admirable work ; and by another, to be dull and dragging in style, unnatural in plot and exaggerated in character, generally spiritless, and, as a whole, a very heavy and uninteresting production, indeed.   Now supposing these writers to be *sincere*, which may, perhaps, be conceding too much, what can be more unfair than to assume, as they thus do, their *own consciousness* as an unfailing standard of truth ?   One of the consequences of this is the formation of *cliques*, who, resolving their united taste to be the only true one, exert upon literature and all the arts an influence equally pernicious, for they only, in fact, extend somewhat the same narrow principles which govern the individual critic, and condemn every thing that does not strike in harmony with their peculiar notices or prejudices.   Who, remembering the exquisite poetry, the profound and beautiful morality, indiscriminately condemned, by a certain set of critics, in the mass, under the absurd cognomen of the " Lake School," does not regret the want of some sure standard in the arts, which might preserve excellence from the blighting effects of arrogance, ignorance, and envy ?   In this same school were ridiculously blended, writers, altogether distinct, in every attribute which can possibly distinguish one elegant and gifted intellect from another.

Wordsworth, it appears, wrote a preface for a volume of poems, to which several of his friends contributed, and among others, the subject of this article.   In this preface, he ventured to put forth some new opinions upon poetry as an art, in which he showed a laudable desire to strip it of its mere tinsel, and teach a host of meanless scribblers that the garniture and flaunting robes of the muses could not compensate for the absence of their living forms.   The critics took offence ; and, in revenge, classed every one who had contributed even a ballad to the work in the same school, upon which they heaped the most unsparing ridicule.   Several of these writers resided near the lakes, and were hence called the " Lake School of Poets."   But Coleridge, neither in theory nor practice, subscribed to all the principles of Wordsworth, but has distinctly recorded in his "Biographia Literaria" his objections, while Southey, who, at this time, wrote epics in holy reverence of the sacred unities, was confounded with both. Wordsworth, the only one who attempted to reduce his views into actual practice, was sometimes led by them to affect a simplicity of language rather too severe, but even this could not destroy the freshness and beauty of the thoughts it so scantily clad. But the critics, and very soon the public also, resolved that all the authors who happened to reside within the vicinity of the lakes, were altogether bad and unreasonable; and years passed away, and custom and fashion became, as usual, too hard for justice, the decision could not be revoked, and *popular* writers were constantly, without the slightest fear of detection, stealing from the excommunicated school.

To return from this digression to the subject before us. The conversational powers of Coleridge, unequalled in his day, though it was even more remarkable for such excellence than when

> "Johnson talked, and Goldy wrote,
> And bustling Bozzy penned his note,"

have never, perhaps, been adequately described, though many an eager listener has recorded his warm and genial admiration of the full, flowing, and finished language which clothed the loftiest thoughts, the subtlest beauty, and the most refined morality. The "Table Talk," collected and published by his relative, can be considered only as the mere "shreds and patches" of those connected and glowing speculations heard by the Lambs, the Hazlits, and the Talfourds, and we have never perused it, without regretting that Coleridge was not so fortunate as to have his Boswell, too, who, by preserving the dramatic effect and spirit of dialogue, might have given us a true picture of his brilliant conversation.

In a previous number, we stated that his "Marvellousness" was larger than Ideality, and that his poetry, in harmony with the fact, proves the accuracy of Spurzheim's examination, and then referred to the "Ancient Mariner," as an appropriate illustration. We would now direct the reader to a strange fragment called "Christabel," which certainly could not have been conceived without the organ large and active. Indeed, it cannot be appreciated without the same endowment. Scott, whose Marvellousness was exceedingly developed, admired it to a degree perfectly incomprehensible to those deficient in the same faculty. Basil Hall tells us, in one of his numerous journals, that until he heard Scott read the poem to his family, "he had always thought Byron's praise of it a mere hoax." The profound observer of American manners and institutions had

en made, perhaps, so often the victim of Yankee hoaxing, that he
id grown over-suspicious. However this be, there can be no doubt
' Byron's sincerity, for he proved it by a very excellent imitation.
oleridge's Adhesiveness was large and active, which, with his other
gh endowments, rendered his attachment to friends as free from the
int of selfishness as is, perhaps, permitted to our nature. All
miliar with his writings, know his success in describing the softer
elings. It would not be easy to select from any author, ancient or
odern, a more thrilling manifestation of this organ, delicately marked
i it is by Marvellousness, and illumined by Ideality, than is to be
und in the exquisite ballad of " Genevieve." The reader, who
ay have perused it, will at once recall, by the mere mention of its
ime, that genial dream of love and beauty. He will remember
iose six or eight concluding stanzas which so truly paint the first
itpouring of a woman's affection, and know that he might turn his
ir in vain to all the bards who have ever sung to the like melting
otes, which, with so much simplicity, such nice discrimination of
ie very essence of feminine reserve vanquished by her love, tremble
om his harp in the following. The reader is aware the lay had
ready been sung which aroused the sympathy of the maid, and
xtorted her weeping confession :—

> All impulses of soul and sense,
> Had thrilled my guiltless Genevieve
> The music and the doleful air,
> The rich and balmy eve—
>
> And hopes and fears that cherish hope,
> An undistinguishable throng,
> And gentle wishes long subdued,
> Subdued and cherished long.
>
> She wept with pity and delight,
> She blushed with love and maiden shame,
> And like the murmurs of a dream,
> I heard her breathe my name.
>
> Her wet cheek glowed; she step'd aside
> As conscious of my look she step'd,
> Then suddenly, with a timorous eye,
> She flew to me, and wept !
>
> She half enclosed me in her arms,
> She pressed me with a meek embrace,
> And bending back her head, looked up
> And gazed upon my face.
>
> 'Twas partly love, and partly fear,
> And partly 'twas a bashful art,
> That I might rather *feel* than see,
> The swelling of her heart.

There was one great defect in his organisation, not so much defect perhaps in itself, as in view of his circumstances, of the difi culties that perpetually surrounded him, and the gross injustice wit which he was treated by some of his contemporaries. We allude t his small Destructiveness and Combativeness. The size and hig cultivation of his moral and intellectual faculties, led him to see th vice of contention, and the folly of resentment, in the abstract, and h constantly strove to introduce the beautiful theories of the closet int the world. A more refined morality, a purer religion, was neve cherished, than that carried into even the minutiæ of his daily lif Hating no one, he restrained the manifestation of a righteous indigna tion, and was ever ready to practise upon the sublime principles o Christianity, and return good for evil.

Yet even this magnanimity, this lofty forbearance, could not protec him from the foul calumny and inveterate rancour of those whom, a has justly been observed, the little finger of recrimination might hav shivered into dust. But he listened to the injustice of critics an smiled, and when, tempted by impunity, the libeller at length invade the sanctity of his humble hearth, though he could not but writh under the wounded sensibility of the husband and father, yet eve then he pitied and forgave.

Had his social position been as elevated as his genius, this meel ness, this truly Christian spirit, would have shed additional lustr upon all his gifts; but his was the iron destiny. He was one o those who, favoured by nature and frowned on by fortune, seer designed to convince us how little, in the present state of society, th highest endowments have to do with worldly success, when com pared with the accidents of birth, or with opulence. For the worlc as it *is*, he was altogether too mild and forbearing. The ruffian i still abroad, and the strong arm of law too weak to arrest, or even t punish the most flagrant violations of private rights, and it mu therefore be rather dangerous to tempt the assassin, by pledging ou selves to turn *both cheeks* whenever he shall choose to attack us.

Amid all his sufferings and disappointments, he projected one grea work, from the successful execution of which, he anticipated th happiest results, and around which he gathered his warmest affection his holiest aspirations, the liveliest interest for the welfare of man, an all the fruits of his profound learning, extensive research, and a lit of meditation. Its object was entirely philanthropic. His own wid intercourse with the first intellects of Europe, had convinced him th there was in truth very little settled belief in man's exalted destiny and that religion, so long disfigured by the grossest superstition, wa viewed by many as any thing but the handmaid of another worlc

He trusted, by a severity of reasoning which no ingenuity coul[
resist, to demonstrate the real capacities of our nature, the truth o
revelation, and the immortality of the soul—to rescue the minds o
thinking men from the blighting influence of unbelief, and fix thei
hopes of eternity upon a basis like the mountain rock, sure, safe, an[
imperishable.　This was the warmth of his heart, the manifestatio[
of his large and active Benevolence, and altogether free from the spiri
of mere controversy.　No man of his day, perhaps, was so well fitte[
to bring about this beautiful union of religion and philosophy.　Ther[
was not a doctrine or creed, from Zoroaster's to Swedenborg's, witl
which he was unacquainted, no system of scepticism, from that of th[
ancients to Spinoza's, whose arguments he had not weighed, sifted
and matured.　But the work was never completed.　The leisure an[
comfort which the wise institutions of society so abundantly afford t[
thousands of its most useless members, were denied to him, and th[
philosopher, who ardently longed to serve his fellows, and the ma[
of genius, who wished only to consecrate the gifts of natuie to th[
great cause of truth and human happiness, continued to fritter awa[
his mind in the service of ephemeral magazines for bread

W.

ARTICLE VII.

PATHOLOGICAL FACT, CONFIRMATORY OF PHRENOLOGY.

Dr. Samuel Jackson, Professor of the Institutes of Medicine in th[
University of Pennsylvania, communicated, in the year 1829, to th[
American Medical Recorder,* the following interesting fact on th[
pathology of the brain.　After some general remarks on the import
ance of a knowledge of the morbid state of the various organs of th[
body, in order to understand correctly their healthy functions, D[
Jackson proceeds as follows :—

Our knowledge of the encephalic organs is wanting in speciality
general conclusions have been arrived at, through the medium o
experiments, of pathological observations, and the study of individu[
peculiarities.　In this way it is known that they are the seats o
organs of the intellectual faculties, of sensation, of locomotion, an[
the expressions ; and the general location of these functions is dete[
mined with some accuracy.　It is a question yet to be decide[

* Volume XVI, page 272.

whether the intellectual and moral faculties have for their variou
modifications distinct organs, or have the brain as a common organ
in which the different faculties may be displayed. This question i
to be mainly resolved, it is most probable, by a careful attention to th
intellectual phenomena in a morbid state. In this view, the following
case, it appears to me, is deserving to be placed on record.

The Rev. Mr. R., the subject of this case, is aged forty-eight years
he is of the sanguine temperament, ruddy complexion, light-coloured
hair and eyes, and has lately manifested a strong tendency to obesity
his health for many years has been excellent; he is not subject to
headach, or to any nervous symptoms. His intellectual faculties are
of a high order, but have not been as actively employed as formerly
and he has experienced some mental anxiety; his temper is placid
with a disposition bordering on gaiety.

On the 5th of September last, early in the morning, he awoke with
headach, after a restless night. He had, the preceding evening, beer
exposed to the night air, which had lowered in temperature, and per-
spiration, which was usually copious, received a sudden check. He
took some castor oil, which acted freely in a short time, after which
he again laid down. About eleven o'clock, the Rev. Mr. H., who
resides in the same dwelling, went into his room to inquire respecting
his health, and was surprised to find Mr. R. could not answer his
questions. Alarmed at this circumstance, he immediately requested
me to visit Mr. R.

I found my patient in bed, evidently in the full possession of his
senses, but incapable of uttering a word. I examined the tongue
and ascertained it was not paralysed, but could be moved in every
direction. All my questions were perfectly comprehended, and
answered by signs; and it could be plainly seen, by the smile on the
countenance, after many ineffectual attempts to express his ideas, that
he was himself surprised and somewhat amused at his peculiar situation.

The face at this time was flushed, the pulse full and somewha
slow, and to my inquiries if he suffered pain in the head, *he pointed
to the front of his forehead as its seat.*

I directed hot water to be brought in a bucket, for a pediluvium
and made preparations to draw blood. Mr. R. exhibited at this time
a strong desire to speak, and, after a great many ineffectual efforts
endeavoured to make me comprehend his meaning by signs. Find
ing I could not understand him, he made a sign that he would write
When furnished with pen and paper, he attempted to convey his
meaning, but I saw he could not recall words, and that he had written
an unintelligible phrase: it was " Didoes doe the doe."

Forty ounces of blood were drawn from the arm, and before the operation was completed, speech was restored, though a difficulty continued as to the names of things, which could not be recalled. The bleeding and pediluvium produced some faintness, and he was placed in bed.

The loss of speech appearing to recur again, in fifteen minutes, ten ounces more of blood were abstracted, and sinapisms applied to the arms, legs, and thighs, alternately; the skin became moist, and the headach was relieved.

Mr. R. now communicated to me, that when he made the attempt to write, he had intended to inform me he had already used a foot-bath, and I might see the floor still wet, where the water had been spilled.

The sleep that night was disturbed by uneasiness and throbbing in the head, which disappeared in the course of the sixth, and no further return of the affection has occurred.

In an analysis of this case, we are presented with the following facts: 1st, Sudden suppression of the cutaneous transpiration, succeeded by cerebral irritation and determination of blood to the brain; 2d, Frontal pain immediately over the eyes; 3d, Perfect integrity of the sensations and voluntary movements; 4, The general operations of the intellect undisturbed; ideas formed, combined, and compared; those of things, of events, of time, recalled without difficulty; 5th, Loss of language, or of the faculty of conveying ideas by words, though not by signs; this defect was not confined to spoken language, but also extended to written language.

The inferences to be drawn from these facts, are, 1st, That as the cerebral irritation produced no general affection or disturbance of the functions of the brain, it was local or limited; 2d, As loss of language was the only functional derangement of the intellectual faculties, that faculty must have been connected with the portion of the brain, the seat of irritation; and 3d, That an organ of language exists in the brain. This case lends a strong confirmation to the general truth of the doctrines of phrenology.

MISCELLANY

—

Phrenology in Great Britain.—The British and Foreign Medica
Review, edited by John Forbes, M. D., F. R. S., for January, 1840, con
tains a very able and elaborate article, extending over 25 closely printe
octavo pages, in favour of phrenology.   This article, coming as it doe:
from high authority, cannot fail to have a powerful influence on th
medical profession in Great Britain, as well as in this country.   Th
Edinburgh Weekly Chronicle for January 25, in noticing this numbe
of the British and Foreign Medical Review, alludes to the article o
phrenology as follows:—

That article, which has interested ourselves intensely, is written wit
a degree of candour, ability, and discrimination, extremely rare, an
breathes the most philosophical spirit.   The only objection we ca
reasonably find is, that the article is unnecessary, and is altogether
work of supererogation; for phrenology, in support of which it is writter
has undoubtedly taken its place, (and a high place it occupies,) amon,
the physiological, ethical, and mental sciences, its foundation being on
rock which can never be moved.   We hold, for instance, that an incom
parably greater number of works on phrenology are bought and studie
than on any other branch of knowledge whatever, except religion.   A!
the thinking and intelligent persons known to us, with few exceptions
are strict believers in the science—appreciate its usefulness—and carr
its doctrines more or less into effect in their own conduct.   Indeed, i
throws so much light on the character of our species, and the menta
philosophy on it is so thoroughly tangible and satisfactory, that w
wonder not that the science itself has become so general an object o
study and belief.   We may farther mention, in proof of our position, th
unrivalled circulation to which one of the leading works on phrenolog
has attained; namely, Mr. Combe's "Constitution of Man," which ha
sold to the amount of 45,000 copies in the United Kingdom alone, exclu
sive of large editions in America, and translations into French an
German; and other able works on the subject, the circulation of whic
has been proportionally great.   Nor is this all.   No course of public lec
tures, however useful or interesting, attracts nearly so large and intell
gent audiences as those which have been given in both divisions of th
empire on phrenology.

—

The Human Brain.—The following interesting facts, in relation t
the brain, are copied from the *Bibliothèque Universelle de Génève.*

The weight of the brain of an European adult, of the male sex, varie
from 3lbs. 2oz. (Troy) to 4lbs. 6oz.   That of men of very distinguishe
talent frequently passes that average.   For instance, the brain of Cuvie
weighed 4lbs. 11oz. 4drs. 30grs.; that of Dupuytren, the celebrated sui
geon, 4lbs. 10oz.   On the contrary, the brain of idiots is below tha
average.   The brain of two cretins weighed, the one, 1lb. 9oz., the othe:
1lb. 11oz.   The brain of women is lighter than that of men.   It varie
from 2lbs. 8oz. to 3lbs. 11oz.   The average difference is, at least, from
to 8oz.; and this difference is perceptible in infants from the moment o
their birth.   The brain arrives, about the seventh or eighth year, at it
complete developement.   It is probable, although it has not been absc
lutely demonstrated, that the brain diminishes in weight and in size at
very advanced age; and that thence may be easily explained the weaken

ing of the faculties by which age is generally accompanied. It cann(
be denied that there is an intimate relation between the absolute weigl
of the brain and the developement of intellect and the mental functions

—.

Lectures of Dr. Buchanan in Louisiana.

Jackson, La., March 4, 1840.

MR. EDITOR,

Sir,—A series of phrenological lectures, marked by much originalit
has been recently delivered in this place by Dr. J. R. Buchanan. At tl
close of the course, the class formed itself into a body for the expressio
of their sentiments in reference to Dr. Buchanan's lectures, when tl
following persons were appointed a committee to draft a report, expre
sive of the class:—

Rev. Jas. Shannon, Prest. Louisiana College,
Prof. H. H. Gird,
Prof. A. D. Wooldridge,
Prof. M. Cubi i Soler, } Committee.
A. M. Dunn. Esq.,
W. B. Forsyth, M. D.,

At a special meeting of the class, the committee presented a repor
which was unanimously adopted; and Prof. M. Cubi was appointed
communicate to Dr. Buchanan the proceedings, with such farther sug
gestions as might be appropriate. Messrs. Jno. M'Vea, Jos. Joor, ar
J. N. Carrigan, were then appointed a committee of publication, and tl
meeting adjourned. In discharge of this duty, we offer you the followic
extract from the report, which presents its spirit and character, accon
panied by the letter of Prof. Cubi.

We should not omit to mention an interesting fact occurring, durin
these lectures, under our observation. We submitted to the inspectio
of Dr. Buchanan the skulls of two negroes—one of whom had bee
executed, and the other had not. The descriptions of their characte:
were entirely satisfactory; and while he pronounced one of them fir
and brave, capable of meeting any punishment, he declared the other
possess the sense of feeling to such a degree that he could not bear co
poreal punishment, but would use great cunning to escape it. We kno
that the former met his death with perfect indifference, as we witnesse
his execution. The latter having done something to merit a chastis
ment, was threatened with a flogging by his master, and fled to tl
woods, where he died. The portion of the brain pointed out by D
Buchanan as the organ of the sense of feeling appeared in this cai
unusually large.

Yours respectfully,

JNO. M'VEA,
JOSEPH JOOR, } Committee.
JOHN N. CARRIGAN,

Extract from the Report.

Firm believers as we are, in the truth of the fundamental principl
of phrenology, we think it by no means unreasonable to suppose th
errors may be found in some of its details, and that there may be man
valuable truths in this department of science yet undiscovered. Cons
quently, we must believe that those who bring talents of a high orde
extensive erudition, and persevering industry, to the cultivation of th
science, the extension of its discoveries, and the correction of its error

if any should be found to exist, ought to be regarded as public bene
factors. In such light do we regard Dr. Buchanan. And although i
would be premature, at least for some of us, to express a decided opinio
relative to what is original in his system, yet we must say, that wit
many of his peculiar views we have been highly pleased.

[Accompanying the above communication, we received a copy of Pro:
M. Cubi's letter to Dr. Buchanan. We have taken the liberty, in pre
senting the letter, to omit a few sentences which seem unimportant; an:
as to the new views advanced, we are unprepared to express any opinion
Prof. Cubi addresses Dr. B. as follows:—Ed.]

Your remarks upon the functions of *Alimentireness*, bearing strongl:
on the importance and necessity of attending to its admonitions, are, ii
a country like this, in which food and diet are so little attended to
uncommonly valuable. They speak louder, and more to the purpose
than volumes upon hygiene. Whatever opinions others may hav:
formed in regard to the organ of *Sense of Feeling*, whose functions an:
locality you have discovered, and so satisfactorily explained, for *my* par
I consider it as filling a great vacuity in phrenology. My late observa
tions, and those of some of my friends, go to prove that your views, ir
that respect, are correct. As to the necessity of man's possessing a cere
bral organ of feeling—an organ to make him conscious of the physica
condition of his body for the time being—no one, even *a priori*, can
reasonably doubt. Viewing the benefits which the positive knowledg:
of the existence of such an organ will produce, your discovery cannot b:
too highly praised.

I have been, and I know that others have been, much entertained and
instructed with your remarks on the organ of the *Sense of Emotion*
which you locate in the intermediate region between the intellectual an:
moral portions of the brain. I always thought, that, as there existed :
power in man of incorporating himself with the state of being of those
around him—a power which abstracting us, as it were, from ourselves
passed into the bosoms of others—there must have necessarily been :
corporeal instrument by which the mind exercises that power. You:
discovery in this respect has explained to me many difficulties, an:
removed from me many doubts, which often beset my path in my phreno
logical investigations. The few practical cases which have come withir
cognisance since you first mentioned the existence and functions of th:
organ in question, have all tended to confirm me in the belief that you:
statement is nothing but an exposition of the operations of nature.

The modified conceptions which you have formed respecting the func
tions of the occipital organs, are, to a very great extent, in accordance
with conclusions at which I may be said to have instinctively arrived
Now, that you have laid open before me your convictions, in regard t:
the action of the back-head, I discover causes and facts which no doub:
operated in forming my conclusions, but which I had not present at th:
time of forming them.

Evidence is not wanting that many phrenologists have had vague an:
indistinct notions of the functions which you ascribe to the back-head, an:
which either perplexed them, or were ascribed to some other region.

Alexander Walker, in his late treatise on Intermarriage, does not hesi
tate for a moment in pointing out the occiput as the seat of the passion:
As I can now perceive what in me, more than any facts or mode of
reasoning, produced the impression that energy, activity, determination
and constancy of purpose, together with deep affection for individua:
objects or places, were functions performed by at least the upper an:
lateral portions of the occiput, it is that in all heads thus organised I

seemed to find these qualities highly developed. Experience had also shown me, without fully appreciating my observations, that in the Araucanians, the Bosques, the Welsh, the Scotish, the Calabrians, the Greeks, and all the people descended from high mountainous districts, from whom the world has derived its notions of national liberty and free institutions, have all comparatively large hind-heads. If we take, retrospectively, a comprehensive view of human society, we shall find, that at one period the Celt, at another the Roman, and at another, which is the present, the Goth, have held universal dominion over mankind. In comparing the heads of these three various species of Europeans, we shall find that they are very much alike in general size; but the Roman has a larger and more elongated back-head than the Celt—and the Goth than the Roman.

Besides, it is only by supposing that the occiput produces feelings of a grasping, secretly impelling, and constantly persevering nature, that we can account for the indomitable and fearful energy of such men as Ximenes, for the cool collected courage of the English, and for the irresistible *go-a-head* of the Americans.

Ideas like these, which had often crossed my mind, and to which I had paid no special attention, corroborating your convictions on the functions of the back-head, have now broke forth with new light upon my mind.

As to the organ of Cautiousness, I was *never* a believer in the functions ascribed to it. I soon saw too many fearless heads with preponderating Cautiousness, without much check, at the same time, from its antagonistic region of Combativeness and Destructiveness, to have much faith in the doctrine that ascribed to it the feeling of fear. I fully concur with you in the opinion, that courage, as well as fear, are feelings produced by a combined action of the whole brain, depending more on quality than quantity of the cerebral organs, and more on results produced by efforts of antagonistic regions simultaneously acting, than as specific functions of any peculiar set of organs. I think with you, that names expressive of a mental operation considered only in a peculiar relation, or to which the mind attaches but one single definite, limited conception, to signify function in all its various degrees of intensity, power, and activity, have retarded the progress of phrenology.

Your attempt in forming a new nomenclature, which will be expressive of the locality and not of the function of the organ, must ultimately redound to simplify and improve the science. By divesting from the mind, for example, the conception of Firmness, and directing it solely to a portion of the brain producing such a function, we shall understand more closely, and retain more lastingly, this function in all its various degrees, modifications, and combinations of action.

Phrenology is destined soon to become the only system of mental philosophy taught in all our literary and scientific institutions; the chief guide to direct us in our efforts for intellectual, moral, and religious advancement. How important it is, then, that in this science the march of its adoption and extension should keep pace with that of its improvements and discoveries.

—

Mr. Combe's Lectures at New Haven, Ct.—The New Haven Record, of March 21st, in noticing Mr. Combe's lectures in that city, has the following very candid and common-sense remarks on the science:—

The course of lectures on phrenology, by Mr. Combe, came to a close this week, having been attended throughout by an audience, for numbers and respectability, such as rarely falls to the lot of a public lecturer in this city. Much interest was felt to hear this subject expounded by its greatest living teacher, and the interest was continued unabated through-

out the course. All who heard the lectures will, we believe, acknow
ledge that they have not only been interested, but profited by hearin
much important truth ably illustrated, and many principles presented o
great practical value. Indeed, we sometimes hear it objected to phrenc
logy, that all the truth it contains was known well enough without i
But, although many of the principles deduced from it commend them
selves to our understanding when fairly presented, yet they are prin
ciples which without it, we have, at least in practice, failed to recognise
When they are demonstrated from the connection of the mind with it
material organs, they become much more tangible, are more likely to b
remembered, and thoroughly realised and acted upon.

The simple fact, that the mind is dependent on the body, and influ
enced by its condition, is by some hardly even recognised at all in prac
tice. If phrenology only fixes this single principle, it will have rendere
an important service. In the daily practice of life, and in our system
of mental philosophy, it is exceedingly important that the fact of th
connection of body and mind be not lost sight of, and that the modes i
which the one affects the other be understood. To this department o
investigation, phrenologists have turned their attention and the attentio
of the public—the *doctrina de fœdere*, as Lord Bacon calls it, a depart
ment in the field of science which his sagacity marked out, but whicl
has been hitherto little explored.

It is perfect folly to laugh at phrenology, when the science of the mind
as taught in other systems, is confessedly in so unsatisfactory and un
settled a state. It is perfect folly to deny its principles, without examin
ing the facts to which it appeals. Considered simply as a system o
mental science, laying out of view its organology, there is no other, w
are persuaded, which will so well account for the actual diversities whic
the human character presents, and so well explain the various phenc
mena of the mind, as this. As a system of mental science, it is indee
very imperfect as yet, having been thus far more employed in externa
observation, (both of men's characters and their heads,) than in menta
analysis. When observation shall have been carried to a sufficien
extent, provided the science is true, there will still be a field for investi
gation, by interrogating consciousness more fully, guided by the ligh
which observation has shed. Phrenologists have begun at the right en
in this study, in beginning with observation. They have adopted th
inductive method; and with facts so many and so well attested as the
produce, the modesty of true science should lead us to inquire, and no
to sneer or to dogmatise.

The most serious objection urged against phrenology is, that it is un
friendly to religion—that it is a system of fatalism, overthrows respons
bility, and leaves no place for the doctrines of the Bible respecting si
and regeneration. Such objections we think are founded in mistake
Few will deny that men are endowed with certain constitutional proper
sities and faculties—differing in relative strength in different individual
—which develope themselves in the character, and are frequently tran
mitted from parents to children. These constitutional traits we know
are so combined in some individuals, as to render it extremely improbabl
that they will ever become virtuous or religious men; while in others
is the reverse. Neither in the subjects of renewing grace, are any c
these constitutional principles eradicated or new ones implanted, but
new direction is given to those already existing. Nor is the characte
of all true Christians shaped in one mould; but their religious characte
receives its cast from their natural character—their constitutional dispe
sitions are retained, though differently directed and modified. Th

character of the apostle Paul differed as much from that of the apostle John, after their conversion, as before.   It is difficult to see that the phrenologist goes a step further towards any dangerous consequences, when he makes these elementary faculties dependent on material organs.

We should distinguish the legitimate tendencies of the science itself from the use which individuals may have made of it.   Phrenologists, too, like all other men, are apt to go to extremes—to take partial views— to exaggerate that which has occupied their attention, and lose sight of other things.   Thus they may place all sin in the violation of organic laws, overlooking our relation to God as a moral governor—they may think so much of the influence of the body on the mind as to forget other more important influences of a moral nature—or they may be so confident in the efficacy of a proper discipline and training of the faculties, that they may think little of the necessity of divine influence.   In doing so, they err by taking truth which is important in its place, and giving it a universality which does not belong to it.   The candid and intelligent inquirer will admit the truth and reject the error.

More than three hundred persons have attended this course of lectures. At the conclusion of the course, some resolutions, complimentary to Mr. Combe, were offered by Gov. Edwards, and seconded by Prof. Silliman, and unanimously adopted by the class.   This is the last course of lectures which Mr. Combe delivers in this country.   The set of casts which he used were purchased by the class, and are to be deposited in the Medical College.

———

Moral Agency.—In our first volume, two articles were presented on the subject of "Phrenology in relation to Fatalism, Necessity, and Human Responsibility."   It appears that there were certain views advanced in those articles, which prove unsatisfactory to some friends of the science, and which, in their opinion, interfere with the Scripture doctrine of moral agency.   We do not deem it judicious, or profitable, to enter into any discussion or controversy on this subject in the Journal; but, at the same time, we take pleasure in acceding to the request of those friends by copying the following remarks on this subject, which are from the pen of Mr. Joel Barlow, of New York, and were published in Zion's Watchman, Sept. 21, 1839.

Moral character, or the virtue and vice of mankind, supposes the moral liberty of man; or, in other words, man is a moral agent.   It would be useless to state the objections to this doctrine, or the general arguments by which it is supported.   I shall attempt a definition which will be the least objectionable.   It is the *ability* of men to choose between motives, to *select motives*, and to act according to their choice.   I do not believe that any other science but phrenology can fairly illustrate or satisfactorily prove this proposition.   With this conviction, I shall proceed to give phrenological arguments, and if I am able to convey my ideas to others in my own language as clearly as I understand them myself, I believe the argument will be perfectly satisfactory to all.

Phrenology establishes the existence, and illustrates the function, of the organ of Language.   It is that primary faculty which applies specific sounds to the things perceived by the mind; both when it apperceives its internal states, and when it uses the senses on the external world.   Its function is correlative, and necessary in the inseparable connection, and organic action of mind and matter; and its terms are specific and well known beyond the possibility of self-deception.   The thing expressed must first be a matter of consciousness, before any term can be applied to it; and whatever thus receives a term, general in its use, an specific in its meaning, cannot be denied an existence.

Now the term *liberty*, and its correlatives, freedom, choice, and agency has a specific meaning in mental philosophy, is used by all mankind and is alike understood by the child and the philosopher. The sense o liberty, to which the term is given which we feel to be what the term expresses, must be a state of mind inseparable from the mental constitu tion, or the term never could have existed. And the apprehension of th term is as general as the consciousness of the state it expresses; so tha the term, either written or spoken, as necessarily awakens our conscious ness of the state, as does the consciousness of the state originate th term, or necessitate Language to give it the term. Thus the phrenolc gical argument is, that man must be a free being, and that the freedon expressed in the term liberty, as applied to choice of, and motives be tween, is inherent in his nature, of which he cannot be divested, an which is self-determined by the consciousness it endures; for the tern liberty is applied to every mental operation, and to each action of life Then man is necessarily free, not from choice, and he who denies this must deny the very necessity which he would prove by denying th liberty in question.

There is yet another phrenological argument which proves this fre agency of man. The terms approval and disapproval, which expres two of the strongest states of mind, and which express half our happi ness or misery, could never have been applied, if we did not know our selves able to choose between the motives which urged us to the action respecting which we feel innocent or guilty. All men, then, are free t choose between motives, and able to act according to their choice. Bu this liberty differs in men, according to the strength and activity of the fundamental faculties. Now, since the faculties can be educated, so als can liberty be educated to good or bad choices; and a man is as much t blame for choosing wrong as for acting wrong.

But it will be objected that "your moral liberty is, in itself, necessity and man is free to be what he is, and nothing else." I reply that a ne cessity to be free, as he is, also involves a necessary freedom to be some thing else. Man is, indeed, necessarily free; but it is the necessity which makes the freedom, and this is the thing contended for. All the dispute which have agitated the philosophic world, have been more about the law of phenomena than about the phenomena themselves. This is eminently true of moral agency. The world admits this state of mind, and acts ac cordingly; none but minds partially organised will deny it. The phreno logist must admit it, or destroy his system of induction, based on the evi dence of consciousness.

—

Material Instruments for Mental Manifestations.—A friend ha placed in our hands the following curious extract from the work o *Jeremy Taylor*, on the *Nativity:*—"For if the soul of man were pu into the body of a mole, it could not see nor speak, because it is not fitte with an instrument apt and organical to the faculty; and when the sou hath its proper instruments, its music is pleasant or harsh, according t the sweetness or unevenness of the string it touches; for David himsel could not have charmed Saul's melancholic spirit with the strings of hi bow, or the wood of his spear. And just so are the actions or disposition of the soul, angry or pleasant, lustful or cold, querulous or passionate according as the body is disposed by the various intermixtures of natura qualities."

Phrenological Society at Albany, N. Y.—About the middle of March, a society was formed in this city for the cultivation and advancement of phrenology, and the following gentlemen appointed officers—Thomas W. Olcott, President; Rufus W. Peckham, Vice-President; John Newland, Secretary; William Combe, Treasurer; Amos Dean, W. A. Hamilton, and Amos Fish, Executive Committee. We would here correct a mistake made in our sixth number, page 238, in the notice of Mr. Combe's lectures at Albany. It should have read "Combe on *Physiology*," instead of "Combe on *Phrenology*," that was used as a text-book in the Albany Female Academy.

—

Phrenology in the Family.—This little work on the Application of Phrenological Principles to Early Domestic Education, by Rev. J. A. Warne, seems to be very favourably received by those who are competent to judge of its real merits. We recently received from a gentleman connected with the Canadian government, a letter, dated Toronto, U. C., March 13th, 1840, in which the writer speaks of Mr. Warne's book, and another work, titled "Woman's Mission," in the following manner:—

Mr. Editor,—

Sir,—On the first day of June last I embarked at New York in the packet ship which sailed that day for London, having that morning purchased, and carried on board with me, a small work on education entitled "Phrenology in the Family," addressed especially to mothers, and written by the Rev. Joseph A. Warne, of Philadelphia.

From my youth upwards, my mind has been more earnestly employed in reflecting on the various modes of improving the human mind than on any other subject whatever. I have read with the most earnest attention, all I found written on the subject for the last forty years, and I have exercised myself much in communicating knowledge to children and to adults during nearly the whole of that period.

The value of this book appeared to me so great, that, after my arrival in London, I went to an eminent publisher and offered him the book if he would republish it. After keeping it for twenty-four hours, he returned it to me, declining to print it. From day to day I offered it to six other publishers, the last of whom accepted the book and promised to republish it, and I have since learned that he did so. This was Mr. Hodgson, No. 111 Fleet street.

On returning to New York in September, I purchased another copy, and have since perused it again with more interest than ever.

While in London, I saw and purchased a small work, also on education, just then published, and addressed especially to mothers, entitled "Woman's Mission," and written, as I was told, by a Miss Lewis. This last is a book of general principles, whilst the former is one of details; together, I think them absolutely invaluable. During my stay in that city, I was many times on the point of addressing a letter to the editor of the Times, subscribed with my proper name, and calling upon every woman in Britain to purchase and study these two works, and devote themselves to the duties and practice recommended in them, with all the zeal of affectionate mothers. But the fear of ridicule, and certain peculiar circumstances in which I was then placed, constrained me to silence.

On arriving in New York, I called on an eminent publisher there with "Woman's Mission," and recommended him earnestly to republish it, and he said he would. He did not, however, do so; but I now learn that Messrs. Wiley and Putnam have republished it, and that Bishop Onder donk, of New York, has published a letter highly recommending it to the public. I have personally recommended and requested of many book sellers in both the Canadas to import and sell these books, and some of them I know have done so, and it may be that all have. If they have not, I now, more earnestly than ever, recommend them to do so on the opening of the navigation.

Many months have since elapsed, and my mind has become more deeply impressed than ever with the vast importance of having those books studied forthwith by every human being at all capable of appreciating their value, and of acting in furtherance of the views of the benevolent writers.

Should any of the readers of this letter entertain opinions unfavourable to phrenology, I nevertheless request of them to give Mr. Warne's book one perusal, at least, and this, I very confidently hope, will convince them that the writer is a sincere Christian, that the book teaches a truly Christian doctrine, and that the lessons given in it, if followed assiduously, will produce results the most happy and delightful to a fond parent.

And here let me add, by way of parenthesis, that in the first ten years of life must the foundation be laid of what is usually called good temper; by giving due exercise to benevolence, justice, and to all the moral sentiments, and by watchfully keeping inactive the animal propensities until they shall become duly enfeebled, and perfectly subjected to the control of the moral sentiments and intellectual faculties. The well-instructed mother and nurse can best accomplish this highest and most important of all duties. Thus will mothers be hereafter the great *formers* of human character, and, with Divine aid, they will become the chief benefactors of our race. A few plain lessons to uneducated mothers, even, will suffice to enable them to do much towards bringing up their infant children in love to God, and love to one another.

I verily believe that by the universal circulation and perusal of these two small books, now selling at half a dollar each, an amount of good would be done to the rising generation, and even to the parents themselves, which would exceed all my expectations, sanguine as I confess I am on this very important subject, to our hitherto discordant and wrongly educated fellow-beings.

I earnestly call on every gentle, generous, noble-minded man and woman to turn their immediate attention to these books—to read them, to study them; and if they shall appreciate them as highly as I hope and believe they must, I am sure they will exert their best energies in recommending them to the rich, and also in employing their money in procuring them for such as can make use of, but may not be able to purchase them.

I entreat of every man, who desires the improvement and happiness of those he loves, and the advancement in goodness of all mankind, to purchase and read these books, even by way of experiment; the cost is small, and the mere amusement will amply repay it. Let benevolent men every where come out from themselves, if I may so speak, and strive to turn the young every where from the ways of vice to the paths of virtue. If there be a duty which may, above all others, be characterised as God-like, it is surely this.

Morbid Activity of Destructiveness.—An interesting article on Insanity, by Dr. Milligen, is published in the last number of the (English) Polytechnic Journal, from which we make the following extracts:—

There cannot be the least doubt that many a murderer has forfeited hi life on a scaffold, when he should have been confined in a lunatic asylum For such is the character of this terrific form of insanity, that the culpri appears of sound mind on every other subject, without any other appre ciable disorder of mind or body.

A young German girl, in the family of Baron Humboldt, begged t speak to her mistress, when, falling upon her knees, she supplicated he to turn her out of the house, or otherwise she felt convinced that sh would tear her infant to pieces; she added, that it was the whiteness o the child's skin that inspired her with the horrible desire.

Marc relates the case of a young lady who, on the approach of thi dreadful propensity to shed blood, begged to have a strait-waistcoat pu on; and Mr. R——, a distinguished chemist, committed himself a pri soner in an asylum, to avoid the commission of some murder. He woul often prostrate himself at the foot of the altar, and implore the Divin assistance to resist this atrocious propensity. When he felt the desir for blood, he always requested the medical attendant to tie his hand together. This unhappy man at last endeavoured to kill one of hi friends, and died in a paroxysm of fury.

Dr. John Abernethy.—This celebrated physician, after a candid an thorough examination of the principles involved in phrenology, made thi public statement:—"I readily acknowledge my inability to offer an rational objection to Gall's and Spurzheim's system of phrenology, a affording a satisfactory explanation of the motives of human action."

Organ of Watchfulness.—In Vol. I, page 467, of this Journal, we pre sented an article containing remarks by Dr. Powell on this organ. W have since received two communications commenting on Dr. P.'s view and suggesting additional considerations. One writer (W. R.) attribute chiefly to Wonder, the functions which were ascribed by Dr. P. t Watchfulness; the other writer (O.) communicates some remarks favou ing the existence of a new organ as described by Dr. P., but regards hi views of its functions as incorrect in part, and offers sundry considera tions for calling it the "organ of Discovery." The reasoning in bot these communications is too speculative and hypothetical, and not suff ciently supported either by positive facts or extended observations; an we cannot conceive that the interests of the science will be promoted b their publication.

Presentation of a Vase to Mr. Combe.—The personal labours of M Combe in behalf of phrenology in this country have closed. The scienc is greatly indebted to the influence of his lectures and writings. W are highly gratified that some individuals in New York have united i procuring and presenting Mr. Combe with a beautiful silver vase, as testimonial of their respect. The New York Signal of March 27th give the following account of its presentation:—

The exquisite vase, subscribed for by the class in attendance on M Combe's phrenological lectures in this city, was presented to the distin guished writer and lecturer, on Monday evening, 23d March, at Howard' Hotel, in presence of the subscribers, by a committee consisting of th following gentlemen:—Mr. E. P. Hurlbut, Rev. T. J. Sawyer, D Foster, Dr. Boardman, Mr. S. W. Dewey, Mr. E. C. Benedict. And a this may be considered the termination of Mr. Combe's lectures in the United States, we present our readers with the following accurate report of the proceedings.

The chairman of the committee, Mr. Hurlbut, thus addressed Mr. Combe:

SIR,—The members of the class who attended your lectures, delivered in this city during the past year, have instructed us to present you with this vase, which, in their names, we now beg you to accept.

It bears upon one side three medallic likenesses, exquisitely wrought: one of Gall, to whose great discoveries in nature we are indebted for the true science of mind; one of Spurzheim, who first aided in illustrating and establishing it; and the other of yourself, their first and favourite British disciple.

This high and just association will ever endure. He who founded, and they who first illustrated and advanced, the true science of intellectual and moral philosophy, will descend the stream of time together, shedding lustre upon future ages, and living in the grateful memories of generations to come after us.

Upon this vase are also presented other medallic likenesses: one of Rush, whose far-seeing eye, penetrating the veil of nature, which Gall afterward lifted, had visions of some of the great truths which he demonstrated; and the other of Caldwell, who was the first among our countrymen to embrace and defend the doctrines of the great German, with a boldness and vigour peculiarly his own.

We feel a patriotic pride in associating the names of two of our own countrymen with the most distinguished names of Europe, connected with mental science.

You are soon to return to your native land—to your and our fathers' country.*

Your visit here has awakened the interest of thousands in your welfare —of thousands who are not wanting in gratitude for the instruction and delight which your discourses have afforded them—but who have had no opportunity to manifest, as we do on this most favoured occasion, their high appreciation of your character and attainments, and the enduring impression which your visit has made upon their minds. Their and our best wishes attend you.

Receive, then, this vase—(the subscription upon which is also graven upon our hearts)—and bear it to your home, a tribute to truth, and to the champion of truth; and rest assured, that in our estimation, we could be called to perform no prouder office, than to render a just tribute of respect and admiration to the author of "The Constitution of Man."

Mr. Combe received the vase, and spoke to the following effect:—

GENTLEMEN,—Although I cannot correctly say that I am unused to public speaking, yet, on occasions like the present, words fail me to express what I feel. I accept of your handsome and generous gift with the highest gratification. The classical elegance of form, the exquisite workmanship, and the appropriate devices which it bears, render it a gem of beauty. As a mere physical object, indeed, its merits in this respect have been appreciated in this city; it has gained the gold medal offered for the encouragement of art, and it will successfully sustain the strictest scrutiny of the distinguished artisans of the country to which I am about to carry it. But it is as a moral monument of your favourable estimation of my labours among you, and of the interest which you have taken in the science of mind, that it possesses to me an inestimable value. To Dr. Gall alone belongs the glory of having discovered the functions of the brain ; Dr. Spurzheim generously devoted his whole life to the extension, improvement, and diffusion of this splendid project of Gall's originality and genius ; and it is difficult to do justice to the noble sacrifice which he made to the cause of truth. When Dr. Spurzheim became the disciple of Gall, no human being defended phrenology except its author ; and he not only stood alone, but encountered the hostility of civilised Europe, from the emperor to the peasant, a few high minded individuals only excepted, who were silenced by the hand of power if they rose superior to the influence of scorn. It is no slender honour to me that you associate me with such men. Mine has been a flowery path compared with theirs. It is true that, when still a young man, without name, fortune, high associations, or any external advantages to sustain me against public disapprobation, I fearlessly risked every prospect which the future held forth to my ambition, and became the defender of phrenology when it had few other friends in the British Isles. Professional ruin was prophesied as the inevitable consequence of this, as it was then styled, rash and inconsiderate step. But for the encouragement of the young and ardent worshippers of truth, I am enabled to say that these auguries never were realised. Many were the shafts of ridicule that were hurled against me, and bitter the taunts poured forth by a hostile press ; but they never penetrated to my soul, disturbed my peace, nor impeded my prosperity. I mention this, not in the spirit of vain glory, but to confirm the young in the assurance, that the path of truth and independence may be safely trodden even against a world in arms, if courage and perseverance be added to prudence in the advance.

I have sojourned among you now for the greater part of two years, and I am about to leave your country. That I have experienced some inconvenience, and encountered several disagreeable incidents during my stay, is only what belongs to the lot of humanity ; but these sink into insignificance when contrasted with the generous cordiality and enlightened sympathy which have been showered upon me by yourselves and your fellow citizens. I have held converse with many enlightened minds in this country—minds that do honour to human nature ; whose philanthropy embraces not only patriotism, but an all-pervading interest in the advancement of the human race in knowledge, virtue, religion, and enjoyment in every clime. Many of these admirable men are deeply interested in phrenology. The gifted individual* to whom Massachusetts owes an eternal debt of gratitude for his invaluable efforts in improving her educational establishments, has assured me that the new philosophy is a light in his path to which he attaches the highest value. You, sir, have shown, in a late valuable work that has issued from your pen, that you are penetrated to the core with this last and best of human sciences ;† and many who now hear me, have expressed similar testimonials to its worth. I return, therefore, highly gratified with much that I have experienced among you, and I shall not need this emblem of your respect to maintain the recollection of such men as I have described, engraven on my affections forever. Allow me to add one brief expression of admiration and gratitude to a young countryman of my own, Mr. William Morrison, from Edinburgh, whose exquisite skill chased these admirable ornaments on your gift. Among his first efforts in art was a wax model, which he executed of my head in Edinburgh. Many years ago he came to this country, was highly esteemed as a man and an artist, and the

* Hon. Horace Mann.
† Mr. Combe here referred to a work recently published by Mr. Hurlbut, "Civil Office and Political Ethics."

embellishment of this vase was almost the last act of his life. Ten day
have scarcely elapsed since he was laid in a premature grave. It woul
have delighted me to have addressed to his living ear, the tribute whic
I now offer to his memory.

Again, gentlemen, I assure you of my heartfelt gratitude and lastin
respect, and with best wishes for your happiness and prosperity, bid yo
farewell.

The vase is of exquisite workmanship, being of Grecian model, wit
three medallic likenesses on one side—one of Gall, one of Spurzbein
and one of Combe, with the motto, " res non verba quæso;" and tw
medallic likenesses on the other—one of Dr. Benjamin Rush, and on
of Dr. Charles Caldwell, with the following inscription:—

Presented
to
George Combe, of Edinburgh,
by the class in attendance upon
his lectures delivered in the
City of New York,
in 1839, on the subject of
Phrenology;
In testimony of their profound respect for the
distinguished Lecturer, and of their
belief in, and admiration of,
the noble science
of which he is the ablest living
teacher and expounder.

Around the base of the vase are chased the heads of several animals
as emblematic of comparative phrenology.

———

Cast of Whitefield.—The character of this celebrated divine is wel
known. He died at Newburyport, Mass., and an accurate cast of his
head was taken at the time of his death. We find in a recent numbe
of Zion's Watchman, of New York, the following observations by Mr
L. N. Fowler, on the phrenological developements of Whitefield as indi
cated by this cast:—

Whitefield had a large, uneven head, and, apparently, an active mind
His character was marked. He was distinguished for originality of
thought, moral discernment, regard for principles, justice, and attach
ment to friends. He was ambitious, loved distinction; had great inde
pendence of feeling and moral courage, sympathy and interest in the
welfare of others.

He was energetic, forcible, and possessed of rather strong passions and
propensities; and had considerable tact and management.

His great fort lay in his persuasive powers, and his success in affect
ing the feelings, which was the result of predominant Language, Cau
sality, Ideality, Conscientiousness, Approbativeness, and Adhesiveness.

He should have been distinguished for his ability to make friends, and
to convert persons to his way of thinking. His strong religious feeling
were manifested through his Benevolence and Conscientiousness. Hi
enthusiasm was greater than his credulity, and his imagination stronge
than his devotional feelings. Veneration is rather weak; he had no
much regard for rank, title, honours, &c.; and even in his religious exer
cises, there could not have been that deep-toned piety, and holy *devotional* feeling, which characterised Payson, Brainard, and some others.

Valuable Testimony.—Dr. John Mackintosh, the author of two octavo volumes on the "Principles of Pathology and Practice of Medicine"—a work which has passed through several editions in Great Britain, as well as in our own country—pays, in Vol. II, page 79, the following just tribute to Drs. Gall and Spurzheim:—

The brain has been divided by those distinguished anatomists and physiologists, Gall and Spurzheim, into a number of organs which they conceive to be separate ganglions; and although I must confess that I have had neither time nor opportunity to examine their system with that care and attention which the importance of the subject demands, and which might enable me to give a decided opinion respecting the truth of all its parts, yet experience obliges me to state, that much of their doctrine appears to be true, and that science owes a great deal to the labours of the gentlemen who have been engaged in phrenological inquiry.

Some years after the above was written, and when Dr. Mackintosh had given phrenology a thorough investigation, we find the following sentiments expressed by him in relation to the science, in a letter addressed to Mr. Combe, at the time the latter stood as a candidate for the chair of logic in the University of Edinburgh. Says Dr. M.:—

The more closely I study nature, in health and disease, the more firm are my convictions of the soundness of phrenological doctrines. I regard phrenology as the true basis of the science of the mind, and as such am persuaded it will be found highly conducive to the successful teaching of logic. * * * I know no one who has devoted the energies of his mind to the careful study of phrenology, who has not become a convert, and I anticipate, at no very distant date, the triumph of truth over the prejudices which have been so assiduously heaped upon the science by crafty men, or those quite ignorant of the subject. * * * I may add, that a great revolution has taken place within these few years, not only in this country, but also on the continent, in favour of phrenological doctrines; the number of opponents has diminished, and the disciples have increased in a remarkable manner—in so much, that in Paris there is scarcely an illustrious name connected with medicine, or any of the sciences, that is not found enrolled in the list of members of the Phrenological Society.

—

Massachusetts State Lunatic Hospital.—We have just received the seventh report of this admirably managed institution, from its superintendent, Dr. S. B. Woodward. As it is our intention to give, in a future number of the Journal, a full account of this institution, and show the application of phrenological principles to the treatment of the insane, we can now make only one extract from this report. The intelligent reader, after perusing so lucid and correct an explanation of the nature of insanity, as is contained in this extract, will not be surprised at the remarkable success which has attended Dr. Woodward's labours. In this report, on page 65, Dr. W. remarks as follows:—"We must not for a moment overlook the fact, that insanity is a physical disease, that the mind, in the most deplorable case, is not obliterated; its integrity is only disturbed; it remains the same; its faculties ready, as soon as the physical structure shall have regained health and soundness, to resume operations, and exhibit the manifestations which legitimately belong to them. If the senses are deluded, false impressions are conveyed to the mind, but the senses are physical organs, and the mind is no more at fault if they lead it astray, than it is in believing the false representations of another individual; so of any other function of the brain; false perceptions, morbid activity, or depression of the animal propensities, or of the higher sentiments, depend upon physical influences wholly beyond the power of the individual to control; as soon, however, as the physical imperfection is removed, and a healthy condition of the brain restored reason again resumes its empire, and the integrity of the mind becomes apparent. It is only when the organic structure of the brain, and its appendages, have undergone such physical changes as to be permanent and enduring, that insanity is utterly hopeless. Death only can then cure insanity. The mind is still unharmed, and as soon as its connection with this diseased incumbrance shall be dissolved, who can doubt that the author of its being will furnish it an immortal medium of action in another state of existence, fitted for the sphere of its future enjoyments? The diseased brain in insanity, the worn-out brain of the aged, and the imperfect brain of the idiot, are the only reasons why the mind is not as active and intelligent in these individuals as in the rest of mankind; in another state of existence all will be changed, 'this corruptible will put on incorruption, and this mortal, immortality.' "

And on page 100, Dr. Woodward, in alluding to the introduction and influence of religious exercises on the insane, speaks thus :—" As I have elsewhere remarked, his whole mind is not always insane; there are cords in his intellect and moral feelings which can be made to vibrate by proper touches, and the response may change his whole character and influence his whole conduct. His moral feelings may be sound and healthy, if his intellect is disturbed by allusions, or his understanding may, to a great extent, be rational, when his feelings are perverted and his moral nature estranged. It is by appeals to the understanding, and the sensibilities through the healthy avenues, that the mind is reached by the moral influence which we exert, and this is also the avenue for religious influence."

——

Address delivered before the Albany Phrenological Society, at its meeting in the Female Academy, on the evening of April 2, 1840. By THOMAS W. OLCOTT, *President of the Society.*

We are indebted to Mr. E. N. Horsford for a copy of this very appropriate and well-written address. In speaking of the progress of the science, Mr. Olcott remarks as follows :—

Phrenology, or the physiology of the brain, considered in connection with its mental manifestations, may be said to have passed in triumph the days of its severest trial, and fiercest opposition. Many of the most distinguished medical men and journals give it a cordial support. It is acknowledged and adopted as a science in the London Hospital, the London Institution, Granger's Theatre of Anatomy and Medicine, and its principles are taught in the London University as applicable to the treatment of insanity, and are advocated by the Medical and Surgical Journal of London. The Medico-Chirurgical Review of the same city speaks of the science "as the most intelligent and self-consistent system of mental philosophy ever presented to the contemplation of inquisitive men, and commends its utility especially in reference to purposes of education, legislation, political economy, criminal jurisprudence, history legal and theological elocution, and above all, to the true philosophy of medicine."

And again: Mr. O., after remarking that, if a single organ of the brain is correctly designated as the seat or instrument of a particular faculty then is phrenology clearly and firmly established, proceeds thus :—

I knew a boy who was born with St. Vitus' Dance, in the poor-house at Hudson, and who could neither read nor write, but who discovered, at an early age, arithmetical powers nearly equal to those of Colburn. Mozart began to compose at the age of four years; Handel, at even an earlier period of life; and several of the most eminent poets, painters, and philosophers of former days, evinced precocious genius in some particular department. Phrenology offers a ready explanation of these phenomena, as also of partial insanity or monomania.

"The Lord God formed man of the dust of the ground, and breathed into his nostrils the breath of life; and man became a living soul, created in the image of God." It is the mysterious operations of the machinery of this wonderfully formed being, that phrenology would study and unfold—a being created but a little lower than the angels, and reflecting in the grandeur of moral excellence, the likeness and glory of the Creator —a being deriving life, and soul, and mind, from the immediate emanation of the Divine perfections. Such was man as originally created, and fitting was Eden as the place of his abode. But from the fall of Adam sin became a constituent element of man's nature, and defaced the heavenly impress of moral rectitude and beauty. Man, to be happy must be virtuous, and doubtless even in this life our enjoyment keeps pace with our advance in holiness. Hence "the proper study of mankind is man," in order that we may know ourselves, and become acquainted with the force and bias of the various springs of human action. Either from its peculiar adaptation, or from adventitious circumstances, phrenology appears to be identified with the cause of education, and it certainly furnishes a convenient nomenclature for the study and illustration of the functions and operations of the mind.

—

Phrenological Association.—There has existed for some years past in Great Britain, what is called the "British Association for the Advancement of Science," being composed of the most scientific men from England, Scotland, and Ireland. Among these are quite a number of phrenologists, who last August united and formed themselves into a society, to be called "The Phrenological Association," which should meet annually at the same time and place of the British Association. The objects of this association, as stated in the January number of the English Phrenological Journal, are these:—"1, The advancement of phrenological science; 2, The diffusion of an accurate knowledge of that science; 3, The elevation of phrenology to that degree of consideration and dignity before the public mind, to which it is entitled as a branch of philosophy; 4, To promote intercourse amongst phrenologists of this and other countries. The ultimate objects of the association to be effected by thus promoting a knowledge of man's mental constitution, is the improvement of the human race in intelligence, morality, and consequent happiness."

—

London Phrenological Journal.—We are requested to mention that this journal is published on the first of January, April, July, and October, regularly, by Messrs. Simpkin, Marshall, & Co., of that city, price in London 2s. 6d. per copy for each number, or $2.50 per annum. Messrs. Wiley & Putnam, booksellers, Broadway, New York, have agreed to act as agents for the work in this country, to the effect of procuring, through their house in London, copies for American subscribers who place the requisite funds in their hands in advance; but they do not receive or execute orders on any other terms.

THE

AMERICAN PHRENOLOGICAL JOURNAL

AND

MISCELLANY.

| Vol. II. | Philadelphia, June 1, 1840. | No. 9. |

ARTICLE I.

REVIEW OF MORTON'S CRANIA AMERICANA.[*]

We hail this work as the most extensive and valuable contribution to the natural history of man, which has yet appeared on the American continent, and anticipate for it a cordial reception by scientific men not only in the United States, but in Europe. The subject is one of great interest, and Dr. Morton has treated it in a manner at once scientific and pleasing, while the beauty and accuracy of his lithographic plates are not surpassed by any of the modern illustrations of science.

The principal design of the work, says Dr. Morton, has been " to give accurate delineations of the crania of more than forty Indian nations, Peruvian, Brazilian, and Mexican, together with a particularly extended series from North America, from the Pacific Ocean to the Atlantic, and from Florida to the region of the Polar tribes Especial attention has also been given to the singular distortions of the skull caused by mechanical contrivances in use among various nations, Peruvians, Charibs, Natches, and the tribes inhabiting the Oregon Territory." His materials, in this department, are so ample that he has been enabled to give a full exposition of the subject. He has also bestowed particular attention on the crania from the mounds of this country, which have been compared with similar relics derived both from ancient and modern tribes, " in order to examine by the evidence of osteological facts, whether the American aborigines, of all epochs, have belonged to one race, or to a plurality of races."

The introductory Essay, " on the varieties of the human species,"

[*] From the American Journal of Science and Arts, No. 2, Vol. 38. Edited by Benjamin Silliman, M. D., LL. D.

occupies ninety-five pages.   It is learned, lucid, and, like the whole work, classically written.   The author notices the great diversity of opinions that have existed among naturalists regarding the grouping of mankind into races ; Linnæus referred all the human family to five races ; Buffon proposed six great divisions ; subsequently, however, he reduced it to five ; while Blumenbach, adopting the arrangement of Buffon, has changed the names of some of the divisions, and designated, with greater accuracy, their geographical distribution.   Cuvier admitted three races only, the Caucasian, Mongolian, and Ethiopian ; while Malté Brun enumerates sixteen.   A French professor, Broc, in his Essai sur les Races Humaines, published in 1836, has attempted to establish several *sub-genera*.   The cause of these wide diversities of opinion obviously lies in the imperfect knowledge yet possessed of the subject.

Dr. Morton adopts the arrangement of Blumenbach in so far as regards the great divisions, substituting, however, the word *race* for the term "variety" of the German author, and changing the order in which Blumenbach considers some of them.   He considers the human species as consisting of *twenty-two* families, which he arranges under the heads of the Caucasian, Mongolian, Malay, American, and Ethiopian races.

I. "The CAUCASIAN RACE is characterised by a naturally fair skin, susceptible of every tint; hair fine, long, and curling, and of various colours. The skull is large and oval, and its anterior portion full and elevated. The face is small in proportion to the head, of an oval form, with well-proportioned features.   The nasal bones are arched, the chin full, and the teeth vertical.   The race is distinguished for the facility with which it attains the highest intellectual endowments."

The subdivisions of this race are into—1st, The *Caucasian ;* 2d, The *Germanic ;* 3d, The *Celtic ;* 4th, The *Arabian ;* 5th, The *Lybian ;* 6th, The *Nilotic*, (Egyptian) ; and 7th, The *Indostanic* families.

II. "The MONGOLIAN RACE.—This is characterised by a sallow or olive coloured skin, which appears to be drawn tight over the bones of the face ; long, black, straight hair, and thin beard.   The nose is broad and short; the eyes are small, black, and obliquely placed, and the eye-brows arched and linear; the lips are turned, the cheek bones broad and flat, and the zygomatic arches salient.   The skull is oblong-oval, somewhat flattened at the sides, with a low forehead.   In their intellectual character the Mongolians are ingenious, imitative, and highly susceptible of cultivation."

The subordinate divisions are into—8th, The *Mongol-Tartar ;* 9th, The *Turkish ;* 10th, The *Chinese ;* 11th, The *Indo-Chinese ;* 12th, The *Polar* families.

III. "The MALAY RACE.—It is characterised by a dark complexion, varying from a tawny hue to a very dark brown. Their hair is black, coarse and lank, and their eye-lids are drawn obliquely upwards at the outer angles. The mouth and lips are large, and the nose is short and broad, and apparently broken at its root. The face is flat and expanded, the upper jaw projecting, and the teeth salient. The skull is high and squared or rounded, and the forehead low and broad. This race is active and ingenious, and possesses all the habits of a migratory, predaceous, and maritime people."

The subdivisions embrace—13th, The *Malay;* and 14th, The *Polynesian* (or South Sea Island) families.

IV. "The AMERICAN RACE is marked by a brown complexion, long, black, lank hair, and deficient beard. The eyes are black and deep set, the brow low, the cheek bones high, the nose large and aquiline, the mouth large, and the lips tumid and compressed. The skull is small, wide between the parietal protuberances, prominent at the vertex, and flat on the occiput. In their mental character, the Americans are averse to cultivation, and slow in acquiring knowledge; restless, revengeful, and fond of war, and wholly destitute of maritime adventure."

The families into which this race is subdivided are two—15th, The *American;* and 16th, The *Toltecan.*

V. "The ETHIOPIAN RACE is characterised by a black complexion, and black, woolly hair; the eyes are large and prominent, the nose broad and flat, lips thick, and the mouth wide; the head long and narrow, the forehead low, the cheek bones prominent, the jaws projecting, and the chin small. In disposition, the negro is joyous, flexible, and indolent; while the many nations which compose this race present a singular diversity of intellectual character, of which the far-extreme is the lowest grade of humanity."

This race is divided into—17th, The *Negro;* 18th, The *Caffrarian;* 19th, The *Hottentot;* 20th, The *Oceanic Negro;* 21st, The *Australian;* and 22d, The *Alforian* families. The latter family is most numerous in New Guinea, the Moluccas, and Magindano.

The map which precedes the work, shows the geographical distribution of the five races of men; and the lines of demarcation are those indicated by Professor Blumenbach, as separating the different races in the primitive epochs of the world. These divisions, of necessity, are only approximations to truth. The *boundary* between the *Caucasian* and *Mongolian* races is extremely vague. The line adopted runs from the Ganges in a northwestern direction to the Caspian Sea, and thence to the river Obi, in Russia. "At a comparatively recent period, however, several Mongolian nations have established themselves in Europe; as the Samoyedes, Laplanders, &c." The *Ethiopian line* is drawn north of the Senegal river, obliquely east and south to the southern frontier of Abyssinia, and thence to Cape

Guardafui, thus embracing the Atlas Mountains. "Of the latter, little is known ; but many negro nations inhabit to the north of them, at the same time that the Arab tribes have penetrated far beyond them to the south, and in some places have formed a mixed race with the natives."

Dr. Morton gives a brief but clear description, extending to his 91st page, of the leading characteristics of each of these families, accompanying his text by references to the authorities from which the information is drawn. The labour and accuracy of the true philosopher are here conspicuous. After perusing these details, however, we are strongly impressed with the conviction that this branch of science is still only in its infancy. The descriptions of the mental qualities which distinguish the different families of mankind, given even by the best travellers, are vague and entirely popular. There is scarcely an instance of the specification of well-defined mental faculties, present or absent in the races, or possessed in peculiar combinations ; nothing, in short, which indicates that the travellers possessed a mental philosophy under the different heads of which they could classify and particularise the characteristic qualities of mind which they observed, as the botanists describe and classify plants, or the geologists minerals. The anatomical characters of the races, also, are still confined to a few particulars, and many even of these have been drawn from the inspection of a very limited number of specimens. The subject, however, possesses so much inherent interest and importance, that we may expect rapid advances to be made in its future developement.

The unity of the human species is assumed by Dr. Morton. It is known that the *black* race possess an apparatus in the skin, which is wanting in that of the *white* race. Flourens states that there "are, in the skin of the *white* race, three distinct laminæ or membranes—the *derm*, and two *epiderms ;* and in the skin of the *black* race, there is, besides the *derm* and the two epiderms of the *white* race, a particular apparatus, an apparatus which is altogether wanting in the man of the *white* race, an apparatus composed of two layers, the external of which is the seat of the *pigmentum*, or colouring matter of negroes."*
"The colouring apparatus of the negro is always found in the mulatto." Flourens adds, "The *white* race and the *black* race, are then, I repeat, two essentially distinct races. The same is true of the *red*, or American race. Anatomy discovers, under the second epiderm of the individual of the *red, copper-coloured, Indian*, or *American* race, (for this race is called indifferently by all these

* Annales des Sciences Nat. t. x, Dec. 1838, pp. 361, &c.

names,) a *pigmental apparatus*, which is the seat of the *red* or *copper colour* of this race, as the *pigmental apparatus* of the negro is the seat of his black colour."

Dr. Morton does not advert to the existence of this pigmental apparatus in the American race. The investigations of Dr. M'Culloh, he observes, "satisfactorily prove that the designation '*copper-coloured,*' is wholly inapplicable to the Americans as a race." "The *cinnamon* is, in Dr. M'Culloh's apprehension, the nearest approach to the true colour" of the native Americans. Dr. Morton considers that the "*brown race*" most correctly designates them collectively. "Although," says he, "the Americans thus possess a pervading and characteristic complexion, there are occasional and very remarkable deviations, including all the tints from a decided white to an unequivocally black skin." He shows, also, by numerous authorities, that "climate exerts a subordinate agency in producing these diversified hues." The tribes which wander along the burning plains of the equinoctial region, have no darker skins than the mountaineers of the temperate zone. "Again, the Puelchés, and other inhabitants of the Magellanic region, beyond the 55th degree of south latitude, are absolutely darker than the Abipones, Macobios, and Tobas, who are many degrees nearer the equator. While the Botocudys are of a clear brown colour, and sometimes nearly white, at no great distance from the tropic; and moreover, while the Guyacas, under the line, are characterised by a fair complexion, the Charruas, who are almost black, inhabit the 50th degree of south latitude; and the yet blacker Californians are 25 degrees north of the equator." "After all," he adds, "these differences in complexion are extremely partial, forming mere exceptions to the primitive and national tint that characterises these people, from Cape Horn to the Canadas. The cause of these anomalies is not readily explained; that it is not climate, is sufficiently obvious; and whether it arises from partial immigrations from other countries, remains yet to be decided."

Buffon defines species—"A succession of similar individuals which reproduce each other." Cuvier also defines species—"The union of individuals descended from each other, or from common parents, and of those who resemble them as much as they resemble each other." "The apparent differences of the races of our domestic species," says Cuvier, "are stronger than those of any species of the same genus." "The fact of the *succession*, therefore, and of the *constant succession*, constitutes alone *the unity of the species*." Flourens, who cites these definitions, concludes that "*unity, absolute unity*, of the human species, and *variety* of its races, as a final result, is the general and certain conclusion of all the facts acquired concerning the *natural history of man*."*

Dr. Morton, while he assumes the unity of the species, conceives that "each race was adapted from the beginning (by an all-wise Providence) to its peculiar local destination. In other words, that the physical characteristics which distinguish the different races, are independent of external causes."

This inference derives support from the fact adverted to by Dr. Caldwell, in his "Thoughts on the Unity of the Human Species." "It is," says he, "4179 years since Noah and his family came out of the ark. They are believed to have been of the Caucasian race." "3445 years ago, a nation of Ethiopians is known to have existed. Their skins, of course, were dark, and they differed widely from the Caucasians in many other particulars. They migrated from a remote country, and took up their residence in the neighbourhood of Egypt. Supposing that people to have been of the stock of Noah, the change must have been completed, and a new race formed, in 733 years, and probably in a much shorter period."† Dr. Morton observes, that "the recent discoveries in Egypt give additional force to the preceding statement, inasmuch as they show, beyond all question, that the Caucasian and Negro races were as perfectly distinct in that country, upwards of three thousand years ago, as they are now; whence it is evident, that if the Caucasian was derived from the Negro, or the Negro from the Caucasian, *by the action of external causes*, the change must have been effected in, at most, one thousand years; a theory which the subsequent evidence of thirty centuries proves to be a physical impossibility; and we have already ventured to insist that such a commutation could be effected by nothing short of a miracle."—p. 88.

Dr. Morton describes the general characteristics of the American under the head of the "Varieties of the Human Species," and then enters on a special description of the "crania" of upwards of seventy nations or tribes belonging to that family, illustrating the text by admirable plates of the crania, drawn from skulls, mostly in his own possession, and of the full size of nature.

He regards the American race as possessing certain physical traits that serve to identify them in localities the most remote from each other. There are, also, in their multitudinous languages, the traces

* Flourens' article before cited, and the Edin. New Philosophic. Journ., Vol. xxvii, p. 358, October, 1839.

† Page 72. Philadelphia, 1830.

of a common origin. He divides the race into the "Toltecan family,' which bears evidence of centuries of demi-civilisation, and into th "American family," which embraces all the barbarous nations of th new world, excepting the Polar tribes, or Mongol Americans. Th Esquimaux, and especially the Greenlanders, are regarded as a pai tially mixed race, among whom the physical character of the Mon golian predominates, while their language presents obvious analogie to that of the Chippewyans, who border on them to the south.

In the American family itself, there are several subordinate groups 1st, The *Appalachian* branch includes all the nations of Nortl America, excepting the Mexicans, together with the tribes north o: the river Amazon and east of the Andes. 2d, The *Brazilian* brancl is spread over a great part of South America, east of the Andes, viz between the rivers Amazon and La Plata, and between the Andes an the Atlantic, thus including the whole of Brazil and Paraguay, nortl of the 35th degree of south latitude. In character, these nations ar warlike, cruel, and unforgiving. They turn with aversion from th restraints of civilised life, and have made but trifling progress ii mental culture, or the useful arts. In character, the Brazilian nation scarcely differ from the Appalachian; none of the American tribes ar less susceptible of cultivation than these; and what they are taught b compulsion, in the missions, seldom exceeds the humblest elements of knowledge. 3d, The *Patagonian* branch includes the nations soutl of the La Plata, to the Straits of Magellan, and the mountain tribe: of Chili. They are for the most part distinguished for their tal stature, their fine forms, and their indomitable courage, of all whicl traits the Auracanians possess a conspicuous share. 4th, The *Fue gian* branch, which roves over a sterile waste, computed to be a large as one half of Ireland. Forster computes their whole numbe. at only two thousand souls. Their physical aspect is altogethe repulsive, and their domestic usages tend to heighten the defects o: nature. The expression of the face is vacant, and their mental opera tions are to the last degree slow and stupid. The difference betweei them and the other Americans, is attributed by Dr. Morton to th effects of climate and locality.

Thus far Dr. Morton has travelled over ground previously occupiec by other naturalists; but we proceed to a field in which he has hac the courage and sagacity to enter boldly on a new path. He ha added to his text numerous and minute measurements of the size an capacity not only of each entire cranium, but of its different parts with a view to elucidate the connection (if there be any) betweei particular regions of the brain and particular mental qualities of th American tribes. In his dedication to John S. Phillips, Esq., o:

Philadelphia,* he observes: "It may, perhaps, be thought by some readers, that these details are unnecessarily minute, especially in the phrenological tables; and again, others would have preferred a work conducted throughout on phrenological principles. In this study, I am yet a learner; and it appeared to me the wiser plan to present the facts unbiased by theory, and let the reader draw his own conclusions. You and I have long admitted the fundamental principles of phrenology, viz. that the brain is the organ of the mind, and that its different parts perform different functions; but we have been slow to acknowledge the details of cranioscopy as taught by Dr. Gall, and supported and extended by subsequent observers. We have not, however, neglected this branch of inquiry, but have endeavoured to examine it in connection with numerous facts, which can only be fully appreciated when they come to be compared with similar measurements derived from the other races of men." We shall state, in a subsequent part of this article, the conclusions at which Dr. Morton has arrived, in consequence of his observations and measurements; meantime it is important to state the principles on which he proceeded.

In a few years, it will appear a singular fact in the history of mind, that in the nineteenth century, men holding the eminent station in literature occupied by Lord Jeffrey and Lord Brougham, should have seriously denied† that the mind, in this world, acts by means of material organs; yet such is the case; and the denial can be accounted for only by that entire neglect of physiology, as a branch of general education, which prevailed in the last century, and by the fact that the metaphysical philosophy in which they were instructed, bore no reference to the functions of the brain. We need not say, that no adequately instructed naturalist doubts that the brain is the organ of the mind. But there are two questions, on which great difference of opinion continues to prevail: 1st, Whether the *size* of the brain (health, age, and constitution being equal) has any, and if so, what influence, on the power of mental manifestations? and 2dly, Whether different faculties be, or be not, manifested by particular portions of the brain?

The *first* proposition, that the size of the brain, other conditions being equal, is in direct relation to the power of mental manifestation, is supported by analogy, by several well known facts, and by high

* Dr. Morton acknowledges himself to be under many obligations to Mr. Phillips in the prosecution of his inquiries, and says that it was he who invented the machines in making the measurements, and executed many of them himself.

† Lord Jeffrey, in the Edin. Review, No. 88, and Lord Brougham, in his Discourse on Natural Theology, p. 120.

physiological authorities.   The power of smell, for example, is grea
in proportion to the expansion of the olfactory nerve on the interna
nostrils, and the volume of the nerve itself bears a direct relation t
the degree of that expansion.   The superficial surface of the mucou
membrane of the ethmoidal bone, on which the nerve of smell i
ramified, is computed in man to extend to twenty square inches ; an
in the seal, which has great power of smell, to one hundred an
twenty square inches.   The optic nerve in the mole is a slende
thread, and its vision is feeble ; the same nerve is large and thick i
the eagle, accompanied by intense powers of sight.   Again, the fac
admits of demonstration, that deficiency in the size of the brain i
one, although not the only, cause of idiotcy.   Although the brain b
healthy, if the horizontal circumference of the head, with the muscula
integuments, do not exceed thirteen or fourteen inches, idiotcy is th
invariable consequence.   Dr. Voisin states that he made observation
on the idiots under his care at the Parisian Hospital of Incurables, an
found that in the lowest class of idiots, where the intellectual mani
festations were null, the horizontal circumference, taken a little highe
than the orbit, varied from eleven to thirteen inches, while the distanc
from the root of the nose backwards, over the top of the head, to th
occipital spine, was only between eight and nine inches ; and h
found no exception to this fact.   If, therefore, extreme defect of siz
of the brain be invariably accompanied by mental imbecility, it is
legitimate inference that size will influence the power of manifestatio
through all other gradations of magnitude, always assuming othe
conditions to be equal.

Physiological authorities are equally explicit on this subject.   Ma
gendie says, " The volume of the brain is generally in direct propoi
tion to the capacity of the mind.   We ought not to suppose, howevei
that every man having a large head is necessarily a person of superio
intelligence ; for there are many causes of an augmentation of th
volume of the head besides the size of the brain ; but it is rarel
found that a man distinguished by his mental faculties has not a larg
head.   The only way of estimating the volume of the brain, in
living person, is to measure the dimensions of the skull ; every othe
means, even that proposed by Camper, is uncertain."

The difference of mental power between young and adult minds, i
a matter of common observation.   The difference in the weights c
their brains is equally decided.

According to Cruveilhier, in three young subjects, the weights c
the brains were as follows :—

In the first, the brain weighed 2 lbs. 2 oz. ; the cerebellum, 4¼ oz.
together, 2 lbs. 6¼ oz.   In the second, the brain weighed 2 lbs. 8 oz

the cerebellum, 3¼ oz.; together, 2 lbs. 11¼ oz. In the third, the
brain weighed 2 lbs. 5 oz.; the cerebellum, 5 oz.; together, 2 lbs.
10 oz.

In the Appendix to Dr. Monro's work on the brain, Sir William
Hamilton states the average weight of the *adult* male Scotish brain
and cerebellum to be 3 lbs. 8 oz. troy.

Again : a difference in mental power between men and women, is
also generally admitted to exist, and there is a corresponding difference in the size of their brains.

Sir William Hamilton states the average weight of the adult female
Scotish brain and cerebellum, to be 3 lbs. 4 oz. troy ; being 4 oz. less
than that of the male.   He found one male brain in *seven* to weigh
above 4 lbs.; and only one female brain in a *hundred* exceeding this
weight.

In an essay on the brain of the negro, compared with that of the
European and the ourang-outang, published in the Philosophical
Transactions for 1836, part II, Professor Tiedemann, of Heidelberg,
adopts the same principle.   After mentioning the weights of fifty-two
European brains, examined by himself, he states that "the weight of
the brain in an adult male European, varies between 3 lbs. 2 oz. and
4 lbs. 6 oz. troy.   The brain of men who have distinguished themselves by their great talents, is often very large.   The brain of the
celebrated Cuvier weighed 4 lbs. 11 oz. 4 dr. 30 gr. troy, and that of
the distinguished surgeon Dupuytren weighed 4 lbs. 10 oz. troy.
The brain of men endowed with but feeble intellectual powers is, on
the contrary, often very small, particularly in congenital idiotismus.
The female brain is lighter than that of the male.   It varies between
2 lbs. 8 oz. and 3 lbs. 11 oz.   I never found a female brain that
weighed 4 lbs.   The female brain weighs on an average from four to
eight ounces less than that of the male ; and this difference is already
perceptible in a new-born child."

We have adduced these proofs and authorities in support of the
proposition that size influences power, because we conceive it to be a
principle of fundamental importance in every investigation into the
natural history of man, founded on the physiology of the brain ; and
also because in the hasty zeal of many of the opponents of phrenology,
to undermine the discoveries of Dr. Gall, it has been denied with a
boldness and pertinacity more allied to the spirit of contentious dispu-
ation, than to that of philosophical inquiry.   Its importance in a disser-
ation on *national crania* is very apparent.   One of the most singular
features in the history of this continent, is, that the aboriginal races,
with few exceptions, have perished, or constantly receded, before the
Anglo-Saxon race, and have in no instance either mingled with them

as equals, or adopted their manners and civilisation.   These phen«
mena must have a cause ; and can any inquiry be at once more int«
resting and philosophical than that which endeavours to ascertai
whether that cause be connected with a difference in the brai
between the native race and their conquering invaders?   Farthe
some few of the American families, the Auracanian, for instanc«
have successfully resisted the Europeans ; and the question is impor
ant, whether in them the brain be in any respect superior to what
is in the tribes which have unsuccessfully resisted ?

It is true, that Dr. Gall's fundamental principle, the size in the brai
(other conditions being equal) is a measure of the power of mentu
manifestation, is directly involved in these inquiries ; but we can di«
cover no reason why it should not be put to the test of an extensiv
and accurate induction of facts.   The unphilosophical prejudice tha
every proposition and fact in physiology must be neglected or oppose«
because it bears on the vexed question of phrenology, has been to
long indulged.   The best interests of science require that it should b
laid aside, and we commend Dr. Morton, for having resolutely di«
carded it.   He does not enter the field as a partisan, for ot agains
Dr. Gall's doctrines, but as a philosophical inquirer, and states car
didly and fearlessly the results of his observations.

Dr. Morton reports the size in cubic inches of the interior of nearl;
every skull described by him.   " An ingenious mode," says he, " o
taking the measurement of the internal capacity, was devised by Mı
Phillips.   In order to measure the capacity of a cranium, the foramin
were first stopped with cotton, and the cavity was then filled wit'
white pepper seed,* poured into the foramen magnum until it reache
the surface, and pressed down with the finger until the skull woul
receive no more.   The contents were then transferred to a tin cylindeı
which was well shaken in order to pack the seed.   A mahogany ro
(previously graduated to denote the cubic inches and parts containe
in the cylinder) being then dropped down, with its foot resting on th
seed, the capacity of the cranium, in cubic inches, is at once read of
on it."

Dr. Morton gives also measurements of particular regions of th
`brain, as indicated by the skull ; and in this portion of his work, th
phrenologists alone can claim precedence of him.

Secondly, The most distinguished philosophers on the mind, divid«
the human faculties into the active and intellectual powers ; and som«

---

* " White pepper seed was selected on account of its spherical form, its hard
ness, and the equal size of the grains.   It was also sifted, to render the equalit;
still greater."

admit even subdivisions of the feelings into propensities common to man with the lower animals, and moral emotions; and of the intellect, into observing and reflecting faculties. Dr. Thomas Brown's division of the intellectual powers into simple and relative suggestion, corresponds with this last classification. If, then, the mind manifest a plurality of faculties, and if the brain be the organ of the mind, it appears to be a sound inference that the brain *may* consist of a plurality of organs. The presumptions which arise, in favour of this idea, from the constitution of the external senses and their organs, are strong. Each sense has its separate nervous apparatus. Nay, when the function of a part is compound, the nerves are multiplied, so as to give a distinct nerve for each function. The tongue has a nerve for voluntary motion, another for common sensation, and the best authorities admit a third nerve for *taste*, although the precise nerve is still in dispute. The internal nostrils are supplied with two nerves, the olfactory, and a nerve of common sensation, ramified on the mucous membrane, each performing its appropriate function. The spinal marrow consists, by general consent of physiologists, of at least two double columns, the anterior pair for voluntary motion, and the posterior pair for common sensation. Sir Charles Bell has demonstrated the distinct functions of the nerves proceeding from these columns. Farther, every accurate observer distinguishes diversities of disposition and inequalities of talents, even in the same individual. The records of lunatic asylums show numerous instances of partial idiotcy and partial insanity. These facts indicate that the brain consists of a plurality of organs, and this idea is countenanced by many high authorities in physiological science. " The brain is a very complicated organ," says Bonnet, " or rather *an assemblage of very different organs*."* Tissot contends that every perception has different fibres ;† and Haller and Van Swieten were of opinion that the internal senses occupy, in the brain, organs as distinct as the nerves of the external senses.‡ Cabanis entertained a similar notion,§ and so did Prochaska. Cuvier says that " *Certain parts* of the brain, in all classes of animals, are *large or small, according to certain qualities of the animals ;*"‖ and he admits that Gall's doctrine of different faculties being connected with different parts of the brain, is no wise contradictory to the general principle of physiology.¶

* Palingénésie, I, 334.   † Œuvres, III, 33.   ‡ Van Swieten, I, 454.
§ Rapports du Physique et du Moral de l'Homme, 2de Edit. I, 233, 4.
‖ Anatomie Comparée, tome II.
¶ Rapport Historique sur les Progrès des Sciences Naturelles, &c. p. 193.

(To be continued.)

ARTICLE II.

An Inquiry concerning the Diseases and Functions of the Brain, the Spinal Cord, and the Nerves. By AMARIAH BRIGHAM, M. D. Published by George Adlard, No. 168 Broadway, New York. 12mo. pp. 337.

The above title is peculiarly calculated to attract the attention of the phrenologist. Whatever is published relating to the structure, organisation, and functions of the brain, however uninteresting to others, cannot fail to excite *his* interest. But we must confess our disappointment, in turning from the title of the work before us to an examination of its contents, to find only three pages (!) devoted to the subject of phrenology. It is unnecessary here to vindicate the merits of its advocates, either by pointing out the particular discoveries which they have made in this department of science, or by showing that we are indebted to their labours for some of the most important and valuable knowledge which we possess of the nervous system. It would seem hardly possible for an individual, acquainted with the history and progress of phrenological discoveries, to write a work of more than three hundred pages on the " Diseases and *Functions* of the Brain," without devoting more than *three* pages to the consideration of phrenology in its bearings on this subject, and we must think that Dr. Brigham, as he himself has frankly acknowledged, has had neither opportunity nor leisure to examine this science thoroughly and do it justice. He shall have, however, full credit for what he has said respecting its merits.

The work is designed more especially for members of the medical profession, though it is by no means devoid of interest to the general reader. The author opens the work with some general remarks on the importance of understanding the structure and functions of the brain, after which he proceeds to examine the various methods which have been employed for determining its functions. The several methods mentioned by Dr. Brigham, such as chemical analysis, dissection, experiments on living animals, comparative anatomy, &c. have each, in themselves, proved entirely ineffectual. He has devoted the chief space of his work, under this head, to pathological observations. Dr. B. has here collected and detailed, at some length, many interesting facts, which afford the strongest possible evidence that the brain is composed of a congeries of organs, and moreover, that the external parts of this viscus perform the functions of mental manifestations, while the more interior parts are intimately connected with the

muscular system, and the powers of locomotion. The last method
noticed by Dr. B. for determining the functions of the brain, is that
of "external examination of the cranium, or phrenology;" and here
we present the reader with his three pages on this subject, which were
alluded to above.   We should not omit to state, that honourable mention is made throughout Dr. B.'s work of the labours of Drs. Gall and
Spurzheim, as anatomists and physiologists.

  Dr. Gall should be considered the first who directed attention to this
method of studying the functions of the brain.   Many, I am aware, have
condemned and ridiculed this method, but it appears to me eminently
deserving of attention.   One of the most distinguished of modern philosophers and metaphysicians observes. "There seems to be but little
doubt that *general* inferences concerning the intellectual capacity may
be drawn with some confidence from the form and the size of the skull,
and it has been imagined by some, that corresponding to the varieties
of intellectual and moral character, there are certain inequalities or prominences on the surface of the skull; *and it certainly is a legitimate
object of experimental inquiry to ascertain how far this opinion is
agreeable to fact.*"*   With such high authority in favour of thus investigating the functions of the brain, surely we should not deem this
method unworthy of our notice.   For my own part, I see nothing unreasonable or unphilosophical in it, but can say in the language of one of
the most celebrated modern anatomists, that " the whole subject of
phrenology appears to me of far too much importance to be discussed
without the most rigid and impartial examination of the immense body
of facts adduced in support of it; and this I have not hitherto had leisure
to undertake.   I shall therefore only say that, so far as I am acquainted
with the subject, I do not see it as otherwise than rational and perfectly
consistent with all that is known of the functions of the nervous system."†
  It appears to me that Dr. Gall proceeded in a philosophical and cautious
manner in forming his system, and that he is entitled to the praise of
fairness and candour, as well as that of unsurpassed industry.   He
acknowledges the difficulties of the subject, and declares that, " to speak
correctly of organology and cranioscopy, it is necessary to acquire a
knowledge of it by a long and practical study."   He fully notices the
objections brought against his system, indeed, he was the first to state
these objections, and that in certain cases the external table of the cranium is not parallel to the inner one, that sometimes the crania of men
of very limited capacity are exceedingly thick, even when this condition
is not the result of advanced age or mental disease, both of which produce variations in the thickness of the cranium, and he declares that it
is impossible to determine with exactness the developements of certain
convolutions by the inspection of the external surface of the cranium.
Besides, Dr. Gall never pretended that he was able to determine the
character of men in general by the external examination of the head.
'I have never pretended," says he, "to distinguish the influence which
modifications of the forms of the cranium slightly marked, may have on
the character, or how its corresponding shades may be traced.   My first
observations have only been made upon persons who were distinguished
from other men by some eminent quality or faculty.   I easily perceived

  * Dugald Stewart on Natural Language
  † Solly on the Human Brain, p. 471.

that it was only in such individuals that I could find striking difference of the head, and that I could distinguish well-marked protuberances." Since the announcement of Dr. Gall's opinions, there have been man discoveries in physiology, and numerous pathological researches bearin upon the functions of the nervous system. These have not shaken th system of Gall, but, on the whole, have strengthened it. In fact, I ar confident that opinions respecting the brain being a congeries of organ exercising different functions, and the probability of learning somethin respecting the functions of the brain by the external examination of th skull, would have been by this time advanced and embraced by many solely in consequence of the physiological and pathological discoverie and researches to which I have alluded.

So far as regards my personal observation on this subject, I am com pelled to say, it has not been great. The attention I have given to i has, however, impressed me favourably. I have never found any strikin instances in contradiction of what Dr. Gall considers established. Fo three years I have been a director of the Connecticut State Prison, an have had abundant opportunity of examining and comparing the heads and learning the character of several hundreds of prisoners. I have no to be sure, embraced the opportunity thus afforded of studying this sub ject as thoroughly as I might. Still, I have not been wholly neglectfu of it, and can state that I have found, in numerous instances, confirma tion of the opinions of Gall.

In conclusion, I consider this method of studying the functions of th brain deserving of the attention of medical men, who, of all others, hav the best opportunity of testing its correctness and determining its value particularly by pathological investigations.

ARTICLE III.

ON THE HARMONY BETWEEN PHRENOLOGY AND THE SCRIPTURE DOCTRIN OF REGENERATION.

Many good people have had their fears excited, lest there should b some discrepancy between the principles of phrenology and the doc trines of revelation. They seem to forget this important fact, that th God of *revelation* is also the God of *nature*, and that, consequently the laws of the latter, when correctly interpreted, must *necessarily* b in perfect harmony with the truths of the former. It is impossible, i the very nature of the Divine attributes, that the will of God, a revealed in his Word, should contradict his will, as manifested in hi works. If there should appear to be any discrepancy between nature and revealed truth, the cause, and of course the error, must originat entirely on the part of the *creature*, and *not* on that of the *Creator*.

The advocates of phrenology have at different times attempted t

* Gall on the Functions of the Brain and each of its Parts, &c., Vol. 3.

show the harmony which subsists between their science and the
essential truths of Christianity. We have presented several articles
of this nature in the Journal, and now take pleasure in copying
another, on the Scripture Doctrine of Regeneration, from the fourth
number of the Edinburgh Phrenological Journal. The writer, (whose
name is not given,) after some prefatory remarks, presents us with the
following excellent essay :—

The first step of our investigation must be to *state distinctly* what
the several doctrines in question are ; if they are once understood, it
will not be difficult to make their consistency apparent.

The following, then, I take to be a correct statement of the respective doctrines :

The doctrine of *phrenology* is, that the strength of the different
propensities, sentiments, and intellectual faculties, with which any
individual is *endowed by nature*, bears a relation to the size of different portions of his brain ; and may be *ascertained* by examining
the configuration and dimensions of his *cranium.*

The doctrine of *Christianity* is, that *all* men, whatever be their
natural character, are called upon to repent, to believe in the Saviour,
and to turn from sin to God and holiness.

Now, the objection drawn from these doctrines has been twofold :

1*st*, In the *first* place, there is an inconsistency said to lie in this—
that if a man is *proved* by phrenology to have a bad natural character,
it is *impossible* for that man to obey the gospel-call, to turn from his
evil ways, and to walk in the paths of righteousness.

To the objection, when thus stated, the answer is extremely
obvious ; and it is this, that, if it be an objection to any thing at all, it
is an objection, *not to phrenology*, but to *Christianity.* Phrenology
does not pretend to *make* men's minds, but simply to *know* them as
they have been formed by the hand of nature. That there *are* great
natural diversities in human character, and that there are some men
naturally very bad, no person will deny ; and if any one chooses to
say that this undoubted *fact* militates *against Christianity*, we refer
him to the divines for an answer to his objection. But to impute the
objection to *phrenology*, which merely asserts, and proceeds upon
this *fact*, already known and allowed by all, is very short-sighted, or
very perverse. Every body knows that there are some men by nature
extremely wicked. Such characters may be discovered by common
observation. Phrenology furnishes another mode of observation by
which they may be discovered. But as to their capacity of embracing
Christianity, we leave that as we found it. If their having bad natural
characters does indeed incapacitate them from embracing Christianity,

the incapacity arises *from their character*, and not from *our becoming acquainted with it*, either by one means or another.

2d, But the objection has been put in another shape, which wil require somewhat more attention. It has been said, if the character of all men are *fixed down* by the boundaries of their *crania*, in th determinate way which phrenology presents, how is it possible tha they should undergo that *total revolution* which Christianity requires When a man is converted, is his whole cranium *new modelled i* Certainly not; and what I now proceed to show is, not only that th doctrine of regeneration, as laid down in Scripture, does *not impl; any* change of the *original* powers and qualities of a man's mind, bu that Scripture most distinctly and expressly declares, that no *suc/* change *does* take place, either at conversion, or at any future perioc of the Christian's course, and that the native elements and constitutior of the Christian's mind remain unaltered till his dying day.

In order that the full import of the proposition now announced may be understood, and that its effect in reconciling the doctrines ol phrenology and Christianity may be distinctly perceived, it will be necessary to expound at somewhat greater length the doctrines of the two systems which have been briefly stated above.

And, *first*, with regard to the doctrines of *phrenology*—I have stated, that the phrenological doctrine is, " that the strength of the different propensities, sentiments, and faculties, with which *nature has endowed* any individual, may be *ascertained* by examining the configuration and dimensions of his *cranium.*" It is the *primary elements* of intellectual and moral character *conferred by nature,* which phrenology proposes to discover, and nothing else. It does not pretend that the *cranium* gives information as to the *actual attainments* which any individual has made either in intellectual or moral pursuits. It reveals a man's *capabilities and tendencies*, but not the extent and manner in which these may have been fostered, controlled, and regulated, or neglected, crushed, and perverted.

Circumstances and education have an extensive power in modifying human character. Both the intellectual powers and the moral qualities are alike subject to their influence; the good may be cherished, or it may be thwarted; the evil may be checked, or it may be pampered and nursed into unnatural activity. *The mode* in which these causes operate upon the human mind, is not very material to my present inquiry. It is obvious, however, to remark, that every mental power and disposition has certain external circumstances which are adapted to its nature, which excite it into activity, and form, as it were, the element in which it naturally moves and acts. By placing any individual, therefore, carefully and constantly, in circumstances which exercise one set of his faculties or dispositions, and by removing and separating him from those circumstances which would exercise a different set of his natural faculties or dispositions, the one class of exercises becomes familiar and habitual, while the individual remains unacquainted with, or becomes estranged from, the other class of exercises. It is moreover possible, indeed it is what is done every day, to *fix in the mind itself* certain maxims, rules, and motives of conduct, which propel and stimulate in one direction, while they restrain or form, as it were, a barrier in another direction. One course may be made to appear to the mind as fit or honourable, or as profitable and satisfactory in the long run; while another course is made to appear unworthy, degrading, unsatisfying, and in the end ruinous. This may be regarded as only a different modification of the influence of circumstances over the mental functions. It is the bringing of *future* and *distant* circumstances, of indirect and remote *consequences* into view, representing these vividly, and impressing them strongly upon the mind. Whether the representations thus made to the mind be true or false, they are taken by the mind to be true—as true as *existing realities;* and it is this impression of their reality which gives them their control over the workings and habits of the mind. But without stopping to illustrate this subject farther, I observe that *the fact*, that circumstances and training have an extensive sway over the human mind, is beyond all dispute. Now, phrenology does not stand opposed to this plain truth; nor does it pretend that a man's whole circumstances, education, and history, are stamped in the shape of his skull. It does not pretend to gather one iota of these from an examination of the cranium; and *the whole effects* which they are capable of producing upon the character are, and are acknowledged to be, utterly beyond its ken. What it has to do with, are the *natural endowments* of the mind.

To speak more correctly, phrenology affords external indications by which we can estimate the relative strength of the different powers of the mind as bestowed by nature, and it thus furnishes a key to the discovery of the effects likely to be produced by any combination of circumstances on the characters and dispositions of different individuals; but it affords no indication by the observation of which we can tell in what circumstances an individual has been placed, or which of the faculties possessed by him have been most cultivated and excited.

But the natural endowments of men's minds are as various as are the natural dimensions and proportions of their bodies. The influence which circumstances and training exercise over mind and body, is great; but it is still limited. It will never make either mind or body anew. A pigmy cannot be converted into a giant; a puny and sickly constitution cannot put on the strength, and be nerved with the power of a Hercules; a clumsy and deformed man will never be made a model of grace, or the champion in athletic exercises. And as it is with the body, so it is with the mind. There are pigmy minds, and there are gigantic minds; minds puny and morbidly weak, and minds of Herculean nerve and prowess; clumsy minds and awkward minds, cripples and deformed; and the variety of these *natural* mental frames and constitutions is, at the least, as great and as conspicuous and undeniable as are the diversities of corporeal form and power.

This, then, is the province of phrenology; and a wide and legitimate province it is, and one which it is easy enough to distinguish from the province of circumstances, education, and habit, with which it has been too often ignorantly or designedly confounded. The phrenologists do not pretend to tell whether a man actually speaks Greek, or writes poems, or commits murders. What they undertake to do, is to tell how far a man possesses the *natural powers* which, *under proper circumstances*, would enable him, with ease or with difficulty, to attain either to high or to moderate excellence in any branch of intellectual pursuit; or how far his natural tendencies, either to good or to evil, are strong or feeble. But whether all or any of the powers and qualities of his mind have had *scope* and *opportunity* to exercise and display themselves, whether the mind has been raised and stimulated, and sustained in its exercises; or whether its good qualities have been damped, or its bad qualities disciplined and brought under control, phrenology does not inform, and the phrenologists do not pretend to tell.

If there is any strong *natural* peculiarity—and every person knows what is meant by a natural peculiarity, and how distinguishable it is from what is acquired and artificial—if there is any strong natural peculiarity in any department of mind, temper, or character, the phrenologist will have no difficulty in detecting it, though nothing should occur in his presence to call it into play, or though it should be habitually concealed, so as altogether to elude the notice of ordinary observers. And it is thus with every one individual faculty and quality, whose separate and independent existence our science has revealed to us. We can say in what degree any person has the *capacity* or *tendency* to exercise or indulge it; but whether it *has been manifested* according to its native strength—that depends not only on the capacity—which we know, but upon circumstances and opportunities—of which we know, and upon which, therefore, we will decide nothing.

The doctrine of phrenology is now, I hope, pretty distinctly understood; and before proceeding, I will only farther observe in passing, that by thus defining the legitimate province of phrenology, it must not be supposed that I am leaving nothing in it that is useful and practical. As has just been observed, it always affords the means of detecting decided peculiarities of natural character, however much they may have been thwarted by circumstances or counteracted by education. And although the science does not give information as to men's circumstances and education, yet, after the phrenologist is informed of these particulars in regard to any individual, he will be enabled, by the application of the science, to analyse his character with a degree of completeness and philosophical precision of which a person destitute of the science can form no conception. But what is infinitely more important to observe, the high pretensions of the science are grounded upon this, that, if it be true, it presents us with an entirely new and a correct delineation of man's intellectual and moral nature. If it be true, it supplies the greatest *desideratum* in the whole range of human science; for the *human mind*, the most noble and interesting of all the subjects of physical inquiry, has hitherto been a mere blank—a barren and unproductive waste, in which men of the most transcendent genius have toiled and laboured absolutely in vain.

But I must now turn to the doctrines of Christianity, and what I have to show in regard to them is, that the change which they require to be produced upon a man's character and conduct is not of such a nature as to alter any of the original or constitutional properties of his mind; or, in other words, to alter any thing which the phrenologists assert is ever discoverable from an examination of the cranium. The cranium remains the same, because the man, in all his natural powers and tendencies, remains the same.

"The change which Christianity is calculated to produce, and which it does produce, upon the minds of men, is certainly very great. It produces this change sometimes rapidly, or almost suddenly, but for the most part slowly and progressively; but whether the effect is produced in the one way or in the other, I apprehend it to be clear that the change is of a nature which leaves the radical and elementary qualities of the mind just as it found them. It works its marvellous renovations and transformations by means of *a regulating and controlling influence, not* by means of *eradication;* and the great superiority of the change which its discipline and training effects upon the heart and character, above that which is produced by any other system, arises from the transcendently superior and divine means which it employs for the attainment of its glorious and heavenly object.

What is the great means which Christianity employs at first for changing and afterwards for improving and perfecting the human character? I need hardly say that it is the principle of a true and living *faith*. Now, observe the nature of this principle, and the mode of its operation. What is faith? The Apostle Paul presents us with a most explicit and pointed definition of it in these words: " Faith *is the* "EVIDENCE *of things* NOT SEEN;" an *abiding* and *realising* belief of the whole truths of revealed religion. Let a man, then, have this faith, which is the gift of God, and the means of his conversion, (for " by grace are ye saved through faith, and that not of yourselves—it is the gift of God;") and observe what a mighty principle you have implanted in his breast, for regulating, controlling, and directing all the principles of his nature. Give a man faith; that is to say, let him have an abiding and realising conviction in the presence of a God, holy, just, avenging, long-suffering, and compassionate, but who cannot look upon sin, and will by no means clear the guilty; of a Saviour, the Son of God, who abased himself, and died that we might live— that we might rise from the degradation and death of sin, and live to God, and walk with him in newness of life, and be made heirs of immortality. I say, let a man have faith in these, and all the other glorious and affecting truths of revelation; let him have " the *evidence* of *these* things not seen," abiding and prevalent in his mind; why, you have placed the man in a new world; " old things are passed away, all things are become new;" you have annihilated in a great measure as to him the things of time and sense; or, at all events, you have placed him in the very midst of a new scene, a new creation of high and holy and heavenly realities, which till that moment were to him as if they had had no existence. He was formerly an irreligious man—" God was not in all his thoughts;" and if his mind was unfortunately constituted, he was an immoral man, indulging his natural propensities and passions without restraint; for there was nothing present to his mind calculated to restrain them. But he has now received *faith*—" he believes in God; he believes also in Christ," and in all the other relative and harmonious truths which go to make up those " glad tidings of great joy," which are proclaimed to fallen, sinful, and abject man. This system of truth is " evidenced" to his mind by faith. It is thereby made present to his mind; it occupies his mind and fills it; calls it off from the world and sin, and fixes it upon God and Christ, and holiness and heaven. No doubt the man is not yet perfect; but he is converted; that is to say, he is turned; his course is changed. He has hitherto gone on in the downward path of sin; he now begins to ascend the upward path of virtue. His descent may have been easy and rapid; his ascent may be difficult and slow. But his face is set heavenward; and he will now go on—

shining as he goes—and "shining brighter and brighter unto the perfect day."

Such, I think, will be admitted, by every one acquainted with Scripture, to be a correct view of the general nature of the doctrine of conversion. But before I ask whether it is not consistent with phrenology, I must clear the ground of a difficulty which arises from the writings of the phrenologists themselves. At one time, there was a certain portion of the brain designated as the organ of faith. It is now, I rejoice to say, a long while since this was altered. But, if I mistake not, in the writings of that individual to whom our science is so greatly indebted, it is still laid down that faith is connected very intimately, if not exclusively, with the organ of Hope. Now, without taking any other way of removing whatever difficulty might be supposed to arise from this opinion, if it were correct, I must, with deference, submit, that it is an opinion which must have been taken up without due consideration of the subject in all its extent. No doubt there is a great deal in the faith of a Christian to awaken and animate his hope, and to make this faculty dwell with delightful anticipation upon the bright futurity which is opened up to its view, and which it may discern and exult in even in the lowest depths of worldly debasement, and in the darkest hours of this world's sorrow. But has Christianity no truths which speak to the *fears* of a believer—which may give exercise to his Cautiousness, his Adhesiveness, his Conscientiousness, his Firmness, his Veneration, his Ideality, and even his Combativeness, seeing he is called to *fight* and to *wrestle?* In short, is there one active principle in human nature to which Christianity does not apply itself in the most urgent and affecting appeals, by means of a genuine and living faith in its truths? There is, it must be allowed, a certain degree of intelligence necessary, in order that these truths may be received into the mind; and without that degree of intelligence there can be no Christian, for there is in fact no man. But if the truths are admitted into the mind, and impressed upon it by genuine Christian faith, it seems obvious that it raises the whole man, and gives ample scope for the exercise of all his natural sentiments and powers.

Having put this matter in what, I hope, will appear to be its just light, I now proceed to observe, that it seems quite manifest, that the principle of faith, which is the great means of turning a sinner from the error of his ways, leaves a man's natural powers and qualities unaltered.

Faith implies that the man who has been made the recipient of it, is placed in a world of new circumstances; it consists in this, that these circumstances, which are of the most affecting kind, and address

every power and faculty of the soul, are habitually and constantl
present to the mind; these affecting circumstances being thus mad
habitually present to the mind, they solicit all its powers, and exerci
them all, habitually, in a new way; but they do not change the natu
of the powers, or alter either the absolute or the relative strength c
any one of them. It is not of the nature of the faith or belief of an
truths to altar or touch the intrinsic quality and constitution of th
mind which believes them. It is the mind, such as it is, which fai
employs and exercises; but it seems inconsistent with the very ide
and conception of it, that it should confer upon the mind a new powe
or take away an old one, or that it should affect in the slightest degre
the inherent character of the powers which actually exist.

But the Scripture doctrine will be seen more clearly, and the whol
subject will be illustrated, if we direct our attention for a moment to
general view of what the Scripture unfolds to us of the future cours
and progress of a Christian, after he has undergone the first great an
decisive change of conversion.

The Christian, then, is not only converted by means of faith, bu
he is sanctified in the same way: by which is meant, that he i
enabled to advance in a gradual and progressive course of mor
improvement. But faith enables him to do so, not by giving him
power to root out any of his natural tendencies, but by empowerin
him practically to subject and subdue them. If a man, at his conver
sion, has an evil tendency, it will remain with him to the last. Ther
is, however, no evil tendency in human nature for which the armour
of faith does not furnish a suitable and tempered weapon wherewith t
combat it. When the tendency is felt, it is met and put down by
Scriptural application suited to the occasion; when it springs u
again, it is watched and put down in the same manner. The Chris
tian gets as familiar with the antidote as with the disease; and th
feeling of the one at length naturally, and without effort, leads him t
the instant and effectual application of the other. He graduall
obtains the mastery over the enemy; and he thus strives to kee
under his whole body, and to bring it more and more into subjectio
to the law of Christ. The tendencies still remain; but all thei
impulses are thwarted and strangled in their first risings. The ma
gradually gets estranged from what he never indulges in; a new an
opposing habit is formed, a new and purer taste is acquired. Th
mind, in one word, though still the same mind, has had its view
elevated from earth to heaven, and expanded from time to eternity.

But still, I repeat it, the Scripture doctrine is, that the Christian'
natural tendencies and dispositions continue always the same. He i
called upon to watch, to pray, to contend, to fight, to wrestle; ther

is no period of his course that he is allowed to think himself secure or safe from any, even the greatest failings and sins. The flesh ever lusteth against the spirit, and the spirit against the flesh. If the Christian is to prevail, it is by being strong in the faith; and in conformity with the contemplations and sentiments which his faith awakens, he must watch, and pray, and strive. If he ceases to be thus exercised at any one moment, his whole strength has departed from him, and there is not one of the feeblest of his spiritual enemies that may not start up and surprise him, and gain an advantage over him. This doctrine cannot be stated in stronger terms than it is represented by the Apostle Paul, in his own experience. "For we know," says he, "that the law is spiritual; but I am carnal, sold under sin." "For the good that I would, I do not; but the evil which I would not, that I do." There is a "law in my members warring against the law of my mind, and bringing me into captivity to the law of sin, which is in my members. Oh! wretched man that I am! who shall deliver me from the body of this death?"

Now, here is no change of the natural powers and tendencies. The whole improvement effected on the believer is, literally, and without any figure of speech, the effect of circumstances, training, and habit. The mind has been awakened by faith to the perception of a new class of objects; it has been made alive to God and heavenly things, to which it was formerly dead and insensible; as faith is strengthened, its sway over the powers and principles of the mind is extended, and its ascendency is confirmed; but the powers which are thus awakened, and quickened, and kept alive, and exercised by faith, are the self-same powers which existed before. The only difference is, that they were formerly devoted to objects less worthy of them, less ennobling, or, it may have been, positively debasing. But by means of the divine principle of faith implanted, and growing stronger in his breast, the Christian is removed from the contact and contamination of whatever is low or polluting. He lives by faith. Though in the world, he is living continually above it. His mind is conversant with the sublime and glorious things revealed to his believing eye; and it is his contemplation of these, and his converse with them, which are not transforming the powers and faculties of his mind, but schooling and exercising them, and which are thus gradually moulding his habits and his tastes into a meetness for the fellowship of the saints in light.

If the view now submitted is scriptural, which nobody, I think, can doubt, it establishes the principle which I am maintaining; and shows that Scripture and phrenology, so far from being at variance, are in entire and beautiful coincidence.

But this is not all. So strong are man's natural tendencies to evil, and so completely does Scripture recognise their permanent hold and seat in the heart of man, that even the divine principle of faith is not sufficient of itself to enable him to overcome them. He must continually ask for, and obtain, the aids of the holy spirit of God, to help his infirmities, and to strengthen his otherwise feeble and vain resistance. He is weak in himself, but when he is weak, then is he strong; for the strength of God is made perfect in his weakness, and he is strengthened with might by the spirit in the inner man.

Is it possible, I ask, to conceive any thing that could convey a stronger idea of fixed and deep-rooted propensities than this doctrine implies?

And if any thing should still be thought wanting, I would appeal to one other doctrine of our holy religion, a doctrine which is eminently peculiar to, and characteristic of, Christianity, which never had a place in any merely human system of faith, which was the subject of mockery and derision to the philosophers of Athens, but which, in the most striking manner, countenances and accords with the whole system of phrenology: I allude to the doctrine of the resurrection, which proclaims, in language not to be mistaken, the dignity and the essential importance of our material part. For we are taught that notwithstanding all that Christian faith and Christian exertion and steadfastness, and the spirit of God himself, can do for us, the victory over the flesh will never be complete on this side the grave. It is not until this body has died, and been changed, and made anew, that the soul is to be completely fitted for its eternal home. "This corruptible shall put on incorruption, this mortal shall put on immortality." "Our bodies shall be fashioned like unto Christ's glorious body," and then shall we ascend and "meet the Lord in the air, and so shall we be for ever with the Lord."

I say, therefore, that the phrenologists are not contradicted, but are most expressly and powerfully confirmed, by phrenology, when they hold that no change is produced upon the original faculties and qualities of the human mind by the reception of Christianity. Phrenologists cannot tell whether a man is a Christian from the examination of his cranium, any more than they can tell whether he has been the subject of human teaching or human training. The effects of Christianity are infinitely greater than what are produced by any merely human teaching, or by any merely human discipline, because the Christian is taught of God, and is sustained by the spirit of the Almighty. Under the influence of such means, the very chief of sinners may be brought from darkness into light, and from sin unto holiness. But the fact, that such means are employed, and are necessary to the last, is the very fact which shows that the innate prin-

ciples and constitution of the mind remain unaltered, and which est
blishes my proposition, that there is an entire accordance between tl
doctrines of Christianity and of phrenology.

ARTICLE IV.

ELEMENTARY PHRENOLOGY.—NO. 2.

BY O. S. FOWLER.

The modified influences of the various faculties, when acting
combination, constitute by far the most important part of practic
phrenology. Without properly estimating these influences, no cc
rect estimate of character can be formed; yet this department of tl
science is not sufficiently understood or appreciated. These infl
ences, as applied to the classes of faculties, are particularly interestin
For example: One in whom the posterior portion of the head—whi
includes the organs of the propensities—greatly predominates over tl
frontal, will manifest proportionally more of feeling than reason; (
passion than intellect; of propelling than directing power; of ef
ciency than of originality and strength of intellect; of zeal, energ
and action, than wisdom, discretion, and judgment; in fine, more (
the animal than of the intellectual and moral qualities. But, on tl
other hand, when the frontal portion of the head predominates in si:
and activity over the posterior, the character will be the reverse.

One in whom the basilar or lower portion of the head—whi
includes the animal propensities and observing powers—predominate
will possess great force and efficiency of character, joined with
ready talent for business or study; strong passions applied to selfi
purposes, and unrestrained by the moral sentiments, sufficient sma
ness, tact, and energy, to conduct large operations and effect importa
undertakings, yet less elevation, magnanimity, and depth of intelle
Many men who have been distinguished in the world, have had tl
organs located in this portion of the head large. These organs gi
the propelling power to be employed by the intellect in attaining i
ends, or by the moral sentiments in promoting moral and philanthrop
objects, or by the selfish sentiments in self-aggrandisement. Th
class of faculties is generally accompanied with a strong and robu
constitution.

One who possesses a much greater developement of the moral a
intellectual organs, than of the propensities, will have goodness, wi

less greatness or force, of character, morality, and virtue, joined with
want of impetus, if not of efficiency ; will have fine talents and a love
for moral and intellectual pursuits, accompanied with so much modesty
dependence, if not actual tameness, of character, that he will not be
likely to rise in the world, unless pushed forward by others, but may
then distinguish himself ; will be amiable and sentimental, if no
eminently pious, yet effect but little.   This organisation is but poorly
adapted to the exigences of the nineteenth century.   It is generally
accompanied with the nervous temperament, a delicate constitution
and fine feelings.

One having large organs of the propensities and of the religious
sentiments, and the reasoning faculties only moderate or full, may
struggle hard against the current of his propensities, yet will be liable
to be often overcome by it ; may endeavour to live a virtuous, Chris
tian life, yet will be sometimes guilty of gross inconsistencies ; will
take contracted views of religious subjects, and indulge, alternately
both classes of organs ; but, with the moral and reasoning organs
equally large, will be obliged to struggle hard, yet will generally
struggle successfully, against " his easily besetting sins," and, in
general, be consistent in his religious belief and practice.

One having the propensities well developed, with *very large* moral
and intellectual organs, will combine great strength of mind with great
energy of character, directed by the humane sentiments, and applied to
the advancement of moral and benevolent objects, and be a talented
and useful member of society, yet have his faults.

One with strong propensities, and the intellectual organs large and
the moral deficient, will combine great power and energy of mind
with great depravity of character, and never lack means by which to
gratify his selfish passions.

One having the perceptive organs generally large, and the reasoning
organs only full, will have a mind well stored with facts, and a desire
to see and know ; a thirst for general information, and a facility in
acquiring it ; an ability to attend to details, and a popular, practical
business talent, but will lack depth, judgment, originality, and pene
tration of mind ; may execute well, but cannot adapt means to ends,
nor superintend complicated operations ; may possess versatility of
genius, be a good scholar, and pass for a man of talents and learning
yet will not think profoundly, nor readily comprehend first principles
nor bear sounding.

One with the reflecting organs large, and the perceptive only mode
rate or small, or with the upper portion of the forehead much larger
than the lower, will think more than he observes or communicates
will have much more to do with *ideas* than with *facts ;* with *funda*

mental principles and the *general bearing* of things, than with their details and minutiæ; with the abstract relations, than with the qualities of things; with the analytical and demonstrative sciences, than with the natural; with thoughts than words; may have great strength, shrewdness, and penetration of intellect, and be a deep and profound reasoner, but will lack versatility of talent, and be unable to employ his powers to good advantage, or show what he is, except in a certain sphere, yet will wear well, have a fund of important ideas, and excellent judgment, and shine in proportion as he is tried.

One having the perceptive and reasoning organs both large, and a large and an active brain, will have a universal talent, and a mind well balanced and well furnished with both facts and principles; will be a *general* scholar, and, with a respectable developement of the propensities, possess a decidedly superior intellect, and be capable of rising to *eminence;* will not only possess talents of a very high order, but also be able to use them to the best advantage, and both devise and execute projects, and succeed in whatever he undertakes, even when most of those around him fail.

One with a round, even head, in which all the organs are respectably developed, will manifest uniformity and consistency of character, opinion, and conduct; have few excesses or defects; take his character from surrounding circumstances; be less under the influence of impulses, and manifest on nearly all subjects good sense and judgment; will have what may be called "a well-balanced mind," and, like the poet's good man, "hold the even tenor of his way." If the brain is large and active, and external influences are favourable, the individual will be a universal genius, great in every thing, and capable of swaying a commanding influence in the world.

One with a head uneven, having many protuberances and depressions upon it, will be equally peculiar, eccentric, and *sui-generis;* will present many strong and weak points of mind and character; be too much the sport of impulses, and the creature of circumstances, thus exhibiting opposite phases of character, and hence will be estimated very differently by different persons. Such an individual will be subject to many changes in passing through the world—will be driven here and there by strong excitements, and manifest but little real self-government. Other conditions being equal in two heads, except that the organs of the one are uniformly developed, and those of the other unevenly, the former is far more preferable than the latter; and parents and teachers, in educating children, should take great pains to preserve as much as possible the harmonious developement of all the mental powers.

ARTICLE V.

PREDOMINANCE OF CERTAIN ORGANS IN THE BRITISH POETS.—NO. 5.

COWPER.

If there ever was a man "too full of the milk of human kindness to catch the nearest way," it was the poet of Olney. Destined by his friends to the bar, his peculiar organisation wholly disqualified him for success in the legal profession. The stormy struggles of life, of the forum, or the hall, were about as genial to his nature as the tornado is to the hare-bell, shaken by a breath. In what, then, consisted his unfitness? Neither in intellectual nor moral deficiency—none will believe it of the author of the "Task"—nor yet in want of ambition, that convenient solution in similar cases, for he has written to perpetuate his name, and possessed all a poet's sensibility to applause and censure. He was not without ambition, but, as Lady Macbeth would say, "without the illness should attend it." Phrenology alone can furnish the true key to his character, and open out all his peculiarities, all his weaknesses, and all his virtues. His head was much above the average size, his temperament chiefly nervous, the intellectual and moral region predominant, Cautiousness and Conscientiousness very large, while Hope, Self-esteem, Combativeness, and Destructiveness, were relatively deficient. Such are the simple data from which, joined with other conditions, a hundred phrenologists, possessing the inductive spirit of their science, would infer the same results. But let us turn to his actual history. He studied, or rather dallied over, law for several years, and was in due time called to the bar. On his first attempt to speak in public, he was seized with such excessive trepidation that he could not articulate, and the failure acting on his sensitive system, produced a severe and dangerous nervous affection. This was not an embarrassment which custom could remove, or even greatly modify, but flowed inevitably from his organisation, which disposed him to great timidity, self-distrust, and morbid exaggeration of difficulties. The same deep sense of his unworthiness we see at a later period of his life, where he appears before us in the character of a Christian, entangled in the metaphysical dogmas of theology, overwhelmed with a consciousness of guilt and shuddering at the prospect of eternal reprobation. Painfully impressed with his inability to practise his profession, he soon entirely abandoned it, and sought peace in obscurity. Buried in the gloom of Olney, he lived for many years in violation of physical and

mental laws, vainly endeavouring to find employment for his highly
gifted mind, in constructing farming utensils, superintending a small
garden, and rearing rabbits—useful occupations enough as mere relaxation, but altogether inadequate to supply the demands of a mind such
as his.   Nor was his social intercourse very nicely adapted to his
nature.   The amiable family of the Unwins, grateful as every friend
of the poet must ever feel for their kindness and care, knew very little
of his real character, and were much better calculated to nourish his
morbid views, than to call forth those energies, the due exercise of
which has enrolled his name with the famous bards of his nation.   A
long and painful period passed in this retreat, and with the exception
of some slight contributions to a hymn-book and an occasional sonnet,
nothing indicated the existence of the poet.   But he was visited by
those better able to understand and appreciate him than his usual
acquaintances.   To Lady Austen and his charming cousin, the Lady
Hesketh, whose refined manners, lively wit, and brilliant intellect,
aroused his higher powers, we are chiefly indebted, not only for the
Task, but for many of his best productions.   To the influence, also,
of these attractive qualities of his accomplished relative, which furnished his mind with the healthful excitement it so much needed, and
to the mental labour thus superinduced, he in all probability owed the
long exemption subsequently enjoyed, from that religious gloom and
melancholy which had been fast gathering like night over his entire
moral nature   .
    This admirably exemplifies the great advantage to health of body and
mind, of calling forth the latter by presenting its appropriate objects.
A few intelligent friends visiting him for a short time, awakened into
wholesome activity faculties which were rusting from disuse, or what
was even worse, were employed upon the subtleties of theology,
which filled his imagination with horrors.   The consequence of this
restored vigour was one of the most beautiful poems in our language,
several excellent fugitive pieces, and the amusing adventures of John
Gilpin.   This last, as every reader knows, was composed in one of
Cowper's darkest moods, and it may be well to call, in passing, attention to this fact, as one of the thousands totally inexplicable upon any
other than phrenological principles.   It demonstrates the multiplex
character of the mind, and shows that the faculty of " Wit" can be in
action, suggesting the most ludicrous incidents, even while Cautiousness, and some other organs, are filling the fancy with these frightful
creations.   But let us turn more particularly to his cranial developements.   The perceptive faculties were very strong, indicated in the
likenesses more by the depth than breadth of his forehead.   Hence
his descriptive power, the graphic vigour of which is equal to Thomp-

son's in accuracy, but, in consequence of his smaller propensities, no
in warmth of colouring.   Comparing him with the author of the
" Seasons," whom he somewhat resembles, we agree with Coleridge
in thinking the latter the " born poet."   There is commonly greater
purity of style, if not more depth of thought, in the " Task," but i
lacks the fervour and intensity of the " Seasons."   Cowper's tempe
rament was finer, and his Causality probably larger.   But the Ideality
Language, and affective faculties of Thompson were much superior
Cowper's productions are usually compact, vigorous, and highly
polished.   They never offend the most cultivated taste, but often
delight it, and on the other hand, seldom move the affections
Thompson seizes the attention, holds it in spite of many faults, rivets
it upon the subject, carries his reader right onward in the current of a
sweeping amplification, and often in a perfect cataract of words
words, however, which frequently, with singular beauty, advance
expand, and enforce the thought.   Comparison, in Cowper, was well
developed, and Ideality, though by no means a ruling organ, was not
deficient.   Language, also, was rather large; in accordance with
which he was not only an excellent linguist, but, in our humble
opinion, his English style is unsurpassed in precision and purity, and
combines to a greater degree strength and beauty with a chastened
simplicity, than that of any writer of the last or present century with
whose works we are familiar.   Benevolence, which was powerful,
together with his small Destructiveness, created that extreme horror
of war, however palliated by the necessity of nations, and that almost
morbid sensibility to the infliction of pain upon any sentient being, so
often manifested in his writings.

> "I would not number in my list of friends,
> (Though graced with polished manners and fine sense,
> Yet wanting sensibility,) the man
> Who needlessly sets foot upon a worm."

Veneration and Wonder, equally large and active, disposed him to see
signs and tokens, and a special providence in the operations of nature,
whenever they deviated from common experience.   Philosophical
solutions of doubtful causes displeased him, and seemed to him
profane.

> " Forth steps the spruce philosopher, and tells
> Of homogeneal and discordant springs
> And principles; of causes, how they work ·
> By necessary laws their sure effects;
> Of action and reaction.   He has found
> The source of the disease that nature feels,
> And bids the world take heart, and banish fear.
> Thou fool! will thy discovery of the cause
> Suspend the effect or heal it ?"

Like all men of high intellectual and moral endowment, he was disgusted with the low standard by which society regulates its actions, and he clung to the pleasing belief of eternal justice manifesting its retributive power in partial and particular instances. Like them, too, he was apt, for the want of a philosophy derived from the nature of things, to confound the physical and moral laws. Thus he beheld, in the great fog which covered Europe in 1783, the workings of an offended Deity. Conscientiousness and Cautiousness constitute, both from their size and morbid actions, the most striking points of his religious character. They were the greater part of his life in diseased action, and the source of much of his suffering, which was rendered frightfully intense by his very active temperament. His correspondence, especially that part of it relating to his religious experience, presents a painful picture of the unhealthy action of these organs. Nor is the gloom they leave upon the reader's mind in the slightest degree lessened, by reflecting upon the manner in which some of his friends replied to those communications. The editor of those letters attempts, in his preface, to refute the notion, rather prevalent after the publication of Hayley's life of the poet, that religion, or his views of religion, led to his mental aberrations; but, as we think, unsuccessfully. He states the poet's gloom and hypochondria were entirely produced by his having in early life imprudently checked an erysipelatous affection of the face. That his health might have been thus injured, and his mind, in consequence, slightly effected, is not denied. But it cannot be received, in the face of more powerful ones, as an adequate cause of Cowper's insanity. That his peculiar notions of religion exercised a most powerful influence over his mind, cannot be contested, since he has himself recorded it. Nor will any unprejudiced inquirer hesitate to acknowledge, after weighing all the circumstances of the case, that that influence was frightfully disastrous. Let us, then, remember his organisation; the predominant nervous temperament, the small Hope, moderate Self-esteem, large Cautiousness and Conscientiousness; and it will at once be conceded that any thing calculated to stimulate unduly the larger organs, and encumber the weaker, could not fail to be extremely pernicious. Now, one of the capital points of belief of the sect to which he was attached, is that of the "elect," and the comparative uselessness of good works to secure salvation. One of this persuasion, with a large endowment of Self-esteem and Hope, will be very apt to think himself one of the chosen, even though his actual vices would make him appear, in the eyes of all others, utterly unworthy of the selection. And on the other hand, one with these same organs small, and believing thus, would, notwithstanding his whole life might have been marked by the severe practice of the higher virtues, fear, in his desponding moments, that he was destined to hopeless punishment The latter was Cowper's case. But to show more clearly the influ ence of such views upon one of his organisation, let us listen to himself.

To the Rev. Mr. Newton.

" My dear Friend,—

" My device was intended to represent, not my own heart, but the heart of a Christian, mourning and yet rejoicing, pierced with thorns yet wreathed about with roses. I have the thorn without the rose My briar is a wintry one, the flowers are withered, but the thorn remains."

Again, some months later :

" I have been lately more dejected than usual ; more harassed by dreams in the night, and more deeply poisoned by them on the following day. I know not what is portended by an alteration for the worse, after *eleven years of misery*."

The eleven years here, makes the time during which he believed himself hopelessly doomed to future punishment; and thus he con tinues, several years after :—

" Adam's approach to the tree of life, after he had sinned, was not more effectually prohibited by the flaming sword, that turned every way, than mine to its great antitype has been now almost *thirteen years*, a short interval of two or three days, which passed about this time twelvemonth, alone excepted. For what reason it is that I am thus long excluded, if I am ever again to be admitted, is known to God only. I can say but this, that if he is still my father, this paternal severity has toward me been such as that I have reason to account it unexampled. * * * If the ladder of Christian experience reaches, as I suppose it does, to the very presence of God, it has nevertheless its foot in the abyss. And if Paul stood, as no doubt he did, on the topmost round of it, I have been standing, and still stand, on the lowest, in this thirteenth year that has passed since I descended. In such a situation of mind, encompassed by the midnight of absolute despair, and a thousand times filled with unspeakable horror, I first commenced author."

In this same letter, he alludes to a fear expressed by some of his religious friends that he might be injured by the gaiety of some of the intelligent acquaintances who surrounded him !

" At present, however, I have no connections at which either you, I trust, or any who love me and wish me well, have occasion to conceive alarm. * * * I do not know that there is among them a single person from whom I am likely to catch *contamination.*"

A month later, he writes in the same strain of hopelessness—

" The dealings of God with me are to myself utterly unintelligible More than a twelvemonth has passed since I began to hope that having walked the whole breadth of the bottom of this Red Sea, I was beginning to climb the opposite shore, and I prepared to sing the song of Moses. But I have been disappointed; those hopes have been blasted; those comforts have been wrested from me. I could not be so duped, even by the arch enemy himself, as to be made to question the Divine nature of them; but I have been made to believe that God gave them to me in derision, and took them away in vengeance."

A long letter follows, of exculpation from certain charges of living *too gay a life*, in which he anxiously assures his friend that riding out with Mrs. Unwin in the carriage and company of Lady Hesketh, has not led him into the *dissipation* his friends had feared. There can be but one feeling experienced by every sane mind towards those who would thus have deprived the unhappy poet of the little pleasure within his reach, and that is unutterable disgust.

Our space admits of no more extracts from that painful correspondence, nor do we suppose more to be necessary to convince the reader that whatever happiness others may have found in the tenets he cherished, to Cowper they brought nothing but gloom and misery.

Phrenologists perpetually urge divines, who possess peculiar opportunities for applying its benefits, to study the only true science of mind. Suppose the Rev. Mr. Newton, the poet's friend and spiritual counsellor, could have been thus enlightened, and consequently been able to detect the peculiarities of Cowper's organisation, its excesses and defects, would he have responded as he did to those gloomy, morbid, hopeless letters? When the poet's fears at length extended even unto the horrid apprehension of eternal punishment— when his overwrought Conscientiousness magnified his venial offences into crimes too deep for the infinite mercy of heaven—could any divine acquainted, as every divine ought to be, with the difference between healthy and diseased manifestations, have balanced—according to all the cold niceties of that merciless creed, which is the offspring of an exterminating spirit, savouring much more of man's destructiveness than of the even-handed justice of God—all the probabilities and improbabilities of such a destiny for his friend, and that friend one who had never injured a human being—no, not a particle of organised matter—one who would not have doomed a Nero or a Caligula to the

fate which, with so much self-abasement, he dreaded for himself
Would he have played and tampered with those insane horrors
instead of appealing to that intellect which, even in detailing them
evinced its strength, and to that sense of justice, never blind no
without charity, but when beholding his own frailties—instead o
demonstrating, by a force of reason which his unhappy friend coul
not have resisted, the total impossibility of his ever suffering th
frightful punishment he so much feared, but which, in the whol
course of his sinless life, he could not have incurred? But the Rev
Mr. Newton was without light; the language which the Author o
man has impressed upon the dome of thought had not then bee
interpreted aright, and the inner mysteries of the sanctuary were ye
unsolved.

The melancholy poet, but too prone to observe the darker shade
of life, required society the opposite to that which Olney or hi
religious associations furnished. And the attentive reader of hi
history cannot fail to discover, in the salutary effects which eve
followed his occasional intercourse with strong and healthy minds, th
absurdity of that philosophy which, by a species of homœopathic treat
ment, would cure with what created the disease—would substitute th
base for the antidote—and attempt to dissipate the mists by extinguish
ing the sun.

During the five or more years when he was engaged upon th
translation of Homer, his health was unusually sound, and his min
proportionately vigorous; but after that work was completed, and al
proper excitement withdrawn from his faculties, he unwisely returne
again to theological mysticism. His intellect began to wander, an
once more became thoroughly overcast; but now, unfortunately, wit
clouds and thick darkness no more to be completely dispelled, an
whence he at last emerged, the dim phantom of himself, with hi
physical energies utterly sapped, his mind emasculate and shattered—
the unhappy victim of religious mania.

ARTICLE VI.

The Philosophy of Human Life: being an investigation of the great Elements of Life—the Power that Acts—the Will that directs the Action—and the Accountability or Sanctions that influence the formation of Volitions; together with Reflections adapted to the physical, political, popular, moral, and religious natures of man. By Amos Dean, Professor of Medical Jurisprudence in the Albany Medical College. Published by Marsh, Capen, Lyon, & Co. Boston: 12 mo. pp. 300.

It is highly gratifying to observe that the number of works published on phrenology is rapidly increasing. This fact shows that not only the advocates of the science are zealously engaged in multiplying their efforts in its behalf, but also that a strong conviction exists in the community generally of the truth and importance of the principles it involves. It is stated, on good authority, that a greater number of works on phrenology have been published and sold in Great Britain for several years past, than on any other one subject, with the exception of religion. And we can see no satisfactory reason why this may not yet be the case in the United States. As an evidence of this, there have been published within the past year, five or six new books by our own countrymen, besides new editions called for of several foreign works on the science.

Among the former, may be mentioned the one heading this article. Its extended title will convey to the reader some idea of the nature and character of the work. Its author was one of the first in the United States to espouse publicly the new science. Nearly ten years since, Mr. Dean delivered a course of lectures on phrenology before an association of young men in the city of Albany. These lectures were afterwards published in a small volume, under the title of "Elements of Phrenology," which met with quite a favourable reception. Mr. Dean has also contributed several interesting articles to the Edinburgh, as well as to the American Phrenological Journal. And we congratulate the friends of the science in the reception of this, his last and most valuable contribution on the "*Philosophy of Human Life.*" Our only regret is, that we cannot possibly do the work justice within the small space in which the limits of a periodical like this necessarily confine us.

The topics discussed in the present work, are among the most difficult and abstruse that have ever come before the human mind. Perhaps it may be safe to say, that no other subjects whatever have

excited as much controversy, or enlisted more talent, than those o
Will, Free Agency, and Human Responsibility. And the principle
involved in them are still very far from being settled, or even a smal
share of the difficulties that beset inquirers on these subjects, fron
being removed. The functions of the brain must be correctly an
thoroughly understood by all leading writers on mental science, befor
these points can be generally settled; and even then, large numbers i
the community will be entirely incapable of understanding the philc
sophy of Free Agency and Human Responsibility. But the pas
history, and the present state of mental science, however, indicat
that the time is not far distant when all views of mind, which ca:
have any permanent influence, or command any tolerable share o
attention and respect, must be based on a knowledge of the structur
and functions of the brain. The number of eminent men who ar
compelled to admit this fact, is rapidly increasing, and it is th
part of wisdom and self-interest for all engaged in the study of th
philosophy of the mind, to examine the facts and principles adduce
on this subject, as they may be found collected and recorded i
various phrenological works.

The work before us on the " Philosophy of Human Life," is base
strictly on phrenological principles, though the technical languag
of the science is not generally used. The author commences b;
defining the number and nature of the primitive faculties of the mind
and then describes, in a very clear and satisfactory manner, what i
understood by the term "*power*"—a term which has elicited no smal
share of controversy, and been greatly mystified by the metaphy
sicians. It is utterly impossible, in our present state of existence, t
have any clear and definite conceptions of the nature of *mental power*
if we consider the mind only *abstractly*, and perfectly *independent* o
the body.

Mr. Dean here devotes forty pages to a consideration of the *Will*
His views on this point are decidedly ingenious and philosophical
being well arranged and clearly presented. He alludes to the erro
neous views which some have entertained on the subject in th
following manner :—

"The will appears to have been considered, by many, not as originatin
from the mind, or as forming a *part* of it, but as introduced *into* i
They seem to have viewed it as a separate, independent agent, findin
an appropriate employment in the coining of decisions or determination
which the mind and material organisation are best occupied in carryin,
into effect. This may be inferred from their speaking of the self-detei
mining power of the will, a power which certainly can be exercised i
no other way than by an act of the will. This act, like every othei
must have a cause; and if the will be self-determining, can be cause

only by an act of itself. This would involve the obvious contradiction of requiring an act of volition to precede every act of volition ; which is the same, in substance, as to require a beginning prior to any beginning.

" It may also be inferred from the power they vest in the will of recalling past ideas. That is a power the will can never directly exercise. If ideas cannot be recalled by the different faculties that originally entertained them, no act of the will can be competent for that purpose. If they can be, and are so recalled, they are then present to the mind, and no act of the will is required.

"If the will be an agent thus introduced, and thus gifted with the power, not merely of controlling mind and matter, but also itself, it would be important to inquire into the manner of its introduction ; into its composition ; into the principles on which its decisions are founded ; and into the authority by which it claims to exercise such illimitable sway over the powers of mind and body, with which its only tie of connection would seem to be that of command on the one part, and obedience on the other.

" All this, however, is an error. The will is not a tyrant, merely introduced into the mind to control. It is no more separate from, or independent of, intellectual action, than are perception, memory, or association. It is a legitimate part of the operation of mind ; and hence its origin, elements, and principles are to be sought in that great concentration of all feeling and of all thought.

" With this view of the origin and nature of will, it may be defined to be, *The decision of the whole mind upon the whole matter.*"

To explain this point briefly in our own words, we would remark that will, 'as connected with free agency, may be considered the decision or assent of a majority of the faculties, in view of all the motives presented to them through the intellect. Three conditions are absolutely necessary to constitute any being a free agent : viz. first, WILL ; secondly, A PLURALITY OF MOTIVES ; and thirdly, POWER in the WILL over the INSTRUMENTS OF ACTION. The faculties of the mind may be considered as constituting a little republic, each possessing a nature peculiar to itself, and affected accordingly, in view of motives, or rather, in accordance with certain fixed relations which the mental faculties sustain to external objects. Now, since the propensities and sentiments, i. e. the animal and moral nature of man, are mere blind instincts in themselves, motives must be addressed to them through the medium of the intellect, which alone is endowed with the powers of perception and reason. It is the intellect which furnishes not only the motives, but judges of their adaptation to the other faculties, and reasons on the consequences of selecting and acting in view of the motives presented. Here a knowledge of the structure of the brain throws great light on the subject of the will, as connected with free agency. The posterior and middle lobes of the brain include the organs of the propensities and sentiments, while the anterior lobe includes those of the intellect.

Sir Charles Bell discovered that two distinct sets of nervous

filaments proceed from the spinal column, and, that though they ar
enveloped in the same sheath, and cannot, in their texture, be distin
guished from each other, yet perform entirely different functions
Those filaments which proceed from the anterior part of the spine
column, are the *voluntary* nerves, or nerves of motion, and those pro
ceeding from the posterior part, are *involuntary* nerves, or nerves o
sensation. Consequently, the latter class of nerves, as far as th
choice or agency of the individual is concerned, must necessarily b
governed or controlled by the former. Hence, it might be inferred
a priori, that the same harmony exists in the distribution of the ner
vous filaments, when applied to the brain. And it has since bee
fully established by phrenological discoveries, that the nerves o
motion, or the *voluntary nerves*, ramify the convolutions of the ante
rior lobe of the brain; whereas, the nerves of sensation, or the *invo
luntary nerves*, ramify the convolutions of the middle and posterio
lobes, which also receive a few nervous filaments of motion, and onl:
a few, compared with the anterior lobe. Accordingly, therefore, wil
depends chiefly upon the anterior lobe, and the propensities, feelings
and sentiments, manifested by the functions of other portions of th
brain, must be governed principally by means of the intellect.

Inasmuch as phrenology proves that there is a plurality of facultie
to the mind, there will necessarily be a plurality of motives; and, b:
the discovery of the connection of the *voluntary nerves* with the ante
rior lobe of the brain, we see that this fact gives man indirectly powe
over the instruments of action, or the organs of sensation and feeling
But the actual power of the will must chiefly depend on the relativ
size existing between the anterior and the middle and posterior lobe
of the brain. There are, then, different degrees of free agency, and
consequently, corresponding variations in the amount of huma
responsibility. In this remark, we simply refer to the *natural* capa
bilities of man, and not to the privileges enjoyed, or the knowledg
acquired, both of which conditions have a powerful influence o
human character and conduct. As the philosophy of the will an
moral agency can never be correctly and fully understood without
knowledge of the structure and functions of the brain, we regret tha
Mr. Dean should have omitted, or passed over so slightly, thi
important part of the subject. And we hope, if a new edition of hi
work is called for, he will not fail to introduce this point, and shov
the dependence of the will on the intellect, and the relations whic
subsist between the different lobes of the brain; for by this mean
only, can a rational and satisfactory explanation be given of the prir
ciples involved in free agency.

Mr. Dean devotes the chief body of the work, under the heads o physical, popular, political, moral, and religious sanctions, to prove and illustrate this point, viz. that the Creator governs the world of mind in the same way that he does the world of matter, i. e. by subjecting it to the operation of general laws.   The physical and organic laws which govern human organisation are severally explained, as well as the nature of the faculties attached to their violation.   Under the head of political, and also of popular sanctions, may be found many excellent remarks, peculiarly adapted to the present state of society and of our free institutions.   We should be pleased to make several quotations, but our limits prevent; and the only amend we can make, is, by earnestly recommending the work to the attention of all our readers.   As to the leading objects of the work, they resemble in many respects the "Constitution of Man," though it is by no means a copy of that work, as some persons might naturally infer from the nature of the subjects discussed.   The style, arrangement, and manner in which the views are presented, are decidedly original, and, in some respects, the work will not suffer in comparison with the great master-piece of Mr. Combe.   Mr. Dean's style is chaste and elegant; and would, in the estimation of some, possess too much polish and embellishment for the discussion of scientific and philosophical subjects.

There is one term of very frequent occurrence in Mr. Dean's work, the use of which we are disposed to condemn, viz. *volition*.   This has always been a favourite word with the metaphysicians, but inasmuch as the term, *volition*, is perfectly unintelligible to the great mass of minds, and even writers themselves on mental philosophy put different constructions upon its meaning, the word, in our opinion, should never be used by phrenologists, or by any writers on mental science, who make any pretensions to simplicity and accuracy in the use of language.

We cannot close this notice without copying at some length, a quotation from Mr. Dean's chapter on the religious nature of man. The remarks contained in this extract need no commendation.   It is quite certain, that when man's whole nature is correctly understood, religion will be more rational and consistent in its manifestations, than the world has ever yet witnessed.   When we become fully acquainted with the physical and mental nature of man, and with the true interpretation of revelation, we shall find a most wonderful adaptation and harmony existing between the laws of the former and the truths of the latter.   The exhibitions of Divine truth will then be accompanied with a power and efficacy which we no where now behold, inasmuch as they will be more in accordance with the will of the Deity, and the means which he has divinely appointed for the conversion and salvation of men. There will then, also, be such a beauty and consistency in the manifestation of religious character and conduct as to excite the admiration, and command the respect of the world. It will approximate to that perfect standard which the Deity designed and Revelation requires.

"To learn the will of God from his works, requires the exercise of an acute, discriminating intellect. That he wills the highest possible degree of happiness to his rational creatures, is obvious from the fact, that he has endowed them with capacities for enjoyment, and spread around them a creation to minister to their desires. To the physical wants of every bodily organ he has furnished their appropriate aliment; to the social wants, companions, friends, and relatives; to the ideal wants, all the beauty, sublimity, and grandeur reflected from his creation; to the benevolent wants, objects of misery, and distress every where to be relieved; to the immortal wants, the apprehension of the eternal rules of right and wrong, and the feeble comprehension of his own infinite self. With such a table spread before him, man is bidden to the feast of life. And yet how often does he transform that feast to a revel, or scene of cruel contentions, or of deep debauch! With him lies the choice of directions, that terminate in the issues of life or of death. He may steep the soul in the action of the propensities so deep, that it can hardly wing an aspiration beyond the mere animal nature; or he may lift its action into higher and nobler natures, and ascend, through his own moral and religious elements, to the infinite source of every thing that is.

"To gratify all the propensities, in subjection to the higher sentiments, enlightened by intellect; 'to use the world as not abusing it;' to place the greatest good in the exercise of the highest thought and most ennobling feeling; to mingle with all the bland socialities of life; to revel amid the deep feelings of the ideal; to obey, in all things, the great and eternal rule of right, the golden rule of the gospel; to indulge in the exercise of a high and heaven-born benevolence; above all, to be thoroughly imbued with the deep and all-pervading feeling of dependence, that with the consciousness of having done all, and done all rightly, casts unhesitatingly and unreservedly all results and consequences upon Him with whom are the issues of things; are the dictates of wisdom, and the revelations of God as disclosed in his word, as proclaimed from his works.

"In what, then, does religion essentially consist? Not, certainly, in the mere obedience yielded to creeds, or forms of worship, or special observances. Not in the assumption of undisturbed gravity, great sedateness, or measured regularity of demeanour. Not in the indulgence of an ascetic spirit, condemning every thing bearing the impress of this world and yet instinctively clinging to every thing earthly. Not in narrowness of mental vision, intolerance of opinion, or severity of judgment upon worldly affairs. Not in such consists the religion revealed in the gospel or in the books of nature. Far other and different is its spirit and mode of exhibition.

"It inspires a deep felt humility, a strong sense of dependence, an unshaken confidence in the Supreme Power. To the pains and penalties of the physical sanction it brings uncomplaining endurance; to those of the political, a meek submission; to those of the popular, the disposition and effort to merit better things; and to those of the moral, the terrible inflictions of an awkward conscience, it brings, not the forgiveness of itself, but of its author. It applies to that self-created, and self-inflicting wound, the balm of a pardoning God. It brings to that deadly leprosy of the immortal nature, the only means of relief, the only unction that can heal. Its spirit is mild, merciful, benevolent. To all the varying grades of suffering, it carries but one thought—to relieve. To all the complications of error, it brings but one purpose—to amend. It seeks to do good to the only end that good may be done, and that irrespective of the agent. In joy it meets the approving smile of its God, and rejoices; in sorrow, the discipline of the same being, and rejoices still. It is purified by affliction, and ennobled by endurance. It finds in every thing around it more of good than of evil. It revenges wrongs committed, by visiting the moral nature of the wrong doer with the vengeance of forgiveness. Meek in its aspect, pretensionless in its claims, charitable in its constructions, it goes forth amid all this world's multiplied activities, and throws around its pains and pleasures, its loves and hatreds, its hopes and fears, its triumphs and defeats, the mild mantle of its own bland spirit. Its merits lay not in profession, but in possession. It is no noisy arguer, nor wordy disputant. It flies from the clash of creeds, and the wrangle of sects, and takes refuge with the lowly in mind. It points to the centre, source, origin, and cause of things, and urges upon every primitive power of man the highest possible motive that can be addressed to it. It invites rather than threatens, and appeals to human fears only as a means of strengthening human hopes. It hallows and sanctifies all within the sphere of its influence, and visits this sleep of the soul during life, with, at least, the dreams of heaven. It is to the spiritual world, what light is to the natural, and in its mild effulgence stand revealed, in their true proportions, all the mighty moral machinery of motive, intention, power, volition, and act. This is the spirit of the gospel, the spirit of nature. It is neither adverse to life, nor to any of its legitimate pursuits. Religion, unfitted and unadapted to this world, never would have been sent here by its author. The language of scorn, derision, contempt, and condemnation of all this world's uses and purposes, is the language of men, not of God. Why scorn the nursery in which the infancy of a limitless being is reared? We do not look back with contempt upon the cradle in which our slumbering infancy was rocked. The cradle is to life what the world is to eternity. All the uses and purposes of which the last is susceptible, may, in some after stage of our being, be viewed by us in the same light that we now look back upon the baubles that decked our infancy. Yet those baubles were real to us then, and so are the uses and purposes of this world now. They were also useful then. They brought into exercise the same powers and faculties that were required in after life. So also are the uses and purposes of this world useful now. They call out our powers and faculties into action, and serve to discipline immortal natures. What! with a physical frame, and mental powers and capacities adapted to the present state of things, to condemn every thing earthly, and to yield to that condemnation the highest possible homage, that of our action; to lay aside all effort and exertion, because every thing here is too mean for attainment, and thus merit heaven by becoming self-destroyers on earth! This would be a doctrine unworthy the reception of man; much more, then, the bestowment of God.

"It is not against the uses, but the abuses of this world, that the mild spirit of religion raises its voice of protestation and warning. Against the unregulated action of the propensities it brings to bear all the machinery of man's higher nature. But their modified, regulated action it invites, encourages, enforces. Its great, leading, and all-controlling object is, to make man fitter for heaven, by rendering him a better tenant of earth; not a more earthly tenant, but a more heavenly occupant of an earthly dwelling-place.

"Religion is emphatically a thing of life, and dwells with living sympathies, and kindles and glows with living emotions. It is caculated not merely for a Sabbath day garment, but for an every day familiar. It is designed to accompany the merchant to his counting-house; the mechanic to his work-shop; the student to his study; and the farmer to his field of labour. It forms the golden dream of youth; the firmer strength of manhood; the supporting staff of age. Without it, fear subsides into dismay, and hope dies in despair; all things contingent are regarded as necessary, and all means transformed into ends; the great mistake is discovered too late to be rectified, and the death that was expected to fold in eternal slumber, on its approach seems rather to awaken to eternal vigilance."

MISCELLANY.

Examination of a Skull.—After a public lecture on phrenology at the Temperance Hall, in this city, on the evening of March 6th, 1840, two skulls were presented to Mr. L. N. Fowler for examination. Mr. Fowler had no knowledge whatever of the character of the individuals to whom the skulls belonged, and was governed in his examination solely by their cranial developements. We can now give only the results of one examination, though the other was by no means less striking and correct, and may be presented in some future number of the Journal. Mr. Fowler's remarks on the first skull, were as follows:—

1st, I should think this was the skull of a male, who had a large brain, and considerable mind, yet was more distinguished for his physical strength and powers of endurance.

2d, His moral sentiments were decidedly weak, particularly Conscientiousness and Hope; and his actions were without reference to the future, or regard for principles of justice.

3d, He had very strong animal feelings and propensities. The strongest of these were Combativeness, Destructiveness, Alimentiveness, and Firmness, which, if perverted, would make him quarrelsome, cruel, desperate, and stubborn in the extreme. He would be disposed to boast, be proud of his strength, and when angry, would be reckless and desperate; was naturally ambitious, yet low-minded, witty, and fond of sport and sensual indulgence; was very self-willed, and had uncommon self-possession and presence of mind; never gave up the object of his pursuit, and would always have his own way, right or wrong. To sum up his character, I should say that Destructiveness and Firmness had a controlling influence, making him cruel, desperate, and possessed of a murderous disposition, and a stubborn, ungovernable will.

Such was Mr. Fowler's examination, after which the gentleman who had obtained the skull from Georgetown, Del., stated to the audience some facts in the character of the person to whom it belonged. It appeared that the individual, whose skull was examined, was Robert Morris, who had been executed for murder. The following document contains briefly the facts in the case:—

Court of Oyer and Terminer, Oct. Term, 1831.

Indictment for Murder.

State of Delaware,	This indictment was found at the October term, 1831, of the court in Sussex County, Delaware, upon the oath of the grand inquest, charging the said Robert Morris with the murder, on board of a brig lying in the Delaware Bay, of the captain by the name of Hilburn; he was convicted at the court above-named, and executed on Tuesday, the eighth day of November, 1831.
vs.	
Robert Morris.	
Witnesses:	
Samuel Allen,	
John O'Berry.	

Remarks.—Robert Morris was an Englishman by birth, was shipped at Philadelphia whilst in a state of intoxication, and on being ordered from his berth whilst opposite Lewistown, in the Delaware Bay, was pulled by the captain from the berth in which he was lying, and then stabbed the captain with a long Spanish knife. He was a man of remarkable muscle, and of great firmness. He walked to the gallows, and adjusted the cord about his neck, telling the sheriff where the best place was to fix the knot. The rope broke, in consequence of his request that the sheriff would make the drop long, to kill him instantly. On being taken up again, he offered to place the rope over the hook, remarking, that he would die like a man, and without a struggle. Such was indeed the fact; he never exhibited the least appearance of fear, nor moved a muscle, that could be discovered.

He stated, after his conviction for murder, that he had no intention to kill Captain Hilburn, but that he shipped on board the brig whilst intoxicated, and when he become more sober, he wanted to be set on shore, as he was not pleased with being on board so small a vessel and weak manned, having been accustomed to being on board of men-of-war, having been on a four years' cruise with Commodore Hull, of the United States service, who could, if present, testify to his good behaviour and undoubted bravery.

I certify the above statements to be truths taken from the record, and personal conversation myself with Robert Morris. In testimony of which, I have hereunto set my hand, this 27th February, 1840, at Georgetown, Del.

JOSHUA S. LAYTON.

—

Character inferred from an Examination of the Skull, by Mr. Deville, of London.—The numerous readers of "Jack Sheppard," have doubtless become familiar with the stern, hardened, infamous, and vindictive character of Jonathan Wild, whose skeleton is now in the possession of Mr. Fowler, a surgeon of Windsor, England. The friends of phrenology, and, indeed, the curious portions of society in general, will doubtless be interested in some account of the craniological developements of so extraordinary a villain. We learn, then, that the skeleton, as it stands in case, is five feet five inches; and several medical men who have seen it, have pronounced that Wild, when living, must have stood about five feet eight or nine inches. The skeleton is in a perfect state, with the exception of the thumb of the left hand, and part of the forefinger of the right hand, which are missing. There are three teeth in the head, which are quite sound. Mr. Fowler, anxious to ascertain if the general character of Wild, while living, was borne out by the phrenological developements of the head, sent the skull, some time since, to Mr. Deville, the well-known phrenologist in the Strand; but without giving the most remote hint as to the name and character of the party "whose shoulders it once fitted." It was returned to Mr. Fowler, with a "certificate" from Mr. Deville, of which the following is a copy :—

This is the skull of an individual possessing some useful faculties for mechanical operations, going about and comprehending things readily ; but he is a singular character, with a large portion of brain in the region of the propensities. And under disappointment of his own importance, pecuniary difficulties, or intoxication, he would be very likely to commit crime. He would be fond of offspring or children, but not a kind parent, as the mandate must be obeyed. He would be the associate of a female, and probably be a married man, but liable to jealousy, being a doubter of the integrity of others towards himself; and while in this state of feeling, if aroused, he would be liable to do injury to those so offending him, and, if opposed, murder might be the result from such an organisation. He would be conceited, self-willed, and obstinate, and, if opposed in his own views, his passions would run very high. He would, without much hesitation, appropriate to his own use the property of others ; but, in so doing, show some ingenuity and cunning, it being difficult of detection. He would, at times, manifest some feeling for religion, and might follow some sect, and at times hold forth upon the subject; but I doubt much the integrity upon it, being more to cover and screen the animal propensities. He would be a talker in his own society—a knowing and conceited individual. He has had some notions of music, and having some command of words, would be likely to become the songster of his society—such an organisation preferring society where he could become the hero of a public-house party. From the character of the bones, it appears to be the skull of an elderly man, whom I consider as having had the power of becoming useful, but from the predominance of the animal, I consider him an aged sinner.

It will be perceived by all those who have read the life of Wild, that the above delineation of his character, according to phrenology, is remarkably correct.

—

Noble Sentiment.—Dr. Spurzheim was emphatically the friend of woman. In conversation with a lady at Boston, on the subject of female education, he remarked that woman would have but little influence on society, till the systems of instruction were improved. "And how can they be improved?" inquired the lady. "By the efforts of yourself, madam, and others of your own sex who take an interest in the subject," he promptly replied. "Men do not, except in very rare instances, feel inclined to promote the mental improvement of females ; they fear that they shall lose their empire over you, if you become as wise as men ; therefore, you must in the first place educate yourselves—lead the way, and show us, by example, the benefits that result from a good and thorough system of instruction. I know that *reason* must be cultivated, in order that persons may understand their moral duties, and the best manner of discharging them ; but my sex do not, as yet, care to have women *reason ;* they think it enough if you can only *feel.* This is wrong; for till women are taught to reason, they cannot cultivate the reasoning powers of their children ; and hence it is, that the passions and selfish feelings are made so predominant in the greater part of our race. But women must themselves take the lead in correcting these errors."

Dr. Gall's Visit to the Prison of Berlin.—Dr. Gall was an excellent practical phrenologist, and scarcely ever failed in his delineations of character. The following interesting account of his visit to the prison of Berlin, was drawn up by some of the gentlemen who accompanied him, and was published at the time in Nos. 97 and 98 of the Freymüthige for May, 1805, and afterward's recopied into Gall's large work on the Functions of the Brain:—

Dr. Gall having expressed a desire to inspect the prisons of Berlin, with a view of making himself acquainted with their arrangements and construction, as well as of observing the heads of the prisoners, it was proposed to him, that he should visit not only the prisons of that city, but the house of correction, and the fortress of Spandau.

Accordingly, on the 17th of April, 1805, Dr. Gall began with those of Berlin, in presence of the directing commissaries, the superior officers of the establishment, the inquisitors of the criminal deputation, the counsellor Thürnagel, and Schmidt, the assessors Muhlberg and Wunder, the superior counsellor of the medical inspection, Welper, Dr. Flemming, Professor Wildenow, and several other gentlemen.

As soon as Dr. Gall had satisfied himself in regard to the regulations and general management of the establishment, the party went to the criminal prisons and to the *salles de travail*, where they found about two hundred prisoners, whom Dr. Gall was allowed to examine, without a word being said to him, either of their crimes or of their characters.

It may here be remarked, that the great proportion of those detained in the criminal prisons, are robbers or thieves; and, therefore, it was to be expected, that if Dr. Gall's doctrine were true, the organ of Acquisitiveness should, as a general rule, be found to predominate in these individuals. This accordingly soon appeared to be the case. The heads of all the thieves resembled each other more or less in shape. All of them presented a width and prominence at that part of the temple where the organ is situated, with a depression above the eyebrows, a retreating forehead, and the skull flattened towards the top. These peculiarities were perceptible at a single glance; but the touch rendered still more striking, the difference between the form of the skulls of robbers, and that of the skulls of those who were detained for other causes. The peculiar shape of the head, generally characteristic of thieves, astonished the party still more, when several prisoners were ranged in a line; but it was never so strikingly borne out and illustrated as when, at the request of Dr. Gall, all the youths from twelve to fifteen years of age, who were confined for theft, were collected together; their heads presented so very nearly the same configuration, that they might easily have passed for the offspring of the same stock.

It was with great ease that Dr. Gall distinguished confirmed thieves from those who were less dangerous; and in every instance his opinion was found to agree with the result of the legal interrogatories. The heads in which Acquisitiveness was most predominant, were that of Columbus, and among the children, that of the little H., whom Gall recommended to keep in confinement for life, as utterly incorrigible. Judging from the judicial proceedings, both had manifested an extraordinary disposition for thieving.

In entering one of the prisons, where all the women presented a predominance of the same organ, except one, (then busy at the same employment, and in precisely the same dress as the offenders,) Dr. Gall asked, as soon as he perceived her, why that person was there, seeing that her head presented no appearance indicative of any propensity to steal. He was then told that she was not a criminal, but the inspectress of works. In the same way, he distinguished other individuals confined for different causes besides theft.

Several opportunities of seeing Acquisitiveness, combined with other largely-developed organs, presented themselves. In one prisoner, it was joined with Benevolence and the organ of theosophy, the latter particularly large. The individual was put to the proof, and, in all his discourses, showed great horror at robberies accompanied with violence, and manifested much respect for religion. He was asked which he thought the worse action, to ruin a poor labourer by taking his all, or to steal from a church without harming any one? He replied that it was too revolting to rob a church, and that he could never summon resolution enough to do it.

Dr. Gall was requested to examine particularly the heads of the prisoners implicated in the murder of a Jewess, which had taken place the preceding year. In the principal murderer, Marcus Hirsch, he found a head, which, besides indicating very depraved dispositions, presented nothing remarkable, except a very great developement of the organ of Perseverance. His accomplice, Jeanette Marcus, had an extremely vicious conformation of brain, the organ which leads to theft being greatly developed, as well as that of Destructiveness. He found in the female servants, Bendendorf and Babette, great want of circumspection; and in the wife of Marcus Hirsch, a form of head altogether insignificant. All this was found to be in strict accordance with the respective characters of the prisoners, as ascertained by the legal proceedings.

The prisoner Fritze, suspected of having killed his wife, and apparently guilty of that crime, although he still stoutly denied it, was next shown to Dr. Gall. The latter found the organs of Cunning and Firmness highly developed—qualities which his interrogator had found him manifest in the very highest degree.

In the tailor Maschke, arrested for counterfeiting the legal coin, and whose genius for the mechanical arts was apparent in the execution of his crime, Gall found, without knowing for what he was confined, the organ of Constructiveness much developed, and a head so well organised, that he lamented several times the fate of that man. The truth is, that this Maschke was well known to possess great mechanical skill, and at the same time much kindness of heart.

Scarcely had Dr. Gall advanced a few steps into another prison, when he perceived the organ of Constructiveness equally developed in a man named Troppe, a shoemaker, who, without any teaching, applied himself to the making of watches, and other objects, by which he now lives. In examining him more nearly, Gall found also the organ of Imitation, generally remarkable in comedians, considerably developed—a just observation, since the crime of Troppe was that of having extorted a considerable sum of money under the feigned character of an officer of police. Gall observed to him, that he must assuredly have been fond of playing tricks in his youth, which he acknowledged. When Gall said to those about him, "*If that man had fallen in the way of comedians, he would have become an actor,*" Troppe, astonished at the exactness and precision with which Gall unveiled his disposition, told them that he had in fact been some time (six months) a member of a strolling company—a circumstance which had not till then been discovered.

In the head of the unhappy Heisig, who, in a state of intoxication, had stabbed his friend, Gall found a generally good conformation, with the exception of a very deficient Cautiousness, or great rashness. He remarked in several other prisoners the organs of Language, Colour, and Mathematics, in perfect accordance with the manifestations; some of the first spoke several languages; those with large Colour, were fond of showy clothes, flowers, paintings, &c.; and those with Mathematics large, calculated easily from memory.

—

Testimony in Favour of Phrenology.—Richard Carmichael, of Dublin, Member of the Royal Irish Academy, as well as of several other learned societies, and who is well known in the medical profession as a valuable contributor to medical science, has devoted some attention to the merits of phrenology. In the volume of Mr. Combe's testimonials, published in Edinburgh, we find Mr. Carmichael expressing the following sentiments in relation to the truth and importance of the science:—

I feel the highest gratification in stating my firm belief in the principles of phrenology, and conceive that it explains better than any other system of mental philosophy the operations of the mind. From it alone we learn why two persons, educated together, and subjected to the same moral and physical impressions, may be widely different from each other as to their dispositions, talents, and acquirements. It alone explains in a satisfactory manner the various degrees of that reasoning faculty with which the lower animals are gifted, and why they should necessarily follow almost blindly their dispositions, so as to have hitherto given these tendencies to certain actions the name of instincts, but which phrenology has satisfactorily explained as depending upon the peculiar organisation of the brain of each species of animal. Phrenology has alone afforded a satisfactory explanation of the long disputed doctrines of free will and necessity—it teaches us to what degree we are necessitated to obey the impulses arising from organisation, and how far and by what means we are free agents, to act as the superior faculties direct. By it also are satisfactorily accounted for many mental phenomena in man, which all the old systems of metaphysics and morals failed to explain; from it alone we learn why certain individuals should excel in one pursuit or branch of knowledge, and be dull in most others; why some are so disposed to commit breaches in the organic and moral laws to which man is subjected, that they can scarcely be considered as accountable persons, and are therefore better fitted for the seclusion of a lunatic asylum, than for the punishment to which the criminal codes even of civilised countries would subject them; and on this account we have sufficient grounds to assume that the principles of phrenology ought to be consulted in criminal legislation.

In the practice of medicine, Phrenology is of the highest utility, as it is manifestly the true and only physiology of the brain, and therefore upon it ought to hinge its pathology also. When the functions of this important organ are disturbed, as happens in acute and chronic inflammation of the brain, general fever, injuries of the head, and the various grades of apoplexy, from vertigo to the annihilation of the intellect, power of motion, and use of the senses, and, lastly, in monomania and general insanity, phrenology may assist us in the treatment, as I have already exemplified in a paper inserted in the Dublin Medical Journal.

THE

AMERICAN PHRENOLOGICAL JOURNAL

AND

MISCELLANY.

Vol. II.   Philadelphia, July 1, 1840.   No. 10.

ARTICLE I.

ON THE MERITS OF PHRENOLOGY.*

The time seems to us to have now arrived when a careful and con
scientious examination of the truth and merits of phrenology ha
become imperative on every intelligent member of the profession, an
when its claims to attention can no longer be safely neglected, eve
by those who are more concerned about their personal reputation tha
about the advancement of science and the improvement of mankind
If phrenology be true, its importance to medicine and to philosoph
can scarcely be overrated, and no one can be more usefully employe
than in advocating its cause; whereas, if it be false, and the observa
tions on which it professes to rest be really incorrect, a great servic
would be rendered to medicine by at once demonstrating their hollow
ness, and directing the able and zealous exertions of its misled fol
lowers into a safer and more profitable channel.   Acting on this con
viction, we have ourselves lately bestowed much attention on the sub
ject; and we feel that no apology can be required for now laying th
results before our readers.

In contemplating the past history of phrenology, the difference o
tone and manner in which it is now spoken of cannot fail to b
remarked.   Five-and-twenty years ago, when the late Dr. Gordo
made his unprovoked and ungenerous attack in the Edinburgl
Review on "the man of skulls," whom he imagined to have bee
slain in the same review twelve years before by the abler hand of th
late Dr. Thomas Brown, the public, then profoundly ignorant of th
merits of the question, went so heartily along with him in the torren
of invective, abuse, and ridicule, in which he so inconsideratel

* From the British and Foreign Medical Review, edited by John Forbes, M. D
F. R. S.   •

indulged, that for years after, the subject was never alluded to without a smile of contempt or a laugh of derision, and the gentlest fate which was assigned for it was that of speedy and eternal oblivion.

How different the state of things is now, few even of its most inveterate opponents require to be told. For years phrenology has ceased to be the subject of drawing-room gossip, or the favourite topic of the ridicule of the shallow.   In mixed society it is as little heard of as any other branch of physiological or scientific inquiry, which the rules of good breeding naturally warn us to reserve for a more fitting occasion; and from this circumstance many imagine that it has wholly disappeared.   But when we examine a little more closely what is passing around us, the signs of its vitality and growth are found so numerous and palpable as to shadow forth rather a long, and vigorous, and useful existence, than the speedy extinction with which it has been threatened.   In proof of this, we would refer, among other things, to the numerous works which have lately appeared, not in this country only, but in America and on the continent, and the titles of some of which are prefixed to the present article, not for review, for that were impossible, but as indications of what is going on.   We would refer, also, to the variety of quarters in which phrenology is already received, and more or less acted upon, as established truth. We confess, indeed, that, although far from inattentive to its later progress, we were not prepared for the numerous evidences of its extended diffusion which forced themselves upon our notice, without inquiry, in a late tour through part of England, Scotland, and the north of France, Paris included.   In asylums, schools, and factories, we found it recognised and acted upon, where ten years before not a trace of its existence was to be heard of.   Not only, however, are works on phrenology rapidly multiplying in number, but they are improving in character; and in accuracy of observation, sobriety of inference, and vigour of thinking, a few of them may bear a comparison with any physiological or philosophical works which have lately appeared.   That these qualities have not been without their natural effect in exciting a widely diffused interest in the public mind, is evident from the extraordinary and steady sale which several of the phrenological works, the best, we believe, of their class, have met with, in the face of the active and influential hostility of the leading journals of the day, led on by Lord Jeffrey himself, in the Edinburgh Review, and also by the Quarterly.   If this demand had lasted only for a year or two, it might have been plausibly enough ascribed to fashion and a love of novelty; but when it has extended, as in the instance of Mr. Combe's books, over a period of twenty years, it is difficult to account for it, except on the supposition of their possessing a real and abiding interest, derived either from the inherent nature of the subject, or from the manner in which it is treated. Not to men tion the wide diffusion of the works of the founder of phrenology, and his colleague, Spurzheim, we have now before us the *sixty-firs* quarterly number of the Prenological Journal, which has been carriee on for upwards of sixteen years, and, as we are told by the editor, i yearly increasing in circulation. We have also before us an adver tisement of the last edition of Combe's " Constitution of Man, con sidered in Relation to External Objects," in which it is mentionee that that work, being an application of phrenology to human improve ment, continues in constant demand, after a sale of *forty-five thousan copies* in Great Britain and Ireland alone, besides large editions ii America, and translations into French and German. The "System of Phrenology" of the same author, which contains the best exposi tion of the doctrine, its evidences and applications, although selling a a guinea, and therefore not likely to be bought without due considera tion, has already gone through four editions, and, as we have learned still continues in increasing demand, to the extent of six hundree copies a year. In like manner, the " Introduction to Phrenology,' by the late Dr. Macnish, have sold, as appears from the advertise ment, to the very large extent of five or six thousand copies withir three years, notwithstanding the increasing number of competitors ir the market. We might mention many other evidences, of a simila nature, to prove the progress which phrenology is making in public opinion ; but for these we must refer the reader to the curious volume of Mr. Hewett Watson, on " The Statistics of Phrenology," in which an account is given of the various works published, and societie: existing, in this country, and in which the reader will find much use ful information, of an authentic kind, relating to the past history and present state of phrenology.

As further evidence, of a very unequivocal kind, we may refer to the numerous courses of lectures given on the subject within the las five years in most of our larger towns, and to the intelligent audience: by which they were attended. Even the frequent display of phreno logical busts in the windows of shops is a sign not without meaning to reflecting minds. But perhaps more than all, the rapid diffusion of phrenological ideas under the cover of ordinary language, and withou any reference to their true source, is a proof not only that the nev philosophy is making progress, but that it is found to be of direc utility in questions of nervous disorder, insanity, education, morals and crime. We are acquainted with medical and educational work which have gained no small repute, from the copious but unacknow ledged use they have made of the doctrines of phrenology, and th reputation of which depends chiefly on their borrowed views. We have sometimes, indeed, been tempted to smile at the ready acceptance which strict phrenological ideas have met with when thus stolen and offered at second-hand, only a little altered in dress to prevent their paternity being traced. But much as we rejoice in the diffusion of useful truth, we cannot refrain from condemning this plan of acquiring a temporary popularity at the expense of science; and we are glad that the risk of detection will soon become so great as to deter most men from such unscrupulous conduct. It may seem at first view a light matter thus to put forth a truth in disguise; but in reality, its forced separation from the principle which alone renders its application safe and advantageous, deprives it of much of its practical value; and it is for this reason, as well as for its dishonesty, that we object to the practice.

If our space permitted, we might further refer to the account given in the last number of the Phrenological Journal of Mr. Combe's progress in the United States, and to the works of Vimont, Broussais, Ferrarese, and other continental authors, to show that, abroad as well as at home, phrenology is exciting the serious attention of men of science. But we must content ourselves with the simple statement that such is the fact; and that, among the more recent of the French medical works, the principles of phrenology are either expressly or tacitly assumed, as if no doubt had been entertained regarding them. Many hesitate, and justly, about the details, but we do not go too far in affirming that a conviction of the truth of the leading principles of the new physiology of the brain is fast diffusing itself over the continent.

With these facts before us, we need scarcely add that our past silence has not arisen either from participating in the contempt with which phrenology was formerly treated, or from having been unobservant of its more recent progress. From the first we saw that, whether true or false, the subject was one of great extent and serious import; and we delayed forming or expressing any opinion till we should have sufficient time and opportunity to verify its principles and scrutinise its details. Having now done so, sufficiently to qualify ourselves for giving an opinion, we should shrink from our duty, both to our readers and to science, were we to hesitate longer in avowing our conviction that phrenology embodies many facts and views of great general interest, and direct practical utility to the physician, the philosopher, and the philanthropist; and that as such, it has established a claim to a more careful, serious, and impartial examination on the part of the profession than it has ever yet received. We do not by this mean to affirm that all the facts and doctrines taught by

the phrenologists are accurate and true; so far from it, we hav‹
satisfied ourselves that many have been admitted without a sufficientlȷ
scrupulous examination; and that not seldom, the conclusions deduce‹
from them have been pushed beyond the limits of strictly logical infer
ence. We are consequently not inclined to adopt either of them with
out due verification. But it would be the height of injustice were w‹
on that account to reject the whole as unfounded, and to maintain tha
they cannot possibly be true, merely because they are in contradictioʳ
to our own preconceived opinions ; and yet, to the most unphiloso
phical and illogical mode of proceeding we have condemned, may b‹
traced almost all the opposition which Gall's discovery has met with

If the functions of the brain had been already ascertained by som‹
method of inquiry of a more satisfactory nature than that resorted t‹
by Dr. Gall, we might have argued, with some fairness, that if hiˢ
observations were inconsistent with those already obtained, they coul‹
not possibly be true. But when it is notorious that all other methodˢ
of investigation *have failed* to unfold the mystery of the cerebral func‑
tions, it is as obvious as the noonday sun, that no information whicʰ
we may possess can enable us to decide, *a priori*, and *without anȷ
examination of the evidence*, that his mode of inquiry is fallacious
and its results untrue. To entitle the judgment of any one to the
least weight, either for or against the reality of the discovery, it musᵗ
be based upon a careful examination of the facts and evidence. If ₐ
man propounds, as a new discovery, that the function of the liver is
to secrete milk, we are logically entitled to disregard his assertion.
because we are already in possession of demonstrative evidence thaᵗ
the function of the liver is to secrete bile. But it is very differenᵗ
with the case of the brain. When Dr. Gall affirms, that by a new
mode of inquiry, easy of practice, he has ascertained that the anterioʳ
lobes of the brain serve for the manifestation of intellect, the posterioʳ
lobes for that of the animal passions, and the coronal region for tha
of the moral feelings, we have no right whatever, either in sense or iʳ
philosophy, to say, " No! this is a mistake." So long as we do no
possess a shadow of information at variance with his assertion, i
would be to assume in profound ignorance the privilege of Omni‑
science to say, that such a thing " *cannot be.*" With regard to the
brain, we are in precisely the same situation as we would be witʰ
regard to the spleen, if some physiologist were to discover that its true
use was to secrete a particular kind of digestive fluid, and were t‹
decribe how he made the discovery, and how it might be verified. Iᶠ
the greatest philosopher that ever lived were thereupon to deny, *with‑
out examination of the evidence*, that the spleen served for any sucʰ
purpose, who would attach any weight to his objection, or who woul‹

care one straw for the adverse opinion of any man who had not thought it worth his while *to test the fact*, before deciding on its truth?   In like manner, when Gall professes to have found out the functions of the brain, and explains how he made the discovery, and how it may be verified, it would be equally childish and futile to satisfy ourselves with the simple denial without direct examination of the fact, that the different organs above specified serve the purposes pointed out by him.   Either we must meet the question of fact by a personal and extensive appeal to nature, or we ought to avow that we are not prepared to speak definitely as to the truth of the doctrine.

We are aware that many talk of phrenology as a mere theory, invented by the fertile imagination of an enthusiast, and under this impression think they treat it with all due respect, when they give it half an hour's consideration before they express an opinion of its merits.   We confess that we ourselves once belonged to this rather numerous class of persons, and that we extracted much amusement from the pages of Gall and Spurzheim, by a playful travestie of some of the curious anecdotes by which they occasionally illustrate their positions ; and which, considered apart from the context, have often a somewhat ludicrous aspect.   But when at length we came into contact with Spurzheim himself, and remarked, instead of the wild enthusiasm of a visionary, the truthful earnestness, the calm and forcible appeals to fact and reason, and the occasionally almost solemn feeling of the importance of his mission, with which he advocated his cause, we felt that the subject was of too grave a nature to be either hastily admitted or slightingly rejected, and resolved to try his positions by the strict test of observation before finally deciding upon their truth. The result was, as we have already said, not the blind adoption of the whole phrenological doctrines, but a growing and conscientious conviction of the soundness of the great principles on which they are based, and of the practical value of many of their details.   But although we see strong grounds for believing that an imperishable foundation has been laid, the edifice itself is still far from being complete, and many years and much labour will be required to bring it to that perfection of which even its present outline shows it to be susceptible, and which, in their short-sightedness, some of its admirers imagine it already to have attained.

Gall's discovery, if such it shall turn out to be, of the functions of the brain was no premeditated invention, but, like that of the principle of gravitation by Sir Isaac Newton, the result of accident.   When he first observed at school that the boys who gained places from him by the facility with which they learned and remembered words and recitations, while they were much inferior to him in general talent, were all remarkable for a peculiar prominence of the eye, like that known by the name of bull's eye, he merely *remarked a fact ;* and when he was removed to another school, and subsequently to college, his atten tion was arrested by the fact that there also the talent of learning easily by heart was accompanied by the prominent bull's eye. At that time he knew nothing of the cause of the prominence, nothing of the posi tion, structure, or functions of the brain, and nothing of the philosophy of mind. He attempted no explanation, and had consequently no theory to support. He satisfied himself with observing that the fact was so.

For a long time Gall remained at this point ; but, as he advanced in years and reflection, it at last occurred to him, *that if one marked quality of mind was thus indicated by a peculiarity of conformation the same might be the case with others.* This was the prelude to all his subsequent examinations. He began to remark with care the dif ferent forms of head, and differences of disposition and talent, by which his companions were respectively distinguished. To facilitate his researches and ensure greater accuracy of observation, he now took casts in plaster of every remarkable head or forehead which pre sented itself; and by comparing the peculiarities of each with what he knew of the mental qualities of their originals, he gradually became possessed of a very interesting series of observations, throwing addi tional light upon the facts with which he started. Occasionally, when he thought he had succeeded in tracing a connection between some marked feature of mind and peculiar form of head, an instance would present itself of the same mental peculiarity with a different form of head, and dash to the ground the conclusion which seemed approach ing to certainty. Not discouraged by these results, he neither hesi tated to give up the opinion which was thus disproved by facts, nor found his faith in the uniformity of nature at all shaken. He sub mitted to the correction, but continued his observations, and rarely failed by perseverance to discover the cause of his error, and to add to the stock of positive truths. The ultimate result of his labours was the gradual developement of the physiological and psychological doctrines now known under the name of phrenology.

Phrenology, then, may be considered in two distinct lights : first. as an exposition of the functions of the component parts of the brain ; and secondly, as a theory of the philosophy of mind. Considered in the former light, the evidences of its truth must be sought for in oft repeated observation of the concomitance and connection of certain functions with certain portions of the brain ; whereas, considered purely as a system of mental philosophy, its truth may be judged of like that of other theories of mind, by the facility and consistency with which it explains the phenomena, and admits of practical applications to the purposes of life. The former kind of evidence, viz. that of *direct observation*, is by far the most conclusive, and, as coming within the strict province of physiology, is that to which medical men ought chiefly, or first, to direct their attention. But the evidence arising from complete adaptation to the phenomena, is also entitled to great weight, and may indeed suffice for those who study it chiefly as a branch of philosophy. The best way of all, however, is to investigate the subject from both points of view, and embrace both kinds of evidence; but on the present occasion we must confine ourselves almost exclusively to its consideration as a branch of physiology.

Taken in its widest sense, phrenology professes to be *a theory of the philosophy of mind, founded on the observation and discovery of the functions of the brain, in so far as that organ is concerned in the mental operations.* Its fundamental principles are the following:

First, That the brain is the organ of the mind, and is concerned in every mental operation, whether of emotion or of intellect.

Second, That the brain does not act as a unit, but consists of a plurality of organs, each serving for the manifestation of an individual faculty of the mind.

Third, That the energy of function or power of manifestation is proportioned, *cæteris paribus*, to the size of the organ; or, in other words, that a large organ will, *all other conditions being equal,* enjoy a power of action proportioned to its size, and consequently manifest the corresponding faculty with greater energy than if it were small.

And lastly, That by observing carefully a sufficient number of cases in which the same part of the brain predominates in size over all the other parts, and ascertaining what particular quality of mind is exclusively in excess in the same individuals, we obtain a direct clue to the discovery of the functions of all the organs of the brain, and require only that the observations shall be so carefully made, and so extensively repeated, as to obviate every chance of error before adopting the inferences as established. Let us now see how far these principles are in accordance with nature, and with previously existing knowledge.

That the brain is the material organ, without the intervention of which the mind cannot operate during life, is so all but universally admitted, that we shall adduce no facts to prove it. It is true that some over-scrupulous men, like Lord Jeffrey and Dr. Abercrombie, still doubt whether the mind acts through the medium of material organs, except in its communications with the external world; but as the proposition is regarded by an overwhelming majority of physio-

logists as demonstrated, we shall, on the present occasion, assume i
to be true.

Nearly the same assumption might be made with safety as to th
brain consisting of a plurality of parts, each performing a distinc
function. But the truth of this principle is put beyond a doubt by
mass of evidence which we cannot stop to detail, and is further con
firmed by the successive additions which the brain receives as animal
rise in the scale of intelligence, and by the successive developemen
of its different parts, as the human being advances from the fœtal t
the mature state, and from a state of unconsciousness to one of sensa
tion, emotion, thought, and action. During this transition, the dil
ferent parts of the brain are developed, not simultaneously, as a uni
would be, but successively and irregularly. In one individual, emi
nent for talent, the anterior lobe is early and largely developed; whil
in another, whose intellect is purely idiotic, it remains small and con
tracted. In like manner, partial insanity, and injuries of the brain
attended with a partial affection of the mental powers, equally affor
a presumption of a plurality of cerebral organs. If necessary, i
would be easy to multiply such indications and proofs; but as th
advocates of the unity of the brain are few and far between, and thei
views are entirely without influence on the thinking part of mankind
we consider it needless to occupy more time and space in proving
what is so rarely and feebly denied.

The *third* principle, and that which it is of most consequence t
explain and demonstrate, is the proposition that *organic size is
cæteris paribus, a measure of functional power*. The first two prin
ciples are common to phrenology and physiology in general; but th
third, in its broad and specific form, is peculiar to, and lies at the ver
foundation of, phrenology, and will therefore require a more detaile
and careful examination. If it be false, phrenology must crumble t
dust like the dry leaves of autumn driven along by the winter's blast
If it be true, those who oppose phrenology on the assumption of it
falsity, must themselves fall, and like decaying leaves around th
living parent stem, even serve to nourish and support that which the
attempt to destroy. To the examination of this point we shall there
fore, without scruple, devote considerable space.

The form in which the above principle is generally expressed b
phrenologists is, that *size of brain is, cæteris paribus, a measure o
mental power*. Inattention to the simple meaning of this propositio
has been the chief cause of the opposition it has encountered fron
scientific as well as unreflecting men. Notwithstanding all that ha
been done by phrenologists to enforce attention to the important con
dition of "other circumstances being equal," almost all the oppo

nents, from the Edinburgh Reviewer down to Dr. Holland—the latest
who has published on the subject—continue to utterly disregard it,
and speak of the proposition as maintaining that *size alone* is the
measure of functional power; or, as Dr. Holland chooses to state it,
that "*the gross condition of quantity represents the intensity of
quality.*" Having set up this phantom of their own imaginations,
like a pyramid on its apex, many of the anti-phrenologists proceed,
with heavy blows and an approving conscience, to knock the support
from under it; and when it topples over in obedience to their efforts,
they turn round in triumph, and claim the merit of having upset
phrenology. We have seen this feat performed again and again in
the presence of phrenologists. On such occasions, their simple
answer was, "You have upset a phantom of your own creation, but
you have left the phrenological pyramid, resting on its basis, untouched and undamaged;" and such is in reality the case.

As it is in general far more easy to make merry with fiction than
with truth, it required no great effort of wit in Lord Jeffrey to divert
his readers, by referring to grandmamma Wolf, in the fairy tale, as a
high physiological authority on the side of the phrenologists, when
she tells little Red Riding Hood that she has large ears to hear her
the better, large eyes to see her the clearer, and a large mouth to
gobble her up with the greater facility. But his mirth did not alter
the substantial fact established by the researches of comparative
anatomists, that where great nervous sensibility is required, whether
for hearing or sight, a proportionally large nerve is an invariable
accompaniment, whatever the shape or appearance of the organ on
which it is ramified. Neither did it alter the fact that the venerable
lady's large external ear was really capable of receiving a larger
number of atmospherical pulses, and her large eye a greater number
of the rays of light, than a smaller ear or eye would have been. His
joke, nevertheless, was a good joke. It possessed the rare merit of
diverting, at the same moment, not only himself and those whom he
misled, but also those against whom it was directed. The only
difference was, that he laughed at what he supposed the absurdity of
his opponents, while they were merry at the absurdity of the egre-
gious blunder into which he had fallen, and from perceiving that, in
point of both fact and argument, the venerable grandmamma had the
great reviewer entirely at her mercy.

If the phrenologists are to be judged by their own statements and
acts, and not by those falsely ascribed to them, we should say that,
so far from having adopted the proposition which Dr. Holland
refutes, they even deserve credit for adding to the evidence formerly
existing, that "gross quantity" or size alone is NOT a measure of the

functional power of an organ. We have taken some trouble to inquire, and have never met with one phrenologist who did not utterly scout the notion of organic size being THE ONLY condition of functional energy; and who was not prepared with *proofs* by the dozen of the absurdity of such a proposition. Dr. Holland says, " This *relation of mere bulk of substance to the perfection or intensity of a faculty is, prima facia, very improbable.*" To be sure it is ; but what surprises us is, that a man of Dr. Holland's good sense should have had any doubts about the matter, when he might have satisfied himself of the fact by half an hour's observation ; or, if he preferred the authority of others, by consulting any good phrenological treatise in his library. Yet, strangely enough, while he stickles about the insufficiency of the evidence in support of phrenology, he does not hesitate to admit opinions unfavourable to it upon no evidence at all ; and in this particular instance really argues against one of its plainest and most easily demonstrable principles, merely because he has not taken the trouble to understand its meaning.

For demonstrative evidence of *organic size being*, cæteris paribus, *a measure of functional power* (a very different proposition from "mere bulk," being a constant relation to " intensity of quality"), we would refer the reader, first, to personal observation in the field of nature; and secondly, to the concurring testimony of every anatomist and physiologist who treats of the relation between structure and function. We are not aware of a single work of any reputation in which the above principle is not tacitly adopted as nearly self-evident. It pervades every corner of comparative anatomy, and is constantly, though not ostensibly, resorted to as a guide to the discovery of function. If, in an unknown animal, the optic nerve is found to be large relatively to the other nerves of the senses, we never hesitate to infer that the power of vision will be greater in proportion than where the nerve is relatively small. In the same way, we never discover a large olfactory nerve and extended nasal apparatus, without inferring that the animal must be endowed with a powerful sense of smell. And when it is affirmed by phrenologists that the brain forms no exception in this respect to the rest of the organisation, they merely state a principle in words which is admitted universally in practice. Indeed, all the modes of discovery hitherto employed, Camper's facial angle among the rest, tacitly assume this very principle as their basis ; while it has been left to Gall and his followers to direct attention to it, and demonstrate its importance, as a specific truth. In proof of this statement, it would be easy to multiply quotations from any accredited work on comparative anatomy ; but one from indisputable authority may suffice : " It appears," says Cuvier, " that *there are always certain relations between the faculties of animals and the* PROPORTIONS *of the different parts of the brain.* Thus, their intelligence appears to be always great in proportion to the developement of the hemispheres and their several commissures. It appears even that *certain parts of the brain attain,* in all classes of animals, A DEVELOPEMENT PROPORTIONED *to the peculiar properties* of these animals; and one may hope that, in following up these researches, we may at length acquire some notions respecting the particular uses of each part of the brain." On another occasion, when speaking of the cerebral lobes being the place " where all the sensations take a distinct form, and leave durable impressions," Cuvier adds, " l'anatomie comparée en offre une autre confirmation dans *la proportion constante du volume de ces lobes avec le degré d'intelligence des animaux ;*" thus admitting the influence of *size* of the cerebral organs upon the power of manifesting the mental faculties as distinctly as Dr. Gall himself could assert it.

But, it may be asked, if the principle of size being, *cæteris paribus,* a measure of power, has been thus virtually and universally admitted by men of science, whence arise the objections advanced against it by such men as Dr. Holland, when it is *specially* brought forward by the phrenologists? The only answer that can be given is, that the full value of the principle as a means of successfully prosecuting inquiry, was unknown till demonstrated by Dr. Gall, and that, consequently, it had never been a subject of serious consideration among men of science as a distinct and specific proposition. Even now, however, its truth is so palpable that it is never objected to, except when confounded with the very different and erroneous proposition that size *alone* is a measure of power; and, in point of fact, Dr. Gall has been the first to explain the apparent anomalies which other physiologists met with in their researches, by drawing attention to the necessary limitation of *cæteris paribus.* And when this is kept fairly in view, it becomes nearly as impossible to deny it, as to deny that a whole is greater than a part. Both phrenologists and anti-phrenologists are agreed, for example, that a large forehead *generally* indicates superior intelligence; but the faith of the former in the influence of organic size, as affecting intensity of function, is not in the least shaken by the fact that there are *some* large foreheads unaccompanied by any intellectual superiority. Nobody, indeed, knows this fact so well as the phrenologist, because he has not only observed it, but alone has examined the cause of the difference, and found that *the other conditions of the brain are not the same,* and, consequently, that so long as cause and effect continue related as such, the results in mental power cannot possibly coincide. The large and healthy expanse of brow which distinguishes the bust of Bacon may be equalled, *in mere size*, by the unhealthy expanse of forehead in the cretin or idiot; but will any one venture to infer from this, that the size of Bacon's *healthy* brain added nothing to its functional power ? A single example of this kind is sufficient to demonstrate that size alone is not a measure of intensity, but it leaves absolutely untouched the phrenological proposition that size is an important condition of functional power. Great energy of mind cannot coexist with a small size of brain, because no other healthy conditions can supply the want of size. But a large brain may coexist with feebleness of mind, because, from original malformation, defective constitution, or disease, its power of action may be also defective. Large muscles, in the same way, may coexist with little bodily strength in a very lymphatic or relaxed constitution, and in certain states of health; and yet it is never doubted that, *all other conditions being equal*, large muscles are more powerful than small ones. For more than this, the phrenologists do not contend.

' Had Dr. Holland attended to the foregoing most obvious distinction, as laid down in all the works on phrenology which we have ever seen, he would scarcely have ventured to misrepresent Gall's discovery as resting " on the presumption of the gross condition of quantity representing the intensity of quality ;" and, when speaking of the small brains of idiots, and the large brains of eminent men, as affording the best proofs of the influence of size, he would have had no difficulty in explaining the *apparent* exceptions to which he alludes, and reconciling them to the general rule. Rightly interpreted, *there can be no exception to a law of nature;* and when we meet with cases which seem to contradict the principle of organic size being a chief condition of functional power, we can come only to one of two conclusions. Either the principle *must be fallacious* and size be wholly uninfluential *in all cases*, or it *must be real and operating in all.* In particular cases its power may be controlled, or its action modified, by causes which have escaped observation; but there is no contradiction in the laws of nature, and we may rest assured, that if the principle under discussion has a real operation in any case, it will exercise an influence in all, whether or not we can detect the causes by which its perceptible results are modified.

We almost feel that an apology is due to our readers for insisting so much on so obvious a truth; but the very fact that science has been retarded by its neglect and misconstruction, compels us to enforce it even at the risk of tediousness. Sometimes in conversation, after we imagined that the question was placed clearly before the mind's eye, we have been met with the triumphant assertion that our proposition was annihilated by the single comparison of the small brain of the intelligent poodle with the large brain of the stupid ox.   But are all the other conditions the same in such a case except size?   No doubt the brain of an ox is a brain as well as that of a poodle; but is there no difference in their structure, no difference in the proportions of their anterior lobes, and no difference in the number and complexity of their convolutions sufficient to exercise an influence on their functions in addition to mere size?   Looking to the philosophical principle of *cæteris paribus*, it is clear that the proper way to arrive at the truth, is to compare the brain of a clever with that of a stupid poodle, and of one ox with another, as nearly as possible of the same age, state of health, and constitution.   If this be done, and the intelligent poodle be found to have the smaller anterior lobe, then by all means denounce the principle of size as untrue, and at variance with fact. But if the reverse be the case, do not attempt to set the truth aside, by comparing two things so essentially different as to make absolute agreement impossible.   If this precaution be kept in view, we venture to affirm that the more the proposition is scrutinised, the more firmly will it be found to rest on the unassailable foundation of truth.

(To be continued.)

ARTICLE II.

FURTHER REMARKS BY MR. SAMPSON ON THE PRIMARY FUNCTION OF IDEALITY.

To the Editor of the American Phrenological Journal.

London, April 14th, 1840.

Dear Sir,—

The editor of the London Phrenological Journal, in reviewing the essay which appeared in No. 9 of your Miscellany, on the organ of Ideality, concludes with the following observation: "For our own part, we cannot avoid the suspicion that there are both physiological and metaphysical difficulties in the way of appointing Ideality to the office of over-looker or drill-serjeant to the other organs; and that, as a matter of fact, individuals endowed with large Ideality are rather more prone than others to run into some extremes, though not into the extremes of brutality and sordid vice."

The plausibility of an objection of this nature had not escaped my attention at the time when I first detailed my views upon the subject, but the narrow space to which a writer is necessarily limited in a periodical work prevented me from touching upon it. Since, however, the objection has proceeded from a quarter which is entitled to the greatest weight among phrenologists, I am anxious to lay it before your readers in connection with the reply which it requires.

From my remark, that "the emotion of *beauty* which gratifies Ideality, arises when an object is presented that appeals harmoniously to all the faculties, and that wherever one faculty is excited to a preponderance above the rest, the idea of beauty is destroyed," your readers will see that I had not any intention to propound a new theory of the function of that organ, but merely to carry the observations already made upon it to the ultimate principles to which they appeared to lead. From the time of its discovery up to the present moment, the true manifestations of Ideality have, perhaps, been the subject of less doubt than those of any other organ; that it imparts the perception of the beautiful, has always been admitted, and it is from the number of observations made to that effect, that Mr. Combe includes it amongst the "ascertained" organs. The question, then, that seemed to arise with regard to it, was not as to its function of creating an agreeable emotion in the mind upon the contemplation of the beautiful, but as to the general laws from the action of which the property of beauty is intrinsically derived.

Now, I think that it is a matter admitting of proof, that the emotion of beauty is more nearly awakened according to the number of mental organs that are simultaneously brought into play, and that its perfect manifestation is only consistent with the harmonious excitement of them all. If this be the case, the objection that persons having large Ideality are "more prone than others to run into some extremes of mental action" militates against the opinion, which, I believe, has never yet been a subject of doubt, viz. that Ideality prompts to an admiration of the beautiful, rather than against the views which I have expressed, and which merely grew out of the question, "What is beauty?"—a question that remains the same, whether Ideality be or be not the organ that adapts man to the cognisance of it. If it is a fact, that beauty is a law of the universe, it proceeds, of course, like all other laws, from fixed principles; and if it be among those principles that harmony and smoothness are essential qualities of the existence of beauty, then it is quite out of the question that an organ which prompts men to excesses by rendering them "more prone than others to run into some extremes of mental action," can be looked upon as the organ which imparts a love of the beautiful and perfect.

With regard, then, to the sense of beauty being dependent upon the harmonious action of all the faculties. It may be stated, as an axiom, that things increase in beauty as they approach towards perfection, and that nothing can be truly beautiful which is not perfect. Now, nothing can appear to man to be perfect which meets the intuitive disapproval of any one of his faculties; and also, as all the faculties (each being fairly developed) equally desire activity, nothing can appear to him to be perfect which withholds action from some faculties, while it excites it in others. This leads us to the point that the full idea of beauty is consistent only with the harmonious activity of the whole mind.

It will not be disputed that man, "the paragon of animals," is, as Shakspeare also called him, the "beauty of the world;" and as man is endowed with a certain number of faculties, all constituting in their active state so many sources of enjoyment, while at the same time they are capable of harmonious action, that object must necessarily appear to him to be most beautiful which awakens at one moment the whole of these sources of delight; and in his own character, too, the attribute of beauty must be more fully apparent when we see him in the exercise of all the powers with which he has been endowed by his Creator, than when he is employed solely beneath the influence of one or two. In the latter case, we might scarcely distinguish him from the brute; in the former, he approaches to the likeness of a God.

I have thus endeavoured to show that it is impossible that a faculty which imparts a sense of the beautiful, can at the same time impart a tendency to irregularity; but it must not be supposed, on the other hand, that it possesses the powers of absolutely repressing all excesses, since, in cases where a person is endowed with a very irregular mental organisation, although he may possess a very considerable developement of Ideality, it would be against all analogy to suppose that the action of this one organ could completely bring into subjection all the opposing elements with which it has to contend. All that could be looked for in such a case would be, not that the party should be free from extremes of conduct, but that he should continually fall into such extremes, yet be at the same time haunted by a sense of their impropriety—the continual victim of self-dissatisfaction, filled with ardent aspirations for better things, yet constantly failing in his struggle to attain them.

And such, in fact, has ever been the fate of those who, most distinguished for the manifestation of Ideality, have been the victims of excesses caused by the disproportionate developement of some other faculty. It was in the full consciousness of painful struggles of this nature, that the following lines fell from the pen of Burns:—

> Oh, gently scan your brother man,
>   Still gentler sister woman;

Tho' they may gang a kennin wrang,
　To step aside is human:
One point must still be greatly dark,
　The reason *why* they do it,
And just as lamely can ye mark,
　How far, perhaps, they rue it.

Who made the heart, 'tis He alone
　Decidedly can try us;
He knows each chord—its various tone,
　Each spring its various bias;
Then at the balance let 's be mute,
　We never can adjust it;
What 's *done*, we partly may compute,
　But know not what 's RESISTED.

　The character of Burns offers, perhaps, the strongest instance tha
can be found of irregular conduct on the part of one in whom the
possession of Ideality was largely indicated, and every page of his
writings teems with evidence of the continued struggles of his mind
between opposing tendencies. It is stated, also, in his biography
that "in the midst of his wanderings he met with nothing in his
family circle but gentleness and forgiveness. He had frequently
acknowledged his follies, promised amendment, and again and again
received pardon for his offences."

　The life of Byron furnishes another striking illustration of the
sufferings endured by those who, with irregular tendencies of mind
possess a large endowment of Ideality. It is scarcely necessary to
quote from his writings in proof of this assertion, for they are al
tinged with the peculiarity in question, and, indeed, disfigured by i
to so great an extent, that it is hardly possible to open a volume of
his works without falling upon an illustration of its effects.

　I might add some further instances, but it is needless; moreover, I
might show that most of those poets who have been very depraved
have exhibited in their writings a great want of good taste, and have
been distinguished more for reckless daring in their poetic aims, that
for those graceful flights that indicate the action of Ideality.

　It must also be remembered, in reference to the fact, that those
who are endowed with this organ, do sometimes, like their fellow
mortals, run into excesses, that they are usually in a greater degree
than others exposed to the influence of temptation—temptation arising
from those two dangerous sources, poverty and love! Among ordi
nary people, the activity of Acquisitiveness is carried to its greates
extreme; and he whose Ideality prompts him to subdue it to a fai
relation to his other and higher powers, will soon find himself behind
hand in the worldly race, and surrounded by all the distractions of
poverty, while his thrifty neighbours hold up their heads, and charge

improvidence upon the children of imagination as one of their incurable "excesses." The chief charge remains to be noticed. Their errors of love, and their frequent unhappiness in marriage. With regard to the first, it may be stated that persons in whom Ideality is a prevailing sentiment, excite more easily the regard of the opposite sex, on account of the grace of thought and manner which that faculty imparts ; and as it is a fact, that the mental constitution of woman is more harmoniously developed than that of man, her society has a double charm for him to whose mind that harmony is of itself a source of the highest gratification. When, in addition to this, it is considered that Ideality gives a perception of the highest order of physical as well as of moral beauty, we shall not wonder that its influence leads its possessor to form friendship with woman, or that those friendships should so often lead to their dangerous and proverbial consequences. Regarding their infelicitous marriages, little need be said, because the causes of them lie upon the surface, and have been so frequently observed. He who pants to share the affections of one who shall harmoniously unite in her own nature all the qualities of the mind, will be apt very early in life to imagine that he has discovered the object of his search. Two young persons casually meet under the influence of these views, they discern some mutual tastes, and therefore imagine that they shall agree in all, and as the season of courtship is not usually the period when irregularities of disposition are very prominently displayed, or stubbornly upheld, it is only after marriage that the illusion is dispelled, and disappointment comes. Perfection is looked for, and too much exacted, on one side, and the sudden change from homage to exaction, is perhaps too keenly felt on the other.

Further, it may be remarked that persons having a large developement of Ideality being frequently the possessors of literary power, their lives are more the subject of public observation than those of other individuals ; and in cases where, united to this faculty, they possess an ill-balanced mental organisation, and are consequently tormented by a distaste for their own errors, these errors usually form the remorseful subject of their most striking effusions, and general attention is thus directed to extremes of conduct, which are as often committed, though not so candidly confessed and repented of by others.

I know of no other excesses than those which have been stated above, which can be charged upon the possessors of large Ideality, since it is admitted that they are usually free from all extremes of brutality and sordid vice—to such an extent, indeed, that the organ is almost invariably found in a low state of developement in the heads of those who fall under the infliction of legal punishment. One peculiarity, however, it may be as well to remark. Persons thus endowed, it is said, have frequently shown a strong desire for solitude; and it is but natural that those whose imagination delights only in the contemplation of a perfect world, should in the present state of society, when the ardour of youth is past, and the lessons of experience have been acquired, find more pleasure in "forgetting altogether the human race, and making society for themselves of perfect creatures as celestial by their virtues as their beauties," than in mixing in the unequal toils and struggles of their fellow-men. But this cannot come under the head of "excesses," as it is merely the natural result of a morbid developement of the faculty which teaches us to shun excesses, and which sees no safeguard from extremes of conduct, but in the total inaction of retirement.

From the present letter, it will be seen that the point for which I chiefly contend, is that moral BEAUTY is consistent only with the harmonious operation of all the powers of the mind, in the same manner as physical beauty is allowed to be dependent on harmonious adaptations. The question, whether Ideality be or be not the organ that gives the taste for the beautiful, I leave to the judgment of those who have made numerous observations, or who have fully studied the various facts that are recorded of its manifestations. Throughout the above remarks I have spoken of it as such, because the testimony which already exists respecting it is, to my mind, sufficiently convincing.

I am, dear sir,
Very truly yours,
M. B. SAMPSON.

ARTICLE III.

LABOURS OF DR. CALDWELL IN BEHALF OF PHRENOLOGY.[*]

The pen of the historian is only true to its design, when, in the simplicity of truth, it faithfully records an act, and leaves it to the judgment which time is sure to award. The bitterest condemnation

[*] The above article was prepared by a young gentleman in Kentucky, for a work on Statistics, &c. &c. of the Western States, but in consequence of the failure of the publication of said work, the article has been placed at our disposal As it constitutes, in part, the history of phrenology in the United States, it is no inappropriate to the pages of the Journal, and even this simple record fails to do justice to the labours of one of the ablest advocates of the science.—ED.

of Nero, is the record of his deeds; and the loftiest eulogy of Washington, is the simple story of his life.   Exaggeration implies a consciousness of the weakness of our theme, as truly as proffered help arises from a knowledge of its need.

In the prosecution of his design, the writer of these pages will keep fully in his view the sentiments just expressed.   The portrait which he shall sketch, will owe to itself alone its power to please.   As a faithful delineator, his business is with the subject before him.   His province is to *represent* an action, not to *adorn* it.   In doing this, he must speak of things as they are, and trust to their own efficacy for the result.   If he is faithful to his theme, embellishments are needless; and if he is not, they are entirely out of place.   He who would sketch an Apollo, needs no other ornament than that which his subject naturally supplies; and he who speaks of an important truth, or details a great achievement, will find that the only excellence in language is clearly to exhibit the one, and faithfully to record the other.   Beyond this, to indulge in polished sentences, or gorgeous imagery, is like adorning a splendid statue, by loading it with the gaudy tinselry of fashion.

Amongst the distinguised names of the founders and earliest promulgators of phrenology, that of Professor Charles Caldwell holds a prominent place.   It was from his teaching that a knowledge of its doctrines was first gained in the United States.   His seed-ground has been the west, more particularly Kentucky, in which, for nineteen years, he has laboured with untiring assiduity.   His efforts have been directed to the great end of extending the bounds of human knowledge, and of expounding the laws which govern the operations of the human mind.   They have had for their object the improvement of his race, and posterity will bestow a just reward.

After his return from Europe, in the summer of 1821, Professor Caldwell delivered to his class, in the mèdical department of Transylvania University, his first course of phrenological lectures.   Up to that time, the science had been unknown in this country; or if heard of, its name was used only as a subject for ridicule, and a mark for the pointless arrows of a bastard wit.   But, influenced by a love of truth, and making the laws of nature his only argument, he opposed a dignified silence to contempt, and the reasonings of a sound philosophy to the shallow sophisms of the objector.   Thus, among those who heard him, the impression was unavoidable, that they were in the presence of a great mind, discussing great principles.   And by this means he has been able to accomplish far more for phrenology than has fallen to the lot of any other man—at least in this country.

From that time, every successive winter has found him repeating

his course to his class, and thus spreading the truths of phrenolog;
through the entire west and south. But this is not all. In th
spring of the following year (1822), he delivered a popular course o
his lectures to the citizens of Lexington, Ky. In the following yea1
that course was repeated in Louisville, Ky. Nor were his labour
confined to oral teaching. He called in the press to aid him in dis
seminating a knowledge of the principles of the science to which h
had so warmly devoted himself, and, in 1824, he published, by invita
tion of his class, a summary of the lectures previously delivered t
them. Of this work, which was reviewed in the Edinburgh Phreno
logical Journal with marked approbation, it is but justice to say, tha
for clearness, strength and profundity of argument, and perspicuit;
and richness of expression, it has no superior. This will be readil;
admitted by those who remember, that, next to a great conception
the highest effort of mind is, *correct condensation*.

In the same year, he visited Nashville, Tenn., and delivered :
course of lectures to the inhabitants of that city. In 1825, he lec
tured to the citizens of Baltimore. The result of these lectures, wa
the formation of a phrenological society in the latter place. At th(
close of this course, he, by invitation, delivered another in the city o.
Washington, which led to a similar result. Before this society, an(
by its invitation, he repeated his course in 1826. In the same year
he produced two papers on the phrenology of the North America1
Indians, compared with that of the Caucasians. Of these papers
which were published in the Edinburgh Phrenological Journal, m;
present plan forbids me to say more than that they were worthy o!
their theme ; and that theme was a great and important one.

In 1827, he published a second and greatly enlarged edition of hi:
" Elements of Phrenology." To this he prefixed, in the form of :
preliminary discourse, a reply to Mr. Jeffrey's attack on that science
employing, for the most part, the weapons of resistless argument
but sometimes using, with great effect, the lighter missiles of wit an(
satire, he left his antagonist completely foiled, on the field from whicl
he hoped to bear the trophies of a victory. And he was far fron
being a common foe.

In 1828, he extended his labours to New England, and delivere(
his first course there, to a Boston audience, in that year. This wa
four years before the arrival of Dr. Spurzheim in this country. S(
that Professor Caldwell had been labouring, as we have seen, mos
efficiently for *eleven years* before the voice of the great pupil an(
co-labourer of Gall was heard on our shores. This statement is du(
alike to each of those distinguished men. Nor would any one resent
more indignantly, the injustice of an attempt to build for himself :

reputation on the labours of another, than the ingenuous and noble-minded Spurzheim.

In the following year, he published his "New Views of Penitentiary Discipline and Moral Reform." This paper was reprinted in Europe, with the most decided approbation. It is one of those efforts which will perish only when truth shall cease to interest mankind, and a recognition of the laws of nature no longer be considered as requisite to a sound philosophy.

In 1831, he published, by request of his class, an "Essay on Temperament," considered in its relation to phrenology. In the following year, he produced an essay, for the Transylvania Medical Journal, on "Mental Derangement;" and another, entitled "Thoughts on True Epicurism." This last was published in the New England Magazine, at Boston. During the same year, he delivered, by appointment, in Lexington, Ky., an "Address on Intemperance." In this address, he gave a view of the phrenology of that vice.

In 1833, he published an essay on "The true Mode of Improving the Condition of Man." The subject is of vital importance to our race, and the essay is imperishable, because it is true to the subject. During the same year, he also published an essay on "Moral Medicine," which subject he considered in its relation to the principles of phrenology. And in an essay on the "Study of the Greek and Latin Languages," published in the New England Magazine, and republished in Europe, he gave a phrenological analysis of mental cultivation. The Transylvania Journal of that year contained, from his pen, a review of the "Principles of Medicine," by Professor Jackson, of Philadelphia, in which he retaliated, with just severity, on that author for a wanton and feeble attack which he made on phrenology.

In the following year, he published an address, delivered by request, to a convention of teachers, held at Lexington, Ky., on the subject of "Physical Education." The subject was treated phrenologically, and with singular ability. This essay was also reprinted in Europe. During the same year, he published two articles, entitled "Phrenology Vindicated." Of these, one was written at the request of the phrenologists of Boston, in reply to an abusive attack on the science in the North American Review, and was published in the Annals of Phrenology, a periodical issued at Boston, Mass.; the other was published in the New England Magazine, in reply to an anti-phrenological article in the same work. In November, of the same year, he delivered, by appointment, at Lexington, Ky., an "Address on Gambling," in which he gave the phrenology of that vice.

In 1835, he delivered a second course of lectures in Louisville, Ky., and also in Nashville, Tenn. During the same year, he published, in the Annals of Phrenology, an article entitled "Phrenology Vindicated," in reply to an attack made on the science by Lord Brougham. Under the same title, he also published a reply to a very virulent attack on phrenology in the "Boston Christian Examiner." All must concede that, in whatever point of view it may be considered, this reply is a master effort. Its strength of argument is equalled only by the keenness of its repartee. And the highest praise of the whole is, that *truth* gives its power to the one, and *justice* imparts its vigour to the other. In that year, he delivered, by appointment, and subsequently published, by request, two addresses of a phrenological character: one at Nashville, Tenn., on the "Spirit of Improvement;" the other at Lexington, Ky., being a second "Address on Gambling."

In 1836, he gave a course of lectures in Natchez, Miss., which was immediately succeeded by another at New Orleans. During the same year, he delivered, by request, an academical address on "Popular and Liberal Education." This was also subsequently published.

In the following year, being in Philadelphia, he delivered, by invitation, a course of lectures to a class of the Summer Medical Institute; and in 1838, and also by invitation, he delivered a course before the Phrenological Society of New York. While in that city, he published, by request of that society, a volume containing two essays: one entitled "Phrenology Vindicated, and Anti-Phrenology Unmasked," being a reply to two lectures by Dr. Sewall, in opposition to that science; the other, the "Phrenology of Falsehood, and its Kindred Vices." During the same year, he delivered at Jeffersontown, Ky., by invitation, an "Address on Education," in which the subject was treated phrenologically.

In the following year (1839), he published, in pamphlet form, a letter to the editor of the American Phrenological Journal, on the "Connection between Phrenology and Religion." In the same year, and as a communication to the same journal, he published an excellent essay on "The most Effective Condition of the Brain, &c.;" and also another very able essay in "Vindication of the Science against the charges of Materialism and Fatalism."

We have thus briefly sketched the history of the introduction of phrenology in the west. Important as it is in itself, and momentous as it is destined to be in its results, it is, in fact, the history of one man. If we have not indulged in tropes or figures, it is because our subject did not need them. The flowers of rhetoric can add no beauty to the wreath of fame. The dignity of our theme is its highest ornament, and studied eulogy can no more add to its worth, than the carpings of envy can detract from its truth.

To conclude. With an energy that has never wearied, and a resolution that has never failed in the most trying emergencies, Professor Caldwell has continued his labours for the advancement of the cause of truth up to the present time. Of his numerous publications, the majority were, by his liberality, distributed gratuitously in the Valley of the Mississippi, for the diffusion of the science of which they treat. And if the unreserved devotion of a rich and powerful intellect to the great cause of nature and of truth, be a sure basis for a reputation which time can never overturn, then is *his* a name which the most distinguished might be proud to own.

ARTICLE IV.

CHRONIC DISEASE OF THE BRAIN.*

Chronic diseases of the brain have been too long considered, both by physicians and the public, as not coming within the *pale* of medicine, and remain to this day the most prominent of the *opprobriæ medicorum*. This has undoubtedly arisen from the obscure notions which we have had of the physiology and pathology of the brain; but the late labours of a Bichat, a Spurzheim, and a Bell, have unfolded to us the anatomy and physiology of the nervous system, while its pathological relations have been as minutely and extensively exposed, by the indefatigable researches of a Meckel, a Lobstein, and a Broussais, so that we are now enabled to detect its diseases, and apply our remedies with as much accuracy and certainty of their remedial powers, as we can to any other internal organ of the body. These reflections, and a strong desire to see a physiological system of treatment established, have induced me to forward for your Journal the following case :—

Mrs. S., of B., Me., aged about twenty-six years, while on a visit to her relations in this city, last July, was attacked with derangement of intellect. The attack was preceded with pain in the head, principally confined to the *anterior part*. At this time, she was treated by Dr. Page, a respectable physician of this city, with a variety of depleting remedies, and with marked benefit; her symptoms became so mild,

---

* From Vol. II, No. 24, of the Boston Medical and Surgical Journal.

that expectations of recovery were indulged by her friends, as well a:
her medical attendant. But upon her return home, she became s(
unmanageably insane as to require, for her own safety, and that o
others, a system of moral coercion. Although she had constant an(
respectable medical attendance, their endeavours proved abortive; an(
I was informed by her relations, that her case was pronounced hope
less, so far as it had relation to medical treatment, but that a systen
of moral treatment, in an insane hospital, might afford some chanc(
of recovery; to which she was going to be sent, when she wa:
brought to this place, and became my patient about the middle of las
November. Upon examining her symptoms, I found that, with th(
exception of costiveness, no functional derangement existed in th(
system, except in the *actions of the brain.* I was informed by her
self, that all her sufferings were located about the *eyes* and *forehead*
and at no time had she suffered much pain in any other quarter
These symptoms, phrenologically considered, would indicate the fol
lowing state of mind—a derangement regarding Time, Number
Colour, Order, Locality, &c., which was actually the case. In on(
of her calm moments, I gave her a quantity of change to count, an(
she would always say that there were a greater number of pieces tha!
there really were: when questioned regarding the colour of a bed
quilt, there was an evident incorrectness in her answers; regardin{
the occurrence of events, although she recollected them, yet she coul(
not tell the time or order of their taking place. These, with a!
exalted state of the imagination, *a desire to travel,* and at times a dis
position to destructiveness, principally exhibited in destroying he
own clothes, constituted the most prominent symptoms. Thougl
not a full believer in phrenology, yet the symptoms in this case cor
responded so well with the doctrines of Spurzheim, that I could no
refrain from attaching some importance to them; and upon the con
clusion that the brain, situated in the anterior part of the skull, wa:
affected with increased excitability, resulting from inflammatory action
the following treatment was determined upon :—

Indication 1st, To reduce the amount of blood in the capillar!
system about the head. This was accomplished by the applicatio!
of twelve leeches to the forehead, daily.

2d, To establish a counter-irritation, or *diverticulum*, to the cir
culating fluids. This was effected by the daily exhibition of tw(
drops of croton oil, and the application of a blister to the head afte
the first week, when the use of the leeches was suspended.

3d, Abstraction of *stimuli*, both moral and physical, by confinin{
her to mild antiphlogistic diet, and restricting her to one attendan!

who was instructed to hold no conversation with the patient, excepting such as would tend to soothe her mind.

4th, To lessen the excitability. This indication was attended to by the administration of fifteen grains of Dover's powders, whenever the mind became unusually excited.

Six days after commencing with this treatment, a favourable change began to take place; and by continuing for three weeks, she became perfectly sane. She was allowed to recover her strength gradually, without the aid of *medicinal tonics*. She resumed the charge of her family, and began to mix with society, of which she is a valuable member, a month ago, and is now enjoying the inestimable blessing of a sound mind in a sound body. This case affords evidence in support of the following conclusions :—That the principles of *phreno- logy* are correct, and that a knowledge of them will greatly aid the physician in forming his diagnosis of the diseases of the brain ; that chronic inflammation of the brain will yield to the same course of treatment as inflammation in any other organ; and that many who now wander about as maniacs, because of the vulgar maxim that it is vain to prescribe for a mind diseased, might, by a persevering and scientific attention, be restored to a state of mental and bodily health.

D. M. R.

Bangor, Me., January, 1835.

ARTICLE V.

PREDOMINANCE OF CERTAIN ORGANS IN THE BRITISH POETS.—NO. 6.

SHELLY.

Were we to yield to the spirit of any of the moods into which reflections upon Shelly's character has often thrown us, and let it dictate the present article, we might fill pages with by-gone notions of the human soul—its manifold mysteries, its strength, its weakness, and its unaccountable contradictions. We might find pleasure, if only from association, in groping once more through the dim caverns of metaphysics. There appeared so much depth in those elevated abstractions, some were really so beautiful, they rendered all experience so useless,' and all careful observation of nature, and were withal so plainly the reveries of no common dreamers, that although we have discovered them to be as baseless as more cherished visions, we could still recall them with interest. By the brilliant theories of

Plato, we might endeavour to ascertain what portion of the ethereal and eternal intelligence was enshrined, during a brief career, in the material personality of Shelly; or by the severer methods of Germany, measure the degree of his *centralisation* or his realisation of the mighty I, or not much more intelligibly descant in good set terms, concerning poetic temperament, genius, and vivid imagination —terms which appear to impart so much, and yet, as commonly employed, mean nothing.   But to neither of these methods are we permitted to resort.   Our science requires us to use such words only as have definite ideas annexed to them; and pleasing as it would be to indulge in speculation, while portraying him who so loved to speculate himself, and in fancy, while describing one who was " of imagination all compact," we must, notwithstanding, restrict ourselves to sober truth, and an humble transcription of the simple language of nature.

His character, as manifested in his life and writings, will be found in striking harmony with his phrenological conditions.   The quality of his whole organisation was of almost feminine fineness, and yet possessed a degree of strength seldom united with a delicacy of structure peculiar to the other sex.   This, for the rough race of life, and all its coarse and grinding cares, was far from favourable; but for the intellectual ideal world, in which he loved to live, and move, and have his being, admirably adapted.   This temperament, blending in different degrees, the bilious, sanguine, and nervous, with the last rather predominant, and not a portion of lymphatic, gave intensity and keenness, life and spirit, to a brain of superior size, in which intellect and the sentiments reigned supreme.   His habits were well calculated to preserve and invigorate these constitutional qualities.   Severely temperate, taking much exercise in the open air, giving free play to his feelings and passions in accordance with nature, rather than subduing them in opposition to her laws, and constantly cultivating his mind, he enjoyed health and regularity in all his functions to an extent seldom known by the studious and sedentary.   A few general remarks upon the direction of his faculties will not be out of place.

Phrenologists are often assailed for assuming that nature does every thing, and art comparatively nothing; that, for instance, an individual endowed with large reflecting organs, a large and active brain, will reason, analyse, generalise, and combine synthetically, although he may never have read a treatise on logic; and that one possessing Ideality, Language, and some other organs, in great developement, can write poetry, though Aristotle's rules, and Horace's art of the same, are to him sealed books.   There is not the slightest force in the objection.   The scholar knows that Aristotle's laws are only deductions from the Iliad, which was written without, perhaps, any further reference to laws of any kind, than such as genius makes for its own guidance in compassing its objects and completing its conceptions. But the phrenologist does not deny that true art is essential to perfection, but concludes that in proportion to the native strength will be the effort to improve it. To illustrate this. Zerah Colburn had an extraordinary developement of the organ of Number, and manifested the appropriate function before any special care had been given to his education. His father's attention was accidently called to the fact, by hearing him whispering with great rapidity, and readily solving all kinds of arithmetical problems. This aptitude was then encouraged—this natural fondness stimulated. The boy seized with avidity, and quickly mastered, treatises upon his favourite science. But this he did because they furnished appropriate objects for his organ of Number, already vigorous and active, and craving its natural element. The same holds good with regard to all the intellectual organs. Shelly as naturally, we might say as irresistibly, sought to gratify his higher powers, as did Zerah Colburn. Endowed with large Causality and Comparison, he mingled minds with such as were in like manner gifted. Having strong perception, he toiled in the fields of knowledge, while reflection enabled him to sift the grain from the chaff. Possessing powerful Ideality, he turned for sympathy to " the quire that cannot die," and searched the works of nature for that harmony and perfection which delight and inspire even more this faculty, and teach it how to create. He passed through the usual routine of collegiate instruction, but by the force principally of his native powers attained mental independence. Despising all petty displays of verbal ingenuity, dignified by the name of reasoning, he inquired elsewhere than in college halls for truths which the place-men of learning have never been paid to teach.

> " And from that hour did I, with patient thought,
>   Heap knowledge from forbidden minds of lore,
> But nothing that my tutors knew or taught,
>   Cared I to learn ; but from that secret store
> Wrought linked armour for my soul."

He early saw that our minds are little strengthened and enriched by being made mere recipients, and that the simplest truth discovered and revolved by ourselves, expands the intellect far more than the highest exercise of memory. To phrenologists, the reason is plain. For merely receiving and recording an idea, or retaining the relation of things, ordinary activity of perceptive intellect will suffice. Whereas to discover one, not only must those organs be more intensely excited, but reflection and the superior powers summoned to their appropriate work to perceive, compare, classify, and deduce. The whole mind is thus put in harmonious action, which constitutes its true labour—"the labour it delights in," and which "physics pain."

Comparison, Language, and Ideality, all large in his head, manifest their proper functions, throughout his writings, with great vigour; illustrating with happy and varied imagery, clothing with rich and choice expressions, and adorning with chaste beauty, some of the loftiest conceptions, the product of his ample Causality, to be found in modern literature. Marvellousness was but indifferently developed; and accordingly we find little of the peculiar character it impresses on an author's style, and which abounds in the works of Scott. Perhaps the inactivity of this organ was a defect in Shelly's character, and made him too prone to reject whatever could not be tested by his senses, or demonstrated by his reason. Approbativeness was not deficient, but its undue action was restrained by his higher powers. As this sentiment covets praise indiscriminately, indifferent to its quality and source, whether it shall inspire its possessor with manly ambition, or make him the victim of mere fugitive vanity, depends, of course, on the developement of other organs, and activity of their functions. In civilised society, no one is more liable to be abused; and unless governed by vigorous intellect, it completely enslaves and prostitutes the mind. Whoever suffers it to become his ruling impulse, may talk of moral courage and mental freedom, but does not possess them—knows not what they are. Its unrestrained action made Goldsmith often ridiculous, Byron sometimes a quack and mountebank, and Rousseau a madman. What, then, must be its pernicious effects upon weaker minds? In the common mind, if uncontrolled, it creates truckling, time-serving, mendicancy—makes him fear censure from the most worthless, and resort to all kinds of servility to avail it. To politicians, professors, writers, and preachers, it perpetually whispers expediency, and prevents them from uttering what they know to be truth. He, therefore, who would exercise the prerogatives of manhood, and possess the very soul within him—who, shuddering at the thought of slavery infinitely worse than that of the body, would employ his best faculties in nobler service than in pandering to others' prejudices, must learn betimes to curb this sentiment, and subject it to the government of reason. This smile-seeking, frown-fearing propensity did not blur the brilliant mind of Shelly. He was inspired by a lofty ambition, but had no "canine love of applause." Hence the unshackled exercise of his powers, his intellectual freedom, and the manly dignity of his character.

Who, acquainted with his history, does not know that benevolence was as characteristic of the man as genius of the author? Any

authentic likeness will show the organ correspondingly large. Conscientiousness was not less striking in developement and manifestation; and to know what was right, and fearlessly pursue it, formed
the noble philosophy of his youth. Destructiveness and Combativeness were but moderately developed; and though some of the incidents of his life supplied them with abundant stimulus, they were ever
restrained from all improper action.

To preserve our benevolence in all its original freshness and fervour,
while floating over the gentle streams of life, when the winds are all
prosperous, and the untried heart responds in its enthusiasm to the
" all good" of the Creator when he gazed upon Paradise, is not difficult, requires no magnanimity, merits no praise. But it is far different, and bespeaks a lofty mind, enlightened by the philosophy that
cannot hate and dare not condemn, to cherish kindness and good-will
towards all—to desire melioration of the mass, and rejoice in individual happiness, when our own course has been, and promises still to
be, through the quicksands, shallows, and miseries of existence.
Shelly received the due quantum of abuse, ever meted out to such as
not only think for themselves, but act in accordance therewith. But
the different effect of calumny upon him and Byron is worthy of
notice, as marking a nice distinction in their characters. In Byron,
it opened a fountain of bitterness, which poured itself forth in satire
and malediction. Shelly it filled with more of sorrow than anger,
pained and wounded Benevolence, but did not destroy it. Byron's
Self-esteem and Approbativeness were deeply offended; Shelly's Conscientiousness, Benevolence, and Intellect. Byron felt abuse chiefly
when aimed at himself; Shelly, whoever was the victim. The one
cursed it as an encroachment on his rights; the other bewailed it as
an outrage on justice.

W.

ARTICLE VI.

PHRENOLOGICAL CHARACTER OF OBERLIN.

The following cut is designed to present a correct likeness of the
head of John Frederic Oberlin, who was greatly distinguished in one of
the cantons of Switzerland for his talents, industry, and piety. There
are many things connected with this head, which are peculiarly interesting to the phrenologist. It possesses all the natural conditions
necessary to render its possessor both a *good* and a *great* man. The

drawing indicates that the individual had an excellent temperament, being a combination of the nervous, bilious, and sanguine, in nearly equal proportions, which would give great physical strength and power of endurance, as well as a decided fondness for mental exercise and improvement. The brain appears to have been large, and was remarkably *well-balanced*. This last condition is one of the highest importance, and it is the leading feature to which we wish to direct special attention in the present character.

Phrenologists have always laid great stress on the *supremacy* of the moral sentiments. They hold that such is the nature of the mental faculties, and their relations to the external world, that in order for man to secure his highest happiness, and effect the great objects of his existence in this world, his *moral* nature should have a predominating, a *controlling* influence. And this is the leading design of Christianity. But the *true nature* of man must be correctly understood, before we can fully perceive the complete and perfect *adaptation* of Christianity to produce this effect, or before we can very efficiently employ the means which God designed for the amelioration and salvation of man. As phrenology *alone* makes known to us the true nature of man's mental and moral faculties, it must ultimately become a powerful hand-maid of religion; for the former is but the *counterpart* of the latter. One is the book of *nature;* the other, of *revelation:* each bears the impress of Divinity. A most wonderful adaptation exists between the laws of the former and the precepts of the latter; and whenever, in the course of time, man shall use those means which are in perfect accordance with the truths of both, for civilising and Christianising the world, then, and not till then, can we rationally expect the blessing of God to follow invariably the means employed. God, in the fulfilment of his plans, can no more consistently suspend or violate the laws of his works, than he can blot out of existence the truths of his Word, which are as eternal and unchangeable as his own Divine existence. A great work, therefore, remains yet to be done in behalf of the regeneration of the race, and that, too, by *human* instrumentality.

In an examination of the character before us, we shall find that the individual obeyed no less the laws of his *mind*, than the commands of *Revelation*. It is true, Oberlin inherited from his parents a remarkable endowment of the moral organs, which rendered him very susceptible of religious impressions. He had not those difficulties to contend with, or overcome, which falls to the lot of the great majority of men. We may correctly and truly say, that he was *naturally* inclined to be intelligent, virtuous, and moral. We will here introduce some remarks by Dr. Spurzheim on the history and character of Oberlin.

This is an extraordinary head, a form that a phrenologist loves to contemplate. There is little brain at the basis, whilst all the upper and front regions are unusually large. The posterior sincipital portion being also in great proportion, independence of mind, steadiness, and perseverance in every pursuit and undertaking, will be prominent features in the exalted moral and religious character, indicated by the rest of the head. Self-esteem will here become dignity; Benevolence and Veneration be blended with, and made inseparable from, wisdom. In a word, such a cerebral organisation approaches in excellence the idea which phrenologists are apt to form of that of Jesus.

This model of Christian piety found the inhabitants of his parish, isolated in five different villages, poor, ignorant, agitated by heinous passions, and without the most necessary means of comfortable existence. But by labouring unremittingly, he, by degrees, succeeded in changing their wretched condition. He taught them to cultivate potatoes, flax, and such vegetables as succeeded best in light and sandy soils. He laid out a nursery, in order to supply the peasants with trees of various kinds, and showed them the advantages they would reap by attending to their cultivation. He gave instructions to the children himself, teaching the younger to read, write, and calculate; while he lectured to the more advanced in age, upon the cultivation of fruit trees, the principles of agriculture, and the noxious and useful qualities of the plants which the country produced. He particularly accustomed them to order and cleanliness.

The good pastor, with his parishioners at his back, actually worked at the formation of convenient ways from one village to another, and of a

good and ready communication with the great road leading to Strasburg
To this city he sent children to become artisans, such as tailors, shoe
makers, smiths, and carpenters, a female to learn midwifery, and a pro
mising youth to study medicine and surgery.   He himself had some
knowledge of the healing art, used the lancet in cases of necessity, and
preserved the most necessary remedies in his house, which he distri
buted as he thought they were required.   He devoted his talents, time
labours, and whole life to the welfare of his flock.   He persuaded a bene
volent family, Legrand, to favour his philanthropic views, and to transfe
their manufactory of ribands from Basle to his parish, and to furnisl
employment to the people.

Besides his vast care of all worldly concerns, he paid the greates
attention to moral and religious instruction, which he enforced in the
most effectual manner by deeds as well as words.   He ended a law-sui
in which the parish had been involved for many years, and he brough
good will and mutual love to dwell with his flock, instead of discord
He well deserves the title *father*, which his parishioners have giver
him.   Their love and gratitude surely will not terminate with his exist
ence, and the good he has done will live long after he is dust.

As Dr. Spurzheim very correctly remarks, respecting the head of
Oberlin, "there is little brain at the basis, whilst all the upper and
front regions are unusually large."   It will be remembered, that the
organs located at the base of the head, are chiefly those of the propen
sities or animal feelings; while those in the frontal and coronal regions
are the organs of the intellect and moral sentiments.   Accordingly
the *intellectual* and *moral* nature will constitute the leading element:
of character.   In case an individual so organised is properly educated
while young, and is placed under correct *religious* influences, he wil
be led to form a character which, in all its features, will approximate
to a more *perfect standard*, than is rarely to be found—a characte
which will correspond, in some good degree, with the requirement:
of the word of God, as well as with the laws of the human mind
Enlightened Benevolence, Veneration, and Conscientiousness, will be
the ruling faculties, teaching their possessor to "do justice, love
mercy, and walk humbly before God."   It is true, *grace* may de
much for such an individual, but *nature* must first furnish the
materials.

We can notice only a few points in the character of Oberlin, in
addition to the clear and condensed summary of his history, which is
contained in the above remarks of Dr. Spurzheim.   Our limits pre
vent a critical analysis of his mental faculties, or extended quotation:
from his biography.   The reader must examine the life of Oberlin for
himself, and, if he be a phrenologist, he will find it a most interesting
and profitable exercise to test the mental manifestations of Oberlin by
the principles of phrenology—analysing each faculty by itself, and ther
considering all their diversified combinations—and he will find such a
beauty, consistency, and perfection of character, as we believe can be

found no where else in the annals of history. It is an example well
worthy of imitation.

Oberlin was blessed with intelligent and pious parents. " He
was," says his biographer, "from his very infancy, the subject not
merely of pious convictions, but of holy affections towards his
Heavenly Father. 'During my infancy,' says Oberlin, 'God often
vouchsafed to touch my heart, and to draw me to himself. He bore
with me in my repeated backslidings, with a kindness and indulgence
hardly to be expressed.' His character, as displayed in the uniform
tenor of his life, presented a remarkable combination of varied excellencies ; for whilst much exalted sanctity and intrepid zeal were conspicuous, an unwearied ardour of doing good, and an habitual willingness to renounce his own interests to promote the well-being of his
fellow-creatures, were equally evident. In addition to this, his
extreme simplicity, conscientious integrity, sweetness of temper, and
refinement of manner, caused him to be both ardently loved and sincerely revered ; whilst his industry, his agricultural skill, his knowledge of rural and domestic economy, and the energy with which he
carried his plans into effect the moment he was convinced of their
utility, rendered him not only an example, but a blessing to the
people among whom he resided, and afforded a delightful proof of the
advantages that may accrue from a union of secular and spiritual
duties."

We have said that, according to the principles of phrenology, the
head of Oberlin was remarkably *well-balanced.* Every mental faculty,
whether of the feelings, sentiments, or intellect, appears to have been
equally developed ; and from a thorough examination of his character,
we cannot point out a *single* excess or deficiency. His social and
domestic feelings were unusually ardent and strong, yet they were
invariably governed by a well-disciplined intellect and enlightened
moral sentiments. The faculties that give force, energy, and independence of character, were decidedly strong, but they were always
directed to the wisest and most benevolent objects. He had naturally
a great deal of tact, management, and shrewdness, but these qualities
were never employed, *only* in advancing the happiness and best interests of his fellow-men. His intellect, both observing and reflecting,
was of a high order. His knowledge of the arts, sciences, and literature, was very extensive. In fact, he was really profound in almost
every department of learning. Had he been ambitious for fame and
worldly renown, few in any profession or business could have
acquired more applause and greater distinction. But Oberlin, cheerfully and unreservedly, consecrated all his talents and attainments to
the good of man, and the glory of his Maker.

His moral sentiments, as may be seen by reference to the likeness, were remarkably well-developed. The manifestations of these constitute the chief, the crowning excellence of his character. He seemed to be almost entirely destitute of selfishness. His whole life was one continued scene of disinterested benevolence. Surely, the remark of Dr. Spurzheim was not profane or irreverent, that such an organisation approaches, in excellence, the idea which phrenologists are apt to form of that of Christ. In character, it certainly is an approximation to what we may rationally suppose was the character of man when he was created in the " likeness and image of God."

In conclusion, we may truly and justly say, that phrenology, when properly understood, teaches the supremacy of man's moral sentiments, and that its principles, when correctly applied, are calculated, in connection with divine grace, to restore to man the moral "likeness and image" of his Creator.

ARTICLE VII.

PATHOLOGICAL FACT.

[The following fact, bearing on the truth of phrenology, was communicated by Dr. Moore, of Claiborne, Ala., to Dr. Powell, who is well known in many of the southern states as an able advocate of the science.—ED.]

DR. POWELL,—

Dear Sir—According to promise, I have endeavoured to procure for you the skull of the negro who was shot in the forehead, as I related to you, but I can find no one who knows the spot where he was buried; possibly I may yet learn. The facts of the case were these. He was shot as near the centre of the frontal bone as you could place your finger. There were some two or three table-spoonfuls of brain discharged from the wound. Every one present thought he would die in a very short time, and left him in the woods accordingly.

The company requested an old gentlemen, by whose house they had to pass, to send his negroes to bury him. They accordingly went; but they found him still living. They returned and informed their master of the fact, who had him brought to his house, supposing that he would die in the course of the night. But, to the great astonishment of all of us, he began to mend, and in a few days he was able to walk about, and steal and roast potatoes at night. When in this condition, if asked a question, he would give a positive or negative answer by nodding or shaking his head, for he had *entirely lost his capacity to use language.* He finally became able to walk about the plantation with ease, and, to the astonishment of every one who knew his condition, he again ran off and committed some small thefts.   He was caught twelve miles from where he started, brought back, and placed in jail, where he died.   He lived a few days over six weeks after he was shot.   The weather was very cold during most of this time.

Yours, &c.,

L. R. MOORE.

ARTICLE VIII.

REMARKS ON THE RELIGIOUS BEARINGS OF PHRENOLOGY.

A very sensible and well-written article on this subject, appeared in the Western Pioneer (published at Rock Spring. Ill.) of December, 1838.   A friend has kindly placed in our hands a copy of said paper, from which we copy the following excellent remarks.   After explaining the elementary principles of the science, and the nature of the evidence on which they are based, the writer proceeds to remark as follows :—

We have now come to the question at issue.   Whether the hereditary principles of phrenology, which are based on established laws of nature, destroy man's free will, agency, or accountability?   And whether the Bible is adapted to the phrenological character of man?

No man is condemned for that which he does not possess, and has not the means of acquiring.   No one is censurable for doing that which he cannot avoid.   We form a notion of right and wrong. That notion may be enlightened and correct—it may be obscure and erroneous.   The animal propensities prompt to action, the superior sentiments give Firmness, Hope, Veneration, Conscientiousness, &c., in executing, and the intellectual faculties are capable of controlling and giving a right direction to action.   The organs of the perceptive and reflecting faculties are employed in reasoning, and are capable of discriminating between right and wrong, when in possession of the requisite means.   The promptings of the propensities are not compulsory; the intellectual faculties are free to choose or reject, to say yes or no.   Suppose a man is prompted to steal, swear, or commit any other crime, it is the prerogative of the reasoning faculties to say,

thus far shalt thou go and no farther.   Suppose a man's head is dis
proportioned, and partakes more of the animal than of the intellectua
developement, for that he is not to be blamed, provided it is not
result of his own procuring.   His progenitor may be censurable
The man who has but one talent, is accountable for only one
Education and the influence of external circumstances, no doubt, hav
much to do in giving the head its peculiar form, and the character it
distinctive features.   So far as means for the formation of a right cha
racter are at our command,· thus far we are accountable : the non
improvement of which is, what gives birth in part to the irregularit;
and disproportion of the mental and physical constitution.   Excess
no doubt, is a powerful agent in producing a disproportion of th
faculties.   When the propensities are excessively gratified, thei
organs increase to an unnatural size, consequently, the organs of th
intellect are enfeebled, diminished in size, and incapacitated for thei
appropriate duties.   On the other hand, the organs of the intellect ar
increased to an unnatural size by intense study and mental applica
tion, the consequence is, that the animal organs are diminished in th
same proportion, and rendered inefficient.   Moderation in anima
gratifications and intellectual pursuits, is imperiously demanded b;
the laws of our nature, a deviation from which is invariably attende
with a disproportion of the mental organs.   There is nothing i
the laws of our nature which compels a man to do wrong.   True
he may be strongly predisposed to vice, to the commission of thi
or that crime, but mark, *predisposition* is not *compulsion*.   Th
will is free to choose or reject.   Reason sits as judge, to decid
all matters of right and wrong.   The propensities are capable o
acquiescing in all decisions.

We have now come to the second question.   Whether the Bible i
adapted to the prenological character of man ?

To discover the adaptedness of the Bible to the principles o
phrenology, it will be necessary to consider the organs which phreno
logy recognises, and their uses.   The first organ we shall notice i
Vitativeness, the use of which is to preserve life.   Alimentiveness
the second organ, its use is to prompt to take food.   Destructiveness
the next, its use to destroy animals for food, and give efficiency o
character.   Amativeness, its use, propagation of the species—affec
tion for the opposite sex.   Philoprogenitiveness, its use, protectio;
of offspring.   Adhesiveness, its use, attachment, friendship.   Con
centrativeness, its use, to give continuity to feelings and intellect
Combativeness, its use, courage, self-defence.   Secretiveness, its use
prudence to conceal.   Acquisitiveness, its use, to provide for presen
and future wants.   Constructiveness, its use, to construct, build, an

invent. These are a part of the feelings or affective faculties, and are termed *propensities.* They are situated in the back part and lower region of the head. Cautiousness, its use, circumspection, care, to keep from danger. Approbativeness, its use, to gain the good will and esteem of others, proper ambition. Self-esteem, its use, proper self-respect. There is also a faculty giving a love of the pathetic, sublime, and awful. Benevolence, its use, mercy, charity, and forgiveness. Veneration, its use, to revere, respect, and reverence laws, parents, the Creator and his laws; and what is great and good Firmness, its use, perseverance, fortitude, and steadiness of purpose. Conscientiousness, its use, perfect justice to all. Hope, its use, to lead one to endeavour to obtain what the other faculties properly desire. Marvellousness, its use, faith, confidence, and proper belief. Ideality, its use, desire of perfection, poetry. Mirthfulness, its use, cheerfulness, mirth, wit, and gaiety. Imitation, its use, natural language—to imitate in nature and the arts. These belong to the affective faculties, and are termed the superior sentiments. They are situated in the upper and frontal region of the head. The organs of the intellectual faculties are the next in course. Individuality, the observing faculty—memory of things. Form, memory of persons—drawing. Size—judges of size, distance, and perpendicularity. Weight—judges of weight and gravity. Colouring—painting, flowers, beauties of nature. Locality, love of travel—memory of places. Order, love of arrangement. Number, love of figures—memory of numbers. Eventuality, love of history—memory of historical events. Time, chronology—time in music. Tune, tones in music—memory of sounds. Language, use and memory of words. These organs are termed the perceptive faculties, and are situated around the eyes and in that part of the cranium. The reflective faculties are the next in order, and the last. Comparison, judgment—logical reason. Causality gives one the power to reason abstractly—a love of metaphysics; and to trace effects to their causes. These organs are situated in the anterior frontal part of the cranium. We have noticed all the organs and their functions which phrenology recognises. That some of those organs are large, and others very small in the same individual, is not unfrequently the case. To rectify this disproportion of the head, and give a proper developement to all the organs, they must be properly educated. The Bible is the great and efficient instrument to be employed in educating these organs, and rendering them subservient to the grand designs of the Creator. There is not a faculty, not a propensity, not a passion, not a sentiment, to which the Bible does not address itself in the most conclusive and striking manner. Are any of the propensities too strong, or inclined to sensuality? the Bible

addresses them by way of warning, reproof, or admonition. The si
which easily besets us, we are exhorted to lay aside. The drunkarc
the glutton, the liar, the thief, the murderer, the profligate, and dis
obedient, are refused admittance to the kingdom, and encouraged t
repent. The Bible also addresses the superior sentiments. It incu'
cates charity, which edifieth and will cover a multitude of sins ; faith
which will work by love ; Hope, which shall be an anchor to the soul
Veneration, which shall duly respect all ; Firmness, which shall perse
vere in well doing ; Self-esteem, which must not be wise in its ow
conceit, or vainly proud and haughty, but possess a just sense of hi
grade—a little lower than the angels, crowned with glory and honour
Approbativeness, which shall regard a good name more than gre:
riches ; Conscientiousness, which shall do justice and judgment t
all ; Ideality, which shall desire to be perfect, even as our Fathe
which is in heaven is perfect ; Mirthfulness, which shall be cheerfi
and apt to teach ; and Imitation, which shall take up the cross an
follow ·Christ.

The Bible addresses the perceptive faculties in the most pointe
manner. "Look unto me, and be ye saved all the ends of the eartl
Behold what manner of love the Father hath bestowed upon ui
Behold the Lamb of God which taketh away the sins of the worlc
Behold I come quickly, and my reward is with me, to give to ever
man according as his work shall be." The reflective faculties ar
also addressed. "Meditate upon these things, &c. Come now an
let us reason together," &c.

Considering the Bible as a whole, and man as a whole, it addresse
him as a physical, intellectual, reasonable, moral, and accountabl
being, with a will free to choose or reject, and a conscience to balanc
between right and wrong, which perfectly accords with the fundamentu
principles of phrenology.

But the *utility* of phrenology is scrupled by many, and especiall
by the religious part of the community. Does the mechanic scrupl
whether he had better examine his tools, and ascertain their uses ; c
whether it is best to sharpen those which are dull, or improve thos
which will admit of improvement ? Does the physician quer
whether it is advisable to acquire a knowledge of the instrument
with which he must amputate a limb, extract a tooth, or probe
wound ? Is it expedient that they know how to arrange those tool
and instruments ? or have a knowledge of the places they occupy
Does the lawyer doubt whether he had better have a knowledge of a
the facts involved in his client's case, or regard any order in th
arrangement of those facts ? Does the farmer question whether h
had better make any efforts to improve the breed of his horses o

cattle ?   Does the dealer in horses think it best to pay no regard to the size and form of the head, temperament, and texture ?

And why so scrupulously conscientious when we come to the study of man ?   " The proper study of mankind, is man."   Yet why so reluctant to examine his own powers and faculties ?   Why shut his eyes against a knowledge of himself, lest he should find some weak organs, or some unruly propensities ?   Herein is the great utility of phrenology, it gives a man a knowledge of himself, and also of others.

There are controlling traits in every man's character, and some not of the most happy and desirable kind.   But before we can apply the remedy, we must know where the organs are situated, the temperament and texture, the causes of those unhappy traits.   Phrenology developes the whole.   The teacher who does not understand the phrenological character of his pupils, is incompetent to adapt his instructions to their several cases, or to designate the proper studies for them to pursue.   The physician who does not understand the temperament and texture, the leading traits of character of his patient, is not master of his profession, and is incompetent to prescribe the most judicious remedies.   The doctor of divinity who does not understand the organs of the mental and physical constitution—what are weak and require milk, and what require meat—is incompetent to prescribe moral remedies adapted to the diseases of the soul.   Those parents who have no knowledge of the ruling propensities of their children, and the causes of certain traits of character, are inadequate to govern or instruct them.

We acquire a knowledge of human nature in part, by observation on the actions of men ; but phrenology developes the causes of those actions, and the combination of circumstances which give the character its leading features.   It puts us in possession of the balancing power, points out the preventative, the antidote, the remedy for that disproportion incident to the mental and physical constitution.   It serves to prepare degenerate man for the renovating and sanctifying influences of the Holy Spirit, and to improve and elevate him, not only as a physical, but as an intellectual and immortal being.   It takes hold of the destinies of eternity, and of millions yet unborn.

MISCELLANY.

Discussion of Phrenology before the Royal Academy of Medicine at Paris.—It appears that, during the last winter, the merits of phrenology were again indirectly discussed before the French Royal Academy

The subject, more particularly, was respecting the existence and locality of the organ of Language. M. Bouillaud introduced the matter, by communicating fifteen cases, in addition to sixty-four cases previously presented, all of which went to prove that the organ of Language was seated in the anterior lobes of the brain. He admitted that many facts had been collected and recorded on this point, which seemed apparently to oppose the principles of phrenology; but, at the same time, insisted that the details of these facts were always unsatisfactory, and insufficient to afford any positive evidence towards settling the question. The discussion was continued during three sittings of the society. and appears to have been conducted with much interest and ability. The leading advocates of phrenology were M. Blandin, M. Ferrus, and M. Bouillaud; the opposers, M. Curveilhier, M. Rochoux, and M. Gerdy. The Medical Gazette of Paris, in closing a notice of the discussion, says—"Certainly we must acknowledge that the phrenological doctrine has, on the whole, very successfully resisted the attacks of its adversaries during this rather protracted ordeal, and that not a little merit is due to M. Bouillaud for his manly and able defence of its positions."

———

British and Foreign Medical Review.—In No. 8, page 369, of the Journal, we alluded to an able and extended article on phrenology, in a late number of the above review. The reader will find a part of this article in the present number of the Journal. It appears that the article has been reprinted from the review in pamphlet form in Great Britain, and is having quite a circulation. The Scotsman, of March 28, (a weekly paper published in Edinburgh, and conducted with much ability,) alludes to it as follows:—"Although long silent, we have not been indifferent spectators of the recent progress of phrenology. We have seen it avowed, or respectfully spoken of, by author after author, and journal after journal, adopted and professed by well-informed persons, whom we meet in almost every company, and its principles reduced to practice in schools, prisons, and lunatic asylums. We who had been beholders to even a slight knowledge of it, as a philosophy of mind and exposition of human nature, for a great addition to our own magazine of thought, power of discrimination, and accuracy of expression, see with much satisfaction the journal of Dr. Forbes, the *British and Foreign Medical Review*, allowed by the medical world to be one of its most influential periodicals, in an admirable article, boldly publishing its adhesion to the leading facts and principles of the new science, and strongly recommending it to the serious, and no longer contemptuous, attention of the profession. We have before had occasion to notice the excellent spirit in which this review is conducted, and the comprehensive, liberal, and candid tone of its criticisms. In its treatment of phrenology, it has acted a part which. for candour and manliness, contrasts greatly in its favour with the timid course pursued by some other journals."

———

Natural Language of the Organs.—It is a settled principle in phrenology, that the manifestation of any particular faculties in one individual is calculated to call into exercise the same class of faculties in another. Thus, if Combativeness or Destructiveness is excited, their exhibition will excite the same faculties in those who witness the manifestation. Many curious phenomena of this kind frequently occur in society, and are entirely inexplicable on any other system of mental philosophy than that of phrenology. A person who understands the science, and is well acquainted with the natural language of the organs, has by this means a very great advantage in understanding human nature, and can sometimes make use of such knowledge for the most important purposes in his dealings with mankind. This knowledge is of the highest importance to parents, teachers, and all who have the care or instruction of the young.

What is meant by the natural language of the faculties, is their external manifestation, as indicated in the movements of the body and the head, and, more especially, as they are expressed in the features of the countenance and tones of the voice. Mr. Combe, in remarking on the natural language of the higher sentiments, in his address before the Boston Phrenological Society, has the following beautiful illustrations. To realise the full force of these illustrations, the reader should be personally acquainted with the individuals referred to:—"Who does not recollect the benignity, the heavenly purity, and the soft and soothing tones of voice of the Rev. Dr. Tuckerman, of this city ? These radiant beams of Christian emotion are the natural language of Benevolence, Veneration, and Hope, which he is constantly calling into play, in ministering, as a home missionary, to the poor, the wretched, and the depraved. Has any one observed a similar expression of Benevolence and radiant joy in the countenance of Dr. Woodward, the superintendent of the Worcester Hospital for the Insane ? It is the natural language of those sentiments of tender sympathy and cheering hope, which he is habitually pouring into minds diseased, and which are the best antidotes to their afflictions. Another practical example may be mentioned. The Rev. Mr. Gallaudet, of Hartford, was for many years head instructor of the deaf and dumb, in the institution near that city. He informed me, that however much annoyed in his own temper, however peevish and even irritable, he might be, the moment he began to instruct his pupils by the language of the higher sentiments, which was the only medium whereby he could cultivate these feelings in them, his evil genius fled, and the spirit of peace and good-will reappeared in his bosom. He added, that he has often subdued the worst passions in his deaf and dumb pupils, solely by radiating on them the natural language of Benevolence, expressed in compassion or regret. He has stifled rage also, and brought forth the beauty of kindly affection, by insisting on the refractory pupil exhibiting the natural language of virtuous feeling. He is so impressed with the importance of natural language as a means of training the feelings, that he has strongly recommended it in his writings.

"Again: Dr. Woodward told me, when I visited the Worcester Hospital, on the 28th of December, 1839, that he finds the activity of the diseased faculties in his patients much increased by the presence or even the insignia of their objects. If a quarrelsome man finds a feather and stick in his hat, he instantly erects his head, and becomes a soldier ; and his diseased propensity rages more fiercely. Dr. Woodward coaxes him to yield up the feather, and to lay aside his military air, saying to him, 'We are all civilians here,' and his pugnacity is mitigated. If a female patient, who fancies herself a queen, gets a shawl or other means of making a robe, with a little finery and embroidery, she puts it on. and instantly struts and sidles about with majestic airs; and her disease is aggravated. He persuades her to part with it, as ' We are all republicans here, and queens might not be properly respected ;' and the intensity of the diseased feeling gradually abates."

———

Classification of the Faculties.—A valuable correspondent has sent us a classification of the mental faculties, with which we have been so much pleased as to be induced to present it in the Journal. There seems to be quite a diversity of opinion among leading phrenologists on this subject; and it will doubtless require considerable time, and farther examination, before any particular classification will meet with a general reception, and become a fixed standard among all the cultivators of the science. The following classification of our correspondent is ingenious, convenient, and, perhaps, not at variance with nature.

Class I.

Propensities or feelings, which correspond with the sensitive tract, or column of the spinal cord, and are supposed to arise from the restiform bodies of the medulla oblongata, viz:

Domestic Group.	*Selfish Group.*
1. Amativeness,	7. Destructiveness,
2. Philoprogenitiveness,	8. Alimentiveness,
3. Adhesiveness,	9. Acquisitiveness,
4. Inhabitiveness,	10. Secretiveness,
5. Concentrativeness	11. Cautiousness,
6. Combativeness,	12. Approbativeness,
Vitativeness.	13. Self-esteem.

Class II.

Sentiments or emotions, which correspond with the middle column of the spinal marrow, and are supposed to arise from the corpora olivaria of the medulla oblongata; giving rise to the *involuntary* emotions, unlike the *feelings* or propensities, viz:

Moral or Religious Group.	*Perfective Group.*
14. Firmness,	20. Constructiveness,
15. Conscientiousness,	21. Ideality,
16. Hope,	? Sublimity,
17. Wonder,	22. Imitation.
18. Veneration,	
19. Benevolence.	

Constructiveness is placed in the above class, though it should perhaps, on some accounts, be ranked among the Intellectual Faculties, yet its organ lies in the middle lobe of the brain.

Class III.

Intellect or will, which corresponds with the anterior column of the spinal marrow, and its organs arise from the corpora pyramidalia; giving rise to volition. These constitute the intellectual faculties, and may be considered under two divisions, viz. perceptive and reflective groups, the names of the particular faculties included, it is unnecessary here to repeat.

Those who are acquainted with the anatomy of the brain, and the spinal columns, will readily perceive how this classification harmonises with it; that the spinal marrow is composed of the anterior, middle, and posterior columns; that the nerves of *voluntary motion* arise from the anterior columns which connect with the organs (Class 3.) of the *will* or intellect, in the *anterior* lobe of the brain; that the nerves of *involuntary* motion arise from the middle columns which connect with the organs of the sentiments (Class 2.) or involuntary emotions in the middle lobe of the brain; and that the nerves of sensation arise from the posterior columns which connect with the *propensities or feelings* in the posterior lobe of the brain. Organs Nos. 7, 8, 9, and 10, (in the middle lobe of the brain,) of Class 1, and perhaps No. 20, of Class 3, are supposed to be spread over the sentiments (Class 2.) like the outer covering of a partially blown rose. The reasons for such a classification are, 1st, Almos the whole of the human system, in its different parts, is made up of a *trinity*. 2d. The trinity of the spinal cord and its nerves, the brain (three lobes), its coverings, ventricles, commissures, medulla oblongata cornua, &c. &c. 3d, The mental actions performed by these three classes are different from each other, being *voluntary, involuntary, and sensitive* or *affective*, corresponding with the three *tracts* or *columns* of the spinal marrow, and the three sets of nerves given off from them; for Mr. Combe, in speaking of the sentiments, says they consist of a different order of feelings from the propensities, joined with what may more appropriately be called an *emotion*, or a feeling of a purer, higher, and more elevated character. 4th, In forming an estimate of character, we have constantly to keep in view the *comparative sizes* of these three classes or, in other words, the *animal, moral,* and *intellectual* nature of the individual examined. Lastly, Its *simplicity* not being nearly so likely to confuse the amateur in science, as the more *minute* divisions mentioned in phrenological works under the head, genus, species, &c. (the writer here refers to the three general classes in the present classification, without so much reference to the *grouping*, which is of no particular consequence).

Again: *Voluntary* motion can be produced independent of, and without affecting sensation or the *senses*, but the latter *seldom*, if ever, act independent of, and without the *direction of voluntary motion;* so also the intellect may be intensely *active*, without arousing the propensities or sentiments, but the propensities and sentiments cannot be *active*, even in a moderate degree, without arousing the intellect and receiving its direction, so that the propensities or feelings themselves are blind instincts or impulses to action, which action receives its direction from the intellect or will, and the sentiments. This teaches us the great importance of cultivating and enlightening the sentiments and the intellect, in order that *these* moving or impelling powers (propensities) may receive a proper direction.

History of Phrenology in Philadelphia.—Dr. John Bell, in a review of Mr. Haskin's History and Progress of Phrenology, in the June number of the Eclectic Journal of Medicine, states some facts of interest respecting the history of the science in this city. As these facts serve to correct some statements already published in phrenological works, and will be valuable for future reference, we deem them worthy of record here. They are as follows:—" The first phrenological society in the United States was founded in this city in the month of February, 1822, of which Dr. Physick was made president, Dr. John Bell, corresponding secretary, and Dr. B. H. Coates, recording secretary. From this time, and not 'twelve years since,' as Mr. Haskins has it, must we date the public advocacy of phrenology by Drs. Coates and Bell. The subject was more formally introduced by Dr. Bell delivering two lectures to the 'Central Phrenological Society, established at Philadelphia,' at its meetings on the 4th and 18th of March, 1822. These lectures, published in the 4th volume of Dr. Chapman's Medical and Physical Journal, were intended to illustrate and enforce the doctrine by various proofs and analogies.

" An interest was manifested to such an extent, as to induce the society to procure an excellent collection of casts from Paris and Edinburgh;

and although the zeal was not maintained by the many, yet the original inquirers and converts after inquiry have ever continued to explain and defend what they believed to be the truth. A stronger proof cannot well be furnished of the fruits of the seed thus sown in Philadelphia, than the fact, that here Mr. Combe had the largest class by far of any which has listened to him in the United States, and it was only exceeded in point of numbers in one of the cities of Great Britain.

"In 1822, Mr. Combe's Essays on Phrenology were republished by Messrs. Carey and Lea, with considerable additional matter furnished by Dr. Bell, viz. a Preliminary Essay, consisting of the lectures already mentioned, and a chapter on the anatomy of the brain, as displayed by Gall and Spurzheim, and another on insanity. A review of these essays will be found on reference to Dr. Chapman's Journal, Vol. 5th, and one of the Transactions of the Phrenological Society of Edinburgh (1824), and of Dr. Caldwell's Elements of Phrenology (1824), in the 8th volume of that journal The last was written by Dr. Bell. In the 7th volume of the same journal, there is an able article entitled *Comparative Phrenology*, from the pen of Dr. B. H. Coates. In the 12th volume of the North American Medical and Surgical Journal, a full review of Dr. A. Combe's work on Mental Derangement, written by Dr. Bell, is preceded by an outline of the science of phrenology, and of the basis, anatomical and physiological, on which it is believed to rest. From the same pen, there is a similar sketch given in the Appendix to the third edition of Broussais's Physiology ; translated by Drs. Bell and La Roche.

"From the year 1823 to the present time, Dr. Bell has given some lectures on phrenology every summer to the class of the Medical Institute, as a part of his course on the institutes of medicine. We ought not to conclude without stating, also, that Dr. Harlan, even then advantageously known for his zealous prosecution of natural history and comparative anatomy, gave a short course of lectures on phrenology in the Philadelphia Museum, during the spring of 1822."

—

Mr. Combe's Address before the Boston Phrenological Society.—A short notice of this address appeared in a previous number of the Journal. It has since then been published in pamphlet form by the request of the society, a copy of which is now before us. Some of the topics discussed are especially important, as connected with the present state and advancement of phrenology. In accounting for the decline of many societies devoted to the interests of the science, Mr. Combe remarks as follows :—

I observe, then, that many phrenological societies have perished from having prescribed to themselves objects of too limited a nature. They have undertaken chiefly the duty of verifying the observations of Drs. Gall and Spurzheim, and other phrenologists, in regard to the organs of the mind, and their functions ; and have too seldom embraced, in their sphere of action, the application of this knowledge to the physical, moral, and intellectual improvement of themselves and their fellow-men ; or, if this aim *have* found a place in the constitution and laws, it has not practically been carried into effect.

A knowledge of the organs and their functions, and of the effects of their combinations, is indispensable as a foundation for the useful application of phrenological science ; and I have long been convinced by observation, that the confidence of each disciple in the power of his principles, and also his capacity of applying them to advantage, bears a relation, cæteris paribus, to his minute acquaintance with organology. Far from undervaluing, therefore, the importance of an extensive series of observations in organology, I emphatically declare my experience to be, that it is the first step towards the formation of a true phrenologist; it is the *second* step; and it is the *third* step towards the formation of a true phrenologist.

But experience induces me to add, that this department is comparatively narrow. In a few years, an individual of ordinary powers of observation may attain to a full knowledge of organology, and a thorough conviction of its truth; and if he stop there, he will resemble a geometrician, who, after having mastered all the demonstrations of Euclid, shrinks from applying them. He would find the constant repetition of them uninteresting, because they had become familiar, and led to no practical results. The same rule holds good in phrenology. To sustain our interest, we must proceed to apply our principles; and here our difficulties commence. The most timid mind may employ itself, in the secret recesses of its own study, in observing casts, or in manipulating living heads, and suffer no inconvenience, except, perhaps, a passing smile of derision from some good-natured friend, who esteems his own ignorance more excellent than our knowledge. But when the phrenologist advances openly to the application of the principles of the science, then the din of conflict arises. He invades other men's prejudices, and sometimes assails what they conceive to be their privileges; for there are persons who claim as a privilege the profits which they may make by public errors. He is then opposed, misrepresented, and abused; and as he is conscious that his object is one of beneficence, he is unwilling to accept a reformer's recompense; discontinues his exertions, and the society becomes dormant. This fate has overtaken several phrenological associations in Britain. They have shrunk from the practical application of their principles, and consequently sleep.

The time is not yet, but will probably soon arrive, for resuscitating them into active existence, as societies for physiological, moral, and intellectual reform; and I venture to prophesy, that whenever they shall embody a reasonable number of members, pledged to the application of the principles of phrenology in these great fields of usefulness, their success will be conspicuous and cheering.

The human mind is regulated by uniform laws, and the same events happen, in similar circumstances, in the United States and in Britain. In several of the cities of this country which I have visited, I have found that phrenological societies have existed, flourished for a brief season, and then fallen into decay; and in general, the cause appears to have been the same. The members soon became satisfied that the great principles of phrenology are true; but they were not prepared to proceed to the practical application of them in any department of usefulness. They saw a public that was either hostile or indifferent to them, and they did not feel in themselves sufficient power to cope with these adverse feelings. The consequence has been that phrenology has seemed to fall asleep. Its enemies have thought that it was dead. But when did any great truth, fraught with blessings to the human race, perish? The ignorant and despotic priesthood which sent Galileo to a dungeon, congratulated themselves that they had cut up, by the root, the heresy of the earth's revolution on its axis. But how delusive was their dream, how absurd their estimate of their own power! The Creator had swung the globe on high, and impelled it in its diurnal and in its annual course. Copernicus, Galileo, and Newton, were guilty only of calling the attention of mankind to what the Creator had done. If the nations were offended, and averted their eyes, worlds did not therefore cease to roll; men, alone, suffered the consequences of their conduct. They remained buried in a stolid and barbarous ignorance, which led them to wage horrible wars with each other; to believe in witchcraft; to bow their necks, in all the helpless imbecility of intellectual darkness, to ruthless tyrants in church and state. So it ever must be when natural truths, in other words, the works of the Creator, are discovered, presented to mankind, and rejected. They do not cease to exist and to act. Truth cannot die. Accordingly, in this country, I find phrenology flourishing in astonishing vigour as a practical art. Wherever I have gone, I have found men who call themselves practical phrenologists, exciting a vulgar curiosity concerning the science; examining heads; predicating character; using it, in short, as a species of palmistry or astrology, and extracting, as I have been told, large sums of money from the people by their skill. I have heard these humble practitioners denounced, by educated and philosophical phrenologists, as the greatest enemies of the science; as having degraded it, and rendered it disgusting to superior minds. I acknowledge the consequences, and lament them; but I am disposed to deal charitably with the offenders. *They* did what higher men left undone. They not only boldly proclaimed their own conviction of the truth of phrenology, but they applied it, to the best of their ability. If the educated phrenologists will do the same, they will be more successful; and they will wipe away this opprobrium from the science, in the only way in which it can be removed, by substituting a better practice in its place.

I repeat, then, my humble conviction that every phrenological society, to be permanently successful, must engage in practical objects; and **I** need not mention how wide is the field for the application of our science. The members of this society are acquainted with many of its departments, such as education, insanity, criminal legislation, prison discipline; criticism, biblical and profane; political economy and moral science. To the successful prosecution of all of these, a knowledge of mind is indispensable.

A knowledge of the location and functions of the several organs, is an important acquisition; but the numerous applications of the science to the advancement of human happiness, and the improvement of the race, are considerations of far greater importance. We need not here repeat nor enforce Mr. Combe's remarks on the absolute necessity of carrying out these applications, in order to sustain and advance the science. It is not necessary, and neither would it be possible, for every person to become a good practical phrenologist; yet most, if not all, by some little study and attention, may be able to judge very correctly from mere observation of the leading features of character. Every person will find even this knowledge of very great advantage in understanding human nature—in knowing at once with *whom* he has to deal, and *how* to adapt himself to the various wants and conditions of those with whom he may have intercourse in the world. *Practical* phrenology is good in *its place*, though it may occasionally fall into bad hands, and a bad use may be made of it. So may every other good thing be perverted. This must be expected until the public generally become better acquainted with phrenology, and until men of character and influence will acknowledge its claims to credence and support, and will take the lead in advocating and promulgating its principles.

Anecdote of a Dog.—A correspondent has sent us the following curious anecdote respecting a dog, and assures us that we may rely on its correctness, as several very respectable and intelligent individuals witnessed the scene, which is thus described:—"A small dog attempted to cross a river, which had a sand-bar in the middle of it, and became entangled in some brush before reaching the bar; a large cur dog seeing his situation from the bank, swam immediately to his assistance, and caught him by the neck and bore him to the bar. The small dog then swam from the bar towards the opposite bank, and was again obstructed by brush; the large dog having remained on the bar, and seeing his situation, swam again to his assistance, and seizing him as before, carried him to the shore, on the opposite side, and then returned to the side of the river from which he started. This scene was witnessed by a large number of persons, all of whom agreed that the large dog could have been actuated by no other motive than that of Benevolence or attachment."

Dr. W. Byrd Powell.—For several years past, this gentleman has been prosecuting the science of phrenology, with untiring zeal and industry, in the southern and western states. He appears to be decidedly popular as a lecturer, original in his investigations, and independent in the expression and defence of his opinions. We have sundry papers before us, containing very commendatory notices of his recent labours in several places in the states of Alabama, Mississippi, and Tennessee.

"We have before us several numbers of the American Phrenological Journal, a publication, issued monthly in Philadelphia, edited with talent and discrimination, and tastefully presented in its externals. 'Let phrenology alone,' said the celebrated Andral, 'and it will throw all obstacles behind it with marvellous force. There is no instance of a truth, fairly launched, having failed to make its way.' Long and arduous has been the conflict, but victory is no longer doubtful. The choicest flowers of vituperation, the most subtle argument and witty sarcasm, have all been unavailing. The often slain now flourishes, to all appearance, in the fulness of youthful vigour, and the calmness of conscious strength. And why has phrenology stood thus unshaken amid the storm of opposition? Simply because it is founded on a rock—the rock of nature. Its doctrines are generalisations of almost innumerable carefully scrutinised and verified facts, and against these no force of argument, nor keenness of sarcasm, nor virulence of bigotry, can prevail."—*Knickerbocker, N. Y.*

"*The American Phrenological Journal* proceeds vigorously: its contents are judiciously selected; and many of the articles are very ably written, and possess great intrinsic interest. Altogether, we have been so much pleased with it, as far as hitherto seen, that we cannot help much regretting the limited circulation it is likely to have in England."—*English Phrenological Journal.*

"I speak literally, and in sincerity, when I say, that were I at this moment offered the wealth of India, on condition of phrenology being blotted from my mind for ever, I should scorn the gift; nay, were every thing I possessed in the world placed in one hand, and phrenology in the other, and orders issued for me to choose one, phrenology, without a moment's hesitation, would be preferred."—*George Combe.*

Mr. George Combe and his lady sailed from New York, for Liverpool, in the British Queen, on the 1st of June.

THE

AMERICAN PHRENOLOGICAL JOURNAL

AND

MISCELLANY.

| Vol. II. | Philadelphia, August 1, 1840. | No. 11. |

ARTICLE I.

ON THE MERITS OF PHRENOLOGY.

(Continued from page 446 of this Journal.)

Admitting the brain to be the organ of the mind ; admitting, also
that the brain is not a unit, but a congeries of organs, each having
its appropriate and peculiar function ; and lastly, admitting that the
energy of every function is proportioned, *cæteris paribus*, to the size
of its individual organ ; it follows, necessarily, as is remarked by
Cuvier, that the size of any cerebral organ affords a direct clue to
the discovery of its function.   Let us suppose, for example, that the
use of the optic nerve was unknown, but that it was invariably found
to be far more largely developed than any of the other nerves of
sense, in animals with powerful vision ; such as the eagle, and much
less so in animals which see very imperfectly, such as the mole ; and
that no instances were to be found in the same species, in which, *all
other circumstances being equal*, powerful vision coexisted with the
smaller nerve, or a larger nerve with feebler vision ; would we not
be justified in at length inferring that the use of the nerve was to
serve for vision ?   In like manner, if a particular portion of the brain
is invariably found to be large, in relation to the other parts of the
same brain, in individuals remarkable for timidity and wariness, and
relatively small in persons remarkable for rashness and the absence
of fear, and no instance can be adduced in which, *cæteris paribus*
the proportion between the feeling and the organ is reversed, are we
not entitled, after sufficiently extensive observation, to hold that the
use of that part of the brain is to serve for the manifestation of the
sentiment of Cautiousness ?   And if this mode of investigation is
applicable to one part of the brain, and to one faculty of the mind
it is obviously applicable to all.   The only indispensable condition
of evidence of this description is, that the coincidence shall be rea

and uniform, and not imaginary or accidental; and here is precisely the grand point of difference between the phrenologists and their opponents, and in regard to which the former have never been fairly met. But as this point is of fundamental importance in determining the truth of phrenology, it will be necessary to devote a little space to its consideration.

The phrenologists affirm, that by observing concomitance of function with size of organ in an infinite variety of instances, as above explained, they have succeeded in tracing a connection between certain faculties of the mind and certain portions of the brain. Whether there are sufficient grounds for maintaining the existence of such a connection, is evidently a *question of fact*, against which *à priori* argument can be of no avail. The only way to meet the phrenologists successfully, is to adduce facts at variance with their conclusions; and even Dr. Holland admits that the conclusiveness of this appeal cannot be denied, for he allows that if the facts tally with the statements of the phrenologists in a large proportion of cases, so as to make reasonable allowance for error or ambiguity, *the improbability must be laid aside, and the whole admitted as a new and wonderful truth.* "Here, then, by common admission, is a direct question of evidence, the amount and strictness of which are solely to be considered."

Dr. Prichard, and other writers on the same side, take a similar view of the subject; but the phrenologists complain, and not without reason, that the very men who are foremost in admitting the question to be one of fact alone, are the first to "turn their backs upon themselves," and attempt to solve it by argument and probabilities, which, considered *as evidences*, are worth nothing. Instead of meeting the followers of Gall by well-observed and hostile facts, Dr. Holland merely says, "Here, I think, it will be found that the phrenologists are yet wanting in what is needful to establish their system, notwithstanding all the obvervation and ingenuity which have been bestowed on its proof;" and in answer to their facts, he contents himself with assigning sundry reasons for quietly setting them aside.

"Look," he says, "at what they have said in aid of their determinations, where the question concerns the relation between a certain outward form of cranium and some faculty or quality of mind, alleged to be in correspondence with it. First, The equal chance of affirmative or negative, as to each particular quality predicated. Secondly, The plea of a balance of some indications by others and opposing ones. Thirdly, The want of exact definition of many of these qualities or faculties, making it difficult to arrest for error where there are so many ways of retreat. And fourthly, The incidental discovery of character by other and more ordinary methods. I well know that the candid disciples of the system will not consciously avail themselves of all these methods. Nevertheless, each one of them has, more or less, been made use of; and looking to the chances and facilities thus obtained, it may be affirmed that the number of true predictions in phrenology is less miraculous than it would be, were this number not to exist."

We admit at once that all this is very plausible, and that, as a reason for exercising caution in observing and in drawing inferences, it is very useful; but *does it in any degree meet the question of fact, and prove that the alleged coincidences are unreal?* We cannot see that it does, and we are of opinion that one well-authenticated fact, opposed to those of the phrenologists, would outweigh a volume of reasoning in a matter of this kind. Dr. Holland states that phrenologists appeal to coincidences between mental power and cerebral developement, but he regards the coincidences as " not sufficiently numerous," and adds that, during his intercourse with Gall and Spurzheim, he had several opportunities of noticing the failure of their judgments upon these particular faculties, as well as in other cases where the doctrine ought to have indicated rightly the relation between faculty and organ. But Dr. Holland does not adduce any details of these failures from which his readers might judge for themselves whether they were real; and if so, whether they resulted from the outward indications being erroneous, or from a mere personal blunder in estimating them, such as may happen, and does happen daily, in the case of a chemist or mathematician, whose science, nevertheless, remains unaffected by the blunder.

We also have heard of erroneous inferences being made by phrenologists, and have taken some trouble to investigate their nature. In some, we should say in most, instances, the error has proceeded from the rash judgment of incompetent persons. In others, we have known a well-qualified phrenologist commit a mistake, either from giving an opinion hurriedly, or from speaking more decidedly than the real difficulties of the case warranted. There are instances, for example, in which a number of organs are so equally developed, and in which the corresponding mental powers are so nearly equal in energy, that it is impossible to assign a marked predominance to any of them. It is in cases of this kind that the influence of education and external circumstances is greatest, and that the quality which is most assiduously cultivated, will assume prominence in the character. Take two men, for example, in whom the selfish and the devotional feelings are originally almost

equally strong, and breed the one to the church, and confine him to
he society of the kind and benevolent, while you place the other in
 counting-room, amidst all the excitement of money-getting—the
ine will assuredly become, not pious and disinterested in the highest
legree, but certainly *more* pious and disinterested than the other;
vhile the phrenologist, who affirmed that they were naturally or
iriginally on an equality in this respect, and that the two faculties
vere nearly equally balanced in both, would most likely be regarded
iy their respective acquaintances as greatly in error.   Again : we
iave known a phrenologist hastily pronounce an organ to be mode-
ate, which was really large, and thus give rise to an apparent con-
radiction.   But although this may happen now and then, *it does not
ilter the reality ;* it leaves the organ of the same size as before, and
f a more careful comparison shows it to be really large, the induc-
ion remains valid, although the manipulator committed a mistake.
This, however, is carefully kept in the back ground by the opponents
if phrenology, who often confound an erroneous estimate of a fact
with hostility of the fact itself, and thence infer that phrenology
nust be in fault, when there has been merely an error on the part of
he individual, for which the science ought never to be made
inswerable.   If the observations made by the phrenologists *are*
ncorrect, surely there can be no great difficulty in obtaining
authentic facts to prove their inaccuracy.   And yet, while all think-
ng men on both sides agree that the question can be authoritatively
iettled only by a reference to fact, it is somewhat remarkable that
he phrenologists alone have taken pains to observe nature, and to
'orm collections of facts, which they have further laid open to
iublic inspection and verification in their museums; while their
intagonists have neither published nor collected any opposing facts,
iut have contented themselves with the vague assertion that such
exist, and with arguing that therefore those of the phrenologists
must be untrue.

   Here, we think, lies the great error of those who contend against
:he truth of Gall's discovery.   All of them—even Dr. Roget, Dr.
Prichard, and Dr. Holland—state, *in a general way*, that their experience is against the alleged concomitance of mental faculty and
:erebral organs.   But instead of themselves specifying facts, and
giving details entitled to confidence, they complain that the observations recorded by the phrenologists are not "sufficiently numerous"
ir accurately made to prove their positions, and argue that hence
:hese must be disbelieved.   This mode of proceeding, when expressed
in plain language, appears palpably absurd.   The phrenologists state
principles, and adduce "some" facts patent to every body, which

tend, *pro tanto*, to prove them. Their opponents, however, say, " No; do not believe one of them, for *we* know facts which do not tally with them, but which *we shall keep to ourselves*, and which you must believe merely on our assurance." The phrenologists have been accused of claiming a large measure of belief on the part of their followers: but their claim is backed, not only by hundreds of published cases, but by museums full of specimens, copies of the more remarkable of which are to be found in almost every large town in Britain. Whereas the anti-phrenologists make a sweeping claim on the public to disregard all these evidences, and to believe them worthless on their own mere affirmation, unsupported by facts of any description! Is it to be wondered at, that opposition so directed has been wholly ineffectual in arresting the progress of phrenology or disproving its truth? We think not; and we suspect that if phrenology is to be put down at all, it must be by an opposition more in harmony with the Baconian rules of philosophising than any hitherto attempted.

Dr. Holland, Dr. Prichard, and Dr. Roget, all have the sagacity to perceive, that, however plausibly the matter may be argued on either side, the truth of phrenology must in the end be decided by an appeal to facts alone; and such being the case, we think our remaining space will be much more profitably occupied with a few remarks on the best mode of testing the phrenological facts by observation, than with comments upon any other parts of the general argument.

If it were necessary, this would be the place to show that there are no insuperable difficulties in the way, to prevent the size and configuration of the brain from being pretty accurately estimated during life, by observing the outward form of the head. In the early days of phrenology, the want of parallelism between the tables of the skull, and the existence of the frontal sinus, used to be rather favourite objections. But they are now nearly abandoned by anatomists. Some parts of the skull are always thicker than others, but the greatest difference in the thickness of the parts, which have reference to phrenology, scarcely ever exceeds one or two lines, whereas, in cases of extreme developement of brain, the difference of external size often exceeds an inch; so that, even after allowing for *the utmost possible* divergence between the tables, enough will still remain to indicate the developement of brain below.

The existence of the frontal sinus generally makes it difficult in mature age, and especially in males, to ascertain the size of two or three of the smaller organs situated, according to the phrenologists, behind it; but we cannot see that it is of the least weight as an

objection to the truth of phrenology in the main.   The sinus rarely.
appears at all before puberty, and consequently cannot interfere with
the accuracy of observations made before that age.   It is also rarely
much developed in females, and therefore an ample field for observation is open, to which no objection of this kind can apply.   But in
this, as in other cases, the scope for controversy would be greatly
narrowed, and truth be far more easily attained, if both parties were
more careful to fix their attention principally upon the real objects
of discussion, and not to lose sight of essentials in their keen pursuit
of mere accessories, which serve only to perplex and mislead.

Admitting, in its fullest force, every thing that can be said about
want of parallelism between the tables of the skull, and about the
existence of a frontal sinus of variable magnitude, all that we can
honestly conclude is, not that the unsoundness of the phrenological
principles has been established, but that a certain amount of difficulty
stands in the way of their universal application.   Thus, in some
cases of chronic disease, the thickness of the skull increases to the
extraordinary extent of an inch or upwards, and in other instances it
diminishes to little more than the thickness of paper.   In old age,
also, the skull is sometimes of very irregular thickness, from the
inner table following the surface of the diminishing brain faster than
the outer.   But during health and in mature age, such aberrations
are never to be met with.   When they do occur, however, it
becomes evidently impossible to determine, *with certainty*, from the
mere examination of the outward form of the head, the size and
form of the contained brain; and, therefore, Dr. Gall expressly
rejects, as inconclusive, all observations made during *old age and
disease*, because they necessarily involve an element of doubt.
Many of such cases afford valuable *illustrations*, but can never be
received as *proofs*.   These must be derived exclusively from the
period of life during which the essential correspondence between the
external indication and the form of the brain can be relied upon.

In investigating the claims of phrenology, in short, it ought never
to be forgotten, by either friend or foe, that the first and grand
object ought to be *to ascertain its truth*; and that till this be done,
it is needless to confuse the question by discussions, referring solely
to the difficulties of applying it to individual cases.   The greater the
facilities afforded for the verification of evidence, the sooner and
more easily will phrenologists succeed in obviating all the difficulties
of mere application; and if the balance of evidence shall turn out
hostile, the matter will be at an end at once, and further discussion
on any part of the question will become altogether superfluous and
unnecessary.

How, then, are the alleged facts of the phrenologists to be most easily verified or disproved? As neither argument nor ridicule can set them aside, our only remaining, and by far the shortest, way is at once carefully to examine nature, and see whether our observations harmonise with, or contradict, those of the phrenologists. If they agree, let us give up prejudice, and adopt them as true; and if they differ, let us at once reject them, and all the inferences deduced from them, as incorrect and untenable.

In surveying mankind, with a view to observe whether the alleged concomitance between certain qualities of mind and configurations of brain holds good, it will be apparent to every thinking inquirer, that a large proportion of society consists of what are called common-place characters, who are not distinguished by any striking mental feature of either a good or a bad kind, and who display an average amount of kindness, piety, conscientiousness, affection, pride, vanity caution, selfishness, and temper, and also about an average amount of acuteness of perception and reasoning power; but who exhibit neither genius nor originality, and never seek to leave the beaten path of every day usefulness in which Providence has placed them On minuter examination, each individual of this large class is found to be distinguished by *shades* of the general character, and to possess a little more of one quality, and a little less of another, than his neighbour, but still to display nothing that marks him as very distinct from the general herd. If, as the phrenologists affirm, the developement of the brain corresponds with the features of the character, it will follow that the mass of mankind, in any one locality will present brains differing little from each other, and equally allied to a common type, as we have seen their characters to be; but that on minute examination, shades of difference will be perceptible in their heads, corresponding to the differences really existing in their minds. But it will also necessarily follow, that the difficulty of observing, and appreciating these minuter shades of cerebral differences must, to an inexperienced person, be equally great, as it would be for a stranger to discover, at a first interview, the slighter shade of character by which each is distinguished from his neighbour.

Influenced by the difficulties of accurate observation amidst general uniformity of this description, the phrenologists wisely advise beginners not to trouble themselves at first by looking for *proofs* among individuals known only for average mental endowments, and in whom, consequently, all parts of the brain may be nearly equally developed. After they have acquired experience in observation, they may obtain additional light by this means; but in *testing the truth* of the phrenological concomitance, it is far more satisfactory to begin with well marked cases, in which one or several of the mental faculties are very strong or very deficient, and in which, consequently, if phrenology be true, we may expect to find the corresponding parts of the brain equally remarkable for size or deficiency, and therefore easy of observation.   For the same reason, they advise that the larger organs of the propensities, or moral sentiments, be selected for verification, in preference to the smaller and more difficult organs of intellect, and that the attention be fixed, at first, exclusively on strongly marked cases, in which no doubt can exist either as to the energy of the mental faculty or the magnitude of the organ.   We would even go farther, and counsel those not much accustomed to precise observation, to commence with cases in which a particular region of the brain, or group of organs, preponderates over the others, and in which the character is broadly marked by the energy of the corresponding faculties; just as in studying the geography of a new country, we should first make ourselves familiar with its leading features, and more general divisions into districts and counties, before seeking to determine minutely the positions of its towns, or the precise courses of its rivers.   When the eye is thus trained to the correct observation of the larger features, it will experience much less difficulty in taking accurate cognisance of details.

According to the phrenologists, the brain, considered as the organ of mind, may be divided into three great regions: the first comprising the anterior lobe, and serving for the operation of the intellectual faculties; the second comprising the coronal region, and more immediately connected with the moral sentiments; and the third comprising the posterior lobes and base, and serving for the manifestation of the propensities common to man with the lower animals.   In a person of a well-constituted mind, these three regions, and the corresponding groups of faculties, are in due proportion to each other; but wherever the character is marked by the predominance of the lower passions and by feebleness of intellect any moral emotion, as in most criminals the posterior and basilar regions will be found in excess, and the coronal and anterior portions narrow and defective, or the "forehead villanous low."   Where, on the contrary, as in Melancthon, the moral sentiments and intellect form the prominent features of the mind, and the passions are weak, the anterior and coronal regions will rise high and arched over a comparatively small base and posterior region.

Here, then, is a good field for a beginner.   To ascertain how far physiologists in general, as well as phrenologists, are right in considering the anterior lobe of the brain to be more immediately connected with the intellectual faculties, it will be easy to compare the expanse of forehead in congenital idiots with that of men of ordinary intelligence, and still more of men of great and general talent.   In most cases of this kind, the idiocy arises from defective developement of the brain, and especially of its anterior portion; and it requires one only to visit a few asylums or workhouses to observe the stinted dimensions of the foreheads of idiots, as contrasted with the lofty brow of a Bacon or a Shakspeare.   The creative genius— the highest attribute of intellect—of Michael Angelo scarcely formed a more striking contrast to the mental inanity of the idiot mentioned in the Phrenological Journal, vol. ix., p. 126, than do their respective foreheads represented from nature.

If we pursue this inquiry throughout the whole family of man, we invariably find the forehead most developed among the races most remarkable for general intelligence, and the reverse.   Lowest in the scale of organisation are, perhaps, the aborigines of some parts of New Holland; and from them we have an almost regular gradation through the Carib, the Esquimaux, the North American Indian, the New Zealander, the Negro, the Sandwich Islander, and the Hindoo, up to the European, who has decidedly the largest forehead and highest intelligence of them all.   It is true that among idiots we occasionally find an example of a very large and prominent forehead and head, as among the cretins of Switzerland; but these are generally cases of hydrocephalus, or of other forms of cerebral disease, in which disorganisation has taken place, and in which the mental faculties have become impaired as the disease advanced.   We have seen small-pox induce idiocy in this manner in a scrofulous subject; and it is not an uncommon termination of long-continued mania. These facts, however, constitute no exception to the axiom, that a brain below a given size is incapable of manifesting the mental faculties in a healthy and efficient manner.

If, to induce us to test the fact by direct observation, we required farther presumptive proof of the connection of the anterior parts of the brain with the intellectual powers, we would refer to the general experience of mankind, and to the many attempts made to measure the one by the other.   Camper's celebrated facial angle, which affords results generally accurate, but presents easily explicable exceptions, is founded on the principle of the anterior lobes being not only the seat of intelligence, but proportioned in developement to the extent of the intelligence; and it fails only from overlooking disturbing causes, which phrenology at once points out, and enables us to avoid.

To ascertain the connection of the animal propensities with the posterior and basilar portions of the brain, we have only to observe the heads of men who are notorious for the fierceness of their passions, for selfishness, cunning, and utter want of principle; and those of men whose delight is in doing good, quietly and unostentatiously, and whose passions are never roused, except in defence of suffering humanity. If, for example, the heads of a Sykes and a Fagin do not form a contrast, in the preponderance of the basilar regions, with those of men like the Brothers Cheeryble of Boz, as remarkable as the contrast between their characters, we need scarcely go further, as it would prove, unexceptionably, the non-existence of the alleged concomitance. But if the contrast is, in reality, as striking as it is said to be, then let us note it well, and continue our observations on characters of a different kind, till evidence shall accumulate sufficient to warrant an opinion on the general truth of the principles on which the phrenological mode of investigation is founded.

Having ourselves bestowed much pains on the verification of the phrenological evidence, and learned, by experience, the best way of surmounting its attendant difficulties, we would earnestly recommend those of our readers who are really desirous of satisfying themselves of the truth of Gall's discovery, to begin by visiting any of the phrenological museums, such as the splendid collection of Deville, in the Strand, and placing, side by side, thirty or forty heads of abandoned criminals, and as many of persons of superior intelligence and morality and contrasting the general features of one class with those of the other. In this way, differences will become palpable, which, viewed singly, might be overlooked; and if, with shades of difference in other respects, the whole of the criminals' heads shall be found to possess a large base of the brain, and a comparatively low and narrow forehead and coronal surface, while those of individuals noted for superior virtue and intelligence show the proportions reversed, it will become very difficult to deny the probability of some fixed relation subsisting between the organisation and the mental qualities. We have tried this test, on a great variety of occasions, in France, in Italy, and in Germany, as well as in this country and in Ireland, and we feel bound to admit, that the general coincidence was very striking. Among the criminal heads we found two or three, on different occasions, which presented a larger fore-head and coronal developement than the rest, and which brought them nearer the type which is considered to indicate average morality and intelligence; but, on further inquiry, we found that these apparent exceptions belonged to criminals superior to their class, by the very traits of character which their heads indicated;

and that they had come under the law of the land, not from the energy of low and brutal passions, but from employing their intellects in schemes of embezzlement or forgery. We are not aware, however, of even one instance of a really ferocious and degraded character being unaccompanied by a decided preponderance in the basilar and posterior convolutions of the brain. Nor have we been able to discover a single example of a person presenting such a developement, being noted in the world for refined morality or elevation of mind.

Having repeated this experiment a sufficient number of times, with different sets of heads, it will be instructive next to compare the skulls of savages with those of any of the European nations, or the least civilised with the more civilised—the New Hollander, for instance, with the Hindoo, or the Carib with the South Sea Islander. The Phrenological Society of Edinburgh possesses, what Tiedemann, after visiting it, admits to be the largest existing collection of national skulls; and many of the societies scattered throughout the kingdom, possess either skulls or casts of skulls from various parts of the world. Deville's museum also contains many, which are accessible to every one. In several of these museums we have tried the same plan of contrasting different races with each other; and, speaking generally, the coincidence of developement of brain, with the known character of the respective races, appeared such as could hardly fail to strike every intelligent and conscientious observer, as affording the strongest presumptive proof of Gall's discovery.

We have seen an exhibition of national skulls arouse attention and excite an interest, which ended in ultimate conviction, in minds prejudiced to the last degree against phrenology; and it may be thought worthy of notice, that the anatomist Dumoutier, who is the Deville of Paris, is at this moment on a voyage round the world, in one of the discovery ships sent out by the French government about a year ago; and that the principal object of his mission is to collect skulls, and take casts or drawings of the skulls and heads of the natives, wherever the ships may touch, for the purpose of serving as phrenological illustrations. We have no doubt that he will return with a rich and valuable collection. In this respect, the conduct of the French government differs widely from that adopted by our own about ten years ago, when the collection of skulls, made for phrenological purposes, by Mr. Collie, Surgeon of H. M. S. Blossom, during a similar voyage of discovery, was taken possession of on his return, and rendered of no use either to science or to himself. Captain Beechey would not even accept the offer of a short report on their phrenological indications, which was volunteered by Mr. George

Combe, and which would have added to the interest, at least, of Captain Beechey's narrative, without possibly doing it any injury.

Having so far prepared himself for making accurate observations, the next step for the phrenological inquirer will be, to examine the general outlines of the heads of those persons whose dispositions are most marked and best known to him; still confining himself, however, to the regions rather than to individual organs. Let him for a time disregard all medium cases, and seek only for extremes. It is from the latter that PROOFS are to be most satisfactorily obtained; for, as yet, the numerous difficulties, inseparable from imperfectly defined cases, would only perplex and confound him. The medical man possesses many advantages in pursuing this inquiry. He not only sees human character and human weaknesses in the confidential intercourse of private life; but in hospitals, in jails, and in schools, he may select the most conclusive cases as evidence, and multiply proofs to his heart's content, before pinning his faith to any man's creed. But in all his proceedings, let him be cautious and steady; neither hasty in adopting evidence, nor precipitate in rejecting it. Some things appear at first sight to be conclusive, for or against a doctrine, while they are so only from being imperfectly known. But wherever, on due examination, facts seem to demonstrate a truth, let nothing turn him away from its adoption: and, on the other hand, let nothing tempt him to retain an opinion which facts appear conclusively to falsify.

It will be found impossible, we think, for any candid person to pursue the above mode of inquiry, for any considerable period, without becoming impressed with the conviction, avowed by other eminent observers as well as by Gall, that the degree of intelligence is, *cæteris paribus*, proportioned to the developement of the anterior lobes of the brain, not in man only, but also in the lower animals. In Vimont's magnificent work on Comparative Phrenology, proofs of this fact superabound; and it is a matter of common observation, that dogs, horses, monkeys, and other animals remarkable for intelligence, have large and rounded foreheads. We are aware, indeed, of supposed exceptions to the rule in persons who present an apparently large and broad forehead, and yet are by no means superior in talent. But in all such cases, where the original constitution or temperament is not very low, and disease has not impaired the cerebral functions, the anterior lobe will be found to be really very moderately developed; and the fallacy to arise from judging of its size by height and breadth alone, *without taking depth into account.* A deep anterior lobe is one which extends far forward over the orbitar plate of the frontal bone, and projects over the eye and

cheek-bones. A shallow anterior lobe, on the contrary, is short
and scarcely advances far enough to protect the eye. The distanc
forward, from the lower extremity of the coronal suture, is a goo
indication of the length of the anterior lobe, and will be found t
vary not a little, even where the mere fronts look equally large
This will be easily understood, by supposing an observer to be place
directly opposite the ends of two logs of wood, each a foot square
but the one twenty feet long, and the other only ten. It is clear
that were he to judge merely from the end view, he would declar
both logs to be equal, although in reality, the one was double th
size of the other. It is the same with the anterior lobe; in order t
avoid mistakes, its depth or length must be reckoned, as well as it
height and breadth. We have heard this called a "loop-hole" fo
the phrenologists; but call it by what name you please, the questior
which concerns us, is simply, whether it is a *fact?* We confess tha
our experience obliges us to admit the reality of the distinction her
pointed out, although at one time we overlooked it; and it is no
where more palpably seen than in the large-looking, but reall
shallow foreheads of the Peruvian skulls, compared with the appa
rently smaller, but much deeper foreheads of the Greeks, French, o
British.

A similar precaution is required in estimating the developement o
the coronal region of the brain. Many of the criminal heads pre
sent rather a broad upper surface; but it extends almost like a fla
plain, and rises little above the level of the points of ossification i
the parietal and frontal bones, instead of forming the high and archec
appearance which we remark in the heads of Sully, Melancthon, anc
others, noted for the energy of their moral feelings. But the bes
way to ascertain the real size of the coronal region, is to compare i
number of heads of persons remarkable for moral endowments witl
those of depraved criminals, or of persons known to be deficient ir
the higher feelings of our nature. If this plan be followed, the diffi
culties will, to a great extent, disappear. But in this, as in othei
comparisons of a similar kind, it ought to be kept in mind, that it ir
not the absolute size of the portion of the brain, in one individual
that is to be compared with its absolute size in a different individual
The true point of comparison is the predominance of a given portior
over the other portions *in the same head*, with a similar preponderance over the other portions in a different head. The comparisor
is, therefore, not a single but a double one; and it is not absolute
size that is to be compared, but the relation between an existing
preponderance in each of two heads, considered with reference *each
to its own standard.* For example, there is a wide difference

between affirming that A.'s nose is larger than B.'s, and affirming that A.'s nose is larger relatively to the rest of his features than B.'s relatively to his. The latter proposition may be perfectly correct, and yet B.'s nose be the larger of the two in absolute size. It ought, therefore, to be distinctly understood, that in all comparisons between different heads, this double standard or comparison is implied—because, if this be overlooked, much confusion may arise.

Having thus made ourselves familiar with the larger divisions of the brain, we next proceed, in our verification of the phrenological evidence, to test the functions ascribed to the individual organs or portion of the brain; and here, also, every precaution must be used to avoid error, and we should be careful to be begin with those organs which, from their size or situation, are most easily observed.

Some of the leading propensities are in great activity in childhood and youth, and, when possessed in a high degree, present very favourable opportunities to the inquirer. In early life, manners are not yet broken into that conventional standard to which most people endeavour to approximate on becoming active members of society, and consequently the natural qualities of the individual stand forth in a more recognisable form than at a maturer age. Hence the facility with which we may then test such propensities as Self-esteem, the love of praise, Cautiousness, Affection, Secretiveness, and Destructiveness. The sly timidity and shyness of one child contrasts strongly with the bold and confident openness of another. In one, a fiery temper rages without control; while another is remarkable for patient submissiveness. Contrasts such as these cannot be mistaken; and if the organisation shall not be found in harmony with each, phrenology must inevitably perish. Facts alone are what it has to stand upon.

It would be out of place, even were it possible, to enter here into a detailed exposition of the mode of observing every individual organ, or of the evidence on which its function is held to be ascertained. For that, we must refer to the works named at the head of our article, and particularly to the " Functions of the Brain" of Gall, the "System" of Combe, the " Human and Comparative Phrenology" and plates of Vimont. All that we can do here, is to point out such things as we found most useful in making our own observations, and to add, that in verifying the individual organs, we derived the greatest assistance from placing side by side, (but always with reference to the principle already explained,) heads and skulls in which the organ in question was possessed in opposite degrees of developement. Thus, in examining Destructiveness, we placed a row of murderers and ferocious savages alongside of a row of virtuous characters and

Hindoos; and in studying the organ of Tune or melody, we contrasted a row of musicians with an equal number of persons indifferent to music. In this way, the larger features come out prominently, and leave no doubt as to the conclusions deducible from them. It is in this way that the collections of skulls and casts of dead and living characters, formed by Deville and many of the phrenological societies, become of great practical value; and we would advise those who, like Dr. Holland, reject the evidence altogether, on the plea that the facts are not numerous enough, to study for three months those which *already* exist in such a collection as Deville's, before they again express an opinion on the subject. We are far from thinking that, after doing so, they will agree in every inference drawn from them by Deville himself, or by other phrenologists; for the latter, like other fallible men, often enough take a step beyond the point of solid support, and in consequence sink into the mud of error. But we should be greatly surprised to meet with any man of average honesty, intelligence, and industry, who did not rise from such an inquiry with a higher respect for the genius and labours of Gall, and with more than a suspicion that the new physiology of the brain is true, in its great principles at least, and requires only to be assiduously cultivated to lead ultimately to a rich harvest of important results. To those who really seek truth, we would say, Do not be too much influenced, either by the successes or the failures of the phrenologists, but *go to nature and observe for yourselves.* Individuals may make "lucky hits" or occasional "mistakes;" but if the main facts are true, they will remain to speak for themselves, in a voice which cannot be misunderstood by any one desirous of understanding them; and will be found to substantiate the opinion of Cuvier, that, as " *Certain parts of the brain attain, in all classes of animals, a developement proportioned to the peculiar properties of these animals,* one may hope, *by following up these researches, at length to acquire some notion of the particular uses of each part of the brain.*"

Before leaving this part of the subject, we must repeat, that in judging of the developement of an individual organ, as a direct test of its function, *its size ought first to be compared with that of the other organs in the same head*, and not with any abstract or ideal standard. A faculty is strong or weak, in proportion to the other faculties of *the same* mind, and the general character takes its hue from *its own* predominant qualities. Hence the obvious necessity of measuring mental power and cerebral developement, with reference to the individual himself, when seeking for *proofs* of the concomitance of the one with the other. It is only by keeping in mind this standard, that we can compare the size of an organ in one head with its size in another.

Long as we have already dwelt on the subject, there are numerous points of much importance, directly connected with it, which we have been obliged to pass over in silence, and others which we have touched upon very cursorily. But as our object is not to teach phrenology, but to draw attention to it as eminently deserving of serious inquiry on the part of the profession, our omissions are of less consequence. At the same time, we wish we could have spared room to state more fully what phrenology is, and to show a few of the numerous applications which may be made of it if it shall prove to be true. In the prevention, discrimination, and treatment of insanity, and of nervous diseases, it already affords great assistance to the physician; and when it shall be freed from some of its accompanying errors, and brought to a maturer state, there will hardly be a possibility of overrating its practical value in education, in legislation, in the prevention of crime, and the treatment of criminals, as well as in medicine. If true, it furnishes the elements of the physiology of the brain and of the philosophy of mind; and no ghost is required to tell us how useful both of these branches of knowledge must be in improving mankind, and adding to human happiness. Although we are not so thoroughly satisfied as to consider ourselves phrenologists, in the full sense of the term, we have paid enough of attention to it to warrant our forming a high estimate of its value, if it shall ultimately prove to be true. That it is rapidly advancing in professional estimation, is evident from many signs, and, perhaps, from none more clearly than the extent to which our best-conducted lunatic asylums are already under phrenological guidance. Every day, indeed, is adding to the number; and the direct evidence, proceeding from many quarters, that phrenology is found of daily and hourly use in the treatment of the insane, certainly affords a strong presumption that, in its great outlines at least, it must be both true and valuable.

We have said nothing about the objections against phrenology, founded on its alleged tendency to materialism, fatalism, irreligion, &c. &c.; because discussions about consequences are utterly superfluous till the truth be ascertained. IF PHRENOLOGY IS A TRUTH, *it is impossible that its use can lead to any thing bad.* If it is true, God is its author, and something more than assertion is needed to prove that HE has connected any one truth with consequences necessarily hurtful to his creatures. IF IT IS FALSE, its consequences may and *must be* bad; but then the way to get rid of them, is to *prove it false*, in which case, the consequences will fall along with it into one common grave, and give trouble to no one. We may add however, that to our minds it seems to leave materialism and fatalism precisely where it found them, and to plant religion on the imperish able basis of adaptation to the constitution which God has given to the mind of man.

ARTICLE II.

ON THE HARMONY BETWEEN PHILOSOPHY AND RELIGION.[*]

The human mind consists of observing and reflecting powers animal propensities, and moral sentiments. The observing facultie: take cognisance of existing objects and events simply as they pre sent themselves; while the reflective powers perceive the relation: existing among them. The reflecting faculties, joined with the moral feelings, constitute man's rational nature, and distinguish him from the brutes. Powers of action are conferred on man, by using which, under the guidance of his observing and reflecting intellect he may subjugate external nature to a prodigious extent to his sway and where this power is denied him, he may still, by studying the order of nature, accommodate his own conduct to its course, so as to reap advantages from its operations. Several conditions are neces sary to render this arrangement beneficial to man: *First*, Externa nature must be regular, both in its elementary constitution and course of action: This we shall assume to be the case; because every well-ascertained fact in philosophy proves it to be so, and because the denial of it implies a charge of want of design and intel ligence in the Creator, which we entirely reject. *Secondly*, The human mind and body must be constituted with a wise adaptation to the course of external nature: Every step in science affords addi tional proof that this proposition is true, and we assume it to be so *Thirdly*, The human faculties must be in harmony with each other If one feeling, legitimately directed, gave us a desire for an object and another, also legitimately directed, an aversion to it; or if one portion of our intellect represented a certain course of action as cal culated to lead to happy consequences, while other faculties induced us to perceive that the result would be disastrous; we could not pos sibly act as rational beings. If our elementary faculties were in

---

[*] From the 32th number of the Edinburgh Phrenological Journal.

their constitution contradictory, they could never enable us to discover which course we ought to follow, nor to feel satisfied with any mode of proceeding after we had adopted it.

The regularity of nature is admitted by every individual in the least acquainted with philosophy.   We have heard Dr. Chalmers, from his divinity chair, expound and illustrate most eloquently the doctrine, that the material universe is regulated by fixed laws, which guide the minutest particles, as well as the most ponderous masses of matter, in their movements.   He distinguished between the unascertained and the uncertain.   The laws of the motions of the planets, for example, have been discovered, and philosophers can with certainty predict their positions and appearances at any future hour. The motions of a minute drop of water dashing over a mountain precipice are not ascertained, and, it may be, not ascertainable, by human observation; but they are equally certain as those of the mightiest orb that rolls in the boundless regions of space.   That atom of matter obeys the laws of gravitation, attraction, and repulsion, as precisely as the earth observes her laws of motion in her circuit round the sun.   In a sermon preached in St. George's church on 22d March, Dr. Chalmers is reported in the newspapers to have said :—" As far as our observation extends, nature has always proceeded in an invariable course, nor have we ever witnessed, as the effect of man's prayer, Nature diverge from her usual course; but we affirm the doctrine of a superintending Providence as wide as the necessities of man."

' The reflecting intellect of man is delighted with this view of the constitution of external creation ; because, if the adaptation of the world to human nature be wise and benevolent, every step in knowledge must necessarily be one in happiness and virtue.   The faculty of Causality, in particular, which has received its desires and powers of perception from the Creator, requires order and arrangement for its satisfaction.   A world in which regularity of cause and effect was designedly wanting, would be in contradiction to a mind in which a faculty of Causality was implanted by the Creator ; and this is a position which appears to us to be unassailable.   There are some brains in which the organ of Causality is so small, that the perception of causation, and the desire to trace it and rely on it, are extremely feeble, and these will probably dissent from our present reasonings ; but it is equally irrational to assume the perceptions of such individuals as standards of philosophical truth, as it would be to determine the importance of music as an art and science, by the opinions of a person extremely deficient in the organ of Tune.

Man has also received from the Creator, sentiments of Veneration,

Hope, Wonder, and Ideality, which, combined with Conscientiousness and intellect, render him a religious being. These faculties prompt him to inquire after, reverence, and love a Superior Being; in short, to acknowledge and obey a God.

The problem which we are now attempting to solve, is to reconcile the perceptions of Causality, which instinctively demands regulated order in all objects and events, with the desires of Veneration and Wonder, which love a God, doing according to his good pleasure in the armies of heaven and among the inhabitants of the earth. It is clear that no opinions in philosophy and religion can become practically useful which do not satisfy both orders of faculties. If we shall embrace a system of necessary causation without a God, our religious sentiments will remain unsatisfied; while, if we shall establish a belief in the superintendence of a particular Providence on such principles as to contradict the perceptions of Causality, we shall offend the strongest dictates of reason; and by neither means can we arrive at that internal harmony of feeling and perception which is essential to enjoyment, and also to the practical direction of conduct.

It appears to us that the Creator has constituted and arranged the external world, and the human mind and body, with admirable wisdom and benevolence in their reciprocal relationship; and that the efficient power of a particular Providence is exercised by the perfect action of the general laws which He has established. In other words, that the general laws are so complete, that they rule every individual case in the best manner; so much so, that the result which they produce in each instance could not be varied without departing from the dictates of benevolence and wisdom. This proposition will be best understood by means of practical illustrations.

Let us suppose that the father of a large family is seized with consumption, and is in danger of dying, and that the prayers of many a believing and loving relative are offered to the Throne of Grace for his recovery; those who contend for a special Providence, independently of general laws, expect that these prayers will be heard, and that, if God see it profitable for the patient and his family, he will restore the sufferer to health.

According to our idea, the first point of inquiry that presents itself is, whence does the condition from which deliverance is craved, originate? Consumption is a diseased affection of the material substance which composes the lungs; and we ask, did God command that organ of the body to depart from its healthy condition, to decay, and, by its imperfect action, to destroy the health of its possessor, with a view merely to show forth the power of his Providence in taking away or restoring to health the patient, according to his good pleasure? or did he imprint a definite constitution on the lungs, one result of which is liability to disease from certain irregularities of conduct, and did this particular affliction arise out of that liability in the ordinary course of physiological action? The latter is our proposition. Physiology shows that the lungs, if originally well constituted, and subsequently wisely treated, will operate in a sound condition till the natural period of decay in advanced age; and that whenever, in individual instances, their substance decays in early or middle life, this evil may be traced to an inherent deficiency in strength, inherited from a feeble parent, or to undoubted infringement of the natural conditions on which healthy action has been made by the Creator to depend. There is nothing arbitrary, therefore, in the state of the sufferer. It is the consequence of departure from physiological laws, instituted apparently of deliberate design by the Deity; and the object of the affliction appears to be to induce men who, having received intellectual faculties, are bound to use them, to study and obey the laws of health, and abstain from all practices tending to impair their lungs; and if they shall have unfortunately violated this duty, to forbear transmitting an enfeebled constitution to posterity. Providence, we may presume, could have entirely prevented the descent of imperfection, if He had seen proper; and some may complain of sufferings arising from inheritance as extremely unjust to the offspring; but whenever the parent has obeyed the organic laws, the children inherit the reward in possessing fine constitutions; and it appears to be part of the Divine plan, that where the parents have violated them, the children should endure part of the penalty in inheriting feeble frames. The parent having received rational faculties, was bound to use them, and he neglected to do so at the highest peril to his offspring.

The recovery of the afflicted parent, in the case supposed, means the cessation of decay in the material organ diseased. Now, as this organ, to adapt it to man's rational nature, has received a definite constitution, in virtue of which it becomes disordered from certain kinds of treatment, and maintains itself in health, in certain other circumstances; the object of the prayer may be, either that Providence will, in this instance, dispense with all the established laws which regulate the condition of the lungs, and restore the patient to health without fulfilment of the natural conditions; or that the patient and his advisers may so study and obey the Divine laws as to discover and apply the established means for bringing back his lungs into a prosperous state. The latter appears to us to be the legitimate object of prayer; and it is calculated to satisfy both

Veneration and Causality. Veneration is gratified by the recognition of Divine Providence in the establishment of the laws which regulate the action of the lungs; and Causality is pleased with the perception that their operations are characterised by regularity, benevolence, and wisdom.

The great error fallen into by those who object to this view, is, that they lose sight of the fact, that the condition from which deliverance is asked by means of prayer, is one brought about by the Creator himself, in the perfect knowledge of all its consequences. If a poor man feel disposed to pray for riches, he ought to consider the causes of his poverty, and he will find that they are incapacity, inattention, ignorance, recklessness, or some other deficiency in himself, in his circumstances, or in those persons with whom he is associated; and according to our view, he ought to set about removing these causes before his prayer can have effect. If a parent is afflicted with a profligate son, and pray for his amendment, he ought first to examine his own conduct, and see whether that child does not date his existence from a day when the parent gave himself up to riot and debauchery, or to passion, or to some insensate pursuit; and if he find this to be the case, he ought to regard his son's immoral dispositions as the personification of his own sin, and view himself as the chief cause. He ought next to consider whether the education bestowed, and example set, have been conducive to the child's improvement. He will discover that his dispositions have an origin which leaves no stain upon the goodness of Providence. It is no disparagement to the Divine Being, to say that he has bestowed on man lungs, which, if properly used, will successfully execute their functions for seventy or eighty years; but which, if improperly treated, will waste at an earlier age; when it is added, that he has also bestowed upon human beings faculties capable, when duly applied, of discovering and fulfilling the conditions necessary to their healthy action, and of avoiding the causes that lead to premature decay. Our view implies that the laws of nature have, every one of them, a beneficial tendency, when properly understood and obeyed; and that every particular evil which afflicts any individual man, arises from infringement of one or more of these laws, in his progenitors, himself, or his associates, perhaps through ignorance, perversity, or incapacity. In many instances this can be demonstrated: Although, owing to the existence of vast regions of unexplored territory in the natural world, many instances of evil occur, in which the precise operation of the natural laws cannot be traced; yet these are the regions of the unascertained, and not of the uncertain. The region of the uncertain would be one in which he elements of nature had received no definite constitution, and acted under no established laws. We have no authority for supposing that the regularity and perfection of the divine government terminates at the point at which our knowledge of it ends. Every generation that unrolls an additional chapter of the volume of natural knowledge, will acquire new proofs of wisdom and goodness, ingrained in the constitution of creation.

If a widow have an only son at sea, and he be overtaken by a storm, and she pray for his deliverance, what will be the effect? We observe, in the first place, that, on the supposition that the Creator has regulated the action of the elements in conformity with his divine goodness and wisdom, the storm is no arbitrary or accidental occurrence. It is a great result of great causes, instituted and directed by Supreme Wisdom, and operating for unquestionable good. Man's intellect is sufficient to inform him that storms do occasionally blow at sea, and he is bound to keep proper instruments for indicating their approach, and also to construct his ship and to manage it with skill sufficient to meet their violence, or stay on dry land. In the general case, the vessel will not sink unless she be too feeble to resist the winds and waves, be unskilfully managed, or have been brought too close upon a rock or shore. The individuals on board may have acted up to the utmost of their knowledge and power; but the course of Providence seems to require, not only that the individuals should do their best, but that they should do all that is necessary by the constitution of nature to bring about the end desired. If they cannot do this, they should not try the adventure. British ships ride triumphantly through seas and storms, in which Chinese junks would sink to the bottom; and since steam-engines were applied to navigation, a new power has been gained to avoid shipwreck, and render shores less fatal to the mariner. "The marine barometer," says Mr. Arnot, "has not yet been in general use for many years, and the author was one of a numerous crew who probably owed their preservation to its almost miraculous warning. It was in a southern latitude. The sun had just set with placid appearance, closing a beautiful afternoon, and the usual mirth of the evening watch was proceeding, when the captain's order came to prepare with all haste for a storm. The barometer had begun to fall with appalling rapidity. As yet, the oldest sailors had not perceived even a threatening in the sky, and were surprised at the extent and hurry of the preparations; but the required measures were not completed, when a more awful hurricane burst upon them than the most experienced had ever braved." "In that awful night, but for the little tube of mercury which had given the warning, neither the strength of the noble ship, nor the skill and energies of the commander, could have saved one man to tell the tale."* I Providence supplied the deficiencies of human skill when the limits of individual knowledge were attained, there would be no premium offered by the order of creation to the advance of the race in the cultivation of their own faculties, and the study of the institutions o nature, duties implied in the very idea of a rational being. If Providence, in answer to prayer, had enabled sailing vessels to move against or without the wind, we should never have had steamboats The destruction by storms of weak and ill-managed ships, leads to higher attention in constructing and navigating vessels; and any relaxation on the part of the Divine Ruler, in enforcing these requisites, would be a premium offered to human sloth and incapacity whereas the design of the Creator appears to be, by the maintenance of a rigid but salutary discipline, to hold out rewards to men to improve themselves in knowledge, virtue, and activity, in the highes possible degree. This end is promoted by the destruction of the careless, when they throw themselves in the way of danger. The widow would have no means of knowing that a storm existed at the distance of thousands of leagues; but waving this objection, the object of her prayer may be supposed to be, either that Providence would arrest the storm before the ends for which it was raised were accomplished, which is not a proper petition; or that her son migh sail in safety, although he had embarked in a ship not strong enough to resist the tempest, or joined himself to an ignorant and incapable crew, or had come too near the shore to be able, according to the laws which regulate the motion of ships, to avoid being driven on a shoal. If the storm be serving a great and beneficial end—if the undeviating regularity of the laws of motion constitutes the very basis of navigation, which could not be interfered with without incalculable mischief to man himself—and if it be the design of Providence to encourage vigorous exertion, and punish rashness, ignorance, and incapacity, then we do not think that the prayer, in this form, could be answered, in consistency with any rational idea o the divine government of the world. The proper prayer, in our opinion, would be one by the young sailor himself and his comrades that they might put forth that skill, perseverance, and exertion, which by the established order of creation, were necessary to meet the dangers of their condition, and to navigate the ship in safety through the storm. Omnipotence and ubiquity are necessarily implied in al adequate conceptions of the Divine Being, and we consider him cog-

* Arnot's Elements of Physics, i. 350.

nisant of every operation that takes place in the physical world; in fact, we regard all its laws as mere emanations of his will; their invariableness being the necessary result of his invariableness, which is inseparable from perfect knowledge and complete power. Change for the better always implies imperfection, and change for the worse is more incompatible still with the notion of perfect wisdom and goodness. The Creator is equally cognisant of the state of mind of the devotee; and hence there is complete communion between him and his intelligent creatures. Obedience to the laws which he has established is conformity to his will; and the beneficial consequences of obedience, are purely gifts of his grace. In all prayers, the qualification, "if it be thy will," is expressed or understood; but the laws impressed by the Creator on external nature have not been generally recognised and taught by religious guides to the people, as manifestations of the divine will. In consequence, they continue to be grievously infringed, and enormous evils ensue.

We are at a loss to discover whether this view differs or not from that which appears to be entertained by Dr. Chalmers. In the notice of his sermon (published in the Weekly Chronicle of 24th March,) he is reported to have said, "There is an infidelity abroad that would expunge the doctrine of a special Providence, and the efficacy of prayer. As far as our observation extends, nature has always proceeded in an invariable course, nor have we ever witnessed, as the effect of man's prayers, nature to verge from her usual course; but we affirm the doctrine of a superintending Providence as wide as the necessities of man. Grant the uniformity of visible nature, and how little does it amount to! We can discover the first step upward in the chain of causation, and call it the proximate, of the next, and call it the remote cause; but there are higher events in the train we try in vain to reach, which will ever lie in deepest concealment from our view; and the Deity may, by a responsive touch at the higher end of the chain of events, give efficacy to the prayer of man without the answer being visible to man, which, if the intervention were at the lower end of the chain, would render it a miracle to the eye of man. In this way, the reaction to prayer is at a place higher than the observation of philosophy can reach. All that man can see, is but the closing footsteps in the series. The domain of philosophy terminates at that which we can reach by human ken. Beyond this, may be termed the region of faith. At this place of supernal command, the Deity can direct matters as he will, without altering any of the visible laws of the universe."

We agree with Dr. Chalmers in affirming "the doctrine of superintending Providence as wide as the necessities of man;" because we consider every position in which man can be placed, t be reached by the laws established by the Creator, and that thes are constituted with such admirable efficiency and wisdom, that the meet every particular case in the best possible manner. Any specia act of Providence that should produce a result different from tha which they would evolve, would be a departure from wisdom. Th Creator does not require to think twice, and correct himself lik men. We conceive ourselves maintaining the greatness, goodness and absolute sovereignty of the Creator, in teaching this view; an we can conceive no other reconcileable at once with the divine pei fection, and with man's rational nature. The experience of lif shows that, in some instances, prayers are followed by the conse quences desired, and at other times not; and it appears to us tho the chief difference between Dr. Chalmers' view and ours, lies i this—that we conceive the established natural conditions to hav been fulfilled in those cases in which the desire of the prayer i granted, and not to have been fulfilled when it is not granted; th order of creation having been so wisely arranged all the while, tha no deviation from it was necessary; whereas he appears to conceiv that the Deity, "by a responsive touch at the higher end of th chain of events, gives efficacy to the prayer of man," independentl of his fulfilling the natural conditions on which his deliveranc depended by the established order of the universe. Dr. Chalmer considers that in this way "the reaction to prayer is at a place highe than the observation of philosophy can reach." We should like t see this idea applied to any specific actual case. Will the Deity, i answer to the consumptive father's prayer, touch any spring c causation which will subvert the established conditions on which th healthy action of the lungs depends? If the answer is in the affirme tive, we inquire whether this does not imply a direct condemnatio of these conditions, as unsuitable and improper in themselves, whic require to be subverted or dispensed with? If the answer be in th negative, and if we are told that the natural conditions must be fu filled, then he and we are agreed. If he say that the Deity, i answer to prayer, will cause the natural conditions to be fulfillec whereas, if there had been no prayer, he would have allowed th neglect of them to go on, and the patient to die; we agree, also, i this opinion, under certain explanations. It appears to us, tha when the organs of Veneration, Hope, and Wonder, are large in a individual, he is naturally disposed to pray; and that the efficacy c prayer results from the established laws of his constitution, whic

ire cognisable by reason.   We shall endeavour to explain this pro-
osition.

Let us revert to the case of the consumptive patient; if the prayer
ie, that he and his advisers and attendants may discover and fulfil
ill the conditions appointed by Divine Providence for the restoration
if diseased lungs, in the full reliance on the Divine goodness, that
ho malady has not been sent vindictively or arbitrarily, but results
rom infringement of physiological laws highly beneficial to man
vhen duly observed, the effects of the prayer would be the follow-
ng:—The feeling of submission to the divine appointment, and of
:onfidence in the divine goodness, and the earnest attention to all
ihysical and moral conditions which could influence recovery, would
iperate in the most favourable manner on the constitution, and
;reatly promote that kind of action in the body from which conva-
escence must proceed.   Prayer, advanced in expectation of divine
iid, independently of fulfilment of the natural conditions, would lead
o indifference and inattention to these appliances—would withdraw
he mind from all consideration of the causes and course of the dis-
:ase, and leave to Providence the duty of performing a miracle, in
irder to supply the deficiencies of an ignorant devotee.

Experience shows that the patient frequently dies, notwithstanding
he most earnest prayers.   Our explanation is, that the physiological
aws, although influenced by the state of the patient's mind, do not
lepend on it alone, but on it and other conditions; and that, in cases
if death, these other conditions have not been fulfilled.   Providence
ippears to be inexorable, where too wide a departure from the
ippointed conditions of health has ensued.   Submission, then, be-
:omes the patient's duty and only resource.

It may be objected, that the cure would take place if the natural
:onditions were fulfilled, as well without prayer as with it.   This
nust mean, that if the lungs should heal by the operation of physio-
ogical causes without prayer, the disease would be at an end; which
s granted.   In like manner, if inflammation should, in any particular
:ase, subside without bleeding, the disease would be gone; but it does
iot follow that there is no need for bleeding in inflammation in
;eneral.   The general rule is, that bleeding tends to cure inflamma-
ion; and also the general rule is, that a pious, submissive, and
:nlightened frame of mind promotes recovery from all diseases, by
:xciting that kind of action in the animal economy which is favour-
ible to health.   Prayer, by exercising the highest and best faculties,
idds to the power of fulfilling the natural conditions on which restora-
ion depends.   The mind, which in sickness has no conviction of the
:xistence of a Supreme Being, no confidence in his power and good-

ness, and no reliance on his administration of the world, must be so shallow, reckless, pugnacious and irrational, that it will be blind at almost every condition calculated to influence health, and will fall a sacrifice to the laws of Divine Providence, which it can neither perceive nor obey. A mind of a high moral and intellectual endowment will trust in the Supreme Governor of the world, and try to obey his laws; and the exercise of the concomitant dispositions will unquestionably promote the progress of the body's cure. In like manner, the sailor whose mind is alive to this view of divine government, who relies implicitly on a benevolent Providence for protection when he does his own duty, will be led to fulfil the natural conditions on which deliverance from shipwreck depends, with greater alacrity and success, than if his mind were obtuse and unthinking, reckless and irreverent, or ignorant and superstitious.

Where the petitioner cannot fulfil the natural conditions necessary for his deliverance, as in cases of incurable diseases and fatal shipwrecks, he ought to pray for a spirit of resignation and submission to the divine will. The rational worshipper who believes in the wise regulation of every object and event in nature by a Supreme intelligence, who perceives that a part is allotted to him to perform on the stage of life, and that faculties are given to him for this purpose, will, in presence of his God, survey the objects of his approaching pursuits, and their relationship to the divine laws, and put forth an ardent wish that he may successfully discharge the duties of his appointed station. If he have faith in the perfection of the divine laws, and in their power to reach him in every position, he will be strongly led to prefer high and virtuous objects, because he must know that these alone meet with divine approval and protection; and he will experience a depth of obligation to improve his whole nature and to acquire strength, activity, and knowledge, that he may be enabled to act rightly, which can scarcely be felt where no such views are entertained. He will look for a specific cure for every specific evil, and always presume himself to be in the wrong when he suffers. Such a worshipper appears to us to be prepared for a higher discharge of duty, as a moral and intellectual being, than i he recognised no God; and his prayers will, according to the esta blished laws of the world, conduce forcibly to their own fulfilment.

We forbear entering into Scriptural discussions, for the reason stated in our article on Scripture and Science, vol. vii. p. 321. By discussing the question on the principles of reason, we avoid wound ing religious opinions, which we treat with the highest respect, and we place such implicit reliance on the harmony of all truth, that we doubt not that if we arrive at sound conclusions in reason and philo sophy, they will harmonise with all sound interpretation of Scripture.   In point of fact, we could cite numerous instances in which views similar to those now advocated have been expounded by divines as Scriptural doctrine.   So far from regarding these principles as inimical to piety, we humbly think that Religion will never put forth half her power until she shall be wedded to Philosophy. Religion springs from Veneration, Hope, and Wonder; and when these sentiments act in opposition to Causality and the observing powers, they must remain unproductive.   If the external world be constituted in harmony with reason, no sentiment, when legitimately directed, can contradict philosophy.   The first and most striking effect of these principles, if carried into practice, would be a deep conviction of the extent and danger of our ignorance, unbounded confidence in the Creator, and an eager desire to discover his laws and to obey them.   Every teacher of religion, who was penetrated by these views, would feel that he was dealing forth mere husks to his people, when he taught them only duties to be performed, without showing them *how* to accomplish them.   In short, science and philosophy would become the pioneers of religion, and religion would constitute the vivifying and presiding spirit of human undertakings.   Man's rational powers will never display themselves in their full might, until his whole moral and intellectual faculties shall combine in one sustained effort to discover and obey the divine laws.   At present, clerical teachers give too little instruction to the people concerning the natural conditions which must accompany religion, to render it efficacious in temporal affairs ; an omission which can be accounted for only by the fact of the present system of religious teaching having been instituted nearly three centuries ago, when science and philosophy were unknown.   At that time, God was scarcely recognised, in any practical sense, as the author of external nature.

There is a vast difference between our doctrine and that which teaches that whatever is, is right.   According to the latter principle, murder is virtuous, because it exists.   According to our view, it is only the faculty of Destructiveness and its legitimate applications which are right; all abuses of it are wrong.   We maintain, farther, that the order of creation, both physical and moral, is arranged in harmony with this faculty, as an existing propensity, and with its proper uses; but at variance with, and calculated to check and punish, its abuses.   Every rational person admits, that, in certain instances, the efficacy of prayer is limited by the natural laws; no old man in his senses prays to be rendered-young again, although the Divine Being could easily perform this change, which would be very desirable for the aged devotee ; nor does any sensible person,

whose leg has been amputated, pray that it may grow on again
The prayers in these instances are limited to a prolongation of life
with the usual accompaniments of age, and to recovery to the
remaining portion of the limb, and to the general health of the
sufferer. The sole reason for this limitation is, that these benefits
appear to be all that the laws of our constitution, appointed by the
Creator, authorise us to expect, as agreeable to his will. Our doc
trine does not teach that an amputated limb is as desirable as a
sound and serviceable one; but only that no limb requires to be cu
off as the direct and proper result of observing the divine laws; or
the contrary, that this necessity springs exclusively from infringe
ment of laws calculated to produce beneficial effects in their legiti
mate sphere of action, although leading to painful consequences
when neglected or infringed. These laws are in themselves so
admirably adapted to the human constitution, that they could nor
now be interfered with, the elements of physical and moral nature
remaining unchanged, without injury to man himself. When we
enter the regions of the unascertained in philosophy and science
many persons conceive that we have then arrived, also, at those of
the uncertain; or that Providence operates, in an unknown territory
in a manner different from that followed by him in the explored
domains of nature. Many men who will not expect an extirpated
eye to grow in again, in answer to prayer, will think it quite reason
able to hope, that, by addresses to heaven, the cholera may be
arrested by a special interference, independently of the removal of
its physical causes; or that these causes themselves may be stayed
by a responsive touch in the chain of causation at a higher link than
man can reach, in answer to their petitions. We humbly think
that if we saw clearly the physical causes of cholera, their modes of
operation, and the natural adaptation of other physical and moral
causes within human reach to modify or arrest them, this expecta
tion would appear as little warranted by true religion, as the hope
that small-pox should be averted by prayer without vaccination, or
that after amputation a new leg should shoot forth.

In these observations, we confine our attention exclusively to the
world as now constituted, after miraculous power has ceased to
operate. Not one word of our argument applies to periods and
places where miraculous interference was the law of the divine
government. There and then every arrangement would be wisely
adapted to that order of administration. If miraculous power still
continued to be exercised, we would yield up reason at once, and be
guided by faith alone; but if it has ceased, and if the order of crea
tion be now adapted to the regular developement and steady improve-

ment of man's rational nature, we subject our faith to our reason, in regard to the action of physical causes, and believe that in doing so we conform ourselves to the will of God.

ARTICLE III.

PATHOLOGICAL FACTS.

[The following pathological facts have been communicated to us by Mr. O. S. Fowler, and, as they have never before been published, we deem them worthy of record in the Journal. Such facts afford evidence so positive and irresistible in proof of the science, that they need no accompanying remarks to enforce their presentation.—ED.]

Whilst lecturing on phrenology in the city of New York in 1837, Dr. Howard, who then lived in Carmine street, called on me, December 27, and stated that, on the evening before, he had been called in great haste to visit a lady who was seized with a most violent local pain, which was so severe as entirely to prostrate her in fifteen minutes by producing fainting. When brought to, she had forgotten the names of every person and thing around her, and almost entirely lost the use of words, not because she could not articulate them, but because she could not *remember* nor *think* of them. She could not even mention the name of her husband, or her children, or of any article she wanted, nor in any way convey her ideas by *words*. Yet she understood all that was said to her, and possessed every other kind of memory unimpaired. "And where is this pain located?" I eagerly inquired. "That is for you to say," said Dr. H. "If phrenology is true, *you* ought to be able to tell *where* it is located." "Then it is *over her eyes*," said I; and he replied, "That is the place." The pain was seated *there*, and no where else. In other words, the phrenological organ of Language had become greatly diseased, and the *faculty* of Language was the *only* mental power that suffered injury, all the others remaining unimpaired.

Dr. Carpenter, of Pottsville, Pa., related to the writer, about two years since, the following fact;—One of his patients fell from a horse, striking the centre of his forehead against a rock, by means of which accident a small portion of brain was lost. As Dr. C. entered the room, the patient recognised him, as he did each of his neighbours, but had forgotten every *fact* and *event*, and them *only*. · He asked the doctor what was the matter with him, and as soon as he was informed, forgot, and asked again. To use Dr. C.'s expression, "Fifty times over he asked what was the matter, and as often as told, forgot, and asked again." He forgot that his brother was coming on that day from a distance to visit him, and that he himself had then started with the design of meeting his brother—a thing which any one would certainly be very likely to remember under those circumstances. Every past event was to him as though it was not, yet all his other mental powers remained uninjured. When depletion was proposed, he objected, and assigned his reasons, showing that his reasoning faculties were unimpaired. After his recovery from this injury, he regained, to a considerable extent, his memory for facts, events, &c. I have seen this individual, examined the scar, and know, from its location, that it was the organ of Eventuality that was injured by this accident.

Dr. Ramsay, of Bloomfield, Pa., reported the following case as having occurred in his practice:—About four years since, a patient of his, in consequence of his horse becoming frightened, was thrown with great violence against a fence, striking the centre of his forehead against the corner of a rail. When Dr. R. was called in, he recognised him, and asked "What all this fuss was about?" As soon as Dr. R. had told him, he forgot, and asked again and again and continued the inquiry many times in succession; and to this day he has not the slightest recollection of this most important event in his life, except the mere fact that his horse became very much frightened.

Another case was related to the writer, in the winter of 1840, by the Rev. S. G. Callahan, an Episcopal clergyman, and a teacher of high intellectual and moral worth, at Laurell, Del. About twelve years ago, the Rev. Mr. C. was intimately acquainted with a Dr Thomas Freeman, formerly a surgeon on board an English man-of-war, who, in an action with the Dutch, received a very severe blow from a rope with a knot in it, which broke in the skull in the centre of his forehead, "here," said Rev. Mr. C., (putting his finger directly on the organ of Eventuality,) "producing a cavity resembling the inside of a section of the larger end of a hen's egg." The accident caused a loss of *memory of facts only*, (which occasioned his dismissal on half-pay for life,) while every other power remained uninjured. Thus, if he went in pursuit of any particular object, he was as likely to get a very different thing, or not any at all, as the object he had in view. Being a good chemist, he was employed to prepare a vat for colouring broadcloths; he constructed every part of the apparatus right, (his Causality, Constructiveness, and other faculties, being unimpaired,) but when he came to the chemical process of dyeing, with which he was as familiar as with the alphabet, he failed repeatedly. Finally, they were obliged to employ another dyer, who pointed out the omissions, or mistakes, which caused Dr. F.'s failures. Although the doctor was an excellent chemist, and perfectly understood every part of the process of dyeing, yet he would omit one thing in one experiment, and another in another, and thus fail in every attempt. He could seldom succeed in any chemical experiments, though passionately fond of the science, because of these omissions, "and yet," said Mr. C., "start him on a train of thought, and he would reason as clearly, and logically, and powerfully, as almost any one I ever knew."

Another fact, similar to the above, occurred in the case of Mr. Robert M'Farland, an innkeeper, who, in 1837, lived in Carlisle, Pa. near the Court House. When about sixteen years of age, in consequence of a fall from a horse, he had a deposition of watery matter collected, which finally settled in the centre of his forehead, forming a sack between the skin and the skull. This remained there for several years, until it became so extremely painful as to render it necessary to have an operation performed upon it. A portion of the skull was removed, and the brain beneath was more or less affected. Before this injury, his memory of circumstances, of what he heard, saw, read, &c., was so excellent that he was often referred to. This kind of memory, and this only, appeared to be destroyed by the accident. On this account he called on me, whilst lecturing in that village, for a phrenological examination, but did not make known his object, waiting to see if I should detect any impairment of memory. On examining his forehead, and perceiving the organs of Size, Form, Individuality, and Locality, quite large, I remarked that his memory of forms, things, persons, places, &c., should be decidedly good; but observing a deep-seated scar where the organ of Eventuality is located, I remarked, that if the wound which caused it had affected the brain there, his memory of events, of little incidents, every day occurrences, &c. must have been impaired. "That is a fact," said he. "If I see a man who called on me ten years ago, I recognise his form and features at once; but if a customer wants any little thing, and another calls for something before I have waited on the first, I forget the first entirely, and thus often give offence; but I cannot help it. And it is of no use for me to read any thing, for I forget it immediately." The location of this scar fixed the injury of the brain precisely on the organ of Eventuality, and that was the only mental faculty impaired.

Another fact occurred in the case of a Mr. Camp, of New Haven Ct. who, by the bursting of a gun, had the end of the barrel driver about an inch into the centre of his forehead, scattering some brair upon the stone wall against which he was leaning. And ever since this accident, his memory of facts, events, &c. has been defective Lawyer Stoddard informed me that more than once he had been com pelled to suspend public business, or cases at law, in which he wa: engaged in behalf of Mr. Camp, in consequence of Mr. C.'s defective memory. I have seen this scar, and can testify that it is located over the organ of Eventuality.

Mr. Nathan Dalby, of Wilmington, Del. is another example o the injury of this organ, and, with it, of the faculty of Eventuality caused by falling from a horse and striking his forehead upon a stone.

The following case affords a striking instance where the organ o Tune was affected, and became preternaturally excited. It wa: reported to me by Dr. Jacques, of Wilmington, Del. who was the attending physician in the case, which occurred in 1821, in the per son of one Robert Hunter, an Irishman, at Young's factory, on the Brandywine, five miles above Wilmington. Mr. Hunter was engaged in blasting rocks ; and having charged a rock with a heavy blast which did not ignite, he swore he would *make* it go off at some rate and jammed with great violence his drill down upon the powder. I struck fire and went off, but did not split the rock. The drill was thrown, no one knows where. Both of Mr. Hunter's hands were torn off by the charge, which, coming up in a body, also struck his head along the superciliary ridge, cutting a furrow in the skull, and carrying away a portion of the *dura mater*, as well as affecting more or less the brain. From his friends, at whose house he boarded and died, (Mr. and Mrs. White,) I learned the precise location of the injury, viz. *along the superciliary ridge* and externally of it. About fifteen minutes after he was carried to the house of Mr. W. " he fell to singing songs," and continued singing almost without inter mission till his death, which took place nine days after the accident. The following description of his singing propensity, I noted down from Mrs. W.'s remarks, and give them in her own words. " He sung the whole time after he was blown up—did not stop one hour, put it altogether. Mr. W. began to read the Bible to him, but he broke out singing and stopped his reading. He was very musical much more so than when he was of himself. I thought this very strange. It was not a quarter of an hour after he was brought in before he began to sing ; and he sung all the time till he died, and stopped only when some one went in to see him, and then began

again directly.   His principal song was "*Erin go Bragh,*" and he
sung it with a better tune than I ever heard it sung before or since.
It beat all how musical his voice was.   He sung very loud, and
seemed to take a great deal of pleasure in it."   Dr. Jacques
observed, that what struck him most forcibly, was to hear him sing
with so much feeling, and pathos, and ecstacy.   Several other persons
also bore testimomy to the same point.   From the description
of Mr. and Mrs. W. who frequently dressed the wound, as well as
from Dr. J. who was the attending physician, I am certain that the
injury of the head occurred on the borders of the organ of Tune,
highly exciting it, though not disorganising it.

Again : Numerous cases have fallen under my observation, where
the brain in particular regions of the head has been preternaturally
excited, so much so as to cause severe pain to the individual, and a
feverish heat externally, which was distinctly perceptible to the
sense of touch.   Two or three cases of this nature I will mention.
A Mr. C. of Boston, Mass. is subject to spells of violent pain in his
forehead, and there only, (the seat of the intellectual organs,) which
is accompanied with an irrepressible desire to read, think, study,
write, &c.   He often sits up whole nights indulging this intellectual
mania.   Nothing but sleep will relieve the pain, and even this remedy
is often prevented by the great activity of the brain ; and not unfrequently he declines seeking repose, because of the extreme delight
experienced in thus gratifying his mind by reading, study, &c.
though fully aware that such a course serves only to aggravate the
disease.

Another striking instance occurred in the case of a distinguished
lawyer, who has been for many years the attorney-general of one
of the New England states.   On examining his head, I found an
unnatural and feverish heat in his forehead, particularly in the
region of the perceptive faculties, and I remarked to him, " Sir, the
brain in your forehead is highly excited and inflamed ; you have
been studying or thinking too hard, or doing too much business of
some kind, and unless you stop at once, and take care of yourself,
you will soon be either a dead man, or a crazy one."   Upon this, he
started upon his feet, and exclaimed, " Who has been telling you
about me?"   "No one, sir."   "But some one *has,*" said he.   "Upon
my honour and my conscience, sir, I neither know you, nor your
occupation, nor your condition in life, nor one single thing about
you, except what I infer from your phrenological developements."
I then pointed out to him the preternatural heat of his forehead ; and
he requested me to proceed in the examination, when at its close, he
" stated that for several weeks he had been dreadfully afflicted with

a most violent and intolerable pain in his forehead, particularly in the lower portion, and on that account had requested an examination." He continued his remarks, saying, "that his memory of business, which, up to that time, had been remarkably retentive, had failed him, and that his intellectual faculties appeared to have sustained some injury; and that this was occasioned chiefly at a recent sitting of the court, when his mental faculties were employed to their utmost stretch, for several days and nights in succession, upon very difficult law cases, both in behalf of the state as well as for private individuals." This gentleman is about sixty years of age, has a strong constitution, and a most active temperament.

ARTICLE IV.

CASE OF INJURY OF THE HEAD CONFIRMATORY OF PHRENOLOGY.

Dr. Drake, now professor in the Medical Institute of Louisville Ky. communicated to the "Western Journal of Medical and Physical Sciences," in the year 1835, an interesting case of the pathology of the brain. The facts involved in this case, afford not only positive evidence of the existence and location of the organ of Language, but serve to throw additional light on the nature of its functions. Dr. Drake then resided at Cincinnati, Ohio; and the individual whose head was affected, was Mr. C. Van Zant, of Louisville, Ky This gentleman called upon Dr. D. for advice, complaining of pain in his head. He had received a contusion upon the head by a ball without a laceration of the integuments, and had suffered by epileptic fits. At this time, "*he had almost entirely lost the power of recollecting proper names, to whatever class of objects they may belong.*" "When he called upon me," says Dr. D. "he could not tell the name of the city (Louisville) where he belonged, nor of the river (Ohio), nor of the steamboat (Michigan) on which he had made the voyage, nor of the city where he then was (Cincinnati), nor my name. To enable himself to find me, he had written my name upon a bit of paper, from which he read it when inquiring for my office." "I at first supposed, for a moment, that he was deranged, or idiotic but soon discovered that his mind was otherwise nearly sound, for his narrative was intelligible and well connected, though when he came to a proper name he stopped, and had to substitute a description of the object." In every interview had with him, the same "phenomena was manifested," though once or twice he succeeded in recalling the name which was desired. He could not recall the names of any place where he had lived, or of any towns around Louisville, his present residence; he could not mention any of the names of the physicians who had attended him, though he could distinctly relate all they had done for him. He could recollect none of the names of the journeymen he employed, though he could state their different qualifications. It was with great difficulty and study only, that he could, on any occasion, recollect his children's names; " but when it came to his own baptismal name, and that of his wife, he could not proceed." Upon putting a slate and pencil into his hands, he was *sometimes* able to write a proper name, and then to read it ; but in one case he wrote " Kentucky" instead of Louisville, for the city in which he resides. He could use common nouns without the least difficulty, such as rivers, town, doctor, medicine, state, boat, &c. and also every part of speech, except proper names. The pain of which he complained, is in *his temple and about the eye.* The left eye is watery, and the sight of both is weak, and their motions unsteady. " Without indulging in conjectures," says Dr. Drake, " I shall direct the attention of the reader to the fact, that the seat of his neuralgic pain is near the part of the brain which the phrenologists regard as the organ of Language, situated immediately behind the globe of the eye."

ARTICLE V.

PHRENOLOGICAL DEVELOPEMENTS OF HENRY COBLER MOSELMAN,

Who was executed in the city of Lancaster, Pa. for the murder of Lazarus Zellerbach, December 20th, 1839. With remarks by Wm. B. Fahnestock, M. D.

History.

Henry Cobler Moselman was a German by birth, about thirty years of age, five feet ten inches in height, broad shouldered, stoutly built, and muscular; of a bilious lymphatic temperament—dark brown eyes and black hair.

The accounts given of him before he came to this country, are of a doubtful character; and although many unfavourable reports were at one time in circulation, they have passed away with the excitement, and but few are now heard of, but what seem to be borne out by circumstances of, at least, a probable nature. Upon his left arm were discovered several large eschars, which reached from near the shoulder to the elbow, and which were said to have been caused by the teeth of a " man-trap," in which he had been caught, whilst committing some of his robberies. That he was obliged to flee his country, there seems to be little doubt ; and the earliest information we have of him in this country, is that which was given of him at his trial by Mrs. Catherine Rowe, from Fell's Point, Baltimore, who testified that he came to her house about thirteen months before in company with his mother, and that, after staying with them all night, they departed for the west. In the months of October and December following, they received two letters from him, directed to their care, for a hired girl in that city. In the first, he stated that he was at work in Ohio, at the depot, and received one dollar and fifty cents wages per day, and requested that if the wages were better in Baltimore, she should let him know, and he would return. The contents of the second were not stated, and witness merely mentioned that they had written him word that the girl had been married.

On the morning of the 5th of February, 1839, he was seen in company with Lazarus Zellerbach, about eight miles above Harrisburg, by Mr. Jacob Koch, to whom Zellerbach then stated that he was on his way to Philadelphia, and that Cobler, who was then his companion, intended to accompany him.

On the evening of the 7th of February, Cobler arrived in the city of Philadelphia, and put up at the house of Christiana Shauffler. He was dressed very shabbily, and had with him a pedler's pack and a tin box. He opened the pack and offered his merchandise for sale ; and when a purchaser was found for a piece of merino, he did not know what price to fix on it, and referred to a tailor who was present to say what it was worth. He sold it for seventy-five cents. Some of his prices were entirely too high and others too low, and it was evident to all present that he was no pedler, and knew nothing about the business. Of his tin box, he said he had lost the key, and not being able to procure one to fit it, broke it open, and when he saw its contents, he seemed frightened, and shut it down 'immediately. Being asked from whence he came, he stated that he had come from Lancaster, and that he had traded for a very large watch upon the road. In the course of the evening, he went out and purchased himself several articles of clothing, and next morning left for the city of Baltimore. On the afternoon of the same day, he arrived at the house of Mrs. Rowe, where he had before put up with .his mother, when they landed from Germany. He was so much improved in his outward appearance, that Mrs. Rowe did not at first recognise him, he being dressed like a gentlemen, and having with him a pedler's pack and a tin box, containing clothes, shawls, hand-kerchiefs, and a variety of jewelry.   He had also a large pocket-book full of bank notes, and gave various accounts of himself, stating that he came from his mother's, who lived in Ohio, and that he had made all his money by keeping boarders and peddling upon the canal ; that he had a store in Philadelphia, and was in partnership with a Jew.   Soon after he arrived, he went up stairs, and in the presence of Mrs. Rowe he opened the tin box, and took from it a bundle of papers, which he burnt; three other papers he gave to her, and requested her to keep them for him.   One was a Hebrew Almanac, which, after trying to decipher, but in vain, he gave to the children to play with.   The second was a pedler's license, which he said he had exchanged with a Jew, the Jew having his and he the Jew's. The third she described as being "a square piece of paper, like a five dollar note, rather narrower, bordered with blue, and written on the inside."   The next day he went out with Willman, and had his note exchanged for gold, which, upon returning, he emptied on the table, and after looking at it for some time, put it away.   On Mon-day, two days after, he took boarding with Mrs. Triste, and on Wednesday he gave her several articles to wash, among which was a white flannel shirt, the wristbands of which were "bloody all round."

On the 19th of February, he hired Lewis Willman as a servant, and soon after returned in company with him to Philadelphia.

On the 25th, he disposed of a parcel of articles to Messrs. Isais Reed & Co. amounting to ninety dollars, for which he received a check, which he afterwards lost, and advertised in the Public Ledger under the name of Henry Cobler.   The check was found; and as the advertisement did not state where the person who found the check should call, it was returned to Mr. Reed, but was never afterwards called for by Cobler.   The evidence of Willman, which will be found in this paper, will give a history of what followed from the time of his employment until after their arrest.   During his confine-ment in prison, Cobler was generally sullen and reserved ; some-times he would sing ; and although evidently ill at ease, he assumed a kind of desperate indifference, together with a duplicity of cha-racter, which seemed to baffle all conclusions respecting his true feelings or his sincerity.

On the morning of the day upon which he was executed, he seemed to desire his end, and passed most of his time in prayer, and in conversing with those who came to visit him.   When led out, he ascended the scaffold with great firmness, and sang a hymn of his own composition, with a loud and clear voice, after which he requested the sheriff to hang him, and protested his innocence to the last moment of his existence.

Tape Measurements of the Skull.

	Inches
Circumference around Philoprogenitiveness, Secretiveness, and Individuality, . . . :	21½
The same around Eventuality, ...	21

Calliper Measurements of the Skull.

	Inches
From Occipital Spine to Individuality, ...	$7\frac{7}{16}$
" Philoprogenitiveness to Individuality, . . .	$7\frac{6}{16}$
" Self-esteem to Individuality, ...	$6\frac{8}{16}$
" Ear to Individuality, ...	$4\frac{6}{16}$
" " Eventuality, ...	$4\frac{7}{16}$
" " Comparison, ...	$4\frac{8}{16}$
" " Benevolence, ...	5
" " Reverence, ...	$4\frac{8}{16}$
" " Firmness, ...	$5\frac{1}{16}$
" " Self-esteem, ...	$5\frac{1}{16}$
" " Philoprogenitiveness, ...	$4\frac{7}{16}$
" Destructiveness to Destructiveness, ...	$5\frac{6}{16}$
" Secretiveness to Secretiveness, ...	$5\frac{6}{16}$
" Acquisitiveness to Acquisitiveness, ...	$5\frac{4}{16}$
" Combativeness to Combativeness, ...	$5\frac{3}{16}$
" Cautiousness to Cautiousness, ...	$5\frac{4}{16}$
" Ideality to Ideality, ...	$4\frac{8}{16}$
" Constructiveness to Constructiveness, . . .	$4\frac{5}{16}$
" Alimentiveness to Alimentiveness, ...	$5\frac{1}{16}$

The skull is of moderate thickness, except in the regions o Destructiveness, Secretiveness, Acquisitiveness, Alimentiveness, Cau tiousness, Combativeness, Causality, Self-esteem, Amativeness, Love of Life, Tune, the front part of Benevolence, and the lower part o Philoprogenitiveness, where it is very thin; and if a lighted taper be introduced into the skull, it is quite transparent over the above organs, whilst all the rest are dark, particularly over the regions o Reverence, Conscientiousness, Hope, Marvellousness, Ideality, Con structiveness, Approbativeness, Inhabitiveness, Adhesiveness, the back part of Benevolence, and the upper portion of Philoprogenitive ness.*

* The above remarks, concerning the thickness of different regions of the skull involve principles in craniology of the highest importance. Abundant evidence we believe, can be deduced both from facts and analogy, as well as from th organisation and growth of the skull, to prove that the constant exercise of an

The following cuts present three correct views of the outlines of Moselman's skull. They were drawn by Mr. John Henry Brown, a very promising young artist of this city.

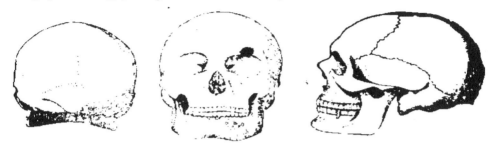

Relative Size of his Organs, on a Scale from 1 to 7.

Alimentiveness, full		5	Marvellousness, small	2
Destructiveness, very large		7	Ideality, average	3 to 4
Amativeness, large	6 to 7		Sublimity, average	3 to 4
Philoprogenitiveness, very large		7	Imitation, moderate	3
Adhesiveness, moderate		3	Individuality, very large	7
Concentrativeness, moderate		3	Form, large	6
Inhabitiveness, full		5	Size, large	6
Combativeness, large	6 to 7		Weight, large	5
Secretiveness, very large		7	Colour, average	3 to 4
Acquisitiveness, very large		7	Locality, large	6
Cautiousness, full		5	Order, large	6
Approbativeness, moderate		3	Calculation, average	3 to 4
Self-esteem, very large		7	Eventuality, rather large	5 to 6
Benevolence, full		5	Time, average	3 to 4
Reverence, full		5	Tune, large	6
Firmness, large	6 to 7		Language, small	2
Conscientiousness, moderate		3	Comparison, full	5
Hope, small		2	Causality, full	5

The head of this individual is of a large size, considerably above the average. The intellectual region is full, the moral rather small, and that of the propensities very large.

Of his intellectual region, the perceptive faculties are the most strongly developed; and he must have had considerable powers of observation, knowledge of facts, places, forms, and a musical taste, &c. The reasoning faculties being only full, his ability to discriminate, illustrate, compare, or to investigate the nature,

mental faculties tend to render those portions of the skull thin which are situated immediately above the organs of these faculties; and, on the other hand, that the skull becomes much thicker where the brain beneath it receives but little exercise or nutriment. We wish to call the special attention of phrenologists to this class of facts, and to the principles which may be established upon them, as they have, thus far, been greatly overlooked by the cultivators of the science.—ED.

causes, and effects of things, could have been only moderate, and would have prevented him from exercising much originality of thought, or logical reasoning. The moral region, though in part full, would be entirely too feeble to have much influence over his propensities, which are all either large, or very large; and consequently, he must have had considerable difficulty in restraining his propensities, and if placed in a situation to favour their activity would have been likely to yield to their influence.

From the combinations of his organs, I should judge that he would be likely to finish what he began, and, as the case might be would strike in the dark, or, Judas like, betray the hand that reared him. His disposition to acquire would be very great, and he would not stop much as to the means by which he might procure it. His compunctious visitings would be "few and far between," and remorse would scarcely ever be felt for the most heart-rending atrocities He would be highly selfish, treacherous, and secretive, but not overly cautious, and would make any sacrifice of friends to gratify his desires. His love of children would be very considerable, and is almost the only trait that illumines the dark catalogue of his propensities.

The evidence of Lewis Willman, the servant of Moselman, and to whom he confessed the deed, will show a recklessness upon the part of the perpetrator, which has few, if any, parallels upon record, and which, I need scarcely add, accords most accurately with his developements. As the language in the evidence which was given in by Willman is broken (he being a German), and from necessity unconnected, I will endeavour to give the facts in such a manner as will make them at least intelligible. Lewis Willman stated to the jury, that he first became acquainted with Cobler at Baltimore; was with him when he got his money changed, and when he purchased a pistol and a knife. That Cobler hired him as a servant on the 19th of February, at twelve dollars per month, and on the same day gave him a coat and a watch. That they traveled from Baltimore to Philadelphia in company, and after remaining there about two weeks, they returned to Baltimore, and got some papers which Cobler had left with Mrs. Rowe.

That he (Willman) saw the papers frequently: one was a Jewish Almanac, the other a check on the bank, and the third was the license of Zellerbach. That he had read it often, and which Cobler afterwards destroyed, by putting it into his gun and shooting it away. Some time after, they returned to Philadelphia, and being indebted to the innkeeper where they had lodged to the amount of twenty-six dollars, and not wishing to discharge the debt honestly,

Cobler by degrees smuggled off all (save his two guns) in his hat and boots, and being unable to remove the guns clandestinely, he told the innkeeper that he intended to go a gunning, and in that way succeeded in getting them off triumphantly. Having crossed the Delaware, and after staying there a few days, they returned to Philadelphia, and from there they traveled to Pittsburg, by the way of Lancaster, Harrisburg, and Chambersburg, and after remaining there a few days, returned as far as Lancaster by the same route.

As they drew near Lancaster, Cobler told him that he had seen his name in the papers, and that he was suspected of being the murderer of Zellerbach. Here Cobler wished to go to Philadelphia, but upon Willman's objecting, he resolved to go to Baltimore, by the way of Strasburg; and when within a mile of Baltimore, he gave Willman a bundle, and told him to hide it under a small bridge, and afterwards to go into the city and ascertain what was said about the murder of Zellerbach, and to say nothing about the license which he had seen in his possession. Cobler remained at the Point, where he had left him, until he returned with his intended father-in-law, who persuaded him to go into the city with them. The next morning, whilst at breakfast, they were arrested, and, after a hearing, were placed in prison, where they remained for ten days, and were then removed to Lancaster.

During their mutual confinement in the Lancaster prison, and after being hardly pressed by Willman, Cobler told him that he was the murderer. That he had traveled with Zellerbach from Cleveland, Ohio, to Pittsburg; that Zellerbach remained in Pittsburg for ten or fifteen days, and that he had then and there enlisted in a company of United States dragoons, from which Zellerbach afterwards persuaded him to desert, and at the same time offered him his assistance, and pecuniary means to pay his passage to Philadelphia. They left Pittsburg in company, and traveled upon the canal as far as Harrisburg, when they proceeded on foot until within about a mile of Lancaster, (where a bridge crosses the Harrisburg pike,) when they both sat down to ease themselves, and he being done first, buttoned up, and whilst Zellerbach was still sitting, he took a stone and struck him upon the forehead, and followed up the blow by stabbing him with a knife. After some time, Zellerbach got up and attempted to make his escape, but was followed, overtaken, and after considerable resistance, was finally overcome by Cobler, and despatched with a knife. After throwing him over the fence, he carried him some distance into the field, where he rifled his pockets, and sat down beside him to examine their contents by the light of the moon. He remained with the body until nearly daylight, and as his own clothes were bloody, he dressed himself in a suit of Zeller-bach's, which he had previously taken from the pack, and after throwing his own into a neighbouring privy, he walked to Lancaster and took the cars for Philadelphia, entering his name on the books as Peter Dill. After going to New York, he returned by way of Philadelphia to Baltimore, and stopped at the house of Mrs. Rowe, where Willman soon after became acquainted with him. The evidence of Willman was corroborated by the rest of the testimony throughout; and the following statement, which I obtained from Mr. Reed, (who was at that time sheriff of Lancaster county,) besides confirming the testimony of Willman, shows in a very strong light the duplicity of Cobler's character.

"As I returned to Lancaster with Cobler," says Mr. Reed, " he positively denied all knowledge of Zellerbach, and declared that he had never known him. Some time after, and whilst under my charge in prison, in conversation with him one day, he told me that he had enlisted in Pittsburg, and as he thought for one month only. He there met Lazarus Zellerbach, who told him that he was mis-taken about his enlistment, and that instead of one month, he had enlisted for five years. Upon ascertaining this fact, Cobler deter-mined to desert, and with the assistance of Zellerbach, who furnished him with clothes, &c. he made his escape, and traveled with him as far as Harrisburg." Upon Mr. Reed's asking him how it came, " that when coming from Baltimore with him, he should have denied all knowledge of Zellerbach, and now confessed that he had traveled with him from Pittsburg to Lancaster? He made no reply, and very abruptly broke off the conversation. Mr. Reed also stated that Cobler was fond of children, and that he had requested him to send his children over to see him once more the day before his execution. Whilst under his care, he described him as being " sullen, very passionate, and easily offended," and that he did not seem to have much friendship for any person, and was very careful to secrete all his papers.

That he had a great disposition to acquire, I presume no person will doubt, after having heard the notorious fact of his having sold his body for the purposes of dissection, about ten days previous to his execution. The following is a copy of the agreement.

"Know all men by these presents : That I, Henry Cobler Mosel-man, now under sentence of death in the common jail of the county of Lancaster, for and in consideration of the sum of five dollars, to me in hand paid by George B. Kerfoot, M. D. of the city of Lan-caster, the receipt and payment of which said sum is hereby acknow-ledged, have bargained and sold, and by these presents do bargain, self, and convey my body unto him the said George B. Kerfoot, after I shall have been duly executed in conformity with the sentence of the court of oyer and terminer of Lancaster county, on Friday, the twentieth day of December next, by virtue of a warrant from the governor of the commonwealth of Pennsylvania, under the broad seal of said commonwealth, directed to the sheriff of the county of Lancaster aforesaid, to have and to hold my said body to the use and behoof of the said George B. Kerfoot, M. D. for the purpose of dissection, and the promotion of anatomical knowledge.

In witness whereof I have hereunto set my hand and seal, this tenth day of December, in the year of our Lord one thousand eight hundred and thirty-nine."

HENRY COBLER MOSELMAN.

Sealed and delivered in presence of
JOHN WISE,
GEORGE FORD, JR.

Through the kindness of the Rev. Mr. Beates, I have been enabled to glean the following from a diary kept by him during his visits to the unfortunate Cobler. At the request of Cobler, Mr. Beates visited him on the 31st of August, 1839, and as he entered his room, found him reading the Bible. After conversing with him for some time, he found that his mind was in such a state as to render him entirely unfit for spiritual conversation. He accused the judge and jury of injustice towards him, denied all knowledge of Zellerbach, and stated that some other person in the neighbourhood had been guilty of the murder.

Sept. 3d. Found him reading the Bible, and asked him if he found any thing in it to interest him. He said, No; and that he merely read it because he had nothing else to do. When asked whether he believed in it, he answered, Yes; and to the question, " Why, then did you not live up to it?" he answered that he did. Persisted in his innocence, and again railed at the judge and jury.

Sept. 5th. Found him indifferent and unconcerned about his situation; and upon being asked what were his feelings when he thought of death, judgment, and eternity, he made no decided reply—said that he was satisfied with what God should ordain—seemed hardened and inexorable, although every thing was tried to bring him to a sense of his duty.

Sept. 11. Found him reading a psalm-book—asked him if he believed that his soul was immortal, and if his conscience did not chide him for what he had done. He answered, Yes; and laughingly remarked, that he was not worried or uneasy, and slept well during the whole night—that he hoped and expected to die happy because he had lived in such a manner that he had every reason to expect it.

Sept. 13th to 30th. Commonly found him reading his Bible, and from day to day persisting in his innocence. Made no answer when asked where he obtained the clothes of Zellerbach; and when asked respecting the scars upon his arm, he said that they were caused by his having taken cold after bathing, and that he had lost some bones out of it. On the 23d, he swore at Willman; and when asked again respecting the clothes, he said they were his.

Oct. 1st. Seemed to be very unconcerned, and more hard-hearted than usual; and upon being asked if he believed in the Bible, he answered, No! and said that Mr. Beates should save himself any further trouble.

Oct. 7th. Found him in a good humour, and after praying for him as usual, Mr. B. desired him to make a prayer for himself. He complied, and made a very pretty prayer for the judge, jury, his mother, and himself.

Oct. 9th. Was requested to pray particularly for himself; but instead of complying, he treated all that was said lightly, and said that he had always led a pious life, and was sure that he would die happy, but would not acknowledge that he was a sinner.

Oct. 11th. Being asked respecting his guilt, he declared as follows—"If this my soul was separated from my body, and stood before the throne of the Almighty, I could say that I was innocent of the blood of this murdered man, and I sometimes think that my heart will burst, when I think that I will have to die, and am innocent." Said he would be twenty-one years of age on Christmas and seemed to wish his end.

Oct. 14th. Appeared to be in good spirits; and when asked whether he still believed that Zellerbach was murdered by one of the neighbours, as he had before stated, he said, No; and that some evil persons had put it into his head to say so, and seemed sorry for what he had said respecting it. This was the first day that he could be brought to say that he was a sinner.

Oct. 16. Appeared to be serious, and said that hanging was too good for the man that committed the murder. "If I had done it," said he, "I would, with bended knee, seek for pardon and mercy."

Oct. 21st. Seemed to be under the impression that he would not be hung, and gave the following reasons for so believing:—1st, That his grandfather had prophesied that he would have to suffer much before he came to be twenty-five years of age, and that after that he would have it good; 2ndly, That in his own country they would not hang any person who did not confess his guilt, or upon whom the murder could not be proven by eye-witnesses; and 3dly, That it was written in the 35th chapter of Numbers, and 30th verse, that " Whoso killeth any person, the murderer shall be put to death by the mouth of witnesses ; but one witness shall not testify against any person to cause him to die." He said no person saw him do it, and if they did hang him, the Bible would not be true.

Oct. 23d. Said the governor was long about sending him his death warrant ; and upon being asked how he received the marks upon his arm, he said he did not know.

Oct. 28th. Found it utterly impossible to make any impression upon him ; and when asked to pray, he laughed out loud, and would not.

Nov. 13th. Death warrant was read to him. Mr. B. remarked that he became pale, but believed that it was more from anger than any thing else. He told Mr. B. that it was not necessary to call any more ; and that if he prayed at all, he should pray for the jury.

Dec. 16. Requested Mr. Beates to administer the Lord's Supper to him ; whereupon Mr. B. after endeavouring to bring his mind to a sense of his situation, but in vain, replied, " that he would do any thing in the world that lay in his power, but that this he could not do, as he did not think that his mind was in a fit state for it." Cobler seemed satisfied ; and upon Mr. B.'s asking him whether he should call again, he said that it was not necessary.

As the head of Moselman is a very remarkable one, and will serve to illustrate a method by which I have been in the habit of ascertaining the developements of the different regions of any given brain, as it were, by a glance, I shall embrace the present opportunity of communicating it to the public.

It is simply as follows : I place one point of a compass in the meatus externus auditorius, and the other to the extremity of the chin, and draw a complete circle around the head, as in the following cuts :—

GALL.

Nº 1

MOSELMAN.
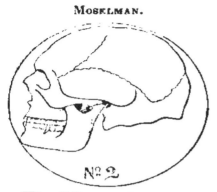
Nº 2.

AN IDIOT.
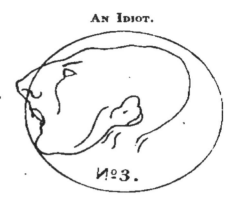
Nº 3.

The difference between the above is very evident; and if the drawing which is intended to represent Dr. Gall be correct, the line will show the exact quantity of intellectual and moral superiority which he possessed over No. 2 and 3.

The same measurement can be taken upon the living subject, by means of the callipers; and I have not yet met with a single individual, over whose head the callipers would pass as they did in the case of the unfortunate Moselman.

In making drawings of the head, I have found the auriculo mental, or chin measurement of considerable importance, and would recommend those who wish to make correct outlines, to use the same means.

The harmony between phrenology and physiognomy has been generally acknowledged, but no positive rules, so far as I know, have ever been laid down, by which that harmony can be practically demonstrated.

I hold, that if phrenology be true, then is physiognomy true also; and that every part belonging to the body, besides being governed by the brain, is in fact an exact representation of the same, differing only in this, that one is mind and the other matter. I have, perhaps, already trespassed too far, and will leave the facts as I found them.

WM. B. FAHNESTOCK.

Lancaster, June 16, 1840.

MISCELLANY.

British Phrenological Association.—We have recently received from a London correspondent, a circular of this association, which is organised for the cultivation and advancement of phrenology as a science. It is to meet the present season at Glasgow, at the same time of the sitting of

the British Association for the Advancement of Science.   The following gentlemen have been appointed officers for the current year:—

George Combe, Esq. President
Sir Geo. S. Mackensie, Bart. F. R. S. L. & E. ⎫
W. C. Trevelyan, Esq. F. R. S. E.   ⎬ Vice
Prof. Evanson, M. D., M. R. I. A.   ⎪ Presidents.
Edward Barlow, M. D.   ⎭

Phrenology in Dublin, Ireland.—Phrenology has long had many
stanch and able friends in this city.   Dr. Marsh and Mr. Carmichael,
who stand at the head of the medical profession, have publicly advocated the science now for more than twenty years.   In an address,
delivered before the "*Medical Society of Dublin*" by one of its committee, and which, by a unanimous vote of the society, was ordered to
be published, the writer alludes to the science as follows:—"On the
importance of the consideration of mental disease, as a subject of medical
education, I candidly express my humble conviction, that, from the further developement of the rapidly advancing science of phrenology, (long
a chosen theme of vituperation, but now gradually acquiring that influence which must arise from truth,) these results (before described) are
to be anticipated, compared with which, the profound discoveries of
Archimedes, Newton, or the wondrous mechanical inventions of a Watt,
sink into comparative insignificance, in point of utility, and practical
benefit to mankind."

Mr. Combe's Visit to Cincinnati.—In the month of April, Mr. Combe
made a hasty visit to Cincinnati, Ohio.   Soon after this, a correspondent
of the "Boston Medical and Surgical Journal" alluded to Mr. C.'s visit
to Cincinnati, saying that he did not "deliver a single lecture, or make
any acquaintance with the medical gentlemen of that city," and expressed
considerable surprise, if not some disaffection, that such should have been
the fact.   The following statement is copied from Mr. Combe's reply to
the above allusion, which was published in the "Boston Medical and
Surgical Journal" of June 17.   "When I came to the United States, in
September, 1838, it was my intention to lecture in the eastern cities in
the first winter, and in Baltimore and the western cities during the
second winter of my stay.   In April or May, 1839, I was waited on in
New York city, by Dr. S. D. Gross, of Cincinnati, who inquired if I
would lecture there.   I explained to him that phrenology is a disputed
subject; that I did not wish to intrude on an unwilling ear; that in
Britain I had never lectured out of Edinburgh, except on invitation, and
to an audience pledged to attend; that in the United States I had followed the same rule; that in Baltimore, after public advertisements, no
adequate class could be mustered, and that I had not lectured there; that
I was willing to lecture in Cincinnati, if one hundred and fifty hearers
could be guaranteed, but not otherwise, and I agreed to keep my arrangements open till the 1st of July, to allow him time to return home and
ascertain the public sentiment on the subject.   He never wrote to me,
and no invitation came.   In consequence, I abandoned my intention of
lecturing in the west, believing that I was not wanted.   My visit to Cincinnati in April, was merely in the course of a rapid excursion to see the
physical aspects of the country before embarking for Europe.   I had then
no intention of lecturing, and had not a single illustration with me for
the purpose.   I had only one month to spare for my whole western excursion, and presented no letters of introduction in any of the cities."

THE

AMERICAN PHRENOLOGICAL JOURNAL

AND

MISCELLANY.

| Vol. II. | Philadelphia, September 1, 1840. | No. 12. |

ARTICLE I.

A New System of Phrenology. By J. STANLEY GRIMES, President
of the Western Phrenological Society at Buffalo.

> "To him who in the love of nature holds
> Communion with her visible forms, she speaks
> A various language."—BRYANT.

Buffalo: Oliver G. Steele. New York: Wiley & Putnam. 1839,
pp. 320, 12mo.

The business of reform and improvement is one of the most difficult and hazardous enterprises in which man can engage. And this
is as true of reform in principle, as of reform in *practice;* because
the *latter* is, or at least ought to be, the product of the *former.* No
one, therefore, whatever may be his calling or profession, should
embark in the enterprise, until, by the most thorough investigation,
and patient, persevering, and matured reflection, he has attained a
positive certainty on two points—viz. that his predecessors on the
subject he is canvassing have been in error, and that he has
possessed himself of unquestionable truth; or that they have been
in some things deficient or wrong, and that he is qualified to supply
their short-comings, and rectify their mistakes.

If these sentiments be correct, (and we doubt whether any one
will venture to gainsay them,) it is at least *improbable*, if not *impossible*, for a young inquirer to be a successful reformer—for one who
is necessarily but an *inquirer* himself, to be fortunate in his effort to
become at once an instructor and an improver of others. To this
general rule, exceptions *may* perhaps occasionally occur; but that
they are exceedingly rare, and altogether unlooked-for, will not be
denied.

As respects reformation and improvement in science, these remarks
may be regarded as settled *canons* in criticism. They constitute an

rthodoxy, from which it is unwise, if not presumptuous, to depart. It may not therefore be altogether amiss to inquire, for a moment, to what *extent* they are applicable, if applicable at all, to the work whose title-page forms the heading of this article, and which professes to be a " *New System of Phrenology.*"

If report on the subject, as it has reached us, be correct, it is not more than from *four* to *five* years since Mr. Grimes commenced the study of phrenology, without having been previously an educated man, or in any degree remarkable for his devotedness to inquiry. Certainly it is *within* that time that he has made himself *known* as a phrenologist. It might well be regarded, therefore, as something more than questionable, whether he could become, in so short a period, an improver of the result of the labours of more than *forty years*, by men of the most distinguished ability and the highest attainments. It is in no degree disparaging to him, nor is it intended to be so considered, to say that, under circumstances so insufficient, and in a case so unpromising, the verdict of the world, if given in the abstract, would be decidedly against him. It would be asserted that, as yet, he could himself be nothing but a *learner*—the more especially if, as is understood to be the case, he has, until recently, dedicated to study but the *fragments* of his time. It is *possible*, however, that the decision might be incorrect; and that, in the short period of four years, our author might prepare himself to remodel and improve, by a single and first effort, the system, in the erection of which nearly half a century has been consumed by Gall and Spurzheim, Combe and Broussais, and many other distinguished fellow-labourers. But success so unusual is *hardly more than possible*. It is certainly not very probable. At any rate, it would be equally unfair in principle, and inconclusive in result, to attempt to settle Mr. Grimes' standing as a phrenologist *potentially* instead of *practically*—by conjecturing what he possibly might have done in four or five years, instead of examining what he actually *has* done. To the latter and more just and satisfactory mode of trial, therefore, it shall be our business to resort. And this we do with the more readiness, in consideration of the writer's invitation to that effect, which we shall regard as sincere, and act on it accordingly. " I appeal," says he, " with confidence to the *justice* and candor of phrenologians. I invite their *criticisms* as a favour; and when I am convicted of error, either in facts or conclusions, I shall take great pleasure in making acknowledgments." This, in our author, is candid and manly, and calculated to make a favourable impression on the public. With the kindest feelings toward him, therefore, as a fellow-labourer in a great cause, we take him at his word, and close with his invitation. And as his more immediate friends an associates will no doubt point out and illustrate the truths an valuable qualities of his work, which are neither few nor small, w shall dwell chiefly on what we consider his errors and faults. And when fairly and competently executed, this, though the most un pleasant, is far the most useful office of criticism. A writer is bu little, if at all, benefited by an enumeration of his excellencies, and descant on his beauties. On the contrary, he is often injured b them. But a candid and judicious representation of his error; wants, and failures, provided he receive it in a becoming spirit, ca never fail to be a source of improvement to him. Though the fact of the "New System," whether reputed or real, shall be our chie concern, we shall not pass all opinions embraced in it entirely un noticed. We shall even begin with a stricture on an opinion, whic' appears to us to be directly opposed to one of the most obvious an operative principles in nature—a principle without whose influence creation would relapse into confusion and chaos.

"Although," says our author, "I have taken some trouble t show that certain organs (of the brain) naturally act together, I can not countenance the idea that some organs were intended as *antago nists* to others. *They all act in harmony.*"

The fallacy of this notion is palpable. The highest perfectior of the *human* mind, and of course one of the chief difference between it and the minds of the inferior animals, consists in th balance created and preserved by the antagonisation of some of it faculties. Under the influence of judicious and well-matured disci pline, the moral and reflecting, especially the former, so antagonis the animal faculties, as to hold them in a state of salutary and prac tical regulation and control. And hence alone results mental har mony. Abrogate this control, and wild disorder and disaster mus follow. Man will become more insidious and thievish than the fo: or the weasel, and more ferocious and sanguinary than the hyena o the tiger. In an individual, for example, whose Destructiveness Combativeness, and Acquisitiveness, are powerful and active, para lyse or extinguish Benevolence, Conscientiousness, Veneration, an the reflecting faculties, and you render him a daring and repulsiv object of profligacy and crime. Revive those faculties, and the' will so antagonise and counterbalance the animal powers, that yo will check vice, and bring back the offender to the paths of virtue Nor is it in the human mind alone, that antagonism preserves an perpetuates harmony and order, and averts the evils of confusio: and misrule. As far as our knowledge on the subject extends, th same is true of creation at large. In dead matter, attraction an repulsion, by antagonising and balancing each other, maintain peace and good order on earth; and throughout the entire range of the heavenly bodies, the centripetal and centrifugal powers do the same. Destroy the latter of the two powers, in each case, and universal consolidation and inaction will ensue in the last instance, and lawless misrule and confusion in the first.

In the living human body, who is ignorant of the necessity and beneficial effects of a well-balanced muscular antagonism? and of the convulsion and distortion, or tonic spasm and permanent rigidity, which follow, when that antagonism is suspended or deranged? But we can pursue this topic no further. Nor is it necessary that we should do so. Enough has been said to prove against our author the charge of error; to show, in opposition to his opinion, that some of our cerebral organs *are*, and of course were "*intended* to be, antagonists to others;" and that is all that was aimed at by us, and all that is necessary for the purpose we have in view.

Another singularly erroneous notion entertained by Mr. Grimes, which shows his deficiency in physiological knowledge, is expressed as follows:—

"These three classes of organs, the *bones*, the *muscles*, and the *nerves*, constitute the *most essential* part of the human constitution."

That the nerves, including the brain, constitute the master tissue of the human body, is true. But next to these stand the *blood-making* and the *blood-circulating* organs, contained in the thorax, and the *digestive* organs, contained in the abdomen. The *bones* and *muscles*, though highly important, hold an inferior rank. So true is this, that the organic contents of the three great cavities, the abdomen, the thorax, and the cranium with their immediate append-ages, especially the nerves, spinal cord, and blood-vessels, constitute so essentially the chief elements of the individual, that they might be almost pronounced the *individual himself.*

But these mistakes, especially the latter, though sufficiently strik-ing, and any thing but flattering to our author's scientific accuracy, are not very serious in their bearing on phrenology. There exists, however, another of a very different character, which comes, if we mistake not, into direct collision with one of the most important truths in anthropology;—we should rather perhaps say, in the phi-losophy of the entire range of living organised matter, from the highest to the lowerst order of it. It relates to the elements or constitution of the *bilious temperament*—that temperament, which bestows on its possessor superior vigour, both mental and corporeal, and unequaled endurance under exposure and hardships, and every form of privation that may befall him, and which can do all this for no other reason but because it is a source of *superior vitality*—that temperament the author ascribes to a predominance in size of the *venous* system, and a superabundant amount of *venous* blood.

In his discussion on this subject, he has, with a view to strengthen his position, or to render it at least more plausible, fallen into sundry minor errors, and has, in several instances, substituted *assertions* for *facts*—at least for what he has not established as facts.

"The blood," he asserts, "is not *so warm* in the veins as it is in the arteries."

Whether is this, we would ask, a fact or a supposition? Has the writer ever made *satisfactory* and conclusive experiments to prove it to be a fact? We fear he has not; nor, as far as our knowledge extends, has any body else. That, under similar circumstances arterial blood, when drawn from the system, retains its temperature longer, and therefore loses it more slowly, than venous blood, is true. Its specific temperature, arising from its greater amount of latent caloric, is the higher. But when circulating in the living and healthy system of man, the temperature of arterial and venous blood is the same. We certainly know of no experiments demonstrative of the contrary. In the reports of experimenters on the subject there is no uniformity. Some have stated that, in passing from the right to the left side of the heart, (or, as others express themselves, from the *venous* to the *arterial* heart,) the blood loses about one degree of heat. Others, again, have asserted the reverse—that the blood, in making the passage, *gains* a degree.

To say the least of it, therefore, the point is *unsettled*, and cannot with positiveness and safety be either affirmed or denied. Individually, however, we are inclined to believe that the temperature of the two varieties of blood, when circulating in the blood-vessels is the same. Again:

"The venous system," says our author, "is developed in different degrees in different persons."

Is he confident, however, that it is always and necessarily developed in a *higher degree* in the bilious temperament than in the sanguineous? What observations has he made on which to found, and what experiments to prove, the position? Or has he, in reality, any thing to found it on, more substantial than conjecture and fancy? If so, he owes it alike to himself and the science he professes, to make it publicly known. For we are inclined to believe that positive facts are wanting on the subject.

"The venous system," he again observes, "becomes more full as people grow older, and at the same time the arteries shrink. *Certain climates also give greater activity to the venous system.*"

In this paragraph are two propositions, one of which is correct, and the other *doubtful*, if not groundless. And both are hostile to our author's hypothesis.

It is true that the " venous system becomes more full as people grow older," especially after the meridian of life—and more especially still in far advanced life—say, after the age of sixty. But will the writer contend, that at that period of advancement, when life and strength are deep in decline, the bilious temperament, with its vigour and endurance, is more completely formed and matured, and therefore in higher perfection, than at an earlier period, when the system was more fresh, its stamina unbroken, and its spirits unexhausted? Surely he will not. Nor will he, we think, allege that, in old age, the venous system contains a greater amount of blood, because it possesses "*greater activity.*" On the contrary, the reverse is true. In advanced life, the veins are more distended with blood, because they are *less* vigorous and active, and therefore less able to empty themselves of the blood, which they receive from the capillaries, than they were in youth, and in the prime of manhood.

As respects Mr. Grimes' assertion, that " certain climates give greater activity to the venous system," we want evidence to convince us of its soundness, and should be pleased to receive it. Is it tropical and other hot climates that thus enlarge the " venous system?" Observation has not yet confirmed us in that belief. On the contrary, the veins of the negro, a native of Africa, are inferior in size to the veins of the European, the size of the individuals being the same. This is, in a particular manner, and in no small degree, the case as respects the veins in the hands and feet. Hence the hand of the African is cooler than that of the Caucasian, because there is less blood in it; and, for the same reason, his feet are more easily injured by frost. Our author, moreover, will hardly assent that cold climates augment the size of the veins; because the assertion would be at war with his hypothesis. Such climates are less productive of the bilious temperament, than the climates of the south. In the north, as far at least as climate avails in the matter, the predominant temperament is the sanguineous; and, other things being equal, we venture to say that there is as much venous blood in the sanguineous temperament as in the bilious—as much, we mean, in proportion to the amount of arterial blood. And in confirmation of our assertion, we appeal to observation. In the sanguineous temperament, the whole amount of blood being unusually large, the whole vascular system corresponds to it—the veins constituting no exception. And if the arteries are small in the bilious temperament, so are the veins; for between these two sets of vessel a fair degree of harmony must prevail in size as well as in action else disease and death will be the unavoidable result. Hence the dangerous character, and the too frequently fatal termination o apoplexy, pneumonia notha, and every form of what is called con gestive fever, in each of which there exists, in some part of the body, a preternatural accumulation of venous blood. To attribute therefore, to the bilious temperament, as its cause, any degree o such accumulation, or any tendency toward the fulness and genera condition of the veins which arise from their exhaustion and debilit; in old age, is to be the advocate of a notion which to us appear altogether groundless.

To speak of it in still plainer and stronger terms, it is a notion held by our author, in direct contradiction of all we know, or have reason to believe, in relation to the design and uses of the blood, ii nourishing the solids of the body, in imparting life to them, and ii maintaining that life in vigour, permanence, and fitness for action These high and important offices, as is known to physiologists, are all performed by the *arterial* blood, not one of them by the *venous* The venous blood contributes nothing toward nutrition, because it is carried *from* the nutritive vessels or tissues, toward the right side o the heart and the lungs, there to undergo the requisite change. I contributes nothing to the vitality of the solids, because it is already too much exhausted of its own vitality, until it receives a fresh supply of it, and is reconverted into arterial blood, by the action o the lungs. Hence, as already intimated, an accumulation of venous blood in an organ never augments any of the vital properties of tha organ, but diminishes them; while, on the other hand, an accumu lation of arterial blood increases them. In confirmation of the truth of this latter proposition, in inflammation, and in all forms o vital erection, where there is necessarily an accumulation of arteria blood, the vital property of sensitiveness, with calorification, and the process of *natural* secretion, are heightened and invigorated, and sometimes a new form of secretory action is set up. But we repeat that, under the influence of venous congestion, the very reverse o this occurs. Instead of an increase of vitality in the part congested a diminution of it takes place.

If this representation be correct, (and no physiologist will deem i safe to question it,) it is physically impossible that the bilious which, of all the *simple* temperaments, is the most high-toned vigorous, and efficient in action, and which has marked, in part a least, the greatest men the world has produced, and has not a little contributed to their greatness—it is absolutely impossible that, ii any degree of consistency with the laws of nature, such a temperament should depend, for its production and maintenance, on a superabundance of the *semi-devitalised* venous blood.   And had Mr. Grimes been a physiologist, as every thorough-bred and philosophical phrenologist *must* be, he would never have involved himself in so fatal a mistake.   As well may he contend that the venous blood is the immediate source of innervation, nutrition, secretion, calorification, and every other vital process, and even of vitality itself, as of the bilious temperament.   We have dwelt somewhat at length on this subject, as it involves important principles connected with phrenology, and Mr. Grimes' views of the temperaments appear to be decidedly erroneous, and, consequently, cannot prove otherwise than injurious to the science.

Another physiological mistake in our author, as palpable and gross as can well be imagined, is where (see page 27) he states the venous system to be one of the " three *nourishing* systems" of the body. As well might he so denominate that branch of the absorbents whose office is to *take up* and *carry away* the substance of organs, instead of *conveying it to them* and *putting it down*, for the purpose of nourishing them.

But a still higher, and, as relates to phrenology, a more important feature in the " New System" of Mr. Grimes, and one on which we apprehend he sets a greater value than on any other, is yet to be mentioned.   It is his classification of the cerebral organs, his supposed discovery of new organs, and his changing the names bestowed on those already known by his predecessors, (not to call them his instructors,) with which all phrenologists had become familiar, and with which but few had expressed dissatisfaction.   And of none of these innovations can we cordially approve, because we do not regard them as *improvements.*   To change the nomenclature of a science, except for the most substantial reasons, and especially without improving it, is worse than useless.   It is an act of arrogance which should never be committed; but of which our author, if we mistake not, is guilty.   In our estimation, instead of improving the nomenclature of phrenology, he has materially injured it.   Forbidden by a want of time and space to assign our reasons at large for this opinion, we can only say, that to ourselves they are satisfactory; and that we hold ourselves prepared to render them hereafter, should it be deemed necessary.

As respects his new organs, (Pneumativeness and Chemicality,) more especially his location of them, we are compelled to deem it a *fancy* rather than a *fact.*   Of this we are confident, that, from the locality he has given them on the " phrenological bust" which constitutes the frontispiece of his book, they can never be detected by the strictest examination of the exterior of the head. No developement of any portion of the brain, consistent with health, can produce the slightest protrusion of the sites he assigns them. They are situated quite too far below the mechanical action of the base of the brain, to be in the least affected by its natural developement. Nor is this all.

The writer's organ of Chemicality is, and must be, (or we are greatly mistaken,) a *creation of his own.* It is a *compound* organ—an anomaly which nature has yet to form. It involves the *perception* of two distinct senses, taste and smell, and performs, therefore, two essentially different functions. But no cerebral organ can do that, any more than the same nerve can subserve sensation and voluntary motion. As well might Mr. Grimes amalgamate in the same organ the sentiments of Veneration and Hope, as the functions of the olfactory and the gustatory nerves. The fancy, in either case, is unnatural and preposterous, and too well calculated to bring down ridicule, not to say disrepute, on its author or his science, if not on both. In this, we hope we are clearly understood. Mr. Grimes, we repeat, in his organ of Chemicality, represents the same portion of brain as the receptacle of two distinct impressions conveyed to it —one by the nerve of taste, the other by the nerve of smell. As soon, we say, shall the same cerebral organ be the seat of the sensation of seeing and hearing—an absurdity which no enlightened physiologist will admit.

The writer's division of the cerebral organs into Intellectuals, Ipseals, and Socials, involves nothing new in either fact or principle, but only in *names.* And with some of his names we are not satisfied. Ipseals we consider affected and pedantic; and the socials are made to include organs which belong of right to different classes. To associate thus closely Amativeness and Inhabitiveness with Veneration and Wonder, is unnatural. Nature herself may be regarded as giving testimony confirmatory of this error, by placing the organs so remote from each other. As to the assertion, that they spring from the same root, and therefore belong to the same class, we receive it as a conjecture, entitled to no weight in a philosophical discussion. It has never been anatomically demonstrated as a fact. In a word, we are compelled to regard Mr. Grimes' classification as, in no small degree, a work of *his own devising* and *constructing;* not as an ingenious and correct exposition of the work of nature. His class of " Ipseals," although they have not been strictly designated to that effect by name, have been always represented as *individual* and *selfish ;* being exercised almost exclusively for the gratification of their possessors. And his "Socials" have been expounded as feelings not centered in self, but as bearing a relation to other beings—some of them chiefly to the inhabitants of earth, and others not only to the same inhabitants, but also to beings of a superior order, rising upward to the Deity himself. The very slight and superficial change which he has made in the intellectuals, we shall so far notice, as to say that it amounts to any thing but an *improvement*. The simplicity of his division of the organs into three classes, he has seriously marred, by the number, complexity, and confusion of his eight " ranges" and three " groups." Nor, as we shall show presently, is his location of the organs in his " ranges" in every case correct. A transfer of some of them to other "ranges," would be an amendment.

The classification by Mr. Combe, which is an improvement on that by Dr. Spurzheim, and embraces all in Mr. Grimes' that is in any degree useful, is the best yet extant. It is the most natural and simple, and therefore the most intelligible, and most easily applied to practical purposes. It has nothing artificial in it, does not appear to have been framed in a *human manufactory*, but to be a plain and judicious exposition of a work of nature.

Man, when viewed in his true character, is manifestly a compound of three natures or modes of being—animal, moral, and intellectual—which glide into each other so gradually, that it is exceedingly difficult, if not impossible, to trace between them well settled and definite lines of demarcation. And such is the representation of him given in Mr. Combe's classification of his mental faculties. In the system of Mr. Grimes, on the contrary, there is an effort made to group the faculties, or rather their organs, too precisely and arbitrarily, and to include them within stricter measures and bounds than nature has prescribed for them, or than she is willing to sanction.

With some of our author's "ranges," we have expressed ourselves dissatisfied. In the title " *rodentia* range," we perceive no shadow of *fitness*, applicability, or *correctness of meaning*. On the contrary, we are inclined to think that there is much error and *unfitness* in it. The only two faculties represented as belonging to it, are Constructiveness and Acquisitiveness. And we cannot regard the assignment of them to it as correct. Many species of the feathered race are distinguished for their Constructiveness, beyond, perhaps, any other of the inferior animals. They have also a sufficient stock of Acquisitiveness to induce them to take possession of places and things, to claim them as *their own*, and to defend and retain them in battle, at the risk of their lives. Yet with no show of propriety or correctness can they be, in any respect, consistently with the principles of science or language, designated by the term "rodentia." That term signifies *gnawers*. It is a name given to a class of animals, on account of the peculiarities of their teeth, and of their habits in the employment of them. They gnaw and cut wood, nuts, grain, and other solid substances. To this class belong beavers, squirrels, rats, weasels, mice, and various other *quadrupeds—but no birds*. Yet do birds, we repeat, surpass in Constructiveness.

Nor is this all. Every species of animals belonging to the "rodentia" tribe have not enough of Acquisitiveness to induce them to hoard, or even to cling to a place of residence, or any other sort of possession, as if they deemed it *their own*. The "rodentia range," therefore, we consider a failure, both in principle and application.

Nor are we inclined to say much less of the "herbivorous range," which our author incorrectly characterises by *Secretiveness*, as if that faculty were predominant in herb-eating animals. But the fact is otherwise. It is much less predominant in them than in carnivorous animals. The reason is plain. The food of herbivorous animals neither hides from them nor flies from them. They have, therefore, no need to exercise secrecy or stratagem in the procurement of it. But with carnivorous animals the case is quite different. They must gain possession of the victims they prey on, by stealth and surprise. In them, therefore, the organ of Secretiveness is much more fully developed than in animals that subsist on vegetables. Nor is our author much more correct in relation to Cautiousness, the other organ which he includes under the "herbivorous range." It is far from being peculiar to vegetable-consuming animals, or even from being bestowed on them in an inordinate degree. In most carnivorous animals it is equally predominant, and more so in some of them. With all his occasional boldness and daring, even the lion has much of it. So have the tiger, the leopard, the cougar, and almost every other animal of the cat kind. Hence they engage in combat with great caution, except when they are confident of their superior strength, or of their possession of some other decided advantage. The lion is extremely shy of the elephant, and is cautious of coming to battle with the royal tiger, a monster of about his own size and strength. Indeed, in the habits, manners, and actions, of most carnivorous animals, Secretiveness and Cautiousness unite their functions, and give aid to each other, at least in as high a degree as they do in the herbivorous tribes—were we to say in a higher, it would not be easy to convict us of error. To other "ranges" we have also objections; but a want of room prevents us from stating them.

Of our author's change in phrenological nomenclature, we cannot approve. Such a measure is justifiable only on one of two grounds, or on both united—*necessity* or *usefulness*. And, in the present case, no plea, we think, can be based on either. The nomenclature of Gall and Spurzheim, and their co-labourers and followers, sufficiently subserved the purposes of the science. It is not *necessary*, therefore, to change it. And we are much mistaken if the change made by Mr. Grimes amounts to an improvement. In most respects, we deem it the reverse. Nor are we satisfied that it is otherwise in any respect. In our remarks on this subject, we must necessarily be brief. We shall limit our observations to two organs.

On the organ heretofore denominated Wit and Mirthfulness, our author has bestowed the name of Playfulness, and considers it as belonging to all animals, from fishes to man, and as being peculiarly predominant in *young animals*. Why? Because all animals play; and young ones play more than old ones. Here our author makes no distinction between playfulness of mind and playfulness of body— between the mirthful exercise of the human brain, and the clumsy muscular gambols of the grampus. He considers the source of the refined and exquisite wit of Shakspeare and Cervantes, Rabelais and Voltaire, the same with that of the frisking of the kitten, the awkward capering of the pig, and the sport of the gosling and the duckling in the mud-puddle! But this topic is really too ludicrous to be introduced and gravely treated of in a philosophical discussion. It is calculated to bring phrenology into disrepute, rather than to benefit it. We therefore decline its farther consideration. Again:

To the organ heretofore called Veneration or Reverence, Mr. Grimes gives the name of Submissiveness. And this organ, also, which all other phrenologists, Broussais perhaps excepted, consider as peculiar to man, and as constituting one of the most prominent marks of distinction between him and inferior beings, Mr. Grimes bestows on dogs, horses, cows, and other animals, characterised by a disposition to submit and be tractable. Nor is this all. He asserts that the sentiment of Veneration is the product of Submissiveness; thus palpably substituting the *effect* for the *cause*. He contends that we venerate men and beings of a superior order, up to the Deity himself, because we submit to them, instead of submitting to them because we venerate them—an opinion which involves as palpable a perversion of cause and effect as can possibly be imagined. Has Mr. Grimes ever discovered in the brains of dogs, cows, and horses, or of any other inferior animals, that convolution which forms the organ of Veneration? Or has he ever found in them the organ of Mirthfulness? He will not reply to these questions affirmatively, and submit his reply to the test of anatomy. The truth is, that the

two organs referred to belong as exclusvely to man, as either Hop
or Ideality, which our author has correctly placed in his "huma
range," but under the names of "Perfectiveness" and "Hopefulness,
without either necessity or usefulness to justify the change, an
therefore, as we conceive, on indefensible ground.

Our author has been at fault in the new names he has bestowe
on several other organs, especially in calling Self-esteem "Impers
tiveness," and Locality, "Direction." The former of these organs
with its sentiment, does not alone constitute the love of empire o
command, although it forms an element of it; and an ability t
remember and recognise places, and steer courses with dexterit
and correctness, is the result of the united action of several organs
Individuality and Size being two of them.

Of Mr. Grimes' calling Benevolence "Kindness," and Wonder
"Credenciveness," we shall only say, that it appears to us to be
change made by him merely from a *love of change.* Assuredly i
is not *necessary*, and no *useful* end is attained by it. With his ne
name of Sanitativeness, and his remarks on the organ thus denomi
nated, we are also dissatisfied. It might be easily made to appear
that a fair analysis of the subject is adverse to his views. But w
can pursue this discussion no farther.

Notwithstanding the numerous exceptions we have taken to Mi
Grimes' "New System of Phrenology," we have no disposition t
disparage the author. Far from it. He possesses a mind of pene
tration and activity, perceives and thinks clearly, and is, we doub
not, an attractive lecturer. But he has written indiscreetly, unde
the ambitious character of a reformer, at too early a period of hi
studies. Many of his views are therefore limited and crude, an
ought not to have been submitted to the public, except as mer
suggestions, until farther reflected on, expanded, and matured. Hi
style, moreover, without being in a high degree faulty, is certainl
neither chaste, vigorous, nor polished. It should therefore be care
fully cultivated and amended by him. And, with his command c
language, the task may be easily accomplished. He is compara
tively young in science, and has before him a flattering prospec
and an honourable career, provided he be true to science and him
self. But as regards the standing and distinction he aims at, an
even thinks, perhaps, that he already possesses, (we mean as
reformer and an instructor of the world in phrenology,) he mus
labour for them many years before he shall have attained them, an
should deem himself fortunate if he attain them at last. With thes
remarks, accompanied by the kindest feelings, and best wishes fo
his success and prosperity, we respectfully take leave of him.

ARTICLE II.

PHRENOLOGICAL DEVELOPEMENTS OF GOTTFRIED, A MURDERESS.

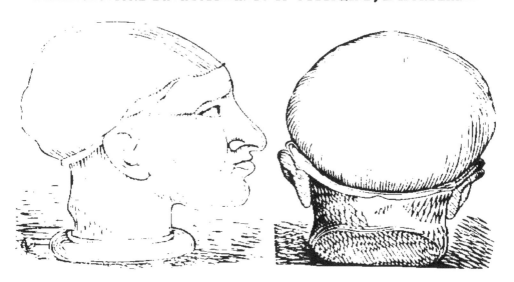

The above cuts are designed to present two different views of the head of Gesche Margarethe Gottfried, who rendered herself notorious as a murderess. She resided at Bremen, Germany, and was executed in September, 1830. Dr. Hirschfeld took a cast of her head, and forwarded it to the Edinburgh Phrenological Society, from whose collection Mr. George Combe brought a copy to this country, and from which the above cuts are drawn. The developements of the cast are so striking, and the character of the individual which it represents is so notorious, that it serves as a most interesting specimen to prove and illustrate the principles of phrenology. An extended article on the subject may be found in the thirty-second number of the Edinburgh Phrenological Journal, the mere substance of which can here only be presented.

The father of Gottfried was a tailor in Bremen, of active and industrious habits, but of a stingy and selfish disposition. Gesche was an only daughter. In the seventh year of her age, she became addicted to stealing, and continued committing thefts at every convenient opportunity through life. When about twenty, she was married to a man by the name of Miltenberg, who is represented to have treated her with much kindness and affection. But she had been married to him only four months before she fell in love with

GOTTFRIED, THE MURDERESS.

Gottfried, her future husband, and soon after, with another man by the name of Kassou. She determined to kill Miltenberg, in order to marry Gottfried, but was defeated in several of her first attempts At last she seized an opportunity, when he was sick, to give him some poison, which took effect and produced his death. But now two serious obstacles stood in the way of her union with Gottfried 1st, Her parents interfered, and forbid the match; and 2dly, He objected to the marriage on account of her children—having had three by her first husband.

About this time, her parents came to reside with her, both of whom she poisoned, and soon after this, each of her children followed in quick succession—the victims of her cruelty. But here, unexpectedly, another obstacle rose—her brother, who had long been absent on a military campaign in Russia, came home unwell, and opposed her marriage. He soon, however, met with the same fate Thus, within a few months, she destroyed the lives of six persons who were bound to her by the nearest and dearest relations in life.

Her marriage with Gottfried proved unhappy, and he, within one year from their union, became also the victim of her cruelty. After this, says her biographer, " she began to poison her acquaintances without any visible motive : a child came to congratulate her on her birth-day, and received a dose on a piece of biscuit ; a friend called one forenoon, and also received a dose ; and she tried the strength of her poison on another of her friends, on whose face it caused blotches to appear." At different times, she had many suitors, several of whom she murdered, besides others of her acquaintances. She was finally detected, convicted, and condemned to death, for murdering thirteen individuals, most of whom were related to her in life by the strongest possible ties of consanguinity and friendship.

The phrenological developements of Gottfried were very marked and striking, as may be seen by the cuts. The chief portions of her brain were located in the lower and posterior regions of the head giving very strong selfish feelings and animal propensities. There was a great deficiency of brain (as the cuts very clearly indicate) in the frontal and coronal regions, showing that she was almost entirely destitute of the moral sentiments. Her strongest faculties appear to have been Amativeness, Secretiveness, Acquisitiveness, Destructiveness, Firmness, and Self-esteem ; and those most deficient, were Benevolence, Conscientiousness, Adhesiveness, and Philoprogenitiveness. The cut presenting a back view of the head, shows very great breadth of head over the ears, indicating exceedingly strong Secretiveness and Destructiveness ; and the great size and breadth of the neck indicates very large Amativeness. The cuts also show

:hat the organs of Benevolence and Conscientiousness were very small, and that the organs of Firmness and Self-esteem were extremely large. The reader is referred to the location of those organs, as indicated by the cuts. We deem it unnecessary to enter into any farther analysis of Gottfried's character, or to attempt to show the harmony existing between her phrenological developements and actual life; our object is simply to present the facts in the case, and leave the reader to make the requisite applications, or to draw his own inferences.

" *Progress of Phrenology.*—Since Mr. Combe took his departure for Europe, very little is said on this heretofore engrossing topic. Still, a few individuals are devotedly pursuing investigations, and accumulating important facts illustrative of the leading principles of the science, which will be regarded, at some future period, with interest by philosophers. Mr. L. N. Fowler, of New York, and his brother, O. S. Fowler, who resides in Philadelphia, are collecting cabinets of casts, which embrace fac-similes of the heads of men, women, and children, who have been distinguished for qualities out of the common order of mankind; and the stranger who visits their collection, is positively astonished at the results of their unobtrusive industry in this department of nature. Through the politeness of Dr. Bond, we had an opportunity of inspecting the Philadelphia Phrenological Museum (for such it actually is) the other day—the rarest assemblage, perhaps, on this continent of unique skulls, and casts of persons now living. Each one is characterised by some developement either a little out of the ordinary course, or so strongly marked by peculiarities as to be considered nearly, if not wholly, unparalleled in the series of cranioscopal formations.

" The art of taking casts has been greatly improved by the Messrs. Fowler. Some of their work is quite equal to the best specimens of clay modeling by Clavenger or Ives. The bust of Dr. Reynell Coates was admirably finished, and altogether superior to any method before known to artists, or, at least, practised by them, in New England. If the progress of phrenology depends on accuracy in copying nature, in amassing specimens of her handy work, in connection with the study of mental phenomena, the science is surely losing nothing in the United States."—*Boston Medical and Surgical Journal, July 8th.*

ARTICLE III.

REVIEW OF MORTON'S CRANIA AMERICANA.

(Continued from page 397 of this Journal.)

If, then, there be reason to believe that different parts of the brain manifest different mental faculties, and if the size of the part influ ence the power of manifestation, the necessity is very evident o taking into consideration the *relative proportions of the differen parts of the brain*, in a physiological inquiry into the connectio between the crania of nations and their mental qualities. To illus trate this position, we present exact drawings of two casts fron nature: one, figure 1 (next page), is the brain of an American Indian and the other, figure 2, the brain of an European. Both casts bea evidence of compression or flattening out, to some extent, by the pressure of the plaster; but the European brain is the flatter of the two. We have a cast of the entire head of this American Indian, an it corresponds closely with the form of the brain here represented.

It is obvious that the absolute quantity of brain, (although probably a few ounces less in the American,) *might* be the *same in both ;* and yet, if different portions manifest different mental powers, the cha racters of the individuals, and of the nations to which they belonged (assuming them to be types of the races,) might be exceedingly different. In the American Indian, the anterior lobe, lying between A A and B B, is small, and in the European it is large, in proportion to the middle lobe, lying between B B and C C. In the American Indian, the posterior lobe, lying between C and D, is much smaller than in the European. In the American, the cerebral convolutions on the anterior lobe and upper surface of the brain, are smaller than in the European.

If the anterior lobe manifest the intellectual faculties—the middle lobe, the propensities common to man with the lower animals—and the posterior lobe, the domestic and social affections ; and if size influence power of manifestation, the result will be, that in the native American, intellect will be feeble—in the European, strong ; in the American, animal propensity will be very great—in the European more moderate ; while in the American, the domestic and social affections will be feeble, and in the European, powerful. We do not state these as established results ; we use the cuts only to illustrate the fact that the native American and the European brains *differ*

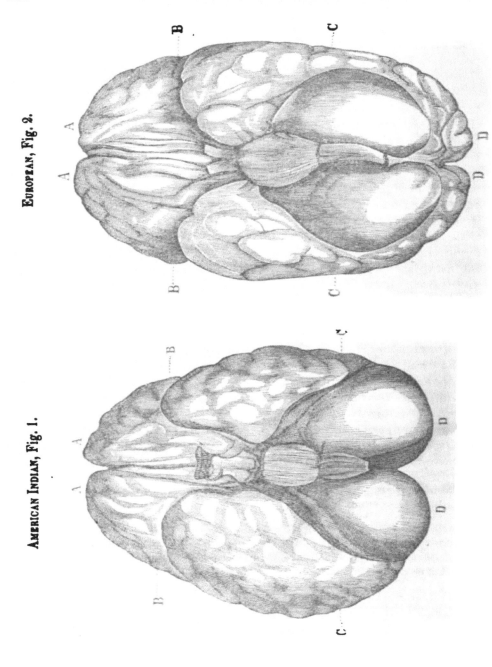

EUROPEAN, Fig. 2.

AMERICAN INDIAN, Fig. 1.

Inches.

widely in the proportions of their different parts ;* and the conclu
sion seems natural, that if different functions be attached to differen
parts, no investigation can deserve attention which does not embrac
the size of the different regions, in so far as this can be ascertained

We have entered more minutely into the reasons why we regar
these measurements as important, because we conceive that the dis
tinguishing excellence of Dr. Morton's work consists in his havin;
adopted and followed out this great principle. It appeared neces
sary to dwell upon it at some length, also, because Professor Tiede
mann, in his comparison of the European with the Negro brain, ha
entirely neglected it, and in consequence has arrived at physiologica
conclusions which we regard as at variance with the most certai
psychological facts, viz. He says that " there is undoubtedly a ver;
close connection between the ABSOLUTE SIZE of the brain and th
INTELLECTUAL POWERS AND FUNCTIONS of the mind;" and proceed
ing on this principle, he compares the weight of the whole brain, a
ascertained in upwards of fifty Europeans of different ages an
countries, with its weight in several Negroes, examined either b
himself or others. He gives extensive tables, showing the weigh
of the quantity of millet seed necessary to fill Ethiopian, Caucasian
Mongolian, American, and Malay skulls ; and adds, that "the cavit;
of the skull of the Negro, in general, *is not smaller* than that of th
European and other human races." The inference which he draw
is, that *intellectually* and *morally*, as well as anatomically, th
Negro is naturally on a par with the European; and he contend;
that the opposite and popular notion is the result of superficia
observation, and is true only of certain degraded tribes on the *coas*
of Africa.†

* From inspecting numerous crania of both races, we cannot doubt of the genera
truth of this proposition.

† Tiedemann's Essay has been critically examined by Dr. A. Combe, in th
Phrenological Journal, (vol. xi.) who shows not only the error of principle com
mitted by the author in assuming the whole brain to be the organ exclusively o
the *intellectual* faculties, but the more striking fact that Tiedemann's own table
refute his own conclusions. Tiedemann's measurements are the following :—

				Inches.	Lines
Average length of brain in 4 Negroes,			. .	5	1½
" " "	7 European males,		. .	6	2 1-7
" " "	6 European females,		. .	5	10½
" greatest breadth in 4 Negroes,			. .	4	8 1-6
" " "	7 European males,		. .	5	1 1-7
" " "	3 European females,		. .	5	4½
" height of brain in 3 Negroes,			. .	2	11½
" " "	7 European males,		. .	3	4
" " "	4 European females,		.	2	9½

The inferiority of the Negro brain in size, is self-evident from these dimensions

We entertain a great respect for Prof. Tiedemann, but we cannot subscribe to his principle, that the whole brain is the measure of the *intellectual* faculties; a proposition which assumes that the animal and moral feelings have no seat in this organ. He does not grapple with Dr. Gall's facts or arguments, but writes as if Gall had never existed. Dr. Morton has followed a different course, and we think wisely. He says, "I was from the beginning desirous to introduce into this work a brief chapter on phrenology; but, conscious of my own inability to do justice to the subject, I applied to a professional friend to supply the deficiency. He engaged to do so, and commenced his task with great zeal; but ill health soon obliged him to abandon it, and to seek a distant and more genial climate. Under these circumstances, I resolved to complete the phrenological table, and omit the proposed essay altogether. Early in the present year, however, and just as my work was ready for press, Geo. Combe, Esq. the distinguished phrenologist, arrived in this country; and I seized the occasion to express my wants to that gentleman, who, with great zeal and promptness, agreed to furnish the desired essay, and actually placed the MS. in my hands before he left the city." He adds, that Mr. Combe provided his memoir without having seen a word of the MS. of the work, or even knowing what had been written, and besides, owing to previous arrangement, he was limited to a given number of pages.

We can afford space only to notice Mr. Combe's illustration of the location of the great divisions of the faculties in the different regions of the brain. It is necessary to give this in order to render the true import of several of Dr. Morton's measurements and results intelligible to the reader.

In this figure (Fig. 3), a line drawn from the point A, transversely across the skull, to the same point on the opposite side, would coincide with the posterior margin of the super-orbitary plate : the anterior lobe rests on that plate. The line A B denotes the length of the anterior lobe from back to front, or the portion of brain lying between A A and B B in figures 1 and 2. A, in figure 3, "is located in the middle space between the edge of the suture of the frontal bone and the edge of the squamous suture of the temporal bone, where these approach nearest to each other, on the plane of the superciliary ridge." We have examined a Peruvian skull of the Inca race, a skull of a flat-headed Indian, an Indian skull found near Boston, and compared them with several skulls of the Anglo-Saxon race, and observe that the line A B is considerably longer in the latter than in the former, and that it corresponds with the length of the anterior lobe, as denoted by the super-orbitar plate. The

Swiss, Fig. 3.

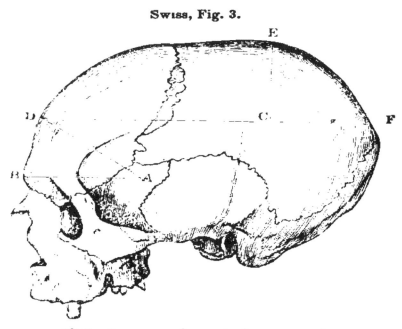

All the figures are drawn to the same scale.

point C is the centre of ossification of the parietal bone, corresponding to the centre of Cautiousness. The line C D is drawn from C
through the centre of ossification in the left side of the frontal bone
This is the centre of Causality. E corresponds with Firmness o
the phrenologist. The space D A B is an approximation to the
department occupied by the intellectual faculties. D C E contains
the organs of the moral sentiments. All the space behind A, and
below the line D C F, is devoted to the animal organs. The space
E C F contains Self-esteem and Love of Approbation, which may
act either with the moral sentiments or animal propensities, according as either predominate. Mr. Combe states that these lines are
only approximations to accurate demarcations of the regions, as no
modes of rigid admeasurement have yet been discovered.

Mr. Phillips invented an instrument, (which he describes,) by
which Dr. Morton and he measured the contents of the space above
D C F, in cubic inches, in nearly all the skulls. This is called the
coronal region. By deducting the contents of this space from the
contents of the whole skull, they give the measurement of the *sub
coronal region.* Mr. Phillips found it impossible to measure D A B
and the space behind A and below D C F, in cubic inches, and Dr
M. therefore measured, as an approximation, the whole space con

tained in the skull anterior to the anterior margin of the foramen
magnum.   He designates this the *anterior chamber*.   He measured
all behind that margin, and calls it the *posterior chamber*.

In addition to these, Mr. Phillips has added tables of thirty-nine
phrenological measurements (which are lucidly described by him) of
each skull.   We quote the following statement as an example of the
spirit of philosophic inquiry which animated Mr. Phillips in his
labours.   "A series of measurements with the craniometer and
compasses, much more extensive than any we had seen published,
had been carefully made on upwards of ninety of the crania, when
Mr. George Combe arrived in this city.   That gentleman immediately pointed out so many erroneous points of measurement,
(arising from the use of a badly marked bust,) that those tables
were condemned, together with the labour bestowed on them," and
new measurements of the whole were substituted in their place!

It is impossible to commend too highly the zeal and perseverance
manifested by both of these gentlemen in their endeavours to do
justice to their subject; and we anticipate that their example, and
the results to which their labours have led, will give a powerful
impulse to others to prosecute this interesting branch of science.

We shall now present a brief view of the manner in which Dr.
Morton applies his own principles, and of some of the conclusions at
which he has arrived.

He divides the native American nations into two great families—
the *Toltecan* and *American*.   "It is in the intellectual faculties,"
says he, "that we discover the greatest difference between them.
In the arts and sciences of the former, we see the evidences of an
advanced civilisation.   From the Rio Gila, in California, to the
southern extremity of Peru, their architectural remains are every
where encountered to surprise the traveller and confound the antiquary; among these are pyramids, temples, grottoes, bas-reliefs, and
arabesques; while their roads, aqueducts, and fortifications, and the
sites of their mining operations, sufficiently attest their attainments
in the practical arts of life." p. 84.   The desert of Atacama divides
the kingdom of Peru from that of Chilé, and is nearly a hundred
miles in length.   A river, abounding in salt, runs through it.   This
desert was the favourite sepulchre of the Peruvian nations for successive ages.   The climate, salt, and sand, dry up the bodies, and
the remains of whole generations of the former inhabitants of Peru
may now be examined, after the lapse perhaps of thousands of years.
Dr. Morton has been enabled to examine nearly one hundred Peruvian crania, and concludes that that country has been, at different
times, peopled by two nations of differently formed crania, one of

which is perhaps extinct, or at least exists only as blended by
adventitious circumstances, in very remote and scattered tribes of
the present Indian race.   " Of these two families, that which was
antecedent to the appearance of the Incas is designated as the
ancient Peruvian, of which the remains have been found only in
Peru, and especially in that division of it now called Bolivia.   Their
tombs, according to Mr. Pentland, abound on the shores and island
of the great lake Titicaca, in the inter-alpine valley of the Desagua
dera, and in the elevated valleys of the Peruvian Andes, between the
latitudes of 14° and 19° 30' south."   Our knowledge of their phy
sical appearance is derived solely from their tombs.   They were no
different " from cognate nations in any respect, except in the con
formation of the head, which is small, greatly elongated, narrow in
its whole length, with a very retreating forehead, and possessing
more symmetry than is usual in skulls of the American race.   The
face projects, the upper jaw is thrust forward, and the teeth are
inclined outward.   The orbits of the eyes are large and rounded, the
nasal bones salient, the zygomatic arches expanded ; and there is a
remarkable simplicity in the sutures, that connect the bones of the
cranium." p. 97.   Dr. Morton presents the following cranium, plate
IV. of his series, " as an illustrative type of the cranial peculiarities
of the people ;" and he is of opinion that the form is " natural
unaltered by art."

ANCIENT PERUVIAN, Fig. 4.

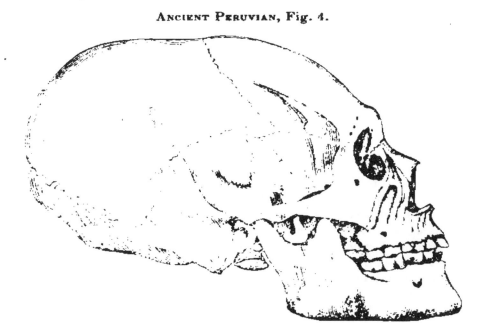

He gives the following description of this cranium :—

"Though the forehead retreats rapidly, there is but little expansion at the sides, and from the face to the occiput, inclusive, there is a narrowness that seems characteristic of the race. The posterior view represents the skull elevated in that region, without any unnatural width at the sides, and the vertical view sufficiently confirms the latter fact.

*Measurements.**

Longitudinal diameter, ...	7.3	inches.
Parietal "	5.3	"
Frontal "	4.3	"
Vertical "	5.3	"
Inter-mastoid arch, ...	14.	"
Inter-mastoid line, ...	4.3	"
Occipite-frontal arch, ...	15.	"
Horizontal periphery, ...	19.8	"
Extreme length of head and face, . .	8.2	"
Internal capacity, ...	81.5	cubic inches.
Capacity of the anterior chamber, . .	31.5	"
Capacity of the posterior chamber, . .	50.	"
Capacity of the coronal region, . . .	16.25	"
Facial angle, ...	73	degrees."

This skull was found by Dr. Ruschenberger, about a mile from the town of Arica, on the south of the *morro*, a cemetery of the

---

* The measurements are thus described by Dr. Morton. The *longitudinal* diameter is taken from the most prominent part of the os frontis to the occiput; the *parietal* diameter from the most distant points of the parietal bones ; the *frontal* diameter from the anterior inferior angles of the parietal bones ; the *vertical* diameter from the fossa, between the condyles of the occipital bone, to the top of the skull ; the *inter-mastoid arch* is measured with a graduated tape, from the point of one mastoid process to the other, over the external tables of the skull ; the *inter-mastoid line* is the distance, in a straight line, between the points of the mastoid processes ; the *occipito-frontal arch* is measured by a tape over the surface of the cranium, from the posterior margin of the foramen magnum to the suture, which connects the os frontis with the bones of the nose ; the *horizontal periphery* is measured by passing a tape around the cranium, so as to touch the os frontis immediately above the superciliary ridges, and the most prominent part of the occipital bone ; the *length of the head and face* is measured from the margin of the upper jaw, to the most distant point of the occiput; the *zygomatic diameter* is the distance, in a right line, between the most prominent points of the *zygomæ* ; the *facial angle* is ascertained by an instrument of ingenious construction and easy application, invented by Dr. Turnpenny, and described by Dr. Morton. Dr. Morton took nearly all the anatomical measurements with his own hands.

ancient Peruvians. "The surface is covered with sand an inch or two deep, which being removed discovers a stratum of salt, three or four inches in thickness, that spreads all over the hill. The body (to which this head belonged) was placed in a squatting posture, with the knees drawn up and the hands applied to the sides. The whole was enveloped in a coarse, but close fabric, with stripes of red, which has withstood, wonderfully, the destroying effects of ages, for these interments were made before the conquest, although at what period is unknown."

Dr. Morton states that the average internal capacity of the Caucasian or European head, is at least 90 cubic inches. In three adult ancient Peruvians, it is only 73. The mean capacity of the anterior chamber is about one half of that of the posterior, or 25 to 47, while the mean facial angle is but 67 degrees.

"It would," he continues, "be natural to suppose, that a people with heads so small and badly formed, would occupy the lowest place in the scale of human intelligence. Such, however, was not the case." He considers it ascertained that "civilisation existed in Peru anterior to the advent of the Incas, and that those anciently civilised people constituted the identical nations whose extraordinary skulls are the subjects of our present inquiry."

There is a discrepancy between this description of these skulls and the civilisation ascribed to their possessors, which is unique in Dr. Morton's work. In every other race, ancient and modern, the coincidence between superior cranial forms and superior mental qualities is conspicuous. On turning to Mr. Phillips's phrenological measurements, however, we find that the *mean* extent of the forehead in this skull, from the point A on one side, to the same point on the other, over B, or the "inter-sphenoidal arch, over the *perceptive* organs," (as ascertained by a graduated tape,) is 6.37 inches; and the mean extent from A to A, over D, or the "inter-sphenoidal arch over the *reflective* organs," is 6.12 inches. The mean of the same measurements of "100 *unaltered* crania of adult aboriginal Americans," of which many are ascertained to be males, are 6.7 and 6.8? inches; showing a superiority in the region of the *observing organs* in the ancient race, and in that of the *reflecting organs* in the modern. This indicates a larger quantity of brain in the anterior lobe in the extinct race, than Dr. Morton's description leads us to infer. This subject obviously requires further elucidation.

If these skulls had been compressed by art, we could have understood that certain portions of the brain might have been only displaced, but not destroyed. The spine, for instance, may be bent, as in hump-back, yet retain its functions; and we might suppose the anterior lobe, in cases of compression, to be developed laterally, or backwards, and still preserve its identity and uses. This, indeed, is Dr. Morton's own conclusion in regard to the brain in the flat-headed Indians. He gives an interesting and authentic description of the instrument and process by means of which the flat-head tribes of Columbia river compress the skull, and remarks that, " besides the depression of the head, the face is widened and projected forward by the process, so as materially to diminish the facial angle ; the breadth between the parietal bones is greatly augmented, and a striking irregularity of the two sides of the cranium almost invariably follows ; yet the absolute internal capacity of the skull is not diminished, and, strange as it may seem, the intellectual faculties suffer nothing. The latter fact is proved by the concurrent testimony of all travellers who have written on the subject." Dr. Morton adds, that in January, 1839, he was gratified with a personal interview with a full blood Chenouk, in Philadelphia. He is named William Brooks, was twenty years of age, had been three years in charge of some Christian missionaries, and had acquired great proficiency in the English language, which he understood and spoke with a good accent and general grammatical accuracy. His head was as much distorted by mechanical compression, as any skull of his tribe in Dr. Morton's possession. " He appeared to me," he adds, " to possess more mental acuteness than any Indian I had seen, was communicative, cheerful, and well mannered." The measurements of his head were these; longitudinal diameter, 7.5 inches ; parietal diameter, 6.9 inches ; frontal diameter, 6.1 inches ; breadth between the cheek bones, 6.1 inches ; facial angle, about 73 degrees. Dr. Morton considers it certain that the forms of the skull produced by compression, never become congenital, even in successive generations, but that the characteristic form is always preserved, unless art has directly interfered to distort it.—pp. 206, 207.*

---

* Mr. George Combe, in his late lectures in New Haven, mentioned that in May, 1839, he had been introduced, in New York, to the Rev. Jason Lee, who had been a missionary among the Indians, 2000 miles beyond the Rocky Mountains, and who had with him Thomas Adams, a young Indian of about 20 years of age, of the Cloughewallah tribe, located about 25 miles from the Columbia river. This young man's head had been compressed by means of a board and cushions, in infancy. Mr. C. examined his head, and found that the parietal was actually greater than the frontal and occipital diameter. The organs in the superciliary ridge of the forehead were fully developed ; the upper part of the forehead was flat and deficient ; his organs of Language and Form, said Mr. C. were large. He had studied the English language for two years, and spoke it tolerably well. Mr. C. added, that in conversation he was intelligent, ready, and fluent, on all subjects that fell within the scope of the faculties of observation, situated in the superciliary ridge, but dull, unintelligent, and destitute equally of ideas and language, on topics

The extinct race in Peru was succeeded by the "INCA, o: MODERN PERUVIANS." This race dates its possession of Peru fror about the eleventh century of our era; and as this period correspond with the epoch of the migration from Mexico of the Toltecas, th most civilised nation of ancient Mexico, Dr. Morton concurs in th opinion expressed by other authors, that the modern Peruvians wer of a common origin with the ancient Mexicans. "The moder Peruvians," says he, "differ little in person from the Indians aroun them, being of the middling stature, well limbed, and with small fee and hands. Their faces are round, their eyes small, black, an rather distant from each other; their noses are small, the mout somewhat large, and the teeth remarkably fine. Their complexio is a dark brown, and their hair long, black, and rather coarse. p. 115. The civilisation and comparative refinement of the Inca was blended with some remains of the ferocity of the savage " Matrimonial engagements were entered into with very little cere mony or forethought, and they were as readily set aside at th option of the parties. Polygamy was lawful, but not prevalent. Among the people, incontinence, sensuality, and child-murder wer common. Their diet was chiefly vegetables. The people wer indolent, filthy, and negligent in their persons. The hair of thei mummies, in many instances, is charged with desiccated vermir Their religious system was marked by great simplicity, and wa divested of those bloody rites which were common with the Aztec of Mexico. They believed in one God, whom they called Viracocha in the immortality of the soul, and in rewards and punishments i the next life. They worshipped both the sun and moon, in whos honour they erected temples and formed idols. They consecrate virgins, in the same manner as practised in modern convents Their funeral rites were barbarous and cruel; when their chief me died, they buried a number of human victims, women, boys, and ser

that implied the activity of the reflecting faculties, situated in the upper part the forehead. Mr. C. considered his mental powers to be in direct harmony wit the developement of his brain. We record this observation, because it is obviou that if different parts of the brain manifest different faculties, it is indispensab that observations on the *manifestations* of the mental powers should be equall minute and discriminative with those on the developement of particular portions the cranium. Mr. C. added, that the only way to ascertain whether the brain we merely displaced by compression, or otherwise altered, was by careful examinatio after death; and that he had recommended to Mr. Lee to call the attention of an medical men who might visit these Indians, to this subject. We observed th death of one of these flat-headed Indians mentioned as having occurred in Ne York. Did any of the phrenologists or anti-phrenologists examine the brain? was an excellent opportunity for Dr. Reese.

vants, to attend on the departed in the next world.   They were con-
quered by Pizarro, with a force which consisted of sixty-two horse-
men, and one hundred and two foot soldiers. p. 124.   The following
is given as a strikingly characteristic Peruvian head.

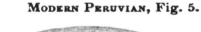

MODERN PERUVIAN, Fig. 5.

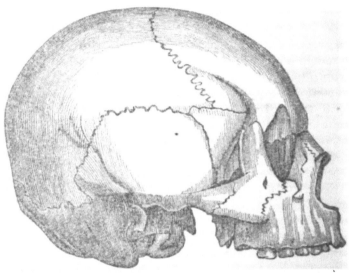

"The skull in these people," says Dr. Morton, "is remarkable for
its small size, and for its quadrangular form.   The occiput is greatly
compressed, sometimes absolutely vertical; the sides are swelled out,
and the forehead is somewhat elevated, but very retreating.   The
skulls are remarkable for their irregularity.   The dimensions of this
skull are as follows ;—

Longitudinal diameter,	6.1	inches.
Parietal "	6.	"
Frontal "	4.7	"
Vertical "	5.5	"
Inter-mastoid arch,	16.	"
Inter-mastoid line,	4.5	"
Occipito-frontal arch,	14.1	"
Horizontal periphery,	19.5	"
Internal capacity,	83.	cubic inches.
Capacity of the anterior chamber,	33.5	"
Capacity of the posterior chamber,	49.5	"
Capacity of the coronal region,	15.75	"
Facial angle,	81 degrees."	

Dr. Morton gives the result of the measurement of twenty-thre adult skulls of the pure Inca race. "The mean of the interna capacity is 73 cubic inches, which is probably lower than that c any other people now existing, not excepting the Hindoos." Th mean of the anterior chamber is 32, of the posterior, 42, of th coronal region, 12 cubic inches. The highest measure of th coronal region is 20.5, and the smallest, 9.25 cubic inches. Th mean facial angle is 75 degrees. The heads of nine Peruvian chi. dren appear to be nearly, if not quite as large, as those of childre of other nations of the same age.—p. 133.

The small size of the brains of this race, compared with that c the Europeans who invaded them, is in accordance with the eas with which the former were overcome and retained in subjectior The deficiency in the posterior region of the brain, in which th organs of the domestic affections are situated, corresponds with thei feeble conjugal attachment and indifference to the lives of their chi! dren. The diameter from Constructiveness to Constructiveness, i stated by Mr. Phillips to be 4.5 inches, and from Ideality to Idealit; 5.1. These organs give a talent for art, and are considerable. Th same measurements in the Naumkeagh, the race which occupie New England, and whose skulls are still dug up near Boston an Salem, and which never made any attainments in the arts, are 4. and 4 inches, respectively. Dr. Robertson, in his history of America mentions that the modern Peruvian race was distinguished for it extraordinary powers of concealment and secrecy. Mr. Phillip states the breadth from Secretiveness to Secretiveness to be 5. inches, which is large; the longitudinal diameter is only 6.1 The region of Combativeness also appears to be deficient in thes skulls.

The IROQUOIS confederacy consisted originally of five nations, th Mohawks, Oneidas, Onondagas, Cayugas, and Senecas. They wer intellectually superior to the surrounding nations, passionately devote to war, and victorious over the other.tribes. They forced thei women to work in the field and carry burdens; they paid littl respect to old age, were not much affected by love, were regardles of connubial obligations, and addicted to suicide. "They wer proud, audacious, and vindictive, untiring in the pursuit of an enemy and remorseless in the gratification of their revenge. Their religiou ideas were vague, and their cautiousness and cunning proverbial They were finally subdued and nearly exterminated by the Angl Americans in 1779. Some miserable remnants of them, ruined b intoxicating liquors, still exist in the state of New York." The fol lowing is the skull of a Huron, one of these nations.

HURON, Fig. 6.

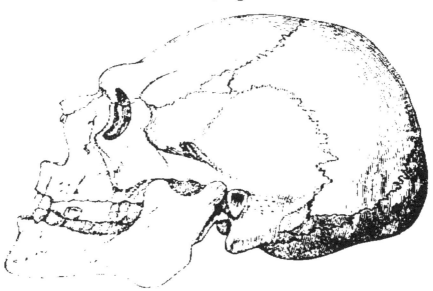

The following are *average* measurements of the five skulls of these nations, given by Dr. Morton : internal capacity, 88 ; coronal region, 15 ; anterior chamber, 31.5 ; posterior chamber, 50 cubic inches.

The ARAUCANIANS are the most celebrated and powerful of the Chilian tribes. They inhabit the region between the rivers Biobio and Valdivia, and between the Andes and the sea, and derive their name from the province of Arauco. "They are a robust and muscular people, of a lighter complexion than the surrounding tribes. Endowed with an extraordinary degree of bodily activity, they reach old age with few infirmities, and, generally, retain their sight, teeth, and memory, unimpaired. They are brave, discreet, and cunning to a proverb, patient in fatigue, enthusiastic in all their enterprises, and fond of war as the only source of distinction." "Their vigilance soon detected the value of the military discipline of the Spaniards, and especially the great importance of cavalry in an army ; and they lost no time in adopting both these resources, to the dismay and discomfiture of their enemies. Thus, in seventeen years after their first encounter with Europeans, they possessed several strong squadrons of horse, conducted their operations in military order, and, unlike the Americans generally, met their enemies in the open field." "They are highly susceptible of mental culture, but they despise the restraints of civilisation, and those of them who have been educated in the Spanish colonies, have embraced the first opportunity to

resume the haunts and habits of their nation." p. 241. The follov
ing is one of three Araucanian skulls delineated in the work.

ARAUCANIAN, Fig. 7.

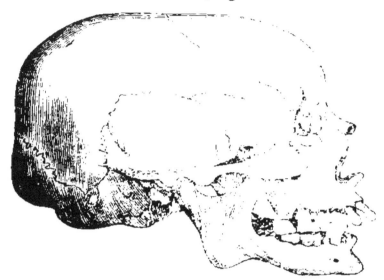

The average measurements of the three skulls are as follows
internal capacity, 79; coronal region, 15.4; anterior chamber, 32.2
posterior chamber, 48.50.

The measurements of the *anterior* and *posterior* chambers, as w
have already mentioned, (p. 549,) are not in accordance with an
phrenological rule. The anterior embraces the whole intellect,
portion of the moral sentiments, and a portion of the animal propel
sities; while the posterior chamber includes the remainder of th
animal propensities, and the remainder of the moral organs. Th
measurement of the internal capacity is free from all objection; an
that of the coronal region approaches to correctness; but the fir
gives merely the aggregate size of all the organs—animal, mora
and intellectual; and the second, that of the moral organs, with
portion of the intellectual organs, and also a portion of the orgar
common to man with the lower animals. The phrenological mer
surements given by Mr. Phillips may probably afford more correr
means of comparing one portion of the brain with another, in th
different nations, but our limits prevent us from analysing then
Unfortunately, also, the letter-press titles to his columns are printe
upside down, which renders it exceedingly laborious to consult then
We therefore only remark, that the application of lines delineated b
Mr. Combe on the skull Figure 1, to those specimens, brings out th

relation between the mental character and cranial developement forcibly to the eye.   Estimating from A to B and D, the ancient Peruvian is seen not to be so defective in the intellectual region as a cursory glance would indicate; while the modern Peruvian is obviously larger in that region.   The space above D C, devoted to the moral organs, is large in the modern Peruvian in proportion to the portion below C D, and behind the ear.   This race was intelligent and comparatively mild, but superstitious and feeble.   It has been subdued by the Europeans, and lives under their dominion. The Hurons, always averse to civilisation, have been nearly exterminated.   The preponderance of the region below C D, (that of the animal propensities,) in them is conspicuous, combined with relative deficiency in the moral and intellectual regions.   The Araucanians have maintained their independence in the open field, but resisted civilisation.   The large developement of the space A B C, devoted to intellect, and also that below C D, and behind the ear, devoted to the propensities, is obvious, while the space below C D, or the region of the moral organs, is proportionally deficient.   This indicates great animal and intellectual power, with imperfectly evolved moral feelings.   To the latter defect, probably, is to be ascribed their aversion to civilised habits.   The inferiority of all these skulls to that of the Swiss, is conspicuous.   The internal capacity of it is 95.5, and that of the coronal region, 21.25.   Dr. Morton does not give the capacity of the anterior and posterior chambers of this skull, but the larger dimensions of the intellectual organs have already been stated.

We have no space to enter into any description of the skulls found in the ancient tombs, or of those of the Flat-headed Indians and Charibs; suffice it to say, that Dr. Morton's materials are full and satisfactory on these topics, and his facts and conclusions highly interesting.   We subjoin a few of the general results at which he arrives from a survey of his entire field.

" The intellectual faculties," says he, " of the great AMERICAN FAMILY, appear to be of a decidedly inferior cast, when compared with those of the Caucasian or Mongolian races.   They are not only averse to the restraints of education, but for the most part incapable of a continued process of reasoning on abstract subjects. Their minds seize with avidity on simple truths, while they at once reject whatever requires investigation and analysis.   Their proximity, for more than two centuries, to European institutions, has made scarcely any appreciable change in their mode of thinking, or their manner of life; and as to their own social condition, they are probably in most respects what they were at the primitive epoch of their existence. They have made few or no improvements in building their houses or their boats; their inventive and imitative faculties appear to be of a very humble grade, nor have they the smallest predilection for the arts or sciences. The long annals of missionary labour and private benefaction bestowed upon them, offer but very few exceptions to the preceding statement, which, on the contrary, is sustained by the combined testimony of almost all practical observers. Even in cases where they have received an ample education, and have remained for many years in civilised society, they lose none of their innate love of their own national usages, which they have almost invariably resumed when chance has left them to choose for themselves." "However much the benevolent mind may regret the inaptitude of the Indians for civilisation, the affirmative of this question seems to be established beyond a doubt. His moral and physical nature are alike adapted to his position among the races of men, and it is as reasonable to expect the one to be changed as the other. The structure of his mind appears to be different from that of the white man; nor can the two harmonise in their social relations, except on the most limited scale. Every one knows, however, that the mind expands by culture; nor can we yet tell how near the Indian would approach the Caucasian after education had been bestowed on a single family through several successive generations." p. 82.*

The following are parts of Dr. Morton's table of "mean results," given from his whole measurements.

	Toltecan nations and skulls from mounds.		Barbarous nations, with skulls from the valley of Ohio.		American race, embracing Toltecan and barbarous nations.		Flathead tribe of Columbia river.		Ancient Peruvians.	
	No. of skulls.	Mean.	No. of skulls.	Mean.	No. of skulls.	Mean.	No. of skulls.	Mean.	No. of skulls.	Mean.
Internal capacity in cubic inches,	57	76.8	87	82.4	144	79.6	8	79.25	3	73.2
Capacity of anterior chamber,	46	32.5	73	34.5	119	33.5	8	32.25	3	25.7
Capacity of posterior chamber,	46	43.8	73	48.6	119	46.2	8	47.00	3	47.4
Capacity of coronal region,	46	14.0	71	16.2	117	15.1	8	11.09	3	14.6
Capacity of sub-coronal region,	46	61.8	71	66.5	117	64.5	8	67.35	3	58.6

Remarks.—"The barbarous nations possess a larger brain by 5½ cubic inches than the Toltecans; while, on the other hand, the Tol-

---

* Dr. Morton adds that the Indians are extremely defective in comprehending every thing relating to numbers, and we may remark that Mr. Combe, in his lectures in New Haven, showed the great deficiency of the organ of number in their skulls.

tecans possess a greater relative capacity of the anterior chamber of the skull, in the proportion of 42.3 to 41.8.   Again : the coronal region, though absolutely greater in the barbarous tribes, is rather larger in proportion in the demi-civilised tribes ; and the facial angle is much the same in both, and may be assumed, for the race, at 75 degrees.

"In conclusion, the author is of the opinion that the facts 'contained in this work tend to sustain the following propositions :—

"1st. That the American race differs essentially from all others, not excepting the Mongolians; nor do the feeble analogies of language, and the more obvious ones in civil and religious institutions and the arts, denote any thing beyond casual or colonial communication with the Asiatic nations; and even those analogies may perhaps be accounted for, as Humboldt has suggested, in the mere coincidence arising from similar wants and impulses in nations inhabiting similar latitudes.

"2d. That the American nations, excepting the polar tribes, are of one race and one species, but of two great families, which resemble each other in physical, but differ in intellectual character.

"3d. That the cranial remains discovered in the mounds from Peru to Wisconsin, belong to the same race, and probably to the Toltecan family."   Dr. Morton subjoins the following,

"NOTE *on the internal capacity of the cranium in the different races of men.*   Having subjected the skulls in my possession, and such also as I could obtain from my friends, to the internal capacity measurement already described, I have obtained the following results. The mean of the American race (omitting fractions) is repeated here, merely to complete the table.   The skulls of idiots, and persons under age, were of course rejected.

Races.	No. of skulls.	Mean internal capacity in cubic inches.	Largest in the series.	Smallest in the series.
1. Caucasian,	52	87	109	75
2. Mongolian,	10	83	93	69
3. Malay,	18	81	89	64
4. American,	147	80	100	60
5. Ethiopian,	29	78	94	65

"1st. The *Caucasians* were, with a single exception, derived from the lowest and least educated class of society.   It is proper, however, to mention that but three Hindoos are admitted in the whole number, because the skulls of these people are probably smaller than those of any other existing nation.   For example, seventeen Hindoo heads give a mean of but seventy-five cubic inches; and the three received

into the table are taken at that average. To be more specific, w
will give, in detail, the number of individuals of each nation, as f(
as ascertained.

Anglo-Americans, ...	6
German, Swiss, and Dutch, ...	7
Celtic, Irish, and Scots, ...	7
English, ...	4
Guanché, (Lybian,)	1
Spanish, ...	1
Hindoo, ...	3
Europeans not ascertained, ...	28
Total, ...	52

"2d. The *Mongolians* measured, consist of Chinese and Eskimaux
and what is worthy of remark, three of the latter give a mean of 8
cubic inches, while seven Chinese give but 82.

"3d. The Malays embrace Malays proper and Polynesians, thi
teen of the former and five of the latter; and the mean of each pr(
sents but a fractional difference from the mean of all.

"4th. The *Ethiopians* were all unmixed negroes, and nine of the(
native Africans, for which I am chiefly indebted to Dr. M'Dowel
formerly attached to the colony at Liberia.*

"5th. Respecting the American race, I have nothing to ad(
excepting the striking fact that, of all the American nations, th
Peruvians had the smallest heads, while those of the Mexicans wer
something larger, and those of the barbarous tribes the largest of al
viz.

Toltecan nations,	Peruvians, collectively, . .	76 cub. i(
	Mexicans, collectively, . .	79 "
	Barbarous tribes, as per table, .	82 "

* Dr. Morton states the mean internal capacity of the European, or Caucasi(
skulls, to be 87, and of the Ethiopian, or Negro race, to be 78 cubic inches. W
observe that Dr. Andrew Combe, in his "Remarks on the Fallacy of Profess(
Tiedemann's Comparison of the Negro brain and intellect with those of the Eur
pean," arrives at results coinciding with those obtained by Dr. Morton. Tied
mann gives the weight of only four Negro brains. "The average European," l
says, "runs from 3 lbs. 2 oz. to 4 lbs. 6 oz.; while the average of the four Neg(
brains rises to only 3 lbs. 5 oz. 1 dr.; or 3 oz. above the lowest European average(
and the *highest* Negro falls 5 oz. short of the highest *average* European, and (
less than 10 oz. short of Cuvier's brain." Phren. Journ. vol. xi. We have alreac
shown, p. 547, that Tiedemann's linear dimensions of the European and Neg(
brain also contradict his theory of equality, and are in harmony with Dr. Morton
results.

"An interesting question remains to be solved, viz. the relative proportion of brain in the anterior and posterior chambers of the skull in the different races; an inquiry for which I have hitherto possessed neither sufficient leisure nor adequate materials."—p. 261.

We now add Dr. Morton's statement in his prefatory letter to Mr. Phillips. "I am free to acknowledge," says he, "that there is a singular harmony between the mental character of the Indian and his cranial developements, as explained by phrenology."

Our readers will discover, in the length and minuteness of this article, the great value which we attach to Dr. Morton's work. We regard it as an honour to the country, and as a proof of talent, patience, and research in himself, which place him in the first rank among natural philosophers. We rejoice to see that he does "not, even now, consider his task as wholly completed;" but hopes to publish a "supplementary volume, in which it will further be my aim to extend and revise both the anatomical and phrenological tables, and to give basal views of at least a part of the crania delineated." We sincerely trust that the favourable reception of this volume will induce him to execute these intentions. Valuable as the materials are in the present work, they lie very much apart. He wrote without systematic relation to phrenology; yet phrenological facts and inferences are presented *passim* throughout the work. Mr. Phillips's phrenological tables are extensive, minute, and interesting, but they are not connected directly with the text; while Mr. Combe's essay was composed and printed without his having seen either the text of Dr. Morton, or the final results of Mr. Phillips's measurements. There is strong evidence, in this course of proceeding, of a very direct love of truth, and a reliance on all its parts harmonising with each other; but much of the effect and instruction are lost to the reader, in consequence of the facts and principles not being brought into juxtaposition by the respective contributors. We shall expect this defect to be supplied in the next edition, which we do not doubt will be called for. The work is remarkably cheap, keeping in view the quantity and quality of the *material* of which it is composed.[*]

---

[*] *Postscript.*—On page 553, we remarked that "there is a discrepancy between the description of the ancient Peruvian skulls and the civilisation ascribed to their possessors, which is unique in Dr. Morton's work." When the present sheet was in the press, we received a letter from Dr. Morton, in which he says, "Since that part of my work which relates to the *ancient Peruvians* was written, I have seen several additional casts of skulls belonging to the same series, and although I am satisfied that Plate IV, (Fig. 4, p. 551,) represents an unaltered cranium, yet, as it is the *only unaltered one* I have met with among the remains of that ancient people, I wish to correct the statement, too hastily drawn, that it is *the cranial type* of their nation. My matured opinion is, that the ancient Peruvians were a branch of the

ARTICLE IV.

Dr. F. J. Gall's System of the Functions of the Brain, extracte
from Charles Augustus Blode's account of Dr. Gall's Lecture
held on the above subject at Dresden, 1805.

L. D. Chapen, Esq. of New York, has in his possession a sma
work on phrenology with the above title. It is probably the onl
copy in this country, and, from the rarity and antiquity of the worl
it is certainly quite a curiosity in the history of the science. D
Gall, in the early course of his labours, wisely determined to publia
no account of his discoveries until he could do the subject justic
and acquit himself with honour. And the first production which b
ever presented to the public, was, in connection with Dr. Spurzhein
a work on the Anatomy of the Brain, offered to the French Institu
in the year 1808. In the mean time, several sketches of Dr. Gall
discoveries were published, either in miscellaneous periodicals, or :
distinct treatises by themselves. In this last class, we find the fo
lowing notices of works: Froriep published one in Berlin, 1802
Martens, in Leipzic, 1802; Walther, in Zurich, 1802; Bischoff, :
Berlin, 1805; Blode, in Dresden, 1805. This last was published i
German, and from which the work heading this article is extracte
and translated into the English language. It was undoubtedl
designed to explain, in some measure, the nature of Dr. Gall's disc
veries, and prepare the public mind for their reception.

The work before us (which Mr. Chapen has kindly loaned us)
particularly interesting to the phrenologist, in a historical point
view. In its looks, typography, and language, it bears the impres
of "olden times," and seems to carry the reader back to the earl
history and labours of the great founder of the science. It is, as
were, a mirror through which we may behold the nature and exten
of Dr. Gall's discoveries in the year 1805. At that time, he ha
been engaged in expounding and defending publicly the science onl
about nine years; but more than thirty years had then elapsed fro
the time of his *first* discoveries touching the functions of the brai
and it is even truly astonishing how much he accomplished within th

great Toltecan family, and that the cranium had the same general characteristi
in both. I am at a loss to conjecture how they *narrowed the face* in such due pr
portion to the head; but the fact seems indisputable. I shall use every exertion
obtain additional materials for the farther illustration of this subject.

Signed, SAMUEL GEORGE MORTON."

Philadelphia, March 3, 1840.

period. He had, even at that date, proved and settled all the great fundamental principles of the science, and discovered a majority of the cerebral organs; and that our readers may become better acquainted with the results of his labours, we will here present a brief synopsis of the work before us.

It opens with an "anatomical introduction," designed to prove not only the *fibrous* structure of the brain, but that it is composed of two distinct sets of nerves—viz. the diverging and converging fibres. After a minute, and somewhat extended, exposition of the anatomy of the brain, he enters upon a discussion respecting its functions, under the following inquiries or propositions :—

"Man and animals are born with certain dispositions and inclinations, and for the exertion of them they have received certain organs, by way of innate instruments, by the means of which they may have an intercourse with the external world. These organs reside in the brain, which, however, must not be considered as a faculty, but merely as a material requisite of it. Nor is the brain the general organ of all the mental faculties, but merely the place of rendezvous of all the single organs, each innate disposition having an organ of its own, which is increased in proportion to the power residing in the disposition. These organs of the innate dispositions are expressed on the surface of the brain, and form certain protuberances on the osseous cover of the skull, by which the existence of the organs may be ascertained under certain strictures. And from these observations arises the special system of the organs, or the system of the skull, as a science entirely new."

Each of the above propositions are discussed at considerable length. For instance, the inquiry respecting a plurality of organs to the brain, is examined under the following heads :—

1. "The existence of sundry single organs of the mental dispositions may with some probability be inferred from analogy; for we observe throughout the whole scale of creation, that whenever nature intends to create a new power, or produce a new effect, she will also take new preparatory arrangements for them."

2. "It is a fact, known and proved, that man can vary the objects of reflection and attention at large."

3. "All men, if the brain were the general organ of the soul, must by nature be endowed with like dispositions; but this is not the case. For experience teaches us, that with regard to their intensity or intrinsic quality, the greatest variety is found, even from infancy, in the dispositions of man."

4. "The single dispositions to most mental powers, innate to man, are, again, found single and detached in the different species of animals."

5. "The dispositions of man cannot reside in one and the same organ for every disposition, because these dispositions are not deve-

loped at one and the same time, but at several different periods (
life."

6. "The existence of sundry single dispositions, and their bein
attended with their respective organs in the brain, likewise is prove
from many phenomena which appear in hurts and distempers of th
brain."*

7. "We lastly may, from many other physiological and psych(
logical phenomena and facts, be led to suppose that every singl
mental power must have its own organ in the brain." Dr. Ga
here enters into an examination of the philosophy of sleeping
dreaming, somnambulism, visions, ecstacies, and the effects of med
cines and intoxicating drinks on the brain, and deduces from each (
these, severally, many important facts and arguments in proof of
plurality of cerebral organs. His remarks on the organisation an
growth of the skull, showing that its general shape and particula
protuberances are occasioned by the brain, and, consequently, the
its external surface corresponds to its internal, and therefore the siz
of the individual cerebral organs may be very accurately ascertaine
by the developements of the skull—his remarks on all these topic
are copious, critical, and satisfactory. After disposing of thes
points, Dr. Gall enters upon the description and an analysis of th
several mental faculties which he had then discovered. In this lis
we find twenty-seven organs mentioned, the names of which are a
follows :—" *The impulse to propagation ; Tenderness for offspring
The organ of the aptness to receive an education ; The organ q
Locality ; Of the recollection of persons ; The disposition for colou*
*ing, and the delighting in colours ; The organ of sound ; Arith
metic ; Words ; Language ; Mechanical skill ; Friendly attachment
Valour ; Murdering ; Cunning ; Larceny ; Weight ; Ambition an(
vanity ; Circumspection ; Comparative perspicuity ; Metaphysica
perspicuity ; Wit ; Inference ; Good-nature ; Theosophy ; Persev(
rance and Mimic.*"

These are the *English* names applied by the translator, and it i

---

* The following curious fact, under this head, is introduced by the compiler (
the work in the form of a note :—" Very remarkable is the instance which th
celebrated *Villers*, in his exposition of Gall's system, relates of a young womar
who, through some accident during her first childbed, lost all recollection of wha
had happened to her ever since her marriage. She would hear neither of her hu(
band nor of her child, constantly endeavoured to remove both from her, an
nothing but repeated persuasions and the authority of the asseverations of he
relatives were able to convince her that she was a wife and a mother. She, how
ever, could never recollect the first year of her wedlock."—*Monthly Mag. Ja*(
1805, *p.* 494.

quite probable that many of them do not clearly express the sense, or just the right shade of meaning which Gall might have intended, as he first described and named the organs in the German language. It will be observed that these names have now been very much changed, and that several additional organs have since been discovered. This might rationally be expected in the farther developements of the science, and it moreover affords evidence of the truth and reality of the discoveries.   Though some changes have taken place in the number and nomenclature of the organs, yet the location and essential functions of *all* the organs which Gall discovered and described, remain now the same that they ever were.

There is abundant evidence to prove that Dr. Gall did not first map out the skull, or merely conjecture the location of the organs, but, on the contrary, that he proceeded slowly, step by step, discovering first one organ, then another, and another.   In proof of this, we quote the following remarks made by Mr. Combe, last year, in his lectures in this city :—" When I was in Germany," says Mr. Combe, " I saw a collection of books describing the science at different stages of its progress, and also skulls marked at different times ; all proving that the organs were discovered in succession. Indeed, I have found in this country a most unexpected corroboration of the fact.   Nicholas Biddle, Esq. of this city, when a young man, and on a visit to Europe, in 1806, attended a course of Dr. Gall's lectures, and was so much interested, that he requested Dr. Spurzheim to mark out the places of the organs on the skull, which he did.   This is the skull, (which Mr. Biddle has kindly presented me, saying that I could make a better use of it than he could,) and you perceive that there are a number of unoccupied places.   You perceive that Hope, Conscientiousness, Individuality, Concentrativeness, Time, Size, and Weight, are not marked upon it, they, at that time, being unascertained."

ARTICLE V.

A Lecture delivered before the Woodville Lyceum Association, by MARIANO CUBI I SOLER, Professor of Modern Languages in the College of Louisiana.   8vo. pp. 24.

This is an address on phrenology, delivered publicly before a large audience at Woodville, by Professor Soler, of the Louisiana College, located at Jackson.   From numerous sources, we have evidence to believe that phrenology not only has many able advocates, but has created a very general interest throughout all classes of the community, in this portion of the United States. The science is taught in several of their public institutions of learning, and not unfrequently is made the theme of popular addresses and lectures. Such is the character of the pamphlet now before us. Though it treats chiefly of the elementary principles of the science, yet they are ably and lucidly discussed, under the following heads ;—First, that *the mind acts through the brain ;* Secondly, that *the mind employs, variously, different portions of the brain ;* and, Thirdly, that *size of brain is a chief element of mental power.*

After disposing of these propositions, Professor Soler discourses in a general manner on the *three* natures of man, *moral, intellectual,* and *animal ;* that there are certain innate faculties or powers pertaining to each, and possessing certain fixed and definite relations to external objects ; that these faculties are all primarily *good in their nature,* though liable to perversion ; that man is, by his creation, a free moral agent, and can direct and control these powers at his will ; that his highest happiness, and the perfection of his being, require that all these faculties should be exercised in *perfect harmony,* and gratified by their *appropriate objects,* and that such a course is no less in accordance with the laws of the nature of man than with the requirements of God. As a specimen of his style and manner of treating the subject, we present below the last two pages of this lecture.

"We must study man as he has been created ; created by supremely perfect wisdom, for supremely perfect ends ; with imperfect but improving elements—with liabilities to sink into vice, but with powers to walk in the path of rectitude—with tendencies to suffer misery, but with capacities to seek and enjoy present and future happiness.

"But religion, as well as philosophy, shows that virtue and happiness, not vice and misery, were the object of the Almighty in the creation of man. Religion, as well as philosophy, shows that virtue and happiness consist in obeying, as far as we can, the laws which God has established for the physical and moral government of the universe ; and that, therefore, it becomes our most imperative duty to discover these laws, that we may act in accordance with the will of our Heavenly Father. Phrenology explains the laws which govern mind here below—mind, as it exists in our present condition, connected with matter. Without a knowledge of it, therefore, we remain, to a very great extent, ignorant of the manner in which we ought to act, in the most important occasions of our lives, to ensure, now and hereafter, happiness to ourselves and others.

"Take marriage for example. Without a knowledge of phrenology—without knowing that God has, by an eternal, unchangeable decree, ordained that man can only be virtuous and happy by *satisfying temperately and harmoniously all his desires,* we may enter into that condition and reap from it ourselves, and communicate or transmit to others, ffliction and misery instead of gratification and joy. Suppose a person, nfluenced only by love of the beautiful and love of property, disregards he cravings of the remaining thirty-three mental instincts, and forms a natrimonial connection with an individual beautiful and rich, indeed, ut incapable of gratifying the other organs. Ideality and Acquisitiveess will no doubt luxuriate for a while, but, like hunger surrounded by ainties, they will soon cease to crave. In this satiated condition, Benevolence, Adhesiveness, intellect, Self-esteem, will cry aloud for atisfaction; and if, instead of finding in the individual with whom we ave connected ourselves for life the proper qualities to appease the ravings of these other mental appetites, we only find there immoral rinciples, levity, ignorance, and undignified deportment, what a harvest f affliction and misery we shall reap, notwithstanding the transcendent eauty and immense property of our partner! On the other hand, if we larry chiefly with a view to satisfy what is termed pure, disinterested ve, and even all our moral sentiments, but disregard Acquisitiveness nd the sense of feeling, thus becoming blind to the known laws of phycal existence and transmission, neither the most exquisite, the most fined satisfaction of all our affections, nor the most sublime and eaven-like enjoyment of all our virtuous cravings, will make up for the iseries of want, or the pangs created by a deformed, sickly, halfarved, suffering progeny.

"As this principle is of universal application, I might multiply, without end, examples in illustration of it. The one offered may suffice for he present. We may smile, or we may be serious, when we hear of ian's possessing thirty-five organs, and of his having various clashing, pposing, and antagonistic desires; but it will nevertheless be certain, at the greater number of them we satisfy in any action, the more ligious, moral, happy we are, and shall be, as far as that action is oncerned; and the fewer we gratify, the more vicious, immoral, and iserable. With a knowledge of phrenology we shall be certain, that marriage, or in any other action, not one but all our organs must be tisfied temperately and in due proportion, and that, therefore, we must udy not only the nature of the action in all its bearings, but also ourlves as connected with that action. When we shall be certain that r animal passions, as well as our intellectual powers and moral feelgs, will all be, by that action, temperately and harmoniously gratified, en, and not till then, shall we be certain that we are right—then, and ot till then, shall we be certain that we obey the laws of God.

"And here, in conclusion, permit me to observe, that power of acting tablishes duty of performance. If it has pleased Infinite Wisdom to stow upon us animal instincts, moral sentiments, and intellectual wers, and to place us in a sphere where these capacities can find nple scope for action and guidance, as all the facts which constitute e sciences of geology, physiology, and phrenology prove, we are in ity bound to give them well regulated exercise. We can, as moral d intellectual beings, discern results, and be anxious to act for the neral good. If we do not use our efforts so to do, as far as in us lies e power, we are responsible to God and man for our neglect, and for l the evil to us and to others, which shall arise from it. He who acts w, without connecting his *present* action with its inevitable *future* sult, and without ascertaining, as far as it is in his power to ascertain, at the *result* will be for present as well as future, for individual as ell as general happiness, acts not like a man, and clearly transgresses e laws of God, which have given him the power, and therefore made his duty to use efforts to become more and more virtuous, useful, and ppy."

ARTICLE VI.

Treatise on the Physiological and Moral Management of Infancy by ANDREW COMBE, M. D. *with Notes and a Supplementar Chapter,* by JOHN BELL, M. D. Published by Carey & Har 12mo. pp. 307.

This is the title of a new work from the well-known pen of Dr. A Combe, and though its contents do not strictly come within the pro vince of phrenology, yet from the intrinsic value of its matter, a well as from its intimate connection with the principles of the science, we deem the work well worthy of a notice in this place From a critical examination of its pages, we predict that this ne' production of Dr. Combe is destined to be as popular, and to have a extensive a circulation, as his former work on the " Principles a Physiology, applied to Health and Education."* The increasin demand for works on the subject of physiology and its practice applications, is a cheering evidence of the advancement of a depar ment of knowledge which, of all others, involves most seriously th happiness and best interests of mankind. The primary cause a this change in the community may be attributed, in no small degree to the interest which the discovery and progress of phrenology hav created. In fact, phrenology is strictly a part of physiology, bein simply the results of an investigation into the true functions of th brain—the most important organ in the human body. The adva cates of this science were the first in Great Britain to proclaim th vast importance of a general diffusion of a knowledge of the laws a physical organisation. They took the lead in expounding thes laws, and showing their various applications, by writing popula essays for sundry periodicals, by the publication of numerous works and the delivery of many public lectures on the subject. Such, also has been the case in our own country.

No person but a believer in phrenology can fully perceive an appreciate the important bearings which the principles of physiolog has on human happiness. It is absolutely necessary to see th *entire dependence of all mental manifestations upon physical organi sation,* before mankind will ever pay that attention to the laws of th animal economy which their nature and importance demand. Thi

* We are informed, on good authority, that the Messrs. Harpers, of New Yorl have sold over *thirty thousand* copies of this work within four years, and they hav recently issued a new edition, considerably improved and enlarged, which will un doubtedly find as great a sale.

is one of the principal causes why these laws have been so little appreciated or understood, both by the learned and the unlearned. And just as long as *mind* is studied and regarded as an *abstract entity*, being entirely independent in its operations of the body, and as long as there exists in the community a certain kind of contempt for the latter, just so long will there be ignorance and violation of some of the most important laws in the moral government of God. Mere dry precepts or verbal directions are not sufficient on this subject. We must become thoroughly acquainted, by observation and study, with the nature of the laws involved, and the consequences of their violation. And this remark applies not only to the laws of organic matter, but also to the *laws of mind*—for the laws of the latter are as fixed and certain as those of the former; and when violated, their penalties are equally unavoidable.

The work before us contains a very clear and faithful exposition of these laws, as applied to infancy. It is one of Dr. Combe's best productions; and we hesitate not to affirm that it is decidedly the most valuable and useful work that has ever been written on the subject. The truth of this remark could be fully substantiated, did space permit; but as we shall take occasion to refer to some topics in this work hereafter, our present notice of it must necessarily be brief. It discusses the following topics :—extent of mortality in infancy ; sources of disease in infancy ; delicacy of constitution in infancy ; conditions in the mother affecting the health of the child ; of the constitution of the infant at birth ; the nursery, and conditions required in it ; the management of the infant immediately after birth—washing and dressing ; food of the infant at birth ; on the choice, properties, and regimen of a nurse ; artificial nursing and weaning ; cleanliness, exercise, and sleep in early infancy ; management of the infant during teething ; management from the time of weaning to the end of the second year ; on the moral management of infancy ; and a supplementary chapter, including some general remarks on the above subjects, with particular reference to this country, by the American editor, Dr. J. Bell. Dr. B. has also appended to the other chapters many valuable notes. We most cordially recommend this work to the attention of all our readers ; it should be not only read, but *studied* by every parent—and most especially by every *mother*—throughout the United States.

MISCELLANY.

—

Philosophy of Mind, developing new sources of Ideas, designating their distinctive classes, and simplifying the faculties and operations of the whole mind. By JOHN STEARNS, M. D. of New York, late President of the Medical Society of the State.

This is the title of a new treatise (in pamphlet form, 8vo. pp. 25) on mental science. The writer, after some general observations on the nature and importance of mental philosophy, proceeds to remark as follows:—"I shall now proceed to give my views on this subject, for which I claim no farther credence than as they may consist with reason and with truth, and be sustained by facts and by satisfactory evidence. Preparatory to more detailed explanations, I now submit the following propositions, as comprehending the fundamental principles of this theory:—

"I. Man consists of three distinct entities.—BODY, SOUL, and MIND.

"II. The ideas of sensation are those carnal ideas which constitute the animal propensities, and which we derive, in common with other animals, from the five senses.

"III. The intellectual, and moral, and religious ideas, which some philosophers ascribe to reflection, and to innate principles, are derived entirely and exclusively from the soul. In the soul is held the high court of chancery, denominated conscience, or the moral sense.

"IV. When the soul operates upon the brain, it produces what may be denominated a *moral mind,* endowed with intellectual and religious faculties; and until excited to operation by this operation, the faculties of the brain remain perfectly dormant.

"V. When the senses operate upon the brain, they produce what may be denominated a *sensual mind,* which man possesses in common with the inferior animals, but which is essentially changed and improved by the accession of the soul to the body."

Dr. Stearns here discusses, at some length, his first proposition, after which he offers sundry remarks in proof and illustration of the remaining propositions. We cannot here present even an analysis of his views, and much less enter into an examination of the merits of his theory of mind. It is altogether too *abstract* and *metaphysical* to discuss in a *phrenological* journal.

—

Aspects of Phrenology on Religion.—In a recent number of the Georgia Argus, (a weekly paper published at Columbus, Ga.) we find the following communication of a correspondent, addressed to the editors:—

"I had the pleasure last Sabbath of attending the very able and learned discourse of the Rev. Dr. Blake, at the Methodist church; his subject was managed with great ability; showing evidently a mind of the highest order of intellect, and studiously cultivated. In the elucidation of a portion of his subject, he incidentally mentioned the science of phrenology; and remarked, that if it was properly understood by divines, and its principles practically taught, great good would result to the church; the idea appeared to the auditors, I have no doubt, as somewhat absurd, as a smile was visible throughout; it struck me, however, as true; in fact, I have for many years believed that the time was not far distant when truths brought to light by philosophy would be called to aid the cause of religion.   It has been unfortunate for the world, however, that so much bigotry should have existed in different ages : Galileo was told from high authority in the church, that his doctrine of the earth's revolution around the sun was at variance with Holy Writ, and that therefore it could not be true ; the same was said to Columbus, upon his intimation of the existence of another continent.   Bishop Butler, Adam Smith, Dugald Stewart, Dr. Huchinson, Mr. Ried, Dr. Thomas Brown, and Judge Blackstone, have all carried out in their teachings the principles of phrenology, though ignorant of the science.   Improvement in the philosophy of the human mind is progressive, consequently the arts and sciences advance in every age.   The discovery of the art of printing greatly aided the cause of religion and the spread of the gospel; so the discovery of phrenology is destined by the Almighty to carry truth into the ranks of error, to scatter that darkness which now enshrouds the intellectual and moral world, to strengthen the cause of God and religion, and to teach mankind that all the faculties of their nature, when brought into harmony with those laws which govern man and external nature, will constitute him happy here, and that a conformity to the will of God will render him happy hereafter.

" The time will come, when it will be seen that phrenology and religion harmonise : that the mysterious truths of the one will be analogically illustrated by the other ; both teach the supremacy of man's moral nature ; revelation addresses the individual powers and faculties which phrenology ascribes to man ; revelation and phrenology alike suppose man designed by the Creator to believe mysterious truths, and capable of believing them, and righteously punished if this disbelief be persevered in ; both agree in the fallen condition of man ; both recognise the moral conflict in the breast of a good man between antagonistic principles; both acknowledge diversity of endowment, and consequent responsibility ; both demand candour and charity in judging others ; both agree in their estimate of virtue, and in exploding the doctrine of human merit.   Truth and error cannot harmonise."

Laws of Hereditary Descent.—It is a settled principle in physiology, that the organisation of children depends very much on that of the parents.   This principle pervades all organic matter, and has long been observed and successfully applied in many departments of the animal kingdom.   But the great mass of mankind have been either profoundly ignorant, or entirely unmindful of the fact, that the *human* race is, in like manner, governed by organic laws, and is susceptible of improvement by precisely the same means.   It would seem at first scarcely possible, that there could exist such ignorance and indifference on a subject that so vitally affects the health, happiness, and best interests of man. Strange that he should not exercise reason and common sense for the improvement of his own race, as well as of that of the brutes !

Phrenology is destined to throw great light on this intricate and all-important subject.   Facts abundantly prove that not only bodily *predisposition* to certain diseases is transmitted from parents to children, but that *mental* peculiarities are also, to a great extent, the result of hereditary descent.   Phrenology, by making known the true functions of the brain, and showing the dependence of mind on matter, enables us to understand the laws which govern the transmission of mental qualities— that, as a general thing, the faculties which predominate in strength and activity in the parents will constitute the leading features of character

in their children. Thus strong animal propensities, selfish feelings, anc
moral sentiments, may severally be transmitted ; or faculties calculatec
to excel in the mechanic arts, fine arts, and poetry, or those bette
adapted to the cultivation of literature, science, and philosophy. These
laws involve interests of the greatest magnitude, and cannot in thei
proper place receive too much attention. They have repeatedly beer
alluded to in the Journal, but will be discussed more fully in its page:
hereafter.

___

Mental Derangement.—The following curious case of insanity we
copy from the Philadelphia Gazette of July 7. The mental phenomena
in the present instance are entirely inexplicable on any other principle
whatever, except that of a plurality of organs to the brain. Only a few
faculties appear to have been deranged ; Combativeness, Destructive
ness, and Cautiousness, were undoubtedly most affected. The intellec
tual faculties as a class, it appears, were unimpaired. The facts in the
case were as follows :—

"Some thirty years ago, a beautiful lady, the only daughter of a noble
house in the north of Germany, from having been one of the most cheer
ful girls, became subject to fits of the deepest melancholy.. All the
entreaties of her parents were insufficient to draw from her the reason o
it ; to their affection, she was cold—to their caresses, rude ; and though
society failed to enliven her, she bore her part in it with a power and a
venom of sarcasm that were as strange to her former character as they
were unbecoming her sex and youth. The parents contrived, during he
temporary absence from home, to investigate the contents of her writing
desk, but no indications of a concealed or disappointed passion were to
be found, and it was equally clear that no papers had been removed
The first news they heard of her was, that the house in which she was
visiting had been burnt to the ground ; that she had been saved with dif
ficulty, though her room was not in that part of the building where the
fire had commenced ; that her escape had at first been taken for granted
and that when her door was burst open, she was found still dressed anc
seated in her usual melancholy attitude, with her eyes fixed on the
ground.

"She returned home neither altered in manner or changed in demeanor
and as painfully brilliant in conversation when forced into it. Within
two months of her return, the house was burnt to the ground, and her
mother perished in the flames ; she was again found in the same state as
on the former occasion ; did not alter her deportment upon hearing the
fate of her mother, made no attempt to console her father, and replied to
the condolence of her friends with a bitterness and scorn almost demo
niacal. The father and daughter removed to a spa for change of scene
On the night of their arrival, the hotel was in flames ; but this time the
fire began in her apartment, for from her window were the sparks firs
seen to issue, and again was she found dressed, seated, and in a reverie
The hotel was the property of the sovereign of the little state in which
the spa was situated.

"An investigation took place ; she was arrested, and at once confessec
that on each of the three occasions she had been the culprit ; that she
could not tell wherefore, except that she had had an irresistible longing
to set houses on fire. Each time she had striven against it as long as
she could, but she was unable to withstand the temptation ; that this
longing first supervened a few weeks after she had been seized with a
sudden depression of spirit ; that she felt a hatred to all the world, bu

had strength to refrain from oaths and curses against it. She is at this
moment in a madhouse, where she was at first allowed some liberty,
but after an exhibition of homicidal monomania towards a child, of a
ferocity most appalling, it was found necessary to apply the severest
restraint. She still possesses her memory, her reasoning powers, her
petulant wit, and observes the most scrupulous delicacy."

Periodicals and Phrenology.—The *North American Review* for July,
has fourteen pages devoted to a review of Dr. Morton's Crania Americana.
This notice is decidedly favourable to the work—compliments it highly
as a production on natural history, but is entirely silent as to its important bearings on phrenology. This review contains only one single
allusion to the science, and that is, in the *writer's opinion,* against it;
whereas, many hundreds of facts and arguments, far more striking and
palpable, might be adduced from the Crania Americana in favour of
phrenology. · The ancient Peruvians are cited, by the reviewer, as having only *average-sized heads,* and yet were far advanced *in civilisation,*
at some future time, we may show *in what* their civilisation consisted
and that it was of such a *character* as to be in *perfect accordance* with
their cranial developements.
    The *Christian Examiner* for May, published at Boston, contained a
notice of the Crania Americana, similar in character to that in the
North American Review, though much shorter.
    The *American Journal of Science and Arts* for July, contains an able
and extended plea in behalf of phrenology, from the pen of its editor
Professor Silliman. This article, vindicating the claims of phrenology
in the first scientific Journal in the United States, is no less creditable
to its conductor, than just to the cause of truth and science.
    The two last numbers of the *Western Medical Journal,* published a
Louisville, Ky. contain a critical and extended review of Morton's
Crania Americana, from the pen of Professor Caldwell. As the subject
is treated in strictly a *phrenological* manner, accompanied with many
interesting and important remarks on the science, we shall copy, at the
first convenient opportunity, some parts of this review into the Journal.
    The *Gentleman's Magazine* for August, has an article "on the *Hum-
bug of Phrenology,* by Russell Jarvis. Esq." The *character* of this
article is such, that we consider it entirely unworthy of notice in our
pages.

Application of Phrenology to Marriage.—In a small work, entitled
"Philosophy of Courtship and Marriage"—first published in Great Britain, and recently reprinted in this country—the author, after giving
some wise and appropriate directions in this matter, thus introduces the
subject of phrenology :—

"A Xantippe may rouge and pearl-powder her face into the semblance
of the meekly patient Griselda, but she cannot obliterate the organs o
Combativeness and Destructiveness. The fair infidel may play the out
ward devotee to perfection, but all her surface orisons will not fill up the
fatal gap in the organ of Reverence. I sincerely pity the anti-phrenolo
gist for many reasons, but for none more than this, that he throws away
the best and most effectual guiding-staff through the quicksands o
courtship and marriage. Combe and Cupid should ever be fellow-tra
vellers; and by trusting in *Gall,* you may escape *wormwood.*"

had strength to re
moment in a ma
but after an exl
ferocity most a
restraint. She
petulant wit, a

Periodica
has fourteen
This notic
as a produ
ant bearir
allusion
whereas,
palpabl,
phreno'
ing on'
at sor
and r
their
     T
not'
No

ai
F
i

had strength to re
moment in a ma
but after an exl
ferocity most *
restraint. She
petulant wit, *

Periodica
has fourteer
This notic
as a produ
ant bearir
allusion
whereas
palpabl
phreno
ing on
at sor
and *
their
　T
not
Nc

a:
F
i

Check Out More Titles From HardPress Classics Series In this collection we are offering thousands of classic and hard to find books. This series spans a vast array of subjects – so you are bound to find something of interest to enjoy reading and learning about.

Subjects:
Architecture
Art
Biography & Autobiography
Body, Mind &Spirit
Children & Young Adult
Dramas
Education
Fiction
History
Language Arts & Disciplines
Law
Literary Collections
Music
Poetry
Psychology
Science
…and many more.

Visit us at www.hardpress.net

Im The Story
personalised classic books

JANE IN WONDERLAND

LEWIS CARROLL

"Beautiful gift.. lovely finish.
My Niece loves it, so precious!"

Helen R Brumfieldon

☆☆☆☆☆

UNIQUE GIFT

FOR KIDS, PARTNERS
AND FRIENDS

Timeless books such as:

Kids

Alice in Wonderland • The Jungle Book • The Wonderful Wizard of Oz
Peter and Wendy • Robin Hood • The Prince and The Pauper
The Railway Children • Treasure Island • A Christmas Carol

Adults

Romeo and Juliet • Dracula

Highly
Customizable

Change
Books Title

Replace
Characters Names
with yours

Upload
Photo (for
inside page)

Add
Inscriptions

Visit
Im The Story .com
and order yours today!

SD - #0005 - 170822 - C0 - 229/152/34 - PB - 9781318508860 - Gloss Lamination